Medieval Perceptual Puzzles

Investigating Medieval Philosophy

Managing Editor

John Marenbon

Editorial Board

Margaret Cameron
Nadja Germann
Simo Knuuttila
Martin Lenz
Christopher J. Martin

VOLUME 13

The titles published in this series are listed at *brill.com/imp*

Medieval Perceptual Puzzles

*Theories of Sense Perception in the
13th and 14th Centuries*

Edited by

Elena Băltuță

BRILL

LEIDEN | BOSTON

The Library of Congress Cataloging-in-Publication Data is available online at http://catalog.loc.gov

Typeface for the Latin, Greek, and Cyrillic scripts: "Brill". See and download: brill.com/brill-typeface.

ISSN 1879-9787
ISBN 978-90-04-40847-0 (hardback)
ISBN 978-90-04-41303-0 (ebook)

Copyright 2020 by Koninklijke Brill NV, Leiden, The Netherlands.
Koninklijke Brill NV incorporates the imprints Brill, Brill Hes & De Graaf, Brill Nijhoff, Brill Rodopi, Brill Sense, Hotei Publishing, mentis Verlag, Verlag Ferdinand Schöningh and Wilhelm Fink Verlag.
All rights reserved. No part of this publication may be reproduced, translated, stored in a retrieval system, or transmitted in any form or by any means, electronic, mechanical, photocopying, recording or otherwise, without prior written permission from the publisher.
Authorization to photocopy items for internal or personal use is granted by Koninklijke Brill NV provided that the appropriate fees are paid directly to The Copyright Clearance Center, 222 Rosewood Drive, Suite 910, Danvers, MA 01923, USA. Fees are subject to change.

This book is printed on acid-free paper and produced in a sustainable manner.

Contents

Notes on Contributors   VII

1   Introduction   1

2   Perceiving As: Non-conceptual Forms of Perception in Medieval
Philosophy   10
Juhana Toivanen

3   The Chameleonic Mind: The Activity versus the Actuality of
Perception   38
José Filipe Silva

4   The Visual Process: Immediate or Successive? Approaches to the
Extramission Postulate in 13th Century Theories of Vision   73
Lukáš Lička

5   *Visio per sillogismum*: Sensation and Cognition in 13th Century
Theories of Vision   111
Mattia Mantovani

6   Spirituality and Perception in Medieval Aristotelian Natural
Philosophy   153
Rega Wood

7   The Escape Artist: Robert Kilwardby on Objects as *sine qua non*
Causes   179
Elena Băltuță

8   Rational Seeing: Thomas Aquinas on Human Perception   213
Dominik Perler

9   Aquinas on Perceiving, Thinking, Understanding, and Cognizing
Individuals   238
Daniel De Haan

10   "Accidental Perception" and "Cogitative Power" in Thomas
Aquinas and John of Jandun   269
Paolo Rubini

CONTENTS

11 Peter John Olivi on Perception, Attention, and the Soul's Orientation towards the Body 304
   André Martin

12 Caesar in Bronze: Duns Scotus on the Sensation of Singular Accidents 335
   Andrew LaZella

13 John Buridan on the Singularity of Sense Perception 364
   Martin Klein

   Index of Names 389
   Index of Concepts 394

Notes on Contributors

Elena Băltuță
Ph.D. (2012), Al. I. Cuza University, is postdoctoral Fellow at the Babeș-Bolyai University. She published a monograph on Thomas Aquinas's theory of intentionality (Humanitas, 2013) and several articles on medieval theories of cognition, intentionality, and causation.

Daniel De Haan
Ph.D. (2014), KU Leuven and University of St Thomas, is a Research Fellow at the University of Oxford. He has published articles in *The Journal of the History of Philosophy*, *Arabic Sciences and Philosophy*, *Documenti e studi sulla tradizione filosofica medievale*, *Quaestio*, and *The Review of Metaphysics*.

Martin Klein
Ph.D. (2016), Humboldt University of Berlin, is a Lecturer (Wissenschaftlicher Mitarbeiter) at the Department of Philosophy at the University of Würzburg. He is the author of *Philosophie des Geistes im Spätmittelalter* (Brill, 2019).

Andrew LaZella
Ph.D. (2010), DePaul University, is Associate Professor of Philosophy at The University of Scranton. His most recent publications include *The Singular Voice of Being: John Duns Scotus and Ultimate Difference* (Fordham, 2019) and the co-edited volume (with Richard A. Lee, Jr.) *The Edinburgh Critical History of Medieval and Renaissance Philosophy* (Edinburgh University Press, forthcoming).

Lukáš Lička
Ph.D. (2016), University of Ostrava, is a post-doctoral researcher at the Institute of Philosophy, Academy of Sciences of the Czech Republic and researcher at the Faculty of Arts, University of Ostrava. He has published several articles on medieval theories of perception; currently, he works on late medieval optics and on disputations at Prague University around 1400.

Mattia Mantovani
Ph.D. (2018), Humboldt University of Berlin, is a post-doctoral fellow at the KU Leuven. He works on Medieval and Early Modern philosophy and science, with a special focus on vision theory and optics. His current post-doctoral project investigates the teaching and reception of Descartes' natural philosophy.

André Martin

is currently a doctoral candidate at McGill University. He is writing a dissertation on the emerging notion of *attention*, especially as something conscious, active, and direct, in 13th and 14th century theories of cognition and the surrounding metaphysical debates.

Dominik Perler

Ph.D. (1991), is Professor of Philosophy at the Humboldt-Universität zu Berlin and Member of the Berlin-Brandenburg Academy of Arts and Science. He has published on medieval metaphysics, epistemology, and philosophy of mind. His books include *Zweifel und Gewissheit. Skeptische Debatten im Mittelalter* (Frankfurt a.M. 2006), *Partitioning the Soul: Debates from Plato to Leibniz* (ed., Berlin, 2014), *The Faculties: A History* (ed., Oxford, 2015), *Feelings Transformed: Philosophical Theories of the Emotions, 1270–1670* (Oxford, 2018).

Paolo Rubini

Ph.D. (2013), Humboldt University of Berlin, is a staff member of the Leibniz Edition at the Berlin-Brandenburg Academy of Sciences and Humanities. He also worked at the University of Helsinki. His fields of interests are natural philosophy and theory of cognition from the late Middle Ages up to Leibniz. He is the author of *Pietro Pomponazzis Erkenntnistheorie. Naturalisierung des Menschlichen Geistes im Spätaristotelismus* (Brill, 2015).

José Filipe Silva

Ph.D. (2009), Porto University, is Associate Professor of Medieval Philosophy at the University of Helsinki and the Director of the ERC research funded project *Rationality in Perception: Transformations of Mind and Cognition 1250–1550*. His research interests are medieval theories of perception, mind, and rationality, on which he has published extensively. He is the author and editor of *Robert Kilwardby on the Human Soul* (Brill, 2012), *Active Perception in the History of Philosophy* (Springer, 2014), *The Senses and the History of Philosophy* (Routledge, 2019).

Juhana Toivanen

Ph.D. (2009), University of Jyväskylä, is an Academy Research Fellow at the same institution, and a postdoctoral researcher at the University of Gothenburg. He has published widely on medieval philosophy of mind, including a monograph, *Perception and the Internal Senses* (Brill, 2013). Currently he is working, among other things, on medieval conceptions of human sociability.

Rega Wood

Ph.D. (1975), Cornell University, is a Professor of Philosophy at Indiana University, Bloomington. She has published critical editions of works by John Duns Scotus, William Ockham, and Adam Wodeham; also many articles on medieval philosophy, particularly the philosophy of Richard Rufus of Cornwall. Most recently she published a critical edition of his *Sententia cum quaestionibus in libros De anima Aristotelis,* with J. Ottman, N. Lewis, and C.J. Martin (Oxford University Press, 2019).

CHAPTER 1

Introduction

1 General Remarks

In our daily lives, we are surrounded by all sorts of things – such as trees, people, cars, madeleines, or books – and perception allows us access to them. Just by being aware of this fact we are provided with a preliminary grasp of the very act of perception. We have thus the possibility to begin investigating it. For instance, we could ask some basic questions about the subject of perception, its object, and the relation between the subject and the object. Or we could resort to more elaborate questions: Do we really perceive things or just some properties, like color or odor? What are the mechanisms of perception? What faculties do we employ in perception? What is the dynamics between these faculties? Is rationality somehow involved in perception? What causal processes are enmeshed in perception? Reaching such a level of complexity when investigating perception presupposes working with more technical concepts. What is more, the meaning itself of the concepts employed can become problematic. What do concepts like *perception, faculty, rationality,* or *causality* actually mean? What would their proper use be? What is their corresponding theoretical framework? Through questions of this sort, the investigation of perception could take a historical turn. After all, concepts in general do not have a fixed meaning. With time, they suffer various semantic shifts. Paying attention to history allows us therefore to get acquainted with other ways of conceiving the world and the things within it, involving other meanings of perception, of its subject and object, or of the relationship between its subject and object. Other concepts, other questions, and other presuppositions come to the fore. The acquaintance with the alterity of history can thus afford a firmer grip on the temporal character of an investigation of perception and even on our own perceptual access to the things in our daily lives.

In order to acquire a steady, historical, perspective on perception, it is, however, not enough to come up with a superficial, readily available, overview of history and put it to work. We need ourselves to do history; we need ourselves to acquire knowledge about the past ways of conceiving perception. Such a task cannot be fulfilled at once. It needs patience and diligence. This latter request implies that, in order to do history, at least a preliminary choice should be made. We should concentrate on particular historical periods. For choosing them, one has at one's disposal a multitude of criteria. For instance, a particular period of time could simply be, for someone, more alluring than others. Someone like this would do history for the sake of it and for her own enjoyment. We could, therefore, say that the criterion she uses is an *aesthetic* one. Another historian might be interested in a particular period of time just because she finds in it some resources for dealing with, say, a specific contemporary issue regarding perception. The main interest in such a case is directed towards the present, the past being conceived as a means for improving the contemporary approach to perception. The criterion employed in this second situation could thus be designated as *pragmatic*. Yet another historian might find the two criteria just mentioned too narrow, and so unacceptable. Instead of focusing primarily on either the past or the present, she seeks to treat both of them with utmost care. The main task she sets for herself would be, in this case, *hermeneutically circular*: to delve into the past without neglecting the inevitable influence exerted on her work by the present situation and, by delving into the past, to make more apparent, and thus more available for questioning, the present situation.[1] Nevertheless, on its own, such a hermeneutically flavored approach does not really provide us with a functional criterion for choosing to investigate a particular historical period. Making a choice like this presupposes taking into account the actual person able to conduct an investigation into the past, the historian herself. What is her background? What are her competences? What are the historical periods she is familiar with? The answers to such questions play a decisive role also in the use of the first two criteria.

As a matter of fact, by taking into consideration the actual person dealing with how past philosophers accounted for perception, we can easily understand that choosing to investigate a particular historical period is not, first and foremost, about applying a selection criterion. The historian herself is never guided, in her choice, solely by enjoyment, nor by some interest in contemporary philosophy, nor by her care to maintain some balance between the past and the present. Most of the time, the choice to investigate a particular historical period is the result of a play of contingencies; it emerges from the interaction of several attitudes towards history, be they aesthetic, pragmatic, or hermeneutic, with the skills at the disposal of the historian herself. Such a picture becomes even more intricate, naturally, if we are to take into account the choice

---

1   Taking into account these possible attitudes towards history owes much to D. Perler, "The Alienation Effect in the Historiography of Philosophy," in M. van Ackeren and L. Klein (ed), *Philosophy and the Historical Perspective*, Oxford, Oxford University Press, 2018, pp. 140–154.

INTRODUCTION

of a group of scholars, each with her own attitudes towards history and her own skills. Apart from the play of contingencies, however, there are historical periods rich enough to meet numerous requirements following from numerous attitudes towards history effective within a group of scholars.

The present collected volume gathers a series of twelve essays that deal with various theories of sense perception from the Latin philosophy of the 13th and 14th centuries. What makes these centuries particularly rich and interesting is that, against the traditional Augustinian background of the 12th century, imbued with Stoic and Neoplatonic ideas, newly Aristotelian writings on natural philosophy and their Arabic commentaries became available, changing and making the discussion about perception more complex. This shifting philosophical landscape prompted a series of debates on the nature of matter, on the plurality or unity of substantial forms, on the epistemic role of representations in cognition, or on the relation between the body and the soul. The Latin philosophy of the 13th and 14th centuries thus reveals itself as most engaging when it comes to investigating medieval theories of sense perception. Various interests, employing various selection criteria for various themes concerning sense perception, are all to be satisfied with the choice of such a historical period. At the same time, given the richness of the 13th and 14th centuries, dealing with theories of sense perception requires from the historian of philosophy a great deal of skills. They are already put to use in the essays that follow. All these aspects, that is, the importance and complexity of the historical period under consideration, the profile of the historians combining their efforts to investigate medieval theories of sense perception, their solid background and skills or their broad interests in history of philosophy, contribute to the strength and diversity of the present volume.

Owing to the philosophical richness of the period and the fair amount of scholarship on medieval philosophy, someone might assume that any new contributions to the field should simply find their rationale in their relationship to the preceding ones. Research on medieval philosophy, in general, should thus consist, today, of noting and trying to fill in some gaps here and there, in the scholarship, addressing some terminological issues, contriving new arguments, and the like. On this view, there would be some aspects of the 13th and 14th centuries' theories of perception that have been neglected in the philosophical secondary literature, and the present volume would be supposed to remedy this situation. But such a line of thought would take a somewhat too optimistic perspective on the matter at hand. Currently, scholars interested in medieval theories of sense perception do not have at their disposal, apart from some primary sources, a substantial literature. They can resort to volumes dealing generally with the history of perception, which include papers on the medieval period, but do not focus particularly on it.[2] More or less extended chapters from companions, monographs, and journal articles dedicated to individual medieval authors can also be of some help. Yet another option would be to look at volumes engaging with themes relevant to medieval philosophy, which deal with perception or perception-related issues only insofar as these are of importance for the themes under investigation. To give but a few examples, there are volumes dedicated to the species debate,[3] to the relation between sensory and intellectual cognition,[4] and, most recently, to the active elements involved specifically in sense perception.[5] Despite these sources of information, it is evident that dealing with medieval theories of sense perception, in a collected volume, cannot be mainly about filling in the gaps in the secondary literature. It is more important to contribute to laying the foundations for solid scholarship, and thus to create the possibility of an overarching approach. That does not mean starting all over again. It is necessary and helpful to use the already existing secondary literature, just as it is necessary and helpful to introduce a more systematic character to the scholarship.

2   Structure of the Volume

The essays gathered in the present volume bring their own valuable contribution to the task of establishing the theories of perception as an important field of inquiry into medieval philosophy. Their approach varies from conceptual analysis to synthetic surveys of topics relevant for the theories of perception, from interventions in the debates between contemporary scholars, proposing new arguments or renewing old distinctions, to bringing to the fore less-known

---

2   See C. Burnett, M. Fend, and P. Gouk (eds), *The Second Sense: Studies in Hearing and Musical Judgement from Antiquity to the Seventeenth Century*, London, The Warburg Institute, 1991; S. Knuuttila and P. Kärkkäinen (eds), *Theories of Perception in Medieval and Modern Philosophy*, Dordrecht, Springer, 2008; J.F. Silva and M. Yrjönsuuri (eds), *Active Perception in the History of Philosophy: From Plato to Modern Philosophy*, Dordrecht, Springer, 2014.

3   See L. Spruit, *Species intelligibilis: From Perception to Knowledge*, vol. 1: *Classical Roots and Medieval Discussions*, Leiden, Brill, 1994.

4   See R. Pasnau, *Theories of Cognition in the Later Middle Ages*, Cambridge, Cambridge University Press, 1997; D. Perler, *Theorien der Intentionalität im Mittelalter*, Frankfurt am Main, Vittorio Klostermann, 2002.

5   See J.F. Silva and J. Toivanen, "The Active Nature of the Soul in Sense Perception: Robert Kilwardby and Peter Olivi," *Vivarium*, vol. 48, no. 3–4, 2010, pp. 245–278; H.T. Adriaenssen, "Peter John Olivi on Perceptual Representation," *Vivarium*, vol. 49, no. 4, 2011, pp. 324–352; Adriaenssen, *Representation and Scepticism from Aquinas to Descartes*, Cambridge, Cambridge University Press, 2017.

INTRODUCTION 5

medieval authors. The volume is divided into two parts. The first part is centered on general themes connected to perception. It starts by addressing, in the first chapter, the architecture and the functions of the faculties involved in perception, goes through the evolution of active theories of perception, in the second chapter, and ends with two chapters revolving around the theories of vision.

Medieval philosophers recognized that perception involves elements which cannot be reduced to the sensory qualities of external objects, such as smells, colors, textures, sounds, and tastes. Just as we are willing, nowadays, to admit that objects are perceived not only as having a certain color or a certain smell, but also as being three-dimensional, as being helpful, harmful, or as being the objects of desires, so did medieval philosophers. Accounting for such qualities that escape our external senses led them to add internal senses to the list of faculties responsible for perception. Juhana Toivanen offers, in the first chapter of the volume, a survey on the conceptions regarding the interplay between the external and internal senses by focusing on different types of "perceiving as" medieval philosophers acknowledged, and by explaining what exactly is being added to perception in these instances of perceiving. He advances two heuristic models for analyzing medieval theories of perception and tries to establish the boundaries between conceptual and non-conceptual perception. The authors brought into discussion are, among others, Albert the Great, Thomas Aquinas, Peter John Olivi, Dominicus Gundissalinus, Roger Bacon, John Blund, John of La Rochelle, and William of Auvergne.

From the level of interaction between the faculties involved in sense perception, the second chapter of the volume descends into the interaction between the subject and the object of perception. José Filipe Silva analyses the development of active theories of sense perception, from Augustine to Duns Scotus, focusing on the manner in which medieval philosophers employed two metaphors: the chameleon and the living wax. Such metaphors were used to make sense of the dual character of perception within the framework of active theories. Unlike their Aristotelian counterparts, Augustinians understood perception as a dual-component account or as a two-step model according to Silva's terminology, consisting of a reception stage, caused by the external object, and a stage establishing the perceptual act, which is caused by the cognitive power. Some of the authors adopting these metaphors, and thus investigated by Silva, are Augustine, Albert the Great, Robert Kilwardby, Peter John Olivi, John Pecham, and William of Auvergne.

The last two chapters of the first part of the volume take a further step and descend even deeper into the process of perception. Lukáš Lička and Mattia Mantovani deal with medieval theories of vision, and both call into question particular aspects of the already existing scholarship on the matter. In his chapter, Lička addresses the commonplace according to which, by the year 1250, extramissive theories of vision, which appealed to rays coming out of the eyes for explaining vision, were a thing of the past. Avicenna, Averroes, and Alhacen supposedly presented such convincing arguments against them, that the intromissive theories became the norm. Lička is challenging this narrative. During the 13th century, philosophers still took extramissionist arguments seriously, whether in an attempt to refute them (Albert the Great), in attempts to combine them with intromissionist ones (Roger Bacon), or in efforts to rethink and reformulate them (Peter John Olivi). In his chapter, Mantovani tries to prove that, in their discussions of perception, the perspectivists Roger Bacon, Witelo, and John Pecham, unlike Aquinas, were not interested in establishing which of the external senses is more spiritual. Rather, they were keener on making the case for a two-stage process of perception: a sensory and a cognitive one. For this reason, they developed theories that took apprehension of proper sensibles, such as light and colour, to be a sensory material stage, and apprehension of common sensibles, such as shape, to be a cognitive stage that involved even syllogisms. If one takes into account the way perspectivists understood perception, and especially the visual apparatus, Mantovani suggests, the famous opposition between "materializers" and "dematerializers," advocated in the Sorabji-Burnyeat debate, is not only overly simplifying, but also misleading.

The second part of the volume is focused more on individual figures from the 13th and 14th centuries and their theories of perception. The chapters are organized chronologically. This option is not aimed, first of all, at pursuing the evolution of particular theories of perception, but, on the contrary, at noticing and underlining the synchronicity of different philosophical traditions and the interaction between them. The diversity, mobility, and effervescence of the philosophical traditions were, after all, among the main arguments for choosing the 13th and 14th centuries as temporal framework for the volume. In the first chapter, Rega Wood proposes refreshing the famous debate between Burnyeat and Sorabji by taking a closer look at a wrongfully ignored 13th century Aristotelian, Richard Rufus of Cornwall (? –1260). Wood starts by explaining the differences between modern and medieval notions of spirituality and then delves into Rufus' particular take on perception. Like Averroes, he took spirituality to come in degrees and used it to explain the physical, albeit immaterial, process of perception. A particular aspect of Rufus' understanding of spirituality is its connection to the theory of light. According to him, light transforms the sensibles' natural way of being into a spiritual one and enables them to be apprehended by the senses.

INTRODUCTION 7

A fellow Oxonian and contemporary of Richard Rufus, Robert Kilwardby (1215–1279), is discussed by Elena Băltuţă in the second chapter. She argues that, in his theory of perception, the external object plays the role of a *sine qua non* cause. While substantiating this claim, Băltuţă also shows that two of Kilwardby's seemingly incompatible claims actually fit together. According to the first claim, what the sensory soul perceives are corporeal objects; according to the second claim, the sensory soul, although it perceives corporeal objects, cannot be acted upon by them. The way out of this apparent inconsistency is to look at Kilwardby's theory of perception from a double, that is, natural and cognitive, perspective.

The next three chapters turn to a more famous contemporary of Rufus and Kilwardby. They focus on three instances in which Thomas Aquinas (1225–1274) addresses the relationship between *vis cogitativa*, an inner sensitive faculty present only in humans, and sense perception. Taking Aquinas' metaphysical background as a starting point, Dominik Perler makes the case that human beings perceive material objects in a rational way. A key role in his argument is played by the workings of *vis cogitativa*, which, according to Aquinas, is always guided by the rational faculty. Hence, states Perler, human perceptions are always conceptually structured, which means that Aquinas' theory of perception can be understood along the lines of what contemporary philosophy calls "transformative rationality." Daniel De Haan, in his chapter, focuses on the relation between *vis cogitativa* and the cognition of individuals. According to him, a proper understanding of *vis cogitativa* can rectify the old narrative about Aquinas not having a real solution to the problem of cognizing individuals. De Haan brings two argumentative lines in support of his claim: (1) in cognitive operations, the powers of the soul do not work individually, but in cooperation, and (2) the key to understanding Aquinas' solution to cognition of individuals is to look at how the external senses, the *vis cogitativa*, and the possible intellect cooperate. Aquinas' conception of *vis cogitativa* is discussed by Paolo Rubini as well, but in a comparative manner, by considering also Jean of Jandun's (1285–1328) take on the matter. The two medieval authors found themselves on opposite sides when it came to understanding the workings of this faculty. As an Aristotelian, Aquinas has, according to Rubini, an intellectualist account, while Jean of Jandun, an early 14th century Averroist, has a radical empiricist account of its working. For Aquinas, *vis cogitativa* is subordinated to the intellect's flow of concepts, while for Jean of Jandun, *vis cogitativa* has to perform its operation separated from the intellect.

Roughly twenty years younger than Aquinas, Peter John Olivi (1248–1298) is famous in the history of philosophy for his refractory stance towards Aristotle's views, including his account of perception. However, André Martin proposes a new reading, focused on the notion of *aspectus*, rendered either as "attention" or as "orientation," which allows Olivi to retain some Aristotelian elements in his theory of sense perception. The apparent tension that arises from Olivi's use of *aspectus*, understood both as selective attention and as an orientation towards lower faculties and corporeal organs, could be dispelled by introducing the distinction between a conscious and a non-conscious *aspectus*.

The last two chapters of the volume address the cognition of individuals in the cases of two philosophers from the High Middle Ages, Duns Scotus (1265/6–1308) and John Buridan (1300–1361). Individuals are intelligible *per se* according to Duns Scotus. However, they are not intelligible *per se* for humans. Andrew LaZella sets out the task of explaining why for Scotus we do not see *this* red or we do not hear *that* C-flat. His investigation reveals that for understanding Scotus' position properly one has to dig deep into his metaphysics and to pay particular attention to the formal distinction between *ratio agentis* and *ratio agendi*. Martin Klein sets for himself the task of defending the claim that, for Buridan, contrary to the common opinion of his contemporaries, the materiality of the senses is not the one responsible for making sense perception a cognition of singulars. In view of this, Klein engages with the present day scholarship on Buridan, and calls attention to the importance of distinguishing between epistemological and metaphysical questions. Such a distinction can prove crucial in understanding Buridan's own stance on cognition of singulars.

Acknowledgements

First, there was the workshop *Theories of Sense Perception in the 13th and 14th Centuries*, for which the Alexander von Humboldt Foundation and the Humboldt University of Berlin generously provided financial support. Dominik Perler was, right from the beginning, highly supportive of the whole project. His guidance was, as usual, invaluable and most welcome. In the preliminary stages of the workshop, Paolo Rubini's and Sonja Schierbaum's involvement was crucial and greatly appreciated. For stimulating very lively debates while chairing the workshop sessions, Han Thomas Adriaenssen, Sonja Schierbaum, Stephan Schmid, and Anna Tropia deserve a huge thank-you. Julia Teske, Carolin Finkemeyer, and Claudio Mazzocchi made sure everything ran, administratively and organizationally, as smoothly as possible.

Now, there is a collected volume. As editor, I am deeply indebted to all the contributors for their professionalism, which made my job easy and enjoyable. Without the constant help and encouragement of John Marenbon the volume would have not seen the light of day. My deepest gratitude goes to him for not losing confidence in this editorial project and for raising my morale when I had no idea I needed it. Marcella Mulder, Nidha Jeddy, and the Brill team helped making the transition from project to product that much easier. Special thanks go to Hannes-Ole Matthiessen, for stepping in at the right moment, and to Sergiu Sava, who offered endless support and assistance.

Bibliography

Adriaenssen, Han Thomas, "Peter John Olivi on Perceptual Representation," *Vivarium*, vol. 49, no. 4, 2011, pp. 324–352.

Adriaenssen, Han Thomas, *Representation and Scepticism from Aquinas to Descartes*, Cambridge, Cambridge University Press, 2017.

Burnett, Charles, Fend, Michael, and Gouk, Penelope (eds), *The Second Sense: Studies in Hearing and Musical Judgement from Antiquity to the Seventeenth Century*, London, The Warburg Institute, 1991.

Knuuttila, Simo and Kärkkäinen, Pekka (eds), *Theories of Perception in Medieval and Modern Philosophy*, Dordrecht, Springer, 2008.

Pasnau, Robert, *Theories of Cognition in the Later Middle Ages*, Cambridge, Cambridge University Press, 1997.

Perler, Dominik, "The Alienation Effect in the Historiography of Philosophy," in M. van Ackeren and L. Klein (ed), *Philosophy and the Historical Perspective*, Oxford, Oxford University Press, 2018, pp. 140–154.

Perler, Dominik, *Theorien der Intentionalität im Mittelalter*, Frankfurt am Main, Vittorio Klostermann, 2002.

Silva, José Filipe and Toivanen, Juhana, "The Active Nature of the Soul in Sense Perception: Robert Kilwardby and Peter Olivi," *Vivarium*, vol. 48, no. 3–4, 2010, pp. 245–278.

Silva, José Filipe and Yrjönsuuri, Mikko (eds), *Active Perception in the History of Philosophy: From Plato to Modern Philosophy*, Dordrecht, Springer, 2014.

Spruit, Leen, *Species intelligibilis: From Perception to Knowledge*, vol. I: *Classical Roots and Medieval Discussions*, Leiden, Brill, 1994.

CHAPTER 2

Perceiving As: Non-conceptual Forms of Perception in Medieval Philosophy

Juhana Toivanen

1   Introduction

Sense perception primarily conveys information about the sensible qualities of external objects; we see colours, hear sounds, taste flavours, and so forth – at least if we accept a (naïve) realist conception of perception. Yet, our experience of the external world contains several elements that cannot be reduced to these qualities. To name but a few, external objects are perceived as three-dimensional things that exist in time, as synthetic wholes that are composed of many different sensible properties, as useful or harmful for the perceiving subject, and as objects of desires, fears, and other emotions, and they are conceptualised in various ways – in short, they are perceived *as* something.

The aim of the present chapter is to take a closer look at medieval discussions concerning the phenomenon of 'perceiving as,' and the psychological mechanisms that lie behind it. In contemporary philosophical literature this notion is usually used to refer to *conceptual* aspects of perception. For instance, when I perceive a black birdlike shape as a crow, I may be said to perceive the particular sensible thing x as an instance of a universal crowness φ, that is, as belonging to a natural kind and falling under the concept of 'crow'. In this sense, perceiving x as φ requires mastering the concept φ.[1] However, I use the term 'perceiving as' in a wider sense and concentrate on various kinds of non-conceptual sensory processes, which can be understood as forms of 'perceiving as'.[2] Even though conceptual perception requires intellectual powers, medieval discussions on cognitive psychology can be understood properly only by taking into account the complex forms of perception that fall short of being truly

---

1   This conception of 'perceiving as' has been applied also to medieval theories. For instance, E. Stump has argued that Aquinas' theory of cognition contains a distinction between seeing and seeing as, and that the latter is possible only because the intellect penetrates sensory cognition (E. Stump, *Aquinas*, London, Routledge, 2003, pp. 260–262).

2   Thus, the role of rationality in perception is set aside here, but this is just a methodological decision. The models for analysing medieval views, which are suggested below, can be applied to conceptual perception as well.

© KONINKLIJKE BRILL NV, LEIDEN, 2020 | DOI:10.1163/9789004413030_003

PERCEIVING AS: NON-CONCEPTUAL FORMS OF PERCEPTION

intellectual, but are nevertheless over and above the simple sensation of sensible qualities of external things. The borderline between simple sensation and conceptual perception is unclear, and quite a lot is going on in the grey area between the two. Instead of presupposing any modern notion of 'perceiving as' and applying it to medieval discussions, my purpose is the opposite: to look at medieval discussions and see if they can be used to broaden modern discussions by including also non-conceptual varieties of perception.[3]

I shall begin the analysis in section two by specifying various types of cognitive processes that were discussed by medieval authors and can be considered as forms of 'perceiving as'. The bulk of the historical work will be done in section three, where I focus on medieval discussions on three interrelated cognitive functions – perceiving different sensible qualities as a synthetic whole, incidental perception of one sensible quality through another, and the possibility of perceiving substances and recognising individuals. The reader should bear in mind that I shall use ideas from several medieval authors without paying much attention to the differences between their theories of perception. Although occasionally radical, these differences are not highly relevant in the context of the present chapter. In section four, I propose two theoretical models that can be used for analysing medieval views concerning these psychological phenomena. Finally, I conclude the chapter by making some remarks on the potential impacts of reading medieval views in relation to the concept of 'perceiving as'.

2   Varieties of Perceiving As

Medieval authors discussed various kinds of psychological processes that together provide a complex perceptual experience. This was done in the context of faculty psychology in which the so-called internal senses played a central role. The number of internal senses and the details of their functions varied from author to author, but the basic principle remained rather stable – each more or less well-defined psychological function was attributed to a distinct power of the soul. Just like the five external senses are distinct powers that have their proper functions, and one may lose one of them without losing others (there are animals that lack sight but are able to hear), the sensory soul

---

3 It goes without saying that in contemporary discussions this aspect of perception is approached from various perspectives. One may begin with W. Wright, "Nonconceptual Content," in M. Matthen (ed), *The Oxford Handbook of Philosophy of Perception*, Oxford, Oxford University Press, 2015, pp. 181–197.

12 TOIVANEN

includes higher cognitive powers that are in this sense independent of each other.[4]

If we look at the various functions that medieval authors attributed to the internal senses, we can find at least six different cases in which a simple perception of a sensory quality turns into a more complex perceptual experience that can be called 'perceiving as':

(1) Perceiving several sensible qualities as forming a synthetic whole.
(2) Incidental perception of one sensible quality through another.
(3) Perceiving a certain individual.
(4) Perceiving something as harmful or useful.
(5) Perceiving temporal succession.
(6) Perceiving three-dimensionality.

These cases originate mostly in Aristotle and Avicenna, and they were widely discussed in the Latin tradition. Modern scholarship has concentrated especially on case (4), which is the main function of the so called estimative power: when one perceives an external object, the estimative power apprehends its relevance to the perceiving subject, and this explains the behaviour of the subject. Usually, this process was accounted for by appealing to insensible affective qualities, the so-called intentions (*intentiones*), that enter the cognitive apparatus of the subject together with the perceptual qualities of the object, even though they cannot be directly perceived.[5] However, there were also philosophers who argued that intentions are not insensible properties of objects but rather are estimative judgements that affect the way external objects are perceived.[6] Further, perception of temporal succession (case 5) was discussed

---

4   In the following, I shall presume that the reader is familiar with the general aspects of medieval theories of the internal senses. The literature on them is voluminous; see, e.g. N.H. Steneck, "The Problem of the Internal Senses in the Fourteenth Century," PhD dissertation, Ann Arbor, Michigan, UMI, 1970; D.N. Hasse, *Avicenna's "De anima" in the Latin West: The Formation of a Peripatetic Philosophy of the Soul, 1160–1300*, London, The Warburg Institute, 2000; C. Di Martino, *Ratio particularis: Doctrines des senses internes d'Avicenne à Thomas d'Aquin*, Paris, Vrin, 2008.

5   See, e.g., Thomas Aquinas, *Summa Theologiae*, P. Caramello (ed), Turin, Marietti, 1948–1950, 1.78.4; Thomas Aquinas, *Quaestiones disputatae de anima*, B.C. Bazán (ed), *Opera omnia 24*, Rome, Commissio Leonina, 1996, q. 13; Di Martino, *Ratio particularis*, pp. 85–101; D. Perler, "Why Is the Sheep Afraid of the Wolf? Medieval Debates on Animal Passions," in M. Pickavé and L. Shapiro (eds), *Emotion and Cognitive Life in Medieval and Early Modern Philosophy*, Oxford, Oxford University Press, 2012, pp. 32–51.

6   Alexander of Hales, *Summa Theologica*, vol. 2, Quaracchi, Collegium S. Bonaventurae, 1928, 1.2, q. 2, 436a; 438b; Peter John Olivi, *Quaestiones in secundum librum Sententiarum*, B. Jansen (ed), Firenze, Collegium S. Bonaventurae, 1922 (hereafter *Summa II*), q. 64, 602–607. For a

PERCEIVING AS: NON-CONCEPTUAL FORMS OF PERCEPTION

in relation to Avicenna's examples of a raindrop appearing as a line as it falls from the sky and of a circle of fire that appears when a torch is whirled quickly around. Instead of seeing a series of still images of the raindrop and the torch, we see a line and a circle, and yet the external world does not contain the line and the circle.[7] Likewise, although the external world is three-dimensional (case 6), that aspect is not immediately present to the sense of sight. In principle, the world is seen as two-dimensional because both eyes receive a two-dimensional image of it. Three-dimensionality becomes a part of our perception only because the cognitive apparatus interprets these images in a certain way.[8] The most radical example of this interpretative activity is familiar to anyone who has ever been to an art museum. Paintings are two-dimensional flat surfaces but they are perceived as if they contained three-dimensional objects. Three-dimensionality is added to bare perception because we have learned that the real things that are represented in a painting are three-dimensional.[9] These three cases can be considered as more complex ways of perceiving external sensible qualities, which are brought about by psychological processes in which the soul actively structures perceptual content by adding new elements to it.[10]

Although these three cases are highly interesting, I am not going to analyse them further in this context. Instead, I focus on the first three cases in the list, which pertain to perception of sensible qualities and an individual substance that is the bearer of these qualities. These three cases have in common that they all are more or less complex ways of apprehending the real properties of external things. It seems at the outset that they do not involve any additional input from the soul, and that the cognitive apparatus does not need to actively

---

discussion on Olivi, see Juhana Toivanen, *Perception and the Internal Senses: Peter of John Olivi on the Cognitive Functions of the Sensitive Soul*, Leiden, Brill, 2013, pp. 327–339.

7 Avicenna, *Liber de anima seu Sextus de naturalibus*, S. van Riet (ed), vol. IV–V, Leiden, Brill, 1968, 1.5, 88–89. For a discussion, see J. Kaukua, "Avicenna on the Soul's Activity in Perception," in J.F. Silva and M. Yrjönsuuri (eds), *Active Perception in the History of Philosophy: From Plato to Modern Philosophy*, Dordrecht, Springer, 2014, pp. 99–116. In addition, medieval philosophers discussed perception of time in relation to *De sensu* 7, 448a19–30. See, e.g., Thomas Aquinas, *Sentencia libri De sensu et sensato, Opera omnia* 45.2, Rome, Commissio Leonina, 1985, 1.17, 94a.

8 For a discussion concerning different historical models, see M. Yrjönsuuri, "Seeing Distance," in J.F. Silva and M. Yrjönsuuri (eds), *Active Perception*, pp. 187–206.

9 This example is presented in Olivi, *Summa II*, q. 73, 99. To be sure, it is not completely clear that seeing a painting and seeing the world as three-dimensional are based on the same mechanism.

10 It would be tempting to say that these ideas resemble the Kantian approach, but there is at least one crucial difference; while medieval authors acknowledged that the soul structures the perceptual content, they argued that it only grasps the world as it is in reality.

structure the perceptual experience in relation to them. However, a closer look reveals that this initial impression is not altogether correct.

These cases can be considered as forms of non-conceptual 'perceiving as' (or so I claim), but it is far from clear that medieval philosophers consider them as such. Each of them was understood as resulting from a *different* psychological mechanism than the other two, and this raises the question of whether they can be treated as instances of a psychological phenomenon that we call 'perceiving as' – especially because medieval authors did not use any single expression that could be identified with any modern notion of 'perceiving as'. It would be anachronistic to apply modern conceptions to different psychological processes in medieval psychology by using the sole criterion that these processes seem to fit what we are looking for.

There are two remarks that I want to make in relation to this methodological concern. First, I am not claiming that medieval authors would have considered these cases as instances of a single psychological phenomenon. Instead, by looking at medieval discussions on the psychological functions of the internal senses, we might find some insights that help us to rethink the modern notion of 'perceiving as'. After all, the modern notion is not unified and well defined either, and there is some room for developing it with the help of historical views as long as we distinguish our interpretations clearly from what medieval authors wrote and meant. This kind of rethinking does not presuppose any strong unity of the psychological functions that figure in medieval theories. Second, for reasons that will become clear below, it seems to me that the different kinds of psychological processes listed above *do* have a sort of unity, which makes it reasonable to consider them together. Namely, they are all processes that modify and enrich our perceptual experience of the external world. If we suppose (at this point simply for the sake of argument) that there is a unified perceptual experience that emerges from the joint action of different powers, the ways in which this experience is modified have the intended kind of unity, even if a detailed analysis shows that there are significant differences in the psychological and physiological mechanisms that brings it about.

3 Perceiving Sensible Qualities and Individual Substances

3.1 *Synthetic Wholes*
Let us now turn to the psychological processes that enrich the perceptual experience. As I already mentioned, each of the five external senses has its proper object, the sensible qualities of colour, sound, flavour, and so forth. When I see a crow, I see directly a black colour in a certain shape, nothing else.

PERCEIVING AS: NON-CONCEPTUAL FORMS OF PERCEPTION

However, if the crow happens to be cawing, I also hear its voice. These two proper sensibles are connected in my experience in such a way that I perceive a black thing that is cawing. (Or to be exact, I perceive this-black that makes this-cawing-sound; whether or not I perceive the substance behind these accidental qualities is another matter.)[11]

In the framework of faculty psychology, the unified experience of different sensory qualities requires an explanation. Colours cannot be heard and sounds cannot be seen, and thus there has to be some single power that apprehends both. Medieval philosophers answered to this problem – known today as 'the binding problem' – by attributing the unifying function to the common sense.[12] The information from the external senses is transmitted to the common sense, which functions as a centre where a unified bundle of properties is formed:

> The proper sensibles are united in the common sense. For, if there was nothing in us where whiteness and sound were united, we would not know that the thing, the sound of which we hear, is white. The unity of whiteness and sound is apprehended neither by the eyes nor by the ears, but by the common sense.[13]

---

11   Aristotle's favourite example is the perception of white and sweet, and he focuses mainly on the ability to tell the difference between the two. Some medieval authors thought that the white and sweet substance in Aristotle's example is milk: "Likewise, they say that just as white and sweet in milk are the same in being and formally different, so is the common sense." "Item, sicut album et dulce in lacte sunt idem subiecto et differunt formaliter, sic dicunt de sensu communi." (Anonymous, *Quaestiones super librum De sensu et sensato*, Paris, BNF Ms. lat. 16160, q. 37, 118va.) In contrast, Albert the Great refers to sugar: "as white and sweet in sugar" "ut album et dulce in zuc[c]aro" (Albert the Great, *De homine*, H. Anzulewicz and J.R. Söder (eds), *Opera omnia* 27.2, Münster, Aschendorff, 2008, q. 35, a. 1, 269.) Although not widely available, sugar was known in medieval Europe. See S.W. Mintz, *Sweetness and Power: The Place of Sugar in Modern History*, New York, Penguin Books, 1986, pp. 19–32; E. Abbott, *Sugar: A Bittersweet History*, London, Duckworth Overlook, 2008, pp. 11–27. A recent study on Aristotle, which shows a similar preoccupation with the contents and structures of perceptual experience as the present essay, is A. Marmodoro, *Aristotle on Perceiving Objects*, Oxford, Oxford University Press, 2014.

12   See, e.g., Averroes, *Long Commentary on the "De Anima" of Aristotle*, trans. R.C. Taylor, New Haven, Yale University Press, 2009, 2.146, pp. 267–268.

13   "[...] sensus communis est, in quo coniunguntur sensata propria. Si enim nihil esset in nobis, in quo coniungerentur albedo et sonus, nesciremus hoc album esse, cuius sonum audivimus. Coniunctionem vero albedinis et soni non apprehendit oculus nec auris, sed sensus communis." (Albert the Great, *De homine*, q. 35, a. 2, 271.) For later discussions on this function, see H. Lagerlund, "Awareness and Unity of Conscious Experience: Buridan on the Common Sense," in G. Klima (ed), *Questions on the Soul by John Buridan and Others: A Companion to John Buridan's Philosophy of Mind*, Dordrecht, Springer, 2017,

At the outset, it might seem that this process cannot be considered as a type of 'perceiving as'. After all, there does not seem to be any additional information over and above the perception of colour and sound. Unifying them does not require classification or interpretation; we just perceive a colour and a sound in connection to each other.

However, a closer inspection shows that the process provides the perceiver with information that is not trivial. It is one thing to perceive two distinct qualities, colour and sound, and it is quite another to perceive them as forming a synthetic whole. The black colour is perceived as a part of the same bundle as the cawing sound and vice versa, and it is precisely the *connection* between the two qualities, the unity of the two, that can be considered as 'perceiving as'. The process that brings about this connection is a real addition, because the unity is not obvious. It is possible to imagine a subject that lacks the ability to perceive different qualities as connected to each other. Her perceptual experience would thus differ radically from normal perception.

The idea that different sensible qualities are perceived as unified synthetic wholes suggests that perception is structured from the very beginning. We perceive the world as divided into separate objects and individual substances. This is to be expected on the basis of medieval acceptance of the idea that the world *is* divided into individual substances. The black colour and the cawing belong to one and the same substance, the crow, and they form a unity in our experience because that unity is a part of reality. However, the five external senses perceive the sensible qualities of these substances separately – in a way, the cognitive apparatus starts by dismantling particular objects into different kinds of accidental qualities. One would expect medieval authors to offer a philosophical explanation for the consequent re-assembly into structured substances or synthetic wholes, which include those properties that belong to a certain substance and exclude all the others. When I have the visual-auditory experience of the crow, I perceive a black cawing thing, but I do not attribute to it any other sensory qualities, such as the fresh smell of the forest, or the gentle feeling of raindrops on my skin. I can perceive these qualities simultaneously with the colour and sound of the crow, but they do not become associated with the crow.

To the best of my knowledge, medieval philosophers do not give an explanation for this bundling of properties; or they do, but only by explaining *how* the originally unified whole is assembled again in the cognitive apparatus. They

---

pp. 149–156; J. Toivanen, "Peter Olivi on Internal Senses," *British Journal for the History of Philosophy*, vol. 15, no. 3, 2007, pp. 427–454.

PERCEIVING AS: NON-CONCEPTUAL FORMS OF PERCEPTION

fail to explain *why* all of the properties of a certain substance, and only those, are united in our experience. The reason for their neglect may be the underlying realistic conception of the relation between the world and our perception of it. The sensory qualities of the crow belong to one substance in reality, and therefore the fact that they appear to us as a unified whole is only natural.[14] To be sure, this does not explain why they merge in the psychological apparatus; it just explains why medieval authors did not raise the question.

In this respect, it is notable that when medieval philosophers analyse perception, they usually do not think of a process by which we come to apprehend the whole surrounding world; they have a tendency to consider the perception of *objects*, not that of a *visual field*. This approach sets the problem aside because the focus is not on the simultaneous perception of qualities that belong to several objects. The ability to perceive several things simultaneously was discussed in relation to Aristotle's *De sensu*, but the fact that the question was raised shows that it was something of an anomaly for the general theory.[15]

The process in which the common sense bundles sensible qualities together is not infallible, however. The Aristotelian maxim states that external senses cannot err in their perceptions, but the more complex forms of sense perception are susceptible to error. For instance, Albert the Great argues that:

> However, in composing the sensibles, there is frequently a great deception: for instance, what the coloured thing is (whether a golden-yellow thing is honey or yellow bile); or where the coloured thing is; or what it is that makes a sound; or where it sounds; and so with the others. I will explain below that the reason for this is that the combining does not belong to external sense but to some higher power, which makes the mistake.[16]

---

14   When Albert the Great argues that two qualities must be perceived simultaneously, because they are simultaneously present in the object, he notes tersely that: "But the judgement is like the thing is." "Iudicium autem est secundum quod res est." (Albert the Great, *De anima*, C. Stroick (ed), *Opera omnia 7.1*, Münster, Aschendorff, 1968., 2.4.10, 162; see also n. 40 below.) Another possibility is that the *intentio* of the crow functions as a kind of a proto-concept that unifies the different sensible qualities together (see below).

15   See, e.g., Aquinas, *Sentencia libri De sensu*, 16–18, 90a–101b. Even some versions of extramissive theories were thought to hold that the base of a visual cone is one object, not the whole visual field (Albert the Great, *De sensu et sensato*, S. Donati (ed), *Opera omnia 7.2A*, Münster, Aschendorff, 2017, 1.5, 26b56–27a5).

16   "In compositione tamen sensibilium magna frequenter est deceptio, sicut *quid* est quod est *coloratum,* ut utrum croceum sit mel aut cholera citrina *aut ubi* est coloratum *aut quid est,* quod *sonat, aut ubi* sonat, et sic de aliis. Et causam *huius* infra *dicemus* esse quoniam sensus *proprius* non habet componere, sed aliqua superior potentia, et illius est error." (Albert the Great, *De anima*, 2.3.5, 103.)

Most of these mistakes are related to the so-called common sensibles and incidental perception (see below), but not all. The "what it is that makes a sound" clearly stands for the ability to connect a certain sound with other sensible qualities that are perceived at the same moment – the connection between the cawing and the black colour, for instance. Albert admits here that the unifying function of the common sense often fails to make veridical bundles of the accidental qualities of objects. The possibility of error underlines that the process adds something to the simple perception of distinct sensible qualities. Perceiving black colour as a colour of a thing that also makes a cawing sound is a process that enriches the perceptual experience in a significant and non-trivial way. Occasionally this aspect fails or is missing, and the resulting experience is radically different in comparison to cases where it is present. It is therefore clear that the unity that the common sense brings to perception is a real addition to, or modification of, the simple perception of singular qualities, and as such it can be called 'perceiving as' in a broad (non-conceptual) sense. It introduces structure into perceptual experience by allowing the perception of two qualities as belonging to the same synthetic whole.

3.2   *Incidental Perception*

A closely related type of non-conceptual 'perceiving as' is what medieval philosophers called accidental perception (incidental perception in modern parlance). Aristotle's examples of this process include perceiving bile as bitter without tasting it and perceiving bile as honey due to the similarity of their colours. Avicenna elaborates on these examples, and Latin authors by and large follow his view.[17] The central idea in the example is that when we perceive one sensible quality (yellow), we often apprehend it in such a way that a sensible quality of some other sense modality (sweet taste) figures in our perceptual experience, even if we do not taste sweetness at the moment. In the words of John of la Rochelle:

> Note, therefore that there are per se sensible and accidentally sensible things. The accidentally sensible things are when an object of one sense is said to be perceived by another, as when it is said that sweetness of an apple is seen. This is accidental perception, because the sweetness is an

---

17   Aristotle, *De anima, The Complete Works of Aristotle*, 2 vols., trans. J. Barnes, Princeton, Princeton University Press, 1984, 3.1, 425a30–b4; *Sophistical Refutations, The Complete Works of Aristotle*, 5, 167b4–5; Avicenna, *Liber de anima* 4.1, 7–8. For a recent analysis of Avicenna's position, see Kaukua, "Avicenna on the Soul's Activity in Perception," pp. 99–116.

object of the sense of taste. It is said to be seen accidentally, that is, through another (namely, through the red colour of the apple); the sweetness is perceived per se and properly only by the sense of taste.[18]

The result of this process can be considered to be a form of 'perceiving as'. When we see a red apple or a jar full of yellow substance, we see nothing but a colour that has a certain shape. But if incidental perception takes place, we see the red as having the taste of an apple and the yellow colour as sweet (if we see it as honey) or as bitter and repulsive (if we see it as yellow bile).

Now, one might have a problem with the idea that the taste of honey is *seen*. It would be more precise to say that when the colour of honey is seen, the perceiver becomes aware of a synthetic whole that also includes other sensible qualities of honey. Supposedly the experience is not similar to actually tasting honey, but closer to imagining sweetness. After all, the sensible qualities are stored in the imaginative power, and they are evoked from there when the yellow colour of honey is seen. Medieval authors clearly accepted the idea that some kind of cognition (or awareness) of sweetness takes place, and they were usually happy to say that the taste is seen, but probably this was just a way to emphasise that the incidental seeing of sweetness is distinct from imagining sweetness.

Incidental perception is a part of perceptual experience. By this I mean that when medieval authors say things like "we say that we see bitter when we see yellow,"[19] they are not referring just to an objective fact (i.e., that the yellow thing we see happens to be bitter), but also and perhaps mainly to a subjective experience – bitterness figures in our experience. Although this is not always made explicit, many texts leave little room for doubt. For instance, Albert the Great continues soon after the previous quotation by referring to a subjective experience: "often when one grasps yellow, one thinks that it is bitter."[20] Moreover, the process takes place on the sensory level and does not involve intellectual powers. It is a non-conceptual form of 'perceiving as'. The yellow

---

18 "Nota ergo quod est sensibile per se et sensibile per accidens. Sensibile per accidens est, cum obiectum unius sensus dicitur percipi ab alio, ut dulce in pomo cum dicitur uideri. Iam hoc est per accidens, quia dulce est obiectum gustus. Dicitur tamen uideri per accidens, id est per aliud, scilicet per colorem coccineum pomi; per se tamen et proprie dulce non percipitur nisi gustu." (John of la Rochelle, *Summa de anima*, J.G. Bougerol (ed), Paris, Vrin, 1995, 2.94, 236–237.)

19 "[...] dicimus nos videre amarum, quando videmus citrinum [...]." (Albert the Great, *De anima*, 2.4.6, 156.)

20 "[...] saepe cum accipit citrinum hoc ipsum putat esse amarum." (Albert the Great, *De anima*, 2.4.6, 156.)

substance does not need to be conceptualised as honey, and one does not need to have a propositional belief that it is honey in order to perceive it as sweet, because these would require mastering the concept of honey, knowing the essence of honey, and so forth. Thomas Aquinas famously argues that there is a radical difference between the way rational human beings and irrational animals perceive the world around them.[21] Only human beings have a cogitative power, which enables apprehending things "as existing under a common nature," because this power has an intrinsic connection to the intellect. Supposedly Aquinas means that humans can perceive individual things as members of natural kinds and as instances of universals. Thus, conceptualising and classifying the perceived yellow thing as honey requires rationality, but the incidental perception of honey as sweet does not.[22]

This point can also be seen in the following argument, which Dominicus Gundissalinus copies almost verbatim from Avicenna's *Liber de anima*:

> If these <qualities> were not connected in the imagination of animals (which lack the intellectual power), they would not desire to eat a thing which has a certain shape and is sweet when they see it, although they are inclined by their own desire to sweetness. [...] Likewise, if animals did not have a power where the forms of perceptible things are connected, it would be difficult for them to live – namely, if smelling did not reveal taste, and if sound did not reveal taste, and if the form of a stick did not remind of a form of pain so that one flees from it. There is no doubt,

---

21 Thomas Aquinas, *Sentencia libri De anima*, *Opera omnia 45.1*, Rome, Commissio Leonina, 1984, hereafter *Sent. DA*, 2.13, 121b–122b. A useful discussion and references can be found in A. Oelze, *Animal Rationality: Later Medieval Theories 1250–1350*, Leiden, Brill, 2018, pp. 57–69. Robert Pasnau writes that: "Whereas we perceive a world full of familiar kinds of objects, animals must lack this level of conceptualization. They see objects, perhaps, but do not see them as members of kinds." (R. Pasnau, *Thomas Aquinas on Human Nature: A Philosophical Study of "Summa Theologiae" Ia 75–89*, Cambridge, Cambridge University Press, 2002, p. 271.) See also A.J. Lisska, *Aquinas's Theory of Perception: An Analytic Reconstruction*, Oxford, Oxford University Press, 2016, pp. 249–254.

22 Aquinas thinks that incidental perception, properly speaking, applies only to properties that are imperceptible by themselves. He is stricter than many others, who claim that we may speak of incidental perception also in cases where one of the sensible qualities is not perceived directly at the moment. See *Sent. DA*, 13, 120b–121a; Lisska, *Aquinas's Theory of Perception*, pp. 239–242. Two different kinds of incidental perception: see, e.g., Albert the Great, *De anima*, 2.4.6, 155; Averroes, *Long Commentary on the "De Anima,"* 2.134, 255–256.

therefore, that these forms must have some one internal thing where they are connected.[23]

Gundissalinus clarifies that the power that provides the required unity is the common sense.[24] The basic idea of his argument is that animals desire to eat sweet things, and the perception of sweetness explains why they pursue certain objects around them. A desire for a certain thing arises only if it is perceived as sweet. We can easily observe that animals often seek things that they are not tasting at the moment. This proves that they are capable of perceiving distant objects as sweet – they incidentally perceive sweetness when they see something that is suitable for their nourishment. Because animals lack reason, however, the process cannot be a rational one.

If the yellow substance is not categorised as honey, what kind of perceptual content does incidental perception bring about? If perception does not include any recognition of *what* the yellow thing is, how does it evoke the perception of sweetness? One possibility is that non-conceptual perception of yellow as sweet is based on association. A perception of yellow stuff just happens to evoke the form of sweetness in the imaginative power, and no further explanation can be given. Another possibility is that the imaginative power does not store isolated sensible qualities but bundles of several qualities; after all, it was considered to be the storehouse for the representations that the common sense brings about, and unifying different sense modalities was one of the functions of the common sense. The process would still be associative, but one that can be explained by earlier experiences. When one sees *and* tastes honey, the two qualities are unified in the common sense and then stored in the

---

23 "Si enim non coniungerentur in imaginatione animalium quae carent intellectu, cum inclinarentur proprio desiderio ad dulcedinem, scilicet quod res quae est huiusmodi formae est dulcis, cum viderent eam non appeterent eam ad comedendum. [...] Item, si non esset in animalibus virtus in qua coniungerentur formae sensatorum, difficile esset eis vivere, scilicet si olfactus non ostenderet saporem et si sonus non ostenderet saporem et si forma baculi non rememoraret formam doloris ita ut fugiatur ab eo. Oportet igitur sine dubio ut formae istae habeant unum aliquid in quo coniungantur intrinsecus." (Dominicus Gundissalinus, *Tractatus de anima*, J.T. Muckle (ed), "The Treatise *De Anima* of Dominicus Gundissalinus," *Mediaeval Studies*, vol. 2, 1940, c. 9, 72. The passage is taken from Avicenna, *Liber de anima* 5.1, 2–3.)

24 He argues that the imaginative power is nothing but a storehouse of sensory forms, and it does not provide any awareness of its contents. See Gundissalinus, *Tractatus de anima*, c. 9, 72–73. There is a considerable fluctuation concerning the attribution of incidental perception to one of the internal senses. The common sense, imagination, estimative power, and cogitative power all have their defenders.

imagination together. Subsequent perception of one of these qualities evokes the complex representation, including the other qualities.

However, there are many yellow things that are not apprehended as sweet, and they do not evoke the incidental perception of sweetness. It seems likely that dissimilar reactions towards different yellow things might be explained simply by appealing to differences in visible qualities of yellow things. If the visible qualities of the representation of honey, which is stored in the imagination, differ from the visible qualities of other representations, the explanation for different reactions upon seeing different yellow things is at hand.

Medieval authors do not take this route, however, probably because they acknowledge that incidental perception can be mistaken.[25] Sometimes the very same yellow substance is apprehended as sweet, sometimes as bitter. This suggests that there is a third option; the yellow substance needs to be recognised as honey before sweetness is attributed to it. It has been suggested that Avicenna's theory presupposes that the process is inferential in this sense. The yellow substance is seen as sweet, *because it is seen as honey*.[26] The estimative power "recognises" the yellow substance as what it is – as a substance that is both yellow and sweet – and the incidental perception of sweetness arises on the basis of this recognition. The *intentio* of honey functions as a "proto-concept" that holds different sensible qualities together in one representation and triggers the incidental perception of sweetness. The *intentio* in this case is not an insensible affective quality on par with harmfulness or usefulness. Instead, it is some kind of non-conceptual representation that functions as the basis for unifying different sensible qualities into a synthetic whole.[27]

Given that this process takes place at the sensory level and can be attributed to non-human animals, it must be non-conceptual (or perhaps pre- or

---

25 See, e.g., Albert the Great, *De anima*, 2.4.6, 156.

26 Kaukua, "Avicenna on the Soul's Activity in Perception," pp. 106–111.

27 Albert the Great uses the term *intentio* precisely in the sense that it signifies the individual thing as such. See Albert the Great, *De anima*, 2.3.4, 102; J.A. Tellkamp, "Albert the Great on Structure and Function of the Inner Senses," in R.C. Taylor and A.O. Irfan (eds), *The Judeo-Christian-Islamic Heritage: Philosophical and Theological Perspectives*, Milwaukee, Marquette University Press, 2012, pp. 316–318; Tellkamp, "Aping Logic? Albert the Great on Animal Mind and Action," in J. Kaukua and T. Ekenberg (eds), *Subjectivity and Selfhood in Medieval and Early Modern Philosophy*, Dordrecht, Springer, 2016, pp. 119–120. Medieval philosophers argued that memory preserves *intentiones* apprehended by the estimative power. At the same time, memory was thought to remember, for instance, what a certain person did in a certain place at certain time, which suggests that *intentiones* represent something more than just affective features such as harmfulness. See John of la Rochelle, *Tractatus de divisione multiplici potentiarum animae*, P. Michaud-Quantin (ed), Paris, Vrin, 1964, 2.10, pp. 76–77.

PERCEIVING AS: NON-CONCEPTUAL FORMS OF PERCEPTION 23

proto-conceptual) in the sense, to use Aquinas' expression, that it does not enable perceiving the individual object under a common nature. However, the psychological mechanism that underlies this experience requires recognising "this-yellow-stuff-that-is-sweet." It is difficult to see how else the incidental perception of sweetness could come about, especially in those cases in which the same sensible quality may be connected to different incidentally apprehended qualities.[28]

It is not easy to grasp how this apprehension falls short of conceptualisation, because medieval authors do not address the issue in so many words. However, the distinction between conceptual apprehension of honey as honey, and the perceptual process of perceiving honey as this-foul-tasting-stuff, was occasionally taken up. Gundissalinus claims, following Avicenna, that:

> The estimation is the more excellent judge in animals. It judges according to the invention of the imagination when it is not certain, just like when a human being thinks that honey is foul because it is similar to excrement. For, the estimation judges that it is so, and the soul follows the estimation even though the intellect disapproves.[29]

It is not altogether clear how this argument should be interpreted, especially the idea that "the intellect disapproves." Probably the point is that although the intellect does not approve the shunning from the yellow stuff, the person (or her *anima*) follows the estimative judgement to shun from it. In other words, there is a conflict between an intellectual consideration of what should be done, and an emotional reaction of the sensory part of the soul.[30] Animals do not have any higher power to guide them, and therefore they necessarily follow estimative judgement, and some humans are similar to animals in this respect because they

---

28   Gundissalinus, again following Avicenna to the letter, distinguishes two kinds of intentions – ones that are insensible by their nature (e.g., harmfulness) and others that are sensible but not actually sensed at the moment. The latter are responsible for incidental perception. See Dominicus Gundissalinus, *Tractatus de anima*, c. 9, 73. Given that sweetness is not the kind of object that the estimative power apprehends, it seems that the role of estimation is to recognise the yellow substance as honey (this point is made in Kaukua, "Avicenna on the Soul's Activity in Perception," pp. 108–109).

29   "Dicimus ergo quia aestimatio excellentior iudex est in animalibus quae iudicat ad modum adinventae imaginationis, cum non est certa sicut cum putat homo mel sordidum quia simile est stercori. Aestimatio enim iudicat ita esse et anima sequitur ipsam aestimationem quamvis intellectus improbet." (Dominicus Gundissalinus, *Tractatus de anima*, c. 9, 77.)

30   *Improbo* has connotations to moral judgement, but also "to overrule an opinion or judgement."

do not follow their reason.[31] The crucial aspect of this argument is that the repulsion does not disappear even if one *knows* that the yellow substance is honey, and the conflict is also between perceptual judgement and an intellectual belief.[32] The intellect has to make a cognitive judgement that the substance is honey, not excrement, because otherwise it would not question the judgement of the estimation. The repulsion remains, and thus the intellectual judgement that the yellow substance is honey does not overrule the non-conceptual misjudgement, the "recognition" of this-yellow-stuff-that-is-repulsive. If there were no intellectual judgement ("In fact, this is honey"), or if the intellectual judgement overruled the estimative judgement, the conflict would not arise. Whether the perceptual judgement is based on a proto-conceptual recognition of this-yellow-stuff that is excrement and foul (or bile and bitter), or just on the association between the sensible qualities of yellow and bitter, the fact remains that the level of perception is not directly affected by intellectual conceptualisation. Knowledge that the yellow substance is honey does not remove the repulsiveness. One still *perceives* it as repulsive excrement.[33]

If this is on the right track, we can see that conceptualisation works on a different level and does not necessarily influence the perceptual content.[34] Perception is not false in the sense that a yellow substance would be seen as something that it is not. It is seen as yellow. The mistake arises either when the imagination spontaneously evokes the incidental perception of bitterness (or some other foul taste), or when the estimation judges that the substance is bile and causes the incidental perception of bitterness. The details of the process are unclear – that is, whether there is a need for "recognising" honey as this-yellow-sweet-substance, or whether incidental perception is associative and therefore more or less arbitrary. At least in the case of those medieval authors who emphasise the role of the estimative power when they describe the process, it seems likely that something more is at stake than simple association of various sensible qualities in the imagination.[35] However, even attributing a

---

31   Dominicus Gundissalinus, *Tractatus de anima*, c. 9, 77–78.

32   Avicenna has been interpreted along these lines. See Hasse, *Avicenna's "De anima" in the Latin West*, p. 137.

33   A more illustrative example concerns snakes: human beings tend to have what medieval authors would have called an estimative repulsion towards snakes. When someone sees a snake, he may *know* that the species to which it belongs is not dangerous. Although this knowledge may change the way he acts in the situation, it does not necessarily diminish the estimative repulsion and fear.

34   This seems to entail that the intellect should be understood in terms of the "addition-model": see section four below.

35   See, e.g., Dominicus Gundissalinus, *Tractatus de anima*, c. 9, 73; John of la Rochelle, *Summa de anima*, 2.4.101, 248.; Albert the Great, *De anima*, 2.3.5, 104. For a discussion on Albert,

PERCEIVING AS: NON-CONCEPTUAL FORMS OF PERCEPTION 25

role to the estimative power does not prove that proto-conceptual recognition takes place, and one might just hope that medieval authors would have been more precise when they wrote about incidental perception. It goes almost without saying that they might have had different opinions on the matter, and it is likely that at least some of them did not even consider the issue in such a detailed manner.

3.3 Substances and Individuals

This leads us to the third type of 'perceiving as', namely perceiving one sensible quality or a synthetic whole of several qualities as a certain individual. Regardless of whether or not external objects need to be recognised as certain kinds of objects before incidentally perceiving the other qualities they possess, medieval authors occasionally discussed the ability to perceive substances as if "behind" the bundles of sensory qualities. They also acknowledged that even animals are capable of perceiving things as certain individuals – they have an ability to recognise *this particular* thing by their estimative powers. Let us briefly consider both of these.

Sense perception was thought to convey information only about the sensible (accidental) qualities of an external object. Substances, to which these qualities belong, cannot be perceived directly. I cannot *see* the crow because I see only its colour and shape. Already John Blund argues along these lines, but he also emphasises that substances can be perceived incidentally: "Qualities such as colours, tastes, heat, and cold are the proper sensibles of sensation. However, their subjects are not perceived through sensation *except by accident.*"[36] William of Auvergne defends a similar position. He emphasises that when we perceive the accidental qualities of external objects, we perceive the substance,[37] but he makes it clear that the apprehension of the substance behind the accidents requires rationality.[38] It is possible to perceive this

---

see D. Black, "Avicenna's 'Vague Individual' and Its Impact on Medieval Latin Philosophy," in R. Wisnovsky, F. Wallis, C. Fraenkel, and J.C. Fumo (eds), *Vehicles of Transmission, Translation, and Transformation in Medieval Textual Culture*, Turnhout, Brepols, 2011, pp. 259–292; Tellkamp, "Aping Logic?," pp. 109–122.

36 "Qualitates, ut colores, sapores, caliditates, frigiditates, sunt propria sensata sensus. Subiecta autem illarum non apprehenduntur sensu *nisi per accidens.* Quod ergo proprie et per se cadit in sensum est qualitas." (John Blund, *Tractatus de anima*, D.A. Callus and R.W. Hunt (eds), trans. M.W. Dunne, *Treatise on the Soul*, Oxford, Oxford University Press, 2013, pp. 124–125, emphasis mine.)

37 William of Auvergne, *De Anima*, F. Hotot (ed), *Opera omnia*, vol. 2, Paris, Andreas Pralard, 1674; reprint Frankfurt am Main, Minerva, 1963; William of Auvergne, *The Soul*, trans. R.J. Teske, Milwaukee, Marquette University Press, 2000.

38 William of Auvergne, *De Anima* 5.18, 143; 7.1, 203 (*The Soul*, 257; 424).

individual crow in addition to its sensible qualities, but apparently only if the intellect contributes to the cognitive process.

Perhaps the strongest support for the ability to perceive substances comes from Roger Bacon, who argues that:

> [...] the claim that substances are not perceived by sense is to be understood with reference to a particular sense and the common sense and imagination; but it can easily be perceived by the estimation, which, although it is not called a sense, belongs none the less to the sensitive soul.[39]

Bacon's motivation for attributing this ability to non-human animals is not altogether clear,[40] but the most important thing to note here is that those authors who emphasise the ability to apprehend the substance in one way or another seem to take seriously the common experience that we (and perhaps other animals) perceive *things*, not bundles of qualities. I see the crow and a cat sees this-black-*something*, instead of seeing only a black shape. Because simple perception pertains only to accidental qualities, the cognitive apparatus adds to the perception and turns it into a more complex experience, which might be called 'perceiving as'.

---

39   "Quod igitur dicitur quod substantie non sentiuntur a sensu intelligendum est quod a sensu particulari et communi et ymaginatione; sed bene potest sentiri ab estimatione, que, licet non dicatur sensus, est tamen pars anime sensitive." (Roger Bacon, *Perspectiva*, D.C. Lindberg (ed and trans.), *Roger Bacon and the Origins of "Perspectiva" in the Middle Ages: A Critical Edition and English Translation of Bacon's "Perspectiva,"* Oxford, Clarendon Press, 1996, 1.1.4, 14–15.)

40   It may be noted that Albert the Great occasionally claims that the perception of "the subject" in which various sensible properties are united is necessary in order to actually apprehend these properties as bundled together – and that this ability belongs to the common sense: "External senses grasp only proper sensibles, such as colour, sound, odour, or something else. But the common sense grasps the substance in which the proper sensibles are united, and thus it combines and distinguishes proper sensibles by saying that this white is sweet and this yellow is bitter like bile." "Acceptio autem sensus particularis non est nisi sensibilis proprii sicut coloris vel vocis vel odoris vel alicuius alterius. Acceptio autem sensus communis est subiecti, in quo uniuntur sensata propria, et ideo componit et dividit sensata propria dicens hoc album esse dulce et hoc croceum esse amarum sicut fel." (Albert the Great, *Physica, libri I–IV*, P. Hossfeld (ed), *Opera omnia 4.1*, Münster, Aschendorff, 1987, 1.1.6, 11.) Cf. "Sight does not provide awareness of colour only, but of a coloured thing; and the species of the coloured thing in sight is the species of the coloured thing *qua* coloured; and judgement is about the coloured thing *qua* coloured. And the same goes for other intentions, regardless of the level of abstraction in which they are grasped." "Non enim accipitur per visum notitia coloris tantum, sed colorati, et species eius in visu species est colorati, secundum quod coloratum est, et iudicium fit de colorato, secundum quod coloratum est. Et sic est de aliis intentionibus, in quocumque gradu abstractionis accipiantur." (Albert the Great, *De anima*, 2.3.4, 102.)

As for the recognition, there is an abundance of texts that deal with the ability to perceive individual things as individuals. It goes without saying that perception is always about individuals; only intellectual powers are capable of cognising universals. The crucial question is whether perception allows recognising *a certain individual* in distinction to others (of the same species). The Aristotelian idea that we are able to recognise individual human beings as sons and daughters of other individuals – perceiving something white as the son of Diares – is a prime example of this ability. One or several sensible qualities are perceived, and through these the person is recognised as a certain individual. Although recognition of a certain person was often thought to be an intellectual process,[41] or a sensory process that needs input from the reason, we find similar processes in non-human animals.

It may be an exaggeration to say that all thirteenth-century philosophers attributed the ability to perceive individuals to irrational beings, but there is no denying that it was widely accepted that animals can do this. The estimative power was thought to be responsible for apprehending harmfulness and usefulness and thus triggering emotional reactions that enable animals to avoid harms and acquire useful things. In addition, Latin authors repeatedly argued that the estimative power allows animals to recognise individuals. A sheep recognises its lamb and vice versa, a dog recognises its master, and so forth. The animal in the example changes, but the overall idea remains the same. In Albert's words: "[...] and a wolf would never feel compassion for its offspring, unless it cognized [1] that particular individual, and [2] that this individual is its offspring."[42] The wolf is able to distinguish its own cub from other things and also from other members of the same species, just by perceiving certain accidental qualities and by incidentally perceiving the substance behind them.[43]

The capacity to perceive substances is not necessary for being able to recognise an individual, however. Even if one perceives only bundles of properties, one might still be able to recognise one bundle and distinguish it from others. For instance, John Blund argues that animals can recognise individual things and distinguish them from other things, but because they lack reason, they cannot pass a conceptual judgement that the thing they are perceiving belongs to a certain class of things – they distinguish but do not discern.[44] Likewise, as mentioned above, Aquinas distinguishes human beings from other animals by claiming that only humans are capable of conceptual perception. Animals do

---

41 See, e.g., Averroes, *Long Commentary on the "De Anima,"* 2.134, 255–256.
42 "[...] nec unquam lupus miseretur nato suo, nisi habeat cognitionem et huius individui et quod hoc individuum est natus eius." (Albert the Great, *De anima*, 3.1.2, 167.)
43 See also Albert the Great, *De anima*, 2.3.5, 104.
44 John Blund, *Tractatus de anima*, 26.2, 226–228.

not perceive things in their surroundings as belonging to natural kinds because they do not grasp universal concepts that would enable recognising them as the things they are. Instead, they perceive external things as objects or causes of their actions or emotions.[45] This does not mean that animals would not be able to perceive other animals as somehow distinct individuals. The object of an emotion or action is not just any sensible quality, but a complex thing that usually consists of a certain set of sensible qualities and is not confused with the background or surrounding objects. Even if irrational animals were incapable of perceiving anything besides bundles of properties, as Aquinas seems to think,[46] they would nevertheless apprehend these bundles as individuals of a sort.

The two levels – perception of a certain individual as *this* individual and conceptualisation that is based on grasping the universal nature of the individual thing – are not exclusive in the sense that medieval authors would not have considered other kinds of perceptual processes that are related to recognition and classification. They discussed apprehension of the so-called "vague individual." When we (and in some cases animals) do not see a distant, say, human being well enough to recognise her, we nevertheless perceive in a vague way that she is a substance and an animal – supposing that she is moving.[47] The fact that medieval philosophers recognised various types of cognitive processes shows how easy it was for them to think that cognition forms a kind of a scale. Perception is never just an apprehension of an isolated sensible quality, or even a set of sensible qualities. It involves different kinds of more complex features that make the external world appear to us (and to animals) *as* something.

4   Two Heuristic Models

On the basis of the foregoing, it should be clear that we are not dealing with forms of perceiving something as conceptually classified. Rather, medieval discussions are about perceiving some sensible quality x in such a way that something else is apprehended alongside it. This "something else" can be another particular sensible quality, a particular substance, or any of the multiple conditions that characterise the x – such as movement, three-dimensionality, individuality, relevance to the well-being of the perceiver, and so forth. It is possible

---

45   Thomas Aquinas, *Sent. DA*, 2.13, 122.
46   Lisska, *Aquinas's Theory of Perception*, pp. 143–144, 243–249.
47   Black, "Avicenna's 'Vague Individual,'" pp. 259–292.

to make a formal description that applies to all these different types of 'perceiving as':

$$P(x) \text{ as } \varphi$$

This formulation means that some subject "perceives x as φ," where x is a sensible quality and φ is any of the possible additional things that are perceived along with x. It should be noted that although I have mostly left aside the cases in which the intellectual powers of the soul enrich the contents of perceptual experience, the formulation itself is neutral with respect to rationality. Conceptual perception is a special case in which the additional element φ is a universal, a natural kind, or something else that is added to perceptual content by the intellectual power. According to some authors, rationality may also be a condition for other kinds of φs – as, for instance, in perceiving individual substances – but the theoretical model is not affected by these differences.[48]

Usually the apprehension of different kinds of φs was attributed to different powers of the soul. Understood in this way, 'perceiving as' is a kind of an information processing model.[49] Information enters the soul in a rudimentary and fragmented form, and after the initial reception of raw information, various powers of the soul process it by either extracting further elements from it or by introducing new aspects. The common sense compiles a unified whole and hands it over to the imagination and the estimative power, which process the information further. This process continues until the intellect abstracts the universal essence of the thing.

There is another way to understand medieval theories, which might be called a "holistic model." Formally it might look something like this:

$$P(\varphi x)$$

This formulation spells things out differently than the previous one, and here the subject "perceives a φx" – a dangerous wolf, sweet yellow, or crow black.

These two models bear resemblance to what Matthew Boyle has called *additive* and *transformative* models of rationality in perception. According to the former, rationality adds a conceptual layer to perception, but perception itself

---

48 Aquinas' argument concerning animals' inability to perceive things as falling under a common nature is a case in point. On the need of rationality, see also Averroes, *Long Commentary on the "De Anima,"* 2.63, 176; 2.65, 178.

49 See, e.g., S. Kemp and G. Fletcher, "The Medieval Theory of the Inner Senses," *American Journal of Psychology*, vol. 106, no. 4, 1993, pp. 568–569.

remains non-conceptual – humans and animals perceive the world more or less in the same way, but humans can conceptualise what they see in addition to seeing it. In the transformative model, by contrast, rationality transforms perception completely, which means that perception is fundamentally different in rational and irrational animals.[50] A similar kind of distinction can be made in relation to different *perceptual* processes that are functions of the internal senses. The first model, $P(x)$ *as* φ, suggests that different powers of the soul do not directly change the other powers' way of operating, and that in principle the internal senses are independent elements that process information in their own ways.[51] In the holistic model, in contrast, perceptual acts are transformed on the very basic level by the presence of various φs from the other powers of the soul. Perceptual experience is either additive (internal senses either add or do not add elements to perception) or transformative (internal senses always affect the process).

The holistic model applies particularly well to theories that posit only one internal sense. I am thinking especially of Peter Olivi, who denies that we should postulate distinct powers to the soul in order to account for the various psychological functions that bring in additional φs at the sensory level. There is only one power, and it acts in different ways. For instance, estimation is nothing but a perception that is affected by a disposition (which can be either innate or learned). This view can be understood in such a way that there is no "pure" act of perception $P(x)$, which may or may not be accompanied by different φs. There is only a single act of perception, which already contains the additional elements that enrich it. Nothing has to be added to the initial perception in order to make it complex.[52]

It seems natural that reducing the powers of the soul entails moving from the first model to the second. However, it is not obvious that defenders of the plurality of the internal senses prefer the $P(x)$ *as* φ model. Faculty psychology can be seen as an analytic project that tries to make sense of a complex psychological experience that is a unified whole at the outset. In this case, the starting point is a phenomenologically unified experience that already contains all of the different φs. This experience can then be analysed according to its simplest

---

50 M. Boyle, "Additive Theories of Rationality: A Critique," *European Journal of Philosophy*, vol. 24, no. 3, 2016, pp. 527–555. E.g., John McDowell has defended the transformative model (J. McDowell, *Mind and World*, Cambridge, Harvard University Press, 1996, pp. 46–65). I am thankful to Dominik Perler for making me aware of Boyle's article.

51 One might think, for instance, that when Aquinas explicitly argues that rationality changes estimative into cogitative power and memory into reminiscence, his point is that none of the other internal senses are affected.

52 For Olivi's theory, see Toivanen, *Perception and the Internal Senses*, pp. 225–344.

PERCEIVING AS: NON-CONCEPTUAL FORMS OF PERCEPTION 31

constituents, which are attributed to different powers of the soul. Understood in this way, the methodological approach of faculty psychology is not that of an information-processing model, and the division of the powers of the soul is not meant to indicate that perceptual experience is somehow divided into components that may or may not be present. To use Aristotle's famous illustration, the intellectual soul contains the sensory soul just like a square contains a triangle. The triangle *is* there, but one can find it only by doing some analytic work. Faculty psychology can be seen in a similar light. A unified perceptual experience contains all the φs, but they can be singled out and distinguished from the experience only through a philosophical analysis.[53]

Some medieval authors flirted with this kind of view. For instance, when Alexander of Hales discusses the relation between the external senses and the common sense, he makes the following remark:

> Moreover, it is shown that the external senses are perfected by the common sense. Namely, because the organs of the external senses are divided into two parts [...] (as in two eyes and two ears), and yet the sense object does not appear to be two but one, it is then necessary to bring it to one internal organ. Since therefore the sense object is perceived at a single moment and as one, the species is at the same time in the internal and external organ. Therefore, the external sense is perfected by the common sense, when it is perfected in the internal organ.[54]

This argument suggests that perceptual experience can be understood only in terms of the holistic model, at least on the very rudimentary level. We have two

---

53   For instance, Avicenna presents different divisions of the internal senses – threefold in medicine and fivefold in philosophy (Avicenna, *The Canon of Medicine* (*Al-Qānūn Fī'l-Tibb*), L. Bakhtiar (ed), trans. O.C. Gruner and M.H. Shah, Chicago, Kazi Publications, 1999, 8.1, § 557, pp. 163–164). This suggests that the division into different powers is an analytical tool that reflects our theoretical needs (Kaukua, "Avicenna on the Soul's Activity in Perception," p. 102). I have argued in favour of this interpretation in relation to Latin authors in J. Toivanen, "Perceptual Experience: Assembling a Medieval Puzzle," in M. Cameron (ed), *The History of the Philosophy of Mind*, vol. 2: *Philosophy of Mind in the Early and High Middle Ages*, London, Routledge, 2019, pp. 134–156.

54   "Praeterea, ostenditur quod sensus particularis perficitur a sensu communi. Cum enim organa sensuum particularium bipartita sint, [...] ut in duobus oculis et duabus auribus, tamen sensibile non apparet duo, sed unum, necesse est tunc deferri ad unum organum interius; cum ergo simul tempore percipitur sensibile et ut unum, simul tempore sit species in organo interiore et exteriore: ergo perfectio sensus particularis est a sensu communi, cum perficitur in organo interiore." (Alexander of Hales, *Summa Theologica*, vol. 2, 1.2, q. 2, 437b; I have amended the punctuation.)

eyes, and therefore two $P(x)$s take place with respect to each colourful object we see, but in our experience the object is seen as one, thanks to the common sense. Despite the fact that the common sense is distinct from the external senses, the perception of the object is unified from the beginning. We can understand that the two eyes contain one image each, but doing so requires rational inquiry. Alexander seems to apply the same approach to other internal senses as well.[55]

There is one important difference between the two heuristic models. In the first model, $P(x)$ *as* φ, it is possible to distinguish pure perception of a single sensible quality, $P(x)$, from the subsequent processing or interpreting of the quality. In contrast, in $P(\varphi x)$ the interpretative φ is an integral part of the complex perceptual act and cannot be removed (although it can be analytically singled out). Perception is always interpretative in the sense that different φs are always part of perception. This means that there cannot be a perceptual act without an estimative element – estimative judgement is always present, but it is neutral when we perceive something that is not relevant to our well-being. Other internal senses are part of perception in the same way, and they form a dynamic unity. If perception is always intrinsically related to imaginative, estimative, and memorative aspects (which sometimes may be "empty"), the picture is radically different in comparison to a view in which these higher powers sometimes act and sometimes do not. This view also provides an explanation for our ability to recognise familiar things. Memory elicits an image of a previously apprehended object when we see it anew, but there is no need to give a reason for its ability to know when to act and when not to because it is always active.

Another difference between the two models is related to the additive and transformative models mentioned above. In $P(x)$ *as* φ, the lower levels do not necessarily depend on what kind of higher cognitive capacities the perceiving subject has. There might be some feedback mechanism that allows the higher powers to influence the lower ones, but this is not built into the theory. In contast, $P(\varphi x)$ entails that it is not possible to have a perceptual experience that lacks the elements that the higher powers add to it, regardless of whether they actually alter the functions of the lower powers.

At this stage it is not possible to say with certainty whether the holistic model can be applied to all medieval theories. It depends, obviously, on the details of each author's theory, and further research is needed in this regard. At any rate, the two heuristic models should be taken as two different perspectives to

---

55   See also Alexander of Hales, *Summa Theologica*, vol. 2, 1.2, q. 2, 431a–b.

medieval theories of perception rather than as two conflicting theories themselves. The information processing model emphasises the physiological and psychological mechanism that brings about a perceptual experience that is enriched by various additional elements. The holistic model, on the other hand, emphasises the phenomenal experience and its unity. Although the models are not mutually exclusive, they serve as useful tools that enable looking at medieval theories from different perspectives.

5 Conclusion

By looking at medieval cognitive psychology below the level of conceptualisation or conceptual perception, it is possible to find highly sophisticated discussions on the various ways in which perceptual experience is enriched and structured. We might bundle these psychological processes under the rubric 'perceiving as', but at the same time we should be careful not to attribute too strong a unity to them. After all, they are functions of different cognitive powers, not all animals have all of them, and so forth. However, medieval theories can be analysed from the viewpoint of perceptual experience, which is brought about and structured by the joint action of the internal senses. In this sense, they can be considered to be unified in a relevant way.

The main reason why I have applied the concept of 'perceiving as' to medieval philosophy is that it enables a reassessment of the borderline between conceptual and non-conceptual perception. In modern philosophy of mind, 'perceiving as' is often used in relation to conceptual perception. It tries to capture our ability to categorise things and to see the world through conceptual lenses. However, this approach leaves out many interesting aspects of perception. For instance, we humans seem to have an innate tendency (to say the least) to perceive the world around us as consisting of distinct individual things. Arguably, there is nothing conceptual in this phenomenon, although it structures our perceptions in such a way that conceptualisation becomes possible.

Medieval authors make fine-grained analyses of different elements that figure in perceptual experience, and we can ask whether some of these elements could be considered conceptual. If we adopt a strict intellectual notion of conceptuality, we might be willing to say that none of the functions discussed above counts as conceptual in the proper sense. In that case, we are led to admit that reasonably complex and sophisticated non-conceptual perception is possible. Another option is to accept a broader notion of conceptuality, which easily leads to hybrid notions such as proto-concepts. Either way, the grey area between simple perception and conceptually structured engagement with the world remains problematic and interesting, and medieval theories are helpful because they bring various non-conceptual/proto-conceptual aspects of perception to the fore.

Medieval discussions can also help us to reconsider the distinction between humans and other animals. Almost all forms of 'perceiving as' discussed above were attributed to animals. According to the first heuristic model, $P(x)$ *as* φ, humans have an additional mental capacity that might add something to perception, namely rational knowledge of the essence of the perceived thing, conceptual classification, linguistic dimension, and so forth. But if this approach is taken strictly, as a version of the additive model, perception itself is similar in humans and animals. In contrast, the second model, $P(\varphi x)$, is easier to see as transformative, so that the intellectual level affects perception from the very beginning. Higher types of cognitive processes cannot be distinguished from perceptual experience, which means that humans and animals might perceive the world differently – although not necessarily, because this depends on what rationality is thought to add and how deep its influence is thought to go.

The impact of the approach adopted in the present chapter – taking 'perceiving as' in the broad sense and applying it to non-rational cognitive processes – can be fully seen only by taking into account *all* of the varieties of 'perceiving as' that were mentioned in the first section. Unfortunately, there is no room for that here. The central claim is that if we take seriously the possibility that medieval discussions can be used to develop a notion of non-conceptual 'perceiving as', then it is possible to achieve a more nuanced picture of the complexity of perceptual experience. The obvious next step would be to ask what the role of rationality is in this picture. I am not going to do that here and now – paraphrasing a famous quote, at this point it would be a tiny hop for mankind, but too big a step for me.[56]

Bibliography

Primary Literature

Albert the Great, *De anima*, C. Stroick (ed), *Opera omnia 7.1*, Münster, Aschendorff, 1968.

---

56   This research was funded by the Academy of Finland and Stiftelsen Riksbankens Jubileumsfond.

PERCEIVING AS: NON-CONCEPTUAL FORMS OF PERCEPTION

Albert the Great, *De homine*, H. Anzulewicz and J.R. Söder (eds), *Opera omnia 27.2*, Münster, Aschendorff, 2008.

Albert the Great, *De sensu et sensato*, S. Donati (ed), *Opera omnia 7.2A*, Münster, Aschendorff, 2017.

Albert the Great, *Physica, libri I-IV*, P. Hossfeld (ed), *Opera omnia 4.1*, Münster, Aschendorff, 1987.

Alexander of Hales, *Summa Theologica*, vol. 2, Quaracchi, Collegium S. Bonaventurae, 1928.

Anonymous, *Quaestiones super librum De sensu et sensato*, Paris, BNF Ms. lat. 16160, fol. 109ra–118vb.

Aristotle, *The Complete Works of Aristotle*, 2 vols., trans. J. Barnes, Princeton, Princeton University Press, 1984.

Averroes, *Long Commentary on the "De anima" of Aristotle*, trans. R.C. Taylor, New Haven, Yale University Press, 2009.

Avicenna, *Liber de anima seu Sextus de naturalibus*, S. van Riet (ed), vol. IV–V, Leiden, Brill, 1968.

Avicenna, *The Canon of Medicine (Al-Qānūn Fī'l-Tibb)*, L. Bakhtiar (ed), trans. O.C. Gruner and M.H. Shah, Chicago, Kazi Publications, 1999.

Dominicus Gundissalinus, *Tractatus de anima*, J.T. Muckle (ed), "The Treatise *De anima* of Dominicus Gundissalinus," *Mediaeval Studies*, vol. 2, 1940, pp. 23–103.

John Blund, *Treatise on the Soul*, D.A. Callus and R.W. Hunt (eds), trans. M.W. Dunne, Oxford, Oxford University Press, 2013.

John of la Rochelle, *Summa de anima*, J.G. Bougerol (ed), Paris, Vrin, 1995.

John of la Rochelle, *Tractatus de divisione multiplici potentiarum animae*, P. Michaud-Quantin (ed), Paris, Vrin, 1964.

Peter John Olivi, *Quaestiones in secundum librum Sententiarum*, 3 vols., B. Jansen (ed), Firenze, Collegium S. Bonaventurae, 1922.

Roger Bacon, *Perspectiva*, D.C. Lindberg (ed and trans.), *Roger Bacon and the Origins of "Perspectiva" in the Middle Ages*, Oxford, Clarendon Press, 1996.

Thomas Aquinas, *Quaestiones disputatae de anima*, B.C. Bazán (ed), *Opera omnia 24*, Rome, Commissio Leonina, 1996.

Thomas Aquinas, *Sentencia libri De anima*, *Opera omnia 45.1*, Rome, Commissio Leonina, 1984.

Thomas Aquinas, *Sentencia libri De sensu et sensato*, *Opera omnia 45.2*, Rome, Commissio Leonina, 1985.

Thomas Aquinas, *Summa Theologiae*, P. Caramello (ed), Turin, Marietti, 1948–1950.

William of Auvergne, *De anima*, F. Hotot (ed), *Opera omnia*, vol. 2, Paris, Andreas Pralard, 1674; reprint Frankfurt am Main, Minerva, 1963.

William of Auvergne, *The Soul*, trans. R.J. Teske, Milwaukee, Marquette University Press, 2000.

Secondary Literature

Abbott, Elizabeth, *Sugar: A Bittersweet History*, London, Duckworth Overlook, 2008.

Black, Deborah, "Avicenna's 'Vague Individual' and Its Impact on Medieval Latin Philosophy," in R. Wisnovsky, F. Wallis, C. Fraenkel, and J.C. Fumo (eds), *Vehicles of Transmission, Translation, and Transformation in Medieval Textual Culture*, Turnhout, Brepols, 2011, pp. 259–292.

Boyle, Matthew, "Additive Theories of Rationality: A Critique," *European Journal of Philosophy*, vol. 24, no. 3, 2016, pp. 527–555.

Di Martino, Carla, *Ratio particularis. Doctrines des senses internes d'Avicenne à Thomas d'Aquin*, Paris, Vrin, 2008.

Hasse, Dag Nikolaus, *Avicenna's "De anima" in the Latin West: The Formation of a Peripatetic Philosophy of the Soul, 1160–1300*, London, The Warburg Institute, 2000.

Kaukua, Jari, "Avicenna on the Soul's Activity in Perception," in J.F. Silva and M. Yrjönsuuri (eds), *Active Perception in the History of Philosophy: From Plato to Modern Philosophy*, Dordrecht, Springer, 2014, pp. 99–116.

Kemp, Simon, and Fletcher, Garth, "The Medieval Theory of the Inner Senses," *American Journal of Psychology*, vol. 106, no. 4, 1993, pp. 559–576.

Lagerlund, Henrik, "Awareness and Unity of Conscious Experience: Buridan on the Common Sense," in G. Klima (ed), *Questions on the Soul by John Buridan and Others: A Companion to John Buridan's Philosophy of Mind*, Dordrecht, Springer, 2017, pp. 149–156.

Lisska, Anthony J., *Aquinas's Theory of Perception: An Analytic Reconstruction*, Oxford, Oxford University Press, 2016.

Marmodoro, Anna, *Aristotle on Perceiving Objects*, Oxford, Oxford University Press, 2014.

McDowell, John, *Mind and World*, Cambridge, Harvard University Press, 1996.

Mintz, Sidney W., *Sweetness and Power: The Place of Sugar in Modern History*, New York, Penguin Books, 1986.

Oelze, Anselm, *Animal Rationality: Later Medieval Theories 1250–1350*, Leiden, Brill, 2018.

Pasnau, Robert, *Thomas Aquinas on Human Nature: A Philosophical Study of "Summa Theologiae" Ia 75–89*, Cambridge, Cambridge University Press, 2002.

Perler, Dominik, "Why Is the Sheep Afraid of the Wolf? Medieval Debates on Animal Passions," in M. Pickavé and L. Spahiro (eds), *Emotion and Cognitive Life in Medieval and Early Modern Philosophy*, Oxford, Oxford University Press, 2012, pp. 32–51.

Silva, José Filipe and Yrjönsuuri, Mikko (eds), *Active Perception in the History of Philosophy: From Plato to Modern Philosophy*, Dordrecht, Springer, 2014.

Steneck, Nicholas H., "The Problem of the Internal Senses in the Fourteenth Century," PhD dissertation, Ann Arbor, Michigan, UMI, 1970.

Stump, Eleonore, *Aquinas*, London, Routledge, 2003.

Tellkamp, Jörg Alejandro, "Albert the Great on Structure and Function of the Inner Senses," in R.C. Taylor and A.O. Ifran (eds), *The Judeo-Christian-Islamic Heritage: Philosophical and Theological Perspectives*, Milwaukee, Marquette University Press, 2012, pp. 305–324.

Tellkamp, Jörg Alejandro, "Aping Logic? Albert the Great on Animal Mind and Action," in J. Kaukua and T. Ekenberg (eds), *Subjectivity and Selfhood in Medieval and Early Modern Philosophy*, Dordrecht, Springer, 2016, pp. 109–123.

Toivanen, Juhana, "Perceptual Experience: Assembling a Medieval Puzzle," in M. Cameron (ed), *The History of the Philosophy of Mind*, vol. 2: *Philosophy of Mind in the Early and High Middle Ages*, London, Routledge, 2019, pp. 134–156.

Toivanen, Juhana, "Peter Olivi on Internal Senses," *British Journal for the History of Philosophy*, vol. 15, no. 3, 2007, pp. 427–454.

Toivanen, Juhana, *Perception and the Internal Senses: Peter of John Olivi on the Cognitive Functions of the Sensitive Soul*, Leiden, Brill, 2013.

Wright, Wayne, "Nonconceptual Content," in M. Matthen (ed), *The Oxford Handbook of Philosophy of Perception*, Oxford, Oxford University Press, 2015, pp. 181–197.

Yrjönsuuri, Mikko, "Seeing Distance," in J.F. Silva and M. Yrjönsuuri (eds), *Active Perception in the History of Philosophy: From Plato to Modern Philosophy*, Dordrecht, Springer, 2014, pp. 187–206.

CHAPTER 3

The Chameleonic Mind: The Activity versus the Actuality of Perception

José Filipe Silva

1

In the history of philosophy there are key texts by central figures that have occasioned numerous interpretative debates. Augustine is such a figure, and among his many writings we find a theological treatise pregnant with philosophical significance, the *De Trinitate*. In the context of his investigation into the divine trinity and the applicability of the trinitarian image to the human soul, Augustine examines the way we come to know the external world. A passage in the *De Trinitate* 11.2.5 (DT hereafter) has received intense scholarly scrutiny, but Augustine's use in the passage of the metaphor of the 'chameleon' to illustrate the workings of the soul in perception has largely been unnoticed. My aim in this paper is not only to consider whether this metaphor serves its purpose as an explanation of Augustine's account of perception, but to investigate its impact in later medieval philosophy. As a result of this investigation, I propose the first systematic categorization of the different models of active perception in the later medieval period.

But to return to the original Augustinian passage and metaphor:

> Since this is so, let us recall how these three, though differing in nature, may be fitted together into a kind of unity, namely, (i) the form of the body that is seen, (ii) its image impressed on the sense, which is vision, or the sense informed, and (iii) the will of the soul which directs the sense to the sensible thing and keeps the vision itself fixed upon it. The first of these, that is, the visible thing itself, does not belong to it in such a way that it arises in the body and through the body in the soul, for it arises in the sense, which is neither without the body nor without the soul. The third, however, is proper to the soul alone, because it is the will. Although the substances of these three, therefore, are so diverse, yet they form together such a unity, that the first two, namely, the form of the body that is seen and its image which arises in the sense, that is, the vision, can hardly be separated from each other, except when reason intervenes as a judge.

© KONINKLIJKE BRILL NV, LEIDEN, 2020 | DOI:10.1163/9789004413030_004

The will possesses such a power in uniting these two that it moves the sense to be formed to that thing which is seen, and it keeps it fixed on it when it has been formed. And if it is so violent that it can be called love, or desire, or passion, it likewise exerts a powerful influence on the rest of the body of this living being. And where a duller and harder matter does not offer resistance, it changes it into a similar form and color. Note how easily the little body of the chameleon turns very easily into the colors that it sees.[1] (trans. S. McKenna, 65–66, emphasis added).

At first glance, Augustine's account is clear. He describes how we come to see an external thing as the result of that thing acting upon our senses, but that such an action is not enough to account for our seeing it. For that to happen, the will must – in addition – focus on the image of the thing, as it were, forcing the sense to take on that form by means of which we become aware of an object standing in front of us. If this was all there is to say about the passage above, there could be no place for puzzlement; and yet there is.

There are two aspects of this account that are in need of further explanation: one, about the ontology of the soul, that is to say, about the nature of this will-power, responsible for the mental and physical transformation; the other, about the causal nature of the process, that is to say how, exactly, is Augustine claiming that we have access to external objects: as the result of the object's

---

1 "Quae cum ita sint, tria haec quamuis diversa natura quemadmodum in quamdam unitatem contemperentur meminerimus, id est species corporis quae uidetur, et imago eius impressa sensui quod est uisio sensusue formatus et uoluntas animi quae rei sensibili sensum admovet, in eoque ipsam uisionem tenet. Horum primum, id est res ipsa uisibilis, non pertinet ad animantis naturam nisi cum corpus nostrum cernimus. Alterum autem ita pertinet ut et in corpore fiat, et per corpus in anima; fit enim in sensu qui neque sine corpore est neque sine anima. Tertium vero solius animae est quia uoluntas est. Cum igitur horum trium tam diuersae substantiae sint, tamen in tantam coeunt unitatem, ut duo priora uix intercedente iudice ratione discerni ualeant, species uidelicet corporis quod uidetur et imago eius quae fit in sensu, id est, uisio. Voluntas autem tantam habet uim copulandi haec duo, ut et sensum formandum admoueat ei rei quae cernitur et in ea formatum teneat. Et si tam violenta est ut possit uocari amor aut cupiditas aut libido, etiam ceterum corpus animantis uehementer afficit, et ubi non resistit pigrior duriorque materies in similem speciem coloremque commutat. Licet uidere corpusculum chamaeleontis ad colores quos uidet facillima conuersione uariari. Aliorum autem animalium, quia non est ad conuersionem facilis corpulentia, fetus plerumque produnt libidines matrum quid cum magna delectatione conspexerint." (Augustine, *De Trinitate*, W.J. Mountain (ed) with the assistance of F. Glorie, Turnhout, Brepols, 1968, XI.II.5, pp. 338–339; *On the Trinity*, books 8–15, trans. S. McKenna, Cambridge, Cambridge University Press, 2002, pp. 65–66.)

action upon the soul, or as the result of the soul's own action? The story told in the passage seems to have implications in terms of both causation and epistemology. The question being asked is twofold: (1) how do we come to know things from their being made available to us; and (2) how do the modes of this availability have certain effects in us, cognitive and otherwise, as embodied cognitive subjects? One of the underlying assumptions is that one should be able to understand (2) in a way that does not endanger one of Augustine's long held claims, found for instance in *De musica* VI, that *absurdum est fabricatori corpori materiam quoquo modo animam subdere*: that "it is absurd that the soul is subsumed to the matter of the body as to an artificer." One of the most recognizable features of Augustine's thought is how strenuously he argues against bottom-up causation, grounded on the ontological superiority of the soul (*praestantior*), and which can be stated in the form of a principle significant for later debates:

> [POH] Principle of ontological hierarchy (or physical containment thesis): physical objects cannot be the cause of cognitive acts of the soul.

What the chameleon metaphor does is to go one step further from POH and show that, not only is the body not able to act on the soul, but also that the strength of the soul subjugating matter is such that, when informing matter of a suitable kind, the soul is able to bring about change in the organization of the matter it informs. The *De Trinitate* text thus presents a striking example of this interaction, and it is worth noting that it is not even the case of *mental* causation, but applies also to the animal *soul*. The claim Augustine makes in the passage is not about the superiority of the soul qua rational entity, which would exclude non-human animals, but its superiority qua principle of life and cognition. Such a claim about the soul's power of intentional action agrees with what he says elsewhere, for instance in *De Musica* (6.5.9), where the soul is characterized as animating the body in the form of the will of an agent (*intentione facientis*) and in DT (11.2.5), where the soul is shown to exert an absolute control over the body (*corpus animantis vehementer afficit*). This tightness of grip, with which the soul holds the body it vivifies, exists precisely because, by being the principle of life, the soul is also the principle of whatever operation takes place in it, whether internally (as in dreams) or externally (as in perception). With the chameleon analogy, Augustine wishes to press on with the main thesis of his theory of mind and cognition: whatever is in the soul is there by means of the action of the soul alone and not the body. By contrast, if something is to be found in the body that is a likeness of an external material thing, this is the result of the soul's intentional action on the body.[2] This expression of the soul's ontological superiority constitutes the backbone of Augustine's explanation of how we come to know material objects in the extra-mental world and, as I have argued elsewhere, that is what intentional awareness looks like in the conceptual framework of dualism.[3]

In the case of the chameleon, this transformative action requires the fulfilment of three conditions: the existence of matter that is capable of undergoing such a change; the existence of the acting principle, the soul, which is able to operate such transformation, reaching beyond its proper realm; the presence to the senses of an external thing that is imitated by the transformative action of the soul upon matter. Of these, all but one requirement can be modified when applied to other sentient beings: matter can be of the kind that it suffers the action of the soul but is not changed. This takes us to the second striking aspect of this account, about how we come to know external things. One way to consider it is what I have elsewhere called the "conformational nature of the soul";[4] that is to say, the soul has this essential capacity to make itself like the images of the objects affecting the sense organs.[5] When we unpack this conception of transformative agency, we find two key features that will play an important role in later theories. First, the immanent nature of the action: the

---

2 Henry of Ghent has noted this with remarkable acuity: "Vocat autem August. illam animi intentionem causaliter, quia ipsam sit sensus animi intentus ad obiecta percipienda" (Henry of Ghent, *Quodlibeta*, Venice, 1608, *Quodlibet* XI, question 5, 195va).

3 J.F. Silva, "Perceptiveness," *Proceedings of the Aristotelian Society*, Supplementary Volume 91, 2017, pp. 43–61.

4 J.F. Silva, *Robert Kilwardby on the Human Soul: Plurality of Forms and Censorship in the Thirteenth Century*, Leiden, Brill, 2012, p. 165.

5 How this *De Trinitate* account relates to what Augustine says in other works, even contemporary ones (for instance the *De Genesi ad litteram*), has been a vexing aspect of Augustine's theory of perception and cannot be addressed here. We find a hint of the explanation, however, in this chameleon analogy and I will argue for the rest of this paper that this is adopted by later medieval thinkers, in some cases under a different metaphor: the soul as living wax. I will also present the anti-chameleon analogies of the menstruating woman (*mulier menstruata*) and the basilisk (*basiliscus*): "Item, videmus quod occulus mulieris menstruose inficit speculum et basiliscus visu interficit hominem, quod non esset nisi virtus visiva esset activa" (Anonymi Magistri Artium, *Quaestiones super librum De anima*, P. Bernardini (ed), Firenze, SISMEL, Edizioni del Galluzzo, 2009, II, q.64, 209). In these two cases, the explanation is grounded on a form of natural causation: the blood in the eyes of the woman or the venom in the eyes of the basilisk "infect" the surrounding air and via this as a continuum, progresses to affect the mirror (*speculo*) and to infect a human being, poisoning him/her in the case of the basilisk. The principle is simple: it is a case of material transmission – or transmission in a material substrate.

soul brings about a likeness of the external thing on the occasion of the presence of the species in the sense organs, which is to say an affection of the body.[6] Second, this action is self-caused: the soul elicits its own act of production of the internal likeness and of awareness of the external thing (and in the case of a changeable matter, its change proportional to what is perceived). In brief:

> [PAC] Principle of auto-causation: cognitive acts are self-caused but determined in what concerns their content by particular things.

It is not the colored external thing that brings about the change in the chameleon but the soul itself, even though the color in the external thing determines the content of that change: what that change is about. But determination of content of the act is not the cause of the act.[7] If POH and PAC are correct, one still needs to explain how determination, but not causation of perceptual acts, takes place. The answer to this question is found in the basic definition of perception: the awareness by the soul of an affection of the body. On the one hand, we have the affection of the body (a sense organ) by an external thing, causing that affection; this consists in a causal interaction between two corporeal entities, an object and a sense organ. On the other hand, we have the soul becoming aware of the affection of the body and by means of it becoming aware of the external thing causing this awareness.[8] By defining it in this way, Augustine wants to stress that the soul is able to bring about the act of perceptual awareness on its own, rather than being caused by the external thing.[9] The decisive point here is the direction of causation, from the soul to the world rather than from the world to the soul, a direction of fit that is expressed in the

---

6 It must be noted that the terminology of immanent action is not found in Augustine but in later authors. It is however clear that both this notion and the associated one of vital acts follows from Augustine's characterization of the relation of the soul to the body *simpliciter*, as the principle of life, characterized by a mode of being he describes as 'vital attention': the soul is wholly in each and every part of the body it vivifies or animates. On this, see J.F. Silva, "Medieval Theories of Active Perception: An Overview," in J.F. Silva and M. Yrjönsuuri (eds), *Active Perception in the History of Philosophy*, Dordrecht, Springer, 2014, pp. 117–146.

7 For an elaboration of this argument, please see Silva, "Perceptiveness," pp. 43–61.

8 That Augustine and Augustinian authors subscribe to an extra-mission account of visual perception can be taken as marginal in the sense that it piggybacks on the impassibility claim.

9 Whether or not it suffices to avoid this accusation of crossing ontological orders in causation to claim, like Albert the Great does, that "sensible things do not act upon the soul, but only in the bodily organs [...] the organs however are animated and therefore the motion from the sensible thing reaches the soul" (Albert the Great, *De anima*, A. Borgnet (ed), *Opera omnia 5*, Paris, Vivès, 1890, II.3.1, 98), is an optional question.

THE CHAMELEONIC MIND: ACTIVITY V. ACTUALITY OF PERCEPTION   43

chameleon, rather than say the basilisk or the menstruating woman metaphor.[10]

One of the common ideas in medieval thought about cognition is the continuation of the ancient idea of knowledge as assimilation: that is to say, by virtue of a likeness, the knower becomes like the known. Assimilation or conformation, whatever the direction of fit (from world to mind or from mind to world), entails causation as part of the explanation for the capacity of the subject of knowledge to become like the object of knowledge. To become like is to take on the form of what is known, but this can be explained by either the object making the knower become like itself or the knower make itself become like the known thing. Returning to the chameleon analogy, the point is that the chameleon is active when, upon the presence of something that is such and such, *(the soul) acts upon the matter subjected to it in such a way as to make the matter like the external object because it makes itself to be like the thing it is in presence of.* It is active in the sense of being productive of an action, the making of itself to be like that external thing. That the body is of the moldable type, so that it is made to be like what is present to it is an afterthought, not the driving force.[11] Augustine toys with two key notions: one, the relation between soul and body is that between artificer and matter subject to it; two, the likeness of an external thing, like color, is in the body because it is primarily in and as the result of the action of the soul. Applying these two notions to perception, it means that the aim of the chameleon analogy is to show the limits to the action of the external thing in the constitution of the visual experience and to reinforce the thesis that any change in the perceiving subject originates in the soul, and so has an outward direction of fit.

What Augustine himself intended by his analogy itself is a different matter from what medieval authors made of it. One way to read them is as sharing Augustine's aims, and William of Auvergne is one such voice. In his *De anima* section of the treatise *Magisterium divinale ac sapientale*, William returns to that Augustinian image:

---

10   This raises many questions but one in particular: if the soul cannot be actualized as the result of the causal action of the object bringing about the actualization of the perceiver's power, what explains that the act of awareness is about a particular thing in the world the species of which is made to be present in the perceiver's sense organs? The soul must be somewhat determined from its general aptitude for knowing to the actual perception of a property of an individual present to the senses, without any strong causal connection.

11   See J.F. Silva, *Robert Kilwardby on the Human Soul* and *Active Perception in the History of Philosophy* for a detailed examination of these claims and references; see also J.F. Silva and J. Toivanen, "The Active Nature of the Soul in Sense Perception: Robert Kilwardby and Peter John of Olivi," *Vivarium*, vol. 48, no. 3–4, 2010, pp. 245–278.

The intellective power, therefore, is by nature able to receive by one excitation, even a slight one, many designations and to become a book of many designations. But the reason for this is that such an excitation applies it to things and joins it to them by a spiritual union. And for this reason the intellective power is like what is said about the animal called the chameleon, which receives into itself the likeness or signs of all the things to which it is joined by such an application. And just as it is evident regarding a monkey that it mimics, as far as it can, the works which it sees are done by human beings and assimilates itself to their actions, so the intellective power is naturally able to make itself like things, when it is applied to them, and to receive the likenesses or signs of them. For it is naturally able to make itself into a book in act for itself of those things to which it is united in that way. [...] Not without reason did that holy and wise man [a reference to Augustine and to the *De Genesi ad litteram* 12.16.33] say that the human mind forms in itself and through itself images or signs of all the things that it understands.[12]

The passage quoted above appears in the context of an important question about whether we know things as the result of their actions upon us and whether the nature of this action is that of an efficient or an occasional one (*De anima*, Chapter 7, Part 8). In this passage, William answers the question by pointing out the natural capacity of the soul to make, in and of itself, the images of the things it cognizes. The soul does so by its natural power and agility, a capacity that overflows from the essence of the soul itself as a fountain of

---

12   "Nata igitur est virtus intellectiva una excitatione etiam levi recipere multas designationes, & fieri liber multarum designationum: causa autem in hoc est, quoniam excitatio huiusmodi applicat illam rebus, atque conjungit conjunctione spirituali. Et propter hoc sicut dicitur de animali quod chamaeleon nominatur; sic se habet, & de virtute intellectiva quae omnium rerum, quibus huiusmodi applicatione conjungitur similitudines vel signa in se recipit: & sicut de simia manifestum est quod opera quae videt ab hominibus fieri prout valet effigiat; & se eis operationibus assimilat: sic virtus intellectiva nata est rebus sic applicata se assimilare, similitudinesque vel signa earum assumere; ad hoc enim nata est naturaliter ut efficiatur liber in effectu sibi ipsi rerum quibus sic conjungitur. [...] Non immerito igitur vir ille sanctus, & sapiens dixit quod mens humana in semetipsa, & per semetipsa formet imagines seu designationes rerum omnium quas intelligit" (William of Auvergne, *De anima*, F. Hotot with *Supplementum* B. Le Feron (eds), *Opera omnia*, vol. 2, Paris, Andreas Pralard, 1674, pars nona, 215b-216a; trans. R.J. Teske, Marquette, Marquette University Press, 2000, p. 456, with changes). On this, see S. Marrone, *William of Auvergne and Robert Grosseteste: New Ideas of Truth in the Early Thirteenth-Century*, Princeton, Princeton University Press, 1983, pp. 66–67.

THE CHAMELEONIC MIND: ACTIVITY V. ACTUALITY OF PERCEPTION 45

knowledge, and ultimately from the fountain of all knowledge, God himself.[13] The soul naturally has this cognitive power that is able *to apply itself* to things and as a result to make itself like them. And this conformational capacity and exercise has an epistemic role, since the soul, by transforming itself into the external thing, becomes aware of that same thing. Perceptual awareness presupposes the natural capacity of the soul to produce an internal representation of whatever it is to be known, because: (i) all knowledge takes place by means of likeness; and (ii) the soul makes itself like things rather than material things making the soul to be like them. For that the soul must receive the likenesses of the accidental features or dispositions of things which, in turn, are signs that indicate and reveal what those things are and can be known by us.[14]

It is clear that William's statement of how causality works between things of different realms is reminiscent of Augustine: corporeal things cannot act upon the soul but the soul can act upon the body that is subjected to its action.[15] To

---

13   This aspect of the theory need not concern us here. One aspect that does concern us, however, is how it has been noted that William is here talking about the intellect, rather than the power of sensation. I think however that William uses here the intellective power as a shorthand for the human soul, which is through and through rational. Only this explains why William offers no independent account of sensation; instead, what the spider, the money-changer, the monkey, and the chameleon all show is that William is talking about sensation which, in the case of human beings, is embedded with reason (William of Auvergne, *De universo*, F. Hotot with *Supplementum* B. Le Feron (eds), *Opera omnia*, vol. 1, c.76, 930a). I am not alone in this reading: see A. Masnovo, *Da Guglielmo d'Auvergne a S. Tommaso d'Aquino*, vol. 3, Milan, Società Editrice Vita e Pensiero, 1945, p. 132.

14   "[...] visionem inquam sensibilem omni illa intuenti pleneque omnia cognoscenti ad intelligibiles dispositiones & ad faciendam visionem intellectualem indubitatamque certitudinem uniuscuiusque subiecti sui intelligibilis intuenti illa, pleneque & clare cognoscenti. [...] quae omnia quemadmodum dixi tibi de sensibilibus dispositionibus non abscondunt nec obnubilant, sed potius indicant, revelant, & notum subjectum efficiunt, necesse est ut intuenti haec faciant claram visionem intellectibilem, plenamque notitiam, ac certitudinem indubitatam de subjecto cuius sunt quod evidenter indicant & ostendunt. [...] quemadmodum cum intueris in Socrate sive circa ipsum omnes sensibiles dispositiones ipsius, & clare vides illas ac perfecte, dicis te clare ac perfecte videre Socratem" (William of Auvergne, *De anima*, 102b).

15   "Sic debes considerare comparationes, & habitudines substantiarum spiritualium ad res corporales, & corpora, videlicet ut quemadmodum corpora ligaturam quandam habent ad substantias spirituales, & velut quandam obdientiam, ut ad earum imperium moveantur; sic & spirituales substantae non omni modo seorsum sunt, sive immunes, aut liberae a comparationibus, & respectibus, sive habitudinibus, ad corporales, ut de dispositionibus earum nihil, ut ita dicatur, sentiant, aut alio modo cognoscant" (William of Auvergne, *De universo*, c76, 930fg).

transform itself or to produce in itself an image of an external thing is the task of the soul constituting the cognitive process. As in Augustine, we find also here that this denial of bottom-up causality introduces something that I will call the *dual component account* (to use an expression from A.D. Smith) or the *two-step model* of perception:[16] a description of perceptual experience requires a basic distinction between the reception of the (object-representing) species in the sense organ and the act of perception caused by the cognitive power itself. The difference, historically and conceptually significant, is between two descriptions of the event we call perception:

(1)   the sense organ receives a species/likeness of what is to be perceived
(2)   the sense receives a species/likeness of what is to be perceived

Procedure (2) has been read so as to equate the reception of the species with the actualization of the power to perceive, meaning that the presence of the species brings about the perceptual act that has the object as its content *and* efficient cause. To receive the species of x is to be caused to perceive x. Procedure (1), however, remains neutral to what follows this reception of the species in the sense organ, but it discriminates between the reception in the organ and the psychological cognitive operation of perception proper. Once we accept this distinction, a wide range of possibilities arises concerning the nature of the relation between reception and operation, with or without causal undertones, and it is those possibilities that I wish to investigate next.

One group of theories that subscribe to this dual component account frame the relation between reception and the perceptual act in terms of excitation. Contrary to what I myself and others have suggested in the past, the terminology of excitation is used in the context of both active and passive accounts of perception.

The first such model is what I shall call [A] *Excitation as passive assimilation*: perception is constituted by a change of the sense organ that excites the soul to action, that is, to perceive the object. The first example of this model is found in the Anonymous, *Lectura in librum De anima*, edited by Gauthier:

> [...] to sense is to be affected. The species of the object seen first changes the medium and then changes the organ [of sense], exciting the visual power; therefore, the species of the object acts upon the organ and the

---

16   A.D. Smith uses it to refer to those theories of perception that distinguish between sensation (i.e. reception of sensory data) and perception (i.e. perceptual judgement). See his *The Problem of Perception*, Cambridge, Harvard University Press, 2002, pp. 67-sqq. In this piece, I do not go into the issue of whether a distinction between sensation and perception can be explicitly found in medieval authors, and therefore treat the two terms as synonymous with regard to the historical sources I consider.

THE CHAMELEONIC MIND: ACTIVITY V. ACTUALITY OF PERCEPTION

power, so as to change the sensitive power and exciting it. And it must be said that the sensitive power is both passive and active: first, [it is passive because] the sensitive power is affected by the species of the object changing the organ and exciting the sensitive or visual power which is in the eye; however, once affected, [the sensitive power] turns itself to the object and acts on it.[17]

I assume that "to act upon the object" in the last sentence of this passage must be taken in a cognitive sense: that the power perceives the external thing, rather as a suggestion of an extra-mission type of action, whereby a visual ray issues from the eye. If this reading is correct, the sense of the passage is to show that the main effect of the external object acting upon the sense is to bring that sense into actuality, which is the exercise of its operation. The power is passive and its operation caused by the action of the external thing.

Another example of this same model can be found in the *Quaestiones super librum De anima* by another anonymous Master of Arts, edited by Paola Bernardini:

As the Commentator says in the second book: the sensible is only an accident and changes the medium and the organ and the sense; and the organ is passive only, as it receives the species. But the sense is passive at first because the sense power is excited by the species received in the organ; once excited, however, it turns itself to the species received and judges it, and in doing so it is active.[18]

---

17   "[...] sentire est quoddam pati [...] species obiecti uisus primo fit in medio inmutando ipsum et postea fit in organo ipsum inmutando et excitando uirtutem uisiuam; agit ergo species obiecti in organum et in potenciam, ut uirtutem sensitiuam inmutando et ipsam uirtutem excitando. [...] Et dicendum quod potencia sensitiua passiua est et actiua est: primo enim patitur uirtus uisiua a specie obiecti inmutante organum et excitante uirtutem sensitiuam uel uirtutem uisiuam que est in oculo, ipsa autem iam passa conuertit se supra obiectum et agit in ipsum" (Anonymi Magistri Artium, *Lectura in librum De anima a quodam discipulo reportata*, R.A. Gauthier (ed), Grotaferrata, Ad Claras Aquas, 1985, II.10, q.3, p. 277).

18   "Sicut dicit Comentator secundo huius: quod sensibile est tantum accidencium et inmutat medium, et organum, et sensum; et ipsum organum tantum passivum est: recipit enim speciem. Set ipse sensus primo passivus est, et hoc quia excitatur talis virtus sensitiva a specie in organo recepta, et ipsa sic excitata convertit se super speciem receptam, et iudicat de ipsa, et in hoc est activa" (Anonymi Magistri Artium, *Quaestiones super librum De anima*, II, q.64, p. 210). See also P. Bernardini, "La passività del senso nei commenti alla *Vetus* del *De Anima*. Le origini della dottrina del *sensus agens*," *Documenti e studi sulla tradizione filosofica medievale*, vol. 25, 2014, pp. 243–288. In this important study, Bernardini traces to the origins of the debate over the activity and passivity of the senses to some

As in the previous passage, the main claim is that the reception of the species in the sense organ causes, by exciting it to action, the operation of the cognitive power. That the active element in this second passage is the act of judging the species does not change the alignment with the traditional causal model of cognition; rather, it reinforces it: in both passages, the causal relationship between the two components or steps of the process is described in terms of our perception of an external object being caused by that external object. There is excitation whenever the species is received in the sense organ, triggering the power to activity; therefore, "excitation" and "triggering" are to be taken as causal expressions, entailing the passivity of the senses. These are passive insofar as they are receptive and insofar as the operations of the sense modalities are caused by the reception of appropriate species.

A contrasting model is what I shall call [B] *Excitation as active assimilation*. In this case, there is also a change in the organ, but this need not be followed by a change in the soul. By eliminating the necessity of this entailment, authors in this model aim at dismissing the underlying causal claim that the necessity entailed: the bodily change is not the cause of the act of the soul. One of the early proponents of this view is the Dominican Robert Kilwardby, who starts his investigation into the nature of perception by asking how the soul comes to have in itself images of external things.[19] Having dismissed the views that these originate in the intellect, he considers two alternatives: that they (1) come from the senses as the result of the causal action of external things; or (2) are produced by the soul on the occasion of the presence to the senses of the things these images represent. Lest there be any doubt, Kilwardby presents these two alternatives as representing the models of (respectively) Aristotle (1) and Augustine (2).

According to Aristotle (i.e. (1)), the object acts via a causal chain, by impressing its likeness in the medium, in the sense organ, and finally in the sensory power itself, which is completely passive.[20] The efficient cause of the perceptual

---

of the first Parisian Masters of Arts in the thirteenth century; in their texts commenting on Aristotle, activity mostly means the judgement the internal sense produces once it has received the sensory information from the external senses.

19   On Kilwardby on perception, please see J.F. Silva, "Robert Kilwardby on Sense Perception," in P. Kärkkäinen and S. Knuuttila (eds), *Theories of Perception in Medieval and Early Modern Philosophy*, Dordrecht, Springer, 2008, pp. 87–99; J.F. Silva, *Robert Kilwardby on the Human Soul*, pp. 131–176; J.F. Silva, "Robert Kilwardby on the Theory of the Soul and Epistemology," in P. Thom and H. Lagerlund (eds), *A Companion to Robert Kilwardby*, Leiden, Brill, 2013, pp. 275–313.

20   There is a vast literature on this: see, e.g., J. Owens, "Aristotle – Cognition a Way of Being," *Canadian Journal of Philosophy*, vol. 6, no. 1, 1976, pp. 1–11. Examples of medieval interpretations of this view can be found in Albert the Great, *De anima* II.1, 96a: "Et dicendum, quod [sense] est in genere potentiae passivae, eo quod *sensus* secundum actum *accidit in*

act is the object in a primary sense but the immediate cause is the sense organ informed by the sensible likeness.[21] As such, it is proper to say that the soul is moved by the external thing because its power is in a state of potentiality to that sensible thing via its species.

Kilwardby's way of proceeding is to separate the questions concerning the nature of the species, which the material object is able to generate, and the kind of action the object is able to bring about in the sense. The reception of the species either (a) causes a change in the organ, or (b) it causes a change in the power, or (c) it causes a change in the organ *and* in the power. This leads us to the second question, which is whether the causal impact of the object (via the species) on the sensory power (and the sensory soul) is enough for producing sensation. Here we have two main options: either the reception of the species is identified as the exercise of the power's act, entailed by (b) and (c), or the act of the power is connected, but causally independent of, the reception of the species, as suggested by (a). It is important to note in this context that it is not the case of inquiring whether the mere production of species is enough for perception because species, whatever their ontological status, exist in the medium, which is not percipient; rather, the question is whether their coming to be *on a subject of a cognitive kind* entails perception of the thing they represent. Whereas in the case of the Aristotelian tradition the object is the agent or efficient cause of both the species and the act of sensation – because reception of the species is the actualization of sense[22] – in the case of the tradition we

---

    ipso moveri organum et *pati* a sensibili obiecto, quod formam suam agit in organum sensus"; II.1, 97a: " [...] sensus non potest perfici secundum sentire in actu sine praesentia sensibilis, quod agit in ipso formam suam, ut illa sentiat in actu"; II.1, 98a: "[...] de sensu, qui efficitur in actu per formam sensibilis in ipso existentem"; and II.3.4, 101b: "Dicimus igitur quod omne apprehendere est accipere formam apprehensi"; and Godfrey of Fontaines, *Quodlibeta XIII*, J. Hoffmans (ed), Leuven, Institut Supérieur de Philosophie de l'Université, 1935, q.3, 193: "[...] actus potentiarum animae non sunt effectiue a potentia animae in qua sunt sed potius ab obiecto"; and *Quodlibeta IX*, J. Hoffmans (ed), Leuven, Institut Supérieur de Philosophie de l'Université, 1924, q.19, 274: "Sed in quantum est vis animalis et sensitiva sola sensatione immutatur; et sic illud, quod per se immutat sensibile in potentia sensitiva ut sensitiva est, non est nisi ipsa potentia secundum talis, et illud secundum quod sensibile ipsam potentiam sensitivam immutat non est nisi sensatio." For references in Thomas Aquinas, please see G. van Riet, "La théorie thomiste de la sensation externe," *Revue philosophique de Louvain*, vol. 51, no. 31, 1953, pp. 374–408.

21   Robert Kilwardby, *De spiritu fantastico*, P.O. Lewry (ed), *On Time and Imagination: De tempore, De spiritu fantastico*, Oxford, Oxford University Press for the British Academy, 1987, hereafter DSF, 97; Robert Kilwardby, *On Time and Imagination*, Part 2, trans. A. Broadie, Oxford, Oxford University Press, 1993.

22   In other words, to move the sense is to produce sensation (Jacopo Zabarella, "Liber de sensu agente," in *De rebus naturalibus libri XXX*, Venice, Apud Paulum Meietum bibliopolam Patavinum, 1590, 848B). Peter of Ailly notes that "sensible species" are

are considering here, there are two distinct even though related independent agents. For Kilwardby, as for Augustine and William of Auvergne, perception requires two agents, each responsible for one activity: the object for the production of the species, by means of which the object is known, and the impressing of it on the sense organ, and the subject for the act of sensation, by means of which it knows the object the species represents. Kilwardby makes the point of clarifying that this is the way Aristotle should be read "when Aristotle says that *sense [sensus] is receptive of the sensible species without matter,* he means the sense organ" (DSF 112).

The Augustinian way (2) is to claim that perception is an awareness of a bodily affection, which is a change in the sense organ caused by the external thing (DSF 103). By turning itself to this bodily change, the soul makes an image of the external thing by means of which it perceives the external thing. The basic idea is that by becoming like the species in the sense organ, the soul sees the external thing. This is so because the soul is now like the species and the species is identical qua representation to the external thing that generated it; thus, by seeing itself like the species the soul sees the external thing.[23]

Our concern – and Kilwardby's – is not however with the issue of representation; rather, his focus is on the relation between the reception of the species in the organ and the operation of the soul. His claim is that the species in the sense organ (the affection of the body) is the *sine qua non* but not the efficient cause of perception; otherwise, the material object and its species would transcend its material nature by acting on, by bringing about, an act of the soul. Instead, the soul is that efficient cause of perception (DSF 103). The general argument is that the bodily change is necessary but not sufficient for perceptual experience, which is explainable primarily by the relation the soul holds towards the body (directly tapping into Augustine's definition of intention), rather than the way it relates to the external world, its objects and their sensible qualities.

---

so called not because they are perceptible in themselves, but because they cause sensation – see *Tractatus de anima*, O. Pluta (ed), *Die Philosophische Psychologie des Peter von Ailly*, Amsterdam, B.R. Grüner, 1987, pp. 48–49.

23   In other words, the two – soul and species – are identical, as the result of this process. But if the soul is identical to the species qua representation of the external thing, by looking at itself, the soul sees the external thing. One can of course doubt that a species can successfully and completely represent the thing it is the species of; or doubt the capacity of the soul to make itself like the species in the organ; but that is another story and one that is not part of the medieval debate I am here investigating (although it is certainly part of another medieval debate).

THE CHAMELEONIC MIND: ACTIVITY V. ACTUALITY OF PERCEPTION 51

The problem with this should become clear, once we consider the consequences of what was just said, indeed, by reflecting on the nature of the two elements involved. On the one side, there is a material thing; on the other, there is the sensitive soul that continues to flow into the body, promoting its well-being, and thus explaining the nature of the operations of that living being. The result of this close connection is that there is a correspondence between the operations of the soul and the affections of the body (DSF 99). But the direction of fit, once again, is not from the world to the soul (the body causing the soul to act in a certain way); rather the soul moves its body according to the diversity of the bodily affections (DSF 100) and it does so (or is able to do so), because there is a continuous state of attention the soul gives to the body. There is a teleological inspiration to the argument, as the soul moves the body in the way that best protects it, while at the same time there is also the need for the soul to act in accordance with the physical state of the body, be that healthy or sick. However, the essential aspect of the model was announced much earlier in the treatise:

> [...] the sentient is constituted by two [elements], the body and the soul, of which the body is as it were the instrument and the soul is as it were the rector and the artificer. (DSF 3)

That the bodily instrument is affected by the material object via the species seems reasonable in view of the fact that the object itself cannot be upon the sense organ and that all cognition is done by means of the likeness of the thing being present in the knower. That the artificer is affected by the material thing is however rather problematic and in contradistinction to Augustine's definition of perception as an affection of the body that does not go unnoticed by the soul. Instead, it is better to say that a body, the sense organ, is affected by another body, the object via the species, and that the soul acts on this affection as if it were a living wax:

> [...] if you place a seal before wax so that it touches it, and you assume the wax has a life by which it turns itself towards the seal and by striking against it comes to be like it, by turning its eye upon itself it sees in itself the image of the seal.[24]

---

24 "Erit autem qualecumque simile ad istud intelligendum, si posueris sigillum coram cera ita quod tangat eam, et posueris ceram habere uitam qua se conuertat ad sigillium, et inpingendo in illud assimilet se illi, et in se aciem reflectendo uideat in se ymaginem sigilli: sic enim spiritus sensitiuus se conuertendo attentius ad suum organum specie sensibili

The meaning of the seal-wax analogy is completely transformed from its original context: whereas in Aristotle it was intended to show that the recipient is affected primarily in a cognitive sense, for Kilwardby it is taken to demonstrate how the action of the seal is made significant in the cognitive sense because of the active (counter-)motion of the soul. The nature of this activity is clear from what was said before about Augustine: this action of the soul results (1) in the production of an internal representation that is just like the species in the organ (thus, like the relevant sensible property of the external thing) and (2) in the awareness of that sensible property, that is to say, perception proper (DSF 102). Having defined the soul as the principle of life and characterized its relational state to the body as continuously paying attention, perception cannot be explained in the causal terms of the reception of the species in the sense organ. Instead, perception originates from the soul qua principle of life that, as a living wax, molds itself to that causing an affection of the bodily sense organ and qua principle of cognition, turns upon itself as being like that external thing and perceives it (DSF 103). The sensory soul is the efficient cause of the perceptual act like a living wax that acts *by pressing itself against the seal.*

Such a view received strong criticism early on from none other than Thomas Aquinas,[25] who identifies it as being that of Plato (and the Platonists), the umbrella designation he often uses for all non-strictly hylomorphic opposing views. In his words,

> He [Plato] also claimed that sense is a power operating on its own: so not even sense itself, since it is a spiritual power, receives an impression from sensible things. Rather, the organs of the senses receive an impression from sensibles, and because of this impression, the soul is somehow aroused to form in itself the species of sensible things. Augustine also seems to come close to this view in *De Genesi ad litteram* XII, where he says that "it is not the body that senses, but the soul thorough the body, using the body as a messenger in order to form within itself the message received on the outside."[26]

---

informatum facit se ei similem, et in se propriam aciem reflectendo uidet se talem" (Kilwardby, DSF 103).

25   I am here making no claim regarding Kilwardby as being the specific target of Aquinas; rather, I am making a weaker claim that such a generic view was targeted by Aquinas.

26   "Sensum etiam posuit virtutem quandam per se operantem. Unde nec ipse sensus, cum sit quaedam vis spiritualis, immutatur a sensibilibus: sed organa sensuum a sensibilibus immutantur, ex qua immutatione anima quodammodo excitatur ut in se species sensibilium formet. Et hanc opinionem tangere videtur Augustinus, XII *super Gen. ad litt.*, ubi dicit quod *corpus non sentit, sed anima per corpus, quo velut nuntio utitur ad formandum*

THE CHAMELEONIC MIND: ACTIVITY V. ACTUALITY OF PERCEPTION   53

Aquinas' objection is grounded on the idea that, according to Aristotle, the senses are entirely passive and that to perceive is an operation of the animal composite, body and soul, and not only of the soul;[27] therefore the reception of the species brings about the operation of the cognitive faculty. In other words, the reception of the species is equivalent to bringing the cognitive subject to the act of cognizing: *facit cognoscentem actu cognoscere* (QDV 10.4). I shall call this (Aristotelian) model, [C] the *Identity-theory of perception*.

As for the objection that others may raise, according to which this implies that what is lower in the ontological hierarchy of being (the object and the species) affects what is higher in that scale (the soul and its cognitive faculties), Aquinas replies that the external sensible thing, since it is in actuality, is ontologically superior to the sense organ of the perceiving animal (*corpus sensibile est nobilius organo animalis*); therefore, respect for ontological hierarchy is not compromised. In fact, Aquinas is here largely repeating an argument found in his teacher, Albert the Great. Albert claims that sensible things themselves are active in bringing about species of their sensible properties in such a way that they are able to affect and actualize the senses relative to their proper sensibles.[28] An external material thing acts by means of its form, not its matter, and as such its action is not inferior to sense.[29] Color is the per se cause of vision (*color per se est motivus visus*: De anima II.6, 106b). All proper sensibles are such – sensible – by their own essence and as such have the power to multiply their own intentions, which have spiritual/intentional being (*esse spirituale/ intentionale*) and thus to act on the senses, without the need for any external

---

 in seipsa quod extrinsecus nuntiatur" (Aquinas, *Summa Theologiae* I, q. 84, 6, trans. R. Pasnau, *The Treatise on Human Nature*, Indianapolis, Hackett, 2002, p. 150, emphasis added).

27 See R. Pasnau, *Theories of Cognition in the Later Middle Ages*, Cambridge, Cambridge University Press, 1997, pp. 126–130 for references.

28 "[...] per se sensibile esse, quod in secundo modo dicendi per se per essentiam suam est causa sui esse sensibilis" (Albert the Great, *De anima* II.6, 106a). In this same passage, Albert points out that the sensible thing does not need to be actualized by something already in act because this principle only applies to what is in potency to the material cause, not what is in potentiality to the formal and efficient cause. The sensible form is able to multiply itself and to act everywhere ("omnis forma inferior universaliter et non particulariter agit et multiplicat seipsam, et sic formae sensibilium se universaliter agunt"), when it acts on its own (*per se solam*: De anima II.6, 106b).

29 Albert the Great, *De anima* II.3.6, 106: "[...] nos superius ostendimus omnem virtutem activam esse per se perfectam ad agendum sine aliquo motivo extrinseco. [...] Forma autem corporalis per se agens nihil supra se confert, quando confert esse intentionale." This argument seems to me "disingenuous" because of what the opposing view would be: that the species representing the external thing is matter.

cause.[30] In this model, the object produces two high-order effects: the species as an entity with spiritual being and the actualization of the power of the soul.

Soon after Kilwardby (and Aquinas), we find John Pecham and his account, which I will be calling "epistemology of compassion". This is a version of [B], the *Excitation as active assimilation* model. Pecham argues that "the species changes the bodily organ and this change excites the soul to change itself in accordance to it."[31] The soul is able to change itself because of the tight connection (*colligantia*) between the visual power and the sense organs, with the power being the perfective element of this unity.[32] The form/power and matter/organ unity allows Pecham to build a non-causal binding model of perception: the soul transforms itself in the likeness of the thing impressed in the organ.[33] He further offers an interesting reading of Aristotle's dictum that "sense is in potency to all sensible things," which he takes to mean that the soul is not affected by the body, but that it suffers with it (*corpori compatitur*: TdA 4.2, 13). The soul joins in compassion with the affection of the body. That is why the epistemic explanation requires a dual component model: the organ being affected by the object and the soul reacting to the affection of the bodily organ. In his words:

> I say at present that it is impossible for the corporeal species to be impressed into the rational soul, as Augustine says in book VI of the *De musica*. But, excited by the sense and enlightened by the eternal light, [the soul] forms in itself and of itself the spiritual images of those bodily likenesses that are in the [organ of] sense [...] I say that because the soul is connected to the body as the perfection to the perfectible, it both naturally turns to the changes in the body and transforms itself into their likeness.[34]

---

30   Albert the Great, *De anima* II.6, 107b. See also the forceful conclusion: "Et quod hic determinamus, hoc est, quod forma sensibilis multiplicat se in esse spirituali et sufficit sibi ad hoc, sicut omnis forma in propria et essentiali actione sibi sufficit."

31   "[...] species immutat organum corporale et organum immutatum excitat animam ad immutationem sibi consimilem suo modo quam anima facit in se ipsa de se ipsa" (John Pecham, *Quodlibet* I.4, *Quodlibeta quatuor*, G.J. Etzkorn and F. Delorme (eds), Grottaferrata, Collegium S. Bonaventurae, 1989, p. 10).

32   It is this binding that explains how the soul is corrupted by the corruption of the body; see Pecham, *Quodlibet* III, q.8, 149. The body affects the soul by resisting its action, an idea of clear Augustinian origin.

33   "Anima transformat se in similitudinem rei cuius species est in organo" (Pecham, *Tractatus de anima*, G. Melani (ed), Firenze, Biblioteca di Studi Francescani, 1948, 4.4, p. 14).

34   "Dico ad praesens quod impossibile est speciem corporalem imprimere in animam rationalem, sicut Augustinus, VI *Musicae*. Sed excitatur a sensu et format in se de se

THE CHAMELEONIC MIND: ACTIVITY V. ACTUALITY OF PERCEPTION 55

Pecham insists in his *Tractatus de anima* (Chapter 2) on how life and sensation are interrelated and subordinated to thought: the first act of life is to persevere in being (*persistere*), closely followed by cognition (*apprehendere*).[35] Human beings naturally desire to know both material and spiritual things, but whereas the occasion arises from the senses, the actual cause of cognition is the soul, infused as it is with eternal light (*lux aeterna*).[36] In this sense, it is not possible for the soul to be acted upon by material things, as a patient;[37] instead, the soul must be the agent of cognition. Referring to Augustine in the *De Genesi ad litteram* (XII) and the *De Trinitate* (X), Pecham insists in this transformative and productive capacity of the soul to form in itself likenesses of material things present to the sense organs via their species – which he takes to be equally material –[38] and the reception of which excites the soul to action:[39] "the soul, excited by the senses, transforms itself into the likeness of all the things."[40] Now, this "excitation" seems to indicate a reaction that has all the appearances of a causal relation from the object (or the reception of the species in the organ) and the act of the soul, as if he were advocating a version of [A]. Pecham is however quick to dismiss this possibility: the intimacy between body and soul – organ and power – cannot make us overlook the fact that these two are not equal partners. Instead, one, the body, is the instrument of the other, the soul; in Pecham's words, "to sense is not of the composite as if the body were to cooperate in the apprehension but rather because [the body] serves the soul in receiving the corporeal species, which does not enter in the

---

     similitudines spirituales illorum quorum similitudines corporales sunt in sensu, illustrante luce aeterna. [...] Dico quod quia colligatur anima corpori, sicut perfectio perfectibili, et advertit naturaliter immutationes corporis et transformat se in illarum similitudinem" (Pecham, *Quodlibet* III, q.9, p. 151). I am deliberately ignoring the phrase that reads "illustrante luce aeterna," which I take to be a reference to the natural capacity of the rational soul to operate in this productive way.

35   "In the human being, the principle of sensitive cognition is intellectual" ("In homine enim sensitiva cognitio principium est intellectuale" (Pecham, *Tractatus de anima*, p. 8).

36   The similarities with William of Auvergne are not mere coincidental.

37   "Item, res corporalis spirituali est penitus improportionalis nec potest virtus finita de re corporali facere rem spiritualem" (Pecham, *Tractatus de anima*, p. 11).

38   "[...] species in organo est corporalis et dimensionata dimensionibus organi" (Pecham, *Tractatus de anima*, p. 11).

39   "[...] ergo species immutat organum corporale, et organum immutatum excitat animam ad immutationem sibi consimilem suo modo, quam anima facit in seipsa de seipsa" (Pecham, *Quodlibet Florentino*, in *Tractatus de anima*, Appendix IV, p. 148).

40   "Omnino enim nobilius est agens patiente, non igitur a corpore anima rerum similitudinem recipit, sed ipsa seipsa excitata a sensibus, in omnem rerum similitudinem se transformat, dicente Augustino, *Super XI Genesis ad litteram*" (Pecham, *Tractatus de anima*, p. 10).

56   SILVA

soul" (*Tractatus de anima* 4.7, 16). The best way to illustrate this is with the (by now) familiar example:

> This agrees with the Philosopher's example which says that the soul is formed from the species like the wax from the seal. And it is clear that the vestige of the seal in the wax is made from the potentiality of the wax, not from something that migrates from the seal. Therefore, the soul is formed from the species as if in a certain way per impossibile the wax would be alive and propel itself to the likeness in the seal.[41]

According to Pecham, to say that the images in the soul would arise as the result of the action of an impressing cause (the object) would be contrary to the intention of Augustine; instead, one should say that the internal representations arise on the occasion of the soul being excited by the species in the organ.[42] The soul is active to the extent that it has this assimilative capacity to produce its own images of the affecting objects represented by the species received in the sense organs,[43] so that there is never the transmission or transference of form from the lower bodily realm to the higher spiritual realm. The *physical impression* is simply the occasion for the *mental operation* of which the soul is the cause. In the case of perception, this outward causation is done with the contributing role of the species, which are united or present to the power as accidents to a subject,[44] as particular determinations of the perceptual act.

---

41   "Cui concordat exemplum Philosophi dicentis quod anima formatur a speciebus sicut cera a sigillo. Et certum est quod vestigium sigilli in cera fit de potentia cerae, non de aliquo quod migrat e sigillo. Unde ita formatur anima a specie quodam modo acsi cera per impossibile viveret et propelleret se in similitudinem sigilli" (Pecham, *Quodlibet Florentino*, p. 148). See also: "[...] sicut alibi comparat Aristoteles animae receptionem receptioni cerae a sigillo, in qua certum est similitudinem fieri sigilli de ipsa possibilitate cerae, quae est omnimode figuralis et non de aliquo migrante a sigillo" (Pecham, *Tractatus de anima*, p. 11).

42   "Ad secundum, quod species illae nascuntur de se per occasionem excitativam, non per causam impressivam; aliter enim esset sibi contrarius Augustinus" (Pecham, *Quodlibet Florentino*, p. 148).

43   "[...] ipsa anima, cuius substantia in nuditate creata, assimilabilis est omni creaturae, vigore enim suo et vi anima transformat se in omnium similitudines, quae sensibus ingeruntur, et facit in se ipsa" (Pecham, *Tractatus de anima*, p. 11).

44   "Sed cognitio est actus intimus animae. Ergo numquam perficitur nisi per intima animae. Item in primo sunt idem ipsum cognoscens et ratio cognoscendi. Ergo quanto aliquid perfectius cognoscit, tanto magia est unum ratio cognoscendi cum cognoscente. Sed in cognitione sensitiva ponunt speciem esse ab extra et unitum potentiae sicut accidens

THE CHAMELEONIC MIND: ACTIVITY V. ACTUALITY OF PERCEPTION

To conclude this section on Pecham, one should note that what makes the reception of the species cognitively conducive is not the causal efficacy of the object but the nature of the soul as something able to mimic and (re)produce in its own realm the species. What makes this production that follows the affection possible is the special relationship between soul and body, power and organ, described under the expression of 'colligantia.' This concept will be of major import in the debates that follow but here I am more interested in noting the change of metaphor, from the chameleon to the living wax.

The three models that have just been presented have it in common that they attribute a cognitive role to the species, which in two cases ([A] and [C]), but not the third, is expressed in causal terms. In [B], the activity of the soul goes beyond the mere judgment of sensory information, because it also has the capacity to select among the stimuli, to produce internal representations of external things, and elicit for itself its cognitive acts. In what follows, I show that it is possible to hold an active account that, contrary to the excitation model, assigns no cognitive role to incoming sensible species. According to such an account [D], the *Self-directing model*, the soul is the absolute efficient cause of perception, able to have direct and *unmediated* contact with the external thing: that is the model of the Franciscan Peter John Olivi.[45] Olivi strongly argues against the view that makes the actualization of the power's potentiality dependent on the reception of sensible species. There are a number of reasons for his refusal, from the impossibility of arguing for their ontological status, the possibility of material things to generate them, and their capacity to represent something other than the species themselves. Olivi argues that if what the perceiver receives are the species, then what the perceiver is able to perceive are those species, rather than the external object.

What matters for my purposes here however is that Olivi grounds this impossibility in a basic principle in the Augustinian philosophy of perception, that the soul cannot be acted upon by external physical objects in order to bring about its cognitive acts [POH].[46] Instead, the principle or source of

---

subiecto" (Pecham, *Questiones de anima*, H. Spettmann (ed), *Questiones tractantes de anima*, Münster, Aschendorff, 1918, 10, p. 96).

45   It is worth noting that there are other theories that do not accept incoming species, like that of William of Ockham; and others that do not accept internal representations, like that of Durand of St. Pourçain and Godfrey of Fontaines. But of these only Durand holds an active view.

46   Peter John Olivi, *Quaestiones in secundum librum Sententiarum*, 3 vols., B. Jansen (ed), Firenze, Collegium S. Bonaventurae, 1922–1926, hereafter *InIIS*, 72, p. 13. See also *InIIS*, 58, 437–439. Olivi takes Augustine's view to entail that (i) the soul makes in and of itself the images of external things and (ii) that the action of the object is limited to the impression

knowing is founded upon the principle of being a living thing, which means that *the cause of a particular perceptual act must be found in the internal operative principle*, rather than in its end-term, the object. What makes an action cognitive is its source being the principle of life. In other words, a cognitive act is a vital act (*actus vitalis*).[47] To see, in particular, and to perceive, in general, are the kind of acts that only living beings can perform, not objects, and thus that can only be caused by the soul of the perceiving subject.[48] Later on, this notion of vital act will become particularly relevant for the active account of perception given by authors such as Durand of St. Pourçain, who similarly argues that the *actus vitae* and *actus vitalis* cannot be elicited to the activity proper to it by something external but only by an internal principle.[49] For Durand,

---

of sensible species on the bodily sense organs; see *InIIS*.58, 462; and also *InIIS*.74, pp. 112–113.

47 "Quarto, quia nihil sic ultimata et actuali ratione habet rationem cognitivi et actus vitalis sicut habet actio cognitiva," (*InIIS* 72, pp. 24–25).

48 Duns Scotus identifies the source of this thesis with Augustine in the *De civitate Dei* (VIII.6); see *Ordinatio*, C. Balic (ed), *Opera omnia*, Vatican, Typis Polyglottis Vaticanis, 1954, I. d.3, p. 3, q.2, p. 249: "[...] ergo operatio vitalis non potest esse nisi a principio agendi vitali vel vivo. Istae operationes cognoscendi sunt operationes vitales, ergo sunt ab ipsa anima sicut a ratione agendi." At roughly the same time as Olivi, also Henry of Ghent makes a passionate defense of this principle, especially in *Quodlibet* XI, q.5. See J.F. Silva, "Intentionality in Medieval Augustinianism," in M. Summa and J. Müller (eds), *Phänomenologische Forschungen*, vol. 2, 2018, pp. 25–44; M. Pickavé, "Causality and Cognition: An Interpretation of Henry of Ghent's *Quodlibet* V, q. 14," in G. Klima (ed), *Intentionality, Cognition, and Mental Representation in Medieval Philosophy*, New York, Fordham University Press, 2015, pp. 46–80.

49 "Quinto, quia, sicut prius dicebatur, inconveniens ualde uidetur quod actus vitalis, ut est sentire et intelligere, sit in nobis effectiue a non uiuente" (Durand of St. Pourçain, *Scriptum super IV libros Sententiarum*, F. Retucci (ed), Leuven, Peeters, 2012, II. 3.5, p. 155); Durand of St. Pourçain: "[...] ridiculum est dicere quod actus vite inquantum huiusmodi sit principaliter uel totaliter ab eo quod nichil est uiuentis, set aduenit ab extrinseco; set intelligere et totaliter cognoscere est actus uite, species autem nichil est ipsius uiuentis, set aduenit ab extrinseco." On Durand, see J.-L. Solère, "Durand of Saint-Pourçain's Cognition Theory: Its Fundamental Principles," in R.L. Friedman and J.-M. Counet (eds), *Medieval Perspectives on Aristotle's "De anima,"* Louvain, Peeters, 2013, pp. 185–248. On vital acts, see also Nicole Oresme, *Expositio et Quaestiones in Aristotelis De anima*, B. Patar (ed), Louvain-La-Neuve-Louvain, Éditions de l'Institut Supérieur de Philosophie, 1995, II.9, p. 272. Albert the Great had already argued against a version of this principle, which he took to be Platonic and Augustinian (*De anima* II.6, 105b), by saying that there is no incompatibility between perceiving being a vital operation (or an operation of the principle of life) and the species being determinants (*specificantia*) in formal and efficient terms of the soul's cognitive operations because the species does not determine the soul with respect to life, but simply with respect to the cognition of external things ("Quod autem dicunt sentire esse opus vitae et in illo esse formalem speciem sensibilem, dicendum, quod sentire est opus vitae, secundum quod egreditur ab anima et non secundum quod specificatur

THE CHAMELEONIC MIND: ACTIVITY V. ACTUALITY OF PERCEPTION

the species in the organ cannot be the cause of the cognitive act; if their reception were enough for this eliciting, then the reception of the sensible species in the medium would lead to perception *by the medium* of the object represented by the species.[50]

Likewise, Olivi strongly denies that objects are causally efficacious with respect to cognitive acts; otherwise, the object's action would go beyond the power of its corporeal nature (*InIIS*.72, 101). For that same reason, Olivi argues against the view found in some of his contemporaries according to which the object acts upon the senses, exciting the soul to action. He describes this process in his own words, as the influx from the body to the spirit as an action that excites the [cognitive] power to its cognitive act.[51]

Olivi denies this because he takes it to imply that triggering corresponds to a form of causation and thus to a form of bottom-up causality. Although this has been thought to be directed at views such as those held by Kilwardby and Pecham (therefore model [B]), it could also be the case that Olivi has in mind something like the view found in the Anonymous texts I have discussed under the heading of model [A], *Excitation as passive assimilation* theories. Olivi's objection, in any case, is that if this account were right, the soul would play the supporting role to that external action. Instead, he argues, the soul, qua principle of life and cognition, must play the role of the primary (and free) cause of cognition, directing its attention to particular objects present in the perceptual field, not unlike a living wax:

> [...] it must be said that an agent of a species cannot in itself and absolutely cause immediate effects that are different in species (...) <as> if one were to think that wax would have in itself the power to apply and impress itself to different seals, so that the seals would simply be the end term of this mode of application and impression rather than something acting upon the wax. Therefore, the wax would produce in itself the images of different seals not in itself and absolutely but only with respect to

---

a forma sensibili; non enim specificatur ab ipso sensibili in speciem vitae, sed potius ad notitiam rei exterioris habendam," Durand, *De anima* II.6, 107a).

50   "[...] ergo si ipsa [species sensibilis] est principium eliciendi actiue operationem sentiendi, sicut per eam sentit oculus, ita per eandem sentiret medium; quod non est uerum; ergo ipsa non est principium eliciendi actiue operationem sentiendi" (Durand, *Scriptum super IV libros Sententiarum* II.3.5, p. 150).

51   "Item, aut influxus factus a corpore in spiritu est actio cognitiva aut principium effectivum ipsius aut est actio excitativa potentiae ad actum cognitivum" (Olivi, *InIIS*.72, p. 24).

60   SILVA

the different seals and to their diverse terminations, applying itself and impressing itself to them.[52]

Olivi makes it clear that the soul is not constrained in its action by external things, but rather that it has in itself the source of its own power to apply itself to the objects, just like the wax by its own power applies itself to the different seals it is directed to. The diversification of the end-terms of its action does not diversify the essence of the power because it is not necessary for there to be as much diversity in the cause as there is in the effects. In other words, there is no restriction as to the number of images of seals the soul is able to produce in itself because the diversity of acts does not arise from the power of the objects but the power of the soul.[53] Although there is no limitation to the power to direct itself to a multitude of different objects and accordingly to produce their images in itself, there is the general constraint that, for each act, the power must be directed to a particular object. Like Kilwardby (and Pecham) before him, Olivi wants to emphasize that the activity of the soul in perception still requires the existence of extra-mental objects that terminate its acts, that is to say, that constitute and determine the content of those acts. Otherwise, the soul could *at will* perceive external things, even in their absence. The object must be there, not as the efficient cause (that is the role of the soul), but as the terminative cause: what the soul's attention (*aspectus*) is about.[54]

I want to note that, even though the above-quoted passage appears in the context of a discussion about the power of the will, the main thrust of the

---

52   "Ad secundum dicendum quod agens unius speciei secundum se et absolute non posset facere effectus immediatos diversos in specie, sed secundum diversos ordines et aspectus ad terminos diversarum specierum hoc potest [...] Esset autem huius rei clarius exemplum, si ponetur quod cera haberet intra se virtutem applicandi et imprimendi se diversis sigillis, sic quod ipsa sigilla essent solummodo termini huiusmodi applicationum et impressionum absque hoc quod aliquid agerent in ipsam ceram. Tunc enim ipsa cera posset in se producere imagines diversorum sigillorum, non tamen secundum se et absolute, sed solum in ordine et aspectus ad diversa sigilla et ad diversas terminationes eorum, applicando se scilicet et imprimendo se eis. Sic enim est in proposito et etiam multo altiori modo, modo scilicet intellectuali et vivo: voluntas enim applicando se libere et virtualiter uniendo suius obiectis producit in se diversa velle, et in hac applicatione ipsa obiecta se habent solummodo in ratione termini nihil agendo in ipsam voluntatem" (Olivi, *InIIS*.58, pp. 415–416).

53   "[...] si cera praedictam virtutem applicandi se haberet, semper in infinitum posset in se producere diversas imagines secundum diversitatem sigillorum et secundum diversos modos applicandi se eis" (Olivi, *InIIS*.55, p. 417).

54   "Licet enim obiecta non producant suas similitudines in ea per modum efficientis, veraciter tamen exiguntur et coadiuvant ad earum productionem per modum termini seu per modum obiecti" (Olivi, *InIIS*.58, p. 421).

THE CHAMELEONIC MIND: ACTIVITY V. ACTUALITY OF PERCEPTION   61

argument is to refute the passivity of the soul and state that the "cognitive powers of the soul are the efficient cause of their own acts."[55] This is a clear adop-
tion of the Augustinian [PAC]. The fact that something is necessary for a given
action, does not mean that it is an efficient cause: in cognitive operations, the
object is necessary as determination (or terminative cause, in Olivi's terminology), but the cognitive power is the efficient cause (*InIIS*.58, 419; 72, 37–8). In a
clear statement of the activity of the soul in cognition, Olivi explains that:

> [...] when an agent acts within itself, by directing its active force to an
> extrinsic object and in doing so also exposing and applying its passive
> power toward that object, as if it were going to grasp that object within
> itself. And it is in this way that the immediate principle of an apprehen-
> sive or volitional action acts within the soul's power.[56]

This passage shows cognition does not have an external cause but that the action that initiates and produces our awareness of external things is the soul
and its attention as directed to a particular external thing. In other words, the
mere presence of the object and its affection on the senses is nothing without
the soul's active attending of the environment, thus making it clear that we
should dismiss the view that perceptual acts are brought about by the external
thing's causal efficacy.

Around the same time as Olivi, we find a similar model in Roger Marston's
Quaestiones disputatae de anima, written c. 1282–1284. Question 8 focuses on
whether the sensitive soul receives the species of the things it knows from the
outside, or whether it forms them in itself and, if that is the case, what is the
nature of this formation? Marston starts by presenting the view, which he will

---

55   That is how Olivi explicitly describes this question in his famous "Epistola ad fratrem R.,"
      S. Piron et al. (eds), *Archivum Franciscanum Historicum*, vol 91, 1998, p. 55: "[...] quod po-
      tencie anime apprehensive sint tota causa efficiens actuum suorum, quanvis obiecta eis
      cooperentur, non per modum efficientis, sed per modum obiecti."
56   "Quartus modus est, quando agens agit intra se, dirigendo vim suam activam in obiectum
      extrinsecum et etiam eo ipso aperiendo et applicando suam potentiam pasivam ad ipsum
      obiectum, acsi deberet illud obiectum intra se capere. Et hoc modo immediatum princi-
      pium actionis apprehensivae vel volitivae agit intra potentiam animae" (Olivi, *InIIS*.72,
      p. 9, trans. R. Pasnau, 1997). The other three are: first, there must be proportionality be-
      tween the agent (and its power to act) and the patient (and its receptivity to be acted
      upon) (Olivi, *InIIS*.72, p. 6); second, the agent, although higher in the ontological hierar-
      chy than the patient, can voluntarily subject itself to the action of the patient (Olivi, *InIIS*.72,
      p. 6); third, when what is affected is affected indirectly by being intimately related to
      something that is directly subject to this affection (Olivi, *InIIS*.72, pp. 6–8).

later refute, according to which the soul receives the species from the outside and that this reception is the cause of the perceptual experience.

Reading Augustine, he says, we find the view that cognition entails the reception of species from external things,[57] and that from these a sequence of species proceeds up to the power of memory. The soul can receive species because such reception does not imply that it is affected or altered, because the species received are not corporeal.[58] According to this account, the issue of materiality is distinct from the issue of receptivity: the soul receives the species although it is not transformed or qualitatively altered by the external thing.

Some, Marston notes, have objected to this in saying that reception should be understood as a form of excitation, leading the soul to transform itself into the form of the external thing.[59] But certainly such a view is incoherent because excitation constitutes a reaction, meaning that in order to react the soul must be affected by material objects – the very point the authors of this view wish to deny.[60] Marston goes on criticizing the active model, noting that if the soul made the species itself, like any other generating thing, then the species would represent the soul more than they represent the external thing.[61] Finally, if the soul were to act as an efficient cause, the relation it would hold with respect to the external things would be that of an occasion.[62] But in that case, the object of the act would be accidental to the operation of the soul, which means that all external things perceived would be sensed by accident. And

---

57 "[...] species recipiuntur a corpore in sensu" (Roger Marston, *Quaestiones disputatae de anima*, Quaracchi, Collegium S. Bonaventurae, 1936, p. 376).

58 "[...] anima species possit recipere, quia in tali receptione nec patitur nec alteratur" (Marston, *Quaestiones disputatae de anima*, p. 378).

59 "Nota quod dicit: 'non est excitatio in anima ut talia formentur in ea,' hoc est non se transformat in species consimiles illis quae recipiuntur in sensu" (Marston, *Quaestiones disputatae de anima*, p. 377). We find this view presented by Nicholas of Cusa in his *Idiota de mente*, R. Steige (ed), Hamburg, Meiner, 1995, Chapter 4, 77: "Sicuti vis visiva animae non potest in operationem suam, ut actu videat, nisi excitetur ab obiecto, et non potest excitari nisi per obstaculum specierum multiplicatarum per compreensiva rerum et notionalis, non potest in suas operationes, nisi excitetur a sensibilibus, et non potest excitari nisi mediantibus phantasmatibus sensibilibus."

60 "[...] quod anima formet in se speciem, excitatur ab obiecto; huiusmodi vero excitatio actio quaedam est cui necessario respondet passio, cum ipsa sit effectus illatioque actionis; ergo si excitatur, patitur" (Marston, *Quaestiones disputatae de anima*, p. 379).

61 "Item, omnis species evidentius repraesentat rem de qua gignitur quam aliquam aliam; ergo species, quam anima format de se ipsa, magis repraesentabit animam quam obiectum extra" (Marston, *Quaestiones disputatae de anima*, p. 379). We find this argument against the species in both Olivi and Ockham.

62 "Si dicas mihi quod tantum occasionaliter est a re extra, ergo, cum per illam sentiat, sentiet tantum per occasionem" (Marston, *Quaestiones disputatae de anima*, p. 379).

THE CHAMELEONIC MIND: ACTIVITY V. ACTUALITY OF PERCEPTION   63

that is simply false. From this "object-as-occasion-account" would also follow that, whenever an object makes itself present to the senses, perception follows, something that is proved to be experientially false.

Against this passivity view, Marston presents a series of scholastic-like objections, using Augustine also here as his authority. In several places, he remarks, Augustine states that the soul makes the images of bodily things in and of itself (*in semetipsa de semetipsa*).[63] Although some have interpreted this as applying primarily to the intellect, Marston explicitly claims that Augustine is talking about the sensitive soul, the part of the soul that form the images of bodily things and that we have in common with non-rational animals.[64] One of the main reasons for claiming that this production in and by the soul takes place is that otherwise one would need to take the objects that are perceived as being able to generate species that can be received in the soul, and thus as having a spiritual nature. But that would be contrary to the basic [POH]. To the reception in the sense organ of an impressing species, the soul produces a species of its own, in an act of self-causation:

> [...] in the same way as the wax, if it were to have the power to apply itself to the seal and conform itself to it, once the seal was present would configure itself to it, much more expressively and efficaciously can the soul, via a sensitive power, conform itself to alterations made in the organ, of which it is the perfection, because it is wholly present in whatever part of the body.[65]

I shall call this [E], the *conformation model of perception*. According to Marston, it is due to the conformational nature of the soul that we perceive the external world and in a way that is caused by that external world, following the path initiated by Augustine in the DT. Marston's view develops in interesting ways, but this is not the place to explore them.

We have seen until now that there are a number of positions on this issue, especially on the active excitation model. Whatever the version of the model, the fact of the matter is that a number of objections were immediately raised

---

63   "Ecce quod dicit imagines factas in anima et de ipsa anima" (Marston, *Quaestiones disputatae de anima*, p. 381).

64   "[...] ut patenter advertissent ipsum loqui non de mente seu intellectu possibili, sed de virtute sensitiva, in qua cum bestiis communicamus. Unde illud in quo fiunt imagines corporum, secundum quod hic de imaginabus loquitur, est solum potentia sensitiva" (Marston, *Quaestiones disputatae de anima*, p. 381).

65   Marston, *Quaestiones disputatae de anima*, p. 394. I present the same passage in Silva, "Perceptiveness," p. 56.

by contemporary authors – in fact, even by some of the proponents of active theories themselves (see Olivi and Marston). These objections can be divided into two camps: one is related to the question of the explanatory value of excitation, as it is dependent on the reception of species in the sense organs; the other concerns the issue of whether a cognitive power is able to bring itself to full actuality, which would go against the metaphysical principle, well-accepted in Aristotelian circles, that one and the same thing cannot be both active and passive (in respect to the same aspect). These objections are in fact directed to all dual component accounts of perception, especially those that do not accept the causal relation between the reception of species and the cognitive act (so, models [B] and [D]).

Some authors attempted to place themselves entirely outside this debate. One of them, John Duns Scotus, strenuously argued against some versions of this "excitation-model of perception," which he explicitly associated with Augustine. Scotus does accept that cognitive operations are vital operations that cannot come except from an internal vital principle, which is the soul;[66] moreover, he finds justification for this claim in *De Genesi ad litteram* where Augustine states that the soul makes in and of itself the images of the things it cognizes.[67] But he takes issue with this account in its assigning to the object via the species impressed in the sense organ the role of inclining or exciting the power into actual cognition.[68] That being the case, Scotus goes on to argue, it becomes difficult to see what this 'exciting' ("Quaero enim quid sit 'excitare'?" p. 253) or 'inclination' ("quaero quid intelligitur per 'inclinationem'?" p. 274) actually means. If, on the one hand, we take it in a causal sense, which is prior to the cognitive act, then this must mean that it is the cause of the cognitive act. If, on the other hand, excitation does not constitute a cause – does not bring about or elicit the act, then how does the act come to be and how is it about this particular (exciting) thing?[69] The problem with this active or

---

66   "[...] ergo operatio vitalis non potest esse nisi a principio agendi vitali vel vivo. Istae operationes cognoscendi sunt operationes vitales, ergo sunt ab ipsa anima sicut a ratione agendi" (Scotus, *Ordinatio* I. d.3, p.3, q.2, p. 249).

67   See Scotus, *Ordinatio* I. d.3, p.3, q.2, pp. 272–273.

68   "[...] quaerens de principio activo actionum vitalium – scilicet sensationis et intellectionis – ponit quod illud principium est aliquid in ipso animato et non obiectum extra. Sic et in sensu point quod species impressa in organo tantum inclinat et inclinando excitat potentiam et quasi evocat ad ipsam operationem" (Scotus, *Ordinatio*, p. 272). Like the editors of the text note, this is a clear reference to Henry of Ghent in his *Quodlibet* XI, q.5. Scotus points out the agreement between this conception and Augustine's statement that "the soul forms in itself the images of the things cognized" ("Ad hoc concordat ratio Augustini, quod anima 'format in se imagines cognitorum,'" *Ordinatio*, p. 273).

69   See Scotus, *Ordinatio*, esp. pp. 252–253.

THE CHAMELEONIC MIND: ACTIVITY V. ACTUALITY OF PERCEPTION 65

self-causation account is that it seems to allow for perceptual episodes to take place without there being any external thing that the sensation is about.[70]

The opposite view, which takes perception to be fully passive, fares no better. According to this view, the senses take on the species from the object and these species constitute the eliciting principle of the power's operations. In other words, the species fully determines the power's potentiality to perceive.[71] Scotus objects to this in general terms by saying that, if the species were to be the formal principle that elicits the power to act, then the species would be superior to the power.[72] That cannot, however, be the case: although the species contributes to the cognitive act in so far as it is a disposition conducive to it, it cannot be the (sole or even main) cause of it. Nor, for Scotus, it will not do to say, as the writer the editors identify as being the Augustinian Giles of Rome holds, that the species is to be identified with the act itself.[73]

There are two authoritative sources for the "Giles of Rome" account. One is Aristotle's statement in the *De anima* that the sensible in act and the sense in act are the same, and the other is Augustine's statement in the *De Trinitate* that the form impressed in the sense by the object is seeing (*visio*).[74] By this account, sensation is directly and efficiently caused by the object, that is to say "to sound is nothing but the generation of the species of sound and hearing is nothing but the reception of the species."[75] Scotus' objections focus on blocking this identification of (reception of) species and (cognitive) act: if sensation were simply the reception, the medium would then have sensations. Instead, we need to have in addition an internal efficient principle, which is the soul via

---

70   "Item, si essent activae, cum hoc quod sunt passivae, sequitur quod sensus posset sentire sine obiecto exteriori" (Scotus, *Quaestiones super secundum et tertium De anima*, B.C. Bazán et al. (eds), St. Bonaventure, The Franciscan Institute, 2006, q.12, p. 97).

71   "Quidam dicunt illas esse passivas primo respectu speciei impressae ab obiecto; illa autem species informans potentiam cognitivam sibi subiectam est principium elicitivum, sicut ratio eliciendi operationem cognoscendi"; and "Item, indeterminatum ad plura non potest determinari ad unum nisi per aliquid impressum sibi determinans; potentiae praedictae sunt indeterminatae, quantum est de se ad actus diversos; igitur in eis est species impressa ipsas determinans ad agendum" (Scotus, *Quaestiones super secundum et tertium De anima* II, q.12, p. 99).

72   "[...] si igitur species est formale principium eliciendi cognoscendi et potentia materiale tantum, sequitur quod actus sentiendi et intelligendi magis debent attribui speciei quam potentiae, quod falsum est; quia species non sentit nec intelligit sicut potentia" (Scotus, *Quaestiones super secundum et tertium De anima* II, q.12, p. 100).

73   "[...] species in potentia cognitiva non est aliud ab actu cognoscendi" (Scotus, *Quaestiones super secundum et tertium De anima* II, q.12, p. 102.)

74   Scotus, *Quaestiones super secundum et tertium De anima* II, q.12, p. 102.

75   "[...] sonatio non est nisi generatio speciei soni; igitur auditio non est nisi receptio speciei" (Scotus, *Quaestiones super secundum et tertium De anima* II q.12, p. 102).

its cognitive powers.[76] These powers are from an internal or intrinsic principle that is also a vital principle, and so the operations of sensing are vital operations that as such are immanent to the agent (the soul via its power) itself.[77] Cognition, as a vital operation, cannot have as its total cause a non-living thing: the cognitive power is necessary to execute the immanent cognitive act.[78] In addition, Scotus argues, there is much evidence for the fact that reception of species cannot be identified with sensation: when asleep or distracted, one's sense organs continue to receive species from objects in the surrounding environment and yet no perception of those objects follows. There are even animals, like rabbits, that sleep with their eyes open, but no visual experience follows because their soul is not active in attending to the visual stimuli.[79] These cases demonstrate the dependency of sensation on attention, which means that the cognitive power must be the main cause.[80]

Scotus goes on to assert that species are needed for perception as determining the power to perceive that which generated the species received in the organ and represented by them.[81] As the passage quoted above shows, the power is not informed and its act is not elicited by the reception of the species but determined in terms of content: by receiving the species, the act is about and intentionally directed to that object out of all the objects in the world.

---

76 "[...] intelligere et sentire sunt actiones immanentes in agente [...] igitur obiectum non est activum talium, sed potius homo sentiens et intelligens, mediantibus suis potentiis animae" (Scotus, *Quaestiones super secundum et tertium De anima* II, q.12, p. 104).

77 "Item, operationes vitales sunt effectivae a principio vitali et intrinseco, si sint naturales; actus sentiendi et intelligendi sunt operationes vitales, et etiam substantiales sentienti et intelligenti; igitur a principio intrinseco effectivo" (Scotus, *Quaestiones super secundum et tertium De anima* II, q.12, pp. 104–105).

78 Scotus, *Ordinatio* I, d.3, p.3, q.2, p. 301.

79 "Item, in organo caeci vel vigilantis ad alia intense distracti vel dormientis oculis apertis sicut leporis imprimitur species visibilis, tamen nullum illorum videt; igitur, etc. Item, dormiens non audit et tamen excitatur ad sonum, quod non faceret nisi in eius organo imprimeretur species soni; igitur *aliud est receptio speciei et auditio*" (Scotus, *Quaestiones super secundum et tertium De anima* II, q.12, p. 103, emphasis added). See also Scotus, *Ordinatio* I, d.3, p.3, q.2, pp. 283–284.

80 "[...] sed per solam potentiam intenditur actus cognoscendi" (Scotus, *Quaestiones super secundum et tertium De anima* II, q.12, p. 100). On the object and soul as the two causes necessary for perception, see R. Cross, *Duns Scotus's Theory of Cognition*, Oxford, Oxford University Press, 2014, pp. 22–27.

81 "[...] potentia recipit immediate secundum actum evocatum, et determinatur a specie sibi praesentata sui obiecti in organo potentiae sensitivae ad sentiendum[...] Item autem secundum actum elicit ipsam potentiam evocante et determinante ad cognoscendum illud obiectum cuius est species, non tamen aliqualiter ipsam potentiam informante" (Scotus, *Quaestiones super secundum et tertium De anima* II, q.12, p. 106).

Perception is not simply being affected by the object,[82] but this affection is required for it: the sense power in its capacity to perceive has in the object via the species the principle of diversification (or specification or determination) of its acts.[83] Scotus' remarks are an important reminder to models of active perception that the specific intentionality of cognitive acts needs to be explained by appeal to an external object that must somehow be constitutive of the cognitive act by determining (*determinat*) its content: what they are about – otherwise, the act could not be a likeness of the object.[84]

Scotus' view is probably best described as [F] the *hybrid model of perception* because for him perception has two causes: the object via the species and the cognitive power.[85] These are not two concurrent causes because they do not have the same ontological standing (they are not "causae ex aequo") – the power, as part of the soul qua principle of life, is ontologically superior. They are rather essentially ordered causes.[86] Scotus gives an illustrative example: if my hand holds a knife, which is sharp, I can cut things. But there is a difference between the motive power of my hand to use (or move) the sharp knife and the sharpness of the knife. Let us imagine now that the sharpness qualifies the hand, rather than the knife; this sharpness causes the hand to be able to cut things, but it does not explain the power of the hand to execute the action of cutting.[87] That capacity is explained by what the subject is and the powers belonging to the subject, of which the hand is a part. In a sense, we are back to the essentials of the Augustinian theory, notwithstanding the weightier role Scotus gives to the object/species: there is an essential distinction necessary to explain perception between the cause of the determination of the content of the cognitive act and the cause of the cognitive act itself.[88] The object via the

---

82 "[...] sentire non tantum est pati ab obiecto" (Scotus, *Quaestiones super secundum et tertium De anima* II, q.12, p. 112).

83 "[...] operationes immanentes intra possunt diversificari ab obiectis" (Scotus, *Quaestiones super secundum et tertium De anima* II, q.12, p. 111).

84 "[...] actus non esset similitudo obiecti" (Scotus, *Ordinatio* I, d.3, p.3, q.2, p. 290; see also p. 326).

85 "[...] si ergo nec anima sola nec obiectum solum sit causa totalis intellectionis actualis [...] sequitur quod ista duo sunt una causa integra respectu notitiae genitae" (Scotus, *Ordinatio* I, d.3, p.3, q.2, p. 296). That the point is valid for perception, see p. 327.

86 "Sunt ergo causae essentialiter ordinatae" (Scotus, *Ordinatio* I, d.3, p.3, q.2, p. 295).

87 Scotus, *Ordinatio* I, d.3, p.3, q.2, p. 296.

88 It seems clear that Scotus attempts to formulate a theory that is, if not Augustinian, at least compatible with Augustine. Scotus goes to great lengths to explain how the different textual passages from Augustine used by proponents of the first view (the excitation theory) can be accommodated into his (Scotus') own account: see *Ordinatio* I, d.3, p.3, q.2, pp. 299–303.

species determines the act to have the content it does but it does not cause the cognitive operation itself: the cognitive faculty is the cause of that act. Whereas Scotus accepts the causal interaction between object and the soul, others (Kilwardby, Pecham, Marston) deny such causal interaction, even though their models seem to presuppose it in practice; others still (Olivi) completely do without it. It seems clear that any of these versions of the dual component account of perception can give the identity-theory of perception a run for its money.

They do so because they provide an account of perception according to which a perceptual act does not come about because of the presence to the senses of an external thing, despite the fact that that act is about that external thing or one of its sensible features. What is particularly significant and worth emphasizing is that at the core of these models is the commitment to the separation of what accounts for the *causality* of perceptual acts and what accounts for the *content* of those same perceptual acts. Determination is not actualization because it is not about bringing the act about, but narrowing its scope. External things explain the about-ness of cognitive acts but not their directedness. To conflate the two is something foreigner to the Augustinian active theory, at least as I understand it.

2

I would like to conclude by going over the structure of my argument. Scholars working on medieval theories of perception have emphasized the debates over the nature or ontological status of the representational devices (species) by means of which, in most accounts, the object and its sensible properties are made known to perceptual subjects naturally endowed with suitable cognitive faculties. These debates focus on (I) the kind of being species have in the medium and in the sense organs and (II) whether these species constitute, or not, the primary objects of perceptual experiences. This is an interesting debate but one in which I do not discuss here. The other main focus of the existing scholarship is on the nature of the mechanisms and the processing faculties that constitute the perceptual cognitive system of the subject: what happens in each power, what sort of coordination takes place, what cognitive resources are available to the system at any given moment, and what is the nature – sensory or conceptual – of these resources. These are very interesting questions, often driven by a desire to understand those theories from a perspective that makes sense to contemporary readers, and thus frequently subordinating the metaphysical perspective (the medieval one) to a more phenomenological one (which is a contemporary concern). Whereas nowadays we are mostly concerned with how we experience a given perceptual situation, for the historical sources the concern is how to explain *the sensitivity of the perceptual system* to certain sensible features (of objects) in the world. How one interprets this difference in focus is important not only for understanding the historical sources but how one understands the relation between those historical sources and the contemporary debates. Notwithstanding the relevance of these questions, however, they were not the focus of my paper. Instead, I wanted to pay close attention to the issue of how medieval thinkers, who accept that material objects are able to make their impression on sense organs, describe the relation between this reception of the species and the perceptual experience properly: is this a relation of identity, of concurrence, or of causation?

Despite differences between the several accounts just presented, the key element is the basic distinction operating in perception between what makes a cognitive act to be about a certain thing and what makes or brings about that cognitive act. For what I have called the "identity account," the reception of the species in the sense is equated with perception, because the object is the efficient cause of that act. On the other hand, for those models I have presented under the general heading of "dual component account" of perception, the reception of the species is not equated with perception but with a part of that cognitive process that may or may not be causally connected to the production of the perceptual act itself. Finally, it is also the case that one can defend the activity (or self-motion) of the soul in the causation of its cognitive acts without accepting the reception of species in the organ, thus not upholding the dual component account; this is the case with Peter John Olivi.

It seems clear, therefore, that the issue of the activity or passivity of perception cannot be reduced to a debate between the pro-species and the no-species theorists, but that it encompasses a wide range of philosophical theories, the details of which still deserve further investigation.[89] It seems that one can talk about many ways of how the soul can be said to be active in perception and that excitation is not enough on its own to qualify such a view as active, if that excitation is explained as simply constituting a reaction. Confirmation on this

---

89 One example of what I am suggesting here is the conflation of some versions of the agent sense model of perception of Averroist origin and the active sensation model of Augustinian origin. The common thread that explains this conflation is the refusal by these two models of accepting a fully passive account of sense perception and to uphold the two-step account: reception in the organ as distinct from, and non-causally related to, the activity of the power. On this, see my "From Agent to Active Sense: Was there an *Augustinianism-Averroisant*?," in A.M. Mora-Márquez and V. Decaix (eds), *Active Cognition*, Dordrecht, Springer, forthcoming.

depends on further research, especially in the so-called Augustinian tradition on the philosophy of perception. Meanwhile, in this article I presented the first attempt to systematically map the models within this tradition and even those opposing it. I have also suggested that what unites these authors into what I call the "Augustinian philosophy of perception" is the attempt to combine two aspects that the Aristotelian tradition takes apart: the intrinsic principle of life is the efficient cause of cognition. For the authors just discussed and notwithstanding their differences, the original Augustinian POH is updated by explaining the superiority of the soul towards the body as being about life rather than about spirituality. The motivation for calling it "Augustinian" issues from the basic principles that can be traced back to Augustine, whom all these authors explicitly quote as authoritative to their own views on the nature of perception.

Acknowledgements

The author would like to acknowledge funding from the European Research Council under the ERC Starting grant agreement n. 637747 for the project *Rationality in Perception: Transformations of Mind and Cognition 1250–1550*.

Bibliography

Primary Literature

Albert the Great, *De anima*, A. Borgnet (ed), *Opera omnia 5*, Paris, Vivès, 1890.

Anonymi Magistri Artium, *Lectura in librum De anima a quodam discipulo reportata*, R.A. Gauthier (ed), Grotaferrata, Ad Claras Aquas, 1985.

Anonymi Magistri Artium, *Quaestiones super librum De anima*, P. Bernardini (ed), Firenze, SISMEL, Edizioni del Galluzzo, 2009.

Augustine, *De Trinitate*, W.J. Mountain (ed) with the assistance of F. Glorie, Turnhout, Brepols, 1968.

Augustine, *On the Trinity*, books 8–15, trans. S. McKenna, Cambridge, Cambridge University Press, 2002.

Durand of St. Pourçain, *Scriptum super IV libros Sententiarum*, F. Retucci (ed), Leuven, Peeters, 2012.

Godfrey of Fontaines, *Quodlibeta IX*, J. Hoffmans (ed), Leuven, Institut Supérieur de Philosophie de l'Université, 1924.

Godfrey of Fontaines, *Quodlibeta XIII*, J. Hoffmans (ed), Leuven, Institut Supérieur de Philosophie de l'Université, 1935.

THE CHAMELEONIC MIND: ACTIVITY V. ACTUALITY OF PERCEPTION 71

Henry of Ghent, *Quodlibeta*, Venice, 1608.

Jacopo Zabarella, "Liber de sensu agente," *De rebus naturalibus libri XXX*, Venice, Apud Paulum Meietum bibliopolam Patavinum, 1590, pp. 582–599.

John Duns Scotus, *Opera omnia*, C. Balic (ed), Vatican, Typis Polyglottis Vaticanis, 1954.

John Duns Scotus, *Quaestiones super secundum et tertium De anima*, B.C. Bazán et al. (eds), St. Bonaventure, The Franciscan Institute, 2006.

John Pecham, *Questiones de anima*, H. Spettmann (ed), *Questiones tractantes de anima*, Münster, Aschensorff, 1918.

John Pecham, *Quodlibeta quatuor*, G.J. Etzkorn and F. Delorme (eds), Grottaferrata, Collegium S. Bonaventurae, 1989.

John Pecham, *Tractatus de anima*, G. Melani (ed), Firenze, Biblioteca di Studi Francescani, 1948.

Nicholas of Cusa, *Idiota de mente*, R. Steige (ed), Hamburg, Meiner, 1995.

Nicole Oresme, *Expositio et Quaestiones in Aristotelis De anima*, B. Patar (ed), Louvain-La-Neuve-Louvain, Éditions de l'Institut Supérieur de Philosophie, 1995.

Peter John Olivi, "Epistola ad fratrem R.," S. Piron et al. (eds), *Archivum Franciscanum Historicum*, vol 91, 1998, pp. 33–65.

Peter John Olivi, *Quaestiones in secundum librum Sententiarum*, 3 vols., B. Jansen (ed), Firenze, Collegium S. Bonaventurae, 1922–1926.

Peter of Ailly, *Tractatus de anima*, O. Pluta (ed), *Die Philosophische Psychologie des Peter von Ailly*, Amsterdam, B.R. Grüner, 1987.

Robert Kilwardby, *De spiritu fantastico*, P.O. Lewry (ed), *On Time and Imagination: De tempore, De spiritu fantastico*, Oxford, Oxford University Press for the British Academy, 1987.

Robert Kilwardby, *On Time and Imagination*, Part 2, trans. Al. Broadie, Oxford, Oxford University Press, 1993.

Roger Marston, *Quaestiones disputatae de anima*, Quaracchi, Collegium S. Bonaventurae, 1932.

William of Auvergne, *De anima*, F. Hotot (ed), with *Supplementum* Blaise Le Feron (ed), *Opera omnia*, 2 vols., Paris, Andreas Pralard, 1674; reprint Frankfurt am Main, Minerva, 1963; trans. R.J. Teske, Marquette, Marquette University Press, 2000.

Secondary Literature

Bernardini, Paola, "La passività del senso nei commenti alla *Vetus* del *De anima*. Le origini della dottrina del *sensus agens*," *Documenti e studi sulla tradizione filosofica medievale*, vol. 25, 2014, pp. 243–287.

Cross, Richard, *Duns Scotus's Theory of Cognition*, Oxford, Oxford University Press, 2014.

Marrone, Steven, *William of Auvergne and Robert Grosseteste: New Ideas of Truth in the Early Thirteenth-Century*, Princeton, Princeton University Press, 1983.

Masnovo, Amato, *Da Guglielmo d'Auvergne a S. Tommaso d'Aquino*, vol. 1, Milan, Società Editrice Vita e Pensiero, 1945.

Owens, Joseph, "Aristotle – Cognition a Way of Being," *Canadian Journal of Philosophy*, vol. 6, no. 1, 1976, pp. 1–11.

Pasnau, Robert, *Theories of Cognition in the Later Middle Ages*, Cambridge, Cambridge University Press, 1997.

Pickavé, Martin, "Causality and Cognition: An Interpretation of Henry of Ghent's *Quodlibet* V, q. 14," in G. Klima (ed), *Intentionality, Cognition, and Mental Representation in Medieval Philosophy*, New York, Fordham University Press, 2015, pp. 46–80.

Silva, José Filipe, "From Agent to Active Sense: Was there an *Augustinianism-Averroisant?*" in A.M. Mora-Márquez and V. Decaix (eds), *Active Cognition*, Dordrecht, Springer, forthcoming.

Silva, José Filipe, "Intentionality in Medieval Augustinianism," in M. Summa and J. Müller (eds), *Phänomenologische Forschungen*, vol. 2, 2018, pp. 25–44.

Silva, José Filipe, "Medieval Theories of Active Perception: An Overview," in J.F. Silva and M. Yrjönsuuri (eds), *Active Perception in the History of Philosophy: From Plato to Modern Philosophy*, Dordrecht, Springer, 2014, pp. 117–146.

Silva, José Filipe, "Perceptiveness," *Proceedings of the Aristotelian Society*, Supplementary Volume 91, 2017, pp. 43–61.

Silva, José Filipe, "Robert Kilwardby on Sense Perception," in P. Kärkkäinen and S. Knuuttila (eds), *Theories of Perception in Medieval and Early Modern Philosophy*, Dordrecht, Springer, 2008, pp. 87–99.

Silva, José Filipe, *Robert Kilwardby on the Human Soul: Plurality of Forms and Censorship in the Thirteenth Century*, Leiden, Brill, 2012.

Silva, José Filipe, "Robert Kilwardby on the Theory of the Soul and Epistemology," in P. Thom and H. Lagerlund (eds), *A Companion to Robert Kilwardby*, Leiden, Brill, 2013, pp. 275–313.

Silva, José Filipe, and Toivanen, Juhana, "The Active Nature of the Soul in Sense Perception: Robert Kilwardby and Peter John of Olivi," *Vivarium*, vol. 48, no. 3–4, 2010, pp. 245–278.

Smith, Arthur D., *The Problem of Perception*, Cambridge, Harvard University Press, 2002.

Solère, Jean-Luc, "Durand of Saint-Pourçain's Cognition Theory: Its Fundamental Principles," in R.L. Friedman and J.-M. Counet (eds), *Medieval Perspectives on Aristotle's "De anima*," Louvain, Peeters, 2013, pp. 185–248.

van Riet, Georges, "La théorie thomiste de la sensation externe," *Revue philosophique de Louvain*, vol. 51, no. 31, 1953, pp. 374–408.

CHAPTER 4

The Visual Process: Immediate or Successive? Approaches to the Extramission Postulate in 13th Century Theories of Vision

Lukáš Lička

1 Introduction

Is vision merely a *state* of the beholder's sensory organ which can be explained as an immediate effect caused by external sensible objects? Or is it rather a successive *process* in which the observer actively scanning the surrounding environment plays a major part? These two general attitudes towards visual perception were both developed already by ancient thinkers. The former is embraced by natural philosophers (e.g., atomists and Aristotelians) and is often labelled "intromissionist," based on their assumption that vision is an outcome of the causal influence exerted by an external object upon a sensory organ receiving an entity from the object. The latter attitude to vision as a successive process is rather linked to the "extramissionist" theories of the proponents of geometrical optics (such as Euclid or Ptolemy) who suggest that an entity – a visual ray – is sent forth from the eyes to the object.[1]

The present paper focuses on the contributions to this ancient controversy proposed by some 13th century Latin thinkers. In contemporary historiography of medieval Latin philosophy, the general narrative is that whereas thinkers in the 12th century held various (mostly Platonic) versions of the extramission theory, the situation changes during the first half of the 13th century when texts by Avicenna, Aristotle (with the commentaries by Averroes), and especially Alhacen, who all favour the intromissionist paradigm, were gradually assimilated.[2] It is assumed that, as a result, since ca. 1250 the intromissionist account was universally accepted by most Latin thinkers while extramission

---

1 For an account of the ancient theories of vision based on this line of conflict see especially D.C. Lindberg, *Theories of Vision from al-Kindi to Kepler*, Chicago, University of Chicago Press, 1976, pp. 1–17, and A.M. Smith, *From Sight to Light: The Passage from Ancient to Modern Optics*, Chicago, University of Chicago Press, 2015, pp. 23–75.
2 For these authors' criticism of extramission, see, e.g., Lindberg, *Theories of Vision*, pp. 44–49 (Avicenna), pp. 53–54 (Averroes), pp. 61–67 (Alhacen).

© KONINKLIJKE BRILL NV, LEIDEN, 2020 | DOI:10.1163/9789004413030_005

came to be regarded as a strange, eccentric, and antiquated theory – and the whole controversy became outdated.[3]

The present paper aims to somewhat amend this narrative. It argues that the extramissionist theory was taken quite seriously by many 13th century thinkers (at least as a more or less sophisticated theory one should deal with and argue against) and even may have some merits in explaining the visual process. The attitudes towards extramission held by the 13th century Latin thinkers investigated in the paper can broadly be divided into three categories: refutation, where the best example is Albert the Great (especially his works written in the 1240s and 1250s); syncretic tendencies to incorporate some extramissionist tenets into a broader intromissionist framework obvious especially in Roger Bacon (in his works written in the 1260s); and, finally, an open-minded rethinking and reformulation of the theory which, as I will argue, may be found in Peter Olivi (especially in various questions he wrote in the 1270s and early 1280s). As I will argue, while the traditional narrative is without doubt true in the general contour, these three figures do not fit into it. It is not true without qualification that the controversy between intromission and extramission had become antiquated already in the mid-13th century due to the "Alhacenian turn" – Bacon and Olivi still take the extramission postulate very seriously later in that century.

2 Extramission, Its Varieties, and Merits

Before these three medieval thinkers' accounts of vision can be considered, it ought to be elucidated (1) what an extramissionist theory amounts to, (2) what kinds of extramissionist involvement are present in theories of vision contemporary to the three thinkers investigated here, and (3) why an extramissionist theory may be challenging and interesting.

What are the distinctive features of extramissionist theories of vision? At least four general tenets can be pointed out:[4]

---

3 For a concise but broadly conceived instance of such a traditional narrative see D.N. Hasse, "Pietro d'Abano's Conciliator and the Theory of the Soul in Paris," in J. Aertsen, K. Emory, and A. Speer (eds), *Nach der Verurteilung von 1277. Philosophie und Theologie an der Universität von Paris im letzten Viertel des 13. Jahrhunderts. Studien und Texte*, Berlin, De Gruyter, 2001, pp. 645–647. For more details, see Lindberg, *Theories of Vision*, pp. 87–121; Smith, *From Sight to Light*, pp. 228–277.

4 For a clear depiction of the grades of extramissive involvement in a visual theory see M.E. Kalderon, "Perception and Extramission in *De quantitate animae*," *Oxford Studies in Ancient Philosophy*, forthcoming.

(1) *The extramission postulate.* These theories share the assumption that visual perception consists in (or at least includes) the perceiver "extending" outwards to the visible object in a special way. This extension is often articulated by postulating an entity that issues from the eyes and reaches the object. In most authors, what is emitted is something material, albeit very subtle – e.g. the inner light of the Platonists, the visual ray of the Euclidians, or the visual spirit or *pneuma* of the Galenists.

(2) *The primacy of visual activity.* As implied in the extramission postulate, the visual organ is active and plays a primary role in the visual process, which begins not because an external object affects the eye (which processes the affection in response), but because the eye itself acts first and reaches the object by means of something emitted. The primacy of the eye's activity is sometimes stressed by advocating the eye movements and the consequent focusing of attention.[5]

(3) *Reducing vision to establishing a cognitive contact.* Vision is explained as establishing a contact between the observer and the object and often interpreted in haptic terms. The contact is ensured by the entity emitted from the eyes and hence vision is very much like a kind of touch: as the famous Stoic metaphor says, we see a thing by means of a *pneuma* just like a blind man "sees" by means of a cane.[6]

(4) *Use of geometry.* Extramissionist theories often (but not exclusively) describe vision in geometrical terms – a visual cone is postulated with the base on the object seen and the apex in the eye.[7]

It is worth noting that several degrees of commitment to the extramission postulate are present in the visual theories commonly known or elaborated in Latin philosophy of the 12th and 13th century. First, there is (A) a genuine extramissionist explanation of vision – visual ray theories. These theories postulate visual rays emanating from the eyes towards the objects. The most

---

5 E.g., Chalcidius, *Timaeus a Calcidio translatus commentarioque instructus*, J.H. Waszink (ed), Leiden, Brill, 1975, hereafter *In Tim.*, 10, § 238, p. 251.

6 This feature of extramissionist theories is stressed, e.g., by Nemesius of Emesa, *De natura hominis, Nemesii episcopi Premnon physicon sive Peri physeōs anthrōpoy liber a N. Alfano archiepiscopo Salerni in Latinum translatus*, C. Burkhard (ed), Leipzig, Teubner, 1917, 7, 75 (who mentions Hipparchus's comparison of the eye with its rays to a hand grasping a thing); Albert the Great, *De homine*, H. Anzulewicz and J.R. Söder (eds), *Opera omnia 27.2*, Münster, Aschendorff, 2008, 187b, 194b, 195b. Cf. Kalderon, "Perception and Extramission in *De quantitate animae*" who stresses that this condition in particular must be fulfilled for a theory to be called "extramissionist."

7 There is no single understanding of the properties of such a visual cone. For a general survey of the issue among late ancient geometricians see H. Siebert, "Transformation of Euclid's *Optics* in Late Antiquity," *Nuncius*, vol 29, no. 1, 2014, especially pp. 90–94, 106–123.

prominent examples are (A1) the works on geometrical optics translated into Latin during the 12th and 13th century – Euclid's *De visu* and *De speculis* with a compilation *De speculis* falsely ascribed to Euclid, Ptolemy's *Optics* and Al-Kindí's *De aspectibus*. The visual theories expounded in these works display all of the aforementioned features.

Medieval scholars extrapolated a slightly different version of the visual ray theory also (A2) from Platonic philosophy, especially Plato's *Timaeus*, where a fiery nature is ascribed to the eyes with the consequence that they emit a special kind of light which coalesces with daylight to form a continuous body between the observer and the seen object. Such a ray theory is also ascribed to Augustine, at least by some Latin thinkers.[8] This Platonic version of the visual ray theory includes tenets (1)–(3) but does not make use of geometry. As Albert the Great points out, this is the main difference between Euclidians and Platonists: whereas Euclidians explain the fact that distant things are seen poorly by the small angle included between the lateral rays of the visual cone, Platonists propose that when the visual ray is obliged to stretch to a distant object, it is weakened and, hence, the vision is poor.[9]

However, the Platonic visual theory can also be interpreted differently – as including not only extramission of visual rays but also an emission from the visible object. (After all, a pure extramissionist theory may lead to the consequence that the visual act is not in the eyes but on the object where the visual ray touches the object.)[10] Such (B) a *syncretic* account is suggested already by Galen who stresses that Platonic theory includes not only an emission of internal light but also a reverse motion from the object to the eyes. In his view, the

---

8   Augustine is commended as a proponent of extramission by Roger Bacon, *Perspectiva*, D.C. Lindberg (ed and trans.), *Roger Bacon and the Origins of "Perspectiva" in the Middle Ages*, Oxford, Clarendon Press, 1996, hereafter *Persp.*, I.7.2, 100, and criticized for the same reason by Peter John Olivi, *Quaestiones in secundum librum Sententiarum*, 3 vols., B. Jansen (ed), Firenze, Collegium S. Bonaventurae, 1922–1926, hereafter *Summa* II, 58, 482–484; 73, 55–58. Roger Marston, *Quodlibeta quatuor*, G.J. Etzkorn and I. Brady (eds), Grottaferrata, Collegium S. Bonaventurae, 1994, I.19, 57–58, believes that Augustine proposed an intromission theory of vision; Peter Sutton (?), *Quodlibeta*, F. Etzkorn (ed), *Franciscan Studies*, vol. 23, 1963, I.24, 111, asserts that extramission was a position upheld by the young Augustine when he was first instructed (*imbutus*) in a Platonic doctrine, but he corrected his view later. The ascription of a full-fledged extramissionist theory to Augustine is convincingly refuted by Kalderon, "Perception and Extramission in *De quantitate animae.*"
9   Albert, *De homine*, 192b–193a.
10   A point ascribed to Augustine and criticized by Olivi, *Summa* II.73, 61–63.

EXTRAMISSION POSTULATE IN 13TH C. THEORIES OF VISION   77

emitted entity is a visual *pneuma* that renders the intervening air an instrument of vision and enables the colours of the object to enter the eye.[11]

Latin scholars elaborated further on such syncretic accounts involving both extramission and intrommision. Two versions may be discerned – a syncretic account with (B1) a primacy of extramission and another one with (B2) a primacy of intromission. The primacy of extramission was stressed by some 12th century Platonists: first, a visual ray of a fiery nature is sent forth from the eyes, then it encounters the object, disperses over its surface, grasps its form and brings the form back to the eye.[12] In the 13th century, the same view was held by the anonymous author of the *Lectura in librum De anima* (Paris, ca. 1246–47)[13] and later attributed to certain *Platonici* and dismissed by Roger Bacon, John Pecham (between 1277 and 79) and Peter Olivi.[14] This kind of syncretic theory includes the extramission postulate and the primary activity of the eye (tenets 1)-2), but does not reduce vision to establishing a contact by means of a visual ray; the form of the object must be transported to the eye. None of its proponents mentioned above elaborates on the geometry of vision (tenet 4); although a visual cone formed by the rays is sometimes mentioned by them.

Another kind of syncretic theory was quite prominent in the 13th century, especially among Franciscan thinkers. According to this theory, vision is basically established by intromission – but the postulate of visual rays emitted from the eyes is preserved (for details see Bacon below). Such a (B2) syncretic theory of vision with a primacy of intromission is suggested by Grosseteste

---

11   An outline of the Galenic account of vision is to be found in Lindberg, *Theories of Vision*, pp. 10–11, and Smith, *From Sight to Light*, pp. 36–43. Constantine the African also points out that the Galenic account is in the middle between extra – and intromission – *De oculis, Collectio ophthalmologica veterum auctorum VII*, P. Pansier (ed), Paris, 1933, IV.2, 177–180.

12   Such a position is defended by Bernard of Chartres, William of Conches, and Adelard of Bath – see Bernard of Chartres, *Glosae super Platonem*, P.E. Dutton (ed), Toronto, PIMS, 1991, II.7, p. 207; Guillelmus de Conchis, *Glosae super Platonem*, E.A. Jeauneau (ed), Turnhout, Brepols, 2006, II.137, pp. 248–249; Guillelmus de Conchis, *Dragmaticon philosophiae*, I. Ronca and A. Badia (eds), Turnhout, Brepols, 1997, VI.19.3–5, pp. 244–245; Adelard of Bath, *Quaestiones naturales, Conversations with his Nephew: On the Same and the Different, Questions on Natural Science*, and *On Birds*, C. Burnett (ed and trans.), Cambridge, Cambridge University Press, 1998, 23, pp. 140–142. See also Lindberg, *Theories of Vision*, pp. 90–94 and Smith, *From Sight to Light*, pp. 237–241.

13   Anonymous, *Lectura in librum De anima a quodam discipulo reportata*, R.A. Gauthier (ed), Grottaferrata, Collegium S. Bonaventurae, 1985, hereafter *Lectura*, II.14.1, 324.

14   Bacon, *Persp.* I.7.3, 102–104; John Pecham, *John Pecham and the Science of Optics: "Perspectiva communis,"* D.C. Lindberg (ed), Wisconsin, University of Wisconsin, 1970, I.46(49), p. 128; Olivi, *Summa* II.73, 55, 59–61.

78   LIČKA

(1220s), in an eclectic manner by Bartholomeus Anglicus (ca. 1240),[15] and also
by an anonymous master whose questions on *De anima* are preserved in MS
Assisi, Biblioteca del Sacro Convento 138 (ca. 1240s).[16] Visual rays are also advocated in the anonymous *Summa philosophiae* once ascribed to Grosseteste
(1265–1275).[17] As I argue below, an elaborate version of this account is proposed
by Roger Bacon (in early 1260s). Bacon's version is adopted by John Pecham
and apparently also by Roger Marston (Oxford, between 1282 and 1284).[18] This
syncretism is mocked as a peculiar novelty by Albert the Great in the 1240s and
1250s[19] and later in a *quodlibet* attributed to Peter Sutton.[20] The position cannot be called "extramissionist" except in a broad sense. Its general setting is
intromissionist and with its stress on the primary activity of the visible object
it is against tenets (2) and (3). However, it preserves (1) the extramission postulate and (4) the use of geometry (albeit in an intromissionist rendering).

It is obvious that the extramission postulate was not a rare and eccentric
feature of 13th century visual theories – rather on the contrary. This list of visual theories more or less committed to the extramission postulate constitutes

---

15   Robert Grosseteste, *De iride seu De iride et speculo*, L. Baur (ed), *Die philosophischen Werke
       des Robert Grosseteste, Bischofs von Lincoln*, Münster, Aschendorff, 1912, pp. 72–73; Bartholomeus Anglicus, *De proprietatibus rerum*, Frankfurt, Wolfgang Richter, 1601, hereafter
       DPR, III.17, 64.

16   Anonymous, *Quaestiones in De anima*, MS Assisi, Bibl. Sacr. Conv. 138, fol. 253vb. On the
       text, see R.J. Long, "The anonymous *De anima* of Assisi, biblioteca comunale cod. 138," in
       A. Musco et al. (eds), *Universalità della ragione. Pluralità delle filosofie nel Medioevo*, vol. 2,
       Palermo, Officina di studi medievali, 2012, pp. 271–280.

17   Pseudo-Robert Grosseteste, *Summa philosophiae*, L. Baur (ed), *Die philosophischen Werke
       des Robert Grosseteste, Bischofs von Lincoln*, Münster, Aschendorff, 1912, XII.15–18,
       pp. 502–508.

18   Pecham, *Perspectiva communis* I.46(49), 128–130; Roger Marston, *Quodlibeta* I.19, 58–59.

19   Albert, *De homine*, 198a; Albert, *De sensu et sensato*, S. Donati (ed), *Opera omnia 7.2A*,
       Münster, Aschendorff, 2017, hereafter *De sensu*, 1.5, 28b ("*novella et fatua … non opinio, sed
       insania*"). Albert may have had some of his contemporaries in mind (Grosseteste and Bartholomeus Anglicus being the most probable options). However, it is possible that Albert
       actually meant a syncretism with the primacy of extramission – then his target would be,
       e.g., William of Conches. For further surmises on the issue, cf. H. Anzulewicz, "Perspektive
       und Raumvorstellung in den Frühwerken des Albertus Magnus," in J. Aertsen and A. Speer
       (eds), *Raum und Raumvorstellungen im Mittelalter*, Berlin, De Gruyter, 1998, pp. 263–264,
       and Hasse, "Pietro d'Abano's Conciliator," p. 649.

20   Peter Sutton (?), *Quodlibeta* 1.24, 110. While the traditional dating of the quodlibet was
       1309–1311, recently it was suggested that it might be from the late 1280s (see M. Pickavé,
       "The Controversy over the Principle of Individuation in Medieval Quodlibeta (1277-ca.
       1320): A Forest Map," in C. Schabel (ed), *Theological Quodlibeta in the Middle Ages: The
       Fourteenth Century*, Leiden, Brill, 2007, p. 56). In such case its author cannot be Peter
       Sutton.

EXTRAMISSION POSTULATE IN 13TH C. THEORIES OF VISION 79

a framework for investigating the attitudes of Albert the Great, Roger Bacon and Peter Olivi to extramission. The most important question for such an investigation is their stance towards tenet 3, namely, whether they agree with extramission as an instrument for establishing a cognitive contact between the perceiver and the object seen. Hence, in examining their theories, a special emphasis is placed on the following two issues regarding the cognitive contact: First, how is the cognitive contact with the external object established? Is it by means of something received in the sight, or rather by something emitted from the eye? And when the cognitive contact is established, is it sufficient for vision to occur, or must a further operation be performed? Second, is there an ontological gap between the material world and the more or less immaterial sensory soul? If so, how is the gap bridged in the visual process?

Besides these questions, the paper is guided by the query whether an extramissionist theory actually has any merits. Why might it be challenging? Why did so many medieval thinkers deal with extramission, if it is empirically doubtful? Several arguments in favour of the theory are often repeated by medieval authors, who seem to have regarded at least some of them as sound and convincing. Besides some anecdotes from the ancient literature (cats seeing in the dark, basilisks killing with their glance, or menstruating women staining the mirror with their gaze), there was also the authority of some ancient thinkers defending (or apparently defending) extramission: besides geometrical optics and Platonists, even Aristotle is sometimes referred to as a proponent of visual rays (especially his *De animalibus* and *Meteorologica*).[21] Theological arguments for extramission can also be brought up.[22]

---

21 See, e.g., Pseudo-Petrus Hispanus, *Expositio libri De anima*, M. Alonso (ed), Madrid, Instituto de filosofía "Luis Vives," 1952, III.10, pp. 393–394 (without justification); Bartholomeus Anglicus, *DPR* III.17, 64; Anonymous, *Quaestiones in De anima*, MS Assisi, Bibl. Sacr. Conv. 138, f. 253vb; Bacon, *Persp.* I.7.2, 100; Roger Marston, *Quodlibeta* I.19, 58. The Aristotelian passage often referred to is *De generatione animalium* V, 1, 781a1–2; however, the belief of medieval scholars that this passage is a statement of extramission seems to be based on a mistranslation – see D.C. Lindberg, *Roger Bacon and the Origins of "Perspectiva" in the Middle Ages: A Critical Edition and English Translation of Bacon's "Perspectiva,"* Oxford, Oxford University Press, 1996, p. 359, note 223. Nevertheless, Aristotle's adherence to an intromissionist approach is not uncontested. The elements of a visual ray theory in Aristotle's writings are briefly listed by S. Berryman, "Euclid and the Sceptic: A Paper on Vision, Doubt, Geometry, Light and Drunkenness," *Phronesis*, vol. 43, no. 2, 1998, pp. 183–184. It is possible that such an attitude to visual theory prevailed in the early Peripatetic school – note that Chalcidius attributes the view that visual rays are emitted by the eye to both geometricians and Peripatetics (*In Tim.*, 10, § 238, 250–251).

22 For medieval thinkers, incorporeal beings such as angels or separated souls cannot be affected by any corporeal impulses from the outside; hence, it is possible that they see by means of extramission. Such a position is mentioned and refuted by Bonaventure,

Further, the extramission postulate was traditionally connected with geometrical description of the visual experience. Hence, the extramissionist approach – with the visual cone demarcating the visual field whose size depends on the angle included between the rays issuing from the eye – was believed to be better equipped to explain how the distance, location and size of an object is perceived. However, the notion of a visual cone can very easily be incorporated into the intromissionist framework, as we will see below – hence, it does not force a thinker to uphold extramission.

Nevertheless, the best argument for extramission is that it may describe some aspects of the visual process more adequately. It seems to be better equipped (than the intromissionist account) to explain some psychological features of the visual experience, e.g., attention focusing, active searching for a thing in the visual field, successive apprehension of a thing exceeding the boundaries of the visual field, etc. In all of these cases, the perceiver's active involvement is needed, as physiologically manifested in the eye-movements, which the extramissionist can easily explain with reference to the movements of the axis of the visual cone.

Take an example of a little penny on the floor, attributed by Nemesius of Emesa to "geometricians." The perceiver may see the whole floor without noticing the penny, until he focuses his attention directly towards it.[23] A conundrum for intromission: if the perceiver sees by virtue of effects caused in his sensory organs by the outside objects, he should see the floor *and* the penny at the same moment. An extramissionist has an advantage here: he may point out that the visual capacity is not distributed homogeneously in the visual cone (and hence, unlike the floor, the penny is not seen in the first moment) and refer to the movement of the axis (which enables the perceiver to see the penny as soon as the axis falls upon it).

Therefore, an extramissionist theory raises questions concerning the temporal and spatial aspects of the visual process. Is vision immediate or successive? And do we apprehend a single entity or a number of things at once? The extramissionist stance is that only one thing is seen at one moment – strictly

---

Aquinas, and Pecham – see Bonaventura, *Commentaria in quatuor libros Sententiarum, Opera omnia* I-IV, Quaracchi, Collegium S. Bonaventurae, 1882–1889, IV.49.2.1.3.2, 1020b; Thomas Aquinas, *Commentum in quartum librum Sententiarum*, Parma, Typis Petri Ficcadori, 1858, IV.44.2.1, 315b-316a; and John Pecham, *Quaestiones tractantes de anima*, H. Spettmann (ed), Münster, Aschendorff, 1918, II.20.6, 164. The position seems to have been preferred to the theory of *species* by Olivi, *Summa* II.58, 489.

23 Nemesius, *De natura hominis*, 7, 75. The same example is also in Pseudo-Euclid, *De speculis*, A.A. Björnbo and S. Vogl (eds), *Alkindi, Tideus und Pseudo-Euklid. Drei optische Werke*, Berlin, Teubner, 1912, 15, 106.

EXTRAMISSION POSTULATE IN 13TH C. THEORIES OF VISION   81

speaking, only the point touched by the axis of the visual cone. The visual apprehension of a thing is completed by a quick transportation of the axis of the visual cone, i.e., successively.[24] On the contrary, Aristotelians insist on the view that vision is immediate – the reception of the object's form is not a result of a local motion but an alteration, and hence instantaneous. Based on the intuition that vision is immediate, some Aristotelians point out that the successive propagation of the visual ray and the consequence that the vision would occur in time is in fact an argument against extramission, because it renders a counterintuitive conception of vision.[25]

Therefore, the third issue considered in the following accounts of Albert, Bacon, and Olivi is their stance towards the temporal and spatial aspects of the visual process.

3   Refutation: Albert the Great

The first theory under consideration here is the Aristotelian approach developed by Albert the Great, which is generally dismissive towards extramission of any kind.[26]

It is worth noting that Albert evidently inclined to extramission in his earliest theological works written in the 1230s and early 1240s. Having a foundation in Plato's *Timaeus* and Chalcidius's commentary on it, he assumes that vision is performed by rays emitted from the eyes coalescing with the external light and that the visual concentration depends on the close connection of the

---

24   This is how the medieval interpreted the Euclidian proposition that "nothing is seen as a whole simultaneously" (Euclid, *De visu*, W.R. Theisen (ed), "*Liber de visu*: The Greco-Latin Translation of Euclid's *Optics*," *Mediaeval Studies*, vol. 41, no. 1, 1979, 1, 62).

25   See John Blund, *Tractatus de anima*, D.A. Callus and R.W. Hunt (eds), trans. M.W. Dunne, *Treatise on the Soul*, Oxford, Oxford University Press, 2013, IX.101, 54; and Peter Sutton (?), *Quodlibeta* I.24, 110. The argument originates from Averroes, *De sensu et sensato*, H.A. Wolfson, D. Baneth, and F.H. Fobes (eds), *Compendia librorum Aristotelis qui Parva naturalia vocantur*, Cambridge, The Mediaeval Academy of America, 1949, p. 34.

26   On Albert's visual theory see, e.g., N.H. Steneck, "Albert on the Psychology of Sense Perception," in J.A. Weisheipl (ed), *Albertus Magnus and the Sciences: Commemorative Essays 1980*, Toronto, PIMS, 1980; L. Dewan, "St. Albert, the Sensibles, and Spiritual Being," in J.A. Weisheipl (ed), *Albertus Magnus and the Sciences*; on the optical issues in his works see Lindberg, *Theories of Vision*, pp. 104–107; C. Akdogan, "Optics in Albert the Great's *De sensu et sensato*: An Edition, English Translation, and Analysis," PhD dissertation, University of Wisconsin-Madison, 1978; and especially Anzulewicz, "Perspektive und Raumvorstellung." On the dating of Albert's writings see H. Anzulewicz, *De forma resultante in speculo*, 2 vols., Münster, Aschendorff, 1999, I, 6–17.

visual rays.[27] Albert's attitude towards extramission changed in the course of his work on the anthropological compendium *De homine* (finished in Paris around 1242) under the strong influence of Aristotle, Avicenna's *De anima* and Averroes's *De sensu* who all argued against extramission. Here Albert dismisses extramissionist theories for the first time and embraces an Aristotelian one.[28] Criticism of extramission is present also in his later *De sensu et sensato* (written in Italy in 1256).[29]

The reason why Albert devoted such a considerable amount of text to arguing against extramission may have been that – in his view – the theory was defended by not a few of the contemporary Latin scholars (*a multis hodie defenditur*).[30] Thus, in his early *De homine* he argues against Plato, Euclid and Al-Kindí (he calls the latter two *aspectivi*, perhaps on the account of the title of Al-Kindí's *De aspectibus*); later in his *De sensu* he uses similar arguments against Empedocles (whom he considers to be a predecessor of Euclid) and again Plato. His reasoning is quite extensive, albeit not particularly original. He heavily relies on Avicenna and Averroes.[31]

From among the extramissionist tenets outlined in the introduction, Albert's main target was the postulate of a material emission itself. If vision was

---

27 A Platonic theory of vision is evident in Albert's *De natura boni* (Germany, ca. 1233–1234) and *De resurrectione* (Paris, before 1242). This seminal change in Albert's visual theory is analysed in Anzulewicz, "Perspektive und Raumvorstellung," pp. 252–267.

28 Albert, *De homine*, 185a-189b and especially the appendix to that question on pp. 189b-202b. Note that the appendix is a later addition to the text, written sometimes before 1246 (see also *De homine* p. xiv). As a consequence of assimilating the Aristotelian framework in *De homine*, Albert abandoned extramission also in his theological works – see Albert the Great, *Commentarii in II Sententiarum*, A. Borgnet (ed), *Opera omnia* 27, Paris, Vivès, 1894, II.13.2, 246b (Paris, around 1246), and Albert, *Quaestio de sensibus corporis gloriosi*, A. Fries, W. Kübel, and H. Anzulewicz (eds), *Opera omnia* 25.2, Münster, Aschendorff, 1993, 2.1, 116b-118a (after 1246 or 1249).

29 Albert, *De sensu* I.7–8, 31a-39a. Albert denies extramission also in his *De anima* (Germany, between 1254–57), C. Stroick (ed), *Opera omnia* 7.1, Münster, Aschendorff, 1968, II.3.14, 119b.

30 Albert, *De sensu* I.5, 27a; I.8, 35a.

31 Albert's borrowings from Avicenna's *De anima* are well documented – see D.N. Hasse, *Avicenna's "De anima" in the Latin West: The Formation of a Peripatetic Philosophy of the Soul, 1160–1300*, London, The Warburg Institute, 2000, pp. 60–69; on vision, pp. 124–126 and especially the analytical index on pp. 270–279 (Albert's borrowings from Avicenna's *De anima* III). Note that Albert did not use Alhacen's *Perspectiva* in his reasoning against extramission (he mentions him only in passing in *De sensu* – see Lindberg, *Theories of Vision*, pp. 106, 252) – in the 1240s and 1250s the assimilation of Alhacen was still in its early stages and was taking place in Oxford, rather than in Paris (see note 62 below).

EXTRAMISSION POSTULATE IN 13TH C. THEORIES OF VISION 83

performed by the emission of a material body that touches the object, a little eye must have the capacity to create an enormously long body reaching up to the stars, which is impossible. Further, since two objects cannot be in the same place, two opposite observers could not see each other, because their visual rays would obstruct one another. For the same reason, every medium such as air or water would have to be porous – filled with vacuous places for visual rays to penetrate them.[32] Albert also assails the extramissionist assumption of the causal primacy of the eye. If the sensory organ were a primary active element in the visual process, the movements of the visual rays would fall under the commands of the will – the beholder would be able to emit the ray and retract it on demand. However, we experience that we are *forced* to see what is in front of us.[33]

All the deficiencies of the extramission theories lead Albert to embrace an intromissionist theory of the Aristotelian kind. Hence, he models the visual process in direct opposition to the extramissionists. The entity endowed with the primary causal activity is not the eye, but the visible object – a colour. The object alters first the medium between itself and the observer and then the eye of the observer, creating its similitude or *species* in the observer's visual power.[34] As a consequence, the cognitive contact between an observer and a visible object is established by the causal activity of the object and the *species* in the visual power is a principle of cognizing the thing seen.[35]

The question yet to be answered is how the ontological gap between the corporeal object and the visual power is bridged. Although Albert is not committed to the view that the visual power is a part of the soul as a spiritual substance, he nonetheless take it to be a potency seated in the material organ[36] and hence a more noble thing than the external object. As a consequence, there arises the problem of the so-called ascendant causality, i.e., how the less

---

32   Albert, *De homine*, 194b, 195a.
33   Albert, *De homine*, 197b.
34   See, e.g., Albert, *De homine*, 146a-b; 185b, 189a (recognition of the Aristotelian position); *De anima* II.3.7, 108; *De sensu* 1.5, 28b; and N. Winkler, "Zur Erkenntnislehre Alberts des Großen in seinem *De anima*-Kommentar als systematische Einheit von sensus, abstractio, phantasmata, intentiones, species, universalia und intellectus," *Bochumer Philosophisches Jahrbuch für Antike und Mittelalter*, vol. 19, 2016, pp. 84–92. For passivity of the senses in general, see, e.g., Albert, *De homine*, 257b; *De anima* II.3.5, 102b-103b, and Steneck, "Albert on the Psychology of Sense Perception," pp. 270–272.
35   Albert, *De homine*, 185a.
36   Albert, *De homine*, 256a.

84   LIČKA

noble object can act upon a more noble one, if the agent is assumed to be more noble than the patient.

Albert deals with the problem in his *De anima*[37] and introduces two possible strategies, both assuming that the *species* (as a causal effect of the object) must be "elevated" and refined by an external agent in order to be able to affect the visual power. In the first account, the external agent is light; in the second it is a power of the soul that proceeds from the observer spiritually (*egreditur spiritualiter*), applies itself to the sensible object (*supponit se sensibili*), and confers being of an incorporeal and spiritual kind on it (*confert ei esse quasi incorporeum et spirituale*).[38]

The former account (held, e.g., by pseudo-Peter of Spain and later by Pseudo-Grosseteste)[39] seems ridiculous to Albert; light has a role only in vision, thus it cannot interfere in the perceptual process of other senses. Besides, the form taken in itself is an immaterial essence – it can act immaterially.[40] The latter account, which Albert attributes to Plato, Augustine, and a few of his contemporaries (*pauci modernorum*),[41] seems a little more probable to him – but he still finds it unintelligible. He confesses that he just cannot imagine how sensory powers could be emitted towards the sensibles.[42]

Thus, Albert dismisses both solutions and declares the question itself to be foolish: in his view, every active potency is (*ex definitione*) perfectly suited to act *without* any external mover. Hence, the sensible form is able to cause its

---

37   Albert, *De anima* II.3.6, 104a–107b; see also Dewan, "St. Albert, the Sensibles, and Spiritual Being," pp. 305–307. As A. Pattin, *Pour l'histoire du sens agent. La controverse entre Barthélemy de Bruges et Jean de Jandun, ses antécédents et son evolution*, Leuven, Leuven University Press, 1988, pp. 1–3, points out, this passage pertains to the early discussions about the so-called agent sense. Albert even refers to the famous passage by Averroes (Averroes, *Commentarium magnum in Aristotelis de anima*, F.S. Crawford (ed), Cambridge, The Mediaeval Academy of America, 1953, hereafter *De an.*, II.60, 220f) from which these discussions originate.

38   Albert, *De anima* II.3.6, 104b–105a.

39   Pseudo-Hispanus, *Expositio libri De anima* II.11, 238–239; II.14, 277–279; Pseudo-Grosseteste, *Summa philosophiae* XII.12, 496–498.

40   Albert, *De anima* II.3.6, 106b.

41   It is not obvious who actually held such a view. Pattin, *Pour l'histoire du sens agent*, p. 3, suggests John Blund (*Tractatus de anima* VI.59, 34) and the anonymous *Lectura in librum De anima* (*Lectura* II.10.3, 277); however, Blund only mentions a *visus agens* and the *Lectura* assumes that the power acts upon the object – but neither uses the terminology employed by Albert. (Moreover, the author of the *Lectura* holds the same position as Albert: he ascribes a role in the spiritualization of the form solely to the medium – *Lectura* II.22.5, 404.) As I argue below, this account is similar to the role attributed to extramission later by Roger Bacon in his visual theory.

42   Albert, *De anima* II.3.6, 106b–107a.

similitude in the medium in spiritual or intentional being, i.e. without its matter. Consequently, the ontological gap between the material object and the ontologically more noble visual power is bridged by the simple fact that the form of the object can create a spiritual or intentional *species* which, having such a refined mode of existence, is able to act on the visual power.[43]

However, the intromissionist account of vision still has some problems to be dealt with. A proponent of Euclidian extramission still has the advantages of the geometrical description of vision on his side and can argue against the Aristotelian theory from this background. Albert is aware of this strategy and presents several arguments against his own position.[44]

For example, if an observer sees a colour by means of an alteration caused by the colour first in the medium and then in his eye, why does the observer not see what is behind him? After all, the colours of objects behind his back alter the medium as well.[45] Albert's general strategy is to preserve optics, but on an Aristotelian foundation: as he notes, although some of the assumptions of geometrical optics are false, it can be modified in a way that both saves the conclusions of the optical science and does not contradict Aristotle.[46] Thus, he makes a concession to the Euclidian: he concedes that there *are* rays involved in vision that in turn make a geometrical description possible. However, these rays are not visual rays emitted from the eyes, but the rays of external light. Light has the power to actualize the colours and these alter the medium in the rectilinear direction. These very rays constitute the visual cone and determine the paths of the *species* the observer receives. The obvious consequence is that the observer can see only what is in front of him.[47] Such a reinterpretation of the nature of the visual cone also enables Albert to preserve the validity of Euclidian geometrical demonstrations and include them in the Aristotelian framework.[48]

Another objection to Albert's position pertains to the issue whether the visible object is apprehended whole at once, or one part after another (and hence in time). The former option is challenged by the example of a coin on a floor

---

43   Albert, *De anima*, 106a; 107a–b.

44   Albert, *De homine*, 187b–189b.

45   Albert, *De homine*, 187b.

46   Albert, *Commentarii in II Sententiarum* 13.2, 246b.

47   Albert, *De homine*, 189a.

48   Albert, *De homine*, 198b. See also 201a and *De sensu* I.8, 39a; I.14, 52b. Such a reinterpretation was popular among the proponents of intromission – one may find it in Avicenna or Alhacen (Lindberg, *Theories of Vision*, pp. 49–50; 71–74); before Albert also in Blund, *Tractatus de anima* IX.93, 50.

(presented above).[49] The way Albert deals with this objection also reveals his opinion regarding the temporal and spatial aspects of the visual process. I consider, first, his criticism of Euclid's position, and second, his explanation of the example with the coin.

In Albert's reading, Euclid's theory is based on the conviction that what is seen at one moment is only one point of the surface of the object – the very point touched by the axis of the visual cone. The vision of the whole object is completed because the axis runs over all the points of the object.[50] However, this "scanning" of the object is so quick that it only takes a portion of time which is insensible to the perceiver. Therefore, the entire object is seen *as if* it were apprehended whole at once.[51]

However, Albert holds that such a view implies an implausible account of vision. All the visual acts would be only *illusory* – every time an object is seen in its entirety, the sight would be *deceived* and the visual representation of the object would be only something fabricated by the perceiver from the infinite partial visions.[52] In such a case, the whole would never be seen – the ray would not be able to run over all the points and grasp the visible object in its entirety.[53]

Albert, on the contrary, is committed to the Aristotelian view that vision is instantaneous (since the change caused by the colour actualized by light is not a local motion but an alteration),[54] the visual power is always altered by one visible object at a time,[55] and hence the entire object is seen at once.[56]

However, the example of the coin on the floor, tailored to Euclidian needs, still calls for an explanation in the Aristotelian framework. Apparently, the only way for Albert is to compromise his Aristotelian tenets a little. He distinguishes between two aspects of the visual process: apprehending the form impressed in the eye (*virtus visiva ... apprehendit formam impressam in oculo*) and "directing" the form to the thing apprehended or focusing on the thing (*dirigit formam illam ad rem, quam apprehendit per ipsam*). Whereas the first phase of the visual process accords with the Aristotelian understanding of vision as passive and receptive, the second phase includes a kind of activity on the part of the visual power. Applied to the example, once the form of the floor is impressed in the eye, the visual power can "direct" (*dirigit*) the form to the floor in

---

49   Albert, *De homine*, 188a. Albert also ponders the problem in detail later in his *De sensu* III.

50   Albert, *De sensu*, III.4, 106a.

51   Albert, *De sensu*, III.7, 110b–111a.

52   Albert, *De sensu*, III.4, 105b.

53   Albert, *De sensu*, III.4, 106b-107a; III.7, 111a.

54   Albert, *De homine*, 180b; 187a.

55   Albert, *De homine,* 176b.

56   Albert, *De sensu*, III.4, 106b; III.7, 111b.

order to apprehend it – either to the whole floor, or only to a part of it. In the latter case, it apprehends one part of the floor after another and sees the coin as soon as it encounters it.[57]

Hence, Albert is willing to introduce a role for attention in his Aristotelian account of vision. The attention is not a presupposition of the vision; it is rather a mechanism for ordering the impressions already received. Surprisingly, the impressions are not understood here as causal vehicles providing the vision, but rather as representations by virtue of which the perceiver apprehends the external things. Whether this does or does not lead to a form of representationalism is a question for another investigation.[58]

4 Syncretism: Roger Bacon

Another attitude to the extramissionist theory is a less dismissive one. Such an attitude may be found in the works of Roger Bacon and other perspectivists. Bacon developed his theory of vision in his early *De sensu*[59] and especially in his mature works based on the optical tradition – *De multiplicatione specierum* and *Perspectiva* (both written in the 1260s).[60] Later, Bacon included the latter

---

57   Albert, *De homine*, 189a–b.
58   For other representationalist implications arguably present in Albert's visual theory, see L. Lička, "What is in the Mirror? The Metaphysics of Mirror Images in Albert the Great and Peter Auriol," in B. Glenney and J.F. Silva (eds), *The Senses and the History of Philosophy*, London, Routledge, 2019, pp. 136–137.
59   While attributing *De sensu* to Bacon is not based on firm evidence, there are no decisive arguments *against* Bacon's authorship. Although S. Donati, "Pseudoepigrapha in the *Opera hactenus inedita Rogeri Baconi*? The Commentaries on the *Physics* and on the *Metaphysics*," in J. Verger and O. Weijers (eds), *Les débuts de l'enseignement universitaire à Paris (1200–1245 environ)*, Turnhout, Brepols, 2013, recently convincingly contested the authenticity of some of Bacon's early Aristotelian commentaries, it does *not* concern the case of *De sensu* (p. 156). The arguments for attributing it to Bacon are gathered in S.C. Easton, *Roger Bacon and His Search for a Universal Science*, New York, Russell & Russell, 1952, pp. 232–235, who inclines (with some hesitation) to a preliminary ascription of the work to Bacon. Since the work bears profound doctrinal similarities to Bacon's mature works, I treat it here as authentic. See also Y. Raizman-Kedar, "Questioning Aristotle: Roger Bacon on the True Essence of Colour," *The Journal of Medieval Latin*, vol. 17, 2007, pp. 372–383, on the colour theory presented in this work. For the dating of *De sensu*, see note 62 below.
60   For Bacon's intellectual biography, see Easton, *Roger Bacon* and the more recent A. Power, *Roger Bacon and the Defence of Christendom*, Cambridge, Cambridge University Press, 2013; cf. also an up-to-date chronology by J. Hackett, "From *Sapientes antiqui* at Lincoln to the New *Sapientes moderni* at Paris c. 1260–1280: Roger Bacon's Two Circles of Scholars," in J.P. Cunningham and M. Hocknull (eds), *Robert Grosseteste and the Pursuit of Religious and Scientific Learning in the Middle Ages*, Dordrecht, Springer, 2016. On Bacon's visual theory, see H. Hoffmans, "La genèse des sensations d'après Roger Bacon," *Revue*

88   LIČKA

work as Part V in his *Opus maius* and also summarized its contents in *Opus tertium*.[61]

At the time of Bacon's life the Latin scholarship witnessed a vast dissemination and assimilation of Alhacen's *De aspectibus* and its intromissionist account of vision – a movement of which Bacon himself was a cutting-edge initiator.[62] At first sight, Bacon's own account of vision seems to have been heavily influenced by Alhacen. After a careful exposition of the anatomy and physiology of the eyes and the psychology of the internal senses in the opening

---

      néo-scolastique, vol. 15, 1908, pp. 474–498; Lindberg, *Theories of Vision*, 107–116; Lindberg, *Roger Bacon*, lxviii-lxxxvii; P.K. Loose, "Roger Bacon on Perception: A Reconstruction and Critical Analysis of the Theory of Visual Perception Expounded in the *Opus Majus*," PhD dissertation, Ohio, Ohio State University, 1979, pp. 179–282; Y. Raizman-Kedar, "*Species* as Signs: Roger Bacon (1220–1292) on *Perspectiva* and *Grammatica*," PhD dissertation, University of Haifa, 2009, pp. 69–101; Smith, *From Sight to Light*, pp. 260–271; cf. also K.H. Tachau, *Vision and Certitude in the Age of Ockham: Optics, Epistemology, and the Foundations of Semantics, 1250–1345*, Leiden, Brill, 1988, pp. 3–26.

61   Roger Bacon, *Opus tertium, Un fragment inédit de l'Opus tertium de Roger Bacon*, P. Duhem (ed), Firenze, Quaracchi, 1909, hereafter *OT* (Duhem), pp. 75–97.

62   The earliest references to Alhacen in the context of psychological literature (known to me) are made by Adam Buckfield in his *De sensu* commentary (late 1230s) and the so-called Oxford gloss on *De sensu* influenced by him (see G. Galle, "Edition and Discussion of the Oxford Gloss on *De sensu I*," *Archives d'histoire doctrinale et littéraire du Moyen Âge*, vol. 75, 2008, pp. 211; 271–272); there are also several excerpts made by Bartholomeus Anglicus in early 1240s (see his *DPR* III.17, 62–64, and Lindberg, *Theories of Vision*, p. 253). Note also Richard Fishacre referring to Alhacen in his *Questio de luce*, written in Oxford between 1245 and 1248 (see J.R. Long and T.B. Noone, "Fishacre and Rufus on the Metaphysics of Light: Two Unedited Texts," in J. Hamesse (ed), *Roma, magistra mundi. Itineraria culturae medievalis*, Turnhout, Brepols, 1998, pp. 520, 532). Nevertheless, a full-fledged assimilation of Alhacen is to be situated not before the early 1260s – putting Bacon's *Perspectiva* aside, Alhacen is often advocated by the Oxford master Geoffrey of Aspall in his *De sensu* commentary – see e.g. Galfridus de Aspale, *Quaestiones super librum De sensu et sensato*, MS Todi, Biblioteca Comunale 23, q. 35, fol. 108r; q. 69, ff. 117r-v. (On this work, see S. Ebbesen, C.T. Thörnqvist, and V. Decaix, "Questions on *De sensu et sensato, De memoria*, and *De somno et vigilia*: A Catalogue," *Bulletin de philosophie médiévale*, vol. 57, 2015, pp. 66–70; I am indebted to S. Ebbesen for sharing with me some images of the Todi manuscript and some portions of his preliminary transcription of the work.) Note that all the references are in works written in Oxford (or – in the case of Bartholomeus – by an Englishman), which is consonant with Bacon's claim, made in the 1260s that *perspectiva* had not been taught in Paris so far and only twice in Oxford (Roger Bacon, *Opus tertium*, J.S. Brewer (ed), *Fr. Rogeri Bacon Opera quaedam hactenus inedita*, London, Longman, 1859, II, 37) and suggests that Bacon received training in this science in Oxford, probably in the early 1250s (see Hackett, "From *Sapientes antiqui*," p. 125) and under the influence of Grosseteste's writings. Furthermore, with respect to numerous references to Alhacen in Bacon's *De sensu*, the work should be dated as being written after that training in the (early) 1250s – rather than in the 1240s, as Easton, *Roger Bacon*, pp. 59–61; 232–235, suggests.

EXTRAMISSION POSTULATE IN 13TH C. THEORIES OF VISION

distinctions of his *Perspectiva*, Bacon introduces the mechanism of vision: the objects issue *species* in all directions and once the *species* are received in the eye, the object is seen. For vision, the *species* of colour and light are required, which is proved by Alhacenian arguments: when exposed to intensive colour or light, the observer experiences afterimages or even pain.[63] The *species* are not forms of the whole object (as in Aristotle or Albert), but rather forms emitted from every point of the surface of the object in all directions along direct lines. In the eye, only the relevant forms are selected – the ones entering the eye along the lines perpendicular to its surface – and a veridical representation of the object is reconstructed. These lines of propagation of the intromitted *species* constitute a visual cone – a notion enabling the use of geometry for explaining vision.[64]

However, Bacon's account should not be labelled "intromissionist" too hastily. Bacon is not a blind imitator of Alhacen – after all, in his own words, although Alhacen is used by some wise Latins, his compendium is nothing other than an exposition of Ptolemy's *Optics*, which is in turn "the true source of the optical science." Further, Bacon stresses that he has also borrowed from another extramissionist authors, such as Euclid, Tideus, or Al-Kindí.[65]

Hence, one need not be surprised when later in Part I of the *Perspectiva* one encounters an explicit *defence* of extramission. Bacon points out that extramission was proposed by many respectable authorities – optical scientists, Christian saints such as Augustine, and even (allegedly) Aristotle.[66] Further, authors such as Avicenna, Averroes and Alhacen who are famous for their criticism of extramissionist theories, should be read as arguing only against a robust version of extramission – against the postulation of a body issuing forth from the eyes that would seize the *species* of the object and bring it back to the eye.[67]

Against such an exaggerated stress on the primacy of extramission, Bacon takes a modest position of syncretism with a primacy of intromission. According to this view, approved also by "experts in Aristotle's philosophy and

---

63   Bacon, *Persp.* I.5.1, 60–62. For the argument from pain, see also Roger Bacon, *Liber de sensu et sensato*, R. Steele (ed), *Opera hactenus inedita XIV*, Oxford, Clarendon Press, 1937, hereafter *De sensu*, 1, 3.

64   Bacon, *Persp.* I.6.1–2, 68–78.

65   Bacon, *OT* (Duhem), 75–76; cf. also *Persp.* I.7.2, 100; *Persp.*, app. 1, 336; and Bacon, *De multiplicatione specierum*, D.C. Lindberg (ed and trans.), *Roger Bacon's Philosophy of Nature*, Oxford, Clarendon Press, 1983, hereafter *DMS*, p. 347. The differences between Alhacen and Bacon are summarized by Smith, *From Sight to Light*, p. 271.

66   Bacon, *Persp.* I.7.2, 100.

67   Bacon, *Persp.* I.7.3, 102.

perspectiva," vision consists in both receiving the *species* of the object in the eye and in propagating something from the eye.[68] In contrast to its many earlier proponents, Bacon presents a different understanding of the extramission postulate. What is emitted from the eyes is not a body of a subtle nature, but a *species* of the eye or of the sight (*species oculi* or *visus*). Such a postulate can be easily justified in the context of his philosophy: if every entity in the universe is constantly multiplying its *species* in the surrounding medium, that is also what the sensory organs should do. And just as the *species* of an object somehow resembles that object as its source, the *species* of the sense of sight somehow resembles the sight and participates in the nature of the visual power to some extent.[69]

Hence, Bacon proposes a syncretic account of vision, in which intromission has a primary role. The emission is not responsible for the multiplication of the *species* of the objects; they are propagated independently of the observer. The cognitive contact between perceiver and object is established by the causal influence of the latter on the former. But Bacon evidently wants to preserve extramission as well. In this strategy, his sources may be Robert Grosseteste or Bartholomeus Anglicus.[70] But does extramission have any role in the visual process, or is its presence in Bacon's theory a residue of an inorganic harmonization of different sources (as seems to be the case in Bartholomeus)?

Scholars have taken various strategies in answering this question. Some emphasize the intromissionist framework of Bacon's account and infer that Bacon's references to extramission are nothing more than *ad hoc* additions incoherent with the rest of his theory, or an unimportant relic of earlier authors, included by Bacon due to his efforts to harmonize all the available sources.[71] Postulating the *species* of the eye would thus be merely a Bacon's way of paying

---

68 Bacon, *Persp.* 1.7.3, 104.

69 Bacon, *Persp.* 1.7.2, 100; *DMS* I.2, 30–32.

70 See note 15 above. Bacon's acquaintance with Grosseteste's works is evident (see, e.g., D.C. Lindberg (ed and trans.), *Roger Bacon's Philosophy of Nature*, Oxford, Clarendon Press, 1983, pp. xviii–xx, xlix–lvi, and Bacon's eulogies of Grosseteste, e.g., in *Compendium studii philosophiae*, J.S. Brewer (ed), *Fr. Rogeri Bacon Opera quaedam hactenus inedita*, London, 1859, 8, 469); Bartholomeus's encyclopaedia was known in Oxford in the late 1240s (see Long and Noone, "Fishacre and Rufus," p. 519) and Bacon refers to it in a passage on magnet in his *Opus minus*, J.S. Brewer (ed), *Fr. Rogeri Bacon Opera quaedam hactenus inedita*, London, Longman, 1859, p. 384.

71 Bacon himself stresses that, when writing on *perspectiva*, he does not want to imitate just one author, but chooses the best parts of every account – *OT* (Duhem), 75.

homage to authors such as Ptolemy, but would not have any significant role in his theory.[72]

However, Bacon's references to extramission are systematic, not merely occasional. A strong affirmation of extramission is found in the *Opus tertium* – Bacon asserts that although the intromissionist account is so "deeply rooted in the hearts of the common scholars that they do not want to hear anything contrary," extramission is the truest (*veracissimum*) position.[73] The work was intended as a brief summary of everything important in the *Opus maius* – would Bacon put so much stress on extramission here, if it was just an *ad hoc* addition to his theory? Besides that, there are numerous places in his optical works where extramission is taken for granted or argued for.[74]

Recently, some scholars have also proposed that Bacon's syncretism may have been motivated by theological concerns. Bacon states that the eye, which not only receives the *species* but also actively cooperates, may serve as a model for spiritual vision, which requires not only the reception of divine grace, but also the cooperation of the recipient's soul and free will.[75] However, I believe that Bacon also had purely philosophical reasons to endorse extramission, which are internal to his visual theory.[76] In my opinion, extramission is not a

---

72   Lindberg, *Theories of Vision*, pp. 114–116; G.B. Matthews, "A Medieval Theory of Vision," in P.K. Machamer and R.G. Turnbull (eds), *Studies in Perception: Interrelations in the History of Philosophy and Science*, Columbus, Ohio State University Press, 1978, p. 196; Raizman-Kedar, "*Species* as Signs," pp. 91–92. Lindberg, *Roger Bacon*, pp. lxxxiii–lxxxvi, suggests that it may also be a result of the fact that Bacon wrote his works "in haste, or in multiple drafts" and left them unrevised.

73   Bacon, *OT* (Duhem), 78–79.

74   See Bacon, *DMS* I.2, 30–32; I.5, 74; *Persp.* I.7.2–4, 100–106; II.1.1, 160–162; II.1.3, 174–176; II.2.1, 176–178; III.1.2, 260–262. The *species visus* is also employed in *DMS* II.5, 128; II.10, 176; *Persp.* I.9.1, 126. Loose, "Roger Bacon on Perception," pp. 205–207, argues that the first two thirds of *Perspectiva* I present a *preliminary* intromissionist account of the visual process, which is later in Part I and especially in Part II specified and modified by the extramission postulate.

75   Bacon, *Persp.* III.3.1, 324; the passage was pointed out by Loose, "Roger Bacon on Perception," pp. 271–272, and Raizman-Kedar, "*Species* as Signs," p. 90; the theological interpretation is embraced by J. Hackett, "Roger Bacon and the Moralization of Science: From *Perspectiva* through *Scientia Experimentalis* to *Moralis Philosophia*," in *I francescani e le scienze*, Spoleto, Centro Italiano di Studi sull'Alto Medioevo, 2012, pp. 384–385; Hackett, "From *Sapientes antiqui*," pp. 133–134.

76   The active component of Bacon's visual theory was stressed already by Hoffmans, "La genèse des sensations," pp. 479–486, but only in order to reprehend the theory for an implicit tendency to subjectivism. A rare acknowledgement of Bacon's syncretism may be found in Loose, "Roger Bacon on Perception," especially pp. 205–225, 244–253.

source of confusion in Bacon's theory, but on the contrary perfectly coherent with Bacon's account. What does Bacon himself say about the role of the *species* of the eye in the visual process? He asserts that the *species* of an inanimate object are ontologically inferior to the eye (as a part of an animated body) and are not suited to act upon the eye just on their own account (*non sunt nate statim de se agere plenam actionem in visum propter eius nobilitatem*); therefore, they must be refined in some way. The *species* of the eye are emitted in the medium, alter and ennoble it and make it commensurate to the visual power. As a consequence, the entrance of the *species* of the object is prepared, because the visual power emitted in the medium ennobles the *species* of the object and renders them commensurate to the eye (*eam nobilitat, ut omnino sit conformis et proportionalis nobilitati corporis animati, quod est oculus*) and consequently able to act upon it.[77]

It is obvious from this passage that extramission (of the sensory power) is Bacon's answer to the issue of the ontological gap between the material world and the cognizer. The conviction that sensory organs are ontologically superior and more noble than material things is asserted already in his *De sensu*. There Bacon expounds the Aristotelian statement that organs are receptive of a certain kind of qualities, because their nature is constituted by the middle between the extremes of these qualities.[78] Bacon explains that it should not be taken that, e.g., the eye is constituted from a colour in the middle of the scale between white and black, but that the elements of organs are elevated above the common status of inanimate objects and have the most noble being possible in nature. Such being is called "spiritual," although not in a sense implying something incorporeal; they are highly refined and subtle, while still material.[79]

Hence, there is a salient gap between the sensory organs and material objects. How can such a gap be bridged? It is worth noting that there is no mention of extramission in *De sensu*.[80] It seems that when Bacon was writing this

---

77 Bacon, *Persp.* 1.7.4, 104; also 1.8.1, 108–110. Another way the sensory power acts on the received *species* is that it forces it to abandon the "laws of nature" and the rectilinear path of multiplication. Once in the animated medium, especially in the nerves, the *species* is not propagated along a direct line anymore but along a "twisted line" (*linea tortuosa*) – see Bacon, *DMS* II.2, 102; Bacon, *The Opus maius of Roger Bacon*, 3 vols., J.H. Bridges (ed), Oxford, Clarendon Press, 1897–1900, IV.2.2, 117; *OT* (Duhem), 78.

78 Aristotle, *De anima* II.11, 424a4–5; Averroes, *De an.* II.118, 313–314.

79 Bacon, *De sensu* 1, 4. Bacon ascribed such an elevation to the powers of the soul and the heavens.

80 *Species* of the eye are mentioned in Roger Bacon, *De sensu* 1, 10–11, but no role in the completion of the visual act is attributed to them. Vision occurs when the sight receives the form of the seen objects and renders them to the ultimate sentient seated at the

work, he was still advocating an Aristotelian theory of abstraction. According to this traditional Aristotelian explanation of how the *species* of a material object can enter the soul's power, the *species* of the object can act upon the senses because they are refined already in the medium and they undergo a continuing abstraction. Indeed, early Bacon remarks several times that the *species* are endowed with spiritual being in the medium and in the organ.[81]

But later in the 1260s, he abandoned the notion of the *species* having spiritual being in the medium.[82] He asserts that it is foolish to deny the material nature of the *species*. They obtain their existence from their causes and since these causes (i.e., the things that generate the *species* on the one hand and the matter from whose potency the *species* are educed on the other) are material, the *species* are material as well.[83] Consequently, Bacon needs another mechanism for bridging the ontological gap. It seems that extramission of the visual power (or "*species visus*") can serve as such a mechanism in the case of vision. Hence, Bacon's concession to extramission is not cognitive, but *metaphysical*: it is proposed in order to deal with the problem of ascendant causality and the need of *species* of material objects for refinement.[84] Bacon seems to endorse the position that *species* are ennobled by the soul's power proceeding towards

---

intersection of the optical nerves – *De sensu* 3, 7–8. (The same assertion is also in *Persp.* 1.5.2, 62–64; however, as we have seen, later it is problematized *how exactly* the forms are received in the sense.).

81 Bacon, *De sensu* 8, 28; 23, 117–118; 24, 124–125. Such a claim is perhaps influenced by Grosseteste – see Robert Grosseteste, *De lineis angulis et figuris*, L. Baur (ed), *Die philosophischen Werke des Robert Grosseteste, Bischofs von Lincoln*, Münster, Aschendorff, 1912, p. 60.

82 And apparently also the whole notion of abstraction, as argued by Y. Raizman-Kedar, "The Intellect Naturalized: Roger Bacon on the Existence of Corporeal Species within the Intellect," *Early Science and Medicine*, vol. 14, no. 1, 2009, pp. 140–145.

83 Bacon, *DMS* III.2, 190. Note that materiality does not imply corporeality here – the *species* are material but they are not bodies *sui generis* – see *DMS* III.1, 178–186. For an interpretation of Bacon stressing that the sensory organs are not only affected materially by *species* but also actually coloured by them, see M. Mantovani, "*Visio per sillogismum*: Sensation and Cognition in 13th Century Theories of Vision," in E. Băltuţă (ed), *Medieval Perceptual Puzzles: Theories of Perception in the 13th and 14th Centuries*, Leiden, Brill, pp. 117–129.

84 Cf. also Loose, "Roger Bacon on Perception," pp. 249–250 who mentions a "vertical causality" and Augustinian influences on Bacon's theory of vision. Another corroboration for such interpretation of Bacon's visual theory may be that it accords with the way some later medieval thinkers understood him. In anonymous questions on optics I found in a 14th century Prague manuscript, Bacon is listed among proponents of extramission along with Euclid and Ptolemy and his metaphysical justification of extramission from *Persp.* 1.7 is analysed there – see Anonymous, *Quaestiones de perspectiva*, MS Praha, Knihovna metropolitní kapituly M.100, ff. 69rb, 69va-b. I am preparing an edition of the treatise.

94 LIČKA

them – a position refuted in Albert's *De anima* – which can perhaps be understood as an early anticipation of the later notion of *sensus agens*.[85]

In Bacon's middle account between intromission and extramission, what is his stance regarding temporal and spatial aspects of vision? Does he prefer an Aristotelian solution or a Euclidian one? Following Alhacen's lead, he dismisses the Aristotelian position, advocates the Euclidian one and gives a reasonable solution to the objections to it that had earlier been raised by Albert.

First, Bacon doubts even the basic Aristotelian claim that alteration occurs immediately – the very multiplication of *species* takes a moment, albeit an imperceptible one for the observer's sensory powers. Hence, it *appears* to him as if the light were propagated in no time.[86] Consequently, sensation also takes place in time.[87] However, the time necessary for completing the visual act is sometimes even perceptible to the observer – Bacon explains this experience by highlighting that the visual act includes not only a reception of the multiplied *species* but also a visual "judgement."[88]

This "judgment," which takes time to be made, is a certification of the vision performed by the movement of the axis of the visual cone travelling over the object. Bacon advocates the Euclidian view that there is a different sensitivity in different regions of the base of the visual cone.[89] However, it should not be understood in the way criticized by Albert, as if some parts of the base were seen and others completely unseen. Euclid's proposition that nothing is seen whole at once should be understood – according to Bacon – with regard to different grades of certainty: the central parts are seen clearly and with certainty and the peripheral ones are unclear and confused.[90] Unlike Aristotelians (and Euclid in Albert's reading), Bacon advocates the view that we see a number of

---

85 The understanding of *sensus agens* as a kind of extramission is mentioned (and refuted) by John of Jandun, *Questio de sensu agente*, A. Pattin (ed), *Pour l'histoire du sens agent. La controverse entre Barthélemy de Bruges et Jean de Jandun, ses antécédents et son evolution*, Leuven, Leuven University Press, 1988, p. 225. The activity of the sensory power is connected with extramission also in Anonymous, *Lectura* II.14.1, 323–324.

86 Bacon, *De sensu* 23, 114–118; *DMS* IV.3, 220–226; *Persp.* I.9.3–4, 134–144 (note that he explicitly associates the multiplication in time also with the *species visus*); *OT* (Duhem), 81. See also Tachau, *Vision and Certitude*, pp. 20–21.

87 Bacon, *De sensu* 23, 120–121.

88 Bacon, *Persp.* I.9.4, 144. "Time" is also included among the conditions of (veridical) vision – an object must not move too quickly in order to be seen properly – *Persp.* I.9.2, 132; *OT* (Duhem), p. 81.

89 Note that according to Bacon, there are two visual cones: one constituted by the *species* propagating from the object and the other consisting of the *species* of the sight. However, these two cones are identical regarding their location – *Persp.* I.7.4, 106; II.2.1, 178.

90 Bacon, *Persp.* I.7.4, 106; II.2.1, 178; also I.6.2, 78.

things at once – but only one thing (or a part of it) is seen with certainty. The vision is completed by the passing of the visual axis (which follows the movements of the eye), by means of which the parts of the thing are certified successively, one after another.[91]

Hence, vision is not a state of being affected, but rather a process in which visual acuity is accomplished by an active scanning of the visual field. A number of things are seen at once, but with a different grade of certainty.

5 Reinterpretation: Peter Olivi

Finally, there is a strategy developed by Peter Olivi in some of his questions (written in the late 1270s and early 1280s) later included in his *Summa*.[92] His attitude towards extramission is an instance of the way he deals with philosophical theories generally – ignoring what is and what is not conceived as plausible by his contemporaries, he often devotes a careful investigation to every theory and uncovers its (often unspoken) foundations and merits, while being determined not to be too dogmatic in philosophical matters.[93]

Although optics and theory of vision witnessed an increasing prevalence of Alhacenian intromission in the 1270s and 1280s (John Pecham and Witelo were composing their works on optics at that time), Peter Olivi does not hesitate to doubt the "Alhacenian turn" and reproaches those who identify a book by "one Saracen" with the whole of optical science for idolatry. Besides, Olivi notes,

---

91 Bacon, *Persp.* II.2.1, 178; also I.7.4, 106.
92 On Olivi's visual theory, see, e.g., Tachau, *Vision and Certitude*, pp. 39–54; R. Pasnau, *Theories of Cognition in the Later Middle Ages*, Cambridge, Cambridge University Press, 1997, pp. 130–134; 168–181; J.F. Silva and J. Toivanen, "The Active Nature of the Soul in Sense Perception: Robert Kilwardby and Peter Olivi," *Vivarium*, vol 48, no. 3–4, 2010, pp. 260–277; H.T. Adriaenssen, "Peter John Olivi on Perceptual Representation," *Vivarium*, vol. 49, no. 4, 2011, pp. 324–352; J. Toivanen, *Perception and the Internal Senses: Peter of John Olivi on the Cognitive Functions of the Sensitive Soul*, Leiden, Brill, 2013, pp. 115–222; and M.E. Kalderon, *Sympathy in Perception*, Cambridge, Cambridge University Press, 2017, pp. 148–177. Olivi's interest in the optical issues was uncovered by Tachau, *Vision and Certitude*, pp. 40–49, and recently partially investigated by D. Demange, "Olivi et les *Perspectivi*," *Oliviana*, vol. 5, 2016, http://oliviana.revues.org/850, accessed February 2019, and L. Lička, "Attention, Perceptual Content, and Mirrors: Two Medieval Models of Active Perception in Peter Olivi and Peter Auriol," *Filosofický časopis*, vol. 65, Special Issue 2, 2017, pp. 103–110, but a complete account is still missing. The dating of Olivi's questions is borrowed from a preliminary chronology of Olivi's works by S. Piron (to whom I express my gratitude for sharing it) – see also S. Piron, "La chronologie des écrits d'Olivi," *Oliviana*, vol. 6, forthcoming.
93 For Olivi's "sceptical" approach to philosophical theories see the classical D. Burr, "Peter John Olivi and the Philosophers," *Franciscan Studies*, vol. 31, 1971, especially pp. 69–70.

indicating his own efforts, that what is explained by "rays coming from things" can be reframed using "virtual rays of the sight itself" – just as Augustine and many others used "corporeal rays of the eye" for the same purpose.[94] Olivi's optical project in its totality cannot be introduced here, thus the focus will be on some aspects of his visual theory in relation to his rethinking of extramission.

Before his visual theory can be outlined, two basic tenets of Olivi's anthropology important for his philosophy of perception need to be recalled. The first one is dualism: the sphere of material objects and the sphere of spiritual souls are radically different. Whereas material objects are extended and inanimate, spiritual souls are unextended and endowed with life and consciousness. Thus, the issue of the ontological gap is of special importance to Olivi. The second tenet is the activity of the soul in its operations: the soul (or its power) is always the first active principle of its operations; otherwise the operations would be necessitated by something external and, as a result, the soul would be passive and not free. Both tenets also presuppose that the soul and its powers are noble and superior to material objects.[95]

The early Olivi perhaps hesitated concerning the intromissionist theory of *species*[96] and later he mentions having taught the common opinion regarding the *species* in schools, or presenting various opinions while asserting none of them.[97] However, the two tenets outlined above make it impossible for Olivi to accept the intromissionist account of vision. If vision occurred by the received *species*, the visual power would not be free but subjected to the objects whose affections it suffers. Further, it is not clear how the *species* of a material and extended object could even enter the sensory power of the spiritual soul.[98]

The extramissionist theory seems to be more suitable for Olivi's demands. In q. 58 (ca. 1277–1278), where he argues for activity of the sensory powers in a digression included in a more extensive reasoning for activity of the will, he

---

94 Olivi, *Summa* II.58, 499.

95 Pasnau, *Theories of Cognition*, pp. 176–181; Toivanen, *Perception and the Internal Senses*, pp. 25–42; J.F. Silva, "Medieval Theories of Active Perception: An Overview," in J.F. Silva and M. Yrjönsuuri (eds), *Active Perception in the History of Philosophy: From Plato to Modern Philosophy*, Dordrecht, Springer, 2014, pp. 132–135.

96 See Olivi, *Summa* II.26, 454–455 (before 1275) where it is taken for granted that vision occurs by means of receiving the *species* (note that the passage is preserved in only one manuscript).

97 Olivi, "Tria scripta sui ipsius apologetica annorum 1283 et 1285," D. Laberge (ed), *Archivum Franciscanum Historicum*, vol. 28, 1935, pp. 128; 404–405.

98 For a detailed account of Olivi's criticism of the theory of *species* see e.g. Toivanen, *Perception and the Internal Senses*, pp. 125–135.

EXTRAMISSION POSTULATE IN 13TH C. THEORIES OF VISION   97

presents a set of counter-arguments based on the tacit assumption that activity of perception implies extramission.[99] He rejects such an assumption and criticizes the emission theory of Augustine, but gradually develops a theory based on some of the less problematic features of Augustine's theory. Later in q. 73 (ca. 1281–1282) focused on extramission, Olivi presents and criticizes the traditional materialistic notion of extramission in a syncretic account with a primacy of extramission, which he ascribes to some Platonists and Augustine, and elaborates his own theory of *aspectus* modelled as a "virtual ray."[100]

Olivi's arguments are targeted especially against the postulate of *corporeal* visual rays. Just as in the case of Albert the Great, Olivi's arguments against extramission seem to have been at least partially influenced by Avicenna. If what is emitted were a corporeal body, it would have to travel extremely fast and reach the stars immediately. Further, the sense of touch would have to be somehow present in the corporeal visual ray – with the absurd consequence that we would *feel* all the changes of the medium, such as hot or cold air or winds, while seeing through it. Also, the changes in the ray and vision cannot be explained with reference to the will since we often see against our will. Finally, Olivi presents an Alhacenian argument against syncretism with a primacy of extramission: if the sole role of the emitted visual ray is to catch the *species* of the object and bring it back to the sight, then – in view of the fact that the *species* of the objects can propagate through the medium by themselves – the visual rays are superfluous.[101] Thus, the extramission postulate is impossible and futile for explaining perception and, as Olivi points out, nobody actually upholds it today (*nullus hodie sequitur*).[102]

---

99   Olivi, *Summa* II.58, 405–407 (counter-arguments) and 486–499 (Olivi's response to them). This kind of assumption seems to have been common among his contemporaries (see the anonymous *Lectura* as in note 85), but, of course, not the sole understanding of the activity of perception (for the others, see Silva, "Medieval Theories of Active Perception").

100 Olivi, *Summa* II.73, 52–106. As it is argued in Lička, "Attention, Perceptual Content, and Mirrors," pp. 105–106, the *Platonici* Olivi criticized are possibly the 12th century proponents of syncretic accounts with a primacy of extramission, such as William of Conches. The role of a Platonic emission theory in developing Olivi's own view was implied already by B. Jansen, *Die Erkenntnislehre Olivis*, Berlin, Dümmlers, 1921, p. 22 (in his summary of q. 73); later mentioned by Tachau, *Vision and Certitude*, p. 41; Pasnau, *Theories of Cognition*, pp. 169–170, Silva and Toivanen, "The Active Nature of the Soul," pp. 272–275; Adriaenssen, "Peter John Olivi on Perceptual Representation," pp. 329–330; and elaborated by Demange, "Olivi et les *Perspectivi*," and Lička, "Attention, Perceptual Content, and Mirrors." Olivi's early thoughts on *aspectus* are present already in his *Summa* II.23, 424–432 (before 1275).

101 Olivi, *Summa* II.73, 59–61.

102 Olivi, *Summa* II.58, 482.

However, there is a grain of truth in the extramissionist theories – the claim (ascribed by Olivi to Augustine) that the sensory powers "touch" (*attingerent*) their objects by a *virtual aspectus* and thus they are at their objects in a metaphorical way.[103] The notion of *aspectus* is at the very core of Olivi's visual theory. In Olivi's view, an *aspectus* is a constituent of every causal action, no matter whether physical or psychological, and manifests its orientation and directedness towards a target (*terminus*). For example, when throwing a stone, the thrower gives an *aspectus* to the stone, an inclination towards an aim. Similarly, when a perceiver is about to see, his sight has an *aspectus* to an object and it is oriented to it.[104]

The first two tenets of extramissionist theories (the extramission postulate and the primacy of the sight) provide inspiration for Olivi's visual theory. The extramissionist emphasis on the activity and primacy of the visual power in the visual process is consonant with his metaphysical principles. The visual process cannot be initiated by the effects of external objects received in the visual power – since the visual power is ontologically superior, objects cannot act upon it.[105] Thus, the primary impulse for vision originates from the observer – Olivi identifies it with the *aspectus*, directedness or focus of the visual power. The visual *aspectus* is understood by him as *attention* – a psychological mechanism enabling the observer to scan the environment and actively grasp perceptual information.[106] It is worth noting that Olivi's notion of attention is completely different from the one proposed by Albert. Whereas for Albert attention is a secondary process of sorting impressions already received, in Olivi's view it is a necessary *preceding* condition of every visual act.[107] The primacy of paying attention is manifested by Olivi's claims that *aspectus* is not necessarily always determined to a specific object.[108] Such an undetermined *aspectus* would occur even in an imaginary scenario where there would be no external object to be seen at all.[109]

---

103   Olivi, *Summa* II.73, 62–63.

104   Olivi, *Summa* II.23, 424.

105   Olivi, *Summa* II.72, 18–27.

106   Interpretation of *aspectus* as attention is quite usual in the literature – see Tachau, *Vision and Certitude*, pp. 41–42; Pasnau, *Theories of Cognition*, pp. 130–134, 168–181; Toivanen, *Perception and the Internal Senses*, pp. 151–161.

107   Olivi, *Summa* II.72, 9.

108   Olivi, *Summa* II.36, 634.

109   On Olivi's thought experiment of a "man before creation," see J. Toivanen, "The Fate of the Flying Man: Medieval Reception of Avicenna's Thought Experiment," in R. Pasnau (ed), *Oxford Studies in Medieval Philosophy*, vol. 3, Oxford, Oxford University Press, 2015, pp. 86–94.

EXTRAMISSION POSTULATE IN 13TH C. THEORIES OF VISION   99

Olivi also exploits a hidden potential of extramissionist theory – the ability to assign a role in the visual process to eye movements, which cannot be explained in the intromissionist framework. According to Olivi, the eye is made round and capable of quick movements on purpose. If it were flat, it would not be able to look around from left to right, but would see only what is in front of it. The roundness of the eye thus contributes to the greater range of visual attention.[110] The eye movements performed on the physiological level manifest attention shifting and focusing on the psychological level.[111]

Besides the primacy of the visual activity, Olivi even holds a version of the extramission postulate – he describes the *aspectus* or attention focusing and shifting as a kind of "virtual ray" (*radius virtualis*).[112] Visual attention is modelled as a ray directed from the eye to the environment. Olivi's description even implies a basic concept of the visual cone: there are imaginary straight lines directed from every point of the pupil to the whole hemisphere demarcating the scope of visual attention.[113] These lines constitute a visual cone – the visual attention stretches forth in the form of a cone (*aciem visivi aspectus ... oportet pyramidaliter acui et protendi*), with the apex in the centre of the eye and the base attached to the quantity of the visible object.[114] Olivi's description of the visual ray and cone reveals that his sources were rather Platonists than Euclidians.[115] Although he once mentions that the apparent size of the object is a function of the size of the angle in the apex of the visual cone,[116] he proposes no geometrical demonstration and focuses more on the dynamic and oscillating nature of the visual ray – attention has an "effort" (*conatus*), a "tendency" (*inclinatio*) and an "onset" (*impetus*) and these dynamic features bring about attentional switching.[117] The shifting of attention (*variatio* or *mutatio*

---

110 Olivi, *Summa* II.73, 95–96.

111 Olivi, *Quodlibeta quinque*, S. Defraia (ed), Grottaferrata, Collegium S. Bonaventurae, 2002, I.4, 17: "[...] *ad uarium motum oculi sequitur uarius aspectus in eius potentia uisiua* [...]"; see also Olivi, *Summa* II.73, 105; II.111, 274.

112 Olivi, *Summa* II.58, 490: "[...] *virtus visiva* [...] *potest dici habere radium virtualem. Qui radius non est aliud quam ipse aspectus sic virtualiter protensus* [...]."

113 Olivi, *Summa* II.73, 65; also II.58, 490.

114 Olivi, *Summa* II.73, 96, also II. 91 and II.58, 497.

115 Olivi, *Summa* II.73, 55–61; on Olivi's sources, cf. Demange, "Olivi et les *Perspectivi*," § 5–10, and Lička, "Attention, Perceptual Content, and Mirrors," pp. 105–106. As far as I know he never mentions Euclid or another proponent of geometrical optics. Note that Demange suggests Al-Kindí as Olivi's source; however, there is no direct evidence for such a claim.

116 Olivi, *Summa* II.73, 91.

117 Olivi, *Summa* II.58, 466, 490.

aspectus) serves as a foundation for Olivi's explanation of optical phenomena such as reflection or refraction.[118]

The most important difference between Olivi's theory of *aspectus* and the visual rays postulated by Augustine and Platonists is Olivi's accentuation of *virtual* and *spiritual* nature of the rays of attention. He explicitly asserts his notion of *aspectus* is a version of Augustinian notion of a visual ray, although the latter is corporeal, whereas the former is "virtual."[119] Olivi also speaks about a "virtual extramission of the visual power" (*extramissio virtualis virtutis visivae*).[120] Nothing is actually emitted (no body, subtle matter, or even a *species* of the power) – the shifting of attention exists really (*tamquam in subiecto*) in the visual power and its organ.[121] However, the dynamics of the visual power has an outward direction and can be metaphorically described as an emission towards the object.[122] The virtual rays are merely imaginary representations of the paths of the attentional switching.[123] Although there is no real emission of the power, no rarefaction or local motion through the medium to the object, the workings of attention are somehow proportionate and analogous to these real properties and can be described as a virtual stretching out, a movement and virtual contact with the object.[124] Also, when attention "touches" the object and is fixed upon it, it is not a material contact but rather a stabilization and "quieting" of the dynamics of attention.[125]

But the movement of *aspectus* or attentional shifting is not vision yet. Against the traditional visual ray theory, Olivi strictly demarcates two phases of the visual process: (1) the visual ray or attention and (2) the visual act itself. The movements of the virtual ray and its fixation upon an object precede the actual vision but are not identical with it.[126] The (1) attention is an

---

118   See Olivi, *Summa* II.58, 498–499; II.73, 69–71; 93, Lička, "Attention, Perceptual Content, and Mirrors," pp. 108–110 (reflection and mirrors), and Olivi, *Summa* II.23, 431–432; II.58, 490–3; II.73, 73–74; 92–93 (refraction).

119   Olivi, *Summa* II.58, 494; *radii virtuales* are mentioned also in II. 58, 490, 494 and 499.

120   Olivi, *Summa* II.58, 488. Note that interpreting the visual rays as spiritual entities was also proposed as a way of preserving the postulate against its criticism by Pseudo-Grosseteste, *Summa philosophiae* XII.18, 507–508.

121   Olivi, *Summa* II.73, 66.

122   On the nature of the virtual *aspectus*, see also Pasnau, *Theories of Cognition*, pp. 172–175.

123   Olivi, *Summa* II.73, 67.

124   Olivi, *Summa* II.73, 104.

125   Olivi, *Summa* II.73, 105.

126   Hence, I do not think that the problem implied in D. Perler, *Theorien der Intentionalität im Mittelalter*, Frankfurt am Main, Vittorio Klostermann, 2002, pp. 136–137, and conceptualized in Adriaenssen, "Peter John Olivi on Perceptual Representation," pp. 331–332, exists: viz., that in order for attention to be fixed upon x, x must already be cognized in a preliminary way; but the cognition of x presupposes a determination of attention to x and,

outwards-directed orientation and dynamic oscillation, while the (2) vision is something created in the visual power of the observer. Once the *aspectus* is fixed upon its object which is "sucked" (*imbibitum*) into the *aspectus*, the visual power efficiently causes its own visual act, which is in turn "conformed and configured" to the object (*conformatur et configuratur obiecto*).[127]

Hence, there are *two* kinds of contact here. The (1) "attentional" contact is outwards-directed and presents a quasi-extramissionist way of reaching out to the visible object. But the visual cognition itself does not occur until the (2) *cognitive* contact is established, which is an inwards-directed determination of the content of the visual act performed by the object once the visual power has created the act.[128]

It is important to note that – since Olivi takes the ontological gap between the object and the soul's power seriously – both contacts are explained without advocating any kind of physical realization or receiving a real entity. As for part (1) of the visual process, having attention fixed upon an object does not mean that the beholder touches it by means of a material extension of himself, but merely that the dynamic efforts of his visual power come to a rest. What is the cause of such a quieting? Olivi stresses that the efficient cause of attentional switching is the cognitive power, or ultimately the will.[129] But the virtual ray of attention must also somehow be affected by the external things. Thus, Olivi introduces a second kind of causation cooperating with the efficient cause – "terminative" or "objective" causality.[130] For example, when attention "bounces back" upon encountering a mirror, the efficient cause of such a change of direction is supposed to be the power and the mirror plays the role of a terminative cause. Having the ontological gap in mind (the mirror is a

---

hence, an infinite regress occurs. On the contrary, in the first moment, the observer just opens his eyes, directs an undetermined *aspectus* outwards and scans the environment, waiting for what will be offered to his *aspectus*. When an object occurs, the *aspectus* is fixed upon it (the virtual ray "touches" the object, which is in the middle of the base of the visual cone) and the second phase of the visual process begins when the visual act is created. For the difference between the undetermined and determined *aspectus*, see Silva and Toivanen, "The Active Nature of the Soul," pp. 275–277; Toivanen, *Perception and the Internal Senses*, pp. 183–187; see also Adriaenssen, "Peter John Olivi on Perceptual Representation," pp. 335–336.

127 Olivi, *Summa* II.72, 35–36.

128 Olivi, *Summa* II.72, 38–39; see also Adriaenssen, "Peter John Olivi on Perceptual Representation," pp. 339–346, who distinguished between the object as a *terminus* of the *aspectus* and as a *terminus* of the act.

129 Olivi, *Summa* II.73, 66; 68; 74.

130 On this notion in Olivi see Pasnau, *Theories of Cognition*, pp. 119–121; Adriaenssen, "Peter John Olivi on Perceptual Representation," pp. 339–346; Toivanen, *Perception and the Internal Senses*, pp. 145–150.

material object and the ray of attention is a spiritual extension of the soul's power), Olivi stresses that the action exerted by the mirror is not a full-fledged ontologically committing efficient causation.[131] Similarly, establishing a (2) cognitive contact between the object seen and the visual act is also not described as an efficient causal influence exerted by the object upon the visual power, but again as merely "terminative causality."[132]

Hence, Olivi's account appears to be a rethinking of the Platonist conception of extramission, or rather a syncretic account with a primacy of extramission. He reinterprets the postulate of a physical extramission in a psychological way as attentional switching and fixation, described as a virtual ray. He reinterprets the "backwards motion" of grasping the form of the object and announcing it to the visual power as establishing cognitive contact, where the visual power efficiently causes the visual act and the object terminatively causes its content.

Finally, the distinction between the two phases of the visual process gives Olivi a good position to deal with the issue of whether vision is immediate or successive. Generally speaking, Olivi seems to be just as suspicious of the

---

131 Olivi, *Summa* II.73, 68; see also II. 73, 66, 89, 103–104.

132 Recently, the problem of whether the determination of the act by the object is to be interpreted in an externalist way (as a special kind of causality of the object) or in an internalist way (as a special kind of "configuration" the power performs itself) was raised by Adriaenssen, "Peter John Olivi on Perceptual Representation," who favours the latter option against the traditional externalist interpretation (e.g. Pasnau and Toivanen as quoted above). I tend to understand Olivi as proposing a special kind of causality here – one that is not ontologically committing (note that Olivi admits that terminative causality can be counted among the efficient causes in the broad sense – *Summa* II.72, 10). Thus, a comparison with the modern Lewisian interpretation of causality as a counterfactual dependence seems useful here. In this view, A causes B, if it holds that (1) if A occurs, B occurs, and (2) if A did not occur, B would not occur. (See D. Lewis, "Veridical Hallucination and Prosthetic Vision," *Australasian Journal of Philosophy*, vol. 58, 1980, pp. 239–249; W. Fish, *Philosophy of Perception: A Contemporary Introduction*, London, Routledge, 2010, pp. 113–118.) Applied to the Olivi's case: the visual act is "caused" by the object in the sense that (1) if the object x occurs then the vision of x occurs and (2) if the object x did not occur, then the vision of x would not occur. Note that Olivi's makes a similar explanation in *Summa* II.72, 10: "[*Vis activa*] *absque tali termino et terminatione non posse agere suum actum et posse hoc cum ipso* [...]." Hence, Olivi's claim that the determination of the visual act is *caused* by the object, although not efficiently but terminatively should be understood as asserting that the visual act counterfactually depends on the object without receiving any actual entity from it (which would compromise the ontological superiority of the visual power). Further, Adriaenssen's internalist reading of the "termination" fits only the second phase of the visual process (determination of the visual content). But Olivi uses the notion of termination also in the first phase (the attention switching and fixation), where the causal interpretation seems to be a better choice.

EXTRAMISSION POSTULATE IN 13TH C. THEORIES OF VISION

successive account of vision as Albert was. If we apprehended just one part of the visible object at one moment, we would never reach a determinate and certain apprehension of the whole thing. Hence, apprehension must be immediate (*in instanti*).[133] If vision is immediate, do we apprehend just one thing or a number of things in one moment? Olivi ponders the question and he presents an argument for the latter solution: if what is seen were solely the place to which the axis of the visual cone is attached, the perceiver would see just one point. However, such a conclusion is implausible: either he sees nothing, or he sees a divisible continuum that has a quantity and hence a plurality of parts.[134] Later he specifies his position: evidently, we see more than just one point, but on the other side, what is seen has to evince some kind of unity. The source of such a unity is the *aspectus* – hence, we see a number of things at once but always under one *aspectus*.[135]

On the other hand, we often experience that we are performing a *successive* scanning of the environment. Is it against Olivi's general conviction that vision is immediate? Not necessarily: he emphasises two phases of the visual process. The first (attention focusing) can be either immediate or successive (*simul vel successive dirigitur aspectus ab oculo*).[136] The simple "propagation" of the *aspectus* is understood as immediate, since it is not a local motion that takes place in time.[137] However, attention focusing can also be successive when it is applied to an excesively large object. In such a case, the observing eye has to oscillate to scan all the parts of the object, which takes some time. The second phase of the visual process (the visual act) is always instantaneous. Hence, Olivi understands vision as immediate or successive, depending on what stage of the process is emphasized.[138]

6 Conclusion

As I have shown, extramissionist theories did not appear as antiquated and obscure to 13th century thinkers as they may appear to us. Although Aristotelians, such as Albert the Great, refuted the theory, it still appeared considerably credible for Roger Bacon and was originally reformulated by Peter Olivi.

---

133   Olivi, *Summa* II.26, 452.
134   Olivi, *Summa* II.37, 660.
135   Olivi, *Summa* II.37, 664.
136   Olivi, *Summa* II.73, 65.
137   Olivi, *Summa* II.26, 451–452; II.89, 209; also Tachau, *Vision and Certitude*, p. 48.
138   Olivi, *Quodlibeta* I.4, 17.

Neither of them upheld the most problematic feature of the theory, viz., the emission of a material entity from the eyes. Both, while open-minded to the extramission postulate, manifest a tendency to "dematerialize" extramission: according to Bacon, what is emitted is the visual power or the "*species* of the sight"; in Olivi's view, there is only a virtual extension of the visual power, best to be described as attention.

Albert the Great refuted extramission, but incorporated the notion of a visual cone into an intromissionist framework; once the observer has received the *species* of the object, vision immediately occurs. However, he also attempts to include a selective attention as "directing" the received *species* to the thing or its part. Roger Bacon presented a syncretic account with a primacy of intromission; extramission has a *metaphysical* function in his account, since it refines the *species* of the material object and helps to bridge the ontological gap between them and the visual organ. Vision is a thoroughly successive process for him – not only the multiplication of the *species* takes time (albeit an imperceptible amount of it), but also the certification of vision performed by passing the axis of the visual cone over the parts of the object seen. Finally, Peter Olivi developed an original rethinking of an extramissionist (predominantly Platonic) visual theory. Extramission has a *psychological* role in his account and the traditional optical conceptual equipment (such as the notion of a visual ray) is used to describe attentional switching. However, the visual process is not completed by the fixation of attention, but by the creation of a visual act (by the power as an efficient cause) and determination of its content (by the object as a terminative cause). Whereas the first phase of the visual process, viz. attentional switching, can be successive, the second phase, viz. the causation of the visual act, is always instantaneous. With a grain of salt, Olivi's account can be described as a Platonic syncretic account with a primacy of extramission.[139]

Bibliography

Primary Literature

Adelard of Bath, "Quaestiones naturales," C. Burnett (ed and trans.), *Conversations with his Nephew: On the Same and the Different, Questions on Natural Science*, and *On Birds*, Cambridge, Cambridge University Press, 1998.

---

139 The research behind this article was supported by the project *The Construction of the Other in Medieval Europe* (University of Ostrava, no. IRP201820).

Albert the Great, *Commentarii in II Sententiarum*, A. Borgnet (ed), *Opera omnia 27*, Paris, Vivès, 1894.

Albert the Great, *De anima*, C. Stroick (ed), *Opera omnia 7.1*, Münster, Aschendorff, 1968.

Albert the Great, *De homine*, H. Anzulewicz and J.R. Söder (eds), *Opera omnia 27.2*, Münster, Aschendorff, 2008.

Albert the Great, *De sensu et sensato*, S. Donati (ed), *Opera omnia 7.2A*, Münster, Aschendorff, 2017.

Albert the Great, *Quaestio de sensibus corporis gloriosi*, A. Fries, W. Kübel, and H. Anzulewicz (eds), *Opera omnia 25.2*, Münster, Aschendorff, 1993.

Anonymous, *Lectura in librum De anima a quodam discipulo reportata*, R.A. Gauthier (ed), Grottaferrata, Collegium S. Bonaventurae, 1985.

Anonymous, *Quaestiones de perspectiva*, MS Praha, Knihovna metropolitní kapituly M.100, ff. 69rb-72rb.

Anonymous, *Quaestiones in De anima*, MS Assisi, Bibl. Sacr. Conv. 138, ff. 251va-261va.

Aristotle, *The Complete Works of Aristotle*, 2 vols., J. Barnes (ed), Princeton, Princeton University Press, 1984.

Averroes, *Commentarium magnum in Aristotelis De anima*, F.S. Crawford (ed), Cambridge, The Mediaeval Academy of America, 1953.

Averroes, *De sensu et sensato, Compendia librorum Aristotelis qui Parva naturalia vocantur*, H.A. Wolfson, D. Baneth, and F.H. Fobes (eds), Cambridge, The Mediaeval Academy of America, 1949.

Bartholomeus Anglicus, *De proprietatibus rerum*, Frankfurt, Wolfgang Richter, 1601.

Bernard of Chartres, *Glosae super Platonem*, P.E. Dutton (ed), Toronto, PIMS, 1991.

Bonaventura, *Commentaria in quatuor libros Sententiarum*, *Opera omnia I–IV*, Quaracchi, Collegium S. Bonaventurae, 1882–1889.

Chalcidius, *Timaeus a Calcidio translatus commentarioque instructus*, J.H. Waszink (ed), Leiden, Brill, 1975.

Constantine the African, *De oculis*, P. Pansier (ed), *Collectio ophthalmologica veterum auctorum VII*, Paris, 1933.

Euclid, *De visu*, W.R. Theisen (ed), "*Liber de visu*: The Greco-Latin Translation of Euclid's *Optics*," *Mediaeval Studies*, vol. 41, no. 1, 1979, pp. 44–105.

Galfridus de Aspale, *Quaestiones super librum De sensu et sensato*, MS Todi, Biblioteca Comunale 23, ff. 99vb-123ra.

Guillelmus de Conchis, *Dragmaticon philosophiae*, I. Ronca and A. Badia (eds), Turnhout, Brepols, 1997.

Guillelmus de Conchis, *Glosae super Platonem*, E.A. Jeauneau (ed), Turnhout, Brepols, 2006.

John Blund, *Tractatus de anima*, D.A. Callus and R.W. Hunt (eds), *John Blund: Treatise on the Soul*, trans. M.W. Dunne, Oxford, Oxford University Press, 2013.

John of Jandun, *Questio de sensu agente*, A. Pattin (ed), *Pour l'histoire du sens agent. La controverse entre Barthélemy de Bruges et Jean de Jandun, ses antécédents et son evolution*, Leuven, Leuven University Press, 1988, pp. 223–234.

John Pecham, *John Pecham and the Science of Optics: "Perspectiva communis,"* D.C. Lindberg (ed), Wisconsin, University of Wisconsin, 1970.

John Pecham, *Quaestiones tractantes de anima*, H. Spettmann (ed), Münster, Aschendorff, 1918.

Nemesius of Emesa, *De natura hominis*, C. Burkhard (ed), *Nemesii episcopi Premnon physicon sive Peri physeōs anthrōpoy liber a N. Alfano archiepiscopo Salerni in Latinum translatus,* Leipzig, Teubner, 1917.

Peter John Olivi, *Quaestiones in secundum librum Sententiarum*, 3 vols., B. Jansen (ed), Firenze, Collegium S. Bonaventurae, 1922–1926.

Peter John Olivi, *Quodlibeta quinque*, S. Defraia (ed), Grottaferrata, Collegium S. Bonaventurae, 2002.

Peter John Olivi, "Tria scripta sui ipsius apologetica annorum 1283 et 1285," D. Laberge (ed), *Archivum Franciscanum Historicum*, vol. 28, 1935, pp. 115–155, 374–407.

Peter Sutton (?), *Quodlibeta*, F. Etzkorn (ed), *Franciscan Studies*, vol. 23, 1963, pp. 68–139.

Pseudo-Euclid, *De speculis*, A.A. Björnbo and S. Vogl (eds), *Alkindi, Tideus und Pseudo-Euklid. Drei optische Werke*, Berlin, Teubner, 1912.

Pseudo-Petrus Hispanus, *Expositio libri De anima*, M. Alonso (ed), Madrid, Instituto de filosofía "Luis Vives," 1952.

Pseudo-Robert Grosseteste, *Summa philosophiae*, L. Baur (ed), *Die philosophischen Werke des Robert Grosseteste, Bischofs von Lincoln*, Münster, Aschendorff, 1912, pp. 275–643.

Robert Grosseteste, *De iride seu De iride et speculo*, L. Baur (ed), *Die philosophischen Werke des Robert Grosseteste, Bischofs von Lincoln*, Münster, Aschendorff, 1912, pp. 72–78.

Robert Grosseteste, *De lineis angulis et figuris*, L. Baur (ed), *Die philosophischen Werke des Robert Grosseteste, Bischofs von Lincoln*, Münster, Aschendorff, 1912, pp. 59–65.

Roger Bacon, *Compendium studii philosophiae*, J.S. Brewer (ed), *Fr. Rogeri Bacon Opera quaedam hactenus inedita*, London, 1859, pp. 393–519.

Roger Bacon, *De multiplicatione specierum*, D.C. Lindberg (ed and trans.), *Roger Bacon's Philosophy of Nature*, Oxford, Clarendon Press, 1983, pp. 1–268; 343–362.

Roger Bacon, *Liber de sensu et sensato*, R. Steele (ed), *Opera hactenus inedita* XIV, Oxford, Clarendon Press, 1937.

Roger Bacon, *Opus minus*, J.S. Brewer (ed), *Fr. Rogeri Bacon Opera quaedam hactenus inedita*, London, Longman, 1859, pp. 311–389.

Roger Bacon, *Opus tertium*, J.S. Brewer (ed), *Fr. Rogeri Bacon Opera quaedam hactenus inedita*, London, Longman, 1859, pp. 3–310.

Roger Bacon, *Opus tertium*, P. Duhem (ed), *Un fragment inédit de l'Opus tertium de Roger Bacon*, Quaracchi, Collegium S. Bonaventurae, 1909.

Roger Bacon, *Perspectiva*, D.C. Lindberg (ed and trans.), *Roger Bacon and the Origins of "Perspectiva" in the Middle Ages*, Oxford, Clarendon Press, 1996.

Roger Bacon, *The Opus maius of Roger Bacon*, 3 vols., J.H. Bridges (ed), Oxford, Clarendon Press, 1897–1900.

Roger Marston, *Quodlibeta quatuor*, G.J. Etzkorn and I. Brady (eds), Grottaferrata, Collegium S. Bonaventurae, 1994.

Thomas Aquinas, *Commentum in quartum librum Sententiarum*, Parma, Typis Petri Ficcadori, 1858.

Secondary Literature

Adriaenssen, Han Thomas, "Peter John Olivi on Perceptual Representation," *Vivarium*, vol. 49, no. 4, 2011, pp. 324–352.

Akdogan, Cemil, "Optics in Albert the Great's *De sensu et sensato*: An Edition, English Translation, and Analysis," PhD dissertation, University of Wisconsin-Madison, 1978.

Anzulewicz, Henryk, *De forma resultante in speculo*, 2 vols., Münster, Aschendorff, 1999.

Anzulewicz, Henryk, "Perspektive und Raumvorstellung in den Frühwerken des Albertus Magnus," in J. Aertsen and A. Speer (eds), *Raum und Raumvorstellungen im Mittelalter*, Berlin, De Gruyter, 1998, pp. 249–286.

Berryman, Sylvia, "Euclid and the Sceptic: A Paper on Vision, Doubt, Geometry, Light and Drunkenness," *Phronesis*, vol. 43, no. 2, 1998, pp. 176–196.

Burr, David, "Peter John Olivi and the Philosophers," *Franciscan Studies*, vol. 31, 1971, pp. 41–71.

Demange, Dominique, "Olivi et les *Perspectivi*," *Oliviana*, vol. 5, 2016, http://oliviana.revues.org/850, accessed in February 2019.

Dewan, Lawrence, "St. Albert, the Sensibles, and Spiritual Being," in J.A. Weisheipl (ed), *Albertus Magnus and the Sciences: Commemorative Essays 1980*, Toronto, PIMS, 1980, pp. 291–320.

Donati, Silvia, "Pseudoepigrapha in the *Opera hactenus inedita Rogeri Baconi*? The Commentaries on the *Physics* and on the *Metaphysics*," in J. Verger and O. Weijers (eds), *Les débuts de l'enseignement universitaire à Paris (1200–1245 environ)*, Turnhout, Brepols, 2013, pp. 153–203.

Easton, Stewart C., *Roger Bacon and His Search for a Universal Science*, New York, Russell & Russell, 1952.

Ebbesen, Sten, Thörnqvist, Christina T., and Decaix, Veronique, "Questions on *De sensu et sensato*, *De memoria*, and *De somno et vigilia*: A Catalogue," *Bulletin de philosophie médiévale*, vol. 57, 2015, pp. 59–115.

Fish, William, *Philosophy of Perception: A Contemporary Introduction*, London, Routledge, 2010.

Galle, Griet, "Edition and Discussion of the Oxford Gloss on *De sensu 1*," *Archives d'histoire doctrinale et littéraire du Moyen Âge*, vol. 75, 2008, pp. 197–281.

Hackett, Jeremiah, "From *Sapientes antiqui* at Lincoln to the New *Sapientes moderni* at Paris c. 1260–1280: Roger Bacon's Two Circles of Scholars," in J.P. Cunningham and M. Hocknull (eds), *Robert Grosseteste and the Pursuit of Religious and Scientific Learning in the Middle Ages*, Dordrecht, Springer, 2016, pp. 119–142.

Hackett, Jeremiah, "Roger Bacon and the Moralization of Science: From *Perspectiva* through *Scientia Experimentalis* to *Moralis Philosophia*," in *I francescani e le scienze*, Spoleto, Centro Italiano di Studi sull'Alto Medioevo, 2012, pp. 369–392.

Hasse, Dag N., "Pietro d'Abano's Conciliator and the Theory of the Soul in Paris," in J. Aertsen, K. Emory, and A. Speer (eds), *Nach der Verurteilung von 1277. Philosophie und Theologie an der Universität von Paris im letzten Viertel des 13. Jahrhunderts. Studien und Texte*, Berlin, De Gruyter, 2001, pp. 635–653.

Hasse, Dag N., *Avicenna's "De anima" in the Latin West: The Formation of a Peripatetic Philosophy of the Soul, 1160–1300*, London, The Warburg Institute, 2000.

Hoffmans, Hadelin, "La genèse des sensations d'après Roger Bacon," *Revue néoscolastique*, vol. 15, 1908, pp. 474–498.

Jansen, Berhnard, *Die Erkenntnislehre Olivis*, Berlin, Dümmlers, 1921.

Kalderon, Mark E., "Perception and Extramission in *De quantitate animae*," *Oxford Studies in Ancient Philosophy*, forthcoming.

Kalderon, Mark E., *Sympathy in Perception*, Cambridge, Cambridge University Press, 2017.

Lewis, David, "Veridical Hallucination and Prosthetic Vision," *Australasian Journal of Philosophy*, vol. 58, 1980, pp. 239–249.

Lička, Lukáš, "Attention, Perceptual Content, and Mirrors: Two Medieval Models of Active Perception in Peter Olivi and Peter Auriol," *Filosofický časopis*, vol. 65, Special Issue 2, 2017, pp. 101–119.

Lička, Lukáš, "What is in the Mirror? The Metaphysics of Mirror Images in Albert the Great and Peter Auriol," in B. Glenney and J.F. Silva (eds), *The Senses and the History of Philosophy*, London, Routledge, 2019, pp. 131–148.

Lindberg, David C. (ed and trans.), *Roger Bacon's Philosophy of Nature*, Oxford, Clarendon Press, 1983.

Lindberg, David C., *Roger Bacon and the Origins of "Perspectiva" in the Middle Ages: A Critical Edition and English Translation of Bacon's "Perspectiva"*, Oxford, Oxford University Press, 1996.

Lindberg, David C., *Theories of Vision from al-Kindi to Kepler*, Chicago, University of Chicago Press, 1976.

Long, James R. and Noone, Timothy B., "Fishacre and Rufus on the Metaphysics of Light: Two Unedited Texts," in J. Hamesse (ed), *Roma, magistra mundi. Itineraria culturae medievalis*, Turnhout, Brepols, 1998, pp. 517–548.

Long, James R., "The anonymous *De anima* of Assisi, biblioteca comunale cod. 138," in A. Musco et al. (eds), *Universalità della ragione. Pluralità delle filosofie nel Medioevo*, vol. 2, Palermo, Officina di studi medievali, 2012, pp. 271–280.

Loose, Patrice K., "Roger Bacon on Perception: A Reconstruction and Critical Analysis of the Theory of Visual Perception Expounded in the *Opus Majus*," PhD dissertation, Ohio State University, 1979.

Mantovani, Mattia, "*Visio per sillogismum*: Sensation and Cognition in 13th Century Theories of Vision," in E. Băltuță (ed), *Medieval Perceptual Puzzles: Theories of Perception in the 13th and 14th Centuries*, Leiden, Brill, 2020, pp. 111–152.

Matthews, Gareth B., "A Medieval Theory of Vision," in P.K. Machamer and R.G. Turnbull (eds), *Studies in Perception: Interrelations in the History of Philosophy and Science*, Columbus, Ohio State University Press, 1978, pp. 186–199.

Pasnau, Robert, *Theories of Cognition in the Later Middle Ages*, Cambridge, Cambridge University Press, 1997.

Pattin, Adriaan, *Pour l'histoire du sens agent. La controverse entre Barthélemy de Bruges et Jean de Jandun, ses antécédents et son évolution*, Leuven, Leuven University Press, 1988.

Perler, Dominik, *Theorien der Intentionalität im Mittelalter*, Frankfurt am Main, Vittorio Klostermann, 2002.

Pickavé, Martin, "The Controversy over the Principle of Individuation in Medieval Quodlibeta (1277-ca. 1320): A Forest Map," in C. Schabel (ed), *Theological Quodlibeta in the Middle Ages: The Fourteenth Century*, Leiden, Brill, 2007, pp. 17–79.

Piron, Sylvain, "La chronologie des écrits d'Olivi," *Oliviana*, vol. 6, forthcoming.

Power, Amanda, *Roger Bacon and the Defence of Christendom*, Cambridge, Cambridge University Press, 2013.

Raizman-Kedar, Yael, "Questioning Aristotle: Roger Bacon on the True Essence of Colour," *The Journal of Medieval Latin*, vol. 17, 2007, pp. 372–383.

Raizman-Kedar, Yael, "*Species* as Signs: Roger Bacon (1220–1292) on *Perspectiva* and *Grammatica*," PhD dissertation, University of Haifa, 2009.

Raizman-Kedar, Yael, "The Intellect Naturalized: Roger Bacon on the Existence of Corporeal Species within the Intellect," *Early Science and Medicine*, vol. 14, no. 1, 2009, pp. 131–157.

Siebert, Harald, "Transformation of Euclid's *Optics* in Late Antiquity," *Nuncius*, vol. 29, no. 1, 2014, pp. 88–126.

Silva, José Filipe and Toivanen, Juhana, "The Active Nature of the Soul in Sense Perception: Robert Kilwardby and Peter Olivi," *Vivarium*, vol. 48, no. 3–4, 2010, pp. 245–278.

Silva, José Filipe, "Medieval Theories of Active Perception: An Overview," in J.F. Silva and M- Yrjönsuuri (eds), *Active Perception in the History of Philosophy: From Plato to Modern Philosophy*, Dordrecht, Springer, 2014, pp. 117–146.

Smith, Mark A., *From Sight to Light: The Passage from Ancient to Modern Optics*, Chicago, The University of Chicago Press, 2015.

Steneck, Nicholas H., "Albert on the Psychology of Sense Perception," in J.A. Weisheipl (ed), *Albertus Magnus and the Sciences: Commemorative Essays 1980*, Toronto, PIMS, 1980, pp. 263–290.

Tachau, Katherine H., *Vision and Certitude in the Age of Ockham: Optics, Epistemology, and the Foundations of Semantics, 1250–1345*, Leiden, Brill, 1988.

Toivanen, Juhana, *Perception and the Internal Senses: Peter of John Olivi on the Cognitive Functions of the Sensitive Soul*, Leiden, Brill, 2013.

Toivanen, Juhana, "The Fate of the Flying Man: Medieval Reception of Avicenna's Thought Experiment," in R. Pasnau (ed), *Oxford Studies in Medieval Philosophy*, vol. 3, Oxford, Oxford University Press, 2015, pp. 64–98.

Winkler, Norbert, "Zur Erkenntnislehre Alberts des Großen in seinem *De anima*-Kommentar als systematische Einheit von sensus, abstractio, phantasmata, intentiones, species, universalia und intellectus," *Bochumer Philosophisches Jahrbuch für Antike und Mittelalter*, vol. 19, 2016, pp. 70–173.

CHAPTER 5

Visio per sillogismum: Sensation and Cognition in 13th Century Theories of Vision

Mattia Mantovani

1 The Aristotelians' Dilemma: "Materialists" and "Dematerializers"

The bedrock of most theories of perception advanced during the 13th and 14th Centuries was Aristotle's claim that knowledge – and thereby sensory knowledge (perception) as well – consists in an "assimilation," and that a cognizer comes to know an object by taking on the object's "form without matter." Despite the widespread reference to these tenets, different thinkers often ended up interpreting Aristotle's statements on the topic in different ways. Some accused their opponents of misinterpreting the true spirit of Aristotle's philosophy; others, conversely, of distorting the plain letter of his texts. The interpretative difficulty that medieval thinkers were confronted with is a real and a tough one, and present-day scholars are still trying their best to puzzle it out. In recent decades, it has indeed been extensively debated whether for Aristotle sense-organs undergo in perceiving a "material" or rather a "spiritual" change. Or, to cast the issue in still more concrete terms, whether the eye (or at least some specific portion of it) literally turns red when faced with a red object – this being what "assimilation" in fact consists in – or not. Richard Sorabji has famously endorsed the former, "materialist" reading, and been strenuously opposed in this by Myles Burnyeat.[1]

In order to substantiate their views, scholars from both sides of this debate have taken advantage of the readings advanced down the centuries by Aristotle's interpreters – especially the "Commentators" of late Antiquity and the Scholastics of the 13th Century – in this case, however, to agree with one another. Both Sorabji and Burnyeat agree, in fact, that leading figures of 13th century philosophy such as Albert the Great (ca. 1200–1280) and Thomas Aquinas (1225–1274) were dyed-in-the-wool proponents of the spiritual change reading. As a matter of fact, the very expression "spiritual change" comes from Aquinas. According to Burnyeat Aquinas was, on this issue, a faithful interpreter

---

1 For a survey of the extensive literature on the topic, see R. Sorabji, *Perception, Conscience, and Will in Ancient Philosophy*, Padstow, Ashgate, 2013.

© KONINKLIJKE BRILL NV, LEIDEN, 2020 | DOI:10.1163/9789004413030_006

of Aristotle, since for this latter too (so argues Burnyeat) "the eye's taking on a color" was just another way of saying "one's becoming aware of some color."[2] "The effect on the organ *is* the awareness, no more and no less," comments Burnyeat, "no more" meaning "without any physiological process" (such as the coloring of the eye-jelly) of the kind described by Sorabji.[3] According to Sorabji, on the other hand, the "spiritual change" account of perception is the result of a centuries-old series of creative misunderstandings and thought-provoking elaborations on Aristotle's actual views: robustly material in Aristotle's own work, the perceptual process (so argues Sorabji) has detached itself more and more from physiology only in the work of his successors.[4] The entity mediating between the object and the perceiver (action at a distance being excluded by Aristotelians) – i.e. what medieval thinkers called a *species* – followed, on this account of things, the same path, gradually forfeiting its originally corporeal nature to become a mere intentional being.[5]

Despite their quarrel over Aristotle, Sorabji's agreement with Burnyeat about how to interpret Aquinas is not surprising. In his commentary on the *De anima* Aquinas in fact makes clear his views in a way that seem to leave no room for doubt:

> It is evident from the kind of change it involves that the sense of sight is more spiritual (*spiritualior*). For in the case of the other senses there is no spiritual change without natural change (*non est immutatio spiritualis sine naturali*). I call a change 'natural' when the quality is received in the patient in accordance with its natural being, as when something is cooled or warmed or moved in space. But a 'spiritual' change is one whereby the form is received in the organ of sense, or in the medium, as an intention, not as a natural form (*per modum intentionis, et non per modum naturalis formae*). That is, the form is not received in the sense in accordance with the being it has in the sensible object. Now it is obvious that in the case of touch and taste – which is a form of touch – there is a natural alteration.

---

2 M. Burnyeat, "Is an Aristotelian Philosophy of Mind Still Credible? A Draft," in M.C. Nussbaum and A.O. Rorty (eds), *Essays on Aristotle's "De anima,"* Oxford, Clarendon Press, 1992, p. 18.

3 Burnyeat, p. 22.

4 R. Sorabji, "From Aristotle to Brentano: The Development of the Concept of Intentionality," *Oxford Studies in Ancient Philosophy*, Supplementary Volume, 1991, pp. 227–259.

5 For a detailed study of the concept of *intentio* in the philosophers of the time see D. Perler, *Theorien der Intentionalität im Mittelalter*, Frankfurt am Main, Vittorio Klostermann, 2002, and, more in general, Perler (ed), *Ancient and Medieval Theories of Intentionality*, Leiden, Brill, 2001.

VISIO PER SILLOGISMUM   113

> In this case, something is in fact warmed or chilled due to contact with a thing that is hot or cold, and there is not only a spiritual change ... But in the case of sight there is nothing but spiritual change (*in immutatione visus est sola immutatio spiritualis*). Whence it is clear that of all senses sight is the most spiritual, with hearing next in line.[6]

The hierarchy that Aquinas establishes running from the sense deepest-seated in matter up to the "most spiritual" sense – that is to say, from touch up to sight – does not need to concern us here, since its main rationale is to be found in the Neoplatonic metaphysics of light rather than in the philosophy of Aristotle (who never, in fact, defended anything like a hierarchy of the senses).[7] The crucial point, nonetheless, is that, according to Aquinas, a "material" (or, as he puts it, a "natural") change in the sense-organs of the sort that Sorabji envisages is neither a *sufficient* nor (at least as far as vision is concerned) a *necessary* condition for perception to occur. Aquinas is not thereby denying that the sense-organ undergoes a change in perceiving.[8] The point, though, is entirely about how we understand this change. Aquinas' setting-up of an opposition between a "spiritual" and a "natural" change should not lead us astray here. Aquinas is not advocating an opposition between soul and body *à la* Descartes and ascribing perception solely and exclusively to the mind: he operates in fact within a hylomorphic framework, in which perception does decidedly count as "one of the doings of the body" (to use Burnyeat's fine phrasing). Aquinas, however, was mindful of the difficulties raised by his teacher, who objected against the claim of a "natural" change that:

> If color were in the air as in a colored thing we ought to see the air colored and the eye colored by the color it receives. And we see the opposite of this. So in abstraction it [color] exists with a different being from that which it has in its own proper matter.[9]

---

6   Thomas Aquinas, *Sentencia libri De anima*, *Opera omnia 45.1*, Rome, Commissio Leonina, 1984, II.14, trans. Burnyeat, "Aquinas on 'spiritual change' in perception," in Perler (ed), *Ancient and Medieval Theories of Intentionality*, pp. 132–133*. Here and thereafter the asterisk (*) indicates that the translation has been modified.

7   Burnyeat, "Aquinas on spiritual change," p. 131. On the importance of Neoplatonic metaphysics for medieval and early modern vision theories, D.C. Lindberg, "The Genesis of Kepler's Theory of Light: Light Metaphysics from Plotinus to Kepler," *Osiris*, vol. 2, 1986, pp. 4–42.

8   Cf. Thomas Aquinas, *Summa theologiae*, P. Caramello (ed), 3 vols., Turin, Marietti, 1963, 1a, q. 75, a. 3: "[...] sentire vero, et consequentes operationes animae sensitivae, manifeste accidunt cum aliqua corporis immutatione, sicut in videndo immutatur pupilla per speciem coloris."

9   Albert the Great, *De anima*, C. Stroick (ed), *Opera omnia 7.1*, Münster, Aschendorff, 1968, II 3.6; trans. Sorabji, "From Aristotle to Brentano," p. 256.

This "different way of existing" is what Aquinas calls "intentional" being, as expressly opposed to the way of existing proper to natural forms. Thus, upon entering the eye, the *intentio* of a red object would not cause the perceiver to "assimilate" the object in question by turning his eye red. Rather, its action would consist simply in directing this knowing subject, by virtue of its intentional nature, to the red object whose *intentio* it is. Nevertheless, the "spiritual" change which the *intentio* thereby induces does still fall, according to Aristotelians, within the purview of physics, since on their view physics encompasses also all psychological activities. For Aquinas, however, only a cognizer can undergo a change which consists in nothing else but becoming cognizant of an object. Tautological as it might sound, the doctrine of a "spiritual" change – as opposed to a "natural" one – was Aquinas' (and not just Aquinas') way of setting cognition apart from all the other manifold activities of which corporeal substances were said to be capable.

Aquinas' influence among the historians of philosophy of the last centuries is difficult to overrate, and for quite a long time scholars of the Middle Ages tended to read all the authors and debates that they were studying through the lens of the *Summa theologiae*. As far as the theory of perception is concerned, Aquinas' doctrine has proven so pervasive as to have almost been taken for self-evident. Accordingly, the thesis that in perceiving the sense-organs – and quite especially the eyes – might undergo a "material" change has been able to be dismissed even by an interpreter as authoritative as Robert Pasnau as "idiosyncratic," "surprising and implausible-sounding," "absurd and confused," if not downright outrageous.[10]

In Aquinas' own era, however, there were still philosophers who maintained that the sense-organs – the eyes included – did indeed undergo such a change. Those who defended such a view, moreover, were neither few in number nor without reputation but rather included the main experts on vision theory of the 13th Century: Roger Bacon (ca. 1214–1294), Erazm Ciolek Witelo (ca. 1230-post 1280) and John Pecham (ca. 1230–1292). In their works on *perspectiva*, written between the 1260s and the '70s, these thinkers argued that light- and color-perception results from a literal coloring of the sentient components of the visual apparatus, both external and internal.[11] Bacon, in particular, insisted

---

10   R. Pasnau, *Theories of Cognition in the Later Middle Ages*, Cambridge, Cambridge University Press, 1997, pp. 66, 94, 90.

11   On the dating of the Perspectivists' works and on the relations between them, see D.C. Lindberg, "Lines of Influence in 13th Century Optics: Bacon, Witelo, and Pecham," *Speculum*, vol. 46, 1971, pp. 66–83. The "anterior glacial humor" – our crystalline lens – was sometimes also referred to at the time as the "pupil," this quite likely being the meaning of *pupilla* in the passage from Aquinas quoted above; see for example Roger

VISIO PER SILLOGISMUM

that there was no other reasonable way of interpreting Aristotle's statements and denounced as "madness" the claim that *species* do not have material being and do not, therefore, bring about material change in the eye.[12]

Sorabji, then, was by no means the first to read the *De anima* and the *Parva naturalia* as making a case for a "material" change. In fact, in a footnote Sorabji himself has already pointed out that the theorist of vision on whom all European Perspectivists depended – Ibn al-Haytham, better known in the Latin West as Alhacen (ca. 965–1039) – held such a view. Shortly thereafter, but once again almost only in passing, Sorabji remarks that this was also true of another, no less influential contemporary of Alhacen: Ibn Sīnā or, as the Latin-speaking intellectuals came to know him, Avicenna (ca. 970–1037).[13] The main reason, however, why Sorabji mentions Avicenna is to introduce the concept of *intentio*, that is to say, the concept that in Sorabji's view was eventually to lead to the complete "dematerialization" of the sensory process.

Intrigued by the grand and compelling narrative presented by Sorabji in his seminal essay, it is easy to fail to appreciate the importance of these marginal remarks, and to form the erroneous impression that the progressive "dematerialization" of the perceptual process advanced substantially unchallenged in the centuries between the Commentators and Brentano.[14] In case, as is argued by Burnyeat, this theory had not been in place right from the beginning.[15] As this paper shows, the controversy between "the dematerializers" (as Sorabji half-jokingly calls them) and the "materialists" was still very much alive during the 13th Century and revolved precisely, and not coincidentally, around the sense that Aquinas had extolled as the "most spiritual" of all. Indeed, had the Perspectivists managed to firmly establish the thesis that the perceiver's eyes become red when apprehending a red object, then *a fortiori* the thesis of a

---

Bacon, *Perspectiva*, D.C. Lindberg (ed and trans.), *Roger Bacon and the Origins of "Perspectiva" in the Middle Ages*, Oxford, Clarendon Press, 1996, I 3, 1, p. 33.

12   Roger Bacon, *De multiplicatione specierum*, hereafter *DMS*, D.C. Lindberg (ed and trans.), *Roger Bacon's Philosophy of Nature*, Oxford, Clarendon Press, 1983, III 2, pp. 91–92.

13   Sorabji, "From Aristotle to Brentano," pp. 228 n. 2, 236.

14   Tellingly enough, Bacon features in the story that Sorabji relates (Sorabji, pp. 244–245, 258) only as a sort of encyclopedia entry to illustrate how the terms *intentio, species, similitudo, phantasma, forma* and the like were used at the time, without a single word about Bacon's or, more generally, the Perspectivists' understanding of the visual process in terms of a "material" change.

15   Burnyeat has not sketched any general history of perception theories comparable to Sorabji's. Nevertheless, in Burnyeat, "Is an Aristotelian Philosophy of Mind Still Credible?" he seems to suggest that the "spiritual" account was intrinsic to Aristotelianism and came to be challenged only in the Early Modern Age, explicitly mentioning Descartes and Hobbes as its opponents.

"material" change occurring in and through perception would have been proven true for all sense-modalities.[16]

In this paper, however, I argue that the Perspectivists were not simply continuing the long-running battle of the "materialists" against the "dematerializers," but brought new life to the debate, contending as they did that if the "material" change they advocated pertained to all the *senses* without exception, it did not, for all that, pertain to all classes of *sensibles*, but only to the *proper* ones. The concept of a proper sensible comes, once again, from Aristotle, who had opened his investigations into the perceptual faculty by drawing a widely-accepted distinction between a first class of sensibles, proper and peculiar to a single sense – such as light and color to sight and sound to hearing – and a second class of sensibles which can be perceived by all of them (or, at least, by both sight and touch). Light and color, shape and motion are all seen; motion and shape, however, are also felt. Therefore, since sensibles belonging to this latter class are common to both sight and touch, Aristotle labelled them *common* sensibles, to be contrasted with the former class of sensibles *proper* (i.e. specific) to one sense only. In what follows, I show that the Perspectivists, nonetheless, did not appeal to the distinction between proper and common sensibles with the intention of studying the senses as a system; their main topic of enquiry remained, in fact, vision, to be investigated in its own right and for its own sake. Aristotle's age-old distinction was reworked to fit the Perspectivists' new philosophical agenda, up to the point of being almost unrecognizable within their list of the twenty-two "visibles" – i.e. of the twenty-two properties of bodies apprehensible by sight. The reason why the Perspectivists relied on this distinction was, indeed, no longer in order to use it to describe the relation between sight and touch. Rather, they used it to distinguish from one another what they took to be the two main *stages* of the visual process, that is, to distinguish the merely sensory stage of this process from its cognitive stage. Or, in their own words, to distinguish "vision by naked sense" from "vision by syllogism." If the debate about the sensory stage revolved around the nature – whether spiritual or material – of the change undergone by the eye, the Perspectivists were also calling into question the standard Aristotelian account of the cognitive process, arguing as they were that the complexity of the operations involved exceeded by far the capabilities of the common sense. As shown in this essay, in their mind the perception of most "common sensibles" required indeed no less than the intellect itself.

---

16 The point is especially clear in John Pecham, *Tractatus de anima*, G. Melani (ed), Firenze, Biblioteca di Studi Francescani, 1948, IV, pp. 12–17.

VISIO PER SILLOGISMUM

2 *Species colorum corporaliter immutant pupillam*

"Light and color are apprehended by naked sense (*comprehendi sensu spolia-to*). They are indeed perceived simply as a result of coloring the ultimate sense" – the brain, roughly speaking; more on this below – after having colored the eyes (*per hoc enim tantum apprehenditur quia ultimum sentiens iis tingitur*).[17] So wrote Pecham, unequivocally stating that for him (like for all the Perspectivists) perception required a "material" change in order to take place even as far as the "most spiritual" of all senses was concerned. In the case of light and color perception, more specifically, this material change was taken to consist in an actual *illuminatio* and coloring of the visual organs. If Pecham spoke generically of a "becoming tinged," Bacon and Witelo were indeed careful to distinguish between *two* different – albeit intimately related – material alterations of the sense-organs, one for each of the sensibles which were said to be apprehended "by naked sense" or "by sense alone" (*solo sensu*):

> The ultimate sense, which is in the common nerve, apprehends light because the common nerve becomes illuminated, as it apprehends color because the common nerve becomes colored, since the forms [i.e. the *species*] of light and color travel through the common sense and become impressed upon it.[18]

---

17 Pecham, *Perspectiva communis*, D.C. Lindberg (ed), *John Pecham and the Science of Optics: "Perspectiva communis,"* Wisconsin, University of Wisconsin, 1970, I 58 {61}, p. 139: "Lucem et colorem comprehendi sensu spoliato. Per hoc enim tantum apprehenditur quia ultimum sentiens iis tingitur." The expression *sensus spoliatus* comes from the Latin translation of Ibn Al-Haytham's *Kitāb al-Manāẓir*, made towards the end of the 12th century by the workshop of Gerard of Cremona (possibly by Gerard himself); cf. Alhacen's *De aspectibus*, A.M. Smith (ed), *Alhacen's Theory of Visual Perception: A Critical Edition, with English Translation and Commentary, of the First Three Books of Alhacen's "De aspectibus,"* Transactions of the American Philosophical Society, vol. 91, no. 4, 2001, I 7, 6.61, pp. 49, 377. Sabra renders the original Arabic term as "pure sensation." See Ibn Al-Haytham, *The Optics of Ibn Al-Haytham, Books I-III: On Direct Vision*, A.I. Sabra (ed and trans.), 2 vols., London, Warburg Institute, 1989, p. 82. The same Arabic expression is translated throughout the second book as *solus sensus* (which Smith renders as "brute sensation" or "brute sense-perception"; Smith, p. 409). Accordingly, the Latin-speaking Perspectivists speak interchangeably of vision "by naked sense" and "by sense alone."

18 Witelo, *Opticae thesaurus ... Vitellionis thuringopoloni Opticae libri decem*, F. Risner (ed), Basel, Officina Episcopiana, 1572, III 22, 95: "Sentiens itaque ultimum, quod est in nervo communi, comprehendit lucem ex illuminatione corporis huius & colorem ex eius coloratione, quoniam horum formae transeunt & figuntur in ipso." For Bacon, see at least *DMS* I 1; Lindberg, pp. 9–11.

Unlike Aristotle, the Perspectivists did not in fact conceive of light as a mere *catalyst* within a transparent medium which enables a subject to perceive colors, but rather ascribed to light a robust causal activity within the visual process. Their understanding of what vision is about changed accordingly. Therefore, whereas Aristotle mentioned nothing but color as the first and proper object of vision – as the only sensible proper to sight – the Perspectivists contended that light itself is perceived, although not in its own right but always as a *colored* light. They accordingly listed both *lux* and *color* as the proper objects of sight.[19]

Whereas this alteration in the list of proper sensibles marks an important point of departure from Aristotle's philosophy, the general claim that color (and light) are apprehended merely as a result of a "becoming colored" (and "becoming illuminated") of the visual apparatus is fully in keeping with the philosophy of the *De anima*, and should not be taken as an instance of crude materialism. The Perspectivists indeed certainly did not conceive of this thing that "becomes colored" as just some random and indifferent material object upon which some light rays happen to fall. In their view, it was indeed nothing else but this very capability of apprehending colors that turned formless matter into the organ of a living being – into an eye. As Aristotle had already made clear, an eye ceases to be an eye as soon as it is no longer able to see (as in the case of a dead animal).[20] No matter how accurate a reproduction of the exterior features of this organ could be achieved, such an apparatus of lenses could not yet be called an "eye," since what makes the eye an eye is nothing but its *function* – that is, its capacity to apprehend colors – not the arrangement of its parts. As Aristotle so vividly put it, "if the eye were a living being, its soul would be its vision."[21] By the same token, Aristotle argued against atomism (and, more generally, against all materialistically-minded psychology) that vision does not amount to the mere mirroring of an image on the eye – nor, analogously, to the simple formation of an image within the eye through reflection

---

19 On Bacon's view on colors see Y. Raizman-Kedar, "Questioning Aristotle: Roger Bacon on the True Essence of Color," *Journal of Medieval Latin*, vol. 17, 2007, pp. 372–385. Aristotle, to be fully accurate, also mentions a further sensible proper to sight, namely, "something which can be described in words, but has in fact no name" (Aristotle, *De anima*, W.S. Hett (ed), *On the Soul, Parva Naturalia, On Breath*, London, Loeb, 1975, B 7, 418^{a}27–28), which proves to be that which is perceptible in the dark. Some of the examples he gives could be explained as phenomena of phosphorescence (419^{a}3–6). Not all of them, though: see *De sensu* 437^{b}6–7.

20 Aristotle, *De anima*, B 1, 412^{b}21–23.

21 Aristotle, *De anima*, 412^{b}19–20.

VISIO PER SILLOGISMUM

or, by the same token, through refraction.[22] The eye, indeed, should not even be taken to be a sort of mirror to which there happens accidentally to be attached a sensitive soul, since an eye (and, more generally, a perceiving organism) is what it is precisely by virtue of this soul. In a rigorous hylomorphic framework, the coloring of the eye and the perception of this color are in fact one and the same thing: if something becomes colored and yet does not perceive this becoming-colored, this thing is simply not an eye, for the eye is, by its very essence, the organ that apprehends color.[23]

Ultimately, therefore, the thesis that the eye must become colored in order for color perception to occur amounts only to the very reasonable claim that an object must leave an impression upon the perceiver's sense-organs if the perceiver is ever to apprehend it. Added to this is the specification that, in the case of vision, this sensory impression is – not very surprisingly – a pictorial impression, *viz.* an image made of colors. By the same token, a hand immersed in water does indeed turn cold, and it is only by itself becoming cold that it can apprehend this quality of the element water. For Bacon and his followers all senses are, in this regard, on a par, contrary to any "hierarchies" of the kind advocated by Aquinas.

As it turns out, the main concern of the Perspectivists in constructing the visual apparatus in the way in which they did was precisely to make plausible the contention that the eye and the portion of the brain from which the optic nerves emerge take on the light and the color of the objects. The Perspectivists did not simply *postulate* that the *species* is of such a nature as to make the perceiver perceive: the doctrine of a material change in perception demanded in fact to its supporters to spell out the *material conditions* in which this process takes place. It is exactly on this point that the Perspectivists' account outdid any other of the time, setting forth an explanation whereas all the "dematerializers" could do was to appeal to a primitive and irreducible capacity of the soul and of the *species*.

The specifics of the arguments with which the Perspectivists shored up their central thesis to the effect that the organs of the visual apparatus (both external and internal) could become tinged with the color of the object they

---

22   Aristotle, *De sensu*, 438ᵃ5–13.

23   Or, at least, the material change of the organ counts in this model as a necessary (albeit by itself maybe not sufficient) condition for perception; on the topic see C.H. Kahn, "Sensation and Consciousness in Aristotle's Psychology," *Archiv für Geschichte der Philosophie*, vol. 48, 1966, pp. 43–81.

perceived are, unfortunately, too subtle and complex to be addressed here in detail.[24] Their explanation proceeded at any rate, in two steps:

(i)   from the object to the anterior surface of the crystalline lens – which they also called the "glacial humor"; and thence:

(ii) from the rear surface of this lens to the brain.

As regards stage (i), the Perspectivists' main concern was to show how it was ensured that the *species*, on entering the eye, did not become blurred. As for (ii), it was to explain how this same *species* was channeled in proper upright order into the hollow optic nerve right up to the *ultimum sentiens*, which Bacon located immediately before the first cerebral ventricle, where the common sense is said to reside or, more precisely, "at the aperture of the skull where the [optical] nerves intersect," also referred to as "the common nerve" or (as we still refer to it today) as the "optical chiasma."[25] According to Bacon, each sense required its own "ultimate sentient power," which Bacon located at the place where the nerves leading to the external sense-organs (for example, to the nose-nodules) join together, the common sense having to be regarded in its turn as the *ultimum sentiens* of all these different *ultima sentientia*.

In order to account for stage (i), the Perspectivists' strategy was basically to argue that, out of all the manifold light rays impinging upon the eye from every direction, only those rays perpendicular to its outermost surface – the cornea – could, being unrefracted, pass through and find their way to the crystalline lens (at least as far as direct vision is concerned). Since only the rays striking the eye's surfaces perpendicularly are said to gain admittance through them, it follows that all the surfaces located before the crystalline lens, as well as the anterior surface of the lens itself, must be concentric to one another.[26] The light rays should then converge at the center of the eye, but are refracted by the rear surface of the crystalline lens and funneled in proper order into the optic nerve.[27]

Such an appeal to perpendicularity and refraction in order to filter out a proper image of the external body is eminently "optical" in nature, but the

---

24   For a detailed account the reader is referred to D.C. Lindberg, *Theories of vision from al-Kindi to Kepler*, Chicago, University of Chicago Press, 1976, and A.M. Smith, *From Sight to Light: The Passage from Ancient to Modern Optics*, Chicago, University of Chicago Press, 2014.

25   Bacon, *Perspectiva* I 5, 3; Lindberg, p. 67.

26   Cf. Bacon, *Perspectiva* I 3, 2; Lindberg, pp. 39–41. Pecham, *Perspectiva communis* I 33 {36}; Lindberg, p. 119.

27   For a more detailed presentation of this point, see A.M. Smith, "What is the History of Medieval Optics Really About?" *Proceedings of the American Philosophical Society*, vol. 148, no. 2, 2004, pp. 184–186.

VISIO PER SILLOGISMUM 121

motivations for arguing along these lines lie elsewhere. This might be proven by simply considering the stage (ii) of the *species* transmission: that from the crystalline lens to the *ultimum sentiens*. Up until the point of their entrance into the nerve's foramen, the focusing of the light rays could still be accounted for by appealing to the shape of the rear surface of the crystalline humor and to its difference in refractive index from the vitreous one, situated immediately behind it. But as soon as the *species* entered the nerve, any such principles of explanation had necessarily to be abandoned. The Perspectivists could try their best, indeed, to argue that the optic nerves were hollow and filled with a transparent body (the visual spirits) which ensured that these nerves were able to transmit colors to the brain.[28] But they could not claim these nerves to be straight since this would have flown too directly in the face of empirical evidence, even according to their own standards in this regard. Unfortunately, however, the entire scientific narrative developed up to that point – up to the foramen of the optic nerve – was based on the principle that light rays travel rectilinearly.

But when forced to decide between the grounding principle of their science and their epistemological commitments, Pecham, and indeed all the Perspectivists before him, seemed to have little doubt about which to choose:

> On the contrary, when the *species* has reached the vitreous humor ... it proceeds more according to the law of spirits than according to the law of transparency. It is indeed curved, following the path of the spirits, all the way to the optic chiasma.[29]

> And in this we admire the power of the soul's excellence, whereby it compels a *species* to follow the twisting of the nerve, so that it proceeds along a twisting line, rather than a straight line as in inanimate bodies of the world. For as long as it is in a single inanimate medium, it always proceeds

---

28   Cf. Bacon, *Perspectiva* I, 4, 3; Lindberg, p. 55. *Perspectiva* I, 2, 1; Lindberg, p. 23. *Perspectiva* I 1, 2; Lindberg, p. 5. Witelo, *Opticae libri decem* III 22; Risner, p. 95. Although it cannot be ruled out that, as is sometimes maintained, ocular anatomists had been led astray by the central retinal artery and vein (which are indeed hollow) or some other nervous structures such as the meningeal covering, it seems quite likely that their claims about the optic nerves had been prescribed in advance by their physiological and philosophical convictions rather than being adopted because of some poorly performed dissections; cf. E. Clarke "The doctrine of the Hollow Nerve in the 17th and 18th Centuries," in L.G. Stevenson and R.P. Multhauf (eds), *Medicine, Science, and Culture: Historical Essays in Honor of Owsei Temkin*, Baltimore, John Hopkins University Press, 1968, pp. 123–141, and, more recently, M. Mantovani, "Eye Anatomy and Perceptual Puzzles from Vesalius to Newton," forthcoming.

29   Pecham, *Perspectiva communis* I 40 {43}; Lindberg, p. 125*.

along straight lines ... but owing to the necessity and nobility of the works of the soul, a *species* in an animate medium follows the course of the medium and abandons the common laws of natural multiplications.[30]

Despite their contradicting one another, the principles concerning the linear propagation of light rays and their refraction (*lex dyaphoneitatis, leges communes multiplicationum naturalium*) and this rather enigmatic *lex spirituum* were nonetheless intended by the Perspectivists to establish the same conclusion: namely, that the visual system was capable of accomplishing its intended task of bringing to the seat of perception an unaltered likeness of the object – its *species*.[31] The contradiction between these two laws was not understood by the Perspectivists as an antinomy between the "optical" and the physiological modalities of light's propagation. It is indeed only in light of the modern understanding of the discipline (largely post-Keplerian, and in the main still our own) that it makes sense to address the issue in these terms. Optics, for Alhacen, Bacon, Witelo, Pecham and all the theorists in the field, was concerned, as its essential theme, with the activity of seeing, and almost only instrumentally with the physical behavior of light rays. Indeed, it is in fact from vision (ὄψις) that the discipline took its name, by taking vision as its object of enquiry. In Mark Smith's elegant phrasing, during the Middle Ages optics was the science of sight rather than specifically of light, as it was to come to be from the Early Modern period onwards.[32] As a consequence, for the Perspectivists both the "law of transparency" and the "law of spirits" were by definition optical in nature, since both had to be posited in order to account for the visual process. Indeed, more than as a science for its own sake, *perspectiva* was mostly cultivated at this period to corroborate an epistemology that had already been accepted on different grounds. It was an epistemology that was taken to require a material change in order for the perceptual process to occur. Therefore, any contrast between the principles of this science and the broader philosophical framework was ruled out right from the outset. It was rather the science of

---

30   Bacon, *Perspectiva* I 7, 11; Lindberg, pp. 97–99. It must, however, be noted that already at stage (i) of the visual process the Perspectivists appealed to the *selective sensitivity* of the crystalline lens (a property the lens was claimed to possess *qua* animate entity) in addition to the principles of refraction in order to single out perpendicular rays; cf. Lindberg, *Theories of vision*, p. 243.

31   On Bacon's theory of natural laws, see Y. Kedar and G. Hon, "Roger Bacon (c. 1220–1292) and his System of Laws of Nature: Classification, Hierarchy and Significance," *Perspective on Science* vol. 25, no. 6, 2017, pp. 719–745.

32   Smith, *From Sight to Light*. See also Smith, "What is the History of Medieval Optics Really About?" pp. 180–194.

VISIO PER SILLOGISMUM

optics that had somehow to accommodate itself to this broader epistemological framework, bending its principles if need be, as it needed to bend light rays
in order to bring colors up to the brain. *Perspectiva* was understood by its own
practitioners as a sort of *ancilla philosophiae* or, with more justice to its merits,
as that science in charge of providing flesh and blood to the abstract claims of
philosophy. Philosophy was understood to demand a coloring of the sense-
organs; *perspectiva* was there to provide it.

As is easy enough to guess, this theory of vision goes hand in hand with an
understanding of the *species* quite different from Albert's and Aquinas.' Bacon
devoted an entire treatise to the topic, wherein he argued vehemently against
the vast majority of the philosophers of his time, for whom *species* had "spiritual existence (*esse spirituale*) in the medium and in the senses."[33] According
to Bacon a *species* is indeed "brought forth out of the active potency of matter
and so has material being."[34] If this were not the case, the metaphysical principle would be violated whereby "no agent is less noble than the thing generated," since "if a *species* is a spiritual thing, it cannot have a corporeal cause,
and consequently no *species* would be produced by bodies, which is contrary
to fact."[35]

Not content with arguing on philosophical grounds, Bacon also wanted to
claim that this was in fact Aristotle's – as well as Avicenna's and Averroes' –
considered view on the topic. Bacon argued that the theory of a "spiritual way
of existing" (*modus existendi spiritualis*) of the *species* – and, accordingly, the
theory of a purely "spiritual" change in the sense-organs – resulted only from a

---

33   Bacon, *Perspectiva* I 6, 3; Lindberg, p. 81.

34   Bacon, *DMS* III 2; Lindberg, p. 191. It has been argued that according to Bacon the same
      would hold true for intellectual *species*; cf. Y. Raizman-Kedar, "*Species* as Signs: Roger Ba-
      con (1220–1292) on *Perspectiva* and *Grammatica*," PhD dissertation, University of Haifa,
      2009, pp. 102–156. Raizman-Kedar, "The Intellect Naturalized: Roger Bacon on the Exis-
      tence of Corporeal Species within the Intellect," *Early Science and Medicine*, vol. 14, no. 1,
      2009, pp. 131–157 (to be seen also for a critical survey of the previous literature on the
      topic). See however to the contrary J. Hackett, "Agent Intellect and Intelligible Species in
      Roger Bacon and John Pecham," in G. Mensching and A. Mensching-Estakhr (eds), *Die
      Seele im Mittelalter. Von der Substanz zum funktionalen System*, Würzburg, Königshausen
      & Neumann, 2018, pp. 149–166.

35   Bacon, *DMS* III 2; Lindberg, p. 189. In what follows, unless otherwise stated, *species* always
      refer to the *species* of the proper sensibles. At the time is was indeed debated (and it will
      be till the 17th century) whether an object issued a *species* of its shape and like features
      besides the *species* of its colors, or the *species* of shape reduced to the *arrangement* of
      colors patches on the crystalline lens; cf. Bacon, *Perspectiva* I 10, 2; Lindberg, pp. 151–52;
      DMS I 2; Lindberg, pp. 39–41. Bacon argued for this deflationary reading mostly from his
      concept of prime matter. This metaphysical theory appears yet to have no major bearings
      on Bacon's epistemology of the perceptual process, and will therefore be left aside.

124 MANTOVANI

gross misunderstanding of Aristotle's statements, so that once this misunderstanding was rectified his contemporaries would no longer have any grounds on which to uphold so "absurd" a theory. Bacon, indeed, was no less contemptuous in rejecting the views of the "dematerializers" than Pasnau was to be some centuries later in rejecting Bacon's:

> It is madness to say that a *species* does not have material being (*insania est dicere quod species non habet esse materiale*) ... [this claim] cannot be saved by any rational judgement, and there is no way to prove it, as it is evident to anyone who wishes to dismiss the foolishness of the majority of people (*stultitia vulgi*) and to follow reason. I therefore state unconditionally that the *species* of a corporeal thing is truly corporeal and has truly corporeal being.[36]

According to Bacon, there was indeed "no evidence to the contrary, except as the result of faulty translations of the words of Averroes, Avicenna, and Aristotle." On a more general level, Bacon insisted that "there are innumerable statements [in the works of the above-mentioned authors] that we cannot take literally ... but must be interpreted and better expressed," providing a few examples of this exegetical strategy:

> Therefore, when the translation imputes to Averroes, in his *De sensu et sensato* and his commentary on Aristotle's *De anima*, the view that the *species* of a corporeal thing has immaterial and spiritual being in the medium, it is replied that this should be understood entirely to refer to insensible being, to which some vulgar [scholar], or the translator, applied the name 'spiritual' because of the similarity between spiritual things and insensibles. For spiritual things are insensibles, and there in common usage we interchange the terms, converting the name 'insensible' to

---

36   Bacon, *DMS* III 2; Lindberg, pp. 191–192*; cf. *Perspectiva* I 6, 4; Lindberg, pp. 87–89. Bacon does indeed hold that "body and spirit are opposites, without intermediary" (III 2); cf. *DMS passim*. On the question of Bacon's Aristotelism – especially in relation to the "Latin Averroists" – see J. Hackett, "Roger Bacon and Aristotelianism," *Vivarium*, vol. 35, no. 2, 1997; J. Hackett, "Roger Bacon and the Reception of Aristotle in the Thirteenth Century: An Introduction to His Criticism of Averroes," in L. Honnefelder, R. Wood, M. Dreyer, and M.-A. Aris (eds), *Albertus Magnus and the Beginnings of the Medieval Reception of Aristotle in the Latin West*, Münster, Aschendorff, 2005, pp. 219–248. On Bacon's attitude towards the philosophical translation of the time, R. Lemay, "Roger Bacon's Attitude Toward the Latin Translations and Translators of the Twelfth and Thirteenth Centuries," in J. Hackett (ed), *Roger Bacon and the Sciences: Commemorative Essays*, Leiden, Brill, 1997, pp. 25–48.

VISIO PER SILLOGISMUM

'spiritual,' so that everything that lacks being sensible to us is said to have intelligible and spiritual being. But this is to use 'spiritual' equivocally [...] Accordingly, as regards what Aristotle says in *De anima* II that sense receives the *species* of sensible things without matter, it is replied that he there uses 'without matter' – i.e., 'immaterial' – to mean 'insensible' rather than 'spiritual,' as opposed to 'corporeal.'[37]

But Bacon's most compelling evidence drawn from earlier authors in favor of his theory did not come from Aristotle or from any of his followers, but from antiquity's most important writer on optics: Ptolemy. Combining Ptolemy's theory of vision with Aristotle's theory of perception, Bacon came to reject, in plain terms, the theory of the *species'* supposed "spiritual way of existing" and to state, in equally plain terms, that *species coloris est color, et species lucis est lux*:

> In the second book of Ptolemy's *De optica* – or *De aspectibus* – it is declared that coloring and illumination come to the medium and the eye from coloring and light (*a colore et luce advenit medio et visui coloratio et illuminatio*). But there can be no coloring except through the being of color, nor illumination except through the being of light [...] Therefore, the *species* of color is color, and the *species* of light is light [...] And therefore Aristotle says in *De anima* II that the recipient of color and sound and every sensible, such as the medium or the sense organs, is of itself uncolored and soundless and lacking the nature of sensibles – meaning thereby that the medium and sense receive color and sound as they receive the *species* of color and sound (*recipiant colorem et sonum ut recipiant species illorum*). And similarly for the other *species* of sensible things.[38]

As Lindberg rightly pointed out, it is only with Kepler (or shortly before) that one can properly begin to speak of "a real optical image within the eye – a picture, having an existence independent of the observer" on a par with the light-images produced by a pinhole camera.[39] But Lindberg pushed his claim too far

---

37 Bacon, *DMS* III 2; Lindberg, pp. 191–92*

38 Bacon, *DMS* I 1; Lindberg, pp. 9–11*. See below n. 51.

39 Lindberg, *Theories of vision*, p. 202. Lindberg's claim about Kepler's priority must be partly revised in the light of Jacopo Zabarella's and Fabrizio d'Acquapendente's accounts of vision, as proven by T. Baker, "Color, Cosmos, Oculus: Vision, Color, and the Eye in Jacopo Zabarella and Hieronymus Fabricius ab Aquapendente," PhD dissertation, Indiana University, 2014. On Kepler's theory of optical images see S. Dupré, "Inside the *Camera Obscura*: Kepler's Experiment and Theory of Optical Imagery," *Early Medicine and Science*,

when he glossed his point by stating that "in the theory of the medieval Perspectivists, the crystalline humor is *stimulated* by the perpendicular rays, but no image or picture is formed there."[40] The fact is that the "stimulation" of the lens did indeed count for Bacon and his followers as a clear instance of a coloring, and the *species* of light and color which were said to be "arranged on the surface of the sentient organ" were indeed held to consist in nothing else but light and color, so that it is no surprise that the "impression" that they form on the lens surface is also described, throughout the treatises of the Perspectivists, in clearly pictorial terms.[41] It was, admittedly, to take centuries, and a completely revised understanding of quite a few basic optical notions (most notably of refraction) for the authors on *perspectiva* to come to equate, without qualification, these orderly color-patches on the sentient surface of the eye with light-images projected onto the rear screen of a *camera obscura*. The understanding of *species* as *intentiones* tended to prevent the identification of the two, since *intentiones* were not considered as entities in their own right, but only as instrumental to the perceptual process and thus endowed only with a somehow "diminished" or "impoverished" form of existence. Even Bacon, despite conceiving of *species* as rigorously material, is committed to positions such as this one.[42] Nevertheless, it is crucial to recognize that the Early Modern understanding of the retinal impression as a *pictura* is largely the result of the Perspectivists' idea of a coloring of the sense-organs, as opposed to any "spiritual" account along Aquinas' lines. Faced with Descartes' famous experiment with a cow's eye located at the aperture of a *camera obscura*, a more traditional thinker of the same era, argued that "the intentional *species* of colors" which the Perspectivists had been speaking about for centuries were indeed nothing else but the *imagines* that Descartes' experiment had just proven to be formed

---

vol. 13, no. 3, 2008, pp. 219–244; Dupré, "Kepler's Optics without Hypotheses," *Synthese*, vol. 185, no. 3, 2012, pp. 501–525; A.E. Shapiro, "Images: Real and Virtual, Projected and Perceived, from Kepler to Dechales," *Early Medicine and Science*, vol. 13, no. 3, 2008, pp. 270–312.

40 Lindberg, *Theories of vision*, p. 202 n. 99 (emphasis added). Cf. Lindberg, p. 243 n. 81.

41 Bacon, *Perspectiva* I 10, 2; Lindberg, p. 153. "species lucis et coloris ... ordinantur in superficie membri sentientis." Cf. *DMS* I 2; Lindberg, pp. 39–41.

42 See for example Bacon, *The Opus maius of Roger Bacon*, 3 vols., J.H. Bridges (ed), Oxford, Clarendon Press, 1897–1900, p. 410 (the passage is discussed and translated in Sorabji, "From Aristotle to Brentano," p. 258*): "In the common usage of physicists this [color] is called an *intentio*, because of the weakness of its being with reference to the thing itself, which declares that this is not truly a thing, but rather the *intentio* of a thing, that is, a likeness (*similitudo*)."

VISIO PER SILLOGISMUM

on the bottom of the eye.[43] Both Bacon and Descartes would have vehemently opposed this claim, and yet Froidmont had a point: even if Bacon's and Descartes' understanding of the *species* was not quite the same, the two agreed at least on what *species* were not. Albert's and Aquinas' contention that the eye does not become colored by the color that it receives was indeed as erroneous a contention for both the *Perspectiva* and the *Dioptrique*.[44]

The theory of a "material change" in perception defended by Bacon became a standard item of doctrine among the writers on optics of the 13th Century and well beyond. Needless to say, different thinkers spelled this doctrine out in slightly different terms. Pecham, for example, put a great deal of emphasis on the role of attention in perceiving and concluded, accordingly, that, although the coloring of the sense-organs is a *necessary* condition for vision to occur, it is not yet a condition sufficient in itself (whereas Bacon seems to have largely treated it as such).[45] The crucial point, though, is that Bacon and Pecham and

---

43 Fromondus to Plempius, 13 September 1637, C. Adam and P. Tannéry (eds), *Œuvres de Descartes*, hereafter AT, Paris, Vrin, 1996, I, p. 405: "Quo modo etiam pag. 5 negat Species Intentionales colorum, cum nihil aliud sint quam imagines illae quas alibi fatetur in fundo oculi depingi, et necessarias esse ad visionem colorum?" Libert Froidmont (1585–1653) was professor of Holy Scripture at Leuven, the editor of Jansenius' *Augustinus* (1640) and the author of the *Labyrinthus sive de compositione continui* (1631), a work much celebrated by Leibniz. His correspondent, Vopiscus Fortunatus Plemp (1601–1671) was later to become professor of medicine at Leuven and the author of an important translation of Avicenna's *Canon*. Both men, therefore, were perfectly aware of the debate between "materialists" and "dematerializers" that had taken place in late antiquity and in the Middle Ages, which makes their exchange even more relevant. On the *species* theory after Kepler see I. Pantin, "*Simulachrum, Species, Forma, Imago*: What Was Transported by Light into the *Camera Obscura*? Divergent Conceptions of Realism Revealed by Lexical Ambiguities at the Beginning of the Seventeenth Century," *Early Science and Medicine*, vol. 13, no. 3, 2008, pp. 245–269; Dupré, "The Return of the *Species*: Jesuit Responses to Kepler's New Theory of Images," in W. de Boer and C. Göttler (eds), *Religion and the Senses in Early Modern Europe*, Leiden, Brill, 2012, pp. 473–487.

44 This historical and conceptual relation was completely missed by Gilson who, in his tremendously influential account of Descartes' rejection of the *species* theory, deliberately restricted himself to the Thomistic tradition; cf. É. Gilson, *Études sur le rôle de la pensée médiévale dans la formation du système cartésien*, Paris, Vrin, 1930. On Descartes' relation with the Perspectivists tradition, see G. Simon, "La théorie cartésienne de la vision, réponse à Kepler et rupture avec la problematique médiévale," in J. Biard and R. Rashed (eds), *Descartes et le Moyen Âge*, Paris, Vrin, 1997, pp. 107–118; D. Perler, "Descartes, critique de la théorie médiévale des *species*," in J. Biard and R. Rashed (eds), *Descartes et le Moyen Âge*, pp. 141–153.

45 Bacon too argues that vision is not a purely passive power. But it turns out that the only "activity" required in addition to the reception of the *species* is, for Bacon, the multiplication of the *species* of the eye itself, "which proceeds through the region occupied by the visual pyramid, altering and ennobling the medium and rendering it commensurable

Witelo, despite the many subtle differences between them, were all forcefully making the case for the occurrence of a genuinely material within the sense-organs, insisting that "the *species* of colors alter in a bodily way (*corporaliter*) the crystalline lens and the internal sense-organs."[46] Indeed, even Pecham's claim that the soul had necessarily to play an active role in order for perception to occur amounted, in the end, only to the contention that the soul must be *attentive* to the material changes taking place in the body. It did not imply (and in fact it explicitly denied) that these "affections of the sense organs" needed somehow to be *cognitively processed* in order for the soul to apprehend them, as Pecham and his fellow Perspectivists argued by contrast to be the case for the common sensibles.[47] Such a cognitive processing, indeed, according to the

---

with sight" (*Perspectiva* I 7, 4; Lindberg, p. 105). It is easy to see here that this multiplication of the *species* of the eye itself unfolds necessarily – according to "the common laws of natural multiplications" – and differs, therefore, altogether from selective attention, which designates the perceiver's ability to direct (at least to a certain extent) the train of her perceptions and thoughts. The main reason why Bacon posits such an "action" is to make room for a certain extramissionist element in his theory. The presence of such an extramissionist element, in its turn, is necessitated mainly by the need to accommodate certain insights found in the treatises on *perspectiva* written prior to Alhacen's (such as Euclid's and Ptolemy's) as well as to reconcile the statements made by Aristotle in the *De anima* with the theory defended in the *Meteorologica* and in the *De generatione animalium*; cf. Bacon, *Perspectiva* I 7, 2; Lindberg, p. 101. For more on the issue, see L. Lička, "The Visual Process: Immediate or Successive? Approaches to the Extramission Postulate in 13th Century Theories of Vision," in E. Băltuță (ed), *Medieval Perceptual Puzzles: Theories of Perception in the 13th and 14th Centuries*, Leiden, Brill 2020, pp. 73–110.

46 Pecham, *Tractatus de anima, ad* 3; Melani, p. 149: "Species tamen colorum corporaliter immutant pupillam et interiora organa sensibilia, et haec vocat Augustinus affectiones sensuum, quia istae vere corporales sunt."

47 On the debate of the time about the role of attention in the perceptual process see in this volume A. Martin, "Peter John Olivi on Perception, Attention, and the Soul's Orientation towards the Body," in E. Băltuță (ed), *Medieval Perceptual Puzzles*, Leiden, Brill, 2020, pp. 304–334. and, more generally, J.F. Silva and M. Yrjönsuuri (eds), *Active Perception in the History of Philosophy: From Plato to Modern Philosophy*, Dordrecht, Springer, 2014. One more appeal to the soul's activity is to be found in thinkers denying bottom-up causation, according to whom the soul perceives what it perceives not *as a result of* a change in the sense-organs but only "on the occasion" thereof. Pecham too makes claims along these lines, most likely under the influence of his predecessor as the Archbishop of Canterbury, Robert Kilwardby; cf. Pecham, *Tractatus de anima, ad* 2; Melani, p. 148: "Species illae nascuntur de se per occasionem excitativam, non per causam impressivam." These problems in the metaphysics of causation can, however, be left aside for the time being, since the activity of the soul evoked by Pecham and others in the case of the proper sensibles was not taken to consist in some sort of *cognitive processing* of the sense-impressions (of the kind required for the apprehension of the non-proper sensibles), but was only intended to make it possible for the soul to experience light and color in the first place. For an overview of the issues at stake and for examination of Kilwardby's specific position, see J.F. Silva, "The Chameleonic Mind: The Activity versus the Actuality of Perception," in E.

VISIO PER SILLOGISMUM

writers on *perspectiva*, was not performed by the sense of vision alone, but required the intervention of the higher faculties of the soul and, more specifically, "of the discriminative faculty, almost imperceptibly intermingled with reasoning" (*virtute distinctiva et argumentatione, quasi imperceptibiliter immixta*), since "no visible ... except light and color is perceived by sense alone."[48] Vision taken in isolation from these higher powers of the soul is in fact precisely what Pecham had in mind when he spoke of a "naked sense." According to the main vision theorists of the 13th Century, light and color are indeed *given* right away to the soul. In their eyes, the only thing that the soul has to do in order to experience light and color (if anything at all) is to direct its attention to the light and colors taken on by the sense-organs.

3   *Non percipimus nos arguere, cum tamen arguamus*

Light and color, however, are not the only features of bodies we human beings apprehend through sight. Already Aristotle had in fact listed quite a few other features of material objects that we experience through this latter sense (as well as through touch), although he appears to have had some doubts about the exact list of these so-called "common sensibles." Around Bacon's time, however, interpreters usually took as canonical the list that is to be found in *De anima* B 6, on which Aquinas (just to name one example) based his claim that *communia sensibilia sunt ista quinque: motus, quies, numerus, figura & magnitudo.*[49]

Already in ancient times, however, Aristotle's list of the sensibles had begun to be reworked and adapted. On at least one important occasion this was precisely in order to better account for visual experience. Never listed by Aristotle among the common sensibles, in his treatise on vision Ptolemy made a point of making room for "position" – as well as for "corporeity" – at the expense of number.[50] Taking his cue from Stoic philosophy, Ptolemy furthermore proposed

---

Băltuță (ed), *Medieval Perceptual Puzzles*, Leiden, Brill, 2020, pp. 38–72. and E. Băltuță, "The Escape Artist: Robert Kilwardby on Objects as *sine qua non* Causes," in E. Băltuță (ed), *Medieval Perceptual Puzzles*, Leiden, Brill, 2020, pp. 179–212.

48   Pecham, *Perspectiva communis* I 56ª {59ª}; Lindberg, p. 137*.

49   Thomas Aquinas, *Sentencia De anima* II 13, 4. Aquinas takes this list from Aristotle, *De anima* B 6, 418ª 17–20. As examples of Aristotle's different versions of these sensibles, see *De anima* Γ 1, 425ª 16–17: "movement, rest, shape, magnitude, number, unity"; *De sensu* 4, 442ᵇ6: "magnitude, shape, rough and smooth, sharp and blunt."

50   Ptolemy, *Optica*, A. Lejeune (ed), *L'Optique de Claude Ptolémée dans la version latine d'après l'arabe de l'émir Eugène de Sicile. Édition critique et exégétique*, Louvain, Publications

130 MANTOVANI

replacing Aristotle's primary tactile qualities (hot-cold and wet-dry) with ἀντιτυπία, and identified the common sense with the ἡγεμονικόν.[51]

But the most fundamental difference with regard to Aristotle here consists in Ptolemy's insistence that visibles other than color are only "secondarily" visible (*videntur sequenter*). Aristotle too had actually claimed at one point that common sensibles are perceived "accidentally" (κατὰ συμβεβηκός) by each specific sense; but he had also insisted that they are perceived, nonetheless, *per se* (καθ' αὐτά) by sensibility, so that his ultimate conclusion remained that there existed a "common sense" above and beyond all particular ones.[52] In none of

Universitaires de Louvain, 1956, II 2, p. 12: "dicimus ergo quod visus cognoscit corpus, magnitudinem, colorem, figuram, situm, motum et quietem."

51   Ptolemy, *Optica*, A.M. Smith (ed), *Ptolemy's Theory of Perception: An English Translation of the "Optics" with Introduction and Commentary, Transactions of the American Philosophical Society*, vol. 86, no. 2, 1996, II 13, pp. 74–75*: "A [sole] proper sensible can be found that is specific to each sense: the quality of "resisting the hand" for touch (*species repulse manus in tactu*) ... But among the things that are common to the senses according to the origin of nervous activity (*secundum principium nervosum*), sight and touch share in all except color." Smith is therefore mistaken in claiming that "in this list of the proper sensibles Ptolemy is simply following Aristotle" as he has failed to notice that Aristotle had never listed position among the common sensibles (Smith, pp. 74, 71; see, however, A.M. Smith, "The Psychology of Visual Perception in Ptolemy's *Optics*," *Isis*, vol. 79, no. 2, 1988, pp. 201–202). Ptolemy further complicates Aristotle's taxonomy of the sensibles by introducing the notion of an "intrinsically (*vere*) visible" feature, identified by Ptolemy with "luminous compactness" (*lucida spissa*). For an explanation of this element of Ptolemy's theory, see Smith's commentary to *Optica* II 3–4; Smith, p. 71. Ptolemy refers even more explicitly to the ἡγεμονικόν – designated as the *virtus regitiva* – in *Optica* II 22–23; Smith, p. 79.

52   See, respectively, Aristotle, *De anima* Γ 1, 425ª16 (to which is to be added Γ 3, 428ᵇ25) and B 6, 418ª7–20. The correct interpretation of these passages – and of the related ones in the *Parva naturalia* – has been a matter of dispute for centuries; for a critical overview of the main positions, see J. Owens, "Aristotle on Common Sensibles and Incidental Perception," *Phoenix*, vol. 36, 1982, pp. 215–236. According to Aristotle the true opposition seems, at any rate, to be that between proper and common sensibles on the one hand and, on the other, what he designates simply as the sensibles κατὰ συμβεβηκός, such as perceiving that that white thing in front of me is, for example, the son of Diares; cf. *De anima* B 6, 418ª7–26. Medieval philosophers, consequently, reserved the designation *sensibila per accidens* for this last class of sensibles alone. The distinction was further complicated by Avicenna's introduction of one more category of sensibles features: the so-called *intentiones*, the usual example being the lamb's perception of the wolf *as* dangerous (*intentio* in this sense being the source of the concept of *intentio* mentioned above in relation to Aquinas, although the two uses of the term should certainly be kept distinct from a conceptual point of view; cf. A.I. Sabra, "Sensation and Inference in Alhazen's Theory of Visual Perception," in P.K. Machamer and R.G. Turnbull (eds), *Studies in Perception*, Columbus, Ohio State University Press, 1978, pp. 70–73); see for example Bacon, *Perspectiva* I 10, 1; Lindberg, pp. 145–149. Below, it is only considered the opposition between proper and common sensibles alone (for an analysis of the concept of "perceiving as" in the authors of the time, the

VISIO PER SILLOGISMUM 131

his writings did Aristotle ever draw a distinction between the *process* through which common sensibles are apprehended and that through which proper sensibles are. In fact, he treated these two classes of sensibles as essentially on a par with one another, so that it seems safe to conclude that, in Aristotle's eyes, there was no difference at all between the manners in which proper and common sensibles are apprehended, or was, at least, negligible enough to simply pass over it in silence.[53] Sorabji and Burnyeat, consequently, have disregarded the distinction between these two classes of sensibles as entirely irrelevant to the issue between them, and rightly so – at least if we consider nothing but Aristotle's theory of perception. (Sorabji went even further and construed the possibility of accounting in terms of "material" change for the perception of proper and common sensibles alike as a strong argument in favor of his reading).[54]

Ptolemy, on the other hand, devoted a substantial portion of his work precisely to spelling out the cognitive operations that the perceiver must perform in order to apprehend the object's size – as well as all other common sensibles – from the differences in light and color that he or she is presented with. He argued, for example, that "the differences in the size of objects must be determined and perceived according to the differences [in the size of] the corresponding visual angles," painstakingly working out the geometrical principles

---

reader is referred to J. Toivanen, "Perceiving As: Non-Conceptual Forms of Perception in Medieval Philosophy," in E. Băltuţă (ed), *Medieval Perceptual Puzzles*, pp. 10–37, Leiden, Brill, 2020, pp. 10–37, in the present volume). As is well known, medieval thinkers referred to all faculties of the sensitive soul beyond the five traditional senses – sight, touch and so forth – as the *internal senses*, whose denomination, number, function and location were a matter of constant debate; cf. H.A. Wolfson, "The Internal Senses in Latin, Arabic, and Hebrew Philosophical Texts," *Harvard Theological Review*, vol. 28, 1935, pp. 69–133.

53 For all these reasons, I think that Smith overstates the similarity between Ptolemy's and Aristotle's account of the visual process, so that his criticism of Lejeune for having neglected the "all-important distinction between primary and secondary visibles" ("The psychology," p. 201, n. 29) backfires against him. Smith, more generally, sees a deep continuity between Aristotle, Ptolemy, and Alhacen as regards the theory of the non-proper sensibles, despite Sabra's apt cautions to keep them distinct; see, respectively, Smith's, pp. 538–541, and Sabra's, II, p. 83, editions of Alhacen. The unqualified identification of Alhacen's *ultimum sentiens* with Aristotle's common sense is on the other hand certainly untenable, *pace* H. Bauer, *Die Psychologie Alhazens. Auf Grund von Alhazens Optik*, Münster, Aschendorff, 1911, pp. 49–50.

54 R. Sorabji "Body and Soul in Aristotle," *Philosophy*, vol. 49, 1974, pp. 63–89; reproduced in Sorabji, *Perception, Conscience, and Will*, Padstow, Ashgate, 2013, p. 49 n. 22; Sorabji, "Intentionality and Physiological Process: Aristotle's Theory of Sense-Perception," in M.C. Nussbaum and A.O. Rorty (eds), *Essays on Aristotle's "De anima*," pp. 195–225; Sorabji, *Perception, Conscience, and Will*, pp. 196–197, 209.

132 MANTOVANI

and theorems which would underlie this perceptual process.[55] Ptolemy's clear-cut distinction regarding how proper and common sensibles are perceived is especially evident if one considers his account of color-perception, which, in contrast to his account of size and such matters, is not claimed to be grounded on trigonometrical principles but rather to result from the mere coloring of the visual ray. (Contrary to Aristotle in his mature psychological writings, and once again revealing Stoic influences, Ptolemy is in fact an extramissionist).[56]

The disparity in the perception of the proper and of the non-proper visibles is not, however, a direct consequence of Ptolemy's extramissionism, but results from some real difficulties in accounting for the perception of size and similar visible features that are not to be found in the case of light and colors. All of the difficulties pointed out by Ptolemy also apply in fact to any intromissionist model. Alhacen, as a consequence, was able to accept the framework of Ptolemy's account of the perceptual process even while replacing Ptolemy's *visual* rays issuing from the eye with *light* rays entering into it. Alhacen's model was, moreover, to face some additional difficulties as far as distance-perception is concerned, since in this case the perceiver could be taken to sense distance by means of the perceived length of the visual rays emanating from her eyes.

There was yet one more point in respect of which Alhacen thought that Ptolemy's theory needed to be adjusted: namely, the list of the visibles, which, according to Alhacen, appeared to fall too far short of our actual experience. Alhacen considered that the basic properties of material bodies that a human being is able to experience through his eyes were indeed no less than twenty-two in number:

> The particular properties that are perceived by sight are numerous, but they are generally reduced to twenty-two, namely: light, color; distance, position, corporeity, shape, size, continuity, discontinuity (or separation), number, motion, rest, roughness, smoothness; transparency, likewise: opacity, shadow, darkness; beauty, ugliness; similarity, and difference among all particular characteristics, as well as among all the forms composed of particular characteristics.[57]

---

55 Ptolemy, *Optica* II 52; Smith, p. 92.

56 Ptolemy, *Optica* II 24; Smith, p. 80*: "The visual flux apprehends color as a result of getting colored. For instance, it apprehends whiteness because it is whitened, whereas it recognizes blackness because it is blackened (*cognoscit albedinem ... quia dealbat, et nigredinem quia denigrat*), and the same holds for each of the intermediate colors."

57 Alhacen, *De aspectibus* II 3; Smith, pp. 438–439*. Cf. A.I. Sabra, "Ibn Al-Haytham's Criticisms of Ptolemy's *Optics*," *Journal of the History of Philosophy*, vol. 4, no. 2, 1966, p. 146.

VISIO PER SILLOGISMUM   133

"These," Alhacen claimed, "are all of the things that are perceived by the sense of sight," under which it is possible to subsume all remaining "visible characteristics;" such as arrangement, for example,

> which will be subsumed under position; [or] writing and drawing, which are subsumed under shape and arrangement; curvature, concavity, and convexity, which are subsumed under shape ... joy, laughter, and sadness, which are included in the shape of the face (and are therefore subsumed under shape); weeping [...][58]

As can be clearly seen here, the terms of Aristotle's common sensibles have not disappeared from Alhacen's list, who included among the visibles also "roughness and smoothness," mentioned by Aristotle in his *De sensu* and yet generally omitted by his followers. Alhacen also integrated Ptolemy's own version of the same list, as shown by his reference to "position" and "corporeity" (although by the latter term the two authors were most probably referring to slightly different concepts). Alhacen, however, did not speak of all these as of "common sensibles." In the same list he mentioned, in fact, physical features such as transparency, which obviously no blind person can experience. That Alhacen's agenda was quite different from Aristotle's and Ptolemy's is even more evident from the fact of his inclusion of "beauty" and "ugliness" among the visibles, a detail praised by a leading art historian of the past century as "a remarkable excursus on what we would call aesthetics."[59] Maybe even as the starting points of this discipline, as has been argued in more recent times by another distinguished expert in the field.[60] (To conclude, it should be pointed out that Alhacen's inclusion of "similarity" and its contrary in his list is most likely derived from the *Theaetetus*).[61]

> Since the goal of this essay is to give an account of Bacon's, Witelo's, and Pecham's theory of perception, I do not discuss here Ibn al-Haytham's original text (by quoting from the Sabra edition) but only its Latin translation, on which the Perspectivists based their accounts. In line with current scholarly practice, I accordingly speak of "Alhacen" rather than of "Ibn al-Haytham," thereby referring to the author of the *De aspectibus*. In any case, as regards this specific issue there are no differences worth mentioning between the Arab and the Latin text; cf. Ibn al-Haytham, *The Optics* II 3 § 44; Sabra, pp. 138–139.

58   Alhacen, *De aspectibus* II 3; Smith, pp. 438–439*.

59   E. Panofsky, *Meaning in the Visual Arts: Papers in and on Art History*, New York, Doubleday Anchor, 1955, pp. 89–90.

60   D. Summers, *The Judgment of Sense: Renaissance Naturalism and the Rise of Aesthetics*, Cambridge, Cambridge University Press, 1987.

61   Plato, *Theaetetus*, W.F. Hicken (ed), *Platonis Opera*, Oxford, Oxford University Press, 1995, 184^d7–185^e9.

134   MANTOVANI

In his *Perspectiva*, Bacon reproduced almost *verbatim* Alhacen's list of the twenty-two visibles, although he erroneously attributed it to Ptolemy.[62] There is, nonetheless, in the *Perspectiva* a clear reminiscence of Ptolemy himself, inasmuch as Bacon presented Alhacen's list as a list of the *common* sensibles, notwithstanding the difficulty mentioned already about features like transparency. The only explanation Bacon felt that he had to give for this concerned the question of how to reconcile his account with the terse list of just five common sensibles which most of his contemporaries took to express Aristotle's considered view on the subject:

> [Besides light and color] there are twenty other sensibles [...] In *De anima* II and the beginning of *De sensu et sensato*, Aristotle lists some of the common sensibles – size, shape, motion, rest, and number – but only as examples. Not only these, but all of the aforementioned, are indeed common sensibles, although vulgar philosophers (*vulgus naturalium*) do not consider this, since they have not investigated the science of *perspectiva*. For the common sensibles are not so called because they are perceived by the common sense, but because they are commonly discerned by all or several of the particular senses – and especially by vision and touch, since Ptolemy says in his *Perspectiva* II that vision and touch share in all twenty of these [common sensibles].[63]

It is, however, very difficult to make sense of Bacon's claim that we can apprehend transparency (as well as opacity, shadow and darkness) by means of touch. All the more so, indeed, since Bacon did not provide any argument in support of this astonishing claim. Nor did Pecham or Witelo trouble to provide any argument in support of it, being content to blindly follow their master on this specific issue.[64] After many centuries, even so competent an expert in the field as François d'Aguilon was still unable to make sense of this claim, which he came to reject as simply indefensible.[65] One would almost be tempted to dismiss the matter as the result of a clumsy confusion of Ptolemy's with

---

62   Bacon, *Perspectiva* I 1, 3; Lindberg, pp. 11–13.

63   Bacon, *Perspectiva* I 1, 3; Lindberg, pp. 11–13*; Cf. *Perspectiva* I 10, 2; Lindberg, p. 149. *Dyaphanitas*, as Lindberg points out, designates in the *Perspectiva* roughly the inverse of what we would call "optical density"; cf. *DMS* II 2; Lindberg, pp. 96–99. On this concept, see also T. Baker, *Color, Cosmos, Oculus*.

64   Pecham, *Perspectiva communis* I 55 {58}; Lindberg, pp. 135–137. Witelo, *Opticae libri decem* III 1, 84; here Witelo openly qualifies these twenty-features as *per accidens visibilia*.

65   François d'Aguilon, *Opticorum Libri Sex*, Antwerpen, Officina Plantiniana, 1613, I prop. XXIX, p. 30: "Maior verò illorum est error, qui transparentiam, opacitatem (quam

VISIO PER SILLOGISMUM 135

Alhacen's line of reasoning, which resulted in the untenable theory about transparency being perceived by hands. Were this the case, then Bacon's theory of visibles would be nothing but the infelicitous result of following different authorities without taking pains to reconcile them, most probably inspired by other Oxford Franciscans such as Adam of Buckfield.[66]

Bacon's statements begin to make sense, however, as soon as one realizes that, despite paying lip service to Aristotle's concept of a common sensible, Bacon was in fact reconceptualizing this Aristotelian notion in the light of Ptolemy's and Alhacen's theories of perception. This is strongly suggested by the entire *Perspectiva*, where, after the remark quoted above from the very first pages of the treatise, the issue of the relation between sight and touch is virtually never taken up again. Bacon, by contrast, devoted many pages of this treatise to spelling out the cognitive processes by means of which a perceiver comes to apprehend visibles other than light and color. Though cast in terms of an opposition between proper and common sensibles, Bacon's distinction between light and color on the one hand and all the remaining twenty visibles on the other was not, in fact, intended to map the relations between different sense-modalities. Rather, what Bacon does here turns out rather to be a matter of articulating a distinction between two different *stages* of the visual process: a bare sensory and a cognitive discursive one.

Once again taking his cue from Alhacen, Bacon distinguished indeed in the *Perspectiva* between three kinds of vision or, more precisely, between "three modes of knowing by means of vision" (*modos cognoscendi per visum*): namely, "by sense alone," "by [previous] knowledge" and "by syllogism."[67] The first of these modes is the vision "by naked sense" discussed in the previous section. Bacon's second mode – "by previous knowledge" – would, on the other hand, consists in the recognition of a light or a color as the light or color of a specific object (of a certain celestial body, say) or of such-and-such a kind by virtue of one already knows about this celestial body and this hue.[68] The crucial point

---

    Alhazenus corporeitatem vocat), obscuritatem & umbram ad hanc classem referunt. Haec enim quo alio sensu percipiuntur, quàm visu?"

66   On the so-called Oxford gloss on *De sensu* and their relation to Adam of Buckfield's commentary see G. Galle, "Edition and Discussion of the Oxford Gloss on *De sensu I*," *Archives d'histoire doctrinale et littéraire du Moyen Âge*, vol. 75, 2008, pp. 271–272 (my thanks to Lukáš Lička for bringing these texts to my attention).

67   Bacon, *Perspectiva* I 10, 3; Lindberg, pp. 155–159. Cf. *Perspectiva* III 3, 2; Lindberg, p. 327: "Triplex est visio, scilicet solo sensu, scientia, et sillogismo."

68   Bacon, *Perspectiva* III 3, 2; Lindberg, p. 327; Bacon, II 3, 2; Lindberg, pp. 203–207. Bacon warns that this "previous knowledge" (contrary to what the expression *visio per scientiam* could suggest) is not based on concepts or on "scientific knowledge," but only on memory

in Bacon's three-fold distinction, however, is the claim that all visibles other than light and color fall into the category of the *third* kind of vision, that all these other visibles are visibles perceived *per sillogismum*.[69]

The complexity of the operations that Bacon believed to be required in order to perceive such visible features clearly emerges in his account of size perception, by way of instance, where in the wake of Ptolemy and Alhacen he argued that "the certification of the magnitude of an object" is the result of a trigonometric reasoning, which requires "to consider the angle and the length of the [visual] pyramid and to compare these with the base of the pyramid, which is the visible object."[70] Significantly enough, it is however the perception of transparency to be singled out by Bacon as the most examplary instance of how *visio per sillogismum* is intended to work in general. To substantiate his claim that the process through which we come to apprehend the common sensibles "resembles a kind of reasoning" (*est quasi quoddam genus arguendi*), Bacon did indeed point out that

> When somebody holds a transparent stone in his hand, he does not perceive (*percipit*) its transparency. But if he should expose it in the air, and if there is a dense object at a suitable distance beyond it and sufficient lights, he will see the light and the dense object beyond the stone. And then, since he cannot see through the stone what lies behind it unless it is transparent, he infers (*arguit*) that it is transparent and pellucid. But this cognition ordinarily occurs suddenly, and we do not perceive that we reason, although in fact we do (*non percipimus nos arguere, cum tamen arguamus*) [...] And it is in this way that the twenty common sensibiles are grasped.[71]

In the course of the treatise Bacon was to show that analogous cognitive operations are required to apprehend distance, shape, the already-mentioned magnitude, motion and rest, implicitly referring the reader to Alhacen for a treatment of the remaining common sensibles. The complexity of the

---

traces. It is therefore available also to non-rational animals: a dog, observes Bacon, does indeed recognize his master; cf. *Perspectiva* II 3, 9; Lindberg, p. 247.

69 Bacon, *Perspectiva* III 3, 2; Lindberg, p. 327: "Per sillogismum quidem cognoscimus omnia que circumstant lucem et colorem secundum omnia viginti sensibilia communia."

70 Bacon, *Perspectiva* II 3, 5; Lindberg, pp. 225–227*. On the topic see, more in general, J. Hackett, "*Experientia, Experimentum*, and the Perception of Objects in Space," in J. Aertsen and A. Speer (eds), *Raum und Raumvorstellungen im Mittelalter*, Berlin, De Gruyter, 1998, pp. 101–120.

71 Bacon, *Perspectiva* I 10, 3; Lindberg, pp. 157*.

VISIO PER SILLOGISMUM 137

operations involved is such that Bacon felt forced to conclude that they exceed
the capabilities of the common sense. This is a truly astonishing claim, since in
the *Perspectiva* Bacon had expressly spoken of such sensibles as falling under
the purview of the common sense.[72] At the very beginning of the treatise Bacon had, however, already suggested that matters could turn out to be rather
more complex. "The making of judgements concerning the twenty kinds of
visibles to be studied in what follows," he wrote, "is attributed by the author on
perspectiva to the discriminative faculty (*virtus distinctiva*)," and Bacon was to
follow "the author" in this. The problem, though, is precisely how this faculty
operates and where it is to be located, these being two of the main questions
that the treatise is intended to answer.[73]

After having distinguished between the three kinds of vision mentioned
above, at the end of the first part of the *Perspectiva* Bacon made it clear that the
third mode cannot be attributed to the common sense, so that the *virtus distinctiva* cannot be identified with it. "Sight in the pupil and the common nerve
as far as the common sense" was indeed, for Bacon, to be identified with vision
solo sensu and nothing more than that.[74] But already the second kind of vision
demanded more than just the common sense, "for unless imagination and
memory of prior vision of the things are present, comprehension in the second
mode cannot occur; but imagination and memory are beyond the common
sense" (this claim being based on a quite standard medieval mapping of the
soul's faculties onto the cerebral ventricles).[75] If this is the case, though, one
has to conclude that

---

72   See, for example, Bacon, *Perspectiva* I 1, 3; Lindberg, pp. 9–13.

73   Bacon, *Perspectiva* I 1, 2; Lindberg, pp. 5–7. As shown by R. Wood, "Imagination and Expe-
      rience in the Sensory Soul and Beyond: Richard Rufus, Roger Bacon, and their Contempo-
      raries," in H. Lagerlund (ed), *Forming the Mind: Essays on the Internal Senses and the Mind/
      Body Problem from Avicenna to the Medical Enlightenment*, Dordrecht, Springer, 2007,
      pp. 27–58, Bacon's frequent appeal to higher faculties of the soul such as the "estimative"
      and the just-mentioned "distinctive" power is a truly distinctive trait of his psychology
      and sets him aside from some of the most influential previous accounts of the topic (such
      as Richard Rufus'). On the medieval concept of a "judgement of the senses" – which does
      not however cover Bacon's specific case – see K.H. Tachau, "What Senses and Intellect Do:
      Argument and Judgment in Late Medieval Theories of Knowledge," in K. Jacobi (ed), *Ar-
      gumentationstheorie. Scholastische Forschungen zu den logischen und semantischen Re-
      geln korrekten Folgerns*, Leiden, Brill, 1993, pp. 653–668.

74   Bacon, *Perspectiva* I 10, 3; Lindberg, p. 159.

75   Bacon, *Perspectiva* I 10, 3; Lindberg, p. 159. For Bacon's account of the ventricles model,
      also in direct relation to previous thinkers, see *Perspectiva* I 1, 2–5. On the role of this
      model in medieval theories of perception and cognition, see A.M. Smith, "Getting the Big
      Picture in Perspectivist Optics," *Isis*, vol. 72, no. 4, 1981, pp. 568–589.

> The third mode [of visual cognition] is further removed from sense alone, since in it more things are considered than in the second mode and comes closer to an operation of reason, for it proceeds inferentially (*magis accedit ad opus rationis propter viam arguendi*).[76]

According to Bacon the *virtus distinctiva* is indeed to be identified with the *cogitatio* or *virtus cogitativa*, traditionally lodged in the middle brain ventricle. Bacon also designates this faculty as the *logistica* or *rationalis*, "not because it makes use of reason," he explains, "but because it represents the ultimate perfection in brutes [i.e. in non-rational animals] as reason does in humans."[77] Bacon points out that non-human animals too are responsive to, say, distance (the distance between them and their prey, for example), from which he infers that they perceive such features as these. But since they are non-rational, Bacon concludes that in animals' distance-perception cannot be the result of an inference in the proper sense of the term, because all reasoning activities pertain to the rational soul.[78] Animal distance-perception is therefore *non-inferential*: in their case, the sensitive soul is so constituted as to *experience* objects at a distance merely as the result of certain color-sensations, a point Bacon expresses by claiming that in animal perception "thinking proceeds as it does by natural instinct alone" (*ex solo instinctu naturali sic decurrit cogitatio eorum*).[79] It is even *non-discursive*. In the case of animals, reasoning (*discursus*) from premises to conclusions amounts in fact for Bacon to a mere perceiving that the conclusion is the case. According to Bacon, distance is indeed *sensed* by animals in the same way that colors are. The only difference between the two is that distance perception does not result from a mere material change in the sense-organs, but from an *ingrained reaction* to this material change (that is, to the organ's becoming-colored). For Bacon, this automatic and naturally determined reaction (*instinctu nature sine deliberatione*)[80] giving rise to distance-sensation counts at the same time as "one of the doings of the body" and as "one of the doings of the soul" (to rephrase Burnyeat's expression). It would be inappropriate to describe it as a "psychophysiological mechanism,"

---

76 Bacon, *Perspectiva* I 10, 3; Lindberg, p. 159*. Cf. Witelo, *Opticae libri decem* III 60–68, 111–15.

77 Bacon, *Perspectiva* I 1, 4; Lindberg, p. 15. I 1, 12: "bruta animalia utuntur solo sensu, quia non habent intellectum."

78 Bacon, *Perspectiva* II 3, 9; Lindberg, p. 247; see also *Perspectiva* I 10, 3; Lindberg, p. 159 (in both passages Bacon expresses analogous concerns about the so-called vision *per scientiam*).

79 Bacon, *Perspectiva* II 3, 9; Lindberg, pp. 247–249.

80 Bacon, *Perspectiva* II 3, 9; Lindberg, pp. 247–249.

however, since the Cartesian divide between mind and body – and, accordingly, between psychology and physiology – makes no sense within the hylomorphic model in which Bacon operates.[81] This ingrained reaction is therefore to be understood as an *operation* of the sensitive soul – Bacon calls indeed upon "animal industry" for its performance – but cannot clearly be described as a *cognitive* operation of the same kind as judgement.[82] Non-inferential, non-discursive, non-cognitive: as far as non-rational animals are concerned, the "syllogism" at stake in animal perception is therefore just an analogical way of speaking (*ac si arguerent; premissis simulantur*)[83] to describe how the sensitive soul naturally happens to experience the non-proper sensibles as a result of having experienced colors. This being the case, Bacon cannot but blame Alhacen – or his translator – for their unfortunate choice of vocabulary.[84]

What is one to make, then, of Bacon's statement about perceiving transparency quoted above, in which he openly invokes inferences? Is cognition *per sillogismum* just an analogical way of speaking even as far as *rational* animals are concerned? Or it is the term to be taken in its rigorous sense, at least in this case? As the rational soul comes in, Bacon thinks that this soul "is primarily and immediately united" precisely to the *virtus logistica*, of which the intellect "makes use as its own special instrument," and which changes accordingly into the *virtus cogitativa*, or simply *cogitatio*.[85] In human beings the perception of the common sensible is indeed, for Bacon (as for Alhacen), the result of a proper inference, albeit of one that is performed so rapidly that it escapes the

---

81 The expression "psychophysiological mechanism" has been used by G. Hatfield, "On Natural Geometry and Seeing Distance Directly in Descartes," in V. De Risi (ed), *Mathematizing Space: The Objects of Geometry from Antiquity to the Early Modern Age*, Berlin, Birkhäuser, 2015, p. 168, to describe a different non-cognitive account of distance perception, namely, Descartes' (in that case the expression being fully accurate). For more on the issue, see below n. 104.

82 The term "cognitive" is here intended in this strictest sense only, as to distinguish between the sensory and the intellectual (rational) stage of the perceptual process. As well-known, the medievals' – Bacon's included – *cognitio* had by contrast a quite wider meaning, so that the thinkers of the time could ascribe "cognitions" to non-human animals while denying them an intellect. This being said, even the 13th century thinkers with the highest appreciation for the skills of non-rational animals (Bacon being without a doubt one of them) ever went so far as to ascribe to "brutes" the capacity to form fully-fledged judgements. On the issue see, recently, A. Oelze, *Animal Rationality: Later Medieval Theories 1250–1350*, Leiden, Brill, 2018, pp. 100–120.

83 Bacon, *Perspectiva* II 3, 9; Lindberg, p. 251.

84 Bacon, *Perspectiva* I 10, 3; Lindberg, p. 159.

85 Bacon, *Perspectiva* I 1, 5; Lindberg, pp. 15–17*.

perceiver's own awareness.[86] Although non-rational and rational animals alike do not perceive that they are reasoning, this happens in the two cases for quite opposite reasons. According to Bacon, beasts do not perceive that they are reasoning simply because they are not doing so, and cannot be. To reason is indeed a chief expression of being rational, but to be rational is precisely what it is to be a man. Humans, by contrast, do not take cognizance of the fact they are reasoning simply because this is just what they do by nature: *homo enim arguit ex natura sine difficultate et labore*.[87] For Bacon the table of syllogisms is just the systematic description *post factum* of how the human mind naturally carries out all its cognitive operations, distance and transparency perception included. In the case of human beings, the expression *visio per sillogismum* is therefore to be taken at face value, the case of transparency discussed above being intended to provide an example of how this is intended to work (whereas Bacon does not unfortunately say much on the epistemological and logical nature of the syllogism's "premises" from a general point of view).

The difference between human and animal perception, however, goes even deeper. According to Bacon rational and non-rational animals are not in fact confronted with one and the same perceptual world. That is to say, Bacon does not envisage the perceptual universe as something that humans have to figure out step by step, making use of processes of reasoning, while "brutes" experience it right from the start in all its complexity simply thanks to their "instinct" and "natural industry." Reason, Bacon believes, does make a difference. Although he rejects the claim that non-human animals cannot perceive distance inasmuch as they cannot perform acts of reasoning, Bacon makes it clear also that quite a few common sensibles are proper to humans alone, as the only animals capable of drawing inferences:

> For surely no argument can disguise the fact that brutes perceive the remoteness of things, as well as motion and rest, *although this is not true of the other common sensibles*.[88]

---

86   On Alhacen's theory of perceptual inferences, see Sabra, "Sensation and Inference." It should be pointed out that, contrary to Bacon, Alhacen never worked out a theory of *animal* perception (at least to the best of my knowledge).

87   Bacon, *Perspectiva* I 10, 3; Lindberg, p. 157. Cf. Pecham, *Perspectiva communis* I 57 {60}; Lindberg, p. 137: "virtus enim distinctiva nata est arguere sine difficultate, que enim aptitudo naturaliter exeritur."

88   Bacon, *Perspectiva* II 3, 9; Lindberg, p. 249: "Nam proculdubio nulla ratione potest dissimulari quin bruta percipiant distantias rerum et motum et quietem, *licet de aliis sensibilibus communibus non sit ita*" (emphasis added).

VISIO PER SILLOGISMUM

For Bacon, then, human and non-human perception are not only differently "structured" or "categorized" in the light of the intellectual notions available only to the former, but differ in *scope* already at the level of common sensibles. This is because most of these visible features can only be *inferred* from the differences in light and color that both rational and non-rational animals are presented with simply as a result of a coloring of their sense-organs (these latter being the same for rational and non-rational animals alike). For Bacon non-rational vision is indeed a diminished form of experience. This is even more relevant if one considers Bacon's keen interest in animal perception and his attribution of a *virtus logistica* to non-human animals, denied to them by most of his contemporaries, Aquinas included.[89] And yet, despite denying such a faculty to non-human animals, Aquinas claimed with most of his contemporaries that "there is no difference between man and animal as regards [the perception of] the sensible forms" – i.e. of both proper *and* common sensibles.[90] Bacon, on his part, was adamant: *perspectiva* is the science *de visu humano* – of *human* vision – and is concerned with the vision of non-rational animals only insofar as the two (partly) overlap.[91] In presenting his treatise to his readers, Bacon averred that whereas that which is perceived by taste, touch or smell is

---

89 Bacon's characteristically high appreciation for the skills of non-human animals has been duly emphasized in recent years by J. Hackett, "Roger Bacon on Animal Knowledge in the *Perspectiva*," in L.-X. Lòpez-Farjeat and J.A. Tellkamp (eds), *Philosophical Psychology in Arabic Thought and the Latin Aristotelianism of the 13th Century*, Paris, Vrin, 2013, pp. 23–42 and Oelze, *Animal Rationality*. Both of whom do not however discuss the – to my eyes, crucial – passage from *Perspectiva* II 3, 9 quoted above.

90 Thomas Aquinas, *Summa Theologiae*, 1a, q. 78, a. 4, *corpore*: "quantum ad formas sensibiles, non est differentia inter hominem et alia animalia, similiter enim immutantur a sensibilibus exterioribus." The difference, according to Aquinas, concerns only the further stages of the perceptual process: "quantum ad intentiones praedictas, differentia est, nam alia animalia percipiunt huiusmodi intentiones solum naturali quodam instinctu, homo autem etiam per quandam collationem." For two different readings of Aquinas' theory of human perception *qua* specifically human, see D. Perler, "Rational Seeing: Thomas Aquinas on Human Perception," in E. Bǎltuțǎ (ed), *Medieval Perceptual Puzzles*, Leiden, Brill, 2020, pp. 213–237 and P. Rubini, "'Accidental perception' and 'cogitative power' in Thomas Aquinas and John of Jandun," in E. Bǎltuțǎ (ed), *Medieval Perceptual Puzzles*, Leiden, Brill, 2020, pp. 269–303.

91 Bacon, *Perspectiva* I 9, 2; Lindberg 131–133. According to Bacon the experience of rational and non-rational animals overlaps in fact only as far as the *proper* sensibles are concerned, and the few common sensibles whose apprehension is said by Bacon to fall under the purview of the automatic reactions ingrained in the sensory soul (which, taken together, constitute the animal's "instinct"). Accordingly, in arguing that non-rational animals too are endowed with a sensitive faculty Bacon could claim that "ita bene videt et audit canis sicut homo, et sicut de aliis operibus *sensitive* virtutis" (*Liber primus Communium naturalium. Partes tertia et quarta*, R. Steele (ed), *Opera hactenus inedita 3*, Oxford, Clarendon Press, 1911, I 4, I, pp. 283–284, emphasis added).

"common to beasts" and human beings, there is something specifically and truly non-brutish in the act of perception through vision: a fact which causes this sense to "attain the dignity of human reason" and makes it worth studying.[92]

The reason why Bacon claimed that "the common sensibles are not so called because they are perceived by the common sense but rather because they are commonly discerned by all or several of the particular senses" was that, according to him, common sensibles are not perceived by the common sense at all. It is not that this faculty of the sensitive soul has no role in the perceptual process. It is precisely in the first ventricle, according to Bacon, that the *species* emerging from different sense-organs are integrated, so that the common sense can still (and actually still has to) perform the tasks attributed to it by Aristotle of making the perceiver aware that he or she is seeing, hearing and so forth, as well as of distinguishing between sensibles emerging from different senses, such as the whiteness of milk as distinguished from its sweetness.[93] For such a color and such a savor are different instances of *proper* sensibles, which no particular sense, but only the common one, can compare. As for the common sensibles of the Aristotelian tradition, however, the cognitive operations that they require in order to be apprehended demand a higher faculty of the soul, in most cases no less than the intellect. For Bacon, in the last analysis, was more acceptable to claim that human beings perceive transparency by touch than a non-rational animal by sight.

4   Conclusions

As has been shown by Katherine Tachau, Bacon's philosophy of perception set the stage for research on the topic for decades to come.[94] Towards the end of the 13th Century, the distinction between vision "by naked sense" and vision *cum quadam adiuncta argumentatione* was also adopted by philosophers whose key themes did not include vision theory: in their *quaestiones de anima*, for example, or while trying to adjudicate whether God's essence can be experienced "by the corporeal eye."[95] Even more unexpectedly, at the beginning of

---

92   Bacon, *Perspectiva* I 1, 2; Lindberg 5. I discuss more in detail this issue in M. Mantovani, "'The Only Sense with a Science of Its Own': Roger Bacon on *Perspectiva*," forthcoming.

93   Bacon, *Perspectiva* I 1, 2; Lindberg, p. 7.

94   K.H. *Tachau, Vision and Certitude in the Age of Ockham: Optics, Epistemology, and the Foundations of Semantics, 1250–1345*, Leiden, Brill, 1988.

95   Both examples are taken from Roger Marston (ca. 1250–1303), who studied in Paris under Pecham. See, respectively, *Quodlibeta quatuor*, G.J. Etzkorn and I. Brady (eds),

VISIO PER SILLOGISMUM   143

the 14th Century we find a thinker like Auriol invoking the Perspectivists' theory about the different kinds of vision in a discussion of whether equality and similarity are or are not real relations.[96] Although thinkers like Ockham ended up rejecting a good portion of the Perspectivists' teachings, it would be an error to imagine that this trend was a general one: during the 14th and 15th Centuries the theory of vision of Bacon and his followers came in fact to hold intellectual sway to such a point that the study of their treatises entered the *curricula* of the universities.[97] Indeed, still in the Early Modern Age a cultivated man was supposed to be conversant with their main doctrines. In his *Encyclopaedia septem tomis distincta* (1630), one of the reference texts of the time, Johann Alsted instructed his readers that, when asked about the number of the visibles, they were to reply: "twenty two," and to go on to specify that only two of these visibles, however, are perceived *sensu spoliato, id est, solo visu*.[98] To attest to the influence of the Perspectivists' treatises, it would be enough to consider that when, in 1572, a student of Ramus' – Friedrich Risner – published his tremendously influential edition of both Alhacen and Witelo, he could still entitle the work "the treasure of optics," as if nothing substantial had been added to the topic during the five centuries in between. With considerable understatement, Kepler was to name his groundbreaking treatise on optics a "Supplement to Witelo," whose *Opticae libri decem* were still referred to by Descartes as a paradigm for science.[99]

Kepler's 1604 *Ad Vitellionem Paralipomena* represents however a true watershed in the history of the discipline. If the Perspectivists had made the optic nerves hollow, and the spirits filling these nerves transparent, in order to permit the *species* to "glowingly travel through the way of spirits up to ultimate

---

Grottaferrata, Collegium S. Bonaventurae, 1994, ql. III, q. XVII, resp.; *Quaestiones disputatae*, Quaracchi, Collegium S. Bonaventurae, 1932, q. II, resp. 5.

96   Peter Auriol, *Commentariorum in primum librum Sententiarum pars prima et secunda*, C. Sarnano (ed), Rome, Typographia Vaticana, 1596, d. XXXI a. II ad 1. Auriol, more specifically, refers to the theory according to which the above-mentioned relations would not be perceived by naked sense but *ex permixtione alicuius virtutis collativae, sicut demonstrat perspectivus*.

97   On the impact of the 13th century perspectivist theories on 14th and early 15th century thinkers, see G. *Federici-Vescovini, Le teorie della luce e della visione ottica dal IX al XV secolo. Studi sulla prospettiva medievale e altri saggi*, Perugia, Morlacchi, 2003, and F. Zanin, *L'analisi matematica del movimento e i limiti della fisica tardo-medievale. La ricezione della "perspectiva" e delle "calculationes" alla Facoltà delle arti di Parigi, 1340–1350*, Padova, il Poligrafo, 2004.

98   Johann Alsted, *Encyclopaedia septem tomis distincta*, Herborn, 1630, *Compendium*, l. XIX § 4, p. 37. See also l. XIX, c. V ii, p. 1177: "Peripatetici sensibilia communia quinque recensent ... Sed Optici numerant visibilia, ac proinde quoq[ue] sensibilia, communia viginti."

99   Descartes, To Mersenne, 27 May 1638, AT III, pp. 141–142.

sense" (*radiose transit per vias spirituum ... usque ad ultimum sentiens*),[100] it was up to Early Modern anatomists to discover that this was not, in fact, at all the case. Kepler admitted that he could not however understand how a light image could possibly be transmitted from the eye to the seat of perception located in the brain by travelling through non-transparent organs (*per opaca corporis ad Animae penetralia*).[101] Descartes' answer to this difficulty, for its part, would have resulted in nothing less than a complete rejection of colors and of all proper sensibles from among the real properties of bodies.[102]

Proper sensibles were not, however, the only sensibles to be overcome by the *novatores*. Although in the *Traité de l'Homme* (1633) and in the *Dioptrique* (1637) Descartes was in fact still working with a revised version of the Perspectivists' theory of the common sensibles,[103] the 1641 *Meditationes* claimed that all sensibles, other than the proper ones, were to be ascribed to the understanding alone, thereby developing with rigorous consistency the trend of thought initiated by Bacon (whose influence on Descartes was already noticed by the first readers of the *Dioptrique*).[104] It did not take long for later thinkers

---

100 Pecham, *Tractatus de anima* 1; Melani, p. 147: "Species corporalis in organo corporali est dimensionata, secundum dimensiones organi; unde angulariter immutatum immutat pupillam et radiose transit per vias spirituum, per nervum opticum et alia media usque ad ultimum sentiens; ergo semper est corporalis."

101 Johannes Kepler, *Optics: Paralipomena to Witelo and Optical Part of Astronomy*, W.H. Donahue (ed), Santa Fe, Green Lion Press, 2000; Johannes Kepler, *The Harmony of the World*, E.J. Aiton, A.M. Duncan, and J.V. Field (eds), Philadelphia, American Philosophical Society, 1997, IV 7, p. 370*. For a valuable analysis of Kepler's attempts to make sense of image transmission, see Simon, "La théorie cartésienne de la vision"; Simon, *Kepler, rénovateur de l'optique*, in D. Bellis and N. Roudet (eds), Paris, Garnier, forthcoming.

102 I argue for this claim in M. Mantovani, "The Eye and the Ideas: Descartes on the Nature of Bodies," PhD dissertation, Humboldt-Universität zu Berlin, 2018.

103 Cf. Descartes, *Traité de l'Homme*; AT XI 159; trans. T.S. Hall, *Treatise of Man*, Amherst, Prometheus Books, 2003, p. 59: "It only remains for me to tell you what it is that will give the soul a way of sensing position, shape, distance, size, and other similar qualities, not qualities related to one particular sense ... but ones that are common to touch and vision, and even in some way to other senses." Cf. *Dioptrique* VI; AT VI 130; trans. J. Cottingham, *The Philosophical Writings of Descartes*, Cambridge, Cambridge University Press, 1984–1991, I, p. 167*: "light and color, which alone properly belong (*appartiennent proprement*) to the sense of sight."

104 Descartes, *Responsiones* VI; AT VII 437–438; (trans.) Cottingham, II, pp. 294–295*. On Bacon's influence on Descartes (the *Perspectiva* had been published in 1614 in Frankfurt), see To Mersenne, November or December 1638; AT II 447. Since according to Descartes non-human animals do not perceive, the problem of how they (being non-rational) can perceive non-proper sensibles does not arise. Descartes was, however, also the first to work out a *non-cognitive* account of distance perception based on a proper "psychophysiological mechanism"; on this topic see Hatfield, "On Natural Geometry" and footnote 81 above. This is not a matter of coincidence, though, but stems directly from Descartes' attempt to

to draw the logical conclusion of this theory, and deny the existence of any "idea or kind of idea common to both senses" – to sight and to touch both.[105] Bacon's theory of the common sensibles had carried within itself the seed of its own destruction: rather than as the *non-proper* sensibles, the common sensibles were to be understood as the *improper* ones. "Things are suggested and perceived by the senses. We make judgments and inferences by the understanding."[106] Although this appears to be a trivial matter to us today, it had taken centuries for *perspectiva* to reject the ancient and medieval concept of a judgment of the senses.

The theories of perception analyzed in this essay have shown that Sorabji's grand narrative regarding the progressive dematerialization of the perceptual process is in need of some qualification. All the more, therefore, must be Burnyeat's. In the course of this study, the opposition between "materialists" and "dematerializers" has revealed itself to be simplistic and potentially misleading, inasmuch as it leads one to assume that the thinkers of the time had just *one* account for all classes of sensibles. The Perspectivists' distinction between a perception "by naked sense" and a perception "by syllogism" has shown that this was not the case. For a thinker like Burnyeat's Aquinas, for whom "the eye's taking on a color is just one's becoming aware of some color," all properties of bodies were indeed substantially on a par with one another, since they were all equally susceptible of becoming the objects of an act of consciousness. For Aquinas there was in the eye, so to speak, nothing but awareness (at least in case Burnyeat is right). Nothing less, but also nothing more – as if the world of colors and shapes were immediately and thoroughly transparent to the perceiver. Thinkers like the Perspectivists, who took into account the corporeal condition in which the perceptual process takes place, were, however, aware

---

      prove that a theory of the mind can dispense with the sensory soul, inasmuch as all the operations usually ascribed to this latter can be explained by appealing either to the intellect or to the body. Descartes carried, consequently, to their extreme conclusions both strands of Bacon's theory of vision: *visio per sillogismum* became in this way purely intellectual; animal instinct a merely bodily mechanism.

105   George Berkeley, *An Essay Towards a New Theory of Vision* (1709), in *The Works of George Berkeley, Bishop of Cloyne*, A. Luce and T.E. Jessop (eds), London, Thomas Nelson and Sons, 1948, vol. I, § 127, pp. 222–223. A decisive premise of the argument is the identification of the mental with the conscious, a thesis that Berkeley derived from Descartes and from which he inferred the impossibility of non-conscious judgement and, more generally, of non-conscious cognitive activities; cf. G. Hatfield and W. Epstein, "The Sensory Core and the Medieval Foundations of Early Modern Perceptual Theory," *Isis*, vol. 70, 1979, pp. 363–384.

106   Berkeley, *The Theory of Vision ... Vindicated and Explained* (1733), § 42; Luce and Jessop (eds), I, p. 265.

that if a light ray impresses the crystalline lens with its color, this patch of color does not establish, just in itself, how far away is the body that reflects that ray. Just as they realized that it is not a trivial matter to reconstruct the shape of a three-dimensional object from the *species* painted on the lens surface. The more the Perspectivists pursued this line of enquiry and insisted that color-perception results from a coloring of the sense-organs, the more sophisticated became the cognitive operations to which they were obliged to appeal in order to account for the perception of shape and other such features. The medieval theories of perception that had taken as their exemplary object of enquiry the most problematic of all the senses were not pressing for a "dematerialization" of the perception of proper and common sensibles alike. Rather, they were *intellectualizing* the perception of non-proper sensibles, and this largely as a result of having understood light and color perception in straightforward "material" terms. For Bacon, in the case of the non-proper sensibles, awareness was not enough. In Bacon's view, something even more "spiritual" was needed in order for the perception of such sensible features to be possible. What was needed was something so spiritual and cognitive in its very nature that, of all living beings, only the one *rational* animal would have the ability to perform it. Perception, Bacon argued, demanded a syllogism.[107]

Bibliography

Primary Literature

Albert the Great, *De anima*, C. Stroick (ed), *Opera omnia* 7.1, Münster, Aschendorff, 1968.

Alhacen, *Alhacen's Theory of Visual Perception: A Critical Edition, with English Translation and Commentary, of the First Three Books of Alhacen's "De aspectibus,"* in A.M. Smith (ed), *Transactions of the American Philosophical Society*, vol. 91, no. 4, 2001.

Aristotle, *On the Soul, Parva Naturalia, On Breath*, W.S. Hett (ed), London, Loeb, 1975.

François d'Aguilon, *Opticorum Libri Sex*, Antwerpen, Officina Plantiniana, 1613.

---

107   The writing of this paper has much profited from the discussions at the workshop organized by Elena Bălțuță which led to this volume. My thanks to Elena and all other participants for their challenges to and discussion of the ideas presented here. I thank Vincenzo De Risi, Sven Dupré, Jeremiah Hackett, Gary Hatfield, Yael Kedar, Dominik Perler, and Paolo Rubini for their helpful comments to drafts of this paper. Part of the research presented here has been carried out while at the Descartes Centre in Utrecht, which provided me with an ideal research environment.

   I dedicate this essay to Alfredo Ferrarin, who many years ago introduced me, first-year student, to Aristotle's *De anima. Grazie di cuore.*

VISIO PER SILLOGISMUM

George Berkeley, *The Works of George Berkeley, Bishop of Cloyne*, A.A. Luce and T.E. Jessop (eds), London, Thomas Nelson and Sons, 1948.

Ibn Al-Haytham, *The Optics of Ibn Al-Haytham, Books I–III: On Direct Vision*, A.I. Sabra (ed and trans.), 2 vols., London, Warburg Institute, 1989.

Johann Alsted, *Encyclopaedia septem tomis distincta*, Herborn, 1630.

Johannes Kepler, *Optics: Paralipomena to Witelo and Optical Part of Astronomy*, W.H. Donahue (ed), Santa Fe, Green Lion Press, 2000.

Johannes Kepler, *The Harmony of the World*, E.J. Aiton, A.M. Duncan, and J.V. Field (eds), Philadelphia, American Philosophical Society, 1997.

John Locke, *An Essay Concerning Human Understanding*, P.H. Nidditch (ed), Oxford, Clarendon Press, 1975.

John Pecham, *John Pecham and the Science of Optics: "Perspectiva communis,"* D.C. Lindberg (ed), Wisconsin, University of Wisconsin, 1970.

John Pecham, *Tractatus de anima*, G. Melani (ed), Firenze, Biblioteca di Studi Francescani, 1948.

Peter Auriol, *Commentariorum in primum librum Sententiarum pars prima et secunda*, C. Sarnano (ed), Rome, Typographia Vaticana, 1596.

Plato, *Theaetetus*, W.F. Hicken (ed), *Platonis Opera*, Oxford, Oxford University Press, 1995.

Ptolemy, *L'Optique de Claude Ptolémée dans la version latine d'après l'arabe de l'émir Eugène de Sicile. Édition critique et exégétique*, A. Lejeune (ed), Louvain, Publications Universitaires de Louvain, 1956.

Ptolemy, *Ptolemy's Theory of Perception: An English Translation of the "Optics" with Introduction and Commentary*, in A.M. Smith (ed), *Transactions of the American Philosophical Society*, vol. 86, no. 2, 1996.

René Descartes, *Œuvres de Descartes*, C. Adam and P. Tannéry (eds), Paris, Vrin, 1996.

René Descartes, *The Philosophical Writings of Descartes*, trans. J. Cottingham, R. Stoothoff, and D. Murdoch, Cambridge, Cambridge University Press, 1984–1991.

René Descartes, *Treatise of Man*, trans. T.S. Hall, Amherst, Prometheus Books, 2003.

Roger Bacon, *Liber primus Communium naturalium. Partes tertia et quarta*, R. Steele (ed), *Opera hactenus inedita 3*, Oxford, Clarendon Press, 1911.

Roger Bacon, *Perspectiva*, D.C. Lindberg (ed and trans.), *Roger Bacon and the Origins of "Perspectiva" in the Middle Ages*, Oxford, Clarendon Press, 1996.

Roger Bacon, *Roger Bacon's Philosophy of Nature*, D.C. Lindberg (ed and trans.), Oxford, Clarendon Press, 1983.

Roger Bacon, *The Opus maius of Roger Bacon*, 3 vols., J.H. Bridges (ed), Oxford, Clarendon Press, 1897–1900.

Roger Marston, *Quaestiones disputatae*, Quaracchi, Collegium S. Bonaventurae, 1932.

Roger Marston, *Quodlibeta quatuor*, G.J. Etzkorn and I. Brady (eds), Grottaferrata, Collegium S. Bonaventurae, 1994.

Thomas Aquinas, *Sentencia libri De anima, Opera omnia 45.1*, Rome, Commissio Leonina, 1984.

Thomas Aquinas, *Summa theologiae*, P. Caramello (ed), 3 vols., Turin, Marietti, 1963.

Witelo, *Opticae thesaurus ... Vitellionis thuringopoloni Opticae libri decem*, F. Risner (ed), Basel, Officina Episcopiana, 1572.

Secondary Literature

Baker, Tawrin, "Color, Cosmos, Oculus: Vision, Color, and the Eye in Jacopo Zabarella and Hieronymus Fabricius ab Aquapendente," PhD dissertation, Indiana University, 2014.

Băltuță, Elena, "The Escape Artist: Robert Kilwardby on Objects as *sine qua non* Causes," in E. Băltuță (ed), *Medieval Perceptual Puzzles: Theories of Perception in the 13th and 14th Centuries*, Leiden, Brill, 2020, pp. 179–212.

Bauer, Hans, *Die Psychologie Alhazens. Auf Grund von Alhazens Optik*, Münster, Aschendorff, 1911.

Biard, Joël and Rashed, Roshdi (eds), *Descartes et le Moyen Âge*, Paris, Vrin, 1997.

Burnyeat, Myles, "Is an Aristotelian Philosophy of Mind Still Credible? A Draft," in M.C. Nussbaum and A.O. Rorty (eds), *Essays on Aristotle's "De anima,"* Oxford, Clarendon Press, 1992, pp. 15–26.

Burnyeat, Myles, "Aquinas on 'spiritual change' in perception," in D. Perler (ed), *Ancient and Medieval Theories of Intentionality*, Leiden, Brill, 2001, pp. 129–153.

Clarke, Edwin, "The doctrine of the Hollow Nerve in the 17th and 18th Centuries," in L.G. Stevenson and R.P. Multhauf (eds), *Medicine, Science, and Culture: Historical Essays in Honor of Owsei Temkin*, Baltimore, John Hopkins University Press, 1968, pp. 123–141.

Dupré, Sven, "Inside the *Camera Obscura*: Kepler's Experiment and Theory of Optical Imagery," *Early Medicine and Science*, vol. 13, no. 3, 2008, pp. 219–244.

Dupré, Sven, "Kepler's Optics without Hypotheses," *Synthese*, vol. 185, no. 3, 2012, pp. 501–525.

Dupré, Sven, "The Return of the *Species*: Jesuit Responses to Kepler's New Theory of Images," in W. de Boer and C. Göttler (eds), *Religion and the Senses in Early Modern Europe*, Leiden, Brill, 2012, pp. 473–487.

Federici-Vescovini, Graziella, *Le teorie della luce e della visione ottica dal IX al XV secolo. Studi sulla prospettiva medievale e altri saggi*, Perugia, Morlacchi, 2003.

Galle, Griet, "Edition and Discussion of the Oxford Gloss on *De sensu 1*," *Archives d'histoire doctrinale et littéraire du Moyen Âge*, vol. 75, 2008, pp. 197–281.

Gilson, Étienne, *Études sur le rôle de la pensée médiévale dans la formation du système cartésien*, Paris, Vrin, 1930.

Hackett, Jeremiah, "Agent Intellect and Intelligible Species in Roger Bacon and John Pecham," in G. Mensching and A. Mensching-Estakhr (eds), *Die Seele im Mittelalter. Von der Substanz zum funktionalen System*, Würzburg, Königshausen & Neumann, 2018, pp. 149–166.

Hackett, Jeremiah, "*Experientia, Experimentum*, and the Perception of Objects in Space," in J. Aertsen and A. Speer (eds), *Raum und Raumvorstellungen im Mittelalter*, Berlin, De Gruyter, 1998, pp. 101–120.

Hackett, Jeremiah, "Roger Bacon and Aristotelianism," *Vivarium*, vol. 35, no. 2, 1997, pp. 129–135.

Hackett, Jeremiah, "Roger Bacon and the Reception of Aristotle in the Thirteenth Century: An Introduction to His Criticism of Averroes," in L. Honnefelder, R. Wood, M. Dreyer, and M.A. Aris (eds), *Albertus Magnus and the Beginnings of the Medieval Reception of Aristotle in the Latin West*, Münster, Aschendorff, 2005, pp. 219–248.

Hackett, Jeremiah, *Roger Bacon and the Sciences: Commemorative Essays*, Leiden, Brill, 1997.

Hackett, Jeremiah, "Roger Bacon on Animal Knowledge in the *Perspectiva*," in L.-X. Lòpez-Farjeat and J.A. Tellkamp (eds), *Philosophical Psychology in Arabic Thought and the Latin Aristotelianism of the 13th Century*, Paris, Vrin, 2013, pp. 23–42.

Hatfield, Gary, "On Natural Geometry and Seeing Distance Directly in Descartes," in V. De Risi (ed) *Mathematizing Space: The Objects of Geometry from Antiquity to the Early Modern Age*, Berlin, Birkhäuser, 2015, pp. 157–192.

Hatfield, Gary and Epstein, William, "The Sensory Core and the Medieval Foundations of Early Modern Perceptual Theory," *Isis*, vol. 70, 1979, pp. 363–384.

Kahn, Charles H., "Sensation and Consciousness in Aristotle's Psychology," *Archiv für Geschichte der Philosophie*, vol. 48, 1966, pp. 43–81.

Kedar, Yael and Hon, Giora, "Roger Bacon (c. 1220–1292) and his System of Laws of Nature: Classification, Hierarchy and Significance," *Perspective on Science*, vol. 25, no. 6, 2017, pp. 719–745.

Lemay, Richard, "Roger Bacon's Attitude Toward the Latin Translations and Translators of the Twelfth and Thirteenth Centuries," in J. Hackett (ed), *Roger Bacon and the Sciences: Commemorative Essays*, Leiden, Brill, 1997, pp. 25–48.

Lička, Lukáš, "The Visual Process: Immediate or Successive? Approaches to the Extramission Postulate in 13th Century Theories of Vision," in E. Băltuță (ed), *Medieval Perceptual Puzzle: Theories of Perception in the 13th and 14th Centuries*, Leiden, Brill, 2020, pp. 73–110.

Lindberg, David C., "Lines of Influence in 13th Century Optics: Bacon, Witelo, and Pecham," *Speculum*, vol. 46, 1971, pp. 66–83.

Lindberg, David C., *Studies in the History of Medieval Optics*, London, Variorum Reprints, 1983.

Lindberg, David C., "The Genesis of Kepler's Theory of Light: Light Metaphysics from Plotinus to Kepler," *Osiris*, vol. 2, 1986, pp. 4–42.

Lindberg, David C., *Theories of vision from al-Kindi to Kepler*, Chicago, University of Chicago Press, 1976.

Mantovani, Mattia, "Eye Anatomy and Perceptual Puzzles from Vesalius to Newton," forthcoming.

Mantovani, Mattia, "The Eye and the Ideas: Descartes on the Nature of Bodies," PhD dissertation, Humboldt-Universität zu Berlin, 2018.

Mantovani, Mattia, "'The Only Sense with a Science of Its Own': Roger Bacon on *Perspectiva*," forthcoming.

Martin, André, "Peter John Olivi on Perception, Attention, and the Soul's Orientation towards the Body," in E. Băltuţă (ed), *Medieval Perceptual Puzzles: Theories of Perception in the 13th and 14th Centuries*, Leiden, Brill, 2020, pp. 304–334.

Nussbaum, Martha C. and Rorty, Amélie Oksenberg (eds), *Essays on Aristotle's "De anima,"* Oxford, Clarendon Press, 1992.

Oelze, Anselm, *Animal Rationality: Later Medieval Theories 1250–1350*, Leiden, Brill, 2018.

Owens, Joseph, "Aristotle on Common Sensibles and Incidental Perception," *Phoenix*, vol. 36, 1982, pp. 215–236.

Panofsky, Erwin, *Meaning in the Visual Arts: Papers in and on Art History*, New York, Doubleday Anchor, 1955.

Pantin, Isabelle, "*Simulachrum, Species, Forma, Imago*: What Was Transported by Light into the *Camera Obscura*? Divergent Conceptions of Realism Revealed by Lexical Ambiguities at the Beginning of the Seventeenth Century," *Early Science and Medicine*, vol. 13, no. 3, 2008, pp. 245–269.

Pasnau, Robert, *Theories of Cognition in the Later Middle Ages*, Cambridge, Cambridge University Press, 1997.

Perler, Dominik (ed), *Ancient and Medieval Theories of Intentionality*, Leiden, Brill, 2001.

Perler, Dominik, "Descartes, critique de la théorie médiévale des *species*," in J. Biard and R. Rashed (eds), *Descartes et le Moyen Âge*, Paris, Vrin, 1997, pp. 141–153.

Perler, Dominik, *Theorien der Intentionalität im Mittelalter*, Frankfurt am Main, Vittorio Klostermann, 2002.

Perler, Dominik, "Rational Seeing: Thomas Aquinas on Human Perception," in E. Băltuţă (ed), *Medieval Perceptual Puzzles: Theories of Perception in the 13th and 14th Centuries*, Leiden, Brill, 2020, pp. 213–237.

Raizman-Kedar, Yael, "Questioning Aristotle: Roger Bacon on the True Essence of Color," *Journal of Medieval Latin*, vol. 17, 2007, pp. 372–385.

Raizman-Kedar, Yael, "*Species* as Signs: Roger Bacon (1220–1292) on *Perspectiva* and *Grammatica*," PhD dissertation, University of Haifa, 2009.

VISIO PER SILLOGISMUM 151

Raizman-Kedar, Yael, "The Intellect Naturalized: Roger Bacon on the Existence of Corporeal Species within the Intellect," *Early Science and Medicine*, vol. 14, no. 1, 2009, pp. 131–157.

Rubini, Paolo, "'Accidental perception' and 'cogitative power' in Thomas Aquinas and John of Jandun," in E. Băltuță (ed), *Medieval Perceptual Puzzles: Theories of Perception in the 13th and 14th Centuries*, Leiden, Brill, 2020, pp. 269–303.

Russell, Gül A., "The Emergence of Physiological Optics," in R. Rashed and R. Morelon (eds), *The Encyclopedia of the History of Arabic Sciences*, London, Routledge, 1996, pp. 672–716.

Sabra, Abdelhamid I., "Ibn Al-Haytham's Criticisms of Ptolemy's *Optics*," *Journal of the History of Philosophy*, vol. 4, no. 2, 1966, pp. 145–149.

Sabra, Abdelhamid I., "Sensation and Inference in Alhazen's Theory of Visual Perception," in P.K. Machamer and R.G. Turnbull (eds), *Studies in Perception*, Columbus, Ohio State University Press, 1978, pp. 160–184.

Shapiro, Alan E., "Images: Real and Virtual, Projected and Perceived, from Kepler to Dechales," *Early Medicine and Science*, vol. 13, no. 3, 2008, pp. 270–312.

Silva, José Filipe and Yrjönsuuri, Mikko (eds), *Active Perception in the History of Philosophy: From Plato to Modern Philosophy*, Dordrecht, Springer, 2014.

Silva, José Filipe, "The Chameleonic Mind: The Activity versus the Actuality of Perception," in E. Băltuță (ed), *Medieval Perceptual Puzzles: Theories of Perception in the 13th and 14th Centuries*, Leiden, Brill, 2020, pp. 38–72.

Simon, Gérard, *Kepler, rénovateur de l'optique*, D. Bellis and N. Roudet (eds), Paris, Garnier, 2019.

Simon, Gérard, "La théorie cartésienne de la vision, réponse à Kepler et rupture avec la problematique médiévale," in J. Biard and R. Rashed (eds), *Descartes et le Moyen Âge*, Paris, Vrin, 1997, pp. 107–118.

Smith, A. Mark, *From Sight to Light: The Passage from Ancient to Modern Optics*, Chicago, University of Chicago Press, 2014.

Smith, A. Mark, "Getting the Big Picture in Perspectivist Optics," *Isis*, vol. 72, no. 4, 1981, pp. 568–589.

Smith, A. Mark, "The Psychology of Visual Perception in Ptolemy's *Optics*," *Isis*, vol. 79, no. 2, 1988, pp. 188–207.

Smith, A. Mark, "What is the History of Medieval Optics Really About?" *Proceedings of the American Philosophical Society*, vol. 148, no. 2, 2004, pp. 180–194.

Sorabji, Richard, "Intentionality and Physiological Process: Aristotle's Theory of Sense-Perception," M.C. Nussbaum and A.O. Rorty (eds), *Essays on Aristotle's "De anima*," Oxford, Clarendon Press, 1992, pp. 195–225.

Sorabji, Richard, "Body and Soul in Aristotle," *Philosophy*, vol. 49, 1974, pp. 63–89.

Sorabji, Richard, "From Aristotle to Brentano: The Development of the Concept of Intentionality," *Oxford Studies in Ancient Philosophy*, Supplementary Volume, 1991, pp. 227–259.

Sorabji, Richard, *Perception, Conscience, and Will in Ancient Philosophy*, Padstow, Ashgate, 2013.

Summers, David, *The Judgment of Sense: Renaissance Naturalism and the Rise of Aesthetics*, Cambridge, Cambridge University Press, 1987.

Tachau, Katherine H., *Vision and Certitude in the Age of Ockham: Optics, Epistemology, and the Foundations of Semantics, 1250–1345*, Leiden, Brill, 1988.

Tachau, Katherine H., "What Senses and Intellect Do: Argument and Judgment in Late Medieval Theories of Knowledge," in K. Jacobi (ed), *Argumentationstheorie. Scholastische Forschungen zu den logischen und semantischen Regeln korrekten Folgerns*, Leiden, Brill, 1993, pp. 653–668.

Toivanen, Juhana, "Perceiving As: Non-Conceptual Forms of Perception in Medieval Philosophy," in E. Băltuță (ed), *Medieval Perceptual Puzzles: Theories of Perception in the 13th and 14th Centuries*, Leiden, Brill, 2020, pp. 10–37.

Wolfson, Harry A., "The Internal Senses in Latin, Arabic, and Hebrew Philosophical Texts," *Harvard Theological Review*, vol. 28, 1935, pp. 69–133.

Wood, Rega, "Imagination and Experience in the Sensory Soul and Beyond: Richard Rufus, Roger Bacon, and their Contemporaries," in H. Lagerlund (ed), *Forming the Mind: Essays on the Internal Senses and the Mind/Body Problem from Avicenna to the Medical Enlightenment*, Dordrecht, Springer, 2007, pp. 27–58.

Zanin, Fabio, *L'analisi matematica del movimento e i limiti della fisica tardo-medievale. La ricezione della "perspectiva" e delle "calculationes" alla Facoltà delle arti di Parigi, 1340–1350*, Padova, il Poligrafo, 2004.

CHAPTER 6

Spirituality and Perception in Medieval Aristotelian Natural Philosophy

Rega Wood

Spirituality and perception are closely linked in medieval accounts of perception. The concept of spirituality is also crucial to a controversy initiated by Myles Burnyeat thirty-five years ago.[1] This paper concerns a later stage of the controversy in which Burnyeat's interlocutor was Richard Sorabji.[2] Burnyeat argued that the alteration required for perception according to Aristotle was not literal alteration strictly speaking and claimed that Thomas Aquinas, in whom he detected a "thoroughly Aristotelian mind at word," espoused a very similar view. As Burnyeat understands Aristotle and Aquinas, perception was rather a spiritual change. Burnyeat concedes that the change is physical, as it must be, since a soul is both the first actuality and the nature of what it ensouls. Nonetheless, Burnyeat holds that "nothing happens" when someone perceives red "save that he sees red."[3] Much has been written about both Aristotle and Aquinas since the debate was originally joined, and I will not attempt to comment on or add to this debate as such. Neither can I claim authoritatively to interpret Aristotle or Aquinas. However, I do think that a better understanding of the history of the concept of spirituality in the thirteenth century may serve to reshape the debate.

1 Major Differences between Medieval and Modern Aims and Concepts

More specifically, I think that the modern concepts of spirituality are so far removed from their medieval counterparts as to make the use of the term

---

1 M. Burnyeat, "Is an Aristotelian Philosophy of Mind Still Credible: A Draft," initially circulated in 1983, but published for the first time in 1992 in M.C. Nussbaum and A.O. Rorty (eds), *Essays on Aristotle's "De anima,"* Oxford, Clarendon Press, pp. 15–26.

2 Burnyeat, "Aquinas on Spiritual Change in Perception," in D. Perler (ed), *Ancient and Medieval Theories of Intentionality,* Leiden, Brill, 2001, pp. 134, 137, 144. Compare R. Sorabji, "Aristotle on Sensory Processes and Intentionality: A Reply to Myles Burnyeat," in Perler (ed), *Ancient and Medieval Theories of Intentionality,* pp. 49–61, esp. p. 53.

3 Burnyeat, "How Much Happens When Aristotle Sees Red and Hears Middle C?" in M.C.Nussbaum and A.O. Rorty (eds), *Essays on Aristotle's "De anima,"* Oxford, Clarendon Press, 1995, p. 421. See also Burnyeat, "Aquinas on Spiritual Change in Perception," p. 130.

© KONINKLIJKE BRILL NV, LEIDEN, 2020 | DOI:10.1163/9789004413030_007

'spiritual' in our times seriously misleading as part of a description of medieval theories of perception. As we use the term, it refers to the holy, to higher moral concerns, and to theological posits. We suppose that the spiritual must be the supernatural. But medievals used the term ambiguously, referring not only to such theological posits as angels, but also to rarefied, immaterial, and intentional objects, and it is this latter use that is relevant here. In the context of medieval theories of perception and sensory cognition, some spiritual entities were considered parts of the physical world and played an indispensable role in scientific explanations of psychological processes.

Also very different are the phenomena spirituality is meant to explain. And if you see what the explanandum is and how spiritual beings explain what happens, you will see why spirituality was a sensible explanatory posit for medievals in ways that would not be likely to occur to us.

I will make my case on the basis of Richard Rufus' thought and its historical basis. Virtually unknown today, Rufus was a famous Aristotelian in the thirteenth century. Or at least the views stated in the forthcoming edition of his *Sententia cum quaestionibus in libros De anima (In DAn)* were so regarded.[4] For a statement of the case for attributing this work to Richard Rufus, see the introduction to *Sententia cum quaestionibus in libros De anima Aristotelis*, ed. J. Ottman et al., Oxford 2019.

Some of Rufus' thoughts were distinctive and original, but most of what I will say here is based on his commentary on *De anima*, where the assumptions

---

4 Richard Rufus of Cornwall, *Sententia cum quaestionibus in libros De anima Aristotelis*, J.R. Ottman, R. Wood, N. Lewis, and C.J. Martin (eds), Oxford, Oxford University Press, 2019, henceforth *In DAn*, 1.4. E1, p. 239; see Ps. Buckfield, *De anima*, henceforth *In DAn*, 1: "Quidam tamen famosi exponunt hoc sic: Quod ipse Plato 'posuit animam secundum [quod] cognoscit esse lineam rectam et secundum quod movet esse quasi linea recta reflexa in circulum sive circulus.' Et est sic anima secundum ipsum primo divisa <? M> 'in duos circulos, intersecantes se secundum angulos acutos, tangentes se in duobus punctis oppositis. Et iterum alterum illorum duorum circulorum posuit <possint M> dividi in septem circulos, scilicet iuxta numerum octo sphaerarum ipsius caeli sumens numerum circulorum animae,' quod totum potest imaginari tam de anima mundi quam de anima humana" (Oxford, Merton College 272, fol. 21vb).

    See also this author's remarks about Rufus' opinion on self-understanding in book 3 (3.E4, p. 537). Ps. Buckfield, *In DAn* 3: "Hic solvit secundam dubitationem, et primo docet quae pars dubitationis est eligenda, dicens secundum quosdam <quasdam M> quod ipse intellectus se ipso est intelligibilis, sicut species in <in mente vel forsan: immediate M> mente comprehensae ab intellectu se ipsis intelliguntur et non per suas species, quia si per species intelligerentur, esset processus in infinitum.... Iste modus legendi satis videtur consonus naturae, translationi et etiam veritati Commentatoris. Et quidam famosi manifeste consentiunt in partem aliam, scilicet quod intelliget se per speciem. Ambae tamen expositiones possunt habere veritatem" (Oxford, Merton College 272, fol.19ra).

SPIRITUALITY AND PERCEPTION IN MEDIEVAL ARISTOTELIANISM 155

he makes were widely shared by other thinkers of the time. That is particularly the case when it comes to the meaning of the term 'spiritual' and the equivalencies he assumed. Thus 'immaterial,' the antonym of 'material,' is a distinctive characteristic of the 'spiritual'; indeed 'immaterial' is sometimes used epexegetically with 'spiritual.'[5] Thus Rufus writes:

> Because a sensible [percept] exists in spiritual, not material being in an organ, it can change an incorporeal substance in some manner.[6]

> But note that sound exists in different [ways]. For in some place[s] sound has material being in the manner of colour in a wall; but in some place[s] it has spiritual being as does colour in the medium or in a [sensitive] organ. And the question is where it has material and where spiritual being and how it goes from material to spiritual being.[7]

> Taste becomes more immaterial and spiritual in its medium.[8]

The subjects of species in spiritual being are successively rarefied.

> Because a tremor is local motion, [and] moreover a tremor disposes a medium for the reception of sound spiritually by rarefying it successively, therefore it generates the species of sound successively.[9]

As sensibles complete or perfect a sensitive faculty, they are intentions. Accordingly when 'sensible' refers not to a distal external object, but to a proximate object or percept, 'intention' is used epexegetically and as a corrective for 'sensible.'

---

5   Since Latin terminology is at issue here, I would have preferred not to translate the following passages.

6   Rufus, *In DAn* 2.11.Q2: "Et quia sensibile est in esse spirituali in organo et non materialiter, ex hoc potest immutare aliquo modo substantiam incorpoream" (ed. J. Ottman et al., p. 441).

7   Rufus, *In DAn* 2.7.Q2: "Sed nota quod differenter est sonus: Alicubi enim est sonus secundum esse materiale per quem modum est color in pariete; alicubi autem secundum esse spirituale sicut est color in medio vel in organo." "Et quaeritur ubi est secundum esse materiale et ubi est secundum esse spirituale et qualiter procedit ex esse materiali ad esse spirituale" (ed. J. Ottman et al., p. 376).

8   Rufus, *In DAn* 2.9.Q1: "... fit sapor in esse magis immateriali et spirituali in medio ..." (ed. J. Ottman et al., p. 403).

9   Rufus, *In DAn* 2.7.Q2: "Quia enim tremor est motus localis, rarefaciendo autem medium successive per tremorem disponit medium ad receptionem soni spiritualiter, ideo generat speciem soni successive ..." (ed. J. Ottman et al., p. 377).

156 WOOD

> A sensitive [faculty] is a power perfectible by sensible [percepts] or [rather] by the intentions of sensible things....[10]

Another closely related passage makes the same point about 'intention,' but now specifies that sensible intentions are species.

> Since he has already shown that the sensitive faculty is a perfectible power, here he shows that this is by sensible [percepts] or the intentions of sensible [objects]. And we should say then that "a sensible power is such as the sensible object [is]" [2.5.418a3–4] – that is, it is a power perfectible by the intentions of sensible [objects] or [rather] by sensible [percepts]. And he makes this manifest, since from what has already been said it is evident that an actual sensible [percept] is the perfection of the sensitive [organ]. And he shows this further with a sign, since the sensitive faculty before it actually senses is unlike the sensible [object], but when it is not potentially receptive but actually has and has received a *species,* then it is like [the sensible object]. And this is a sign that the sensible [percept] is the perfection of the sensitive – namely a second perfection – such that a sensitive [organ or faculty] is a power perfectible by sensible [percepts].[11]

What matters most here are the terms 'spiritual' or 'spirituality' and their twofold construal. They are (1) characterized physically as rarefied or immaterial, and (2) their end is specified: being a potential object of apprehension that ultimately actualizes a sensitive faculty. This second aspect of spirituality is part of an explanation of perception that describes something, not nothing, happening, when we sense, contrary to the suggestion that awareness is a primitive.

---

10   Rufus, *In DAn* 2.4.D1: "Sensitivum est potentia perfectibilis a sensibilibus sive per intentiones sensibilium ..." (ed. J. Ottman et al., p. 333).

11   Rufus, *In DAn* 2.4.E3: "Cum enim iam declaratum sit quod sensitivum est potentia perfectibilis, hic declarat quod a sensibilibus sive intentionibus sensibilium.... Et dicendum tunc quod 'sensitivum est potentia ut sensibile,' id est, est potentia perfectibilis per sensibilium intentiones sive a sensibilibus. Et hoc manifestat, quia ex iam dictis patet quod sensibile actu est perfectio iam ipsius sensitivi. Et hoc magis declarat per signum, quia sensitivum, antequam actu sentiat, est dissimile ipsi sensibili; cum autem non est in potentia receptiva sed iam actu habet speciem et receperit, tunc est ei simile, et hoc est signum quod sensibile est sensitivi perfectio, scilicet secunda, et ita quod sensitivum est potentia perfectibilis a sensibilibus" (ed. J. Ottman et al., p. 345). There is ambiguity in the term 'sensibile' that refers both to the distal and proximate objects of perception. In the translation above I have disambiguated calling the distal object a 'sensible object' and the proximate object a 'sensible percept.'

SPIRITUALITY AND PERCEPTION IN MEDIEVAL ARISTOTELIANISM   157

Of course, Rufus did not invent the concept of spirituality he used without explanation. It was a standard theoretical posit frequently adduced in the medical literature from ancient times. Neither was Rufus the first to apply the concept in explaining perception.

Rufus' much admired guide to Aristotle, Averroes, was the first to introduce the concept of spirituality into Western Peripatetic accounts of perception through the Latin translations of his works.[12] Whereas *intentio* comes from the Arabic *ma'nà* and derives ultimately from the Greek λογος, Averroes' spirituality or rather the spiritual is related to the Arabic *rūh̲ aniyya*.[13]

A particularly clear statement of the role of spirituality in cognition and its increasing purity occurs in an early work that circulated in thirteenth century Paris, the *Compendium libri Aristotelis de memoria et reminiscentia,* Versio Parisina.[14]

> Therefore among the aforesaid faculties and their objects there are different orders, in accordance with the order and degree of their corporality and spirituality. Among these the first [in the series] pertains to the sensible form outside the soul in the thing whose form it is, and this is purely corporeal, the pure hull, as it were, containing within itself the marrow, which the comprehending faculties should perceive. The second pertains to the form in the medium, for example colour in air, and it is intermediate between purely corporeal and purely spiritual; the third, to the form in the common sense, and that is purely spiritual; the fourth, to [the form] in the imaginative faculty, and it is more spiritual than the preceding [kind of form]; the fifth, in the discriminating faculty; the sixth, in the memorative faculty, and this is maximally spiritual, since it receives the marrow which the three preceding or antecedent faculties separate from the hull.[15]

---

12 Probably the first Western use of this Averroistic concept occurs in the anonymous circa-1230 *De potentiis animae et obiectis*, D. Callus (ed), "The Powers of the Soul: An Early Unpublished Text," *Recherches de théologie ancienne et médiévale*, vol. 19, 1952, pp. 150–152.

13 D. Black, "Averroes on the Spirituality and Intentionality of Sensation," in P. Adamson (ed), *The Age of Averroes, Arabic Philosophy in the Sixth/Twelfth Century*, London, The Warburg Institute, 2011, pp. 159–162 and the notes thereto.

14 Averroes, *De somno et vigilia*, A.L. Shields and H. Blumberg (eds), *Compendium librorum Aristotelis qui Parva naturalia vocantur,* Cambridge, The Medieval Academy of America, 1949, pp. 58–59. Hereafter cited as *Compendium*.

15 Averroes, *Compendium*: "Sunt igitur in virtutibus predictis et earum obiectis ordines, secundum ordinem et gradus corporalitatis et spiritualitatis diversi; inter quos est primus forme sensibilis in re ipsa extra animam, cuius est forma; et iste est pure corporalis, quasi

This is an account of the changes in a percept as it moves through the sensory process. At the outset, there is the purely corporeal form itself in the external world as it appears in the outer surface of the thing seen; then there is the percept in the medium, which is in an intermediate state, neither fully spiritual nor fully corporeal. The percept is purely spiritual for the first time in the common sense, still more spiritual in the imagination, and most spiritual in memory.[16] As items move from body to soul, or become psychological rather than somatic, they become successively more spiritual.

Sometimes the percept is assigned different names at each stage of the process: *idolum* in the common sense, *imago* in the imagination, and *intentio* in memory.[17] However, though its being varies as it moves from the medium and through the substantially distinct faculties in different parts of the cerebrum, it is in some manner the same percept, since otherwise it would not produce cognition of the object perceived.

Averroes makes this clear with his analogy between a material form – that is, the form of a material body – and a seed in a hull. Just as it is the same seed with and without its hull (or the same marrow inside and outside a bone), so it is in some sense the same form both when incorporated and when unincorporated. Moreover, the changes in this form do not cease when it becomes fully immaterial or spiritual, but rather it becomes increasing spiritual as it gains the capacity to perfect superior, more spiritual faculties.

Like Averroes, Rufus holds that spirituality comes in degrees and that a percept in the sense organ is more spiritual than it was when transmitted or multiplied across the medium.[18] This has to be the case, because at each stage in the process the receiver is more rarefied, at least in the case of the senses whose medium is external, and the nature of what is received must correspond to the

---

purus cortex, continens in se medullam, quam virtutes comprehensive debent sapere ab ipso. Secundus est illius forme in medio, ut coloris in aëre; et iste est medius inter pure corporalem et pure spiritualem. Tercius est forme in sensu communi; et iste est pure spiritualis. Quartus est in virtute ymaginativa; et iste est magis spiritualis quam precedens. Quintus est in virtute distinctiva. Sextus in virtute memorativa; et iste est maxime spiritualis; recipit enim medulam eius quod tres virtutes precedentes vel antecedentes separant a cortice" (pp. 58–59).

16 For an early Western statement of this point, influenced by Averroes, see *De potentiis animae et obiectis*, p. 150.

17 Averroes, *Compendium*, p. 54.

18 Rufus, *In DAn* 2.6.E5: "Dicit igitur quod ad indigentiam medii simile est in sono et odore, quia nec sonus nec odor tangens instrumentum proprium quo sentitur facit sensum, sed media prius moventur ab his et organa a medio sic moto. Et huius causa est, quia oportet haec fieri in esse magis spirituali in medio antequam recipiantur in organis, quia omne organum est quaedam media proportio suorum sensibilium" (ed. J. Ottman et al., pp. 361–362).

SPIRITUALITY AND PERCEPTION IN MEDIEVAL ARISTOTELIANISM 159

nature of the recipient.[19] By contrast, in current usage, though people are said to become more spiritual as they turn their attention to higher things, few of us suppose that their substance is thereby rarefied or dematerialized or that their forms undergo alteration and are released from incorporation so that they can serve a different purpose.

This is the first aspect in which our conception of spirituality as it might apply to perception differs radically from medieval conceptions. For Averroes and Rufus the forms undergo alteration, becoming more spiritual as they enter the medium and are released from incorporation. And at the same time the medium is changed. Rufus is most explicit about the change in percepts as they traverse the medium in the case of sound. Sound results from the collision of parts of air previously separated and/or by the separation of parts previous conjoined. This sets up a tremor that rarefies the air, not the air where the collision occurs, but the air some slight distance away from the collision; that tremor violently pulls one part of the succeeding air away from another, rarefying it. Accordingly as the sound goes from the struck air, through the rarefied air, to the sensitive organ, it becomes less material and more spiritual.[20]

A second difference can also be observed in the *Compendium* quotation above. As the reader will note, and as Deborah Black points out, for Averroes the primary explanandum is "the kind of abstraction that differentiates one level of cognition from another." Unlike Burnyeat and modern philosophers,[21] Averroes is not concerned with "individual human conscious awareness of an apprehended object."[22] Rather he is explaining a cognitive achievement, what causes the senses to see and the intellect to understand.

---

19 *Liber de causis*, A. Pattin (ed), *Tijdschrift voor philosophie*, vol. 28, 1966, p. 160, 9 (10), 98–99, ut citatur apud *Les auctoritates Aristotelis*, 11.12: "Quicquid recipietur ab alio recipitur per modum rei accipientis et non receptae" (J. Hamesse (ed), Leuven, Publications Universitaires, 1974, p. 232).

20 Rufus, *In DAn* 2.7.Q2: "Ad quod notandum quod omnis sonus aut fit ex violenta separatione et fractione partium prius coniunctarum, aut ex collisione partium prius separatarum.... Eius autem duratio fit quandoque per hoc quod corpus percussum remanet in tremore, et ex hoc movet aerem tremefaciendo ipsum. Et puto quod in aere illo percusso vel diviso per percussionem est sonus materialiter. In aere autem consequenter rarefacto per talem motum tremoris est sonus in esse suo spirituali; tremor enim ex hoc quod per violentiam distrahit unam partem ab alia rarefacit ipsum aerem et subtiliat eius materiam. Et per naturam qua aer est subtilior quam prius fuit potest recipere sonum in esse spiritualiori quam in aere percusso materialiter et corporaliter" (ed. J. Ottman et al., p. 376).

21 Burnyeat, "Aquinas on Spiritual Change," p. 141.

22 D. Black, "Models of the Mind: Metaphysical Presuppositions of the Averroist and Thomistic Accounts of Intellection," *Documenti e studi sulla tradizione filosofica medievale,* vol. 15, 2004, p. 320.

Like Averroes, Rufus was not trying to explain awareness or consciousness of a percept. He was trying to explain a physical process, albeit an immaterial physical process, that leads to sensation. Like Averroes, he explained that percepts were successively altered in the medium, the sense organs, the senses themselves, the common sense, and other apprehensive faculties, so that they could actualize our apprehensive capacities. Awareness is not the focus. Many phases of the process involve items of which there is no specific or independent awareness. The end result of the perceptual process is awareness of colour (of red, for instance). But there is, for example, no awareness of colour in the air, or of colour in the eye. The focus of the entire account is not on what the perceiver is aware of, but on how the perception of red is generated by physical (somatic and spiritual) processes. Modern theories might similarly deal with retinal images, neural processes, etc. Nobody would think we are specifically aware of the retinal image, still less of what is going on in the optic nerve. It is the same with the medieval theories. The background assumption might be of course that the whole process results in awareness of red, for example, but that awareness is not the focus of the explanatory account, only how the properties of a red material object get transferred perceptually into the soul.

This second major difference is between medieval and modern aims. Taken together these two differences indicate that for Rufus and Averroes perception is not a case where nothing happens, but rather a process in which forms are altered and faculties are perfected.

Supposing the reader will agree that setting out to describe how an organ or sense is affected or perfected by a received percept is different from explaining awareness, let us look now at why Rufus and his contemporaries regard perception as a spiritual process. Below we list several reasons why it was sensible to do so.

2 Reasons for Positing Spirituality in Explaining Perception

2.1 *Action over Great Distances*
One comparatively minor reason it was sensible to adopt the view that our percepts have spiritual being is that they are sometimes able to act over a great distance. Rufus and his contemporaries adopted this proof of the spirituality of percepts from Averroes,[23] who held that vultures perceiving scent at great

---

23 Responding to Aristotle, *De anima* 2.9.421b12–13.

SPIRITUALITY AND PERCEPTION IN MEDIEVAL ARISTOTELIANISM   161

distances (*quingenta milaria*), distances to which the material subject of corporeal odour could not extend, was evidence that perceived scent was spiritual.[24] As Burnyeat puts the point in his discussion of Aquinas, "there is not enough material for the job"; spiritual odor "in the medium extends beyond the point" where material odor is exhausted.[25]

What is most important about this passage, however, is that in it Averroes generalizes to all cases in which the medium through which percepts are perceived is external. Not only are odors present in the medium in spiritual being, but so too are sounds and colours. In such cases, too, we must distinguish between the corporeal and spiritual modes of percepts; the latter Averroes here calls 'intentions.'

2.2   *Bridging the Gap between Material and Immaterial Beings*

If action at a distance is a reason why it is sensible to posit percepts in spiritual being, a more basic reason is to address a major problem about how objects in the material world affect immaterial beings. To some extent Aristotle is concerned with the question what makes sensible objects capable of producing sensation.[26] But it was a particularly bothersome problem for medieval thinkers, since there is a general Neoplatonic and Augustinian principle according to which the spiritual is superior to and more powerful than the material, and hence an inferior cannot act on a superior.[27] More specifically, nothing material could affect an immaterial soul. Instead, as Rufus and his somewhat older contemporary, William of Auvergne,[28] explained, in apprehension, though nothing is received, the presence of a percept excites the soul and thereby

---

24   Averroes, *Commentarium magnum in Aristotelis De anima*, henceforth *In DAn*, 2.97, F.S. Crawford (ed), Cambridge, The Medieval Academy of America, 1953, pp. 277–278, here agreeing with Algazel; see *Algazel's Metaphysics*, J. Muckle (ed), Toronto, St. Michael's College, 1933, p. 165. But note that these vultures get around. In his history of the concept of intentionality, Sorabji notes their appearance first in Philoponus, *In Aristotelis De anima libros commentaria*, Michael Hayduck (ed.), Berlin, Reimer, 1897, 392.11–19. Making the opposite point, Avicenna claimed that odorous effluences could be carried far enough for vultures to sense them; see *Liber de anima* 1.2.4, S. van Riet (ed), pp. 148–154. For these and other interesting observations see R. Sorabji, "From Aristotle to Brentano: The Development of the Concept of Intentionality," *Oxford Studies in Ancient Philosophy*, Supplementary Volume, 1991, pp. 227–259.
25   Burnyeat, "Aquinas on Spiritual Change," pp. 138–139.
26   Aristotle, *Sense and Sensibility*, 3.439a16–17.
27   Augustine, *De libero arbitrio* 1.10–11, 3.1, W. Green and K. Daur (eds), Turnhout, Brepols, pp. 224–225, 275.
28   William of Auvergne, *De universo*, F. Hotot (ed), *Opera omnia 1*, 1674, 2.2.65, 74–75, pp. 914, 927–928.

makes it the case that the sensitive soul that is potentially a species or similitude becomes an actual similitude. But this is possible, according to Rufus, only because that percept has spiritual being in the sense organ.[29]

As we have said, Averroes introduced the concept of 'spirituality' into discussions of perception, but he was by no means the first to posit spiritual entities to bridge the gap between the material and the immaterial realms. This form of explanation has its origins in ancient and medieval medicine. In medieval medicine, spirits serve as intermediaries between corporeal and incorporeal things, or between dense and rarefied bodies.[30] And as instruments of the soul as it acts on the body.[31] The medical spirits were the most widely accepted: vital (associated with the heart), animal (associated with the brain), and natural (associated with the liver).[32]

---

29   Rufus, *In DAn* 2.11. Q2: "Et dicendum ad hoc quod plus est in anima sensitiva; cum fit enim sensibile in esse spirituali, immutat organum sensus. Et quia sensibile est in esse spirituali in organo et non materialiter, ex hoc potest immutare aliquo modo substantiam incorpoream, non quia aliquid coloris transmittitur in animam, sed species sensibilis in organo recepti aliquo modo alterat animam secundum quod unitur organo. Et alterando ipsam excitat ipsam ut convertat se supra se ipsam ut est eius similitudo. Anima ergo sic alterata a coloris specie convertit se supra se ipsam ut est eius similitudo, nihil eius recipiendo sed solam eius similitudinem actualem" (ed. J. Ottman et al., p. 441).

30   Avicenna, *Liber de anima seu Sextus de naturalibus* 5.8: "Primo igitur dicemus quod virtutum animalium corporalium vehiculum est corpus subtile, spirituale, diffusum in concavitatibus quod est spiritus.... Comparatio autem huius corporis ad subtilitatem humorum et evaporationem est sicut comparatio membrorum ad spissitudinem humorum" (S. van Riet (ed), Leiden, Brill, 1968, p. 175). Note that for Avicenna, spirits are corporeal, but they are less dense than humors, which are in turn less dense that our members.

    Roger Bacon, *Quaestione supra libros Primae Philosophiae Aristotelis*, R. Steele and F. Delorme (eds), *Opera hactenus inedita 10*, Oxford, Clarendon Press, 1930, p. 287, henceforth *OHI*: "Quod querit utrum sine medio vel non, dico quod anima potest considerari ad corpus, aut quantum ad actum uniendi, et sic nichil requiritur medium, aut quantum ad operationes suas, sic habet medium, scilicet spiritum, licet Aristoteles non loquatur de spiritu."

31   Galen, *De placitis Hippocratis et Platonis decretis*, I. Mueller (ed), Leipzig, Aedibus B.G. Teubneri, 1874, I, 603: "Consentaneum igitur est spiritum hunc in cerebri ventriculis, oriri atque idcirco eo coire arteriarum et venarum non parvam multitudinem, unde complexiones illae, quae choriodes appellantur, exsistunt, atque ipsum esse primum animi, ut dixi, instrumentum." Bacon, *Liber primus Communium naturalium* 1.4: "[S]piritus in animali est quoddam simile vapori qui fluit a corde in omnes partes animalis quod est instrumentum anime. Et cor continue ... emittit vapores subtiles ad confortacionem tocius corporis, qui vapores sunt spiritus subtiles generati ex sanguine puro" (R. Steele (ed), Oxford, Clarendon Press, 1911, *OHI* 3: 279).

32   Constantine the African, *Pantegni, Theorica* 4.19, *De spiritibus*: "Omnis ergo spiritus est tripertitus. Est enim naturalis, est vitalis vel spiritualis, est et animalis. Naturalis nascitur in epate, unde per venas ad tocius corporis vadit membra, virtutem naturalem regit et augmentat, actiones eius custodiens.... Spiritualis qui et vitalis spiritus dicitur in corde nascitur, vadens per arterias ad tocius corporis membra, spiritualem virtutem seu vitalem

SPIRITUALITY AND PERCEPTION IN MEDIEVAL ARISTOTELIANISM 163

Specifically, Galen connected sense with the animal spirit.[33] So when Rufus says that sensation is produced by animal spirits in conjunction with heat, he is thinking of a material cause, natural heat.[34] In so doing, he is appealing to generally accepted truths in medieval medicine.

Indeed, despite offering a materialist account of sensation, even Rene Descartes retains the animal spirits and like Galen connects them with the brain to serve as intermediaries between the brain and parts of the body.

Like Roger Bacon's version of spirits,[35] Descartes' animal spirits are associated with blood. And though like Bacon,[36] Descartes holds that such spirits are material, rather than immaterial, they are characterized by extreme rarefaction like Rufus' spiritual percepts in the medium. Here it is interesting that Descartes seeks to adapt to a purely mechanistic, materialist theory some of the features of the medieval theory that explained the interaction of body and soul in terms of immaterial, spiritual entities. Since Descartes sees animal spirits as communicating with the sense organs, not unexpectedly they function in some of the same ways as Galenic spirits.[37]

The influence of Galen in medieval Europe dates from at least as early as the eleventh century, when Constantine the African translated his works into Latin, and was reinforced in the twelfth century, when Gerard of Cremona translated Avicenna's great medical work as the *Canon*, a work greatly influenced by

---

augmentans atque regens actionesque eius custodiens. Spiritus animalis in cerebris nascitur ventriculis, per nervos tendens ad membra tocius corporis, unde animalis virtus regitur et augmentatur actionesque eius custodiuntur" ("The Chapter on the Spirits in the Pantegni of Constantine the African," in C. Burnett and D. Jacquart (eds), *Constantine the African and Ali ibn al-Abbas al-Magusi: The Pantegni and Related Texts*, Leiden, Brill, 1994, p. 114). How generally accepted these spirits were is evident from their description by the encyclopedists described by M.J. Ortúzar Escudero, "The Place of Sense Perception in Thirteenth-Century Encyclopaedias: Two Different Reading of Aristotle," *Revista Española de Filosofia Medieval*, vol. 25, 2018, pp. 101, 103, 107.

33 Galen, *On the Usefulness of the Parts of the Body (De usu partium)*, trans. M. May, Ithaca, Cornell University Press, 1968, pp. 402–403. Galen's pneuma psychikon, usually translated as 'animal spirit,' is translated as 'psychic pneuma' by C.U.M. Smith, E. Frixione, S. Finger, and W. Clower, *The Animal Spirit Doctrine and the Origins of Neurophysiology*, Oxford, Oxford University Press, 2012, p. 37.

34 Rufus, *In DAn* 2.11. E4.2: "Ignis autem nulli instrumento appropriatur, sed est communis omnibus, quia nullum organum est sensitivum sine calore. Et hoc est quia sensus fit per spiritus animales, cum quibus semper simul est calor naturalis" (ed. J. Ottman et al., p. 447). In support of the light thesis, *In DAn* 3.12.E4.1, ed. J. Ottman et al., pp. 612–613, maintains that animal spirits are lucid.

35 Bacon, *Liber primus Communium naturalium* 1.4, as quoted above.

36 Bacon, *Quaestiones supra libros octo Physicorum* 7, F. Delorme and R. Steele (eds), Oxford, 1935, *OHI* 13: 352, pp. 358–359.

37 René Descartes, *Les passions de l'ame, Œuvres de Descartes*, C. Adam and P. Tannéry (eds), Paris, Vrin, 1996, 1.7–13.

164   WOOD

Galen. So spirit and spirituality perform an essential explanatory function in linking immaterial souls with the material world.

According to medieval thinkers, not only do spirits serve as instruments of the soul that enable its apprehension of external things, but they are also instruments that allow the soul to act on the body. Thus the animal spirit responsible for sensation is also responsible for wakefulness; being awake is the result of animal spirits flowing to the senses, but not all effects of the ebb and flow of spirits are benign,[38] and paralysis can result from the restriction or obstruction of spirit.[39] Given that spirits are responsible for these sort of changes, we should remember that spiritual changes make quite a lot of things happen. True, in perception once percepts have been abstracted from their corporeal subject, nothing material is acting or being acted on. But the spirit world is going about its business: percepts are becoming more spiritual, species are being transmitted, and spirits are flowing. It is true that no "underlying material change" is posited in many medieval accounts of perception, or more precisely, material change is often reduced to an occasional cause of some sensations. But the physical changes medieval thinkers attributed to spirits are far different from those we think of today. And hence the very general function of spirits both shows how different medieval and modern concepts of spirituality are and explains why it makes sense for medievals to postulate them to bridge the gap between the external world percepts we perceive and our perceptual faculties.

For Averroes, who was not a Neoplatonist, bridging the gap between the material and immaterial realms was not the same kind of problem as it was for his Christian successors. Perhaps for that reason, spirituality does not play as much of a role in his *De anima* commentary as it does in Rufus.' And though Averroes was the first to introduce spirituality into discussions of perception

---

38   Avicenna, *Avicennae Canon medicinae*, vol. 1, Venice, Junctae, 1595, Fen 1, tr. 4, 3.4: "Vigilia quidem est dispositio animalis cum effunditur spiritus animalis ad instrumenta sensus et motus ut eis utatur. Sahara vero est superfluitas in vigilia et egressus a re naturali. Et eius quidem causa complexionalis est caliditas et siccitas propter igneitatem spiritus ... Et dicitur quod ille in quo sahara sit fortis deinde accidit ei tussis, moritur" (f. 201v). Henceforth *Canon*.

39   Avicenna, *Canon*, Fen 2, c. 2: "Cumque paralysis accipitur cum intentione mollificationis absolute, ... Et est sicut illud quod non communicat plurimae parti corporis aut uni lateri ipsius absque latere alio. Immo si necessarium fuerit, accidet uni membro, et videtur quod paralysis et mollificatio secundum plurimum fit propter retentionem spiritus. Causa vero retentionis est oppilatio aut separatio pororum ... Oppilatio autem aut est secundum semitam constrictionis pororum, aut secundum semitam prohibitionis ... aut secundum semitam rei aggregantis ambas res, et est apostema quare causa mollificationis et paralysis faciens abscisionem spiritus a membris est constrictio pororum" (f. 213v).

SPIRITUALITY AND PERCEPTION IN MEDIEVAL ARISTOTELIANISM 165

and apprehension, Rufus applied it more systematically and discussed it at much greater length. Nonetheless, we need to say more about what Rufus and his successors owe to Averroes.

2.3 Distinguishing Apprehensible Immaterial Forms from Material Forms

Perhaps most basically, Rufus owes to Averroes a claim about the respects in which the spiritual forms we immediately perceive are the same as and different from the forms that shape matter in the external world. And this is a departure from Aristotle as interpreted by Burnyeat, who holds that the form that sense organs "receive without matter is the very same form as exists with matter in the object perceived."[40] By contrast, Rufus agrees with Averroes that the forms we perceive are importantly different from the forms that shape matter. They are unincorporated, dehulled in Averroes' analogy so that though the marrow or essence remains the same, they have been spiritualized so that they serve another purpose and inhere in different subjects. According to Averroes there is a difference in being, in "definition and subject," or just "definition."[41] For Rufus in *In DAn* the difference is in 'being' (2.11.E1); in later works he also frequently adopts Averroes' phrase, "in name and definition."[42]

---

40 Burnyeat, "Aquinas on Spiritual Change," p. 149. Burnyeat, "*De anima II 5*," *Phronesis*, vol. 47, 2002, p. 76.

41 Averroes, *In DAn* 2.97, 2.121, F.S. Crawford (ed), pp. 232, 317; Averroes, *De memoria*, A.L. Shields and H. Blumberg (eds), *Compendium*, pp. 55–56.

42 See for example Rufus, *Contra Averroem 1.11*: "Et forte iubes similiter dicere de natura obiecta et sua idea recepta in intellectu <intellectum E>, scilicet quod sit eadem essentia et quod idea sit alia ipsa natura, et hoc est quia <vel forsan: quod E> nihil est aliud idea quam natura expressa in speciem vel idolum, modo tamen aliquo numerabiliter non est eadem essentia numero.... Et propter intellectus imbecilitatem grossum subiungatur exemplum: Intelligas per impossibile te unum et eundem numero simul et semel mortalem et glorificatum; nonne sic potero intelligere aliquo modo ideam esse idipsum quod natura obiecta, sed secundum esse alteratum? Aut iterum, dulcissime Deus, quod sit et maneat essentia coloris vel cuiusvis alterius obiecti, ipso tamen colore penitus destructo secundum suum nomen et definitionem? Videtur quod sic" (Erfurt UB, CA Q312.83va-vb).

Rufus, *Scriptum in Metaphysicam Aristotelis* 3.3.E2: "Consequenter ostendit quod non sunt formae intelligibiles actu per se exsistentes, convenientes tamen cum sensibilibus nomine et definitione" (S2322.72vb).

Rufus, *Sententiae Oxonienses* 2.13: "Quid de specie coloris hic in medio dicam? An color est? Nec color nec alia natura quam color; non res alterius praedicamenti. Haec species nomen et definitionem amisit albedinis, scilicet parentis, propter esse alterum, scilicet spirituale, quod comparative habet in medio et adhuc magis spirituale in organo et sensu. Vide an possit dici quod haec species propter praedictam convenientiam sit color, quia scilicet non alterius naturae est. Possit etiam insimul dici quod non sit color, eo quod nomen et definitionem coloris amisit; et hoc, quia nobilius esse adquisivit" (B62.132ra-rb).

Though different in their being – that is, being spiritual, rather than corporeal or incorporated – such forms are essentially the same as the forms that shape matter, but since their subject and purpose differs so does their definition. As spiritual beings they have the potential to produce psychological processes that cause apprehension.

Here Rufus and his successors owe to Averroes an explanation of how essentially the very same form can produce both corporeal colours and the apprehension of such colours. It is something of a mystery how the same form that produces natural changes in the external world of material subjects causes apprehension in the internal world of immaterial subjects. Why is cognitive assimilation so different from ordinary change? The colour red, for example, advening to external-world composites makes all of them red or redder. But, as Burnyeat points out, Aristotle's reliance on a difference in subjects to explain the difference in effect is precisely parallel to other purely natural differences caused by forms such as heat. Heat advening to some subjects solidifies them, while when applied to other subjects, it melts or liquifies them, as *Meteorology* 4 teaches. Hence no further explanation of the difference is necessary – at least if the form and the subject is material.

With Averroes we get a further explanation, however, and the apparent mystery is resolved. Immaterial, incorporeal subjects require spiritual forms. Thus the forms that produce cognitive assimilation are not entirely the same as those that act on material bodies, only essentially the same as those that act in the external world. The forms we apprehend are the precise spiritual or intentional counterparts of material forms we apprehend in virtue of them. And if this were not so, if the colour sensed were the same as the colour that makes an apple red or green, sensing would not produce apprehension. The eye might turn red, but the observer would not see red. Averroes argues this point from *DAn* 2.5.418a3–4, but of Rufus' earliest contemporaries, seemingly only Adam Buckfield adopts this argument, and though he repeats it, he does not explain it.[43]

Thus with the introduction of the concept of intentionality into Western scholasticism, the mystery shifts. We wonder how intentional forms are produced, how they differ from natural forms, and why they can cause cognitive assimilation of the corresponding natural forms.

Richard Rufus offers general answers to these questions. Of those offered in *In DAn*, one is the same answer as that provided by Averroes: the removal or abstraction of colour from a coloured object results in spiritual, not natural,

---

43   Adam Buckfield, *In DAn* 2.39, rrp.stanford.edu/BuckfieldDAn2.shtml, accessed February 2018.

SPIRITUALITY AND PERCEPTION IN MEDIEVAL ARISTOTELIANISM

colour that can act on the organ of sight by perfecting it. Rufus modifies that answer, however, to explain what causes that abstraction or release – namely, the presence of unincorporated light (*In DAn* 2.6.Q1, ed. J. Ottman et al., pp. 353–354). Rufus' *light thesis,* as I designate it, generalizes from the case of vision, claiming that for all percepts the presence of unincorporated light causes the change from natural to spiritual being.

2.4   Solving the Problem of Impedance

As Rufus points out, here assuming what Averroes states explicitly, another advantage of positing spiritual and incorporeal percepts is to avoid the problem of impedance. That is, if corporeal colour were present in the air when we see something, then it would be difficult for me to see a red object whose colour was transmitted through the same medium through which you see a green object, since two bodies cannot occupy the same place, and therefore corporeal greenness in the medium would apparently impede the reception of redness in the medium.

Rufus makes this point when discussing echoes at *In DAn* 2.7.Q1. He is responding to a problem that arises because echoes seem to involve local motion in opposite directions at the same time in the same place. Rufus' first response is to suppose that the sounds we hear in echoes – that is, both the initial sound and its reflection – are in spiritual being, and spiritual beings can move in opposite directions in the same place. Rufus assumes but does not state explicitly here that contraries in spiritual being are compatible.[44] Probably, the absence of an explicit statement is because this was generally assumed and very clearly stated by Averroes.[45]

On this account, echoes result from a spiritual change that releases sound into the medium in spiritual being. *In DAn* 2.7.Q1:

> His definition of echo seems to indicate that Aristotle intended to imply that there was local motion with sound, since there would not be reflection and return from an obstacle unless there were something direct that was prior....

---

44   Rufus himself takes it for granted in stating an objection in his *In Aristotelis De generatione et corruptione* 1.6.2: "Et dicet forte quod haec impressio sic recepta habet esse immateriale sicut species coloris in medio. Et propterea compatitur suum contrarium, nec destruitur ab illo" (N. Lewis and R. Wood (eds), Oxford, Oxford University Press, 2011, pp. 155–156).

45   See, for example, Averroes, *Libri Aristotelis De sensu et sensato* (*versio vulgata*), A.L. Shields and H. Blumberg (eds), *Compendium,* pp. 29–32.

On the contrary, opposite sounds produced in opposite directions are in the same expanse of air and are, as it were, borne away by the same air. But there cannot be simultaneous opposite local motions in the same expanse of air. Therefore local motion is not connected with sound.

To this it would be easy to reply, if we made one assumption – namely, that all sensibles are rooted in light as in one root, not that they are light; for we should not say that colour is light but rather that it is rooted in light.... Therefore we could say that some *being of incorporated light evolves into colour, and some being of incorporated light evolves into sound*, and so on for the other sensibles. And thus we could say that this change is not corporeal, but rather a spiritual change in the light itself.[46]

As the reader will note, Rufus is here making a statement not based on and, indeed, contrary to Averroes' account. He is stating what I called above the light thesis – namely, the claim that light is what enables sensible percepts to prompt apprehension in the senses, and moreover, it is light that is responsible for the transformation of sensibles from natural to spiritual or intentional being. And, in fact, the quotation above is Rufus' first statement of the light thesis as a general account of sensible qualities: all sensibles are rooted in light;[47]

---

46 Rufus, In DAn 2.7.Q1: "Per definitionem eius quod est echo [2.8.419b25–27] videtur quod velit Aristoteles innuere quod motus localis sit cum sono; non enim fieret reflexio sive reditio ad obstaculum nisi aliquid esset directum usque ad illud prius. Et non videtur quod sit ibi aliquid quod posset repercuti ad obstaculum nisi hoc fuerit aer, et ita ibi erit motus localis....

Contra: Soni oppositi facti in partes oppositas sunt in eadem particula aeris et quasi deferuntur per eundem aerem. Sed motus locales oppositi non possunt esse in eadem particula aeris simul. Ergo motus localis non est coniunctus cum sono.

Ad hoc posset faciliter responderi uno quodam supposito, scilicet quod omnia sensibilia radicantur in luce tamquam in una radice, non quod ipsa sint lux; non enim debet dici quod color sit lux sed radicatur in luce. In luce enim sunt duo, scilicet substantia lucis et suus splendor. Splendor autem lucis incorporatae color est. Et sicut dicitur de colore, similiter dicitur de aliis sensibilibus. Posset igitur dici quod aliquod esse lucis incorporatae cedit in colorem, et aliquod esse lucis incorporatae cedit in sonum, et sic de aliis sensibilibus. Et sic posset dici quod haec immutatio non est corporalis, sed mutatio spiritualis ipsius lucis. Sed illud non consonat sententiae verborum Aristotelis; non enim dicit Aristoteles 'cum lux depellitur' sed 'cum aer depellitur'" (ed. J. Ottman et al., pp. 372–373).

47 But note that the rooting of sensibles ultimately in the nature of light does not exclude their initially being rooted in something common to all the sensibles of a particular sense – sounds, for example, in the case of hearing. See Rufus, In DAn 2.10.Q2, ed. J. Ottman et al., pp. 420–423.

SPIRITUALITY AND PERCEPTION IN MEDIEVAL ARISTOTELIANISM

some being of incorporated light evolves into each of the sensibles, and specifically its splendour, but not its substance, evolves into colour, a claim which is probably chiefly important for its denial that sensible percepts evolve from light as substance. According to *In DAn* 2.7.Q1, as they inhere in external-world objects, all sensibles evolve from incorporated light, not just colour, but also sound and every other natural, external sensible. And, as we saw above, the presence of unincorporated light releases them into spiritual being.

What is the spiritual change at issue here? Not the evolution of light into colour or sound, but the evolution of light incorporated as sound into unincorporated or spiritual sound. If this were not what Rufus means, then his reply would not resolve the problem of contrary motions in the same place. So here we have Rufus speaking of light rather than air as a bearer of percepts and generalizing from the case of colour to the cases of sound and other sensibles. Seeing that this explanation is not in accord with Aristotle, *In DAn* also offers an alternative account, but disavows this first account only as an interpretation of Aristotle's discussion of echoes. And as we saw above, this is Rufus' answer to the question, what causes the transformation of natural percepts into spiritual beings capable of perfecting and actualizing sense organs, which once moved, prompt the senses to act.

2.5 *Offering a Unifying Characteristic for the Percepts of the Common Sense*

Postulating spiritual percepts and defending the light thesis advocated by two of Rufus' most influential predecessors[48] has another advantage.

Aristotle's account of perception stipulates a single distinctive kind of percept for four of the five special senses. At least on Rufus' account, they are colour for sight, sound for hearing, odor for hearing, and flavour for taste. The only case in which the percepts of a sense cannot be reduced to a single nature is touch, which is sensitive to a wide range of qualities. But according to Rufus, even the percepts of touch can be reduced to two pairs of contrary qualities: the hot and the cold, and the dry and the wet.[49]

---

48   Alexander of Hales, *Quaestiones disputatae "antequam esset frater"* 18.37, BFS, 19: 31. More extensive is Grosseteste's discussion in his *Hexaëmeron*, which differs from Rufus' perhaps principally because it assumes that vision is by extramission. See particularly Robert Grosseteste, *Hexaëmeron*, R. Dales and S. Gieben (eds), London, British Academy, 1982, 2.10.1, p. 98, and his *Commentarius in Posteriorum analyticorum libros*, P. Rossi (ed), Firenze, L.S. Olschki, 1982, 2.4, pp. 386–387.

49   Rufus, *In DAn* 2.10.E2: "[Q]uamvis ipsius auditus sint plures contrarietates, non tamen sic sunt plures quin reducantur ad unum aliquid, ut ad naturam soni, et similiter est in visu. Ipsius autem tactus sic sunt plures contrarietates quod non sunt ad aliquid unum

However, Aristotle offers no common characterization of the percepts of the common sense and indeed has little to say about that sense. Rufus, by contrast, explains that there is one nature in virtue of which all the percepts of the common sense act on it; it is unincorporated or spiritual light.[50] Of course, according to the light thesis, this is the nature in virtue of which all the percepts of the special senses act as well. But in the case of the common sense, this is the single unifying characteristic for a sense whose percepts do not otherwise share a unifying character.

For Rufus, there is another, more important manner in which the common sense is common – namely, that it is the cause or root in which the proper senses are founded. Moreover, what is common to the percepts of the common sense should not be confused with the common sensibles – motion, rest, magnitude, shape, and number – that are called common because they are sensed by more than one particular sense.[51] Nonetheless, Rufus surely took it to be an advantage of the light thesis that it allowed an account of the common sense that more closely paralleled the accounts of the five special senses.

2.6 *Making the Process of Perception Fit the Faculties of Perception*

Medievals did not regard sensation as a material process, but rather as a case in which immaterial percepts act on unextended senses or sensory faculties. They associate immateriality with apprehension. Why is that? No doubt an adequate answer to that question would be complex. For our purposes, however, it suffices to say first that the association was widely assumed. Indeed, some scholars today hold that this is Aristotle's own view.[52] Second, we should note that most Aristotelians suppose that our apprehensive faculties are incorporeal and unextended. Thus it is an advantage of postulating spirituality that it describes the objects that perfect and actualize them as equally unextended and immaterial.

---

    reducibiles; duae enim contrarietates primae, scilicet calidum/frigidum, humidum/ siccum, non sunt ulterius ad unum reducibiles" (ed. J. Ottman et al., p. 406).

50 Rufus, *In DAn* 2.12.Q2: "Sed tamen omnia sensibilia per naturam unius immutant instrumentum sensus communis, quod tamen unum nihil est de illis sensibilibus, sed simpliciter aliud secundum essentiam, ut per naturam lucis" (ed. J. Ottman et al., p. 473).

51 Rufus, *In DAn* 2.5.N1: "Et intelligendum quod alio modo communitatis dicitur sensus communis esse communis et sensibilia communia esse communia. Sensus enim communis dicitur communis communitate causae, scilicet quia sensus communis est una radix in quo tamquam in radice fundantur proprii sensus. Communia autem sensibilia dicuntur communia quia pluribus sensibus propriis sentiuntur" (ed. J. Ottman et al., p. 350).

52 P. Adamson, "Avicenna and His Commentators on Human and Divine Self-Intellection," in D.N. Hasse and A. Bertolacci (eds), *The Arabic, Hebrew and Latin Reception of Avicenna's Metaphysics*, Berlin, De Gruyter, 2012, pp. 99–100.

SPIRITUALITY AND PERCEPTION IN MEDIEVAL ARISTOTELIANISM

Taken together, the advantages of positing spirituality and unincorporated light are most basically that it bridges the gap between the external material world and the internal immaterial world, and it explains how the forms that shape sensation and thought differ from the forms that shape matter. In the external world, it solves the problems of impedance and the great distance over which some sensibles act. Within the soul, it offers a unifying description of the objects of the common sense, objects that are naturally appropriate to the immaterial apprehensive faculties.

3   What Is Left if There Is No Material Process Underlying Perception?

As Burnyeat indicates, many medieval thinkers explained perception as a process that has no "underlying material process."[53] Perhaps for Rufus there is a minimal material basis – namely, the physicians' *calor naturalis*:[54] "the natural warmth that was life-maintaining when balanced with the *humidum radicale* or quintessential moisture."[55]

Supposing that even in Rufus' case, what material basis there is is minimal, the question naturally arises, what is its basis? With Aristotle, Rufus holds that the percepts of every sense are transmitted across a medium. With Averroes, Rufus postulates a series of increasingly immaterial faculties. Within the body, there are sense organs. As Rufus expounds Aristotle's saying that every sense is a kind of mean between opposite percepts [2.11.424a4],[56] this saying pertains to our sense organs. Thus every sense organ is essentially constituted as a mediate proportion of all its percepts in spiritual being.[57] According to Rufus,

---

53   Burnyeat, "Aquinas on Spiritual Change," pp. 137, 144.

54   Rufus, *In DAn* 2.11.E4.2: "Ignis autem nulli instrumento appropriatur, sed est communis omnibus, quia nullum organum est sensitivum sine calore. Et hoc est quia sensus fit per spiritus animales, cum quibus semper simul est calor naturalis" (ed. J. Ottman et al., p. 447).

55   See L. DeMaitre, *Medieval Medicine: The Art of Healing, from Head to Toe*, Santa Barbara, Praeger, 2013, p. 37.

56   Aristotle, *De anima* 2.11.424a4: "sensus enim est quasi medium inter contrarietatem in sensibilibus" (in Averroes, *In DAn* 2.118, F.S. Crawford (ed), CCAA 6.1, p. 313). Cf. Aristotle, *De anima*, versio deterior: "tanquam sensu ut medietate quadam existente in sensibilibus contrarietatis" (in Anonymous, *Lectura in librum De anima*, R. Gauthier (ed), p. 399).

57   Rufus, *In DAn* 2.10.Q2: "Sed contra hoc videtur quiddam quod dicit inferius [2.11.422b24–25], scilicet quod omnis sensus est medietas quaedam suorum sensibilium, id est, organum cuiuslibet sensus gratia suae ultimae completionis" (ed. J. Ottman et al., p. 421). See also *In DAn* 2.4.Q1: "Dicendum quod omne organum virtutis sensitivae est quaedam media proportio omnium suorum sensibilium spiritualiter exsistentium" (ed. J. Ottman et al., p. 337).

when they reach the sense organs' mediate proportion of contraries in spiritual being, all percepts have acquired spiritual being, most of them as they traverse the medium.

Within the sense organs, this mediate proportion of the relevant percepts is potentially capable of beginning the process of perception. Being intermediate, this proportion is neutral, such that it is equally capable of being affected by white and black, sharp and flat, bitter and sweet. When percepts in spiritual being reach an organ's mediate proportion, it is altered, but this is not ordinary alteration. The alteration that completes the sense organ is not natural alteration, or alteration properly speaking, in which one contrary is corrupted and replaced by another, but rather it is reception or perfection without corruption; it perfects the sense organ by conferring a previously non-existent disposition.[58] Percepts in spiritual being perfect sense organs. This kind of alteration, alteration broadly considered, realizes a perfection in the sense organ that is a first actuality or disposition.

Once a sense organ is perfected, the sense that is rooted in this organ is itself altered in another special way.[59] The percepts in the sense organs are not transmitted to the sense faculties, and hence the senses do not thereby acquire new forms from outside themselves. Rather, the senses are prompted by the alteration in their organs actually to consider the preexisting forms that correspond to the percepts or sensible species in the sense organs that excited them. Prior to this excitement, such sensible species were already present in these senses,

---

58 Rufus, *In DAn* 2.4.E2.2: "Sequitur pars tertia in qua dividit hoc nomen 'pati': Proprie enim dictum pati consistit in corrumpendo dispositionem praehabitam et recipiendo dispositionem non prius habitam; pati autem non proprie dictum sed communiter consistit in altero dictorum, scilicet solum in recipiendo dispositionem prius non habitam. Et huiusmodi pati ab eo quod est actu est magis salus eius quod est in potentia sic passiva quam corruptio vel passio simpliciter....

  Et subiungit exemplum de secundo modo in simili (scilicet, sicut habens scientiam non actu considerans est in potentia passiva respectu eius quod est speculari, et fit speculans), subiungens quod huiusmodi pati aut non est alterari, cum in patiente non sit alicuius corruptio sed solum modo perfectionis inductio, aut est alius modus alterationis ab alterari proprie dicto .... [A]ut non dicendum est illud esse pati quod dicitur pati iam dicto modo secundo, aut dicendum duos esse modos alterationis secundum duplex pati (scilicet, unum mutationem a contrario sive a privatione in dispositionem oppositam, alterum autem esse mutationem alicuius in maiorem perfectionem)" (ed. J. Ottman et al., pp. 341–342).

59 Rufus, *In DAn* 2.4.Q1: "Verum est quod immediate non agit, sed mediante organo in quo radicatur ipsa anima, quo alterato per consequens alteratur et anima" (ed. J. Ottman et al., p. 337). See also *In DAn* 2.11.Q2, ed. J. Ottman et al., pp. 435–436.

SPIRITUALITY AND PERCEPTION IN MEDIEVAL ARISTOTELIANISM 173

but not being considered. In this case of alteration broadly considered, the perfection realized is second actuality, and the sense operates.[60]

For the sake of an example, consider the case of a vulture who finds dead animals by smell. In this case the sensible organ receives a percept, the scent of rotting carrion in spiritual being; this species perfects the organ by conferring on it a new disposition that it did not have before. When the organ is in that state, the sense of smell, which previously only had the potential to smell carrion, is stimulated actually to sense the same species. In other words, it smells dead animals. In the process the sense organ that was in pure potential acquires first actuality, and the sense itself that was already in first actuality gains second actuality.

Miles Burnyeat sees a closely related distinction regarding alteration in Aristotle,[61] but instead of speaking of first and second actuality, he speaks of potentiality. Second potentiality is what we here call first actuality. Burnyeat would call the alteration that perfects the sense organ unordinary alteration; its exercise, extraordinary. Following Aristotle, Burnyeat like Rufus considers the example of a human knower. A human being who has not learned anything is a knower in first potentiality. Once she learns something she can call to mind, she has achieved second potentiality or first actuality. When she exercises her knowledge, she is in second actuality.[62]

Of all our senses, vision is the most spiritual according to Rufus.[63] It is the most spiritual because its percepts are maximally spiritual according to Rufus, probably because unlike other percepts, colour is transmitted instantly and

---

60   Rufus, *In DAn* 3.6.N1: "Et intelligendum quod sicut duplex est perfectio [cf. *DAn* 2.1.412a10–11], scilicet una quae consistit in adquisitione formae et alia quae consistit in exeundo ad operationem per formam prius adquisitam, similiter est duplex motus, scilicet vel in perfectionem primam, et sic non movetur sensitivum a sensibili, aut in perfectionem secundam, scilicet ut ex forma habita egrediatur suus actus, et de huiusmodi motu intendit hic" (ed. J. Ottman et al., p. 558).

61   M. Burnyeat, "*De anima II 5*," *Phronesis*, vol. 47, 2002, pp. 48–66.

62   For a more extended discussion of Rufus on the difference between different kinds of potentiality and actuality see Rega Wood and Michael Weisberg, "Interpreting Aristotle on Mixture: Problems about Elemental Composition from Philoponus to Cooper," *Studies in History and Philosophy of Science*, vol. 35, 2004, pp. 681–706.

63   Rufus, *In DAn* 3.2.E5: "Et hoc quia sensus visus est subtilissimus sensuum sive maxime sensus, propter quod in Graeco accepit nomen a luce, et quia etiam melius permanent sensibilia in animo quae comprehenduntur per visum quam quae per alios sensus. Et hoc quia ipsa sensibilia sunt similia suis sensibus, colores autem inter omnia sensibilia maxime habent esse spirituale, et sensus visus de numero sensuum maxime spiritualis est, et propterea melius conservantur visibilia" (ed. J. Ottman et al., p. 496).

does not have material being in its medium, diaphanous air or water.[64] By contrast with colours, sounds and other percepts require a medium in which to achieve spiritual being.[65] They have material being as they initially enter their medium, and so they can be affected by natural material changes. The maximal spirituality of unincorporated colours in the medium Rufus presumably attributes to their not being subject to natural change.

4 Conclusions

Not every medieval thinker offers as completely spiritual an account of perception as Rufus. According to Roger Bacon, for example, percepts in the medium have material being and are only spiritual in a qualified sense.[66] However, for the most part, medieval thinkers like Rufus and like Aquinas offer a thoroughly spiritual account of perception. And, as we have seen, this was a sensible account, given the constraints within which they operate. However, since having spiritual being meant such different things to medieval thinkers than it does today, and it neither does, nor was intended to, explain principally awareness of the sensible world, it is an account that can easily mislead.

Was it Aristotelian? That depends in part on whether you think that Aristotle was primarily concerned to explain awareness rather than the process that leads to it. If so, neither Rufus nor any of his contemporaries was an Aristotelian. Neither was Rufus an Aristotelian in the sense that he principally sought accurately to interpret Aristotle. But if you suppose that Aristotle's aim was to explain what happens when we see, hear, touch etc., why animals do and plants do not sense, and so on, then Rufus shared Aristotle's aim.

The light thesis, however, was certainly not Aristotelian, and spirituality is not an Aristotelian concept; Galenic spirituality is rather a post-Aristotelian concept. However, immateriality is an Aristotelian concept, and spirituality was part of the best medical theory of the time, which one is tempted to think

---

64   Rufus, *In DAn* 2.7.Q2: "Ex his patet ratio quare sonus non generat speciem suam in medio subito, sed successive. Quia enim tremor est motus localis, rarefaciendo autem medium successive per tremorem disponit medium ad receptionem soni spiritualiter, ideo generat speciem soni successive; non forte quia non possit sonus subito immutare quantum esset de se si esset medium sufficienter dispositum. Et potest ista successio imaginari sicut si successive illuminaretur medium ad receptionem speciei coloris, et diaphanum illuminatum solum reciperet sicut successive illuminaretur, tunc successive reciperet" (ed. J. Ottman et al., p. 377).

65   Rufus, *In DAn* 2.6.E5, as quoted above.

66   Bacon, *Quaestiones supra libros octo Physicorum* 7, *OHI* 13, pp. 352, 358–359.

would have at least interested Aristotle if he had lived centuries later. And though Aristotle did not claim that vision was the most spiritual sense, he did hold, at least in the translation available in 1230–1240, that vision is the maximal sense, and accordingly its sensations are the most persistent.[67] Moreover, Rufus is definitely following Aristotle in distinguishing the changes that occur in perception from those involved in ordinary alteration.

Perhaps, however, we might be better advised to address other questions, such as the impact of Neoplatonism on the gap Rufus posited between the spiritual and the corporeal. Or still better, we might ask whether Rufus was an Averroist, and here the answer is clearer. Rufus took from Averroes his explanation of how apprehended forms differ from the forms that shape the material world. He was concerned like Averroes with impedance and with the problem of sensation over a great distance. As Reńe Gauthier would put it, Rufus was part of the first Averroism of the early thirteenth century.[68]

And finally, Rufus was also an independent thinker. In his later works, he developed a distinction that enabled him not to concern himself further about a gap between the material and the immaterial in perception.[69] He further developed Aristotle's distinction between ordinary change and the alteration involved in perception. Similarly, his version of the theory of spirituality was further adumbrated and more systematic than Averroes.' And Rufus came to believe that spiritual forms did not belong to the categories Aristotle described. Instead, Rufus held that the distinction between the substances and accidents of the natural world and what he later preferred to call the species forms of the immaterial world was necessary and useful. Indeed, ignorance of it was a dangerous source of error.[70]

However, Rufus could not have developed this theory of perception without the close study of Aristotle's *De anima* he presented in his *Sententia cum quaestionibus in libros De anima,* with the guidance of Averroes. And in this sense Rufus certainly was a Peripatetic philosopher. He was also an insightful interpreter of Aristotle, and particularly for readers sensitive to the differences between ancient, medieval, and modern concepts and terminology, his *Sententia*

---

67 Aristotle, *De Anima* 3.3.429a2–4.

68 R.-A. Gauthier, "Notes sur les débuts (1225–1240) du premier 'averroïsme,'" *Revue des sciences philosophiques et théologiques*, vol. 66, 1982, pp. 321–374. Cf. B.C. Bazán, "Was There Ever a 'First Averroism'?" in J. Aertsen and A. Speer (eds), *Geistesleben im 13. Jahrhundert*, Berlin, De Gruyter, 2000, pp. 31–53.

69 For the later works see M. Etchemendy and R. Wood, "*Speculum animae*: Richard Rufus on Perception and Cognition," *Franciscan Studies*, vol. 69, 2011, pp. 53–115. Henceforth *SAn*.

70 Rufus, *SAn* 2, pp. 124–125.

cum quaestionibus is well worth consulting as they seek to understand Aristotle's *De anima* themselves.[71]

Bibliography

Primary Literature

Adam Buckfield, *In De anima, Liber 2*, rrp.stanford.edu/Buckfield*DA*n2.shtml, accessed February 2018.

Alexander of Hales, *Magistri Alexandri de Hales Quaestiones disputatae "antequam esset frater,"* Quaracchi, Collegium S. Bonaventurae, 1960.

Aristotle, *De anima, translatio vetus, versio deterius*, R. Gauthier (ed), *Anonymi Magistri Artium* (1245–1250), *Lectura in librum De anima a quodam discipulo reportata*, Ms. Roma Naz. V.E. 828, Grottaferrata, Collegium S. Bonaventurae, 1985.

Augustine, *De libero arbitrio*, W. Green and K. Daur (eds), Turnhout, Brepols, 1970.

Averroes, *Commentarium magnum in Aristotelis De anima*, F.S. Crawford (ed), Cambridge, The Medieval Academy of America, 1953.

Averroes, *Compendium librorum Aristotelis qui Parva naturalia vocantur*, A.L. Shields and H. Blumberg (eds), Cambridge, The Medieval Academy of America, 1949.

Avicenna, *Avicennae Canon medicinae*, vol. 1, Venice, Junctae, 1595.

Avicenna, *Liber de anima seu Sextus de naturalibus*, S. van Riet (ed), vol. IV-V, Leiden, Brill, 1968.

Constantine the African, *Pantegni*, in C. Burnett (ed), "The Chapter on the Spirits in the Pantegni of Constantine the African," in C. Burnett and D. Jacquart (eds), *Constantine the African and Ali ibn al-Abbas al-Magusi, The Pantegni and Related Texts*, Leiden, Brill, 1994.

De potentiis animae et obiectis, D. Callus (ed), "The Powers of the Soul: An Early Unpublished Text," *Recherches de théologie ancienne et médiévale*, vol. 19, 1952, pp. 411–445.

Galen, *De placitis Hippocratis et Platonis decretis*, I. Mueller (ed), Leipzig, Aedibus B.G. Teubneri, 1874.

Galen, *On the Usefulness of the Parts of the Body (De usu partium)*, trans. M. May, Ithaca, Cornell University Press, 1968.

Ghazalli, *Algazel's Metaphysics*, J.T. Muckle (ed), Toronto, St. Michael's College, 1933.

John Philoponus, *In Aristotelis De anima libros commentaria*, Michael Hayduck (ed.), Berlin, Reimer, 1897.

---

71 Thanks for helping me understand this subject go to my colleagues on the Richard Rufus Project, to Alan Code and Santiago Melo Arias, and to my fellow editors, Christopher J. Martin, Neil Lewis, and Jennifer Ottman.

Liber de causis, A. Pattin (ed), *Tijdschrift voor philosophie*, vol. 28, 1966, pp. 90–203.

Ps. Buckfield, *De anima*, Oxford, Merton College 272.

René Descartes, *Les passions de l'ame*, in *Œuvres de Descartes*, C. Adam and P. Tannéry (eds), Paris, Vrin, 1996.

Richard Rufus of Cornwall, *Contra Averroem* 1.11, Erfurt, Bibl. Univ., Amplon. Q312, fol. 81va-86rb.

Richard Rufus of Cornwall, *In Aristotelis De generatione et corruptione*, N. Lewis and R. Wood (eds), Oxford, Oxford University Press, 2011.

Richard Rufus of Cornwall, *Sententia cum quaestionibus in libros De anima Aristotelis*, J.R. Ottman, R. Wood, N. Lewis, and C.J. Martin (eds), Oxford, Oxford University Press, 2019.

Richard Rufus of Cornwall, *Sententiae Oxonienses*, Oxford, Balliol College, Codex 62.

Robert Grosseteste, *Commentarius in Posteriorum analyticorum libros*, P. Rossi (ed), Firenze, L.S. Olschki, 1982.

Robert Grosseteste, *Hexaëmeron*, R. Dales and S. Gieben (eds), London, British Academy, 1982.

Roger Bacon, *Liber primus Communium naturalium. Partes tertia et quarta*, R. Steele (ed), *Opera hactenus inedita 3*, Oxford, Clarendon Press, 1911.

Roger Bacon, *Quaestiones supra libros octo Physicorum*, F. Delorme and R. Steele (eds), *Opera hactenus inedita 13*, Oxford, Clarendon Press, 1935.

Roger Bacon, *Quaestiones supra libros Primae Philosophiae Aristotelis*, R. Steele and F. Delorme (eds), *Opera hactenus inedita 10*, Oxford, Clarendon Press, 1930.

William of Auvergne, *De universo*, F. Hotot (ed), *Opera omnia 1*, Paris, 1674; reprinted Frankfurt am Main, Minerva, 1963.

Secondary Literature

Adamson, Peter, "Avicenna and His Commentators on Human and Divine Self-Intellection," in D.N. Hasse and A. Bertolacci (eds), *The Arabic, Hebrew and Latin Reception of Avicenna's Metaphysics*, Berlin, DeGruyter, 2012, pp. 97–122.

Bazán, Bernardo Carlos, "Was There Ever a 'First Averroism'?" in J. Aertsen and A. Speer (eds), *Geistesleben im 13. Jahrhundert*, Berlin, De Gruyter, 2000, pp. 31–53.

Black, Deborah, "Averroes on the Spirituality and Intentionality of Sensation," in P. Adamson (ed), *The Age of Averroes, Arabic Philosophy in the Sixth/Twelfth Century*, London, The Warburg Institute, 2011, pp. 159–174.

Black, Deborah, "Models of the Mind, Metaphysical Presuppositions of the Averroist and Thomistic Accounts of Intellection," *Documenti e studi sulla tradizione filosofica medievale*, vol. 15, 2004, pp. 319–352.

Burnyeat, Myles, "Aquinas on Spiritual Change in Perception," in D. Perler (ed), *Ancient and Medieval Theories of Intentionality*, Leiden, Brill, 2001, pp. 129–153.

Burnyeat, Myles, "*De anima* II 5," *Phronesis*, vol. 47, 2002, pp. 48–66.

Burnyeat, Myles, "How Much Happens When Aristotle Sees Red and Hears Middle C?" in M.C. Nussbaum and A.O. Rorty (eds), Essays on Aristotle's "De anima," Oxford, Clarendon Press, 1995.

Burnyeat, Myles, "Is an Aristotelian Philosophy of Mind Still Credible: A Draft," in M.C. Nussbaum and A.O. Rorty (eds), *Essays on Aristotle's "De anima,"* Oxford, Clarendon Press, p. 1992.

DeMaitre, Luke, *Medieval Medicine: The Art of Healing, from Head to Toe*, Santa Barbara, Praeger, 2013.

Etchemendy, Matthew and Wood, Rega, "*Speculum animae*: Richard Rufus on Perception and Cognition," *Franciscan Studies*, vol. 69, 2011, pp. 53–115.

Gauthier, René-Antoine, "Notes sur les débuts (1225–1240) du premier 'averröisme,'" *Revue des sciences philosophiques et théologiques*, vol. 66, 1982, pp. 321–374.

Hamesse, Jacqueline (ed), *Les auctoritates Aristotelis. Un florilège médiéval. Étude historique et édition critique*, Leuven, Publications Universitaires, 1974.

Ortúzar Escudero, María José, "The Place of Sense Perception in Thirteenth-Century Encyclopaedias: Two Different Readings of Aristotle," *Revista Española de Filosofía Medieval*, vol. 25, 2018, pp. 99–123.

Smith, C.U.M., Frixione, Eugenio, Finger, Stanley, and Clower, William, *The Animal Spirit Doctrine and the Origins of Neurophysiology*, Oxford, Oxford University Press, 2012.

Sorabji, Richard, "Aristotle on Sensory Processes and Intentionality: A Reply to Myles Burnyeat," in D. Perler (ed), *Ancient and Medieval Theories of Intentionality*, Leiden, Brill, 2001, pp. 49–61.

Sorabji, Richard, "From Aristotle to Brentano: The Development of the Concept of Intentionality," *Oxford Studies in Ancient Philosophy*, Supplementary Volume, 1991, pp. 227–259.

Wood, Rega and Weisberg, Michael, "Interpreting Aristotle on Mixture: Problems about Elemental Composition from Philoponus to Cooper," *Studies in History and Philosophy of Science*, vol. 35, 2004, pp. 681–706.

CHAPTER 7

The Escape Artist: Robert Kilwardby on Objects as *sine qua non* Causes

Elena Bălțuță

My aim in this chapter is to shed light on the causal role played by external objects in Robert Kilwardby's theory of sense perception. This issue is highly puzzling because of two premises that Kilwardby is commited to: 1. The sensory soul perceives corporeal objects. 2. The sensory soul cannot be acted upon by corporeal objects. The problem with the two premises is that they appear to be mutually inconsistent. On the one hand, if the sensory soul perceives corporeal objects, then Kilwardby is not entitled to say that corporeal objects cannot act upon the sensory soul; on the other hand, if the sensory soul cannot be acted upon by corporeal objects, then Kilwardby is not entitled to say that the sensory soul perceives corporeal objects. To avoid inconsistency, Kilwardby could choose one of the two premises and reject the other. He could either say that the sensory soul perceives corporeal objects, and hence it can be acted upon by them, or that the sensory soul cannot be acted upon by corporeal objects, and hence it does not perceive them. However, Kilwardby instead manages to find a viable third solution to escape this difficulty. According to my reading, the solution is to understand the corporeal object as playing the role of a *sine qua non* cause for perception. A *sine qua non* cause is, as its name suggests, a cause without which something is not the case. The corporeal object is that without which perception cannot take place, but, at the same time, it plays no active role in eliciting perception. To argue in favour of my reading, I will (§ 1) analyse the manner in which Kilwardby appropriates the principle of ontological hierarchy, which does not allow corporeal objects to act upon the sensory soul, (§ 2) spell out the kind of agent the sensory soul is and how much its activity extends, and (§§ 3, 4) elaborate on the causal role played by the corporeal object. Developing this argument will also allow me to dispel some apparent insufficiency that Kilwardby's theory of sense perception was accused of in contemporary scholarship.[1]

---

1 I have in mind José Filipe Silva's contention that Kilwardby is not able to account consistently for the proportionality between the change produced in the body by the corporeal object and the corresponding activity of the sensory soul. See J.F. Silva, *Robert Kilwardby on the Human Soul: Plurality of Forms and Censorship in the Thirteenth Century*, Leiden, Brill, 2012, p. 159.

© KONINKLIJKE BRILL NV, LEIDEN, 2020 | DOI:10.1163/9789004413030_008

1 The Principle of Ontological Hierarchy

My analysis begins with the assumption that Kilwardby grounds his epistemology on ontology. By this, I mean that the ontological framework sets certain margins within which he can build his epistemology. In the particular case of sense perception, I hypothesize that Kilwardby's ontology imposes a limit on causation: as a direct consequence of endorsing the principle of ontological hierarchy, upwards causation, that is an ontologically inferior entity causing an act in another entity that is ontologically superior, does not have a place in his theoretical edifice. This is why he has to adopt a particular strategy when accounting for the content of perception. For example, compared to the naturalist approach of his fellow Dominican, Thomas Aquinas, he has to stress different attributes of the soul, like its activity. The first step in my investigation of the causal role the corporeal object plays in Kilwardby's theory of sense perception will thus consist in the examination of his ontology. I will continue pursuing this task in a comparative manner.

1.1 Kilwardby and Aquinas: Comparative Analysis of the Principle of Ontological Hierarchy

I will, of course, not dive too deep into Kilwardby's ontology. Such an endeavor would require a study of its own. Instead, I will focus mainly on the abovementioned principle of hierarchy, which cuts through his entire view of the world and bears relevance on how causation works. The principle is very common among medieval philosophers, especially among those indebted to Augustine, and its main claim is that the world is hierarchically structured into different, irreducible, levels. The criterion for distinguishing between levels is their degree of being. But one should be careful with ascribing such a view exclusively to Augustinians. In fact, the same architecture of the world was also adopted by someone like Aquinas, who is rather an Aristotelian.[2] He too accepts, like his contemporaries, that there is an ontological difference between God, angels, and corporeal creatures. However, even though Kilwardby's and Aquinas' worlds are structurally similar, the way they understand the causal interaction between entities from different ontological levels is quite dissimilar. While in an Aristotelian picture, like that of Aquinas, causation, by transfer of form, works both bottom-up and top-down,[3] in an Augustinian framework, like that

---

2   Thomas Aquinas, *De substantiis separatis, Opera omnia 40*, Rome, Ad Sanctae, 1968, cap. 8, co.

3   For Aquinas, corporeal objects emit species which transfer the form of the object to the sense organ of sentient beings and thus to the soul. It is in this way that perception occurs. The

of Kilwardby, causation works only top-down. The gist of this difference lies in the way Aristotelians and Augustinians, in this case Aquinas and Kilwardby, understand the nobility of the agent over the patient.[4] This is an important aspect, because it can help us understand better Kilwardby's concept of causation, particularly the reason for which he thinks objects cannot act upon souls.

According to Aquinas, there are two requirements for an agent to act upon a patient, that is, for it to transfer a form: (1) the agent has to possess in act a form and (2) the patient has to possess in potentiality the same form. The actual possession of the form is what makes the agent nobler than the patient. Think, for instance, of a hot cup of tea affecting the hand of a person. For that to happen, the cup of tea needs to possess in act the form of hotness. Furthermore, the same form of hotness must be in potentiality in the hand, meaning the hand must be able to receive the form of hotness.[5] Otherwise, the transfer of form is not possible. Differently put, the hand has to be able to possess the form of hotness, without actually possessing it before touching the cup. But the causal process does not stop here. The form of hotness is transferred from the hand to the sensory part of the soul which perceives it. Of course, this

---

process could, however, not take place if such a transfer of form would not be possible, and the transfer of form in itself is a consequence of the fact that Aquinas' ontology imposes no restrictions to upwards causation. For details on causation in the scholastic period, see P. Rosemann, *Omne agens agit sibi simile: A "Repetition" of Scholastic Metaphysics*, Louvain, Louvain University Press, 1996. On Aquinas' theory of cognition, intellectual and perceptual, see L. Spruit, *Species Intelligibilis: From Perception to Knowledge*, vol. 1: *Classical Roots and Medieval Discussions*, Leiden, Brill, 1994; R. Pasnau, *Theories of Cognition in the Later Middle Ages*, Cambridge, Cambridge University Press, 1997; D. Perler (ed), *Ancient and Medieval Theories of Intentionality*, Leiden, Brill, 2001; J. O'Callaghan, "Aquinas, Cognitive Theory, and Analogy," *American Catholic Philosophical Quarterly, vol.* 76, no. 3, 2002, pp. 451–482; E. Stump, *Aquinas*, London, Routledge, 2003; E. Băltuţă, "Aquinas on Intellectual Cognition: The Case of Intelligible Species," *Philosophia, vol.* 41, no. 3, 2013, pp. 589–602; A. Lisska, *Aquinas's Theory of Perception: An Analytic Reconstruction*, Oxford, Oxford University Press, 2016.

4 This take on the difference between the requirements for agency in the Augustinian and the Aristotelian frameworks is not new. It has been suggested by other scholars, such as Rosemann, *Omne agens agit sibi simile* and J.-L. Solère, "*Sine qua non* Causality and the Context of Durand's Early Theory of Cognition," in A. Speer, F. Retucci, Th. Jeschke, and G. Guldentops (eds), *Durand of Saint-Pourçain and his "Sentences" Commentary: Historical, Philosophical, and Theological Issues*, Leuven, Peeters, 2014, pp. 185–227.

5 This description of Aquinas' account of the causal process of perception is very schematic. One should consider that Aquinas distinguishes between accidental and substantial forms, and between the types of change a form can exert on a patient, which can be material or immaterial. However, these details do not change the core idea that is of interest for my paper. For details about Aquinas' understanding of types of change and types of forms, see H.T. Adriaenssen, *Representation and Scepticism from Aquinas to Descartes*, Cambridge, Cambridge University Press, 2017, pp. 13–29.

means that the sensory part of the soul has also the potentiality to possess the form of hotness before actually possessing it.[6] Consequently, in Aquinas' framework, even if there is an ontological difference between corporeal objects and the sensory part of the soul, corporeal objects can act upon the latter. This is possible by virtue of objects possessing in act what the sensory part of the soul possesses only in potentiality, that is the forms of objects. The criterion for something to be an agent in Aquinas' philosophy is the actual possession of a form. Differently put, if X actually possesses a form, F, and Y potentially possesses F, then X can act upon Y, regardless of X's or Y's ontological degree. I will call this type of nobility of the agent *local nobility*, because the overall ontological degree of an entity is not defining for its role as an agent. Within such a framework, which requires only local nobility for something to be designated as an agent, the efficient cause, that is the principal source of a change, will also require only local nobility for exercising its power. The efficient cause of vision, for instance, is the visible object. Through the sensible species it emits, the form of the object is transferred to the eye. Once the eye receives the form, the sensory part of the soul can sense the corporeal object. Even though the object is corporeal and the soul is immaterial, hence there is an ontological difference between the two, the object can be an agent in relation to the soul. The object is thus the efficient cause of perception.

In Kilwardby's case, local nobility is not sufficient for defining an agent. His ontology is, in this respect, more rigid than Aquinas.' According to the latter, a form is a form, regardless if the composite it is part of is a spiritual or a corporeal substance. This means that all forms existing in the created world have the same ontological degree.[7] For instance, the form of an angel and the forms angels can possess are of the same ontological degree as the form of a human being and the forms human beings can possess. According to Kilwardby, not all forms have the same ontological degree. The form of an angel is ontologically superior to the form of a human being, and the form of a human being is superior to the form of a corporeal entity.[8] The same can be said about the forms an angel, a human being, and a corporeal entity possess. The way the ontological

---

6   See, for example, Thomas Aquinas, *Summa Theologiae* I, *Opera omnia 5*, Rome, Ad Sanctae, 1889, q. 78, a. 3.

7   See Thomas Aquinas, *De malo*, *Opera omnia 23*, Rome, Ad Sanctae, 1982, q. 16, a. 1.

8   For details on Kilwardby's ontology, see A.D. Conti, "Semantics and Ontology in Robert Kilwardby's Commentaries on the *Logica vetus*," in P. Thom and H. Lagerlund (eds), *A Companion to the Philosophy of Robert Kilwardby*, Leiden, Brill, 2003, pp. 65–130; S. Donati, "Robert Kilwardby on Matter," in P. Thom and H. Lagerlund (eds), *A Companion to the Philosophy of Robert Kilwardby*, pp. 239–275.

hierarchy of forms is reflected in the relationship between an agent and a patient consists in the idea that the transfer of forms can take place either horizontally, within the limits of the same ontological level (for instance, a hot liquid warms a cup), or vertically, top-down, from a higher ontological level to a lower one (for instance, the soul acts upon the body). In short, X can act upon Y if X and Y have the same ontological degree or X's ontological degree is higher than Y's, X actually possesses a form, F, and Y potentially possesses F. I will call this type of nobility required from the agent *global nobility*, because the overall superior ontological degree of an entity is presupposed for its role as an agent. But how does this supplementary condition imposed on an agent affect Kilwardby's way of conceiving efficient causality? As a preliminary answer, it can be said that, within such a framework, which requires global nobility for something to be designated as an agent, the efficient cause will also require global nobility for exercising its power. In other words, an entity, X, can efficiently cause a change in another entity, Y, if X has the same or a higher ontological degree than Y. I will call this the *efficient causation criterion* (ECC).[9]

1.2 *Kilwardby's Architecture of the World*

Now that I have determined the criterion for efficient causation, I can look at how the structure of the natural world is affected by the ontological principle of hierarchy. This will allow me to map the ontological consequences that shape causation, focusing on what is relevant for the process of sense perception.

One consequence of Kilwardby's type of ontology, particularly his understanding of the nobility of an agent as global, is that a corporeal object cannot act upon the sensory soul. For this to happen, the object would have to have the same ontological degree as the soul. That is, since the soul is spiritual, the object would have to be spiritual as well. But the object is corporeal, which means that the form it emits through the sensible species, is also corporeal, being efficacious only in relationship to corporeal entities. In DSF 58, Kilwardby addresses this issue and says that:

> [...] because the sensible species in the sense organ is nothing but a certain inflow from the sensible thing, this inflowing will not be said to effect something which the sensible thing itself does not effect primarily.

---

9 For the principle according to which something superior cannot be acted upon by something inferior, see also Robert Kilwardby, *Quaestiones in librum secundum Sententiarum*, G. Leibold (ed), München, Verlag der Bayerischen Akademie der Wissenschaften, 1992, q. 160, p. 445.

184   BĂLTUȚĂ

Because what flows into a power acts by means of it, and the power does not act except in so far as an action is performed by means of it.[10]

The efficacy of sensible species will not cross the boundaries of the corporeal realm, because they are, after all, species of corporeal things.

The architecture of the natural world, described by Kilwardby as a hierarchic construction in which the distinguishing criterion is the ontological degree, is best expressed in paragraph 56 of the DSF. I quote it in full because it is representative of Kilwardby's ontology:

> Moreover, since a man is a sort of world, it is probable that the kinds of different existence which are ranked some above and some below man, are related to activity, passivity, governance, and influence, in the way in which they are related in the greater world. But in the greater world the situation is such that a nature that has a lower existence is entirely governed and acted upon by a nature that has a higher one, and does not act upon that higher existence. Therefore it will be like that in man. Here is a clarification of the minor premise. In the greater world, a created thing has a lower grade of existence than the creator, and the created thing is moved, governed and acted upon by the creator, and the converse does not hold. Moreover, in the created order, bodies have a lower existence than angels have, and bodies are moved, governed, and acted upon by angels, and the converse does not hold. Moreover, among bodies, straight ones are lower than circular ones, and the straight ones are moved and acted upon by the circular ones, and the converse does not hold. Moreover, in straight bodies matter has a lower existence than form has, and matter is acted upon, moved and governed by form, and the converse does not hold. Likewise with spiritual creatures. The human soul in this life is in a certain way inferior to the angles, and hence it is moved and governed by that latter, and the converse does not hold. Therefore this is how it will be in man, where the body has a lower existence than the mind has, and the sense organ has a lower existence than has the soul

---

10   Kilwardby, *De spiritu fantastico*, P.O. Lewry (ed), *On Time and Imagination: De tempore, De spiritu fantastico*, Oxford, Oxford University Press for the British Academy, 1987, *hereafter* DSF, 58: "[...] quia cum species sensibilis in organo sentiendi non sit nisi quedam influentia sensibilis, non dicetur hec influentia aliquid efficere quod ipsum sensibile non efficiat principaliter, quia influens uirtutem agit per ipsam, et ipsa non agit nisi quantenus per ipsam agitur." English translation: Robert Kilwardby, *On Time and Imagination*, Part 2, trans. A. Broadie, Oxford, Oxford University Press for The British Academy, 1993, hereafter OTI, p. 84, modified translation.

which vivifies the organ. And since the sensible body which is external, has the same grade of existence as the organ, for each can be acted on and each is composed of contraries, though the corporeal body is more distant <than the sense organ is> from the sensory soul as regards the order of acting and being acted upon, the sensory soul is not acted upon by the corporeal body, just as it is not acted upon by the sense organ.[11]

One can notice here the use of two principles: the principle of ontological hierarchy and the principle of ontological dependency. According to the first principle, all beings in the world are arranged following a strict sequence: God has the highest ontological degree, then come the spiritual beings, that is, angels and human souls, and, last in this order, the corporeal entities, which have the lowest degree of being. This ontological hierarchy is closely linked to the principle of ontological dependency: beings that occupy a hierarchically lower place depend on beings that are placed higher, in the sense that they are ruled, acted upon, and affected by higher beings. It seems thus that Kilwardby, in line with his understanding of nobility, acknowledges that the ontological degree of a being is proportional to the efficient causality it can exert.

But how safe is this ontological framework when it comes to understanding the interaction between the sensory soul and corporeal objects? Someone might raise a doubt as to whether the hierarchy of entities in the created world is as strict as Kilwardby claims it to be. She could begin by admitting that there is an ontological difference between the object, its sensible species, and the sensory soul. Nevertheless, she would continue, while the difference between

---

11 Kilwardby, *DSF* 56: "Item, cum homo sit mundus quidam, uerisimile est naturas diuerse existentie, que ordinatur sub et supra in homine, eo modo se habere quantum ad actionem et passionem et regimen et influentiam quomodo sese habent in maiori mundo. Set in mundo maiori ita est quod natura inferioris existentie omnino regitur et patitur a natura superioris existentie et non agit in illam. Ergo sic erit in homine. Declaracio minoris hec est: In maiori mundo creatura est inferioris gradus existencie quam Creator, et / hec a Creatore mouetur et regitur et patitur, et non econuerso. Item, in creatura corpora sunt inferioris existencie quam angeli, et hec mouentur et reguntur et patiuntur ab illis et non econuerso. Item, in corporibus sunt corpora recta inferior circularibus, et hec ab illis mouentur et patiuntur, et non econuerso. Item, in corporibus rectis est materia inferioris existentie quam forma, et hec a forma patitur et mouetur et regitur, et non econverso. Similiter eciam ex parte spiritualis creature: Anima humana secundum hunc statum est aliquo modo inferior spiritu angelico, et hec ab illo mouetur et regitur, et non econuerso. Igitur sic erit in homine, vbi corpus est inferioris existentie quam anima et organum sensitiuum quam spiritus ipsum animans. Et cum corpus extra sensibile sit eiusdem gradus existencie cum organo, quia utrumque passibile et ex contrariis compositum, remotius tamen a spiritu sensitiuo quo ad ordinem agendi uel patendi, non patietur spiritus sensitiuus ab illo, sicut nec ab organo." *OTI*, p. 84.

the object and the sensory soul cannot be suppressed, the one between the sensible species and the sensory soul can. The reason for such an assumption would be that, while assimilating the sensible species, the sensory soul also elevates its ontological degree, bestowing on it its own ontological weight. In fact, it would be easy to reach this conclusion, because there are passages where Kilwardby makes statements like the following one:

> [...] in respect of spirituality and corporeality, there is so great a distance between the aforementioned extremes that the extremes are not naturally fitted to be united so as to produce and receive a cognition except via the media. In those media the species of the sensible thing is rendered subtle and is elevated so that it comes into harmony with a power which ought to know, so that by means of the species a cognition comes into existence.[12]

Such an elevated species could thus act upon the sensory soul, one might think. Though apparently strong, there are two problems with this argument. First, once the species is assimilated, it exists in a different receptacle and in a way different than the initial one. Even if the species in the sensory soul would have the same content as the sensible species in the medium or as the one in the organ, there would still be an ontological difference between them. Consider this as an example: an object emits a sensible species, S_1, which passes through the medium and informs the organ. By being assimilated by the sensory soul, S_1 becomes S_2, an S with an ontological weight that enables it to act upon the sensory soul. But the problem is that S_1 is neither numerically nor ontologically identical with S_2. So, it would not be correct to say that S_1 acts upon the sensory soul, because, in fact, only S_2 can act upon the sensory soul in accordance with the ontological requirements of an agent. Second, even if Kilwardby would agree to a scenario in which S_2 could somehow act upon the sensory soul as a result of the ontological elevation of S_1, performed by the sensory soul, he would then end up with a sensory soul possessing two intermediary entities: images, as the standard intermediary entities, and species. Regardless if their contents match or not, this would be an unnecessary multiplication of intermediary entities, representing the same thing. If the sensory soul possesses two intermediary entities, why would it not possess three, or four, or thirty-six, for that matter? The actual intention behind passage 140

---

12 Kilwardby, *DSF* 140: "[...] extremorum tanta est distancia in spiritualitate et corporalitate quod non sunt nata coniungi ad cognicionem faciendam et suscipiendam nisi per dicta media, in quibus quasi subtilietur et sublimetur species rei sensibilis ut fiat conueniens uirtuti que cognoscere debet, ut per illam fiat cognicio." *OTI*, p. 106.

from DSF was to show that between the ontological levels the distance is so great that we need intermediaries. But it is not the species that crosses the border between corporeality and spirituality. Something like this can never be possible. The species itself, according to Kilwardby, can never be an agent in relation to the soul without infringing on the hierarchy of the natural world.

1.3   *Summary of Relevant Consequences*

After the brief overview of Kilwardby's configuration of the world and understanding of an agent, I am now able to synthesize the main consequences for the interaction I am concerned with – that between the corporeal object and the sensory soul perceiving it – and to anticipate the next steps of my analysis. First, the consequences:

(1)   Corporeal entities can be agents only in relationship to other corporeal entities.

(2)   Corporeal entities cannot be agents in relation to spiritual entities, like the sensory soul.

(3)   Spiritual entities, like the sensory soul, cannot be patients in relationship to corporeal entities.

(4)   Spiritual entities can be agents in relationship to corporeal entities.

Allow me now to spell out the next steps of my analysis. I begin by noticing that, given the principles of ontological hierarchy, the principle of ontological dependency, and the global nobility condition, the causal role the corporeal object plays in perception is far from being clear. Nonetheless, the main parts of the problem I am dealing with are now on the table. On the one hand, considering that corporeal entities have a lower ontological degree than spiritual ones, it is clear that efficient causation from corporeal objects to the sensory soul is not possible. On the other hand, we do perceive corporeal objects. What then is the role played by these in perception? To answer this question, I will follow three main steps: first, I will show that the efficient cause of perception is the sensory soul; second, I will spell out the kind of agent the sensory soul is; third, in a lengthier step, I will analyze the operations performed by the sensory soul in perception. This should allow me to map the causal interactions involved in perception, facilitating thus the identification of the causal role played by the corporeal object.

2   Causation in Perception

How is perception possible? How does Kilwardby account for it? More specifically, how does he come to point out the sensory soul as the efficient cause of perception? How, then, is he able to justify such an approach to perception?

188   BĂLTUȚĂ

Let us first have a look at the efficient cause. Kilwardby states that there are only four possible candidates fit to play this role. These are the intellect, the imagination, the body, and the sensory soul:

> [...] if when the sensory soul senses, it begins to have impressed upon it an image or likeness of a sensible thing, it does not seem that the efficient causing of the impression can be done otherwise than by the intellect, the imagination, the body, or the sensory soul itself.[13]

On the one side of the ontological spectrum, we have the corporeal realm, represented by the body. But notice, first, that Kilwardby does not even mention the corporeal object among the possible efficient causes of perception. The reason is that the object is the entity most remote from the sensory soul, so it cannot comply with the requirements of the efficient causation criterion (ECC).[14] Following the same logic, the body also cannot be counted as an efficient cause of perception.[15] The body, too, is corporeal, which means it cannot affect the sensory soul. There simply cannot be such a relation of efficient causation because the body is not, at least, on the same ontological level as the sensory soul. It is important, though, to bear in mind that the causal interaction between body and corporeal object, in virtue of them being situated on the same ontological level, is perfectly possible. It is the corporeal object through its sensible species that efficiently causes the body to possess its form. This is an aspect deserving attention, since it offers a hint about the real import of the causal role exercised by the object, but for now, I will not get into details, and will return to this issue later. The sensible species is also not mentioned by Kilwardby, in DSF 63, among the possible causes of perception. We find the reason in a couple of other places where he states that, since sensible species

---

13   Kilwardby, DSF 63: "Si spiritus sensitiuus, dum sentit, incipit habere impressam sibi ymaginem uel similitudinem rei sensibilis, et hec non uidetur aliunde imprimi posse efficienter nisi uel ab intellectu uel a fantasia uel a corpore uel ab ipso spiritu sentiente," OTI, pp. 85–86.

14   Kilwardby, DSF 55: "Verisimilimus est quodcumque corpus posse pati a corpore alio quam spiritum a corpore. Set corpus circulare quod regit et continet corpora recta non potest aliquid ab eis pati, set eis pocius influit actionem. Ergo multoforcius spiritus senciens qui presidet organo sensitiuo ab illo pati non potest, set in illud actionem influit. Et si ab illo non patitur, multofortius non patitur a corpore sensibili extra distante, quia illud non habet ordinacionem ad spiritum sensitiuum nisi per organum quod animatur illo spiritu."

15   Kilwardby, DSF 47: "[...] quia si actione corporis imprimerentur ymagines corporum spiritui sencienti, tunc ageret corpus in spiritum et spiritus pateretur a corpore tamquam subiecta ei materia." See also DSF 48–50.

ROBERT KILWARDBY ON OBJECTS AS SINE QUA NON CAUSES

are non-self-subsistent accidents emitted by the corporeal object, their causal efficacy is restricted to the corporeal realm, just as their source is.[16] The whole dismissal of the entities belonging to the corporeal realm is, in fact, a direct consequence of Kilwardby's ontology. Efficient causation can take place either horizontally, between entities of the same ontological degree, or vertically, top-down, being exercised by an entity of a higher ontological degree in relation to an entity of a lower ontological degree.

On the other side of the ontological spectrum, we have the spiritual realm. The first possible candidate is the intellect. Being purely spiritual, it complies with the ECC. It can thus be causally efficacious with respect to both corporeal and spiritual entities. But satisfying the ECC is only a necessary, not also a sufficient, condition for being the efficient cause of perception. Perception is predicated univocally of human beings and animals, this being enough reason for Kilwardby to deny to the intellect the status of efficient cause of perception:

> Moreover, the mode of sensing does not seem equivocal in ourselves and beasts. But in beasts the species of sensible things are not supplied <sc. by the intellect> to the sentient soul, since they do not have an intellect. Therefore neither in us are they supplied to the sentient soul <by the intellect>.[17]

If the intellect would be the efficient cause of perception, given the univocal predication of perception, animals would have to have an intellect. But animals do not have an intellect. The efficient cause of perception must, therefore, be another one, one that is the same in animals and humans. Animals have imagination. So, maybe imagination, as a sensory-cognitive faculty present in all animals, rational or otherwise, is the efficient cause of perception. This also cannot be the case, according to Kilwardby, because imagination is, in fact, the same faculty as the sensory soul.[18] The only difference between the

---

16   See Kilwardby, DSF 58.

17   Kilwardby, DSF 44: "Item, non uidetur equiuocus modus sciendi in nobis et brutis. Set in brutis non exhibetur species sensibilium spiritui sentienti, quia non est ibi intellectus, ergo nec in nobis." OTI, p. 81.

18   Kilwardby, DSF 52: "Si enim phantasticus spiritus et sensitiuus sunt idipsum in substantia, licet in modo different, ut premissum est [2]." And DSF 2: " [...] tamen pars fantastica et sensitiua non differunt secundum essentiam set solum secundum officium uel potentiam et usum. Que enim sensitiua est in presentia sensibilis, fit fantastica uel ymaginatiua dum absente sensibili ymagines sensibilium apud se reconditas considerat et per illas absentia ymaginatur."

two is that, when engaged in an operation whose object is present, we refer to the faculty as the sensory soul, and, when the object is absent, not within the range of the sensory organs, we refer to it as imagination. In short, imagination is rejected because it does not deal with actual objects of perception.

From all the candidates for being the efficient cause of perception – the body, the imagination, the sensory soul, and the intellect – only the sensory soul remains unrejected. Kilwardby thus concludes that the sensory soul is the efficient cause of perception.[19] However, even with the efficient cause identified, the problem of perception is far from being solved. The sensory soul is the fficient cause of perception, but knowing this does not also respond to the question of who is responsible for the sensory soul's actualization. It is possible that the soul is actualized by another, and only afterward is able to perform the perceptual operation.[20]

The way I see it, Kilwardby has three possible scenarios for solving this part of the problem of perception: the sensory soul is actualized by another, and this other remains to be identified (1), there is no secondary causation in the world, God being the only real cause (2), the soul changes itself from potentiality to actuality, being thus a self-actualizing agent (3). Let me consider them one at a time. If the soul is self-actualizing, the activity and its degree must be so defined that Kilwardby's theory of perception avoids falling into scepticism with respect to corporeal objects. If, on the other hand, the sensory soul is actualized by another, this might leave some room for some type of causation on the side of corporeal objects. If, finally, the sensory soul is neither self-actualizing nor actualized by another, and God is the only real cause in nature, then it is only fair to admit that corporeal objects are also devoid of causal powers.

Fortunately, for the most part, the job of identifying the right scenario was done while ruling out possible candidates for the efficient cause of perception. On the one hand, I have already shown that the corporeal object, or its sensible species, the body, the imagination, or the intellect cannot efficiently cause a change in the sensory soul that would lead to perception. The reasons for this conclusion also invalidate the first scenario under examination. On the other hand, the passages we have looked into thus far make it clear that Kilwardby is

---

19   Kilwardby, DSF 63: "Recoligamus igitur summatim superiora [42–46] sic: Si spiritus sensitiuus, dum sentit, incipit habere impressam sibi ymaginem uel similitudinem rei sensibilis, et hec non uidetur aliunde imprimi posse efficienter nisi uel ab intellectu uel a fantasia uel a corpore uel ab ipso spiritu sentiente, et non potest imprimi ab aliquo trium prius nominatorum, restat, ut uidetur, quod a quarto. Et ita ipse spiritus sensitiuus in se format huiusmodi ymaginem."

20   The Aristotelian principle "omne quod movetur ab alio movetur," discussed predominantly in *Physics* III.3, VII.1, and VIII.4–5, is present in Kilwardby's writings, even if the wording differs. (See Silva, *Robert Kilwardby on the Human Soul*, p. 52.).

ROBERT KILWARDBY ON OBJECTS AS SINE QUA NON CAUSES

not excluding secondary causation from the natural world, since he states that objects are causally efficacious with respect to the body, in virtue of having the same ontological degree, and, even more, that there are causal interactions between entities of different ontological levels.[21] The simple fact that he addresses the causal activity entities can exert is reason enough to reject the second, occasionalist, scenario mentioned above.[22] The scenario which remains standing is the third one, in which the sensory soul is (a) the efficient cause of perception, and (b) self-actualizing.

Before making any further inquiries into the causal roles assigned to the sensory soul and, eventually, to the object, let me take a look at Kilwardby's own words when describing perception:

> For there are two things in sensing, namely the more attentive action of the soul in the body which is acted upon and the perception of this action. Therefore, while the soul attends to the body which is acted upon so that it moves the body according to the requirement of its passivity, <the soul> assimilates itself to what is acted upon according as it is acted upon. But such assimilation is just the formation of the image of a sensible thing by which <formation> the sense organ finds in itself what has been affected, since the affecting of the organ by the sensible object is the being-acted-upon of which we speak. And this is just the impression, made in the organ itself, of a likeness of the object. But since the soul turns its eye upon itself when thus informed by the image, the more attentive action by means of which the soul is informed is not concealed from the soul. And that is to sense in itself the image which it has formed in itself by acting more attentively upon the body. [...] for in this way the sensory soul, by turning itself more attentively to its sense organ which has been informed by a sensible species, makes itself like the species, and by turning its own eye upon itself it sees that it is like the species. And thus it senses the sensible object outside by means of the image which it has formed in itself.[23]

---

21   See, for example, Kilwardby, *DSF* 56 or, below, *DSF* 103.

22   For now, I take *occasionalism* in its strongest meaning, that is nothing except God has efficacious power in nature. However, one should be careful not to conflate occasionalism with occasional cause. (See S. Nadler, „Descartes and Occasional Causation," *British Journal for the History of Philosophy*, vol. 2, no. 1, 1994, pp. 35–54.) Certainly Kilwardby did not make use of such a distinction, but I nonetheless find it useful for understanding the causal role of the object. I will return to this point later on, in the fourth section of the paper.

23   Kilwardby, *DSF* 103: "Duo enim sunt in sentiendo, scilicet attencior operacio spiritus in corpore passo et huius actionis percepcio. Dum ergo attendit corpori passo ut illud

What Kilwardby is saying here is that, for perception to take place, the sensory soul needs to perform two operations: (1) attending to the change produced in the body by the sensible species of the corporeal object and (2) reflecting on itself and becoming aware that it is attending to the bodily change. The result of the first operation is the formation of an image of the change produced in the body by the corporeal object through its sensible species. By reflecting on itself, at the level of the second operation, the sensory soul realizes that it has formed an image and that this image is similar to the sensible species, and so comes to perceive the corporeal object emitting the species.[24]

Such an epistemological framework seems to leave the object with no causal role whatsoever in the process of perception. It follows, then, that the same framework should possess the proper resources to keep Kilwardby safe from the scepticism that might result from denying a causal role to the object. The same framework should allow satisfactory answers to the following questions: (1) If the object (including the sensible species and the bodily changes) does not exert any causal power on the sensory soul, how can the sensory soul know when to attend to the bodily change? (2) If the object plays no causal role, no matter how remote, in image formation, how does the sensory soul know when to form an image? (3) If the sensory soul can form images without being actualized by another, why does it not actualize itself – that is, form images – at will?

---

moueat secundum exigenciam sue passionis, assimilat se passo secundum quod passum est. Assimilacio autem / talis non est aliud quam formacio ymaginis rei sensibilis qua inuenit affectum suum organum in seipso, quia ipsa affectio organi ab obiecto sensibili est passio de qua loquimur. Et hec non est nisi impressio similitudinis obiecti in ipso organo facta. Quia uero spiritus aciem conuertit ad se sic ymagine informatum, ideo non latet cum attentior actio per quam formatus est. Et hoc est sentire in se ymaginem quam in se formauit attencius in corpus operando. (...) sic enim spiritus sensitiuus se conuertendo attentius ad suum organum specie sensibili informatum facit se ei simile, et in se propriam aciem reflectendo uidet se talem. Et sic sentit sensibilie forinsecum per ymaginem quam in se formauit. *OTI*, pp. 94–95, modified translation.

24 Although it is not of relevance for this paper, it is worth noticing that neither the image nor the sensible species are the proper objects of perception. The sensible species is that through which the sensory soul forms the image, while the image is that through which the sensory soul becomes aware of itself as a sensory soul which vivifies a body and is able to extend its intentionality outwards, reaching the corporeal object. There are interesting issues stemming from this account, such as the epistemological access to the corporeal object or the similarity between the sensible species and the image, but these do not concern the present approach, so they remain to be solved on a different occasion.

ROBERT KILWARDBY ON OBJECTS AS SINE QUA NON CAUSES 193

To be fair, the first question is formulated in a slightly misleading way. It makes it seem as if the sensory soul's attending to the body is accompanied by awareness. In fact, Kilwardby treats this first operation of the sensory soul quite differently, as a natural activity of which the sensory soul is not aware. The relation between the soul and the body, he says, is that of form to matter, and form acts continuously on the matter "in accordance with the power which was granted to it for its purpose."[25] In the particular case of the sensory soul, the action exerted on the body consists of the inflow of vital inspiration, power of growth, preservation, sensation, health, and natural organization of the body. The action of the soul on the body, Kilwardby goes on saying, is necessary for preserving the integrity and the health of the body in accordance with the different passivities and affections it undergoes.[26] This means that the sensory soul "adapts" its activities according to the state of the body. If the body is healthy, the sensory soul acts in a certain way on it; if the body is ill, the sensory soul acts differently. But this adaptation on the part of the sensory soul is performed naturally, which also means non-consciously:

> For nature, acting without either art or its own cognition, is directed by higher cognitive principles as if they were principles of skill, in the way in which an instrument is directed by the artificer using his skill.[27]

The sensory soul acts naturally, continuously and non-consciously, and is led in its actions by a sort of instinct.[28] Keeping this in mind, the first question

---

25 See Kilwardby, *DSF* 99: "Vt autem intelligatur eius sententia, nota quod spiritus sensitiuus, eo quod forma est, continue operatur et agit influendo in corpus quod est ei materia, et hoc continendo, uniendo, saluando et ordinando illud secundum posse sibi ad hoc datum. Et quia est forma que est uita sensitiua, agit influentiam uitalis inspiracionis, uegetacionis et sensificacionis et conseruacionis et salutis et naturalis ordinacionis quantum sibi datur. Et sicut continue operatur sic influendo corpori, sic diuersimode operatur secundum diuersas affections uel passions corporis. Sicut enim saluti et conseruacioni et ordinacioni corporis necessaria est actio anime et influencia eius, / sic continuitati salutis, continuitas actionis, et diuresis passionibus et affeccionibus correspondent. Inde est quod aliter agit anima in corpore sano, et aliter in egro, aliter in calefacto, aliter in frigefacto, et huiusmodi."

26 Kilwardby, *DSF* 99.

27 Kilwardby, *DSF* 127: "Natura enim operans absque arte et cognitione propria dirigitur principiis superioribus cognitiuis et quasi artificibus, per modum quo dirigitur instrumentum ab artifice per artem." *OTI*, p. 101.

28 Kilwardby, *DSF* 128: "Ex his [127] manifestum est quod spiritus sensitiuus formans in se ymaginem rei sensibilis, etsi hoc fecerit non sentiens neque apprehendens adhuc ipsam, non facit hoc causaliter set naturaliter, et prout a superioribus causis cognicionem et

should be reformulated, since the sensory soul does not properly *know* when to orient itself towards this rather than that part of the body affected by a corporeal object. The soul is naturally oriented towards the body, in virtue of being its form, and whenever the body is affected, the sensory soul instinctively focuses its attention more on the affected part of the body. In brief, given the form-matter relationship between the sensory soul and the body, the sensory soul does not know, and does not even need to know, when to orient itself towards the body, because this orientation is what it does naturally; it also does not need to know when a part of the body has been affected, because it reacts instinctively when such an affection takes place. If a part of the body undergoes a more intense affection, the soul will pay more attention to that particular part, and if the affection is less intense, the soul will pay less attention.[29] To use an analogy, the soul is like a computer program designed to maintain the same intensity of light in a room. Whenever someone shuts the blinds, the artificial light becomes stronger. When the blinds are being opened and natural light floods the room, the intensity of the artificial light is lowered. The program does not adjust the light level consciously, but only because it is programmed to do so. We could say that the program possesses built-in intentionality and the ability to adapt its output according to the changes of external conditions.

Before coming to the second question, notice that, as such, the sensory soul's orientation towards the body, its own built-in intentionality, is not subject to change. What seems to change is only the content of the act of the sensory soul. Depending on the bodily changes, which are efficiently caused by the sensible species of different objects, the sensory soul creates different images, corresponding to the sensible species affecting the body. The sensory soul's orientation towards the body is the same, its content differs. Returning to the analogy with the computer program, although the natural light is not the one actually operating the program, the resulting changes in how the program performs are related to it. The sensory soul attending to an unaffected body is

---

    artem regitiuam habentibus directus, instinctu naturali ducitur. Et ideo non accidit in opere suo nisi forte ex aliquo inpedimento accidentali, sicut accidit in aliis operibus nature multociens."

29   Kilwardby, *DSF* 102: "Hinc est quod, cum instrumentum sentiendi patitur ab obiecto sensibili, huic passioni qua afficitur instrumentum occurrit spiritus sensitiuus attentus in omnibus que instrumento accidunt, et secumdum quod maior uel minor est affectio corporis, erit et maior uel minor attencio spiritus occurrentis."

like a program on sleep mode, not out of function, just needing not to intervene to adjust the intensity of light in the room, while the sensory soul attending to an affected body is like a program actually adjusting the intensity of light. Although it is accurate to say that the sensory soul is not actualized by the object, that it is not set into motion by the object, it would not be accurate to say that the sensory soul is not undergoing any change; just as it would be accurate to say that the program does not run because of the light, but in virtue of being constructed in a certain way, and also that, depending on the lighting conditions, the working of the program undergoes certain changes. In other words, there is indeed no relation of upwards efficient causation between the body affected by the object and the sensory soul, but from this to denying the existence of any causal link between them is a big step, which one is not yet entitled to take, especially since Kilwardby specifically states that the sensory soul acts according to the bodily changes produced by the sensible species of the corporeal object.

The second question went as follows: If the object plays no causal role, no matter how remote, in image formation, how does the sensory soul know when to form an image? It should be clear by now, after the specifications occasioned by the first question, that the second question, too, needs to undergo a change and actually be reformulated: If the object plays no *efficient* causal role in image formation, how does the sensory soul know when to form an image? Finding an answer requires keeping in mind that the first operation of the sensory soul, that is, attending to the bodily changes, is not performed accidentally, but naturally, as if guided by a higher power. It would thus be fair to assume the same applies to the outcome of this operation: the resulting image is not formed by the sensory soul accidentally, but naturally. This implies that the answer to the second question is that the soul does not know when to form an image because it does not need to know. The sensory soul is naturally endowed with the disposition to pay attention to the body and its changes, on the one hand, and to form images as it attends to the body, on the other. Another analogy might prove helpful here. Imagine the sensory soul attending to the body is like a surveillance camera facing the front entrance of a house. The camera will continuously record images of the front entrance without having to be conscious of doing so. It performs such an activity simply because it was designed this way. As long as the camera operates within the manufacturer's specifications, it will record images.

Knowing that the soul forms images naturally, non-consciously and continuously, therefore also when the body is affected by a corporeal object, I can now focus on addressing the third question: If the sensory soul can form images without being actualized by another, why does it not actualize itself – that is, form images, at will? The answer is simple, and it has to do, again, with the nature of the sensory soul. From the outset and continuously, the sensory soul is actually oriented towards and actually attending to the body and its eventual changes; from the outset and continuously, the sensory soul forms images. Returning quickly to the analogy with the surveillance camera, I would underline that what the camera does is actually to film, not just to take pictures from time to time. Nonetheless, someone might reply that there is a difference between the efficient cause of the sensory soul being oriented towards the body and the efficient cause of it forming the image of a bodily change. She might admit that the efficient cause of the soul's orientation towards the body is the soul itself, but might have a hard time admitting that the object is not the efficient cause of the soul's forming an image. After all, if the image is similar to the sensible species of the object, it means that there must be some causation exerted by the object, and therefore some passive moment of the soul in its interaction with the object.

Such a line of thought would, however, be inconsistent with the most basic premises of Kilwardby's philosophy, and noticing this inconsistency is sufficient for not taking shelter too easily in a different account of perception, as well as for advancing with my analysis in a reasonably charitable manner. In the end, the idea of some causation exerted by the object does not necessarily lead to some passive moment of the sensory soul or to the identification of the object with an efficient cause. Sticking with Kilwardby's theory of perception, I would reiterate that the soul, acting naturally – and so from the outset and continuously – always actively attends to the body. But such an answer to the objection above, though providing support for my analysis, does not really solve the problem of the similarity between the image formed by the soul and the sensible species of the object affecting the body. In the end, is the similarity between the image and the species not a sign of some causal role played by the object? The move from noting a vague causal role the object apparently plays in perception to understanding the object as efficient cause, and the soul as passive, might not bear the mark of necessity, but neither does the reiteration of some tenets of Kilwardby's philosophy bear the mark of sufficiency. The best solution would thus be to come up with a clear-cut answer as to what is the causal role played by the object in perception.

It is important, for reaching such an answer, to keep in mind that the sensory soul is the protagonist in the process of perception, which means the role of the object remains to be determined within the framework set by the acts of the sensory soul. For this reason, it would be helpful to return to the two operations the sensory soul performs while perceiving that is, (1) attending to the changes produced in the body by the sensible species of the corporeal object, and (2) reflecting on itself and becoming aware that it is attending to the bodily change. The first operation is built on the sensory soul's primary act, whose intentional object is the body. The goal of this first operation is to watch over and protect the body. By doing this, the soul produces images, including of the potential affections of the body – that is, of the sensible species of the objects with which the body comes into contact. One should be careful not to put too much epistemological weight on the object here, since the sensory soul does not properly perceive while producing the images. The primary act of the sensory soul is non-conscious and non-cognitive.[30] The second operation of the sensory soul is the one reaching a cognitive level. It is comprised of the sensory soul's orientation towards itself, noticing that it came to possess an image of an affection of the body. At this stage, the sensory soul is able to discriminate between itself and its product. For the first time, the sensory soul becomes aware of itself, due to becoming aware of undergoing a change from non-possessing to possessing an image of an affection of the body. This is how an extension of the sensory soul's intentionality is brought about: at first, the sensory soul was oriented towards the body; now, through the image it has formed, it orients itself towards the corporeal object. The reason for the extension of intentionality lies, naturally, in the soul's task to watch over and protect the body. Getting acquainted with the objects affecting the body allows the soul to fulfil its task.

Given this framework, what can be said about the causal role played by the corporeal object in perception? A few details can be underlined: (a) the corporeal object is the efficient cause of the bodily change, (b) without the bodily change, the soul could not form the image of a corporeal object; (c) without forming the image of a corporeal object, the soul could not become aware of itself; (d) without becoming aware of itself, the soul could not discriminate between the image and itself; (e) without discriminating between itself and the image, the soul could not extend its intentionality outwards and perceive, through the formed image, the corporeal object. For the second operation to take place, the first one has to have already taken place. But the first operation, understood now as the formation of an image of an object affecting the body, cannot take place if an object does not affect the body. Consequently, there is

---

30 The sensory soul, being ontologically superior to the body, forms images naturally, and it can also naturally compare them to the sensible species in the body – sensible species to which it has access due to its ontological superiority. By stressing the natural function of the soul, Kilwardby is actually able to avoid charges of scepticism. If the soul acts naturally, according to its design, it cannot make any mistakes; hence, scepticism is out of the question.

at least a relation of counterfactual dependency between the object and the process of perception. In a few passages, Kilwardby addresses the issue of the causal role played by the object, and he makes use of the following terminology: *necessary cause* or *necessary occasion, efficient cause per accidens, necessary condition,* or *sine qua non cause.*[31]

My analysis of Kilwardby's theory of sense perception is prompted by the attempt to shed light on the causal role played by the object in the process of perception. At this point, I can rephrase the issue in more specific terms and ask: what does it mean that the object is a *sine qua non* cause of perception? A survey of the existing secondary literature will allow me to lay out more sharply my own reading of the issue.

3   Literature Survey

There are two main interpretative lines with respect to the causal role played by the corporeal object in Kilwardby's theory of perception. First, there is Mary Sirridge's reading, who addresses the issue only tangentially in an article on the relationship between divine understanding and divine speaking.[32] She takes the object to play the role of an efficient cause in perception, and then concludes that the sensory soul's role is passive. Now, although this reading contradicts the principle of ontological hierarchy, one must take into account the passages Sirridge refers to. In *Sentences commentary* I, q. 35–36, Kilwardby does indeed allow for such an approach, indebted to Aristotle, in which perception is not an active process, but a passive one.[33] Based solely on these

---

31   See Kilwardby, *DSF* 57, 117, 123, 129–134, 143. I consider the denomination *sine qua non cause* to be the most comprehensive one, therefore, I will use it through the remainder of this chapter, except, obviously, when the discussed authors use a different name.

32   M. Sirridge, "*Utrum idem sint dicere et intelligere sive videre in mente*: Robert Kilwardby, *Quaestiones in librum primum Sententiarum,*" *Vivarium,* vol. 45, no. 2–3, 2007, pp. 253–268.

33   Kilwardby, *Quaestiones in librum primum Sententiarum,* J. Schneider (ed), München, Verlag der Bayerischen Akademie der Wissenschaften, 1986, q. 35, 152–161: "Similiter in sentiendo ubi non est vere actus, ut dicit Aristoteles in III *De anima,* sensibile agens imprimit suam similitudinem in sensitivo et sic generat sentiens in actu, quod est unum compositum ex sensitivo in potentia tamquam materia et specie sensibilis eidem impressa tamquam forma, et est sensibile in actu gignens sentiens genitum. Quod autem sentiens sit genitum vel sensitivum in actu quod est idem quod sentiens, patet secundum Aristotelem. Dicit enim in II *De anima* quod sensus in actu alteratio quaedam est. Ex quo patet quod sensitivum in actu vel sentiens est alteratum. Sed in I *De generatione* docet quod alteratio est generatio quaedam et alteratum generatum quoddam. Quare patet quod sentiens sive sensitivum in actu est quoddam genitum."

questions from the *Sentences commentary*, one has to agree with Sirridge's reading.

But how, then, does such a take on perception fit with what I have identified as Kilwardby's position? A possible solution to the problem would be to say that Kilwardby changed his mind about perception. Although historically possible, such a radical change, from first understanding perception as active to later understanding it as passive, would create major systematic difficulties. Embracing a passive account of perception would presuppose that his ontology as well undergoes radical changes. For instance, a corporeal thing, composed of corporeal matter and corporeal form, would be able to act upon the spiritual matter and spiritual form of the sensory soul. Such a scenario would be possible if the corporeal form would somehow be transferred from the object to the soul. But this would have further consequences on how the principle of ontological hierarchy should be interpreted. It would have to be so softened as to allow a kind of Thomistic view. For something to act upon another, local nobility would have to be sufficient: something would be able to be an agent just by actually possessing a form potentially possessed by another, regardless of this other's eventual ontological superiority. This would mean that the global nobility condition I have talked about in the beginning of this paper would have to be given up. Even more, it would lead Kilwardby to distance himself from Augustine's authoritative role, a move he does not seem ready to make. Not even in the *Sentences commentary*. What, then, should my take on the passage discussed by Sirridge be? It is clear it does not fit with the results of my analysis until now or with Kilwardby's philosophy in general. For this reason, coming to a satisfying answer requires further research. Given the isolated character of the passage and the limited space at my disposal, I will not try to undertake such a task now.[34]

The second reading can be found in Broadie[35] and Silva.[36] Their main claim is that, in the process of perception, the object plays the role of a *sine qua non*

---

34   For Silva's position on the same topic, see *Robert Kilwardby on the Human Soul,* p. 202.

35   A. Broadie, "Introduction," in Robert Kilwardby, *On Time and Imagination*, pp. 1–20.

36   Silva, "Robert Kilwardby on Sense Perception," in S. Knuuttila and P. Kärkkäinen (eds), *Theories of Perception in Medieval and Early Modern Philosophy*, Dordrecht, Springer, 2008, pp. 87–99; Silva, "The Human Soul in Robert Kilwardby's Natural Philosophy and Theology," PhD dissertation, University of Porto, 2009; J.F. Silva and J. Toivanen, "The Active Nature of the Soul in Sense Perception: Robert Kilwardby and Peter John of Olivi," *Vivarium*, vol. 48, no. 3–4, 2010, pp. 245–278; Silva, *Robert Kilwardby on the Human Soul*; Silva, "Robert Kilwardby on the Theory of the Soul and Epistemology," in H. Lagerlund and P. Thom (eds), *A Companion to the Philosophy of Robert Kilwardby,* Leiden, Brill, 2013, pp. 275–313.

cause and the sensory soul that of an efficient cause. Broadie points only to the distinction Kilwardby makes, in DSF 117,[37] between accidental and *per se* efficient causation. He reduces *sine qua non* causation to accidental efficient causation which can be understood along the lines of the famous wax example with certain modifications:

> Thus, for example, properly speaking and by its nature it is the person who impresses the seal on the wax who is the efficient cause of the figure on the wax; the seal itself is not such a cause of the figure. However, commonly and by accident the seal is indeed the efficient cause of the figure because by means of the seal the figure is effected.[38]

Broadie does not go deeper in spelling out the particular features of this type of cause and its role in perception. However, it is only fair to acknowledge that Broadie's overall goal is just to introduce the reader to DSF, so, in fact, he does not need to go to such depths to reach his target.

Silva, on the other hand, approaches Kilwardby's theory of perception in several articles and chapters of his books. He focuses on the activity of the soul in the process of perception and highlights the strong Augustinian heritage. From this perspective, Silva accepts the reading according to which, on the one hand, the soul is the efficient cause or the efficient cause *per se* of perception and, on the other hand, the object could be understood as a necessary but insufficient condition or cause, as a necessary occasion, a *sine qua non* cause, or an efficient cause *per accidens*.[39] Such an overview is faithful to Kilwardby's theory and terminology. Unfortunately, Silva takes the causal role of the object

---

37 Kilwardby, *DSF* 117: "Responsio. Est efficiens proprie et per se uel communiter et per accidens. Primo modo non efficit sigillum figuram in cera, set imprimens sigillum cere. Ille enim qui inprimit est per se causa et propria impressionis. Secondo modo efficit sigillum figuram quia ipsum est per quod efficitur. Set ipsum non efficit nisi quantenus ab imprimente mouetur. Vnde sicut instrumentum artificis non est motor uel effector artificii nisi per accidens ex extenso nomine, sic est in exemplo predicto. Eodem modo intelligendum este ymagine / sensibilis in organo et de ymagine facta in spiritu sensitiuo. Ymago enim in organo efficit ymaginem in spiritu sensitiuo communiter accepto nomine efficientis et per accidens, quia per illam efficitur. Set ipse spiritus mouens et sibi applicans et secum inuoluens illam ymaginem in organo repertam efficit se ei simile et in se facit ymaginem illi simile, que postea uocatur 'fantasia.'"

38 Broadie, "Introduction," p. 14.

39 For details on understanding the object as necessary but insufficient cause, necessary condition, or necessary occasion, see Silva and Toivanen, "The Active Nature of the Soul in Sense Perception," p. 256; for details on understanding the object as efficient cause *per*

and even the activity of the soul at face value, just as consequences of a historical heritage, and fails to address them philosophically – that is, for the puzzles they really are. The same descriptive treatment is applied to the problems of intentionality or consciousness. One is thus left wondering whether Kilwardby did, in fact, propose a solid theory of perception. This is furthermore an issue since Silva directly expresses concerns about Kilwardby's ability to solve the following difficulty:

> Kilwardby seemed to follow the principle of proportionality of the reaction with respect to the change in the sense organ. The problem with this is that it implies a causal relation that goes against everything Kilwardby wanted to admit in suggesting that the attention of the soul is stimuli driven.[40]

However, one has to concede that Silva's descriptive approach, although failing to delve into questions that would allow the reader to understand the inner consistency of Kilwardby's theory of perception, can still be informative.

In brief, while the causal role played by the corporeal object in Kilwardby's theory of sense perception is present in the literature, it is not addressed principally and it certainly is not analysed in detail. Sirridge, Broadie, and even Silva discuss the causal role of the object only in a tangential or superficial manner. Regardless of the reasons for this situation, the bottom line is that many decisive aspects remain open to investigation. More is thus to be gained by simply returning to my own analysis. The main goal is to have a better grasp of what it means that the corporeal object plays the role of a *sine qua non* cause in the process of perception.

4 The *sine qua non* Cause of Perception

Having seen how the issue of the causal role of corporeal objects in perception is treated in the secondary literature and having in mind the conclusions from the second section about *sine qua non* causation, I can advance with the analysis and delve deeper into understanding how this type of causation works. Allow me now to pull the threads together and draw a picture of the causal

---

accidens, sine qua non cause, necessary occasion or condition, see Silva, *Robert Kilwardby on the Human Soul, pp.* 153–156.

40   Silva, *Robert Kilwardby on the Human Soul*, p. 159.

interactions at play in the process of sense perception.[41] I am focused on proving that, despite not being an efficient cause, the object is still a cause, albeit a *sine qua non* one, and that Kilwardby's theory of perception is still consistent. A secondary goal of this section is to defend Kilwardby's account of perception against Silva's criticism. My point is that although, *prima facie*, Silva's assessment seems valid, if we look closer at Kilwardby's theory of perception, from a legitimate double perspective, it becomes evident that the criticism is actually harmless.

4.1   *Two Descriptive Levels*

The way I see it, perception requires, according to Kilwardby, two events: one bodily, the other spiritual. The bodily event starts with the object emitting the sensible species and ends with the sensible species informing the sense organ. The spiritual event consists of the two operations of the soul, that is, attending to the affected body and reflecting on itself. Together, the two operations amount roughly to four steps: (1) the sensory soul's attention to the body and its sense organs as they are affected by the sensible species, (2) the formation of an image of the affection of the body, (3) the sensory soul's reflection on itself and on the formed image, and (4) the perception of the corporeal object through the formed image. My preliminary claim is that Kilwardby makes use of two descriptive levels when talking about perception, and only by acknowledging this dual descriptive perspective can we capture the whole causal picture and dispel some apparent inconsistencies. The first descriptive level I will call *natural*, the second *cognitive*.

At the natural descriptive level, Kilwardby deals with the bodily event and a part of the spiritual event, that is, the first operation of the sensory soul. He depicts the object as naturally endowed with the ability to emit sensible species, the ability of the sensible species to inform the sense organs, the sense organs as being able to actually possess the sensible species, and the sensory soul's capacity to pay attention to the changes in the sense organs and to form images of the sensible species affecting the sense organ. The cognitive level of description begins with the second operation of the sensory soul, which allows for the resignification, and thus for the recovery in a new context, of the acts pertaining to the natural descriptive level. The sensory soul is endowed with the ability to reflect on itself, while attending to the sense organs that have changed from potentially to actually possessing a sensible species, and to

---

41   In this section of my paper I will have to repeat some information from the second section. I kindly ask the reader's patience, because, as will become clear, I am not simply reproducing bits of information, but adding new interpretative layers.

perceive the object by extending its intentionality. Although they are part of the natural powers of the soul, I do not take these other acts, belonging to the second operation of the sensory soul, to be part of the natural descriptive level. The reason for this is that self-reflection and perception are essentially cognitive acts, and such a feature cannot be captured by the natural descriptive level. While the sensory soul reacts instinctively to the bodily changes and thus produces images, the second operation requires more than simple machinery. The sensory soul reflects on itself and, in particular, on the images it has formed. Then chooses one image, and perceives a particular object, corresponding to the chosen image.[42] Only once the sensory soul is engaged in this second operation can we speak of cognition.

The causal relations delineated at the natural descriptive level are efficient: the object is the efficient cause of the sensible species, the sensible species is the efficient cause of the sense organ being informed, and the sensory soul is the efficient cause of the image. In a diagram, the natural descriptive level would look something like this:

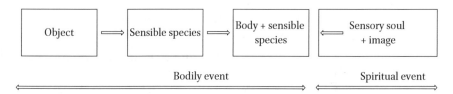

The diagram reveals three features of the bodily event relevant for causation: (1) change as form transfer, (2) the transience of change, and (3) the ascending direction of efficient causation. The first two features are supported by Kilwardby's ontological framework: since the object, the sensible species, and the body share the same ontological degree, there can be a formal transfer between them, and this transfer takes a transient form. Although the direction of causation is, ontologically speaking, taking place at the bodily level, I called the direction ascending because there is a difference in degree between an inanimate entity and an animated one. During the spiritual event, the direction of causation is from the sensory soul to the body affected by the sensible species of an object. The sensory soul being ontologically superior to the body, we can

---

42   For an explanation of the process by which the sensory soul chooses a particular image, see Silva, *Robert Kilwardby on the Human Soul*, p. 150, and Bălțuță, "Selective Attention beyond Activity: Robert Kilwardby's and Thomas Aquinas' Theory of Perception," in A.M. Mora-Márquez and V. Decaix (eds), *Active Cognition*, Dordrecht, Springer, forthcoming.

designate the direction of causation as descending. Because the soul does not pass a form to another, the change present at the spiritual level, albeit productive, is not transient, but immanent. The soul is the efficient cause of the image, but the image, which has the same spiritual matter as the soul, does not come to exist in another; it continues to exist within the soul.[43]

The cognitive level of description is based on the natural level depicted in the diagram above, but is not reducible to it. It goes, so to speak, a step further by adding a cognitive feature to both the bodily and the spiritual events. The object, through its sensible species, efficiently causes a change in the sense organ, but the change itself does not have cognitive value. The natural formation of an image, by the sensory soul in its first operation, as the sense organ is affected, also lacks cognitive value. It is only with the sensory soul performing its second operation, reflecting on itself and its products, that the image, the informed body, the sensible species and the object acquire a new feature – a cognitive one. One fundamental trait of the cognitive relation between the sensory soul and its object is that it is asymmetrical: the object *could* acquire a cognitive feature, but *actually* acquires a cognitive feature only when the sensory soul is oriented towards it cognitively. In other words, if the sensory soul is not cognitively oriented towards the object, the two events, the bodily and the spiritual one, will take place in virtue of their protagonists being endowed with specific natural powers; once the soul is cognitively oriented towards them, the object, the sensible species, and the image acquire a cognitive feature. This feature enriches the causal picture of perception by connecting the object and the sensory soul in a new way. The object remains the efficient cause of the sense organ's affection, but it also *occasions* its being perceived by the sensory soul.[44]

The cognitive descriptive level builds on the natural one, in the sense that it would not be possible without it, and adds to it a new intentional dimension, that was originally lacking. To make more sense of this second level of description and of what it amounts to, it is useful to approach it precisely from the

---

43   See *DSF* 103 above.

44   Here I understand the object occasioning its being perceived by the sensory soul in a manner similar with Nadler's understanding of the occasional cause. He takes the occasional cause to be a real cause which "unites one thing or state of affairs with an effect wrought (through efficient causation, immanent or transeunt) by another thing. Thus, the term denotes the entire process whereby one thing, *A*, occasions or elicits another thing, *B*, to cause *e*. Even though it is *B* that *A* occasions or incites to engage in the activity of efficient causation in producing *e*, the relation of occasional causation links *A* not just to *B*, but also (and especially) to the effect, *e*, produced by *B*. In other words, *A* is the occasional cause of *e*, not of *B*." See Nadler, "Descartes on Occasional Causation," p. 39.

point of view of intentionality. Think of the two operations of the sensory soul, each belonging to one level of description, as being distinguished by two corresponding types of intentionality: (1) natural, built-in intentionality and (2) cognitive intentionality. During the first operation, pertaining to the natural level, the sensory soul is oriented towards the body and forms images of the sensible species that affect the body. During the second operation, after it reflects on itself and on the images it has formed, which is what makes possible the cognitive level, the sensory soul orients towards the corporeal object. The cognitive intentionality is different from the natural intentionality precisely because it passes beyond the limits of the body towards the corporeal objects. At the natural descriptive level, the change in the organ does not lead to perception, and neither does the formation of the image. But the organ and the image lead to perception when the sensory soul chooses to focus on one image and to direct its attention towards the corresponding corporeal object. If we were to represent visually the cognitive descriptive level, it would look something like this:

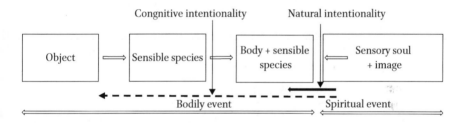

The cognitive dimension is the result of the sensory soul's second operation. The continuous black arrow, extending from the sensory soul to the body, represents the natural intentionality, while the dotted arrow, extending from the sensory soul to the object, stands for the cognitive intentionality. At the cognitive level of description, a new causal picture emerges. Becoming part of a larger scheme, initiated by the sensory soul through the extension of its intentionality, the object acquires a new causal role. The sensory soul maintains its role of efficient cause of perception, but the object turns into a *sine qua non* cause. The cognitive act of the sensory soul could not take place if the object would not act upon the body, which means that, without the change in the body, the sensory soul could not become aware of itself as vivifying the body and could not perceive the object. For the sensory soul to exert the second operation, the object must affect the body.

An appropriate analogy for understanding the *sine qua non* causation is the one used by Aristotle to describe the manifestation of natural inclinations.[45] He believes, and Kilwardby embraces the same position, that things are naturally inclined to fulfil certain ends. For example, objects are naturally inclined to fall on earth when dropped. But if there is something impeding them from falling, like a net, then they will not be able to reach their end. The fulfillment of their natural inclination will resume once the impediment is removed. In this case, the object will fall without its action being triggered by the removal of the net as by an efficient cause. In a similar argumentative vein, I think that, for Kilwardby, the absence of corporeal objects can be interpreted as being an impediment for the sensory soul's manifestation of its natural inclination to perceive. Once the object is present and affects the body, the sensory soul encounters no impediment against the exercise of its ability to perceive. And, of course, what it perceives is the very object responsible for the removal of the impediment, which plays, in this equation, the role of a *sine qua non* cause. An example would be helpful for grasping this meaning of the *sine qua non* cause. Imagine you are in a dark room facing a wall. Whenever an image is displayed on the wall, you have a visual experience. But it is not the image that is triggering the visual experience, because you are already, from the beginning and continuously, exercising your ability to see. The reason why you are not able to have a visual experience in the absence of an image being displayed on the wall is that there really is nothing to see. The absence of an image thus impedes you from actually seeing something. Once the image appears, the always and already activated ability to see passes from potentially seeing to actually seeing, without the image actually affecting the ability to see other than by offering content to the act of vision.

4.2   *The Consistency Claim*

A secondary claim I made right at the beginning of my paper was that, by analyzing Kilwardby's theory of sense perception, I will be able to dispel some apparent insufficiency he was accused of in contemporary scholarship. The criticism I pointed to is raised by Silva.[46] First, I should mention that the context of

---

45   See Aristotle, *Physics*, *The Complete Works of Aristotle*, 2 vols., trans. J. Barnes, Princeton, Princeton University Press, 1984, VIII.4, 255 b30–31; *De anima*, *The Complete Works of Aristotle*, II. 5. For an understanding of the *sine qua non* causation along the same lines, but with respect to a different context, see P.J. Hartman, "Causation and Cognition: Durand of Saint-Pourçain and Godfrey of Fontaines on the Cause of a Cognitive Act," in A. Speer, F. Retucci, T. Jeschke, and G. Guldentops (eds), *Durand of Saint-Pourçain and His "Sentences" Commentary: Historical, Philosophical, and Theological Issues*, Leuven, Peeters, 2014.

46   See Silva, *Robert Kilwardby on the Human Soul*, pp. 29, 150, and, especially, 159.

ROBERT KILWARDBY ON OBJECTS AS SINE QUA NON CAUSES

the criticism is Silva's endeavor to find out what is, according to Kilwardby, the criterion followed by the sensory soul when selecting an image, out of many, as a focal point. Reaching a final answer is, for Silva, only one reference away. The passage he points to is from DSF. There it is said that if multiple rays of light reach our eyes, only the most intense one will be perceived.[47] Thus the criterion sought after is found: it is intensity. The images formed by the sensory soul bear the mark of the intensity of the stimuli affecting the body, and, from all the images, the soul chooses the most intense one. Furthermore, Silva draws the consequence that Kilwardby's theory of sense perception complies with the principle of proportionality: the more intense the stimuli affecting the body, the more intense the reaction of the sensory soul. According to Silva, this is where Kilwardby's thoughts no longer add up. Proportionality should have been kept out of the theory of perception: "The problem with this [with proportionality] is that it involves a causal relation that goes against everything Kilwardby wanted to admit in suggesting that the attention of the soul is stimuli driven."[48] The way I understand it, Silva's worry is that Kilwardby falls into inconsistency when stating both that (1) the sensory soul cannot be acted upon by the object, due to the ontological difference between them, and (2) the sensory soul reacts proportionally to the external stimuli affecting the body. But, although I understand it, I do not share the view.

There are two fallacies lurking in Silva's criticism: a faulty generalization and a straw man. Let me expose them one at a time. First, the textual evidence for the identification of Kilwardby's answer to the problem of selective attention is fairly thin. It amounts to only one passage. In a situation like this, at least, one should resort to a systematic approach. In a way, this is exactly Silva's impulse. He takes a look at the idea of the passage from DSF and realizes it is inconsistent with everything else Kilwardby had to say on the matter. But stops right there. Intensity thus maintains its position as the criterion the soul uses when choosing to focus on one image instead of another. Though inconsistent with the basic tenets of his own philosophy, this is, according to Silva, Kilwardby's answer. Such an interpretative approach is puzzling. If, in general, there is indeed an inconsistency between one passage and the rest of a text, should one not try to adopt (without being unreasonable) a more charitable approach? Should one not read the passage again and seek for an interpretation that

---

47 Kilwardby, DSF 203: "Tamen potest dici quod sicut multa lumina et multi radii simul sunt, et tamen contingit quod vnum uel vnus tantum sensibiliter apparet, propter eius excellentiam que absorbet apparentiam aliorum, sic forte multorum sensatorum species simul sunt in uno spiritu corporeo, de quibus non apparent nisi ille in quas aliqua occasione dirigitur intencio animi."

48 Silva, *Robert Kilwardby on the Human Soul*, p. 159.

would manage to restore some consistency? A few phrases from a larger text should not be looked at as having a perfectly autonomous meaning.

For more clarity on my own side, let me return to the problematic passage from DSF. How should one understand the proportionality between the intensity of the stimuli affecting the body and the reaction of the soul? If we take into account the example of the multiple rays of light affecting the eyes, it might seem, indeed, that proportionality should be understood quite strictly, as involving some form of upwards causation. But is it legitimate to extrapolate this understanding of proportionality to the situations in which selective attention comes into play? Should proportionality always be understood as a sign of upwards causation? I think not. To justify my answer, I turn now to another of Silva's texts on Kilwardby, where he acknowledges that the proportionality of the reaction to the external stimuli is grounded in the soul's task of protecting and preserving the body.[49] Keeping this in mind, I notice that for fulfilling its task, the soul is equipped not just with the ability to distinguish, consciously or not, between the more and the less intense stimuli affecting the body, but with other abilities as well. One of them is the ability to distinguish between harmful and harmless stimuli. Accordingly, if confronted simultaneously with two equally intense stimuli, one harmful for the body and the other pleasant, the reaction of the soul to the two stimuli will not be equal. It is only natural to assume that, given its task, the sensory soul will pay more attention to the harmful stimulus. Such a case leads me to believe that, in the end, proportionality in general should not be understood too strictly. It is not as if a certain degree of intensity of the stimuli affecting the body is always associated with a reaction, on the part of the sensory soul, whose intensity is always the same. The reaction as such of the sensory soul has a more contingent flavor to it. It does not depend only on the stimuli affecting the body, but, first of all, on the task and the situation of the sensory soul. So, if Kilwardby does indeed follow, in his theory of perception, some principle of proportionality, this is not as straightforward as Silva takes it to be. Consequently, the causation involved in the proportionality between the stimuli affecting the body and the reaction of the soul should not be understood too strictly, that is, as a clear sign of upwards causation. Not even when it comes to some rays of light affecting the eyes. This will become evident as I expose the second of Silva's fallacies.

Let us simply admit that we are entitled to speak of some kind of proportionality between the intensity of an image and the reaction of the soul, or, to go even deeper, between the affection of the body and the reaction of the sensory soul. Does this go against Kilwardby's philosophy? Does proportionality

---

49   Silva and Toivanen, "The Active Nature of the Soul," p. 260.

involve a causal relation that would jeopardize its consistency? In my opinion, proportionality is not Kilwardby's worry – *affectionism* is. And proportionality does not necessarily involve affectionism. Consequently, when raising his criticism, Silva commits a straw man fallacy. If we stay true to an approach of perception from a dual perspective, natural and cognitive, the criticism becomes groundless. At the natural level, Kilwardby has no problem in accepting the proportionality between the stimuli affecting the body and the reaction of the sensory soul. In this case, the proportionality does not rest on a bottom-up direction of causation, but on the nature of the sensory soul and its workings. The soul, from the outset and continuously, watches over the body. It does so by creating images, also of the eventual affections of the body. And while the images are proportionate to the eventual affections of the body, they are not the result of a bottom-up causal process; the images are not the result of some affection of the soul. No, the attention and the formation of the image are only the result of the soul's continuous activity, according to its design. What, then, is the situation at the cognitive level? Is there some new activity of the soul triggered by the object affecting the body? As I have already shown in my reading of Kilwardby, nothing like this occurs. The object is just the *sine qua non* cause of perception. It simply offers content to the perceptual acts of the soul – it does not cause them. Consequently, even at this level, we are entitled to speak of proportionality, because the soul perceives as much as it can, without falling into some sort of affectionism. And if there is much more to perceive than it actually can, then the soul has to choose, but always on the grounds of its design and tasks. In fact, it never reacts. It acts.

5   Conclusion

The aim of this chapter was to spell out the causal role of the external object in Kilwardby's theory of sense perception. To do so, I started by comparing Aquinas and Kilwardby's ontological frameworks. The comparison showed that from the two different ontological architectures of the world, two different understandings of agency follow: one driven by local nobility (Aquinas), the other driven by global nobility (Kilwardby). Because of this understanding of agency, Kilwardby cannot follow the same route as Aquinas when explaining perception and causation. This leads him to ascribe different properties to the sensory soul and a different causal role to the object: the sensory soul is self-actualizing and the object plays the role of a *sine qua non* cause of perception. For an understanding of all intricacies of Kilwardby's account of the perceptual processes, I have shown that one has to look at his theory from a double perspective: a natural and a cognitive one. This way, by understanding perception as a two-level process, with two different causal chains and two types of intentionality involved, one can fully appreciate Kilwardby's theory of perception and see that behind apparent insufficiencies there is a consistent thought.[50]

Bibliography

Primary Literature

Aristotle, *The Complete Works of Aristotle*, 2 vols., trans. J. Barnes, Princeton, Princeton University Press, 1984.

Robert Kilwardby, *De spiritu fantastico*, P.O. Lewry (ed), *On Time and Imagination: De tempore, De spiritu fantastico*, Oxford, Oxford University Press for the British Academy, 1987.

Robert Kilwardby, *On Time and Imagination*, Part 2, trans. A. Broadie, Oxford, Oxford University Press for the British Academy, 1993.

Robert Kilwardby, *Quaestiones in librum primum Sententiarum*, J. Schneider (ed), München, Verlag der Bayerischen Akademie der Wissenschaften, 1986.

Robert Kilwardby, *Quaestiones in librum secundum Sententiarum*, G. Leibold (ed), München, Verlag der Bayerischen Akademie der Wissenschaften, 1992.

Thomas Aquinas, *De malo, Opera omnia 23*, Rome, Ad Sanctae, 1982.

Thomas Aquinas, *De substantiis separatis, Opera omnia 40*, Rome, Ad Sanctae, 1968.

Thomas Aquinas, *Summa Theologiae I, Opera omnia 5*, Rome, Ad Sanctae, 1889.

Secondary Literature

Adriaenssen, Han Thomas, *Representation and Scepticism from Aquinas to Descartes*, Cambridge, Cambridge University Press, 2017.

Bălțuță, Elena, "Aquinas on Intellectual Cognition: The Case of Intelligible Species," *Philosophia*, vol. 41, no. 3, 2013, pp. 589–602.

Bălțuță, Elena, "Selective Attention beyond Activity: Robert Kilwardby's and Thomas Aquinas' Theory of Perception," in A.M. Mora-Márquez and V. Decaix (eds), *Active Cognition*, Dordrecht, Springer, forthcoming.

---

50   I would like to thank the reviewers for their very helpful suggestions. Deepest thanks go to Katie Keller and Sergiu Sava for careful reading and ruthless criticism. All remaining errors are due solely to my stubbornness.

ROBERT KILWARDBY ON OBJECTS AS SINE QUA NON CAUSES 211

Broadie, Alexander, "Introduction," in Robert Kilwardby, *On Time and Imagination*, Part 2, trans. A. Broadie, Oxford, Oxford University Press for The British Academy, 1993.

Conti, Alessandro D., "Semantics and Ontology in Robert Kilwardby's Commentaries on the *Logica vetus*," in P. Thom and H. Lagerlund (eds), *A Companion to the Philosophy of Robert Kilwardby*, Leiden, Brill, 2003, pp. 65–130.

Donati, Silvia, "Robert Kilwardby on Matter," in P. Thom and H. Lagerlund (eds), *A Companion to the Philosophy of Robert Kilwardby*, Leiden, Brill, 2003, pp. 239–275.

Hartman, Peter John, "Causation and Cognition: Durand of Saint-Pourçain and Godfrey of Fontaines on the Cause of a Cognitive Act," in A. Speer, F. Retucci, T. Jeschke, and G. Guldentops (eds), *Durand of Saint-Pourçain and His "Sentences" Commentary: Historical, Philosophical, and Theological Issues*, Leuven, Peeters, 2014, pp. 229–256.

Hartman, Peter John, "Durand of St.-Pourçain on Cognitive Acts: Their Cause, Ontological Status, and Intentional Character," PhD dissertation, University of Toronto, 2012.

Lisska, Anthony, *Aquinas's Theory of Perception: An Analytic Reconstruction*, Oxford, Oxford University Press, 2016.

Nadler, Steven „Descartes and Occasional Causation," *British Journal for the History of Philosophy*, vol. 2, no. 1, 1994, pp. 35–54.

O'Callaghan, John P., "Aquinas, Cognitive Theory, and Analogy," *American Catholic Philosophical Quarterly*, vol. 76, no. 3, 2002, pp. 451–482.

Pasnau, Robert, *Theories of Cognition in the Later Middle Ages*, Cambridge, Cambridge University Press, 1997.

Perler, Dominik (ed), *Ancient and Medieval Theories of Intentionality*, Leiden, Brill, 2001.

Rosemann, Philipp, *Omne agens agit sibi simile: A "Repetition" of Scholastic Metaphysics*, Louvain, Louvain University Press, 1996.

Silva, José Filipe and Toivanen, Juhana, "The Active Nature of the Soul in Sense Perception: Robert Kilwardby and Peter John of Olivi," *Vivarium*, vol. 48, no. 3–4, 2010, pp. 245–278.

Silva, José Filipe, "Robert Kilwardby on Sense Perception," in S. Knuuttila and P. Kärkkäinen (eds), *Theories of Perception in Medieval and Early Modern Philosophy*, Dordrecht, Springer, 2008, pp. 87–99.

Silva, José Filipe, *Robert Kilwardby on the Human Soul: Plurality of Forms and Censorship in the Thirteenth Century*, Leiden, Brill, 2012.

Silva, José Filipe, "Robert Kilwardby on the Theory of the Soul and Epistemology," in H. Lagerlund and P. Thom (eds), *A Companion to the Philosophy of Robert Kilwardby*, Leiden, Brill, 2013, pp. 275–313.

Silva, José Filipe, "The Human Soul in Robert Kilwardby's Natural Philosophy and Theology," PhD dissertation, University of Porto, 2009.

Sirridge, Mary, "*Utrum idem sint dicere et intelligere sive videre in mente*: Robert Kilwardby, *Quaestiones in librum primum Sententiarum*," *Vivarium*, vol. 45, no. 2–3, 2007, pp. 253–268.

Solère, Jen-Luc, "*Sine qua non* Causality and the Context of Durand's Early Theory of Cognition," in A. Speer, F. Retucci, Th. Jeschke, and G. Guldentops (eds), *Durand of Saint-Pourçain and his "Sentences" Commentary: Historical, Philosophical, and Theological Issues*, Leuven, Peeters, 2014, pp. 185–227.

Spruit, Leen, *Species intelligibilis: From Perception to Knowledge*, vol. I: *Classical Roots and Medieval Discussions*, Leiden, Brill, 1994.

Stump, Eleonore, *Aquinas*, London, Routledge, 2003.

CHAPTER 8

Rational Seeing: Thomas Aquinas on Human Perception

Dominik Perler

1 Introduction: Human and Non-human Seeing

Suppose that you have a dog and that you go out with him for a walk, the way you do every morning. You leave your apartment and reach a bridge nearby that goes over a small river. But the bridge has been flooded after a severe storm and is now closed to the public. So both you and your dog stop walking. Why do you stop? It seems natural to give two different explanations, one for you and one for your dog. The dog, a non-rational animal, stops walking because he has a perception that immediately triggers a bodily reaction. He does not think that he is standing in front of a bridge, nor does he think that it would be dangerous to step on the bridge. Merely seeing and hearing the cascading water makes him stand still. You also have a perception, just like the dog, and it might also provoke an immediate reaction. But you have more than that. Since you are a rational animal, you spontaneously engage in a number of acts of thinking and reasoning. For example, you think that the bridge is closed, you also think that this is due to the storm last night, and you reason that you would be in great danger if you tried to step on the bridge. This complex bundle of rational activities makes you stand still. The important point is that you share something with your dog, namely perceptual sensitivity, while possessing something in addition, namely rationality, which makes you special. Rationality is exactly what becomes manifest in your acts of thinking and reasoning, not in your basic acts of seeing and hearing.

One might think that medieval authors in the Aristotelian tradition subscribed to this conception of rationality when they distinguished different types of souls in different types of animals. Dogs and other non-rational animals, they famously claimed, have just a vegetative and a sensory soul. Thanks to the sensory soul, they are clearly capable of cognition, for this soul enables them to have many acts of perceiving, imagining, and remembering. All these acts are produced through natural causal processes, and they in turn naturally produce bodily movements. Human beings also have a sensory soul and are therefore also capable of perceiving, imagining, and remembering things with which they have been in contact. But in addition to that, they possess a rational

© KONINKLIJKE BRILL NV, LEIDEN, 2020 | DOI:10.1163/9789004413030_009

soul that enables them to produce concepts, judgments, and chains of reasoning.[1] If we want to understand what makes human beings so special we simply need to look at the activities of the rational soul. That is, we simply need to analyze what conceiving, thinking, and reasoning amount to. But there is no need to pay attention to the acts of perceiving, for these acts are more or less the same in non-rational and rational animals; both types of animals perceive external things by receiving sensible forms and producing sensory representations, so-called phantasms.[2] It would therefore not make sense to ask what is so special about the sensory soul in human beings. Just like the sensory soul in a dog, it is simply responsible for the production and use of phantasms.

On this way of going, of course, one could still hold that there is considerable difference as far as the accuracy of phantasms is concerned. For instance, dogs have a better sense of smell than human beings and can therefore produce more accurate phantasms when receiving an olfactory input. And there is also a clear difference between various non-rational animals. For example, cats have a better sense of sight than dogs, and dogs in turn have a better sense of sight than moles. It is therefore important to assign different types of sensory souls to different types of animals.[3] But, one might suppose, there is no need to highlight the sensory soul in human beings and to characterize it in a special way. It works exactly like the equivalent soul in non-rational animals and differs from it only insofar as its material implementation is concerned, not its range of activities. Hence one should only look at the rational soul when spelling out the characteristic features of human beings.

---

1   These are the three "operations of the intellect," which were frequently mentioned in debates about distinctively human activities. For an extensive overview, see T.W. Köhler, *Homo animal nobilissimum. Konturen des spezifisch Menschlichen in der naturphilosophischen Aristoteleskommentierung des dreizehnten Jahrhunderts*, 2 vols., Leiden, Brill, 2014.

2   To be sure, rational and non-rational animals do not simply receive sensible forms, both proper and common ones, but they also assimilate them, thereby undergoing a special type of change. That is why perception involves not only a passive reception, but also an active adaptation to what is received. For a short analysis of this complex process, see Dominik Perler, "Perception in Medieval Philosophy," in M. Matthen (ed), *The Oxford Handbook of Philosophy of Perception*, Oxford, Oxford University Press, 2015, pp. 51–65.

3   Medieval authors were clearly aware of these differences. Some even tried to establish a taxonomy of different types of sensory souls by distinguishing different types of cognitive achievements. See C.G. Steel, G. Guldentops, and P. Beullens (eds), *Aristotle's Animals in the Middle Ages and Renaissance*, Leuven, Leuven University Press, 1999, and B. Roling, "Die Geometrie der Bienenwabe: Albertus Magnus, Karl von Baer und die Debatte über das Vorstellungsvermögen und die Seele der Insekten zwischen Mittelalter und Neuzeit," *Recherches de théologie et philosophie médiévales*, vol. 80, 2013, pp. 363–466. On the cognitive activities ascribed to animals, see A. Oelze, *Animal Rationality: Later Medieval Theories 1250–1350*, Leiden, Brill, 2018.

RATIONAL SEEING: THOMAS AQUINAS ON HUMAN PERCEPTION 215

It is tempting to approach medieval theories in this way and to assume that Aristotelians were only interested in the rational soul as some kind of "extra ingredient" that makes sophisticated "extra activities" possible. But we should resist this temptation. When comparing non-rational to rational animals, many medieval authors claimed that there is already a striking difference at the level of the sensory soul. Some even went so far as to claim that the sensory soul in human beings is so closely linked to or interwoven with the rational soul that it is somehow imbued with rationality. Thomas Aquinas is a clear example. In his *Questions on De anima* he defends the following thesis:

> ...the sensory soul in a human being is more elevated than in other animals, because in a human being it is not just sensory, but also rational.

> ...the sensory soul in a human being is not a non-rational soul, it is rather at the same time a sensory and a rational soul.[4]

Obviously, Aquinas does not hold that the sensory soul in human beings is more or less the same as in non-rational animals. Since it is closely tied to the rational soul, it participates in the rational soul and therefore works in close cooperation with that soul.[5] Hence it differs from the sensory soul in other animals not just as far as its material implementation is concerned, but also in its very functioning. It would therefore be inappropriate to assume that you and your dog have the same type of seeing when you approach the bridge. Rather, you see the bridge in your own, typically human way by using a sensory soul that is right from the beginning under the guidance of the rational soul. Or for short, you are capable of *rational seeing* while the dog is confined to sensory seeing, and this is the case irrespective of acts of judging and reasoning you might produce in addition to your act of seeing.

But what does it mean for human beings to engage in rational seeing? How does it differ from purely sensory seeing? And in what sense is the soul that is responsible for this type of seeing more than a mere sensory soul? These are the questions I would like to discuss in this paper by focusing on some key texts in Aquinas. I will proceed in three steps. First, I will consider the metaphysical

---

4 Thomas Aquinas, *Quaestiones disputatae de anima* (= QDA) q. 11, ad 12, B.C. Bazán (ed), *Opera omnia 24.1*, Rome, Commissio Leonina, 1996, p. 103: "... anima sensibilis est nobilior in homine quam in aliis animalibus quia in homine non tantum est sensibilis, set etiam rationalis." QDA, q. 11, ad 15: "... anima sensibilis in homine non est anima irrationalis, set est anima sensibilis et rationalis simul."

5 Aquinas explicitly speaks about participation. *Sentencia libri De anima* (= SDA) II.13, *Opera omnia 45.1*, Rome, Commissio Leonina, 1984, p. 122: "... uis sensitiva in sui supremo participat aliquid de ui intellectiua in homine, in quo sensus intellectui coniungitur."

framework and, in particular, examine how Aquinas explains the intimate relationship between the sensory and the rational soul. Then I will look at the epistemological consequences of his metaphysical model and analyze his account of rational seeing by paying close attention to the functioning of the *vis cogitativa*. In the third and last step, I will build a bridge to contemporary debates and make a methodological suggestion for characterizing Aquinas's approach to the problem of human perception.

2 The Metaphysical Inclusion Model

It is well known that in his theory of the soul Aquinas defends a unitarian thesis, claiming that there is a single substantial form and hence a single soul in a human being. He thereby rejects the pluralist position that accepts several substantial forms, which are not just conceptually but really distinct from each other.[6] Much more interesting than this often-quoted thesis is the way Aquinas argues for it, since it is in his controversy with the pluralists that he outlines the relationship between sensitivity and rationality. Let me therefore look at the three most important arguments he adduces to defend the unitarian thesis.[7]

The first argument could be called *the argument from unity*.[8] In order to be a unified substance that is distinct from other substances, a human being needs to have a principle of unity that combines all the parts, thus making a whole out of them. If there were several substantial forms or souls, there would be several principles of unity, which would be responsible for different wholes. For instance, the vegetative soul would be responsible for a whole consisting of the heart and the lungs, the sensory soul would be responsible for a different whole consisting of the sensory organs, and the rational soul would be respon-

---

6 See Aquinas, *Summa theologiae* (= *STh*) I, q. 76, art. 3, P. Caramello (ed), Turin, Marietti, 1952; *Summa contra Gentiles* (= *ScG*) II.58, C. Pera (ed), Turin, Marietti, 1961; *QDA*, q. 11. On the thirteenth-century controversy between pluralists and unitarists, see R. Zavalloni, *Richard de Mediavilla et la controverse sur la pluralité des formes*, Louvain, Éditions de l'institut supérieur de philosophie, 1951, and B.C. Bazán, "Pluralisme de formes ou dualisme de substances?" *Revue philosophique de Louvain*, vol. 67, 1969, pp. 30–73. This controversy shaped medieval debates far beyond the thirteenth century, as R. Pasnau, *Metaphysical Themes 1274–1671*, Oxford, Oxford University Press, 2011, pp. 574–605, shows in his wide-ranging analysis.

7 For an analysis of the general framework of these arguments, which will not be discussed here, see R. Pasnau, *Thomas Aquinas on Human Nature: A Philosophical Study of "Summa theologiae" Ia 75–89*, Cambridge, Cambridge University Press, 2002, pp. 73–99, and more extensively Jeffrey E. Brower, *Aquinas's Ontology of the Material World: Change, Hylomorphism, & Material Objects*, Oxford, Oxford University Press, 2014, pp. 103–184.

8 See Aquinas, *STh* I, q. 76, art. 3, corp.; *ScG* II.58, n. 8–9.

RATIONAL SEEING: THOMAS AQUINAS ON HUMAN PERCEPTION   217

sible for still another whole. But there would be no single whole that integrates all the parts. A complete whole is only possible if there is a single soul that unifies all the parts, whether they are responsible for vegetative, sensory, or rational functions.

A pluralist may remain unconvinced. Of course, he might say, there needs to be a single whole. Consequently, there also needs to be something that integrates all the parts. But why is an all-encompassing soul required for that? Why could we not assume that there is a vegetative, a sensory, and a rational soul, each of them having its own function, and still hold that a single, unified whole results, because all three forms are present in a single body? The body is the common basis for all the forms and therefore the required principle of unity.

In Aquinas's eyes, this reply is unsatisfactory, because it presupposes that a body is an actually existing thing that can serve as the unifying basis for all these forms. But there is no such thing as the body without a form. In fact, it is only because of a form that matter, which in itself has only potential existence, becomes something actual and hence an actually existing body.[9] It would therefore be wrong to assume that there is, right from the beginning, a ready-made body in which various forms can be interconnected and unified.[10] On the contrary, we need a form right from the beginning that makes the body an actual thing. And there can only be *one* actual thing if there is *one* form. The vegetative, the sensory, and the rational elements, therefore, cannot be associated with distinct forms. They can only be different aspects or manifestations of a single form.

This argument clearly shows that Aquinas rejects a compositional model according to which three souls are simply combined in a given body. This also becomes evident in his second argument, which could be called *the argument from predication*.[11] When we make a predicative statement like 'A human being is an animal,' he says, we clearly do not make an accidental predication, for we

---

9   See Aquinas, *STh* I, q. 75, art. 1; *SDA* II.1, Leonina 45.1, pp. 71–73.

10   A pluralist could reply that there is in fact a ready-made body because there is a special form of corporeality that structures matter, thus making it a particular body; a number of additional, hierarchically ordered forms can then be implemented in the body. There were indeed a number of pluralists, among them Richard of Mediavilla and William Ockham, who chose this line of argument (for a discussion, see M. McCord Adams, *William Ockham*, Notre Dame, Notre Dame University Press, 1987, pp. 647–667). However, it does not really solve the unity problem. It rather gives rise to new questions. How are the additional forms connected with the basic form of corporeality? Why should they be hierarchically ordered? And why do all the forms together constitute a unity and not just a bundle or assemblage of forms? As long as these questions remain unanswered, the unity is postulated rather than metaphysically grounded.

11   See Aquinas, *STh* I, q. 76, art. 3, corp.; *QDA*, q. 11, corp.

do not affirm that a human being happens to be an animal right now but could also be something different. We rather say that a human being is essentially an animal, thus making an essential predication. And in this kind of predication we do not merely speak about a general essence, which needs to be further determined. We rather speak about a specific essence, that is, we say that a human being is an animal of a certain type, namely one that has vegetative, sensory, and rational functions. There could be no such essence without a single form that is responsible for all the functions. Hence there must be a single form that determines the full essence.

Here, again, a pluralist could object that this argument is not compelling. Of course, he might say, I agree that 'A human being is an animal' is an essential predication. But in this predication we simply indicate the general genus to which a human being belongs. This genus is fixed by the sensory soul, which makes a human being a living thing with sensory organs. However, we need another form to explain the fact that a human being also belongs to a particular species, namely that of thinking animals. Only when we add this further form do we get a full-fledged human being for which we can spell out the full essence.

When arguing in this way, the pluralist assumes that we can somehow compose an essence, just as we can compose a meal. We start with the most basic ingredient and then add other ingredients until we arrive at the finished product. But from Aquinas's point of view, this compositional method will never yield a unified essence. It will only yield an assemblage of some features – an assemblage that could always be taken apart when the forms are separated. But in the case of a human being, there is no mere assemblage. When one of the key features is taken away, the whole essence collapses. For instance, when we take away rationality, we do not simply have a truncated human essence. We rather lose this essence completely. That is why it is all-or-nothing: either we have a human essence that includes all the relevant functions, ranging from digesting up to thinking, or we do not have a human essence at all.

Finally, Aquinas presents a third argument for the unitarian thesis, which could be labeled *the argument from coordination*.[12] We often notice, he says, that a human being engages in several activities and that one of them is so intensive that it hinders the other activities or even makes them impossible. This can easily be illustrated. Imagine a mathematician who is so absorbed by her abstract thinking that she ignores all the things around her. She no longer hears the bell that is ringing at the door, and she no longer notices the people who come into her apartment. Her activity of thinking is so strong and

---

12   See Aquinas, *STh* I, q. 76, art. 3, corp.; *ScG* II.58, n. 10.

RATIONAL SEEING: THOMAS AQUINAS ON HUMAN PERCEPTION   219

dominant that it leaves no room for other activities. Now this would be impossible, Aquinas argues, if there were not a single soul that produces and coordinates all these activities. Whenever this soul engages in a certain activity more intensely, it reduces its engagement in all other activities. In fact, this soul is the principle of coordination that makes it possible to give priority to a specific activity while hindering or even suppressing other ones.[13]

How might a pluralist react to this argument? He could agree that Aquinas describes a phenomenon we often encounter. But he could give a different account of it. When someone engages in a certain activity more intensely and thus hinders others, there are simply different forms or souls inside that person – souls that act with different force. Thus, in the case of the mathematician there is a rational soul that acts so powerfully that it prevents the sensory soul from functioning. This is the reason why the rational activity predominates while the sensory activities fade out. Indeed, the simple fact that there are different activities with differing degrees of intensity shows that there need to be different souls that bring them about.[14]

This reply would hardly be acceptable to Aquinas. He would immediately point out that it does not suffice to simply refer to different souls. As long as one does not explain why and how these souls are coordinated, it remains a mystery why increasing the intensity of an activity in one soul goes along with a decrease in the activities of another soul. Why, for instance, should the fact that the mathematician's rational soul is engaged in intense abstract thought have an impact on her sensory soul? Why should there be a causal relation? Can the rational soul somehow act upon the sensory soul and prevent it from acting? If so, how can it do that, and, more broadly, how is it possible for the two different types of soul to interact? After all, the rational soul is fully

---

13   Of course, sensory activities need not be suppressed in every situation. For instance, while thinking about a theorem the mathematician may be looking very intently at a paper in a scientific journal. In that case her thinking is supported and strengthened by a sensory activity. Hence, the increasing of a rational activity does not necessarily go along with the decreasing of a sensory activity. All that matters is the coordination of the two types of activity.

14   This is in fact the argument Ockham adduces. He even points out that different souls can bring about contrary activities. Thus, the sensory soul can desire a certain object, while the rational soul can reject it. Which soul will dominate simply depends on the strength of the activities at stake. If, for instance, the rational rejection turns out to be stronger than the sensory desire, the rational soul will win. See *Quodlibeta* I, q. 10, J.C. Wey (ed), *Opera Theologica IX*, St. Bonaventure, The Franciscan Institute, 1980, p. 157. For an analysis, see Dominik Perler, "Ockham on Emotions in the Divided Soul," in K. Corcilius and D. Perler (eds), *Partitioning the Soul: Debates from Plato to Leibniz*, Berlin, De Gruyter, 2014, pp. 179–198.

immaterial, while the sensory soul is present in the sensory organs and therefore material.[15] The causal relation between them seems to be postulated rather than argued for. That is why the pluralist model cannot give a solid account of the problem of coordination. Only a model that accepts a single soul and hence a single principle of activity can explain why all the relevant activities are mutually responsive in the manner seen in the case of the mathematician. This is simply due to the fact that they all have the same cause.

This argument shows again that Aquinas rejects a compositional model, for whenever there is a composition we not only need to give an account of what binds all the components together, we also need to explain why the components fit together and interact. These problems can be avoided if we assume right from the beginning that there are no really distinct components or souls. There is just one soul that acts in different ways, thus bringing about different types of activities. Or as Aquinas himself says: "Therefore, one should say that numerically the same soul in a human being is sensory, intellectual, and nutritive."[16]

However, this unitarian position gives rise to the question of how the single soul can act in different ways. What makes functional diversity possible? Aquinas is not at a loss for an answer. There is functional diversity because the soul has different faculties that are responsible for different types of activities. And faculties are not substantial forms, but powers *inside* the single form. Technically speaking, they are qualities of that form. Aquinas hastens to add that they are not contingent qualities but necessary ones that always belong to the substantial form and that cannot be separated from it.[17] This means that the vegetative, the sensory, and the rational faculties necessarily belong to the human soul. Even after death, when the soul is separated from the body, none of these faculties are destroyed. The vegetative and the sensory faculties simply become inactive, that is, they cease to produce acts of digesting or perceiving because they lack the necessary material basis. But they persist together with

---

15   A pluralist like Ockham concedes that the sensory soul is not just present in the material organs but that it is itself "extended and material"; see *Quodlibeta* I, q. 10, *Opera Theologica IX*, p. 159. This aggravates the problem: how can two souls that belong to two different realms interact?

16   Aquinas, *STh* I, q. 76, art. 3, corp.: "Sic ergo dicendum quod eadem numero est anima in homine sensitiva et intellectiva et nutritiva."

17   Faculties are therefore not simple accidents but *propria*, i.e. qualities that immediately derive from the essence of the soul. See Aquinas, *STh* I, q. 77, art. 1, and *QDA*, q. 12, ad 7. For a detailed analysis, see Dominik Perler "Faculties in Medieval Philosophy," in D. Perler (ed), *The Faculties: A History*, Oxford, Oxford University Press, 2015, pp. 97–139 (especially pp. 105–114).

RATIONAL SEEING: THOMAS AQUINAS ON HUMAN PERCEPTION   221

the rational faculty and eventually become active again when the soul is re-united with the body. Being necessary qualities, they remain inside the soul and are never lost.[18]

But how do they exist inside the single soul? One may have the suspicion that Aquinas reintroduces the compositional model through the back door. Instead of speaking about different forms, he refers to different qualities. But they seem to be really distinct entities that are somehow assembled; and what is assembled can also be separated. So, how and why do they form a unity? Aquinas is fully aware of this problem and attempts to solve it by adducing two arguments. First, he insists that these faculties are not separable. As we have just seen, all the faculties are necessary qualities that are inseparable from each other and from the soul itself. In fact, they exist together as a *totum poten-tiale*.[19] This is not a potential whole, as one might think, but a power-whole, i.e., a complex unity of powers or faculties.[20] This unity can never be taken apart because the different powers are necessarily interconnected and coordinated in their activities. Thus, whenever the sensory faculty produces acts of percep-tion, the rational faculty becomes active on that basis and produces acts of thinking and willing. There is, as it were, a network of powers that act in ac-cordance with each other, because they are all parts of a power-whole.

The second argument Aquinas adduces in order to solve the unity problem is based on his explanation of how the various powers of the soul are related to each other. Borrowing a comparison from Aristotle, he points out that the fac-ulties or powers of the soul are interrelated in the same way as geometrical figures.[21] Just as a pentagon includes a quadrangle, which in turn includes a triangle, so the human soul includes many interconnected powers. We might call this the *inclusion model*, which stands in clear opposition to the assem-blage model.[22] The crucial point is that faculties or powers are not simply

---

18   See Aquinas, *STh* I, q. 77, art. 8; *QDA*, q. 19, corp.

19   Aquinas, *STh* I, q. 77, art. 1, ad 1.

20   Note that all the powers have actual existence, even if not all of them are actually used all the time. It would therefore be misleading to contrast a *totum potentiale* with an actually existing whole. A *totum potentiale* is an actual whole, not a mere potential whole. On this specific type of whole, which should not be conflated with other types, see A. Arlig, "Is There a Medieval Mereology?" in M. Cameron and J. Marenbon (eds), *Methods and Meth-odologies: Aristotelian Logic East and West, 500–1500*, Leiden, Brill, 2011, pp. 161–189 (espe-cially pp. 165–167).

21   See Aquinas, *SDA* II.5 (Leonina 45.1, p. 90), which is a commentary on *De anima* II.3 (414b19–31).

22   In Aquinas, *STh* I, q. 76, art. 4, corp., Aquinas holds when rejecting the pluralist position: "Unde dicendum est quod nulla alia forma substantialis est in homine, nisi sola anima intellectiva: et quod ipsa, sicut *virtute continet* animam sensitivam et nutritivam, ita *vir-*

gathered or mixed up in the soul, similar to the way apples and oranges are mixed up in a basket. They rather form a well-structured whole with a hierarchical structure. Thus, the sensory faculty is subordinated to the rational one, just as a triangle is subordinated to and included in a quadrangle. Hence the sensory faculty never acts as an isolated faculty. All its activities are carried out in close relation to the activities of the rational faculty. Aquinas even uses teleological language when characterizing this dependency relation. He claims that there is a "natural order" among the faculties so that the lower one always acts for the sake of the higher one.[23]

Given this inclusion model, we can now understand the claim that looked so puzzling at the beginning, namely the claim that "the sensory soul in a human being is not a non-rational soul, but at the same time a sensory and a rational soul."[24] This does not mean that our sensory soul is a hybrid soul, composed of a sensory and a rational element. Nor does it mean that this soul goes back and forth between being sensory and rational. It rather means that our sensory soul, unlike that of a dog, is a faculty or power that is always subordinated to the rational power and included in an all-embracing soul. Consequently, its activities are always closely linked to and shaped by those of the rational faculty. Or for short, they are always imbued with rationality.

3 The Functioning of the Cogitative Power

Let us now examine the consequences this metaphysical model has for the analysis of human perception. When explaining the activities of the sensory faculty, Aquinas distinguishes between the external and the internal senses, and he enumerates four internal senses: (1) the common sense, which unifies the sensible forms that have been received by the external senses, (2) the phantasy or imagination, which produces a sensory representation on that basis, (3) the memory, which stores and eventually reactivates this representation, and

---

tute continet omnes inferiores formas... " (emphasis added). Note that the intellectual or rational soul does not "virtually contain" all other souls, as some interpreters suggest with their translation (for instance R. Pasnau, *The Treatise on Human Nature: Summa Theologiae ia 75–89*, Indianopolis, Hackett, 2002, p. 35). There is not simply a virtual containment as opposed to an actual one. Rather, the rational soul contains in its power (*virtus*) all other souls, which are partial but nevertheless actual powers.

23 Aquinas, *STh* I, q. 77, art. 4, corp.
24 See note 4.

RATIONAL SEEING: THOMAS AQUINAS ON HUMAN PERCEPTION 223

(4) the cogitative power (*vis cogitativa*).[25] It is the fourth internal sense that deserves special attention, for it differs from what can be found in non-rational animals. These animals have nothing more than an estimative power (*vis aestimativa*), while only human beings have a cogitative power. This claim makes clear that there is indeed a structural difference at the sensory level. But what exactly is the difference? And what consequences does it have for perception?

Let me answer these questions by first looking more closely at the estimative power. Aquinas claims, following a long tradition initiated by Avicenna, that non-rational animals do not only receive and combine sensible forms. They also receive so-called "intentions" (*intentiones*), which are of crucial importance for their behavior.[26] He presents the famous example of the sheep that faces a wolf in order to explain what these intentions are.[27] When the sheep sees the wolf, it does not simply receive sensible forms such as those of size and color; nor does it simply produce a phantasm that represents the wolf as something big and gray. It also perceives the dangerous character of the wolf, and it is precisely this perception that makes it flee. The important point is that the sheep perceives something in the wolf itself, not just something attributed to it, and that it immediately reacts to what it perceives. One could speak about a *normative property* it grasps, a property that is as much part of the metaphysical make-up of the wolf as its descriptive properties. And this property cannot be directly received by one of the external senses, because it is not a special sensible form that is apt to be grasped by, say, sight or smell. It is rather transported along with all the sensible forms and needs to be detached from them and grasped by a special sense, the estimative power.[28]

---

25 See Aquinas, *STh* I, q. 78, art. 4; *QDA*, q. 13, corp. (Leonina 24.1, pp. 117–118). For a detailed analysis of all four senses, see J.A. Tellkamp, *Sinne, Gegenstände und Sensibilia. Zur Wahrnehmungslehre des Thomas von Aquin*, Leiden, Brill, 1999, pp. 218–294. In his *Sentencia libri De anima*, Aquinas sometimes uses '*phantasia*' as an umbrella term for all the inner senses. But he does not introduce *phantasia* as an additional fifth sense, as some commentators have assumed. For a critical discussion, see A.J. Lisska, *Aquinas's Theory of Perception: An Analytic Reconstruction*, Oxford, Oxford University Press, 2016, pp. 219–226.

26 On the Avicennian theory of intentions and its reception in the thirteenth century, see D.N. Hasse, *Avicenna's "De anima" in the Latin West: The Formation of a Peripatetic Philosophy of the Soul, 1160–1300*, London, The Warburg Institute, 2000; C. Di Martino, *Ratio particularis. Doctrines des sens internes d'Avicenne à Thomas d'Aquin*, Paris, Vrin, 2008, pp. 65–101.

27 See Aquinas, *STh* I, q. 78, art. 4, corp.; *QDA*, q. 13, corp.

28 Given Aquinas's claim that intentions are not grasped by a special external sense, some commentators assume that they are not empirically acquired. Thus, A.J. Lisska, *Aquinas's Theory of Perception*, p. 258, affirms "that a degree of intentional content is attained by some means other than direct sensation in the classical empiricist manner. Once again,

224   PERLER

No doubt, this characterization of intentions as normative properties poses a number of questions concerning their status both in the perceived object and in the perceiving animal. But right now I do not want to tackle these metaphysical problems.[29] All I want to point out is Aquinas's basic thesis that non-rational animals immediately perceive normative properties and react to them in a uniform way. Thus, every sheep flees when it perceives the dangerous character of the wolf. It is, as it were, hard-wired to react with a certain bodily behavior to the normative property it grasps.

Now this is different in the case of human beings, who do not have an estimative power, but a cogitative power. In the *Summa theologiae*, Aquinas describes the relevant difference as follows:

> For other animals perceive these intentions only through a kind of natural instinct, whereas a human being also makes a kind of comparison. And so that which in other animals is called the natural estimative power is called the *cogitative power* in a human being; it discovers such intentions through comparison. Hence it is also called *particular reason* (to which physicians have assigned a definite organ, the middle part of the head), because it compares individual intentions just as intellective reason compares universal intentions.[30]

---

the concept of some form of nativism is suggested." This conclusion is too hasty. Aquinas only claims that intentions are not apprehended by one of the five external senses. But this does not rule out that they can be apprehended insofar as they are attached to sensible forms. For example, neither the sheep's sense of sight nor its sense of smell apprehends danger as such. But danger can very well be apprehended insofar as it is attached to size, figure and sound: a grim look and loud growling manifest danger. That is why an intention such as danger can very well be received together with sensible forms. Metaphorically speaking, it can enter the gate of the external senses by riding on the back of sensible forms. In any case, there is no hint in Aquinas's texts that he accepts innate intentions. This form of nativism would contradict his thoroughgoing empiricism.

29 I discuss them in detail in "Why is the Sheep Afraid of the Wolf? Medieval Debates on Animal Passions," in M. Pickavé and L. Shapiro (eds), *Emotion and Cognitive Life in Medieval and Early Modern Philosophy*, Oxford, Oxford University Press, 2012, pp. 32–52. See also Oelze, *Animal Rationality*, pp. 57–69.

30 Aquinas, *STh* I, q. 78, art. 4, corp. (trans. R. Pasnau, p. 76): "… nam alia animalia percipiunt huiusmodi intentiones solum naturali quodam instinctu, homo autem etiam per quandam collationem. Et ideo quae in aliis animalibus dicitur aestimativa naturalis, in homine dicitur *cogitativa*, quae per collationem quandam huiusmodi intentiones adinvenit. Unde etiam dicitur *ratio particularis*, cui medici assignant determinatum organum, scilicet mediam partem capitis: est enim collativa intentionum individualium, sicut ratio intellectiva intentionum universalium." See also *QDA*, q. 13, corp.

RATIONAL SEEING: THOMAS AQUINAS ON HUMAN PERCEPTION 225

Two points are noteworthy about this statement. First, Aquinas emphasizes that human beings, unlike non-rational animals, do not (or at least not always) immediately grasp intentions. They rather compare different items, most probably sensible properties, going from one to the next and making connections. That is how they discover intentions. Thus, when seeing a wolf a human being makes a connection between the properties "grey," "furry," and "growling," and thereby uncovers the normative property "dangerous." Unlike a sheep, a human being can even actively look for connections that might not be visible at first sight, thereby discovering normative properties that are not immediately evident. For instance, when seeing a snake, he or she can make a connection between "biting" and "poisonous" and thereby discover the normative property "dangerous." This is the reason why the cogitative power in human beings can be understood as a "discursive power," as some commentators have convincingly suggested.[31] Of course, it is not discursive in the same way as the rational faculty, which connects different concepts or propositions. It is discursive in a more basic sense, namely insofar as it "runs through" (*discurrit*) several properties, linking them together. This paves the way for a wide range of reactions, as the sheep example shows. Suppose that the sheep is accompanied by a shepherd and that both of them are facing a wolf. As we have seen, the sheep has no choice: it perceives the dangerous character of the wolf and flees. By contrast, the shepherd can compare the size and the shape he perceives in the wolf with the size and the shape he has seen in other animals. Perhaps he realizes that this wolf is much smaller than other wolves and therefore less dangerous. Perhaps he even becomes aware of the fact that this wolf is injured and in need of help. He therefore perceives it as a rather harmless animal. Consequently, he does not flee. He rather approaches the wolf and tries to help it. The important point is that the shepherd, unlike the sheep, is able to compare various properties and to assess what he perceives. This makes it possible for him to adjust his reaction and to overcome the initial desire to flee. He is not internally programmed to react with one and only one behavior.

There is a second point to be noted in Aquinas's statement. He calls the cogitative power "particular reason," thereby drawing a parallel with reason in the strict sense. Of course, it is not part of reason in the strict sense since it is materially implemented (following the Galenic tradition, Aquinas locates it in a special part of the brain) whereas reason or the rational faculty has no specific

---

31   See G. Klubertanz, *The Discursive Power: Sources and Doctrine of the "vis cogitativa" according to St. Thomas Aquinas*, St. Louis, The Modern Schoolman, 1952, and, following him, J.A. Tellkamp, "*Vis aestimativa* and *vis cogitativa* in Thomas Aquinas's *Commentary on the Sentences*," *The Thomist*, vol. 76, 2012, pp. 611–640 (especially pp. 624–627).

material basis. And it differs from reason in its function, because it deals with intentions, which are particular properties, whereas reason is concerned with universal concepts. Nevertheless, there is a striking similarity. In his introduction to the Leonine edition, René-Antoine Gauthier points out that Aquinas is influenced by Averroes, who already spoke about a cogitative power and compared it to reason by saying that it combines and separates different items, thus making judgments.[32] Of course, the cogitative power does not make judgments in the strict sense, because it cannot make use of a predicative structure and produce a judgment of the form 'x is F.'[33] But it can make judgments with an associative structure, namely by combining and comparing various intentions. To return to my example, we could say that thanks to his cogitative power the shepherd can compare the danger the wolf in front of him presents with the danger posed by another wolf he saw earlier and realize that it is less dangerous. Or for short, he can grasp F as being weaker than F*. To do that, he clearly needs to make use of an associative structure, for he needs to relate F to F*. He even needs to adopt something like a doxastic attitude, for he needs to give his assent to the fact that F is weaker than F*.[34] Otherwise he could not decide how to react.

---

32   See Aquinas, SDA, Leonine 45.1, p. 225*, and more extensively J.A. Tellkamp, "*Vis aestimativa* and *vis cogitativa*," pp. 632–633.

33   Consequently, it cannot produce chains of reasoning that would combine various judgments. Aquinas remarks that the cogitative power is linked to the power of memory, which inquires into past experiences "as if syllogistically" (*quasi syllogistice*); see *STh* I, q. 78, art. 4, corp. This might suggest that there is a logical combination of real judgments, namely of a major and a minor premise. Note, however, that Aquinas does not refer to a real syllogism, but only to a quasi-syllogism. The inner senses associate various perceptions and memories and thereby reach some insight, yet without forming premises and without drawing conclusions. Thus, the shepherd might associate the perception of the properties "big," "furry" and "growling" with the memory of the same properties he perceived yesterday and thereby realize that he is now facing the same type of dangerous animal as yesterday. But he does not make use of a major and a minor premise in order to draw a conclusion. He simply follows a pattern of association.

34   To be sure, this type of assent needs to be distinguished from an assent in the strong sense, which is always a doxastic attitude with respect to a proposition. Nevertheless, the cogitative power can make some kind of affirmation or non-propositional assent. One could speak about an object-related assent (affirming of x that it is F) as opposed to a proposition-related assent (affirming that x is F). In any case, Aquinas clearly ascribes judgments and hence doxastic attitudes to the inner senses. He speaks about "natural judgments," thus distinguishing them from predicative judgments. On natural judgments, see K.H. Tachau, "What Senses and Intellect Do: Argument and Judgment in Late Medieval Theories of Knowledge," in K. Jacobi (ed), *Argumentationstheorie. Scholastische Forschungen zu den logischen und semantischen Regeln korrekten Folgerns*, Leiden, Brill, 1993, pp. 653–668.

RATIONAL SEEING: THOMAS AQUINAS ON HUMAN PERCEPTION 227

At this point one might object that this is simply the case because the shepherd is a human being who uses his rational faculty when facing the wolf. He conceives of the property he perceives as being F, and he judges that F is weaker than F*. Conceiving and judging are obviously rational activities. So there seems to be no difference between the shepherd and the sheep as far as their sensory faculty is concerned. At that level they both form a phantasm and perceive an intention. The only difference between them lies in the way they use the intention. The sheep uses it as an immediate trigger for its behavior, whereas the shepherd uses it as a basis for rational activities, in particular for acts of judging and reasoning, which make a wide range of reactions possible.

As enticing as this explanation seems to be, it does not capture Aquinas's view, for he clearly says that a human being does not simply differ from the non-rational animal because of some additional acts of judging and reasoning. There is already a crucial difference at the level of the sensory faculty. In his *Commentary on De anima*, Aquinas describes this difference as follows:

> The cogitative and estimative powers stand differently in this regard. For the cogitative power apprehends an individual as existing under a common nature. It can do this insofar as it is united to the intellective power in the same subject. Thus it cognizes this human being as it is this human being, and this piece of wood as it is this piece of wood. But the estimative power apprehends an individual, not in terms of its being under a common nature, but only in terms of its being the end point or starting point of some action or affection. It is in this way that a sheep recognizes the lamb not inasmuch as it is this lamb but inasmuch as it can nurse it.[35]

This is a rather dense passage. Let me try to unpack it by distinguishing different cognitive states. There is, first, the state of the sheep that sees a lamb or a wolf. Since it lacks a rational faculty, it is in a purely sensory state. It perceives an individual, namely *this* needy thing (in the case of the lamb) or *this*

---

35   Aquinas, SDA 11.13, Leonina 45.1, p. 122 (trans. R. Pasnau, *A Commentary on Aristotle's De anima*, New Haven, Yale University Press, 1999, pp. 208–209): "Differenter tamen circa hoc se habet cogitatiua et estimatiua: nam cogitatiua apprehendit indiuiduum ut existentem sub natura communi, quod contingit ei in quantum unitur intellectiue in eodem subiecto, unde cognoscit hunc hominem prout est hic homo et hoc lignum prout est hoc lignum; estimatiua autem non apprehendit aliquod indiuiduum secundum quod est sub natura communi, set solum secundum quod est terminus aut principium alicuius actionis uel passionis, sicut ouis cognoscit hunc agnum non in quantum est hic agnus, set in quantum est ab ea lactabilis...".

dangerous thing (in the case of the wolf), and immediately goes for that thing or flees from it; the perceived thing is a mere trigger for a bodily behavior. This can schematically be put as follows:

(1)   x apprehends the trigger F.

Note that the trigger is not categorized or conceptualized. That is why the sheep does not apprehend F as being an instance of F-ness. Nor does it judge that some object is F since it can neither form a proposition nor assent to it. It simply grasps a bundle of properties that are present in an object. Now compare this cognitive state to that of the shepherd. Since he apprehends an individual "as existing under a common nature," as Aquinas says, he does categorize the trigger. His cognitive state can be described as follows:

(2)   x apprehends the trigger F as being an instance of F-ness.

To do that, the shepherd obviously needs to activate his rational faculty since it is thanks to this faculty that he can grasp a common nature and form a general concept. But he does not simply switch from a sensory to a rational activity. He rather combines the two activities, namely by structuring what he perceives. He is therefore still active at the sensory level, but what he is doing there is shaped by what is going on at the rational level. This becomes evident when we compare this case with another one, in particular the case in which the shepherd merely attempts to understand what danger amounts to. In such a case, he no longer perceives this or that dangerous thing, he rather deals with the pure concept of danger. This could be summarized as follows:

(3)   x apprehends F-ness.

The crucial point is that it is only here that we have a purely rational state, the kind of state an angel – a purely immaterial being – could also have. But when standing in front of the wolf, the shepherd does not have this state. He rather has (2): he immediately applies a general concept to a particular object and therefore sees it as an object of a certain type. And he does so without focusing on the pure concept of danger. Perhaps he never tries to understand what danger amounts to because he is not interested in conceptual analysis. Being a person who pursues no purely theoretical projects, he simply wants to deal with the particular object he encounters in his environment. Nevertheless, in this and in many other cases, he spontaneously applies general concepts, whether he intends to do so or not, because he immediately classifies what he sees by using his rational faculty.

To avoid misunderstandings, one should point out that this rationally shaped activity does not always lead to a correct, much less a perfect, classification of the object that is perceived. In a famous passage, Aquinas affirms that the rational faculty cannot go wrong in the grasping of the common nature or

RATIONAL SEEING: THOMAS AQUINAS ON HUMAN PERCEPTION 229

essence of an object.[36] But this does not mean, as one might think at first glance, that reason is some kind of magical faculty that can always fully understand what an object is and so produce a full-fledged, entirely adequate concept. Aquinas concedes that one can, and in fact should, make progress in one's understanding and gradually improve a concept.[37] Thus, the shepherd, who is obviously not a trained biologist, does not possess a detailed, scientifically approved concept of what it is to be a wolf. He does not fully understand what the nature or essence of a wolf amounts to. Nor does he possess a detailed concept of danger. Perhaps he has a very vague concept and ignores the subtle difference between mere danger and threat. But he has at least some concept that captures the nature of danger to some degree, and it is this concept that he inevitably applies when he is facing the wolf. And he can make progress in his understanding: the better he works out his concepts of wolf and danger, the better able he will be to see the wolf as a particular kind of animal with a particular kind of normative property. In any case, rational seeing comes in degrees and does not presuppose the existence of a large stock of sophisticated concepts.

The important point is that rational seeing *always* takes place in a rational being, no matter how crude or modest the available concepts may be.[38] This is the case because the sensory faculty is *always* subordinated to the rational one. Consequently, activities of the sensory faculty are *always* shaped by rational activities. Using metaphorical language, Aquinas states that the rational activity somehow flows into the sensory one:

> The cogitative and memory powers have their superiority in a human being not through something proper to the sensory part, but through a kind of affinity and closeness to universal reason, in virtue of some kind of spillover.[39]

---

36 See Aquinas, *STh* I, q. 85, art. 6, corp.

37 For a detailed analysis of this crucial assumption, see N. Kretzmann, "Infallibility, Error, and Ignorance," *Canadian Journal of Philosophy*, suppl. vol. 17, 1991, pp. 159–194.

38 To be precise, it always takes place in a rational being that makes use of its rational faculty. Newborn human beings may not yet engage in acts of rational seeing, simply because they have not yet activated their rational faculty. But even these beings radically differ from non-rational beings, because they have rational seeing in a *potential* form.

39 Aquinas, *STh* I, q. 78, art. 4, ad 5 (trans. R. Pasnau, p. 77): "... dicendum quod illam eminentiam habet cogitativa et memorativa in homine, non per id quod est proprium sensitivae partis; sed per aliquam affinitatem et propinquitatem ad rationem universalem, secundum quandam refluentiam."

Strictly speaking, there is even a "flowing back" (*refluentia*) and not just a spillover. That is, the descriptive and normative properties present in the sensory faculty first "flow" to the rational faculty, where they are conceptually evaluated, and then the concepts "flow back" to the sensory faculty, where they are immediately applied to what is present. Because of this application, there is no such thing as naked seeing that would consist in the mere grasping of properties and the use of phantasms. Or, to be more precise, there is no such thing in a healthy, well-functioning human being. When discussing the passions, Aquinas grants that there can be situations in which there is hardly any application of concepts. For instance, when people are completely drunk or when they suffer from mental illness, the rational faculty is extremely reduced in its activities.[40] In these cases a person can be said to have a sensory state that is hardly influenced by the use of concepts. A similar situation is possible in the case of perception. A person who is, say, under the influence of heavy drugs may be so severely handicapped that she can hardly apply any concepts. But this is an exceptional case, due to the temporary malfunctioning of the rational faculty caused by the body's being in an odd state. One could even say that this is the case of a temporarily dysfunctional person. In a well-functioning person, where the sensory faculty is subordinated to and influenced by the rational faculty, concepts are spontaneously applied. That is why it does not make sense to speak about a "mere seeing" to which higher rational activities are eventually added. In a well-functioning human being, seeing is always permeated by rational activities.

It is also important to note that a well-functioning person is under no constraint to use one and only one concept when seeing an object. Thus, the shepherd seeing the wolf is not forced to see it as a dangerous animal. Since he has a large stock of concepts and a large number of sensory inputs, he can conceptualize what he sees in many ways. If he realizes that the wolf is on a leash, he can conceptualize it as a tamed animal; and if he further realizes that it is accompanied by a trainer, he can conceptualize it as a friendly animal. Here again, there is a crucial difference with the sheep. The sheep *necessarily* apprehends danger when seeing the wolf, while the shepherd only *contingently* apprehends danger. What he actually apprehends in a given situation depends on the way he conceptualizes what is present to him. And even if he initially apprehends danger because he conceptualizes the wolf as a wild and threatening animal, he can change his cognitive state. After assessing the whole situation he can come to the conclusion that the wolf only appears to be dangerous at first sight, but that it is in fact friendly. This rational activity will have an

---

40   See Aquinas, *STh* I-II, q. 10, art. 3, ad 2.

RATIONAL SEEING: THOMAS AQUINAS ON HUMAN PERCEPTION

immediate impact on his sensory activity: he will come to see the wolf as a friendly companion. This is again a consequence of the metaphysical setting. If reasoning and seeing are activities performed by one and the same soul, not by two souls that may come apart, then every new way of reasoning will inevitably lead to a new way of seeing a given object.

4 Conclusion: Additive and Transformative Theories of Rationality

I hope it has become clear that Aquinas's metaphysical theory of the soul has an immediate impact on his understanding of human perception. In fact, it is because of the inclusion model that he can maintain that there is a crucial difference between rational and non-rational seeing.[41] I also hope that it has become evident why the simple story, which I told at the beginning, cannot be an adequate story for Aquinas. When you and your dog approach the bridge that has been closed after the storm, you do not simply add acts of thinking and reasoning to your acts of seeing; and you do not differ from the dog only because of this extra activity. Rather, you see the bridge in a different way, namely as an object of a certain type to which you attribute a number of descriptive and normative properties. The important point is that you have this kind of seeing naturally and without any effort, in many cases also without reflecting upon it. Or for short: rationality naturally "kicks in," no matter what you perceive.

In recent debates on rationality, the question of how rationality is related to sensitivity has again become an important topic. In his influential book *Mind and World*, John McDowell remarks that many philosophers take rationality to be something that is added to sensitivity as some kind of "extra faculty" or

---

41   The inclusion model is well grounded in Aquinas's unitarism, as has been pointed out in section 2. Note, however, that unitarism is not the only possible foundation. Even a pluralist could try to defend a version of the inclusion model. He could say, for instance, that the forms that are combined in a human being are not simply assembled. Rather, the lower forms are somehow incomplete and need to be completed by higher forms; hence the lower sensory form is completed by the higher rational form and cannot act on its own. This way of arguing was sketched by Richard of Mediavilla, who explicitly spoke about incomplete forms and referred to a hierarchical order among them; see *De gradu formarum*, in R. Zavalloni (ed), *Richard de Mediavilla et la controverse sur la pluralité des formes*, Louvain, Éditions de l'institut supérieur de philosophie, 1951, pp. 143–144. However, this argumentative strategy relies upon a theory of metaphysical incompleteness, which needs to be spelled out. And if the incomplete forms are characterized as mere powers that need to be completed by other powers in a complete form, the pluralist position will collapse into unitarism.

"extra module." Consequently, many philosophers hold that human beings have something in common with non-rational animals, namely sensitivity, while possessing rationality as an additional element, and they assume that human and non-human sensitivity can be accounted for in the same way. McDowell vigorously rejects this view, claiming that there is an alternative:

> But it is not compulsory to attempt to accommodate the combination of something in common and a striking difference in this factorizing way: to suppose our perceptual lives include a core that we can recognize in the perceptual life of a mere animal, and an extra ingredient in addition. [...] Instead we can say that we have what mere animals have, perceptual sensitivity to features of our environment, but we have it in a special form.[42]

We have sensitivity "in a special form" because it is always permeated by rationality; whenever we see or hear something, we do it in a conceptualized way. This is the case because rationality is not simply added to sensitivity but something that determines our nature all the way down. It is therefore incorrect, McDowell claims, to assume that we have an animal-nature with rationality as some kind of bonus element. Rather, right from the beginning we have a *human* nature that is fully rational.

Matthew Boyle spelled out this claim by saying that there are two ways of explaining the relationship between rationality and sensitivity.[43] According to the "additive theory," which is shared by many contemporary philosophers (especially by those who subscribe to the modularity theory of mind), rationality is simply added to sensitivity, yet without affecting it.[44] Rationality is then an encapsulated module that has its own way of functioning without changing or affecting sensitivity. By contrast, according to the "transformative theory" sketched by McDowell, rationality is present in sensory activities and changes them. It makes them genuinely human activities by conceptualizing their content. Most importantly, this model does not posit sensitivity and rationality as two separate modules. It rather conceives of sensitivity as something that is subordinated to and guided by rationality within a single system. That is why the transformative theory avoids the two problems that threaten the additive theory, namely the unity problem and the interaction problem. It does not

---

42   J. McDowell, *Mind and World*, Cambridge, Harvard University Press, 1994, p. 64.

43   M. Boyle, "Additive Theories of Rationality: A Critique," *European Journal of Philosophy*, vol. 24, no. 3, 2016, pp. 527–555.

44   A clear advocate of this model is Peter Carruthers, who assigns different types of mental activity to different modules. See his *The Architecture of the Mind: Massive Modularity and the Flexibility of Thought*, Oxford, Oxford University Press, 2006.

need to explain how two separate modules or systems can form a unity, nor does it need to give an account of the way these two systems can interact. All it needs to do is to spell out the rational transformation of sensory states *inside* a single system.

While mostly discussing contemporary approaches to the problem of rationality, Boyle explicitly mentions Aquinas's theory of the soul as a historical root of the transformative theory.[45] It is easy to see why he chooses Aquinas (besides Aristotle) as the founder of this modern theory. Just like modern proponents of the transformative theory, Aquinas emphasizes that the rational and the sensory faculty form a unity within a single soul. There is no such thing as an interaction between two autonomously acting souls. Moreover, Aquinas stresses that sensory activities are always subordinated to and guided by rational ones. There is no such thing as "pure sensitivity" that would not be shaped by rationally produced concepts. Is it therefore legitimate to call Aquinas a defender – or perhaps even a founder – of the transformative theory? An answer to this question depends on how the transformative theory is spelled out. At least two versions of this theory need to be distinguished.

According to an *extreme* version, rationality transforms every sensory activity so thoroughly that the entire content of a perception is fully conceptualized. Or for short, perceptual content becomes fully conceptual. This means that, returning to the wolf example, a human being seeing the wolf has a perception that is fully structured by concepts such as "grey," "wild" or "dangerous." Seeing the wolf then involves nothing but seeing it as something that falls under these concepts. If one accepts this extreme version of the transformative theory, it does not make sense to speak about non-conceptual perceptual content, since every element would be conceptualized. To put it crudely, one could say that every sensory element is completely wiped out. By contrast, according to a *moderate* version, rationality transforms every sensory activity insofar as everything present in a perception is subsumed under a concept or even a number of concepts. But this does not necessarily mean that perceptual content becomes fully conceptual. There may be some elements in this content that remain truly sensory. Thus, a human being seeing the wolf subsumes it under the concepts "grey," "wild" and "dangerous," but she has more in her perception than a mere bundle of concepts. Her perception also has some sensory elements that are not fully conceptualized. For instance, she grasps a certain shade of color, which she does not immediately conceptualize as this or that type of color. And she smells a very special odor, which she does not immediately conceptualize as this or that type of odor. In fact, there are some sensory

---

45   See Boyle, "Additive Theories of Rationality," pp. 551–552.

elements that resist full conceptualization. Or for short, there are some non-conceptual elements that are immediately present and that co-exist with the conceptual elements.

McDowell seems to defend the extreme version of the transformative theory, for he suggests that it does not make sense to speak about a non-conceptual element that can somehow co-exist with a conceptual element. In fact, he rejects the very idea of non-conceptual perceptual content.[46] By contrast, Aquinas only subscribes to the moderate version. Although he holds that a human perceiver subsumes an object under concepts, he does not claim that perception has nothing but conceptual content. Why not? As we have seen, he refers to four internal senses when he explains the perceptual process. The important point is that the cogitative power is just one of the four senses. And the activity of this power, namely subsuming an object under concepts, is just one of the relevant activities. All other activities are also relevant and also have an impact on the content of a perception. In particular, the common sense that unifies all the sensible forms and the imagination that produces a phantasm on that basis also shape the content. Since these two internal senses deal with sensible forms that are *not* conceptualized, the content of a perception also has a non-conceptual element. Aquinas's point is not that this element is somehow wiped out, but that it co-exists with the conceptual element, for which the cogitative power is responsible. Thus, when seeing the wolf a human perceiver captures a special shade of grey and smells a special odor. In that respect she is just like the sheep that has access to the wolf's color and odor in a non-conceptualized way. But the human perceiver has more than that. Thanks to her cogitative power she also subsumes what she sees and smells under some concepts and therefore perceives the wolf as a certain type of animal. Or for short, she does not only catch some sensible forms, but also categorizes them in light of some concepts, and therefore perceives something as something. But the activity of the cogitative power does not eradicate the activity of the other internal senses. Hence sensory content – the mere presence of some sensible forms – persists.

I hope these remarks make clear that it would be inadequate to present Aquinas as a proponent of an extreme transformative theory. Rational perception does not amount to a purely conceptual perception. Perception, be it

---

46   He rejects Gareth Evans' idea of non-conceptual content and claims that there is no difference between a perception and a judgment as far as the content is concerned: "A judgment of experience does not introduce a new kind of content, but simply endorses the conceptual content, or some of it, that is already possessed by the experience on which it is grounded." (*Mind and World*, pp. 48–49).

non-human or human, always has a non-conceptual element because it always involves the presence of sensible forms that are not fully conceptualized. But the important point is that human perception necessarily has at least some conceptual element because it involves the use of a special power that is always under the guidance of the rational faculty. It is this rational guidance, which is naturally built into every human being, that makes human perception so special.[47]

Bibliography

Primary Literature

Thomas Aquinas, *Quaestiones disputatae de anima*, B.C. Bazán (ed), *Opera omnia 24.1*, Rome, Commissio Leonina, 1996.

Thomas Aquinas, *Sentencia libri De anima*, *Opera omnia 45.1*, Rome, Commissio Leonina, 1984. English translation: *A Commentary on Aristotle's De anima*, trans. Robert Pasnau, New Haven, Yale University Press, 1999.

Thomas Aquinas, *Summa contra Gentiles*, C. Pera (ed), Turin, Marietti 1961.

Thomas Aquinas, *Summa theologiae*, P. Caramello (ed), Turin, Marietti, 1952. English translation: *The Treatise on Human Nature: Summa Theologiae 1a 75–89*, trans. Robert Pasnau, Indianapolis, Hackett, 2002.

William of Ockham, *Quodlibeta septem*, J.C. Wey (ed), *Opera Theologica IX*, St. Bonaventure, The Franciscan Institute, 1980.

Secondary Literature

Arlig, Andrew, "Is There a Medieval Mereology?" in M. Cameron and J. Marenbon (eds), *Methods and Methodologies: Aristotelian Logic East and West, 500–1500*, Leiden, Brill, 2011, pp. 161–189.

Bazán, Bernardo Carlos, "Pluralisme de formes ou dualisme de substances?" *Revue philosophique de Louvain*, vol. 67, 1969, pp. 30–73.

Boyle, Matthew, "Additive Theories of Rationality: A Critique," *European Journal of Philosophy*, vol. 24, no. 3, 2016, pp. 527–555.

Brower, Jeffrey E., *Aquinas's Ontology of the Material World: Change, Hylomorphism, & Material Objects*, Oxford, Oxford University Press, 2014.

---

47   I am grateful to Elena Bălțuță, Paolo Rubini, Stephan Schmid, and Joseph Stenberg for detailed comments on various versions of this paper. An earlier German version was presented in Innsbruck and Regensburg, an English version in Berlin. I am grateful to the audience in all three places for stimulating questions.

Carruthers, Peter, *The Architecture of the Mind: Massive Modularity and the Flexibility of Thought*, Oxford, Oxford University Press, 2006.

Di Martino, Carla, *Ratio particularis. Doctrines des sens internes d'Avicenne à Thomas d'Aquin*, Paris, Vrin, 2008.

Hasse, Dag N., *Avicenna's "De anima" in the Latin West: The Formation of a Peripatetic Philosophy of the Soul, 1160–1300*, London, The Warburg Institute, 2000.

Klubertanz, George, *The Discursive Power: Sources and Doctrine of the "vis cogitativa" according to St. Thomas Aquinas*, St. Louis, The Modern Schoolman, 1952.

Köhler, Theodor W., *Homo animal nobilissimum. Konturen des spezifisch Menschlichen in der naturphilosophischen Aristoteleskommentierung des dreizehnten Jahrhunderts*, 2 vols., Leiden, Brill, 2014.

Kretzmann, Norman, "Infallibility, Error, and Ignorance," *Canadian Journal of Philosophy*, suppl. vol. 17, 1991, pp. 159–194.

Lisska, Anthony J., *Aquinas's Theory of Perception: An Analytic Reconstruction*, Oxford, Oxford University Press, 2016.

McCord Adams, Marilyn, *William Ockham*, Notre Dame, Notre Dame University Press, 1987.

McDowell, John, *Mind and World*, Cambridge, Harvard University Press, 1994.

Oelze, Anselm, *Animal Rationality: Later Medieval Theories 1250–1350*, Leiden, Brill, 2018.

Pasnau, Robert, *Metaphysical Themes 1274–1671*, Oxford, Oxford University Press, 2011.

Pasnau, Robert, *Thomas Aquinas on Human Nature: A Philosophical Study of "Summa theologiae" Ia 75–89*, Cambridge, Cambridge University Press, 2002.

Perler, Dominik, "Faculties in Medieval Philosophy," in D. Perler (ed), *The Faculties: A History*, Oxford, Oxford University Press, 2015, pp. 97–139.

Perler, Dominik, "Ockham on Emotions in the Divided Soul," in K. Corcilius and D. Perler (eds), *Partitioning the Soul: Debates from Plato to Leibniz*, Berlin, De Gruyter, 2014, pp. 179–198.

Perler, Dominik, "Perception in Medieval Philosophy," in M. Matthen (ed), *The Oxford Handbook of Philosophy of Perception*, Oxford, Oxford University Press, 2015, pp. 51–65.

Perler, Dominik, *Theorien der Intentionalität im Mittelalter*, Frankfurt am Main, Vittorio Klostermann, 2002.

Perler, Dominik, "Why is the Sheep Afraid of the Wolf? Medieval Debates on Animal Passions," in M. Pickavé and L. Shapiro (eds), *Emotion and Cognitive Life in Medieval and Early Modern Philosophy*, Oxford, Oxford University Press, 2012, pp. 32–52.

Roling, Bernd, "Die Geometrie der Bienenwabe: Albertus Magnus, Karl von Baer und die Debatte über das Vorstellungsvermögen und die Seele der Insekten zwischen Mittelalter und Neuzeit," *Recherches de théologie et philosophie médiévales*, vol. 80, 2013, pp. 363–466.

Steel, Carlos, Guldentops, Guy, and Beullens, Pieter (eds.), *Aristotle's Animals in the Middle Ages and Renaissance*, Leuven, Leuven University Press, 1999.

Tachau, Katherine H., "What Senses and Intellect Do: Argument and Judgment in Late Medieval Theories of Knowledge," in K. Jacobi (ed), *Argumentationstheorie. Scholastische Forschungen zu den logischen und semantischen Regeln korrekten Folgerns*, Leiden, Brill, 1993, pp. 653–668.

Tellkamp, Jörg Alejandro, *Sinne, Gegenstände und Sensibilia. Zur Wahrnehmungslehre des Thomas von Aquin*, Leiden, Brill, 1999.

Tellkamp, Jörg Alejandro, "*Vis aestimativa* and *vis cogitativa* in Thomas Aquinas's *Commentary on the Sentences*," *The Thomist*, vol. 76, 2012, pp. 611–640.

Zavalloni, Roberto, *Richard de Mediavilla et la controverse sur la pluralité des formes*, Louvain, Éditions de l'institut supérieur de philosophie, 1951.

CHAPTER 9

Aquinas on Perceiving, Thinking, Understanding, and Cognizing Individuals

Daniel De Haan

Among Thomas Aquinas's 13th and 14th century critics, some of them targeted his Aristotelian view that the human intellect does not cognize individuals of a material nature. To many of his readers, Aquinas's stance on this point seems to be indefensible for it is an obvious fact that we think about individuals. In this essay, I argue Aquinas's view has been misunderstood, both by his critics and by many Thomists that have come to his defense. I distinguish two important aspects of Aquinas's approach to this problem. First, I highlight the co-operative function different cognitive powers perform with respect to the unified cognitive operations of the human being. Second, I examine in detail Aquinas's account of human sensing, perceiving, understanding, reasoning, thinking, and cognizing individuals by the co-operative cognition of their external senses, the cogitative power (*vis cogitativa*), and the possible intellect. I show that a proper understanding of the coordinated operations of the possible intellect and cogitative power reveals that Aquinas in fact has a complex and coherent account of how the human being – but not the possible intellect – perceives, thinks, understands, and reasons about individuals.

1 Some Terminological Caveats

First, I employ the English term "cognition" and its cognates in much the same way that Aquinas uses the term *cognitio* and its cognates, namely, as an analogical term that captures diverse forms of apprehension including sensation, perception, imagination, memory, thought, understanding, and reasoning.[1]

---

1   Unlike Peter King and other exegetes of medieval thinkers, I am suspicious of interpretations of medieval accounts of *cognitio* that emphasize or even suggest there are broad similarities between *cognitio* and contemporary computational and information processing accounts of *cognition*, which are characteristic of cognitive science and cognitive psychology. Cf. P. King, "Thinking about Things: Singular Thought in the Middle Ages," in G. Klima (ed), *Intentionality, Cognition, and Representation in Medieval Philosophy*, New York, Fordham University Press, 2015, pp. 104–121.

© KONINKLIJKE BRILL NV, LEIDEN, 2020 | DOI:10.1163/9789004413030_010

AQUINAS ON COGNIZING INDIVIDUALS

Second, for Aquinas, there are two different problems concerning human intellectual cognition of individuals. This is because there are individuals that are pure immaterial entities and there are individuals that are form-matter composites by their very essence. This essay is about the second problem and so I employ the terms "individual" and "singular" to mean individuals that are form-matter composites by their very essence.

Aquinas's position on human intellectual cognition of individuals is crystal clear.

> Our intellect abstracts intelligible species from individuating principles; hence the intelligible species of our intellect cannot be a likeness of the individual principles. And for this reason our intellect cannot cognize singulars.[2]

These individuating principles are bound up with the materiality of form-matter composite entities. The natural operation of the human intellect requires abstracting the principle of its operation from the materiality that is needed to cognize an object as an individual. The human intellect does not have cognition of form-matter composite individuals *qua* individuals. Elsewhere Aquinas distinguishes the aforementioned two kinds of individuals that can be cognized, and makes this point perfectly pellucid.

> A singular thing is not opposed to being intelligible insofar as it is singular, but insofar as it is material, because nothing is [intellectually] understood except [what is] immaterial. And therefore if something singular is immaterial, as is the intellect, this is not opposed to being intelligible.[3]

It is not individuality that is an impediment to intellectual cognition, it is materiality. Aquinas develops at length and in many works a fuller explanation for why materiality individuates and is an impediment to intellectual cognition, but we do not have space to rehearse these points here.[4] With these terminological caveats in mind, let us proceed to Aquinas's approach to Aristotelian psychology.

---

2   Thomas Aquinas, *Summa theologiae* (= *STh*), 1.14.11, ad1, Editio Leonina Manualis, Rome, Editiones Paulinae, 1962. All translations are my own unless noted otherwise.

3   Aquinas, *STh* 1.86.1, ad3. See also *Questiones disputatae de veritate* (= *DV*) 2.6, ad1; 10.5, *Opera omnia 22.1–3*, Rome, Commissio Leonina, 1970–1976.

4   See J.F. Wippel, *The Metaphysical Thought of Thomas Aquinas*, Washington, The Catholic University of America Press, 2000, IX, 4, pp. 351–375.

240   DE HAAN

2   Aquinas's Approach to Aristotelian Psychology

Aquinas endorses the Aristotelian view that theoretical inquiry begins with
what is more known with respect to us and transitions from there to knowledge of what is more known in itself. Following Aristotle, the application of
this distinction to the investigation of human psychology is specified by two
additional principles. First, what is more known to us are psychological *operations* and their *objects*, and it is through an adequate analysis and differentiation of them that we arrive at what is more known in itself, namely, the psychological *powers* that ground these operations, and the substantial *nature* that is
the ground (*radix*) of these different psychological powers.[5] Second, even
though this mode of theoretical analysis lends itself to forms of synecdoche –
such as vision sees, memory recalls, and the intellect understands – it is more
accurate to say the human being sees, recalls, and understands in virtue of
their powers of vision, memory, and intellect.[6] In short, Aquinas's philosophical anthropology begins and ends with the unity of human psychological experience enabled through different psychological operations and powers grounded in the unity of the rational animal; a unity that is hylomorphically constituted
from a rational soul and organic body. We must keep in view Aquinas's point
of departure from the unity of psychological experience that is more known
to us, as we follow his theoretical analysis of this unity into its different objects, operations, and powers of a unified nature, which are more known in
themselves.

Thus far I have summarized a few of the moves Aristotle makes in *De anima*
I-II – which Aquinas adopts – that are relevant to our investigation of Aquinas's account of human sensation, perception, thought, understanding, reasoning, and cognition of individuals of a material nature. A few more points
are needed before we move forward, and the first concerns the many levels of
analysis at which Aquinas might approach a topic in his anthropology.

It is crucial to appreciate the varieties of levels of analysis at which Aquinas
might describe in a more coarse-grained or fine-grained manner the relevant
operations and powers to the topic at hand. In some cases, a topic requires
great precision on a fine-grained issue so Aquinas employs a very technical
vocabulary to demarcate between different powers and operations. On other

---

5   See Aquinas, *STh* I.77.8.
6   See Aquinas, *DV* 2.6, ad3; 10.9, ad contra 3; 22.13, ad7; *STh* I.75.2, ad2; 75.4; I-II.17.5, ad 2; II-
    II.58.2; *Sentencia libri De anima* (= *In DA*), I.10, *Opera omnia 45.1*, Rome, Commissio Leonina,
    1984; *Quaestiones disputatae de anima* (= QDA), 12, ad 13, B.C. Bazán (ed), *Opera omnia 24*,
    Rome, Commissio Leonina, 1996.

AQUINAS ON COGNIZING INDIVIDUALS 241

occasions, a topic at a few levels higher, as it were, might permit looser forms of metonymy, or require technical terms that refer to an assembly of powers functioning in co-operation instead of mentioning each power and its distinctive contribution. For instance, on most occasions Aquinas employs the terms practical reason, imagination, phantasia, and phantasm in this last way. Contrary to what many readers suppose, practical reason rather rarely refers exclusively to the operations of the possible intellect.[7] Strictly speaking, "practical reason" in Aquinas denotes the co-operative coordination of at least two powers: the cogitative power as *particular reason*, which supplies the minor, and the possible intellect as *universal reason*, which supplies the major of the practical syllogism.[8] Practical reason is partially universal and is partially particular (*Ratio autem practica quedam est uniuersalis et quedam particularis*).[9] Similarly, Aquinas does on rare occasions employ the terms imagination, phantasia, and phantasm to denote the power of imagination and the terminus of its operation in contradistinction to the internal senses of cogitation and memory. But Aquinas more typically follows the practice of many medieval Aristotelians and employs these terms generically to capture some combination of the powers of imagination, cogitation, and memory.[10] It is important to keep these

---

7   See Aquinas, *STh* I.79.11 for *intellectus practicus*.

8   "Alio modo secundum quod motus qui est ab anima ad res incipit a mente, et procedit in partem sensitivam prout mens regit inferiores vires, et sic singularibus se immiscet mediante ratione particulari quae est potentia quaedam sensitivae partis componens et dividens intentiones individuales, quae alio nomine dicitur cogitativa, ... universalem enim sententiam quam mens habet de operabilibus non est possibile applicari ad particularem actum nisi per aliquam potentiam mediam apprehendentem singulare, ut sic fiat quidam syllogismus cuius maior sit universalis quae est sententia mentis, minor autem singularis quae est apprehensio particularis rationis, conclusio vero electio singularis operis, ut patet per id quod habetur in III De anima." Aquinas, *DV* 10.5 (Leon., 309: 81–99). See also *STh* I.81.3; 86.1, ad2; *In DA* III.10 (Leon., 251: 128–133, ad 434a16).

9   Aquinas, *In DA* III.10 (251: 128–29). See also *In DA* III.10 (Leon., 251: 128–145, ad 434a16–21); *DV* 14.5, ad 11.

10   "... sed a virtutibus in quibus sunt phantasmata, scilicet imaginativa, memorativa et cogitativa ..." Aquinas, *Summa contra Gentiles* (= *SCG*), II.73, C. Pera (ed), Turin, Marietti, 1961. "... in viribus sensitivis, scilicet imaginativa, cogitativa et memorativa ... Actus autem intellectus ex quibus in praesenti vita scientia acquiritur, sunt per conversionem intellectus ad phantasmata, quae sunt in praedictis viribus sensitivis." *STh* I.89.5. Despite the view of most recent interpreters of Aquinas, many medieval Aristotelians and all the major Thomist commentators held that the typical meaning of phantasia was generic and included a number of internal sense powers, not just imagination. "Nomine phantasiae intelligit Aristoteles tres vires animae interiors excepto sensu communi. Est enim phantasia nomen genericum, quod distinguitur in tres species, quarum una propter penuriam nominum remansit nomine generis, sicut aepe contingit." Domininus Báñez, *Commentaria in primam partem angelici doctoris S. Thomae*, sumpt. Ph. Borde, L. Arnaud, P. Borde, and

points in mind when examining a particular discussion in Aquinas.[11] The questions we must keep in mind are: What level of analysis is his investigation working on? Is he addressing the way a human achieves something through the coordinated exercise of different powers? Or, is he investigating what a single power's distinct contribution is to the human being's activities that are comprised of the coordinated exercise of different powers?

We will return to these questions later on in our examination of *STh* I.86.1 and similar texts wherein Aquinas addresses cognition of singulars – or *singular cognition*, as many contemporary exegetes call it. At this point we can turn to Aquinas's philosophical approach to the differentiation of objects, operations, and powers which follows and expands Aristotle's own approach in *De anima*, II.6.

3   Aquinas on *per se* and *per accidens* Sensibles in *De anima* II.6

Aristotle held all knowledge begins in the senses. Accordingly, his first division of the polymorphic object cognized by humans starts with sensible reality as differentiated into *per se* sensibles and *per accidens* sensibles.[12] Aquinas's interpretation of Aristotle's division of sensibles and their corresponding cognitive operations and powers owes much to Avicenna's innovative developments.[13] Indeed, it is on the basis of Avicenna's amplifications to Aristotle's psychology of the apprehensive or cognitive powers that Aquinas will articulate his own doctrine of the five external senses (vision, audition, olfaction, gustation, tactility), four internal senses (*sensus communis*, imagination, cogitation

---

G. Barbier, Rome, Lugduni, 1663, *In STh* I.78.5.dub.5, p. 279 (a); John of St. Thomas, *Cursus philosophicus thomisticus*, R.P. Beatus (ed), Turin, Marietti, 1930, *Phil. Nat.*, IV. P., Q. 8. A. 2, Reiser, T. III, 252b-253a. See also Alexander of Hales, *Summa theologica*, Quaracchi, Collegium S. Bonaventurae, 1924–1948, Pars Ia, lib. 2, inq. 4, tract. 1, Sect. 2, quaest. 2, tit. 1, memb. 2, cap. 2, 358, p. 435; Albert the Great, *De anima*, C. Stroick (ed), *Opera omnia 7.1*, Münster, Aschendorff, 1968, III.1.3, p. 168b, pp. 72–76.

11   Another illustration is provided by the way the agent intellect and possible intellect both concurrently contribute to an act of understanding. See Aquinas, *QDA* 4, ad 8: "Ad octauum dicendum quod duorum intellectuum, scilicet possibilis et agentis, sunt due actiones. Nam actus intellectus possibilis est intelligibilia recipere; aetio autem intellectus agentis est abstrahere intelligibilia. Nec tamen sequitur quod sit duplex intelligere in homine, quia ad unum intelligere oportet quod utraque harum actionum concurrat." (Leon., 36–37: 255–262).

12   See D. Perler and P. Rubini in this volume.

13   For the details of Avicenna's and Aquinas's interpretations of Aristotle on this front, see D. Black, "Imagination and Estimation: Arabic Paradigms and Latin Transformations," *Topoi*, vol. 19, 2000, pp. 59–75.

AQUINAS ON COGNIZING INDIVIDUALS 243

in humans or estimation in other animals, and memory), and the possible and agent intellects.[14] Let us examine in detail the way Aquinas works out his own account of cognizable objects and cognitive operations on the basis of the Aristotelian division between *per se* and *per accidens* sensibles in his commentary on *De anima* II.6.

Like Aristotle, Aquinas distinguishes *per se* sensibles into proper and common sensibles. Proper sensibles differentiate sensible objects that are uniquely apprehended by one sense power – color by vision, sound by audition, odors by olfaction, flavors by gustation, and tangibles by tactility. These proper sensibles are contrasted with the common sensibles of movement, rest, number, shape, and size.[15] Common sensibles, like proper sensibles, are also *per se* sensibles, but they are apprehended by more than one sense power. For instance, visible shaped movement is cognized by vision just as audible movement and tangible movement are cognized by audition and tactility, respectively. Aquinas employs this account of *per se* sensibles to present his own account of the objects and operations of the five external sense powers and that of the *sensus communis*, the first internal sense power. Contrary to some interpretations of Aristotle, Aquinas maintains that the proper object of the *sensus communis* is not the *per se* common sensibles, but the *per se* sensibles as such, that is, the essentially sensible manifold of proper and common sensibles presented to the sensing animal.[16] The *per se* sensible manifold cognized by the *sensus communis* is then received and retained by the internal sense power of imagination, which is able to re-present isomorphic and innovative combinations of retained *per se* sensible imagery. These *per se* sensibles are, by definition, essentially sensible; they are sensible forms in themselves and constitute the third species of the Aristotelian category of quality. Sensible forms sensed by the external senses and *sensus communis* are all individuated by the material substances in reality they inhere within; *per se* sensibles that are imagined by the power of imagination remain under the conditions of matter insofar as the power of imagination is itself embodied in one of the ventricles of the brain.[17]

After clarifying the division of *per se* sensibles into proper and common sensibles, the remainder of *De anima* II.6 concerns the nature of *per accidens* sensibles, which Aquinas expands into one of his most detailed treatments of the way the intellect and cogitative power in humans can be intimately bound up with the *per se* sensation of *per se* sensibles. Said otherwise, Aquinas's

---

14 See Aquinas, *STh* I.78–79; *QDA* 13.
15 See Aquinas, *In DA* II.13 (Leon., 119: 44–54, ad 418a17).
16 See Aquinas, *In DA* II. 13. (Leon., 119–120: 71–59); *STh* I.78.3–4.
17 See Aquinas, *STh* I.78.3–4.

244 DE HAAN

commentary on the doctrine of *per accidens* sensibles in *De anima* 11.6 presents arguably his most thorough investigation of empirical cognition in humans and nonhuman animals. Since the focus of this essay is especially concerned with Aquinas's view on cognition of individuals, including empirical cognition of singulars, this text warrants close attention. Given the length of Aquinas's commentary on *per accidens* sensibles in *De anima* 11.6, I will divide his commentary into pericopes and examine each in turn.

> [Aristotle] says that something is said to be sensible *per accidens*, for example if we were to say that Diares or Socrates is sensible *per accidens* because it is accidental to him to be white. For that is sensed *per accidens* that is accidental to the thing sensed *per se*. It is, however, accidental to white (which is sensible *per se*) that it belongs to Diares. Hence Diares is sensible *per accidens*. Thus [the sense] is not at all affected by Diares as such.[18]

The individual man, Diares, is just as real as his being white; the *white* skin – but neither *skin* nor *Diares* – is apprehended by the power of vision since the color white is a *per se* sensible. *Diares*, a human, is concurrently apprehended but not by any of the external senses because they only apprehend *per se* sensibles, and *Diares*, *qua* object of cognition, is a *per accidens* sensible. Aquinas will provide some additional examples of *per accidens* sensibles beyond that of *Socrates* and *Diares*, but it is not difficult for us to expand the inventory of *per accidens* sensibles; it includes all the objects of cognition that are apprehended concurrently with our sensation of *per se* sensibles, but which are not *per se* sensibles. It is worth emphasizing how far-reaching the category of *per accidens* sensibles is; it comprehends the full ambit of objects cognized concurrently with sensation which are of central concern in our everyday lives. It is rare that our conscious attention is merely focused on the color, sounds, tangibles, size, shape, and movements of extra-cognitive objects. Ordinary empirical cognition is far richer than awareness of *per se* sensibles. What we primarily cognitively attend to are the *per accidens* sensibles of objects that are potables, edibles, humans and other animals, and the range of affordances these and other objects in the environment have for us.[19] The relevance of *per se* sensibles to an animal are dependent upon the kind of thing these *per se* sensibles

---

18   Aquinas, *In DA* 11.13 (Leon., 119: 56–63). (Pasnau, p. 205, mod. trans.).

19   "The *affordances* of the environment are what it *offers* the animal, what it *provides* or *furnishes*, either for good or ill." (J. Gibson, *The Ecological Approach to Visual Perception*, Boston, Houghton Mifflin, 1979, p. 127.)

AQUINAS ON COGNIZING INDIVIDUALS   245

belong to; bright colors can be indicative of ripe fruit that afford consumption, but they can also be indicative of toxic plants or animals that afford avoiding and not consuming. It is therefore surprising how many exegetes of Aquinas have completely overlooked the role these *per accidens* sensibles have in Aquinas's account of human cognition of individual material things, especially for his general account of empirical cognition of individuals.

Aquinas provides the following criteria for *per accidens* sensibles.

> [I]t is important to know that for something to be sensible *per accidens*, the first thing that is required is that it be an accident of something sensible *per se*. For example, being a human being applies accidentally (*accidit*) to what is white, as does being sweet. The second thing required is that it be apprehended by the thing that is sensing. For if there were some accident of the sense object that was hidden from the thing sensing, that would not be said to be sensed *per accidens*. It must then be cognized *per se* by some other cognitive power belonging to the thing sensing; this will, of course, be either another sense, intellect, or the cogitative power, or the estimative power.[20]

Aquinas presents two conditions for *per accidens* sensation of *per accidens* sensibles. First, all *per accidens* sensibles necessarily belong to and are presented concurrently with *per se* sensible objects. Second, these *per accidens* sensibles must be cognized by the same animal concurrently with its sensation of the *per se* sensibles of the same cognizable object. If while sensing the colored shapes of a painting I *recollect* an amusing episode from the last time I visited this museum, this act of remembering concurrent to my sensation of *per se* sensibles does not qualify as a kind of *per accidens* sensation. Significantly, the *per accidens* sensing animal must be deploying some cognitive power other than the external senses or *sensus communis* (or imagination and memory) to cognize these *per accidens* sensibles. It must be a cognitive power of the animal that can operate concurrently with the animal's sensation of *per se* sensibles to cognize other cognizable features of the present *per se* sensible object. What are these *per accidens* sensible objects in their own right, that is, what kind of cognizable objects are they essentially or *per se*? And, what cognitive powers have these present cognizable objects as their *per se* or essential object? Aquinas addresses this last question first.

Aquinas mentions four cognitive powers whose *per se* operations apprehend these *per accidens* sensibles and so have them as their *per se* object; he

---

20   Aquinas, *In DA* II.13 (Leon., 120: 164–174.) (Pasnau, pp. 207–208, mod. trans.).

246 DE HAAN

lists another sense, the intellect, the cognitive power, and the estimative power. He immediately qualifies the first.

> I speak of "another sense" as if we were to say that sweet is visible *per accidens* insofar as sweet is accidental to white, which is apprehended by sight, whereas sweet is apprehended *per se* by taste. But, to speak strictly, this is not something altogether sensible *per accidens*, but rather something visible *per accidens* and sensible *per se*.[21]

Given the criteria for being a *per accidens* sensible, the color of an object that is seen is a *per accidens* sensible with respect to the same animal hearing a sound produced by the object that is colored. In this instance, color can be understood as being a *per accidens* sensible with respect to sound; however, since both color and sound are *per se* sensibles Aquinas distinguishes them from a still stricter meaning of a *per accidens* sensible, which only includes cognizable objects that are *not per se* sensibles. Aquinas seems to introduce here a third criterion for being a *per accidens* sensible, namely, the cognizable objects that are *per accidens* sensibles cannot also be *per se* sensibles. This entails that *per accidens* sensibles in this strict meaning of the term cannot be the *per se* object of the external senses, *sensus communis*, imagination, or memory. This leaves the three other cognitive powers Aquinas listed: intellect, cogitative power, and estimative power. Let us consider Aquinas's account of *per accidens* sensation by the intellect.

> What is not cognized by a proper sense is, if it is something universal, apprehended by intellect. Still, not everything that can be apprehended by intellect in something that has been sensed can be called sensible *per accidens*, but [only] that which is apprehended by intellect right when [*statim*] the thing that has been sensed is encountered. For example, right when [*statim*] I see someone speaking or moving, apprehending through intellect his being alive, I can say on this basis that I see that he is living.[22]

If the object cognized as a *per accidens* sensible concurrently with the external sensation of the *per se* sensibles of the same object is a *universal*, then the act of *per accidens* sensation of the *per accidens* sensible is achieved by the intellect. Again, note well the conditions obtained here for *per accidens* sensibles

---

21   Aquinas, *In DA* II.13 (Leon., 120–121: 175–181) (Pasnau, p. 208, mod. trans.).
22   Aquinas, *In DA* II.13 (Leon., 121: 182–190) (Pasnau, p. 208, mod. trans.).

AQUINAS ON COGNIZING INDIVIDUALS   247

and *per accidens* sensation. Not all apprehensions of universals through the
cognitive operations of the intellect are forms of *per accidens* sensation of *per
accidens* sensibles. Only intellectual cognition of the universal features of the
cognizable object that is also immediately (*statim*) and concurrently being
cognized by the external senses meets the conditions for being a form of *per
accidens* sensation of *per accidens* sensibles. How does this form of intellectual
per accidens sensation differ from the form of *per accidens* sensation Aquinas
attributes to the cogitative and estimative powers?

> If, however, [the object] is apprehended as an individual – e.g., when I see
> something colored I perceive *this* human being or *this* animal – then this
> sort of apprehension in a human being is produced through the cogita-
> tive power. This is also called particular reason (*ratio particularis*), be-
> cause it joins individual intentions (*intentionum individualium*) in the
> way that universal reason joins universal concepts (*rationum*). But all the
> same, this power is in the soul's sensory part. For the sensory power, at its
> highest level, participates somewhat in the intellective power in a human
> being, in whom sense is connected to intellect. In an irrational animal, on
> the other hand, the natural estimative power brings about the apprehen-
> sion of an individual intention. It is in virtue of this that a sheep, through
> hearing or sight, recognizes its offspring or anything of that sort.[23]

If a human or other animal cognizes an *individual* while concurrently apprehending by *per se* sensation that individual's *per se* sensible qualities, then its
act of *per accidens* sensation of the *per accidens* sensible *qua* individual is
achieved by the cognitive power or estimative power. Notice the way Aquinas
contrasts *per accidens* sensation of individuals by the cogitative power from
per accidens sensation of a universal by the intellect. I can attend to the object
I apprehend by *per se* sensation either *qua* individual or *qua* universal. The
colored, shaped object in motion I see can be concurrently cognized *qua* this
individual man via the cogitative power or *qua* a universal human via the intellect. Aquinas presents a similar account in his commentary on the *Sentences*,
which references Aristotle's example from this passage in *De anima* II.6.

> A *per accidens* [sensible] that is sensed does not affect the sense, neither
> inasmuch as it is a sense, nor inasmuch as it is this sense, but as con-
> joined to those things that affect the sense *per se*. As [for example]

---

23   Aquinas, *In DA* II.13 (Leon., 121–122: 191–205) (Pasnau, p. 208, mod. trans.). See also *DV* 14.1,
      ad9.

"Socrates," and "the son of Diares," and "friend," and other similar things, which are *per se* cognized in the universal by the intellect, and in the particular [they are *per se* cognized] by the cogitative power in human[s], and by the estimative in other animals. In this way then the external sense is said to sense, although *per accidens*, when from that which is sensed *per se*, the apprehensive power, whose [capacity] it is to cognize *per se* this thing cognized, apprehends it immediately without hesitation or discursion (*statim sine dubitatione et discursu apprehendit*). As [for example, when] we see that someone is alive from the fact that he speaks.[24]

In his commentary on *De anima* II.6, Aquinas introduces another name for the cogitative power. He says it is sometimes called the "particular reason" because, even though it is a sensory power, the cogitative power in humans is connected with the intellectual power. This dynamic connection enables the cogitative power to perform operations that share or participate in operations similar to the rational operations of the intellect. Just as the intellect collates (*collativa*) universal intentions or notions (*rationum*), the cogitative power *qua* particular reason collates (*collativa*) individual or particular intentions. We have here in one text Aquinas's answer to both of our earlier questions. Particular intentions are the *per se* object of the *per se* operations of the cogitative power and universal intentions are the *per se* object of the *per se* operations of the intellect, and both particular and universal intentions can be *per accidens* sensibles that are cognized concurrently with the sensation of *per se* sensibles. Aquinas rehearses this comparison in many passages, including in the *locus classicus* for Aquinas's *ex professo* treatment of the internal senses in *STh* I.78.4. Here he again takes note of the reason why the cogitative power is sometimes called the particular reason, for it collates or compares individual intentions, just as the intellectual reason collates or compares universal intentions (*Unde etiam dicitur ratio particularis, ... est enim collativa intentionum individualium, sicut ratio intellectiva intentionum universalium.*)[25] We will return to some of the details of this doctrine later, but it is important to point out that Aquinas is a realist about these natural *intentions* no less than he is a realist about *per se* sensible forms. Just as cognizable sensible forms are the very manifestation of the sensible qualities of a thing *in re*, so also are intentions the very manifestation of the cognizable but nonsensible features of a thing *in re*. These features

---

24   Aquinas, *Scriptum super libros Sententiarum* (= *In Sent*), IV. d. 49, q. 2, a. 2, book IV, Parma,Typis Petri Fiaccadori, 1852–1873. (Parma, vol. VII, pt. 2, pp. 1201–1202). See also *STh* III. Suppl. 92.2.

25   Aquinas, *STh* I.78.4.

AQUINAS ON COGNIZING INDIVIDUALS

can be cognized as individual intentions by the cogitative power and as cogitative experiences they are – like the images retained in imagination and intentions of *pastness* retained by memory – potentially intelligible phantasms. Once these potentially intelligible intentions are abstracted as actually intelligible universal intentions they can be cognized by the intellect.[26]

Aquinas distinguishes the enhanced abilities of the cogitative power in humans from the more limited, but still impressive, abilities of the estimative power in nonhuman animals. The estimative power in nonhuman animals, like sheep, enables sheep to apprehend the individual intentions that the cogitative power enables humans to apprehend. In other words, sheep, like humans, are not just interested in the colors, sounds, smells, flavors, and tangible qualities of moving, small or large, shaped objects in their environment, they are also concerned with concurrently apprehending individual intentions *qua per accidens* sensibles like "offspring" and "anything of that sort." Anyone who has spent time raising sheep will know that sheep – in comparison to other ungulate quadrupeds, like cows and pigs – are among the most unintelligent and skittish livestock around. Nevertheless, Aquinas's "anything of that sort" includes a great deal. We should not underestimate the wide range of diverse individual intentions that sheep can estimate. Elsewhere Aquinas, following Avicenna's own treatment of sheep and wolves, mentions the way sheep apprehend particular intentions like "enemy" (*inimicum*), or "predator," and "harmful" (*noxium*) when they encounter and then flee a wolf seen or heard.[27] Interestingly, he points out that the sheep does not flee the wolf on account of the *per se* sensibles of *color* or *shape* that are sensed *per se*, but because the sheep's *per accidens* sensation *qua* estimation of the individual intentions of the wolf as being a natural predator. This is because sensing and "... imaging forms without any estimation of fittingness or harmfulness does not move the sensitive appetite...."[28] It is not the *per se* sensibles of *per se* sensation that move the sheep to flee the wolf. The sheep's *per accidens* sensation via estimation of the wolf's *per accidens* sensible features *qua* individual intentions of being a *predator* and *harmful* are what motivates the appetites of the sheep that cause it to flee. Aquinas also notes that birds gather straw, not because of any *per se* sensibles they sense, but because birds can estimate the individual

---

26 See Aquinas, *Expositio libri Posteriorum*, II.20, *Opera omnia I*,2*, Rome, Commissio Leonina, 1989; *In duodecim libros Metaphysicorum Aristotelis exposito*, M.-R. Cathala and R.M. Spiazzi (eds), Turin, Marietti Editori, 1950, I, lect., 1, n. 13–15.

27 "Cuius ratio est, quia appetitus sensitivus in aliis quidem animalibus natus est moveri ab aestimativa virtute; sicut ovis aestimans lupum inimicum, timet." Aquinas, *STh* 1.81.3. See also *STh* 1.59.3; 1-11.29.6; *DV* 25.2; *SCG* II.48; *QDA* 13.

28 Aquinas, *STh* 1-11.9.1, ad2.

intentions of utility in the straw, namely, that straw affords being useful for constructing a nest. But we need not restrict the inventory of individual intentions *qua per accidens* sensibles estimated by sheep to those mentioned by Aquinas. Aquinas's straightforward account of individual intentions and estimation can be expanded to include a variety of individual intentions and operations performed by clever critters like dogs, dolphins, cephalopods, corvids, and great apes. What distinguishes the way individual intentions are cogitated by humans from the way they are estimated by nonhuman animals? Aquinas provides some clarification to this question in his final remarks taken from his treatment of *per se* and *per accidens* sensibles within his commentary on Aristotle's *De anima* II.6.

> The cogitative and estimative powers stand differently in this regard. For the cogitative power apprehends an individual as existing under a common nature. It can do this insofar as it is united to the intellective power in the same subject. Thus it cognizes this human being as it is *this* human being, and this piece of wood as it is *this* piece of wood. But the estimative power apprehends an individual, not in terms of its being under a common nature, but only in terms of its being the end point or starting point of some action or affection. It is in this way that a sheep recognizes the lamb not inasmuch as it is *this* lamb but inasmuch as it can nurse it. It recognizes *this* grass inasmuch as it is its food. Thus its natural estimative power in no way apprehends any individual to which its acting or being affected does not extend. For the natural estimative power is given to animals so that through it they are directed toward the proper actions or affections that should be pursued or avoided.[29]

This rich text adds important clarifications to the differences between human and nonhuman animal cognition of individual intentions, but it also leaves ambiguous one significant point. What the text clarifies is that the union of the cogitative power with the intellect in the human enables the cogitative power to apprehend, not only individual intentions, but to apprehend individual intentions as falling under the universal intentions of a common nature. Children first learn to apprehend and discriminate between an individual human and an individual dog, as well as between an individual human and another individual human, between Socrates and Diares. In this respect, the human child's use of the cogitative power to apprehend individual intentions does not differ from the dog's use of its estimative power to discriminate between the

---

29   Aquinas, *In DA* II.13 (Leon., pp. 122: 205–222) (Pasnau, pp. 208–209, mod. trans.).

AQUINAS ON COGNIZING INDIVIDUALS 251

individual intentions afforded by individual humans or individual dogs. But eventually the child's cogitative power will be transformed through its participation and co-operation with the child's intellect, and this will enable the child to employ the cogitative power to appreciate individual intentions *qua* instances of universal intentions. That is to say, the human child will become able to exercise both powers together – the cogitative power and intellect – to form propositions like "This individual man is an animal" or "Socrates is a human," which combine a singular subject with a universal predicate.

Aquinas clearly contrasts this intellectual transformation of the cogitative power's ability to apprehend individual intentions with the natural range of abilities that belong to the estimative power in nonhuman animals. Nonhuman animals, lacking intellectual powers, cannot use their estimative power to apprehend individual intentions as being under a common nature. The scope of the individual intentions apprehended by the estimative power in nonhuman animals is fixed by their relevance to being the aim (*terminus*) or starting point (*principium*) of some action or passion of the animal. A hungry nonhuman animal, like a scrub-jay, might employ its estimative power, albeit not as a *per accidens* sensation, to cognize the *aim* of retrieving food from one of its distant caches. A rabbit fleeing a fox might encounter a burrow that it estimates as affording safety which serves as starting point of action to achieve the aim of escaping the predator.

Aquinas states that the estimative power is unable to apprehend any individual intentions that fall outside the range of actions or reactions required for the animal to survive by pursuing or fleeing some object. Said otherwise, and again using the language of the ecological psychologist James Gibson, if the individual intentions of an object do not *afford* any action or reaction for the animal, then the animal will not estimate those intentions. Aquinas's contrast between apprehending individual intentions under a common nature and merely apprehending individual intentions as they are relevant to the aims or initiation of action or passion suggests a difference between "theoretical" and "practical" pursuits. The estimative power in nonhuman animals only apprehends individual intentions that fall within a "pragmatic" horizon of action and passion, but, due to the intellectual transformation of the cogitative power in humans, the cogitative power can go beyond this "practical" horizon to apprehend individual intentions that need not be relevant to any action or passion on the part of the human. The human cogitative power can be employed both to apprehend individual intentions pertinent to human action or passion, and to apprehend individual intentions in a disinterested way that is required for theoretical forms of apprehension. Theoretical cognition necessitates not merely apprehending individuals *qua* individuals relevant to action, but also *qua* connected to universals that transcend the *hic et nunc* of action and passion.[30]

Even though this passage does clarify Aquinas's contrast between the apprehension of individual intentions by the estimative and cogitative powers, it nevertheless leaves unresolved an important feature concerning the way the estimative power apprehends individual intentions. Aquinas states that "a sheep recognizes the lamb not inasmuch as it is *this* lamb but inasmuch as it can nurse it. It recognizes *this* grass inasmuch as it is its food."[31] There are two ways we might interpret this statement. Given Aquinas's emphasis on the relevance of action and passion that surrounds this statement, we might read Aquinas as excluding from the estimative power the ability to apprehend individual intentions *qua* individuals, by restricting the estimative power to the apprehension of individual intentions *qua* the principles or aims of action or passion. On this reading, sheep do not apprehend individuals like *this* lamb, but only apprehend individual actions or passions to be pursued with respect to *this* lamb. Alternatively, given the contrast Aquinas makes between apprehending individual intentions as falling under a common nature versus their being apprehended without any connection to universals – qualifications which also surround this passage – we might read Aquinas as simply claiming nonhuman animals can only estimate individual intentions *qua* individuals relevant to action or passion.

There are two interconnected problems with the first reading of this passage. First, it suggests that the reason the estimative power cannot apprehend *this* lamb or *this* grass is because these individual intentions can be connected with universals, which would undermine Aquinas's contrast between the estimative power and the cogitative power. But this is no less true of individual intentions that afford actions or passions, like being nursed or being edible; these too can be connected with universals. Accordingly, I take Aquinas's qualification of "can nurse it" over "*this* lamb" and "food" over "*this* grass," to be emphasizing that the sheep cannot estimate *this* lamb and *this* grass as falling under a common nature or as instances of a universal. The sheep's estimation

---

30   This contrast between theoretical and practical requires some qualification with respect to Aquinas's doctrine. As we will see later, unlike the "practical" activities of nonhuman animals, human practical reason requires, like theoretical reason, the application of universal principles to particulars. In short, the ascription of "practical" to nonhuman animals does not involve the apprehension and application of universal intentions, whereas both practical and theoretical human endeavors require the apprehension of universal and individual intentions.

31   Aquinas, *In DA* II.13 (Leon., 122, 215–217) (Pasnau, p. 209, mod. trans.).

of *this* lamb and *this* grass is restricted to them as individual objects that afford some action or passion.

Second, the first reading would exclude from Aquinas's quite nuanced view of nonhuman animal estimation a rather obvious feature of nonhuman animal behavior, namely, that the estimated relevance of the same individual to the action or passion of an animal frequently changes. In different circumstances a body of water affords drinking, cooling off in, and swimming across. In some situations, a mare estimates her colt or filly as affording being nursed, but, at least typically, not another mare's foal as affording being nursed; in fact, some mares can be quite aggressive towards the foals of other mares. But if a predator is encountered, a mare will estimate her own foal as requiring protection. Despite different contexts that require estimations of different actions or passions, the mare apprehends the same individual, its offspring, as affording these distinct actions or passions. Why would we conclude that Aquinas intended his already subtle account of nonhuman animal estimation to exclude these more obvious examples of nonhuman animal behavior?

It is for these reasons that I endorse a version of the second interpretation. Nonhuman animals can estimate individual intentions like *this* offspring, *this* lamb, and *this* grass, but they are always apprehended *qua* individuals-to-be-acted-on or individuals-to-be-affected-by, that is, as relevant to some behavioral aim; they are never apprehended as being connected to universals. Aquinas's texts do not explicitly resolve this issue, but I think this interpretation provides the best reading of the text insofar as it harmonizes all of his qualifications about nonhuman animal estimation and it does not render his account incapable of explaining some obvious features of nonhuman animal behavior.

Let us conclude this examination of Aquinas's treatment of *per se* and *per accidens* sensibles and sensation with a consideration of its relevance to Aquinas's account of cognition of individuals. Despite the technical and idiosyncratic features of Aquinas's treatment, the phenomenon captured by the doctrine of *per se* and *per accidens* sensibles and sensation is utterly quotidian. His example of intellectual *per accidens* sensation consists in a human simultaneously sensing the *per se* sensibles of an object – its color, sounds, movements, etc. – and also intellectually apprehending that this object is a living thing. Our daily life is replete with ordinary forms of discourse and intellectual recognition of the objects we sense in which we identify the universal characteristics of these objects. This is no less true of our cognition of the individual intentions of things that Aquinas ascribes to the cogitative power in humans. Indeed, our primary focus in these cases is rarely directed to the colors, shapes, sounds, or movements of these objects, but to the universal or individual characteristics of these objects that are simultaneously being sensed. We attend to the universal and individual *meanings* of words read or spoken, not to their colors, sounds, shapes, size, or movement. The deep interfusion and confluence of our *per accidens* sensation of *per accidens* sensibles bound up with our concurrent *per se* sensation of *per se* sensibles lends itself to forms of expression that unite in words the unity of the human's cognitive apprehension, which consists in the coordinated exercise of their intellectual and sensory powers. Hence, I can say that I see that he is alive (*unde possum dicere quod video eum vivere*). But neither the universal nor the singular characteristics of *life* are *per se* sensibles and so they cannot be *seen* strictly speaking. Here *seeing* means both the *per se* sensation of visual sight (which is *seeing* properly speaking) and the concurrent apprehension of *life* as universal by the intellect or as singular by the cogitative power, both of which are *seeing* in the extended sense as *per accidens* sensation.

I think it is helpful to draw attention to the way Aquinas's treatment of this topic is similar to Wittgenstein's brief reflections on seeing an aspect; indeed, they seem to be discussing the same phenomenon. Similar to the account given by Aquinas, Wittgenstein distinguishes two uses of the world "see" and provides a number of illustrations of each that track phenomena akin to Aquinas's example. "I contemplate a face, and then suddenly notice its likeness to another. I see that it has not changed; and yet I see it differently. I call this experience 'noticing an aspect'."[32] The different aspects under which we can see, i.e., *per se* sense, the same *per se* sensibles is equivalent to the phenomenon Aquinas describes as *per accidens* sensation of *per accidens* sensibles. These different aspects are the individual and universal intentions Aquinas ascribes to the cogitative power and intellect. We can streamline our language about these two ways of seeing without sacrificing any clarity by stipulating a sharp distinction between "sensation" and "perception." I call all acts of *per se* sensation of *per se* sensibles acts of "sensation," and call all acts of *per accidens* sensation of individual or universal *per accidens* sensibles by the cogitative power and intellect acts of "perception."

4 Aquinas's Approach to Singular Cognition

The central contention of this essay is that a proper understanding of Aquinas's doctrine of human cognition of individuals requires first and foremost

---

32   Ludwig Wittgenstein, *Philosophical Investigations*, trans. G.E.M. Anscombe, G.E.M. Anscombe and R. Rhees (eds), Oxford, Basil Blackwell, 1958, p. 193.

AQUINAS ON COGNIZING INDIVIDUALS 255

grasping the central framing role this account of sensation and perception has for his treatment of human thought, understanding, reasoning, and knowledge of individuals. For Aquinas, all cognition begins in the senses, and as we have seen Aquinas distinguishes sensibles objects into *per se* and *per accidens* sensibles which are sensed and perceived, respectively. This distinction and account of empirical cognition of sensibles, individual meanings, and universal meanings, frames the point of departure for Aquinas's own division of different forms of cognition of individuals, and so also for any adequate interpretation of Aquinas on the problem of singular cognition. The approach adopted here is therefore radically different from the approach common to Aquinas's many of defenders and critics on the problem of cognition of singulars, which read Aquinas's texts on cognition of singulars in isolation from the way Aquinas, following Aristotle, works out the differentiation of psychological objects, operations, and powers in his commentary on *De anima* II.6.

Peter King's essay on singular thought in Aquinas, Scotus, and Ockham nicely illustrates what I mean by the common approach to Aquinas. King summarizes Aquinas's reception of Aristotelian psychology before turning to early criticisms and defenses of Aquinas's claim that the human intellect does not cognize individuals. Following his brief examination of *STh* I.86.1 – which is the *locus classicus* in the *Summa theologiae* for Aquinas's view on human intellectual cognition of individuals – King states: "There are reasons to be skeptical that an account of singular cognition is available to Aquinas – at least, singular thought of material composite substances."[33] King's skeptical contention would be reasonable if he, and others, had mentioned, addressed, and raised problems with Aquinas's account of *per accidens* sensation of *per accidens* sensibles and his nuanced doctrine of the cogitative power and its apprehension and collation of individual intentions. But there is no mention of these topics by King – nor by many of Aquinas's other critics and defenders. However, as we have seen, Aquinas himself clearly took these topics to be central to the issue of human cognition of singulars.[34] Furthermore, King and others seem to

---

33 King, "Thinking about Things," p. 110.

34 King is not alone in this respect. But it is noteworthy that in one of his earlier articles King draws attention to the relevance of the cogitative power to Aquinas account of the emotions, wherein he presents a very rich and accurate account of the way the cogitative power or particular reason cognizes individual intentions and forms singular propositions. King writes, "it is a fundamental thesis of Aquinas's philosophy of mind that sense deals with particulars and intellect with universals; reason joins universal concepts together in propositional judgment. But singular propositions can follow from universal ones, and particular reason is the faculty that draws such inferences. Furthermore, particular reason may supply singular propositions that are combined with other

assume that the only cognitive power Aquinas attributes "thought" and "thinking" to is the intellect. Already our examination of Aquinas's commentary on *De anima* II.6 and other related passages show this assumption is mistaken. Aquinas unequivocally ascribes to the cogitative power the ability to perceive and apprehend individual intentions of things as under a common nature as well as to collate these individual intentions and form singular propositions. It would be difficult to imagine a more straightforward account of "singular cognition" than this, but Aquinas in fact has a great deal more to say about the diverse ways in which the cogitative power enables the human to have singular cognition. In the remaining sections of this essay I present a digest of Aquinas's account of the diverse ways the cogitative power performs operations of thinking, understanding, and reasoning with respect to singulars, beginning with a re-reading of the text from *STh* I.86.1. I hope this arsenal of textual evidence helps put to rest the charge that Aquinas does not provide any explanation for how human singular thought takes place.

5   Re-reading *Summa Theologiae* I.86.1

It is important to be clear about both Aquinas's overt aim in *STh* I.86.1 and the way his aim in this article fits within his treatment of human nature in the

---

propositions, singular or universal to draw conclusions." P. King, "Aquinas on the Passions," in S. MacDonald and E. Stump (eds), *Aquinas's Moral Theory*, Ithaca, Cornell University Press, 1999, pp. 101–132, 129. Given the accuracy of King's own presentation of Aquinas's view that singular propositions are formed and reasoned with by virtue of the particular reason, it makes it all the more peculiar that in his later article on singular thought in Aquinas, Scotus, and Ockham King omits any mention of the cogitative power and individual intentions in his summary of Aquinas, and even endorses William de la Mare's view, who "charges Aquinas with not being able to provide a mechanism that allows singular thought to take place." King, "Thinking about Things," p. 109. There are many readers of Aquinas, both defenders and critics, who either entirely omit or neglect the role the cogitative power clearly plays in Aquinas's account of cognition of singulars. See, for instance, G. Pini, "Two Models of Thinking: Thomas Aquinas and John Duns Scotus on Occurrent Thoughts," in G. Klima (ed), *Intentionality, Cognition, and Representation in Medieval Philosophy*, pp. 81–103; S. Boulter, "Aquinas and Searle on Singular Thoughts," in C. Paterson and M.S. Pugh (eds), *Analytical Thomism: Traditions in Dialogue*, London, Routledge, 2006, pp. 59–78; A. Kenny, *Aquinas on Mind*, London, Routledge, 1993, chs. 3, 7, 9; N. Kretzmann, "Philosophy of Mind," in N. Kretzmann and E. Stump (eds), *The Cambridge Companion to Aquinas*, Cambridge, Cambridge University Press, 1993, pp. 128–149; H. McCabe, *On Aquinas*, New York, Continuum, 2008, chs. 10, 11; C. Normore, "The Invention of Singular Thought," in H. Lagerlund (ed), *Forming the Mind: Essays on the Internal Senses and the Mind/Body Problem from Avicenna to the Medical Enlightenment*, Dordrecht, Springer, 2007, pp. 109–128; E. Stump, *Aquinas*, London, Routledge, 2003, pp. 244–276.

AQUINAS ON COGNIZING INDIVIDUALS

Prima pars of the *Summa theologiae*. The problem addressed in *STh* 1.86.1 is not about whether humans or even whether the cogitative power can cognize or achieve "singular thought of material composite substances," but whether the human intellect *qua* intellectual power can cognize individuals. The query in *STh* 1.86.1 is: "It seems that our intellect cognizes singulars." (*Videtur quod intellectus noster cognoscat singularia.*).

Consider the context of this question. *STh* 1.86 belongs to Aquinas's treatment of human nature in *STh* 1.75–89. Aquinas states that these questions *de homine* are approached from a theological order instead of the philosophical order of the *De anima*.[35] In other words, theology provides a re-ordered appropriation of the inquiries and conclusions of philosophy. The intelligibility of the *Summa*'s theological presentation of human nature (*STh* 1.75–76), powers (*STh* 1.77–83), and investigation of intellectual operations and objects (*STh* 1.84–89), presupposes the intelligibility of the philosophical order of inquiry which proceeds from a differentiation of objects, to operations, to powers, and then onto an investigation of the nature that grounds them.[36] Understanding the theological order of the *Summa* requires an appreciation of its appropriation and transformation of the philosophical inquiry followed in the *De anima*. This inquiry begins in earnest with the division of cognizable objects into *per se* and *per accidens* sensibles in the text we examined above, namely, *De anima* II.6. It is in his commentary on *De anima* II.6 where Aquinas's shows how to appreciate that all of the operations of the cognitive powers are rooted in the sensible objects in one way or another. All cognition, not just sensation, truly begins with the diverse ways in which we empirically cognize *per se* and *per accidens* sensible objects – a point developed at length in *STh* 1.84. So where does *STh* 1.86.1 fit within this theological presentation of human nature?

Aquinas presents his division of sensory and intellectual cognitive powers in *STh* 1.78–79, but in *STh* 1.84–89 he focuses exclusively on the cognitive operations and objects of the intellect. This unit of questions commences with a surprisingly extended prologue.

> We have to consider, first, how the soul has intellective understanding when it is conjoined to the body (questions 84–88), and, second, how the soul has intellective understanding when it is separated from the body (question 89). The consideration of the first topic will have three parts: We will consider, first, how the soul has intellective understanding of corporeal things, which are below it (questions 84–86); second, how it has intellective understanding of itself and of what is contained within itself

35 See Aquinas, *STh* 1.75, proem.
36 See Aquinas, *STh* 1.77.3; *In DA* II. 6; *QDA* 13.

258 DE HAAN

(question 87); and, third, how it has intellective understanding of immaterial substances, which are above it (question 88). As for the cognition of
corporeal things, there are three matters to be considered: first, by what
means (*per quid*) it has cognition of them (question 84); second, in what
manner and order (*quomodo et quo ordine*) it has cognition of them
(question 85); and, third, what (*quid*) it has cognition of in them (question 86).[37]

It is noteworthy that *STh* 1.84–89 treat the different objects cognized by the
power of *intellect*, not the way these objects are cognized by *human*s or other
human cognitive powers. Given everything Aquinas has said from *STh* 1.75–85,
including his division of eleven cognitive powers that contribute to human
cognition, it is clearly contrary to Aquinas's aim to read *STh* 1.86.1 as King and
others do, namely, as presenting Aquinas's view on the way "human cognition"
or even "cognition in general" apprehends singulars of a material nature. The
total package of what the other cognitive powers along with the intellect contribute to human cognition is precisely what Aquinas says *STh* 1.84–89 leaves
out, for these questions are concerned with what the intellect uniquely contributes to human cognition.

In *STh* 1.84–85 we learn, among other things, that the objects of intellectual
knowledge are acquired through abstraction from the senses and complete
knowledge of truth requires that the intellect turn to the phantasms. Given the
dependency of all intellectual cognition on the cognition of the external and
internal senses – a point reiterated in *STh* 1.84 and which is the hallmark of
Aquinas's empirical psychology – his extended presentation and near exclusive focus on intellectual cognition in *STh* 1.84–89 presupposes Aquinas's
broader account of the objects and cognitive operations of sensory powers
that provide intellectual cognition with its object – an account that we find
worked out in his commentary on the *De anima* but that Aquinas explicitly
states he is leaving out in the *Summa*.[38] Hence, to read *STh* 1.86.1 within the
wider context of Aquinas's psychology requires appreciating what Aquinas
himself states needs to be supplemented in *ST* 1.86.1, namely, an account of
human empirical cognition akin to what we find in his commentary on the *De
anima* and elsewhere. With these contextual caveats in mind, let us proceed to
re-read *STh* 1.86.1.

In *STh* 1.86 Aquinas investigates what our *intellect* cognizes in material
things (*Deinde considerandum est quid intellectus noster in rebus materialibus*

---

37 Aquinas, *STh* 1.84, proem. (Freddoso, mod. trans.).
38 See also Aquinas, *DV* 10.5.

AQUINAS ON COGNIZING INDIVIDUALS

cognoscat).[39] The first article concerns whether our intellect can cognize singulars. Aquinas presents four objections that all contend the human intellect can cognize individuals. Aquinas's *sed contra* cites Aristotle as holding that reason cognizes universals and sense cognizes singulars. As for whether the human intellect *qua* intellectual power can cognize individuals, Aquinas's own answer could not be clearer.

> Our intellect cannot have a direct and primary cognition of the singular in material things. The reason for this is that the principle of singularity in material things is individual matter (*materia individualis*), while, as was explained above (q. 85, a. 1), our intellect has intellective understanding by abstracting the intelligible species from individual matter. But it is the universal that is abstracted from individual matter. Hence, our intellect has direct cognition only of the universals (*directe est cognoscitivus nisi universalium*). However, our intellect can have cognition of the singular indirectly and, as it were, by a sort of turning back (*indirecte et quasi per quandam reflexionem*). For as was explained above (q. 84, a. 7), even after it has abstracted intelligible species, it cannot have actual intellective understanding except by turning itself to the phantasms, in which it has intellective understanding of the intelligible species, as *De anima* 3 says. So, then, our intellect understands the universal itself directly through the intelligible species, whereas it indirectly understands the singulars that the phantasms are phantasms of. And it is in this way that it forms the proposition "Socrates is a man."[40]

In this text, and in many others, Aquinas straightforwardly denies that the human intellect can cognize individuals. His reasons for doing so are also perfectly clear. As was detailed before, individual matter is the principle of singularity in material things, the human intellect understands by abstracting its intelligible species from this individual matter, and so the very nature of human intellectual cognition precludes its cognition of individuals that are individuated by matter. We must be cautious if we are to understand accurately what Aquinas has stated so clearly here and elsewhere. Many of Aquinas's readers conflate the question of whether there can be cognition, thought, understanding, or reasoning about individuals with the question of whether the human intellect *qua* intellectual power can have cognition, thought, understanding, or can reason about individuals. Aquinas explicitly addresses the latter question in *STh*

---

39   Aquinas, *STh* I.86. proem.
40   Aquinas, *STh* I.86.1 (Freddoso, mod. trans.).

260   DE HAAN

1.86.1, but he does not tackle the former here. Nevertheless, given the preceding questions on the internal senses in *STh* 1.78.4 and his presentation of the way the estimative and cogitative powers cognize individual intentions – which are also relevant to the way the sensual concupiscible and irascible appetites obey reason (See *STh* 1.81.3)[41] – it is clear that Aquinas does maintain humans have powers that cognize individuals and so the human can cognize individuals. Indeed, he makes this point explicit in a parallel text to *STh* 1.86.1 found in *De veritate* 2.6.

> Humans have prior cognition of singulars through imagination and sense, and therefore can apply universal cognition, which is in the intellect, to a particular; for properly speaking neither sense nor intellect cognize but the human through both, as is clear in *De anima* 1.[42]

Aquinas does, however, state in *STh* 1.86.1 and elsewhere that the intellect has indirect cognition of singulars through a reflection or conversion to the singulars cognized by phantasia, that is, by imagination, memory, and most importantly, the cogitative power.[43] Many defenders and critics of Aquinas have focused their attention on this indirect intellectual cognition of singulars, taking it to be Aquinas's sole explanation for the fact that *humans* cognize singulars. But as we have seen, this reading is deeply at odds with the expressed aims of *STh* 1.86.1 and Aquinas's account of the cogitative power's apprehension of singulars as well as his broader understanding of what different cognitive powers contribute to the unity of human cognitive operations. It is only within this wider framework – which includes the way a human being's different cognitive powers can be coordinated to co-operate – that we can

---

41   "Loco autem aestimativae virtutis est in homine, sicut *supra* dictum est, vis cogitativa; quae dicitur a quibusdam ratio particularis, eo quod est collativa intentionum individualium. Unde ab ea natus est moveri in homine appetitus sensitivus. Ipsa autem ratio particularis nata est moveri et dirigi secundum rationem universalem, unde in syllogisticis ex universalibus propositionibus concluduntur conclusiones singulares. Et ideo patet quod ratio universalis imperat appetitui sensitivo, qui distinguitur per concupiscibilem et irascibilem, et hic appetitus ei obedit. Et quia deducere universalia principia in conclusiones singulares, non est opus simplicis intellectus, sed rationis; ideo irascibilis et concupiscibilis magis dicuntur obedire rationi, quam intellectui. Hoc etiam quilibet experiri potest in seipso, applicando enim aliquas universales considerationes, mitigatur ira aut timor aut aliquid huiusmodi, vel etiam instigatur." Aquinas, *STh* 1.81.3.

42   Aquinas, *DV* 2.6, ad3 (Leon., 66–67: 127–133). My translation. See also *DV* 10.5.

43   See Aquinas, *DV* 2.6; 10.5; M. Stock, "Sense Consciousness According to St. Thomas," *The Thomist*, vol. 21, no. 4, 1958, pp. 415–486.

AQUINAS ON COGNIZING INDIVIDUALS

properly understand Aquinas's appeal to indirect intellectual cognition of singulars.[44]

Thus far we have seen that even though Aquinas denies that the human intellect has singular cognition, he unequivocally does ascribe to the cogitative power or particular reason the ability to perceive individual intentions, to cognize individuals, and to form propositions about singulars. Indeed, despite its frequent omission by his defenders and critics, we even find the last claim in Aquinas's reply to the second objection in *STh* 1.86.1! The second objection maintained the intellect does cognize individuals because the practical intellect directs us to singular action, and this requires cognition of singulars. Aquinas's reply to this objection does not deny the need for singular cognition for practical reasoning and action.

> [T]he choice of a particular action (*electio particularis operabilis*) is, as it were, the conclusion of the practical intellect's syllogism. But a singular conclusion cannot be inferred directly from a universal proposition; rather, it is inferred by the mediation of some assumed singular proposition. Hence, as *De anima 3* says, the practical intellect's universal conception effects movement only through the mediation of a particular apprehension by the sentient part of the soul.[45]

We find a more developed presentation of the same claim in *De veritate* 10.5, where Aquinas touches on the dynamic conjunction among psychological powers that are grounded in the nature of the human being.

> [T]his conjunction is found in the movement from the soul to things, which begins from the mind and moves forward to the sensitive part in the mind's control over the lower powers. Here, the mind has contact with singulars through the mediation of particular reason, a power of the sensitive part, which composes and divides individual intentions, which is also known as the cogitative power, and which has a definite bodily

---

44 For more detailed studies on Aquinas's treatment of intellectual reflection and conversion on the phantasms, see B. Lonergan, *Verbum: Word and Idea in Aquinas*, D.B. Burrell (ed), Notre Dame, University of Notre Dame Press, 1967; G. Klubertanz, "St. Thomas and the Knowledge of the Singular," *New Scholasticism*, vol. 26, 1952, pp. 135–166; T. Cory, "What Is an Intellectual 'Turn'? The *Liber de causis*, Avicenna, and Aquinas's Turn to Phantasms," *Tópicos*, vol. 45, 2013, pp. 129–162; D. De Haan, "Moral Perception and the Function of the *Vis Cogitativa* in Thomas Aquinas's Doctrine of Antecedent and Consequent Passions," *Documenti e studi sulla tradizione filosofica medievale*, vol. 25, 2014, pp. 287–328.

45 Aquinas, *STh* 1.86.1, ad2 (Freddoso, mod. trans.).

262 DE HAAN

organ, a cell in the center of the head. The mind's universal judgment about things to be done cannot be applied to a particular act except through the mediation of some intermediate power which apprehends the singular. In this way, there is framed a kind of syllogism whose major premise is universal, the judgment of the mind, and whose minor premise is singular, an apprehension of the particular reason. The conclusion is the choice of the singular work, as is clear in *De anima* III.[46]

These clear statements pertaining to the way the cogitative power cognizes individual intentions and forms singular propositions do not disappear in Aquinas's later works. Indeed, some of the clearest ascriptions of singular cognition to the cogitative power or particular reason occur in Aquinas's most mature works.

In Aquinas's treatment of prudence in his commentary on book six of the *Nicomachean Ethics* and the *Secunda Pars* of the *Summa theologiae*, he ascribes to the cogitative power a critical role to play in the virtue of prudence due to the cogitative power's capacity for *singular reasoning* and *singular understanding (intellectus qui est circa singularia)* whereby it forms unconditional judgments about singulars (*secundum quod habet absolutum iudicium de singularibus*) akin to the intellect's unconditional judgments about universals.

The reasoning of prudence terminates, as in a conclusion, in the particular operable, to which it applies universal cognition ... But the singular conclusion is syllogized from universal and singular propositions. Hence, the reasoning of prudence must proceed from a twofold understanding. One [kind of understanding] cognizes universals, which pertains to the intellect ... But the other [kind of] understanding, as stated in book six of the *Ethics*, cognizes an extreme, that is, of some primary singular and contingent operable, namely, the minor premise, which must be singular in the syllogism of prudence ... Now this primary singular is some singular end ... Hence, the understanding that is posited as part of prudence is a right estimate of some particular end.[47]

---

46 Aquinas, *DV* 10.5. Modified English translation from Thomas Aquinas, *On Truth*, (trans.) R.W. Mulligan, J.V. McGlynn, and R.W. Schmidt, 3 vols., Chicago, Henry Regnery Company, 1952–1954. For the Latin text, see *supra* n. 8. See *In Sent.*, IV, d. 50, 1. a. 3, ad 3 *in contrarium* (Parma ed, vol. VII, pt. 2, p. 1251).

47 Aquinas, *STh* II-II.49.2, ad 1.

AQUINAS ON COGNIZING INDIVIDUALS   263

The right estimate concerning a particular end is called both understanding, inasmuch as it [pertains to] a principle, and sense, inasmuch as it [pertains to] a particular. And this is what the Philosopher says in book six of the *Ethics*, "Of these, namely, of singulars, [we] must have sense, and this is understanding." But this is not to be understood [as indicating] the particular sense by which we cognize proper sensibles, but [as indicating] the interior sense by which we judge of a particular (*sed de sensu interiori quo de particulari iudicamus*).[48]

This interior sense whereby humans *estimate* or *judge* of a particular is, of course, the cogitative power or particular reason, as the parallel texts from the commentary on the *Nicomachean Ethics* and other passages make explicit.[49]

Thus far we have presented texts wherein Aquinas unequivocally ascribes to the cogitative power diverse forms of singular cognition including perceptions, judgments, understanding, reasoning, and the formation of singular propositions. But there are also texts in which Aquinas attributes *thinking* or *deliberative thought* to the cogitative power as well. In the *Summa theologiae* Aquinas distinguishes three meanings of thinking or to think (*cogitare*). The first is more general and denotes any act of intellectual considering. He distinguishes this from the form of thinking which is proper to the intellectual act of consideration that is characteristic of inquiry prior to arriving at any determinate understanding.

---

48   Aquinas, *STh* II-II.49.2, ad 3.
49   Aquinas's parallel treatment of prudence is found in his commentary on the *Nicomachean Ethics* VI, especially his seventh and ninth lectures, wherein he explicitly ascribes singular understanding and reasoning to the cogitative power. "Et, quia singularia proprie cognoscuntur per sensum, oportet quod homo horum singularium quae dicimus esse principia et extrema, habeat sensum non solum exteriorem, sed etiam interiorem, cuius *supra* dixit esse prudentiam, scilicet vim cogitativam sive aestimativam quae dicitur ratio particularis; unde hic sensus vocatur intellectus qui est circa singularia, et hunc Philosophus vocat in III *De anima* intellectum passivum, qui est corruptibilis..." *Sententia libri Ethicorum* (=*In Ethic*), *Opera omnia 47.1–2*, Rome, Commissio Leonina, 1969, VI, 9, p. 367: 178–186, ad 1143a35. "Est autem considerandum circa ea quae hic dicta sunt quod, sicut pertinent ad intellectum absolutum in universalibus iudicium de primis principiis, ad rationem autem pertinent discursus a principiis in conclusiones, ita etiam circa singularia vis cogitativa hominis vocatur intellectus, secundum quod habet absolutum iudicium de singularibus ; unde ad intellectum dicit pertinere prudentiam et synesim et gnomyn ; dicitur autem ratio particularis secundum quod discurrit ab uno in aliud, et ad hanc pertinet eubulia, quam Philosophus his non connumeravit nec dixit eam esse extremorum" *In Ethic* VI, 9 (Leon. Ed, p. 368: 239–251, ad 1143b11).

264   DE HAAN

> Accordingly, the act of thinking something through is properly speaking a movement of the soul during the time in which it is deliberating and in which it has not yet been brought to perfection through a full vision of the truth. However, since such a movement can belong to the soul either (a) when it is deliberating with respect to universal intentions, which belong to the intellective part of the soul, or (b) when it is deliberating with respect to particular intentions, which belong to the sentient part of the soul, it follows that 'the act of thinking something through' (*cogitare*) is taken in the second sense for an act of the deliberating intellect, whereas 'the act of thinking something through' is taken in a third sense for an act of the cogitative power.[50]

This text demonstrates that, contrary to his many critics, Aquinas *does have* a straightforward account of singular thought of individual intentions. Why has this account been overlooked by his critics and defenders? It is because they have assumed *thought* is proprietary to the intellect. If we adopt this mistaken assumption and restrict our search for a doctrine of singular thought to Aquinas's treatments of the human intellect, then we will certainly come up empty handed. Aquinas, however, never gave the slightest impression that his account of the human intellect is where we should look for it; indeed, he presented unambiguous statements that claimed the human intellect cannot cognize individuals. But even if he had made such suggestions, this last passage from *STh* II-II.2.1 – which is arguably the *locus classicus* on thinking (*cogitare*) in Aquinas – would have set the record straight for those interesting in Aquinas's doctrine of thinking. For in this text they would have discovered that Aquinas does not ascribe singular thought to the human intellect, but *does* attribute singular thinking and deliberation about particular intentions to the human cogitative power.

6   Conclusion: Aquinas on the Diverse Forms of Singular Cognition in Humans

In this essay I have presented extensive textual evidence from the works of Thomas Aquinas to demonstrate that Aquinas has a clear and substantive

---

50   Aquinas, *STh* II-II.2.1 (Freddoso, mod. trans.). "Et secundum hoc cogitatio proprie dicitur motus animi deliberantis nondum perfecti per plenam visionem veritatis. Sed quia talis motus potest esse vel animi deliberantis circa intentiones universales, quod pertinet ad intellectivam partem; vel circa intentiones particulares, quod pertinet ad partem sensitivam: ideo cogitare secundo modo sumitur pro actu intellectus deliberantis; tertio modo, pro actu virtutis cogitativae."

account of human cognition of singulars. This evidence undermines the well known criticism that Aquinas's psychology fails to provide any explanation for the basic fact that humans cognize and think about individuals. I argued that the root error behind this critique is the assumption that singular thought can only be achieved by the human intellect. This mistaken assumption, however, lacks any basis within the texts of Aquinas. From our detailed explication of empirical cognition in his commentary on *De anima* II.6's distinction between *per se* and *per accidens* sensibles, to our re-reading of *STh* I.86.1 and other texts on the intellect and cogitative power, a unified and coherent account of Aquinas's doctrine of singular cognition has come to light. Aquinas unequivocally maintains that there is no human *intellectual* cognition or thought about individual material objects, but he does contend that there is human *cogitative* cognition and thought about singulars. This essay's extended exegesis of Aquinas's many treatments of the cogitative power's diverse forms of singular cognition has established that, far from lacking any account of singular cognition in human beings, Aquinas has a complex account of the many ways in which the cogitative power enables the human being to perceive, understand, reason, think, and cognize singulars, that is, individuals that are matter-form composites. What unites these diverse cognitive operations of the cogitative power in humans are the individual intentions which constitute the *per se* object of the cogitative power. If we want to understand Aquinas's doctrine of singular cognition we need to look to his account of the cognitive power that cognizes these individual intentions for his own doctrine of singular cognition, and not his account of the intellect which only cognizes universal intentions. Of course, as Aquinas frequently reminds his readers, strictly speaking it is neither the cogitative power that thinks about individuals nor the intellect that thinks about universals, rather it is the human being that thinks about individuals and universals by deploying their powers of cogitation and intellection.

Granting this, one might think the real problem with Aquinas's account of singular cognition is the absence of any explanation of how the operations of these different powers are coordinated to contribute to the unified operations of the human being.[51] This essay has not tackled this vexing issue, which raises questions about the prospects for any powers psychology. For if the operations of psychological powers cannot be coordinated and united for the unity of a human operation, then all powers psychologies have a problem, not just Aquinas's. But even if this is a real problem for Aquinas, it is different from the

---

51 Aquinas does confront this issue in his treatment of human action (*STh* I-II.17.1–9) and in his many treatments of the connection of the virtues (*STh* I-II.65.1–5).

problem of singular cognition addressed in this essay. And this essay has demonstrated that the problem of singular cognition is not a problem for Aquinas.[52]

Bibliography

Primary Literature

Albert the Great, *De anima*, C. Stroick (ed), *Opera omnia 7.1*, Münster, Aschendorff, 1968.

Alexander of Hales, *Summa theologica*, Quaracchi, Collegium S. Bonaventurae, 1924–1948.

Domininus Báñez, *Commentaria in primam partem angelici doctoris S. Thomae*, sumpt. Ph. Borde, L. Arnaud, P. Borde, and G. Barbier, Rome, Lugduni, 1663.

John of St. Thomas, *Cursus philosophicus thomisticus*, Reiser P. Beatus (ed), Turin, Marietti, 1930.

Thomas Aquinas, *Expositio libri Posteriorum*, II.20, *Opera omnia 1.2*, Rome, Commissio Leonina, 1989.

Thomas Aquinas, *In duodecim libros Metaphysicorum Aristotelis exposito*, M.R. Cathala and R.M. Spiazzi (eds), Turin, Marietti, 1950.

Thomas Aquinas, *Quaestiones disputatae de anima*, B.C. Bazán (ed), *Opera omnia 24*, Rome, Commissio Leonina, 1996.

Thomas Aquinas, *Quaestiones disputatae de veritate*, *Opera omnia 22.1-3*, Rome, Commissio Leonina, 1970–1976. English translation: *On Truth*, trans. R.W. Mulligan, J.V. McGlynn, and R.W. Schmidt, 3 vols., Chicago, Henry Regnery Company, 1952–1954.

Thomas Aquinas, *Scriptum super libros Sententiarum*, book IV, vol. VII, Parma, Typis Petri Fiaccadori, 1852–1873.

Thomas Aquinas, *Sentencia libri De anima*, *Opera omnia 45.1*, Rome, Commissio Leonina, 1984. English translation: *A Commentary on Aristotle's De anima*, trans. R. Pasnau, New Haven, Yale University Press, 1999.

Thomas Aquinas, *Sententia libri Ethicorum*, *Opera omnia 47.1-2*, Rome, Commissio Leonina, 1969.

---

52   I would like to thank Elena Băltuţă for organizing an excellent conference on the theme of medieval accounts of perception and editing this volume of papers on the same. I am especially grateful to her, the conference participants in Berlin, and an anonymous reader for many helpful comments on earlier drafts of this paper.

AQUINAS ON COGNIZING INDIVIDUALS

Thomas Aquinas, *Summa contra Gentiles*, C. Pera (ed), Turin, Marietti, 1961.

Thomas Aquinas, *Summa theologiae*, Editio Leonina Manualis, Rome, Editiones Paulinae, 1962.

Secondary Literature

Black, Deborah, "Imagination and Estimation: Arabic Paradigms and Latin Transformations," *Topoi*, vol. 19, 2000, pp. 59–75.

Boulter, Stephen, "Aquinas and Searle on Singular Thoughts," in C. Paterson and M.S. Pugh (eds), *Analytical Thomism: Traditions in Dialogue*, London, Routledge, 2006, pp. 59–78.

Cory, Therese, "What Is an Intellectual 'Turn'? The *Liber de causis*, Avicenna, and Aquinas's Turn to Phantasms," *Tópicos*, vol. 45, 2013, pp. 129–162.

Gibson, James, *The Ecological Approach to Visual Perception*, Boston, Houghton Mifflin, 1979.

De Haan, Daniel, "Moral Perception and the Function of the *Vis Cogitativa* in Thomas Aquinas's Doctrine of Antecedent and Consequent Passions," *Documenti e studi sulla tradizione filosofica medievale*, vol. 25, 2014, pp. 287–328.

Kenny, Anthony, *Aquinas on Mind*, London, Routledge, 1993.

King, Peter, "Aquinas on the Passions," in S. MacDonald and E. Stump (eds), *Aquinas's Moral Theory*, Ithaca, Cornell University Press, 1999, pp. 101–132.

King, Peter, "Thinking about Things: Singular Thought in the Middle Ages," in G. Klima (ed), *Intentionality, Cognition, and Representation in Medieval Philosophy*, New York, Fordham University Press, 2015, pp. 104–121.

Klubertanz, George, "St. Thomas and the Knowledge of the Singular," *New Scholasticism*, vol. 26, 1952, pp. 135–166.

Kretzmann, Norman, "Philosophy of Mind," in N. Kretzmann and E. Stump (eds), *The Cambridge Companion to Aquinas*, Cambridge, Cambridge University Press, 1993, pp. 128–149.

Lonergan, Bernard, *Verbum: Word and Idea in Aquinas*, D. B. Burrell (ed), Notre Dame, University of Notre Dame Press, 1967.

McCabe, Herbert, *On Aquinas*, New York, Continuum, 2008.

Normore, Calvin, "The Invention of Singular Thought," in H. Lagerlund (ed), *Forming the Mind: Essays on the Internal Senses and the Mind/Body Problem from Avicenna to the Medical Enlightenment*, Dordrecht, Springer, 2007, pp. 109–128.

Pasnau, Robert, *Thomas Aquinas on Human Nature: A Philosophical Study of "Summa theologiae" Ia 75–89*, Cambridge, Cambridge University Press, 2002.

Pini, Giorgio, "Two Models of Thinking: Thomas Aquinas and John Duns Scotus on Occurrent Thoughts," in G. Klima (ed), *Intentionality, Cognition, and Representation in Medieval Philosophy*, New York, Fordham University Press, 2014, pp. 81–103.

Stock, Michael, "Sense Consciousness According to St. Thomas," *The Thomist*, vol. 21, no. 4, 1958, pp. 415–486.

Stump, Eleonore, *Aquinas*, London, Routledge, 2003.

Wippel, John, *The Metaphysical Thought of Thomas Aquinas*, Washington, The Catholic University of America Press, 2000.

Wittgenstein, Ludwig, *Philosophical Investigations*, trans. G.E.M. Anscombe, G.E.M. Anscombe and R. Rhees (eds), Oxford, Basil Blackwell, 1958.

CHAPTER 10

"Accidental Perception" and "Cogitative Power" in Thomas Aquinas and John of Jandun

Paolo Rubini

1   Introduction

In *De anima* II.6, Aristotle outlines his analysis of sense perception from the point of view of the contents we become aware of in our perceptual acts. In few lines, he sketches a conception of perceptual experience that has been largely debated in late medieval and early modern philosophy.[1] His analysis is well known, but it is worth-while to recall it.

Aristotle classifies perceptual contents according to the causal explanation of sense perception he has previously delivederd in *De anima* II.5: acts of sense perception are described there as passive processes in which the sentient is acted upon and affected by the objects of the perceptual acts; as a result, in acts of sense perception the sentient (formally) assimilates to its objects. According to this explanation, Aristotle in *De anima* II.6 divides perceptual contents into two main classes. The first class (a) encompasses entities that *per se* (*kath'hautá*) or according to their nature can affect the sentient. Such entities can either affect (a1) one single sense modality, or (a2) more than one. The subclass (a1) encompasses sensible qualities such as colors, sounds, smells etc., which Aristotle influentially calls "proper" objects of perception. Members of the subclass (a2) are in turn entities such as motion, magnitude, number, etc., addressed by Aristotle under the label of "common" objects of perception. The second main class (b) encompasses entities that, on Aristotle's view, only "accidentally" (*katà symbebekós*) can be objects of acts of sense perception, that is, not *per se* or according to their nature, but in a derivative and indirect way. His own example for an object of this kind is a property such as "being the son of Diares". According to Aristotle's causal explanation of sense perception, it is plain why entities of this kind can become objects of perceptual acts only *per accidens*: "being the son of Diares" is a (complex) relational property that *per se* or according to its nature cannot affect our senses. Such a non-sensible property can be object of an act of perception only because it

---

1   See Aristotle, *De anima*, II.6, 418a7–25, D. Ross (ed), Oxford, Clarendon Press, 1961.

© KONINKLIJKE BRILL NV, LEIDEN, 2020 | DOI:10.1163/9789004413030_011

happens (*symbébeke*) to be joined in the same thing to a sensible (colored) shape.

My aim is not to discuss Aristotle's classification. I only want to emphasize that for any full-fledged account of perceptual experience it is crucial to explain how entities of class (b) are perceived. A philosophical theory of sense perception has to account for the phenomenological fact that, in our perceptual acts, we do not just become aware of sensible qualities and of their magnitude, number, shape, spatial arrangement, but we become aware of a broader range of properties and, ultimately, of "things" as their bearers: Diares' son gently smiling to us; our friend Pekka complaining about the rainy weather; the superb oak in front of the window losing leaves in a windy autumn day. Even if in sense perception we are primarily acquainted with sensible properties (as Aristotle's classification of perceptual contents seems to suggest), in fact we usually perceive them as linked to properties of a different kind: we perceive a sensible x as a non-sensible P, Q etc. It is a merit of Aristotle's classification of perceptual contents to have acknowledged this phenomenological fact.

However, Aristotle is reticent about the psychological mechanism through which entities of class (b) become contents of *perceptual* acts. His causal account of sense perception seems actually not to allow for any perceptual grasping of such objects. If a property has to affect a sense organ in order to become a content of an act of sense perception and if only sensible properties fulfill this condition, then it is hard to understand how non-sensible properties of class (b) can be grasped in acts of *sense perception*. To avoid this conclusion Aristotle should explain how, in the framework of his theory of cognition, non-sensible properties can enter as "accidental" contents into acts of sense perception.

One possible strategy is to assume that the entities belonging to class (b) are primarily apprehended by some *other* cognitive power(s) of the perceiver and only secondarily joined to proper contents of perceptual acts. This would explain how entities of class (b) become available as cognitive contents in spite of their being non-sensible qualities and in which sense they are contents of perceptual acts *per accidens*: *per se* and according to their nature they are actually contents of different cognitive acts, and only additionally they get involved in acts of sense perception. As a result, however, the mechanism responsible for our (full-fledged) perceptual contents appears to be a more complicate process than Aristotle's causal account suggests at first glance.

I am not going to ask whether Aristotle adopted this strategy in order to explain perception of class (b) objects or, for brevity, "accidental perception."[2]

---

2 For a recent discussion of this topic, see A. Marmodoro, *Aristotle on Perceiving Objects*, Oxford, Oxford University Press, 2014, pp. 156–188.

"ACCIDENTAL PERCEPTION" AND "COGITATIVE POWER"

For sure, late medieval Aristotelians did. They usually explained accidental perception by referring to higher cognitive faculties that, in accordance with Avicenna's influential terminology, were called *internal senses*. As the label suggests, these faculties were taken to be "powers" of the sensitive part of the soul, but different from the five external senses in virtue of their localization: their corresponding organs were supposed to be inside the body, for instance in the brain or the heart. Accordingly, the internal senses were supposed to be affected by external objects not directly, but via the external senses being first affected. Medieval Aristotelians commonly regarded these internal faculties as responsible for grasping and making available the non-sensible contents that are involved in acts of accidental perception.[3]

In spite of this common reference to inner senses, however, not much agreement is to be found on this topic among medieval Peripatetics. Controversies arose about their number, their denomination and their localization inside the body. But the most controversial point was their individual function: Which precisely are the objects of the inner senses? How are they apprehended? In this respect, particular attention was paid to the "cognitive power," often regarded as the faculty of the sensitive soul specifically responsible for grasping the non-sensible contents involved in accidental perception. The function of this power was a topic of debate among late medieval Aristotelians.

To make things even more complicated, a further question lurked in the background: Are the internal senses – and in particular the cogitative power – somehow connected with the rational soul? The major reason for this question was that the non-sensible contents involved in accidental perception appear to pertain, at least partially, to the sphere of objects medieval philosophers usually ascribed to intellectual cognition, namely essences of things. To recognize a sensible *x as* the son of Diares, for instance, seems to entail an apprehension of *x as* a human being, which is an apprehension of *x*'s essence, and apprehension of essences is usually regarded in Aristotelianism as the domain of the intellect. Is the intellect involved in acts of accidental perception?

In the following I will explore and compare two different strategies adopted by late medieval Aristotelians for explaining the complex content of accidental perception. In the next section I will first focus on Thomas Aquinas' strategy, in section 3 on the strategy chosen by John of Jandun, a 14th century master of the Parisian faculty of arts known for his Averroist views in psychology. My choice of these two authors is not arbitrary. Both Aquinas and Jandun account for accidental perception by referring to the contribution of inner senses and by emphasizing the role of the cogitative power. According to both of them, it

---

3 On this point, see C. Di Martino, *Ratio particularis. La doctrine des senses internes d'Avicenne à Thomas d'Aquin*, Paris, Vrin, 2008, p. 14.

272 RUBINI

is the cogitative power that, by means of quasi-rational inferences, grasps and makes available the non-sensible contents involved in accidental perception. But when it comes to explain how the cogitative power operates, they adopt almost opposite strategies. Aquinas emphasizes the contiguity between cogitative power and intellect and accounts for the special capacities of the cogitative power by appealing to a flow of information from the intellect. The ontological framework of his psychology – his hylomorphism – makes such an explanation plausible. By contrast, Jandun's Averroism does not allow for a similar strategy of explanation. As a unique and super-personal entity, the intellectual power is not ontologically connected with the individual hylomorphic compounds that human beings are. Accordingly, Jandun cannot plausibly account for the function of the cogitative power by appealing to any influence of the intellect, as Aquinas did. Instead, he regards the cogitative power as an autonomously operating faculty of the human sensitive soul. In particular, Jandun seems to describe the function of the cogitative power in terms of a complex, automatic mechanism of association.

If my suggestion is correct, Jandun's explanation of the psychological mechanism underlying accidental perception emphasizes the empirical character of sense perception (and, ultimately, of human cognition in general). By contrast, Aquinas' empiricism is significantly mitigated by his appeal to an intellectual origin of the "accidental" contents of perception. I will come back to this point in the conclusive section.

2   Aquinas on Accidental Perception: Cogitative Power and Intellect

If we want to know Aquinas' views about accidental perception,[4] we have first to look at his commentary on Aristotle's *De anima*, in particular at the section

---

4   The topic of "accidental perception" in Aquinas has already captured the attention of historians of medieval philosophy, particularly in the Anglophone world. The most recent and most articulated contribution on this topic is A. Lisska, *Aquinas's Theory of Perception: An Analytic Reconstruction*, Oxford, Oxford University Press, 2016. This study gives an overview on the relevant secondary literature of the last decades and engages in a detailed analysis of manifold passages in which Aquinas displays his ideas about sense perception. Aquinas' account of accidental perception is specially addressed in chapters 10–12 of Lisska's monograph. There, the author correctly insists on the central role the cogitative power plays in Aquinas' account; in particular, he takes the apprehension of individual (primary) substances to be the essential contribution of the cogitative power to accidental perception. Although the basic direction of Lisska's interpretation is by and large correct, his approach falls short of explaining what the operation of the cogitative power exactly consists in. Especially Aquinas' idea of a dependence of the cogitative power on the intellect is neglected in Lisska's

where he discusses Aristotle's classification of perceptual contents (book II, chapter 13). There Aquinas first explains – in line with Aristotle's causal account of perception – that only entities which are able to affect the external senses can be perceptual contents *per se*, that is, only sensible qualities (proper sensible objects, a1) and their modes (common sensible objects, a2). After having proved that, he addresses the topic of accidental perception by asking "why something is said to be sensible *per accidens*."[5] This amounts to the same as asking how it happens that contents of sense perception also encompass non-sensible objects (our class b). Aquinas' answer focuses on two "requirements" that must be fulfilled for accidental perception.[6]

The first requirement pertains to Aquinas' epistemic realism: the non-sensible property grasped in accidental perception needs to be ontologically linked to a *per se* sensible property; otherwise the non-sensible property could not become the *accidental* content of an act of perception. In other words, both the sensible and the non-sensible property need to belong to the thing perceived (the same substance). The second requirement concerns the psychological mechanism underlying accidental perception: the non-sensible property needs to be "apprehended" by the perceiver in some way; otherwise it could not be an accidental *content* of an act of perception – indeed, it could not be a content of cognition at all. The non-sensible property, as Aquinas writes, "must then be cognized *per se* by some other cognitive power belonging to the thing sensing; this will, of course, be either another sense, intellect, or the cogitative/estimative power."[7] The non-sensible content involved in an act of accidental perception is actually a *per se* content of another cognitive act, being added to the *per se* sensible content secondarily. Aquinas indicates three cognitive powers from which the *per se* apprehension of the non-sensible

---

    analysis. Accordingly, my understanding of the operation of the cogitative power differs substantially from Lisska's. More similar views to those I am going to present in this section can be found in Di Martino, *Ratio particularis*, pp. 85–101. However, Di Martino is more engaged in an historical approach to the topic and does not really attempt at explaining the operation of the cogitative power. The topic of accidental perception in Aquinas is also touched upon in D. Perler's and D. De Haan's contributions to this volume.

5 Thomas Aquinas, *A Commentary on Aristotle's De anima*, translated by R. Pasnau, New Haven, Yale University Press, 1999 (hereafter *Commentary*), p. 207; correspondent original text according to *Sentencia De anima* II.13, R.A. Gauthier (ed), *Opera omnia 45.1*, Rome, Commissio Leonina, 1984 (hereafter *Sentencia* II.13), p. 120, ll. 162–163: "[...] restat uidendum qua ratione dicatur aliquid sensibile per accidens."

6 See Aquinas, *Commentary*, pp. 207–208; *Sentencia* II.13, p. 120, ll. 164–174.

7 Aquinas, *Commentary*, p. 208; *Sentencia* II.13, p. 120, ll. 173–174: "Oportet igitur quod [sensibile per accidens] per se cognoscatur ab aliqua alia potencia cognoscitiua sencientis, et hec quidem uel est alius sensus, uel est intellectus, uel uis cogitatiua aut uis estimatiua."

content can originate: (1) a different sense, (2) the intellect, (3) the cogitative viz. estimative power. It is worthwhile to consider these three cases in some details since they depict three different modalities of accidental perception.

Aquinas takes into account case (1) in order to explain what I would call "synesthetic perception."[8] His example is an act of vision in which something white is *seen as sweet*. According to him, a synesthetic perception of this kind is only possible because the sweetness of a white substance, for instance milk, has been previously apprehended (as a *per se* object) by the sense of taste. As a result, a non-visible content of taste is made available for being "accidentally" involved in an act of vision. When we see milk, for instance, the previously tasted sweetness can be associated to the whiteness that is presently affecting our eyes. As Aquinas correctly remarks, this is rather an instance of "accidental vision" than of accidental perception. For sweetness is *per se* a sensible property, but just non-visible. Strictly speaking, the phenomenon addressed in this case is association among sensory contents and not accidental perception, where a sensible x has to be perceived *as a non-sensible P, Q,* etc. Furthermore, Aquinas in his *De anima* commentary delivers an incomplete description of the associative mechanism underlying synesthetic perception, as we will see later.

In case (2) the accidental content of an act of perception is genuinely a non-sensible entity of class (b), namely a universal property such as, for instance, "being alive." In this case a sensible object is *immediately* perceived *as* having such a universal property, for example when we see something as being alive. According to Aquinas, an episode of accidental perception in which an immediate connection of this kind occurs, requires the intellect to perform an act of understanding in the same moment in which the sensible object is perceived: "For example, right when I see someone speaking or moving, apprehending through intellect his being alive, I can say on this basis that I see that he is alive."[9] Here Aquinas clearly suggests that, on account of properties of the sensible object presently perceived, the intellect apprehends a universal property and ascribes it as a universal predicate to the perceived object. Since the perceptual and intellectual acts are simultaneous, the result is an immediate judgment of the form "This x is a (universal) P."

We can take this judgment to be a genuine episode of accidental perception, as Aquinas maintains in his *De anima* commentary. For it involves two synchronic acts of cognition with contents of different kind: (α1) an act of

---

8 See Aquinas, *Commentary*, p. 208; *Sentencia* II.13, pp. 120–121, ll. 175–181.

9 Aquinas, *Commentary*, p. 208; *Sentencia* II.13, p. 121, ll. 187–190: "[...] sicut statim cum uideo aliquem loquentem uel mouere seipsum, apprehendo per intellectum uitam eius, unde possum dicere quod uideo eum uiuere."

"ACCIDENTAL PERCEPTION" AND "COGITATIVE POWER"

sense perception in which x is apprehended as having some (individual) properties, in the first place sensible properties, and ($\alpha2$) an act of intellectual understanding in which x is apprehended as having a universal property P. Synchronic acts of this kind are surely common in our everyday perceptual experience. However, it seldom happens – if at all – that a mere bundle of sensible qualities x is apprehended by the intellect as having a universal property P. In our perceptual experience it is rather the case that *individuals* of some kind are apprehended by the intellect as having a universal property: we perceive *Diare's son* as politely smiling, *our friend Pekka* as complaining about the weather. In other words, accidental perception involves immediate judgments of the form "This (individual) F is a (universal) P." Accordingly, the act of sense perception ($\alpha1$) needs to be in itself an act of cognition in which a mere bundle of sensible qualities x is firstly apprehended as an individual instance of a property F.

Case (3) is presented by Aquinas in the following way: "If, however, [the accidental object of perception] is apprehended as an individual – e.g. if, when I see something colored, I perceive this human being or this animal – then this sort of apprehension in a human being is produced through the cogitative power."[10] In case (3) the non-sensible content of accidental perception is apparently an *individual* entity belonging to our class (b). In perceptual acts of this kind a (not yet determined) sensible x is apprehended as an individual instance of a property F. This is exactly the form perceptual acts ($\alpha1$) commonly have in our everyday experience – whether they are linked to acts of intellectual understanding ($\alpha2$) or they occur in isolation. The kind of apprehension which takes place in case (3) is ascribed by Aquinas to the *cogitative power*, a special faculty of the sensitive soul: an *internal sense*. As an explanation, he immediately adds that the cogitative power is a special internal sense:

> [1] This is also called particular reason, because it compares individual intentions in the way that universal reason compares universal concepts. But all the same, this power is in the soul's sensory part. For the sensory power, at its highest level participates somewhat in the intellective power in a human being, in whom sense is connected to intellect.[11]

---

10 Aquinas, *Commentary*, p. 208 (translation modified); *Sentencia* II.13, p. 121, ll. 191–194: "Si uero [sensibile per accidens] apprehendatur in singulari, ut puta ⟨si⟩, cum uideo coloratum, percipio hunc hominem uel hoc animal, huiusmodi quidem apprehensio in homine fit per uim cogitatiuam [...]"

11 Aquinas, *Commentary*, p. 208 (translation modified); *Sentencia* II.13, pp. 121–122, ll. 195–201: "[Uis cogitatiua] dicitur etiam ratio particularis eo quod est collatiua intentionum indiuidualium sicut ratio uniuersalis est collatiua rationum uniuersalium, nichilominus tamen hec uis est in parte sensitiua, quia uis sensitiua in sui supremo participat aliquid de ui intellectiua in homine, in quo sensus intellectui coniungitur [...]"

276   RUBINI

Apparently, thus, the cogitative power possesses a *twofold status:* as any other sensory power, it is a corporeal cognitive power (linked to a bodily organ) and can for this reason have only individual contents.[12] But because of its participation in the intellective power, its contents are somehow conceptual in kind; they are, more precisely, individualized conceptual contents. As Aquinas writes, "The cogitative power apprehends an individual as existing under a common nature. [...] Thus it cognizes *this* human being as it is this *human being* and *this* piece of wood as it is this *piece of wood*."[13] In other words, the cogitative power performs a kind of *conceptual recognition of individuals* in virtue of which "individual intentions," as Aquinas calls them in quotation [1], become available by means of inferences. In this way, the sort of contents that are involved in "accidental" perception – objects of class (b) – becomes available to perceptual acts (α1).

This account of accidental perception, sketched by Aquinas in his *De anima* commentary, remains obscure in at least one point: the special function ascribed to the cogitative power. What exactly means the analogy between the "universal reason" that operates on account of universal concepts and the cogitative power as a "particular reason"? In order to better understand Aquinas' account of accidental perception, it is useful to consider his theory of the internal senses as it is developed in particular in *Summa theologiae* I, q. 78, art. 4.

There, Aquinas is not primarily concerned with an account of sense perception in general or of "accidental" perception in particular, but with the problem of a correct classification of inner senses. His first aim is apparently to defend a four-members taxonomy against the five members taxonomy proposed by his master Albert the Great.[14] But the general conception of internal senses which underlies his taxonomy is immediately relevant for our topic:

> [2] Because nature does not fail in necessary things, there must be as many actions on the part of the sensory soul as are adequate for the life of a complete animal. And all of those actions that cannot be reduced to a single principle require distinct powers: for a power of the soul is nothing other than the proximate principle of an operation belonging to soul.[15]

---

12   See Aquinas, *Commentary*, pp. 199–200; *Sentencia* II.13, p. 115, ll. 71–94.

13   Aquinas, *Commentary*, p. 208 (emphasis added); *Sentencia* II.13, p. 122, ll. 206–211: "[Uis] cogitatiua apprehendit indiuiduum ut existentem sub natura communi [...] unde cognoscit hunc hominem prout est hic homo et hoc lignum prout est hoc lignum."

14   According to Albert, the internal senses are: *sensus communis, imaginatio, aestimativa, memoria, phantasia.* See Albert the Great, *De anima*, C. Stroick (ed), *Opera omnia* 7.1, Münster, Aschendorff, 1968, pp. 156b–157b.

15   Aquinas, *The Treatise on Human Nature: Summa theologiae Ia 75–89*, trans. R. Pasnau, Indianapolis, Hackett, 2002 (hereafter *Treatise*), p. 74, ll. 41–46 (translation modified);

"ACCIDENTAL PERCEPTION" AND "COGITATIVE POWER"

Aquinas' principle of classification apparently rests on the assumption that the inner senses have to provide a full-fledged account of the cognitive behavior of (complex) animals, whose nature is essentially characterized by the possession of sense perception.[16] With this target in mind, Aquinas attempts to establish both the number and the nature of the single inner senses by applying the notion of the soul's powers as "proximate principles" of living (and cognitive) functions.

First, animal (and human) cognitive behavior requires a distinction between (aP) *apprehensive* and (rP) *retentive* powers of the sensitive soul. According to Aquinas it is evident that (complex) animals not only react to properties of things they immediately perceive, but also to properties of things they have previously experienced.[17] Accordingly, we have to assume that animals are provided with two different kind of sensitive powers: aP powers are responsible for apprehending properties of present objects; rP powers are responsible for storing the apprehended properties and making them available at a later moment.

The second distinction concerns the content of cognitive acts involved in animal (and human) behavior and is immediately relevant for our topic of accidental perception. As Aquinas correctly notices, (complex) animals not only react to sensible properties that can be apprehended along with a feeling of pleasure or pain. Rather, they are also able to *evaluate* apprehended properties of things according to "some further benefits and uses, or harms. Thus [...] a bird collects straw, not because that pleases its senses, but because it is useful for nest building."[18] In conformity with a basic principle of Aristotelian

---

correspondent original text according to *Summa theologiae*, P. Caramello (ed), Turin, Marietti, 1963 (hereafter *STh*) 1, 78.4, corp.: "[C]um natura non deficiat in necessariis, oportet esse tot actiones animae sensitivae, quot sufficiant ad vitam animalis perfecti. Et quaecumque harum actionum non possunt reduci in unum principium, requirunt diversas potentias, cum potentia animae nihil aliud sit quam proximum principium operationis animae."

16 Human beings, too, belong to this class, but their cognitive behavior can only be accounted for by assuming intellectual capacities in addition to their external and internal senses.

17 See Aquinas, *Treatise*, pp. 74–75, ll. 49–53: "Otherwise, since the movement and action of an animal follow apprehension, the animal would not be moved to seek anything absent. The opposite of this is evident above all in complete animals, which move from place to place: for they are moved toward something absent that has been apprehended." *STh* 1, 78.4, corp.: "Alioquin, cum animalis motus et actio sequantur apprehensionem, non moveretur animal ad inquirendum aliquid absens; cuius contrarium apparet maxime in animalibus perfectis, quae moventur motu processivo; moventur enim ad aliquid absens apprehensum."

18 Aquinas, *Treatise*, p. 75, ll. 68–72; *STh* 1, 78.4, corp.: "[Sed necessarium est animali ut quaerat aliqua vel fugiat, non solum quia sunt convenientia vel non convenientia ad

epistemology, Aquinas apparently thinks that such an evaluation rests on the apprehension of an appropriate content: in order to evaluate whatever thing as useful for building the nest, this property ("being useful for building the nest") needs to be grasped. Drawing on a terminology introduced into western medieval philosophy through the Latin translation of Avicenna, Aquinas distinguishes two kinds of cognitive contents that appear to be accessible to animals in acts of sense perception: sensible properties *stricto sensu* – more precisely, "forms perceived by the senses"– and *intentions*, or properties "which the external senses do not perceive."[19] These two different kinds of contents require two different kinds of cognitive powers for grasping (or storing) them: *sP* powers that are responsible for the apprehension (or retention) of sensible properties and *iP* powers that are responsible for grasping (or retaining) intentions, contents which cannot affect the sense organs. Note that the distinction between sensible properties and intentions is exactly equivalent to Aristotle's distinction between objects of sense perception *per se* and *per accidens*, that is, between objects of class (a) and objects of class (b). Aquinas' explanation of how intentions become contents of perceptual acts is thus, at the same time, an explanation of accidental perception. Note, moreover, that the evaluative acts that require intentions such as "useful for nest building" are based on acts in which only sensible qualities are grasped. A swallow evaluates straw or clay as "useful for nest building" on account of the (immediately or previously) apprehended sensible properties of straw or clay. The point is that these sensible properties are not evaluated with regard to their immediately sensible pleasantness or unpleasantness, but with regard to other non-sensible contents, grasped by a different power of the kind *iP*. I will return to this point later.

Aquinas' classification of sensitive powers results from the combination of the two distinctions we have just seen:

> (*asP*) "[T]he proper senses and the common sense are directed at receiving sensible forms."

---

sentiendum, sed etiam propter] aliquas alias commoditates et utilitates, sive nocumenta, sicut [...] avis colligit paleam, non quia delectet sensum, sed quia est utilis ad nidificandum."

19 Aquinas, *Treatise*, p. 75, l. 65 ("formas quas percipit sensus") and ll. 73–74 ("intentiones, quas non percipit sensus exterior"); *STh* I, 78.4, corp. For this distinction see Avicenna, *Liber de anima* IV.1, S. van Riet (ed), Leiden, Brill, 1968, p. 8, ll. 2–3. About Avicenna's contribution to the development of the theory of internal senses in medieval philosophy, see D.N. Hasse, *Avicenna's "De anima" in the Latin West*, London, The Warbung Institut, 2000, pp. 127–153.

"ACCIDENTAL PERCEPTION" AND "COGITATIVE POWER"

(*rsP*) "Phantasia or imagination (the two are the same) is directed at the retention or preservation of these forms. For phantasia (or imagination) serves as a kind of treasury for forms grasped through the [external] senses."

(*aiP*) "The estimative power is directed at apprehending intentions that are not grasped through the [external] senses."

(*riP*) "[T]he power for memory, which is a kind of treasury for intentions of this kind, is directed at their preservation."[20]

Apart from the five external senses, all other powers mentioned by Aquinas in his classification are internal senses.[21] The common sense (*asP*) is responsible for the unification of all different sensible properties apprehended by the external senses while being affected by a particular thing. The complex sensory content apprehended by the common sense is in turn stored in the power of imagination (*rsP*) – a sort of purely sensory memory – and can thus be reactivated even when the external senses are not affected by that particular thing or by anything at all. To this end imagination needs a complex representation of the sensible properties of a particular thing that has been previously perceived; from other texts we know that Aquinas, drawing on Aristotelian terminology, calls *phantasms* this kind of representations.[22] Accordingly, phantasms stored and reactivated in the power of imagination are responsible for all synesthetic associations that take place in our experience. Let us pick up Aquinas' example in his Commentary on *De anima*: When we or our cat, along with the whiteness of milk, "accidentally" see its sweetness, this synesthetic experience rests on a

---

20 Aquinas, *Treatise*, p. 75, ll. 78–86; *STh* I, 78.4, corp.: "[A]d receptionem formarum sensibilium ordinatur sensus proprius et communis [...] Ad harum autem formarum retentionem aut conservationem ordinatur phantasia, sive imaginatio, quae idem sunt, est enim phantasia sive imaginatio quasi thesaurus quidam formarum per sensum acceptarum. Ad apprehendendum autem intentiones quae per sensum non accipiuntur, ordinatur vis aestimativa. Ad conservandum autem eas, vis memorativa, quae est thesaurus quidam huiusmodi intentionum."

21 Lisska remarks that the *sensus communis* has a kind of double status, being at the same time both one of the internal senses and a part of the "external sensorium." See Lisska, *Aquinas's Theory of Perception*, pp. 212–214.

22 Aquinas characterizes phantasms as sensory representations (*similitudines*) of individual things, e.g., in *STh* I, 84.7, ad 2; *STh* I, 85.1, ad 3. For a detailed, but not entirely satisfactory analysis of the concept of phantasm in Aquinas, see Lisska, *Aquinas's Theory of Perception*, pp. 299–328.

phantasm previously stored in imagination and automatically reactivated during the act of vision.[23]

The two inner senses responsible for apprehension and retention of intentions also draw on the phantasm originating from common sense and stored in imagination. On account of the particular sensible properties this phantasm represents, the estimative power (*aiP*) apprehends intentions, non-sensible properties of the represented external thing. For instance, a swallow apprehends the straws it sees in its environment as useful for building the nest. The act of perception performed by the bird at this point is a genuine example of "accidental perception." In a further step, the apprehended intention and its link to an individual phantasm is stored in memory (*riP*) for possible future reactivations. Thus, a swallow can later remember particular patterns of sensible properties – what we would call individual instances of straw – as useful for building the nest and can try to find them again.

In this way, the four internal senses allow for an explanation of the cognitive behavior of animals. At this point, however, a significant dis-analogy appears with regard to human beings:

> [3] One must recognize [...] that with regard to sensible forms there is no difference between a human being and other animals. For they receive a similar impression from external sensible things. But there is a difference with regard to the intentions under discussion. For other animals perceive these intentions only through a kind of *natural instinct*, whereas a human being also makes a kind of *comparison*. And so that which in other animals is called the natural estimative power is called the *cogitative* power in a human being; it discovers such intentions through comparison. Hence it is also called *particular reason* [...] because it compares individual intentions just as intellective reason compares universal intentions.[24]

---

23   For this example, see above, footnote 8. Now we can see why, besides the common sense, imagination is required for an explanation of synesthetic perception.

24   Aquinas, *Treatise*, pp. 75–76, ll. 91–102 (emphasis added); *STh* 1, 78.4, corp.: "Considerandum est autem quod, quantum ad formas sensibiles, non est differentia inter hominem et alia animalia, similiter enim immutantur a sensibilibus exterioribus. Sed quantum ad intentiones praedictas, differentia est, nam alia animalia percipiunt huiusmodi intentiones solum naturali quodam instinctu, homo autem etiam per quandam collationem. Et ideo quae in aliis animalibus dicitur aestimativa naturalis, in homine dicitur cogitativa, quae per collationem quandam huiusmodi intentiones adinvenit. Unde etiam dicitur ratio

"ACCIDENTAL PERCEPTION" AND "COGITATIVE POWER"

As far as just sensible properties of things are involved, animal and human perception do not differ in any significant way. Their contents are essentially the same because the affections that occur in the sense organs are, in turn, the same. By contrast, animal and human perception are relevantly different with regard to intentions, the non-sensible properties involved in acts of "accidental" perception. Let us try to figure out what this difference consists in.

It is important to remark that Aquinas in quotation [3] does not emphasize the difference between singular and universal contents of cognition. As he clearly states, the intentions grasped by the *aiP* faculty of human beings – the cogitative power – are as *individual* as the intentions grasped by the estimative power of animals. On the other hand, it is evident that also these latter somehow involve *universality*. A swallow ultimately evaluates individual straws as instances of the universal property "being useful for building a nest" (all straws are in this respect equivalent or interchangeable for the swallow). As Aquinas points out, the difference rather regards the way in which intentions are apprehended. Let us first consider the case of animals.

According to quotation [3], the intentions apprehended by the estimative power of animals rest on a natural instinct. Animals are disposed by their specific nature to apprehend certain non-sensible contents whenever phantasms represent perceived things as showing certain patterns of sensible properties. For instance, swallows are naturally disposed to perceive straws *as* useful for building the nest. Aquinas does not say much about the mechanism underlying this instinctual apprehension of intentions. He probably thinks that the estimative power of animals first checks the sensible properties of things represented by phantasms; if these properties fulfill some particular conditions, a corresponding intention is automatically grasped by the estimative power; as a result, the perceived thing is *evaluated* in a particular way (e.g. as useful for building the nest). If the sensible properties of the thing represented by a phantasm do not trigger any reaction of the estimative power, then no intention is grasped; the perceived thing remains unqualified with regard to intentions. Since it is difficult to imagine that contents like "useful for building the nest" can be "received" from the things perceived, we have to assume that the repertoire of intentions available to the estimative power is originally stored in this power and automatically activated when common sense or imagination deliver appropriate phantasms. Instinctual apprehension of intentions ultimately amounts to such an automatic activation of non-sensible contents inscribed in

---

particularis [...] est enim collativa intentionum individualium, sicut ratio intellectiva intentionum universalium."

the estimative power. As a result, Aquinas' account of accidental perception in animals appears to rest on the assumption of inborn intentions and of a rigid mechanism of evaluation.[25]

By contrast, the cogitative power of humans does not operate in virtue of a natural instinct, but through a way of *reasoning* through which individual non-sensible contents are apprehended *discursively*. This characterization of the cogitative power as a *ratio particularis* is familiar from the *De anima* commentary, but having Aquinas' general theory of internal senses in view we are now in a better position to understand the operation of this faculty of the human sensitive soul. Aquinas' opinion is clearly that the cogitative power evaluates given sensible patterns by drawing inferences about them. In particular, as suggested in quotation [3], the cogitative power apprehends intentions *by comparing* the sensible properties represented by phantasms. For instance, by comparing the sensible properties of a wolf and by drawing conclusions from that, the cogitative power apprehends the wolf's dangerousness, a property that cannot be apprehended by the common sense. Such a mediate cognition by means of inferences is what Aquinas usually describes as *discursus*, or discursive (intellectual) knowledge.[26]

The superiority of the human cogitative power over the estimative power of animals is, for Aquinas, evident. The human cogitative power is neither bound to any automatism or rigid mechanism of apprehension nor restricted to any innate repertoire of intentions. Starting from the sensible properties of perceived things, the cogitative power can grasp as many intentions as can be inferred through its discursive way of apprehension, that is, through its comparisons. For instance, our cogitative power may apprehend the dangerousness of a wolf in front of us, but also that this wolf is too weak to harm.[27] However, two pressing questions require an answer. First, what does the cogitative power in its discursive grasping of intentions exactly *compare*? Second, how can a (corporeal) power of the sensitive soul be able to draw inferences that resemble intellectual inferences in any respect, except for the fact that

---

25 Lisska, too, remarks that the operation of the estimative power of animals, on Aquinas' view, rests on inborn contents. See Lisska, *Aquinas's Theory of Perception*, p. 241. For a detailed analysis of evaluative judgments in animal cognition according to Aquinas, see A. Oelze, *Animal Rationality: Later Medieval Theories 1250–1350*, Leiden, Brill, 2018, pp. 106–111.

26 See, e.g., Aquinas, *STh* I, 58.3, arg. 1: "Discursus [...] intellectus attenditur secundum hoc quod unum per aliud cognoscitur."

27 See on this point Dominik Perler's contribution to this volume. My interpretation of the operation of the cogitative power in Aquinas in nevertheless significantly different from Perler's.

"ACCIDENTAL PERCEPTION" AND "COGITATIVE POWER"

the latter encompass universal concepts, whereas the inferences of the cogitative power encompass individual (perceptual) contents? Both questions find an answer in Aquinas' account of the discursive operation performed by the cogitative power.

His account is partially already known to us from his *De anima* commentary: the cogitative power "apprehends an individual as existing under a common nature."[28] But once again the *Summa* adds a relevant detail:

> [4] The cogitative and memory powers have their superiority in a human being not through something proper to the sensory part, but through a kind of affinity and closeness to universal reason, in virtue of some kind of *refluentia*. Consequently they are not different powers, but the same ones, more perfect than in other animals.[29]

The essential difference between the estimative power of animals and the human cogitative power is the latter's link to the intellect. In fact, the cogitative power apprehends a particular pattern of sensory properties *as* an individual instance of a "common nature," that is of a universal concept such as "human being," "wood" or "wolf." In this way the set of general properties apprehended by the intellect as belonging to a "common nature"– short: the *conceptual content* – becomes available to the cogitative power. As a result, this faculty can draw inferences from it; for instance: this is a wolf, ergo this can be dangerous. Although inferences of this kind are always referred to individuals, they would not be possible without the support of conceptual contents. In quotation [4] Aquinas explains that this support rests on a *refluentia*, a *flow* of "information" from the intellect *back* to the cogitative power. Despite the intellect being incorporeal and the cogitative power corporeal, intellect and cogitative power are both faculties of the same soul (they are rooted in the same essence) and "contiguous" in the hierarchy of cognitive faculties. This contiguity is a reason to assume that conceptual contents grasped by the intellect can also be

---

28 See above, footnote 13.

29 Aquinas, *Treatise*, p. 77, ll. 144–148 (translation modified); *STh* I, 78.4, ad 5: "[E]minentiam habet cogitativa et memorativa in homine, non per id quod est proprium sensitivae partis; sed per aliquam affinitatem et propinquitatem ad rationem universalem, secundum quandam refluentiam. Et ideo non sunt aliae vires, sed eaedem, perfectiores quam sint in aliis animalibus." I have not translated the word *refluentia*. What Aquinas addresses with this metaphor is not just an *overspill*, as Pasnau translates, but some *influx* of the intellect *backwards* onto the cogitative power, as it will become clear later on.

available to the cogitative power, which in turn can link them to individual sensory patterns (bundles of sensible qualities) represented by phantasms.[30]

Aquinas does not say much about the mechanism through which the cogitative power *recognizes* that a certain sensory pattern corresponds to a certain "common nature." But we know from quotation [3] that "comparisons" are required for that. Accordingly, we can assume that the cogitative power compares, on the one hand, individual sensory patterns and, on the other hand, conceptual contents "flowing back" from the intellect; as a result, a certain sensory pattern can be *subsumed* under a certain "common nature" or – what amounts to the same – recognized as an instance of a universal essence.[31] This mechanism appears to be a necessary condition for the kind of "rationality" exhibited by the cogitative power. For, in a further step, inferences can be drawn from the conceptual contents that belong to the "common nature"; in turn, through such inferences further non-sensible contents (intentions) may be apprehended by the cogitative power. For instance, once the cogitative power has recognized this pattern of sensible properties x as an instance of the common nature "wolf," it may inferentially apprehend that x can be dangerous. But the cogitative power may also recognize x as an instance of the common nature "weak animal," and from this it can inferentially apprehend that x cannot be dangerous. By this way, the whole repertoire of intentions required for human "accidental perception" becomes available; through acts of recognition and inferences performed by the cogitative power under the influx of the intellect, all objects of our class (b) can be employed (as predicates) in judgments of the form (α1).

We see now why Aquinas emphasizes the influx of the intellect in his account of the operation of the cogitative power. It is this influx which, in the end, explains why rationality is to be found in human "accidental" perception. Aquinas' connotation of this influx as a *refluentia* should not irritate. For, according to his general picture of human cognition, it is in the first place the cogitative power which exerts an "influx" on the intellect. The cogitative power

---

30   The "metaphysical inclusion model" of the soul and its relevance for Aquinas' theory of sense perception is lined out in Dominik Perler's contribution to this volume.

31   In turn, such a comparison seems to require that the cogitative power be able to "translate" conceptual contents (flowing from the intellect) into *rules of composition* of patterns of sensible properties. In other words, the cogitative power must be able to translate a set of abstract general properties (e.g., those encompassed by the *concept* of a wolf) into a corresponding set of sensible properties (e.g., those belonging to the *phantasm* of a wolf). In this way the cogitative power can recognize whether a pattern of sensible properties apprehended by the lower sensible powers (a phantasm) can be subsumed under a "common nature" (a concept), or not.

delivers those sensory representations of things (phantasms) which are specifically required by the human intellect for abstraction of "intelligible species" and, in the end, for concept formation.[32] Considering this basic contribution to intellectual cognition, the *refluentia* that enables the cognitive power to act as a "particular reason" is indeed a "flux of information" *back* from the intellect to the cognitive power. In the general framework of Aquinas' epistemology, the *refluentia* he mentions in quotation [4] is just a segment of a complex and "dynamic" interaction that takes place between intellect and cognitive power – an interaction required for a full-fledged account of human cognition in general, and of human perception in particular.[33]

As a result, Aquinas is committed to assume that there is no linear "bottom up" acquisition of knowledge in human beings. A purely empirical explanation of human cognition is only possible up to the level of "accidental" perception. In order to explain the acquisition of non-sensible "intentions" that are involved in accidental perception, a *refluentia* from the intellect to the cognitive power needs to be assumed. At this point the "bottom up" (empirical) account of human cognition needs to be completed by a "top down" account. On the one hand it is true that, on Aquinas' view, the cognitive power supports the intellect by delivering the kind of empirical material that is required for intellectual cognition. But on the other hand, the intellect supports the cognitive power by delivering the conceptual contents that are required for the *conceptual recognition of individuals* on which "accidental" perception and, more in general, human experience rest. This requirement of a "top down" (intellectual) support in order to explain the non-sensible contents of human perception restricts the empirical character of Aquinas' epistemology. This restriction becomes more evident if we consider that, on Aquinas' view, the fundamental operation of the human intellect – apprehension of essences – ultimately rests on the divine light God has implanted into the active power of the human rational soul, the "agent intellect."[34] Concept formation requires for Aquinas

---

32   See Aquinas, *Summa contra Gentiles*, C. Pera (ed), Turin, Marietti, 1961–1967 (hereafter *SgC*), II.73, n. 1503: "Virtus cogitativa non habet ordinem ad intellectum possibilem, quo intelligit homo, nisi per suum actum quo praeparantur phantasmata ut per intellectum agentem fiant intelligibilia actu et perficientia intellectum possibilem." See also *ScG*, II.60, n. 1370; II.81, n. 1625 (a).

33   I have borrowed the metaphor of a "dynamic" interaction (or "contact") between the cogitative power and the intellect from G. Klubertanz, *The Discursive Power: Sources and Doctrine of the "Vis Cogitativa" According to Thomas Aquinas*, Saint Louis, The Modern Schoolman, 1952, pp. 166–167 and pp. 285–286. In general, my interpretation of the operation of the cogitative power in Aquinas is strongly influenced by Klubertanz' monograph.

34   On this point, see Aquinas, *STh* I, 79.4, corp. See also Aquinas, *ScG*, II.77, n. 1584.

apprehension of essences; this, in turn, requires "abstraction" of intellectual representations (intelligible species) from the sensory representations (phantasms) "prepared" by the cogitative power; but abstraction – the very step from sensible cognition to intellectual cognition – requires the efficacious intervention of the agent intellect, that is, a contribution independent from sensory cognition and experience. In Aquinas' epistemology a full-fledged account of sense perception – an account in which the phenomenon of "accidental" perception is explicitly addressed – rests in the end on the meta-empirical, semi-divine capacities of the human intellect.

3 John of Jandun on Accidental Perception: The Autonomy of the Cogitative Power

After having seen how Aquinas accounts for "accidental perception," now I am going to examine what explanation of the same phenomenon can be given in a theoretical framework in which appealing to an influx of the intellect on the cogitative power is no available option. To this end, I will focus on the account of accidental perception we find in John of Jandun.[35] As an Averroist, Jandun takes the intellect to be separated from, and external to, the individual soul of human beings. How can he account for the non-sensible contents involved in accidental perception, if no influx of the intellectual power can be assumed?

At first glance one could even think that John of Jandun is not particularly interested in the phenomenon of "accidental perception." In his commentary on Aristotle's *De anima*, probably written between 1317 and 1319, no special *quaestio* deals with this topic.[36] But a closer look reveals that things are different. We find, scattered in his commentary, several passages that are relevant to our topic. On that basis we can try to reconstruct Jandun's general theory of accidental perception.

---

35 Whereas Aquinas is a most studied medieval philosopher, John of Jandun is a much less known author. See on his life and work S. McClintock, *Perversity and Error: Studies on the Averroist John of Jandun*, Bloomington, Indiana University Press, 1956, pp. 1–9; and J.-B. Brenet, *Transferts du sujet. La noétique d'Averroès selon Jean de Jandun*, Paris, Vrin, 2003, pp. 11–32.

36 I quote John of Jandun's commentary according to the following edition: *Super tres libros De anima quaestiones subtilissimae*, Venice, Iunta, 1544 (hereafter *Quaestiones*). All translations are mine. About the composition of the treatise, see Brenet, *Transferts du sujet*, p. 13 (with references to further secondary literature).

"ACCIDENTAL PERCEPTION" AND "COGITATIVE POWER"

In question 18 of book II, while discussing about "whether common sensible objects are *per se* sensible objects," Jandun describes what accidental contents of perception are:

> [5] Something is an accidental object of perception in two ways [...] In the first way, something is an accidental object of perception because it is not cognized by any particular sense and no proper sensible is necessarily linked to it by a proximate or remote necessity. An individual substance such as Socrates and things of this kind are accidental objects of perception in this [first] way [...] In the second way, something is an accidental object of perception because the sense is not naturally disposed to cognize it insofar as it is a sense, or through the nature that is common to all or to several senses, but insofar these senses are of a particular kind, that is, human senses. In this way, too, the essential differences of individual substances are accidental objects of perception. For, although they are cognized by several senses somehow, nonetheless the senses do not cognize them insofar as they are senses of an animal, *but insofar as they are senses of an intelligent animal, that is, of a human being.*[37]

According to the "first way," *sensibilia per accidens* are entities that essentially – *per se* – cannot affect the external senses. For instance, individual substances (Diare's son, our friend Pekka) are entities of this kind. This non-specific way of being an accidental content of perception is found in human and non-human animals. By contrast, the "second way" is specifically found in human beings. In this case, for non-sensible properties (e.g. "essential differences of individual substances") to be "accidentally sensible" specifically means that they are grasped in perceptual acts of "intelligent animals," animals provided with intellect.

---

37   Jandun, *Quaestiones* II.18, p. 34rb (emphasis added): "Modo aliquid est sensibile per accidens duobus modis [...] Uno modo aliquid est sensibile per accidens ex eo quod non cognoscitur a sensu particulari, nec sensibilia propria sunt ei necessario coniuncta ex necessitate propinqua nec remota. Et sic individuum substantiae est sensibile per accidens, ut Socrates et huismodi [...] Alio modo dicitur aliquid sensibile secundum accidens ex eo quod sensus non est natus ipsum cognoscere secundum quod sensus, id est per naturam commune omnibus sensibus vel pluribus, sed secundum quod sunt tales sensus, scilicet hominis. Et hoc etiam modo differentiae substantiales individuorum substantiae sunt sensibiles secundum accidens; quia licet cognoscantur a pluribus sensibus aliquo modo, tamen sensus non cognoscunt eas secundum quod sunt sensus animalis, sed *secundum quod sunt sensus animalis intelligentis, scilicet hominis.*"

At first glance, then, Jandun seems to suggest a similar explanation of accidental perception as Aquinas: in order to account for the non-sensible contents of class (b) that are involved in perception, higher cognitive faculties need to be considered, namely the internal senses – in particular, the cogitative power – and ultimately the intellect; for it is the intellect that, in the case of human beings, delivers the non-sensible contents grasped in accidental perception, whereas the function of the cogitative power is to join these contents to the sensible contents apprehended by the external senses. After all, human beings are "intelligent animals" because they have an intellect, and this is what Jandun seems to address in his description of the "second way" of being accidental contents of perception.

As we are going to see, it is surely true that the internal senses of humans play a central role in Jandun's account of accidental perception. But with regard to the intellect, things are less clear than in Aquinas. For reasons which should become clear later, Jandun is not entitled to assume any influx of the intellect on the internal senses. If this is true, then Jandun has to provide a different explanation of the "accidental contents" in human perception, an explanation according to which the internal senses prove to be *of their own* the "senses of an intelligent animal." In the following, I will first summarize Jandun's views on the internal senses (with particular focus on the cogitative power). Then I will explain why Aquinas' "intellectualistic" solution is not available for Jandun. Finally, I will present some evidences in favor of the idea that Jandun conceives of the quasi-rational function of the cogitative power in terms of an automatic mechanism of association.

If we want to reconstruct Jandun's views on the internal senses and their different cognitive functions, our most relevant source is question 37 from the second book of his *De anima* commentary. The "official" topic of question 37 is "whether phantasy is the same as sense," but the real discussion is about the right taxonomy of the internal senses, as we have already seen in Aquinas. In presenting his views as based on Averroes' exegesis, Jandun abides by a taxonomy according to which there are four internal sense: common sense, imagination, cogitative power and memory.[38] In other words, Jandun agrees with Aquinas in rejecting a taxonomy according to which a fifth internal sense, namely phantasy, is required for combining sensible "forms" and non-sensible "intentions" – a taxonomy which Jandun (correctly) ascribes to Albert the

---

38   Jandun develops his four members taxonomy in *Quaestiones* II.37, pp. 45rb-45vb. Eventually, he explicitly confirms its conformity to Averroes' doctrine; see *Quaestiones* II.37, p. 45vb.

Great.[39] Not only is the list of the internal senses the same as in Aquinas, but also the ratio according to which the list is made up. First, we need to assume internal powers of the sensitive soul for two different kinds of contents, namely (sP) powers for the "sensible accidents, proper and common," and (iP) powers for the "properties which are not cognized by any particular senses," that is, "non-sensed intentions."[40] Second, we need to assume internal powers of the sensitive soul which are (aP) apprehensive of contents and powers which are (rP) retentive of the apprehended contents.[41] The result is a taxonomy very similar to Aquinas':

(asP) common sense: apprehensive of sensible properties (forms);
(rsP) imagination: retentive of sensible properties (forms);
(aiP) cognitive power: apprehensive of non-sensible properties (intentions);
(riP) memory: retentive of non-sensible properties (intentions).

As already in Aquinas, so in Jandun too an account of the non-sensible contents (intentions) involved in accidental perception rests essentially on the function the *cognitive power* (in its cooperating with the other internal senses, in particularly with imagination and memory). Jandun is even more generous than Aquinas in presenting it as a discursive cognitive power capable of drawing inferences about its objects, namely non-sensible intentions. Taking inspiration from Averroes' scattered remarks in his *De anima* commentary, Jandun lists following operations of the cognitive power:[42]

---

39 About Albert's taxonomy see above, footnote 14. Correcting Albert, Jandun (*Quaestiones* II.37, p. 46ra) remarks that Aristotle "per phantasiam quandoque intelligit imaginativam et quandoque cogitativam." On Albert as a source for Jandun's theory of internal senses (besides Averroes), see Brenet, *Transferts du sujet*, pp. 197–203.

40 See Jandun, *Quaestiones* II.37, p. 45rb: "[I]n individuis substantiarum, et praecipue in hominibus, non solum sunt accidentia sensibilia, propria et communia, sed etiam in eis sunt quaedam proprietates quas non cognoscunt sensus particulares, sicut in Socrate est bonitas vel malitia vel paternitas vel filiatio, et mansuetudo vel iracundia vel sanitas vel aegritudo, et quando et ubi et huiusmodi formae quas nullus particularium sensus cognoscit. Et ideo dicuntur intentiones non sensatae."

41 See Jandun, *Quaestiones* II.37, p. 45rb: "[N]on est unius et eiusdem virtutis animae bene recipere species et bene retinere seu conservare <eas>."

42 The following list is based on Jandun's lengthy description of the operations of the cogitative power in *Quaestiones* II.37, pp. 45rb–vb. For a more detailed analysis, see P. Rubini, *Pietro Pomponazzis Erkenntnistheorie. Naturalisierung des menschlichen Geistes im Spätaristotelismus*, Leiden, Brill, 2015, pp. 499–504.

290   RUBINI

- it apprehends individual non-sensible relational properties (intentions) such as paternity, friendship etc.
- it apprehends individual forms or individual intentions that belong to all ten categories, e.g. Socrates' individual substantial form, his individual whiteness, paternity etc.
- it draws deductive inferences and thereby apprehends unknown individual properties from known individual properties.
- it combines sensible forms stored in imagination with non-sensible intentions stored in memory.[43]
- it apprehends unknown individual properties or states of affairs by means of inductive inferences from known individual properties or states of affairs.

It should be evident from this list that, according to Jandun, the cogitative power is exactly the internal sense that apprehends the kind of contents required for accidental perception. The following example, in which the capacity of the cogitative power to draw inductive inferences is particularly emphasized, clearly shows that it is the context of accidental perception Jandun has in sight:

> [6] Further on, Averroes in the same III book of his *De anima* says that the cogitative power, when it is supported by memory and imagination, will sometimes present an individual, that is, the cogitative power will have cognition of an individual that has not been perceived by the person who is cogitating, such as cognition of a future individual or of a past individual. We can for instance understand [this suggestion] in the following way: When a good physician (a) by means of his cogitative power cognizes this illness in this patient and its cause and the [patient's] complexion and age and place and particulars of this kind, and (b) by means of his memory he remembers to have seen or cognized that such an illness or a similar one was followed by [those patients'] death, and (c) by means of his imaginative power he imagines the [present] patient's death, then it happens that (d) the physician judges by a true judgment that the person is going to die, *as if he presently perceived that the person is dying.*[44]

---

43   For this reason, according to Jandun, there is no need to follow Albert the Great in assuming phantasy as a further, fifth inner sense.

44   Jandun, *Quaestiones* II.37, p. 45va (emphasis added):"Amplius de cogitativa inquit Commentator in eodem tertio quod, cum ipsa fuerit adiuta per memorativam et imaginativam, ipsa praesentabit aliquando individuum aliquod, id est, accipiet aliquam cognitionem individui quod non fuit sensatum ab illo homine cogitante, utpote cognitionem

"ACCIDENTAL PERCEPTION" AND "COGITATIVE POWER"

As the last sentence clearly shows, the physician's judgment that his patient is going to die is embodied in an act of sense perception (vision). Jandun presents this judgment as the result of a chain of inferences based on induction and analogy and encompassing the contribution of all inner senses: (a) the common sense apprehends the sensible properties of the patient, a particular sensory pattern; (b) memory recollects intentions that have been previously apprehended (by the cogitative power) in accordance with similar sensory patterns; (c) imagination delivers a new image of a similar sensory pattern. But the central role is given to the cogitative power, which (d) combines all those elements and draws from them an inferential judgment about the patient who is the present object of sense perception. This is exactly the task of the cogitative power, as Jandun – echoing Averroes once again – remarks: "The scope of cogitation (supply: dealing with past or future things, or with present things that are nevertheless remote from the senses) is nothing but this, namely that the cogitative power sets up a thing that is not present to the senses *as it were a sensed thing*."[45]

It is remarkable that this task, according to Jandun, can only be accomplished because of the rational-like nature of the cogitative power:

> [7] Averroes says about the cogitative power [...] that this power is a kind of reason. I understand this in the following way. As reason is an abstract apprehensive power that reasons about things it has apprehended in a universal manner, this noble [cogitative] power similarly reasons about things apprehended in an individual manner and draws inferences from one thing to another in order to cognize an unknown thing. From this it

---

alicuius futuri aut alicuius praeteriti; verbi gratia sic intelligendo: cum aliquis bonus medicus per suam virtutem cogitativam cognoscit hanc aegritudinem huius hominis et eius causam et complexionem et aetatem et locum et huiusmodi particularia, et per virtutem memorativam memoratur se vidisse seu cognovisse ex tali aegritudine et consimili secutam fuisse mortem, et per virtutem imaginativam imaginatur mortem istius hominis, tunc contingit quod ipse iudicat vero iudicio hunc esse moriturum, *ac si praesentialiter sentiret ipsum mori.*" See Averroes, *Commentarium magnum in Aristotelis De anima*, F.S. Crawford (ed), Cambridge, The Mediaeval Academy of America, 1953 (hereafter: *Commentarium magnum*), III.30, pp. 475–476, ll. 41–57.

45 Jandun, *Quaestiones* II.37, p. 45va (emphasis added): "[I]ntentio cogitationis (supple: negotiantis circa praeterita aut futura, aut praesentia quae tamen remota sunt a sensu) nihil aliud est quam hoc, scilicet quod virtus cogitativa ponit rem absentem a sensu *quasi rem sensatam.*" See Averroes, *Commentarium magnum* III.30, p. 476, ll. 57–59.

292 RUBINI

follows that the cogitative power properly belongs to human beings, since only human beings reason.[46]

As belonging to the sensitive soul, the cogitative power is bodily localized; hence, its sphere of cognition is restricted to individuals.[47] But this restriction does not prevent the cogitative power from operating as a *ratio particularis*, a rational faculty which draws inferences about individuals, as we already know from Aquinas. As well as Aquinas, however, Jandun needs to explain what enables the cogitative power to act rationally. His appeal to the rational character of human beings in quotation [7], or to their being "intelligent animals" in quotation [5], seems to suggest that Jandun, in accordance with Aquinas, assumes some kind of transfer of contents from the intellect to the cogitative power. But this solution turns out to be unavailable to Jandun. Let me try to explain why.[48]

As a follower of Averroes, Jandun rejects Aquinas' view that the human intellect is part of the hylomorphic compound every individual human being consists in. More precisely, the intellect cannot be considered as (a part of) the soul – or substantial form – of individual human beings.[49] According to Averroists such as Jandun, the cognitive function of the human intellect – namely, apprehending essences as universal objects of knowledge – requires immateriality; consequently, the intellect cannot be a *virtus in corpore*, a cognitive power implemented in, and ontologically depending on, the human body, but it must be a separate entity: a unique intellect for the whole human kind. Jandun actually abides by Aquinas' "inclusive" psychological model;[50] but, as an Averroist, he rules out that the intellect can be a part of the human soul. Qua

---

46 Jandun, *Quaestiones* II.37, p. 45va: "Rursus dicit Commentator de ista virtute [...] quod ista virtus est aliqua ratio. Et ipsum intelligo sic, quod sicut ratio est virtus apprehensiva abstracta, ratiocinans de rebus universaliter apprehensis, sic ista nobilis virtus ratiocinatur de rebus individualiter apprehensis et discurrit de uno in aliud ad cognitionem ignoti; et ex hoc sequitur eam esse propriam homini, quia solus homo ratiocinatur." See Averroes, *Commentarium magnum* III.20, p. 449, ll. 175–176.

47 An implicit presupposition for Jandun (as well as for Aquinas) is that corporeal cognitive powers such as the faculties of the sensitive soul can only have individual entities as their objects. Universal contents of cognition require an immaterial cognitive power such as the intellect.

48 Jandun's views about the cognitive operation of the cogitative power are subtly and usefully analyzed in Brenet, *Transferts du sujet*, pp. 270–273. Nevertheless, Brenet does not suggest any interpretation similar to the one I am going to develop in the rest of this section.

49 On this point, see Jandun, *Quaestiones* III.3, pp. 47va-48ra, especially p. 47vb: "Potentia receptiva quae est in substantia animae intellectivae, non est idem penitus essentialiter cum ipsa substantia animae." See also *Quaestiones* III.7, pp. 54ra–56vb.

50 About Aquinas' conception of the human soul see above, footnote 30.

"ACCIDENTAL PERCEPTION" AND "COGITATIVE POWER"

substantial form of the human body, the human soul is essentially specified by its highest cognitive faculty, which is the cogitative power.[51] Since the intellect is not a constituent part of the human soul, Jandun cannot appeal to a common root in order to explain how the intellect grounds the discursive nature of the cogitative power. The kind of "dynamic" interaction Aquinas assumes between intellect and cogitative power seems not to be available in Jandun's account of accidental perception.

In fact, when Jandun presents his ideas about the inner senses and describes in particular the function of the cogitative power, he does not – at least not explicitly – appeal to any influx of the intellect. He rather emphasizes the special capacities of the cogitative power. For this reason, and considering that he takes the cogitative power to be the substantial form of individual human beings, we can assume that, on his view, the possession of the cogitative power *alone* makes human beings "intelligent animals" capable of accidental perception in which non-sensible properties are apprehended inferentially.

However, one might argue that Jandun surely excludes a common ontological root, but maintains a functional interaction between intellect and cogitative power – a functional interaction in which intellect and cogitative power are so tightly unified with each other that the intellect can be described as a "second human form."[52] In fact, Jandun conceives of this interaction as follows: On the one hand, acts of the cogitative power are always required for the intellect to perform acts of understanding in which universal contents are apprehended; more precisely, the (individual) contents apprehended by the cogitative power in its acts determine the (universal) contents apprehended in turn by the intellect. On the other hand, exactly because of this functional dependence of the intellect on acts of the cogitative power, the universal acts of understanding performed by the unique intellect are shared in return by the individual human beings who are subjects of the acts of cogitation.[53] On account of this functional interaction – one might argue – Jandun could plausibly

---

51 See Jandun, *Quaestiones* III.5, p. 51vb (emphasis added): "[H]omo distinguitur ab animalis per intellectum proprie dictum tanquam per operans intrinsecum quod in operando unite se habet ad corpus secundum naturam; et per animam cogitativam distinguitur ab animalis sicut *per formam constituentem ipsum in esse substantiali specifico*. Et sic utraque est eius forma diversimode." Furthermore, see *Quaestiones* III.12, pp. 60vb–61ra.

52 Jandun's characterization of the intellect as a *secunda forma hominis* has been emphasized in J.B. Brenet, "Âme intellective, âme cogitative. Jean de Jandun et la *duplex forma propria* de l'homme," *Vivarium*, vol. 46, 2008, pp. 318–341. See for textual evidence Jandun, *Quaestiones* III.5, pp. 51vb–52ra.

53 On this central tenet of Averroist psychology and epistemology, see, e.g., Jandun, *Quaestiones* III.10, pp. 59ra–va.

294 RUBINI

assume that intellectual contents are accessible to the cogitative power and can be implemented in its cognitive acts. If this is so, then Jandun could also plausibly explain the inferential operation of the cogitative power in a similar way as Aquinas.

Although this line of thought may be attractive at first glance, at a closer look it turns out not to work. The real obstacle appears to be the way in which Jandun conceives of the functional dependence of the intellect on acts of the cogitative power. In fact, while discussing the mechanism of intellectual cognition and the role of the internal senses in it, Jandun commits himself to the bold view that, whatever object the intellect ought to apprehend as a universal content of cognition, the very same object needs to be first apprehended by the cogitative power as an individual content of cognition. In his detailed discussion of the internal senses in book II, for instance, he remarks that, if the intellect has to understand an intention distinctly, then "the cogitative power must first cogitate it individually."[54] As a result, Jandun cannot assume any conceptual content flowing from the intellect back to the cogitative power. On his view, it is *always* the cogitative power that has *first* to grasp "intentions" individually in order for the intellect to grasp them – in a second step – distinctly and universally. Therefore, the cogitative power must be able to grasp its contents *autonomously*, without any support from the intellect. This means, in turn, that in Jandun's epistemology accidental perception cannot be explained by appealing to an indirect contribution of the intellect. At least the basic form of accidental perception – what I have called "conceptual recognition of individuals" in section 2 – must be explained simply by reference to the internal senses and, in particular, to the cogitative power.[55]

If Jandun cannot refer to any flow of conceptual contents from the intellect to the cogitative power, how can he account for the inferential operation of this sensitive, corporeal power? One possible strategy is appealing to natural teleology. The way in which Jandun emphasizes the exceptional character of the human inner senses – and of the cogitative power in particular – seems

---

54   Jandun, *Quaestiones* II.37, p. 45va: "Ad hoc enim, quod intellectus distincte intelligat aliquam huiusmodi intentionem non sensatam, oportet quod virtus cogitativa distincte cogitet eam individualiter, ut patebit ex III huius." For a more extensive treatment of this point, see *Quaestiones* III.15, pp. 62vb-63va; III.35, p. 84ra-b. The role plaid by the cogitative power in the act of intellection is discussed in Brenet, *Transferts du sujet*, pp. 258–264.

55   Note that Aquinas, with regard to the dependence of the intellect on the cogitative power, does not face the same difficulty as Jandun. For Aquinas is, as we have seen above, surely committed to the view that acts of the cogitative power are always required for acts of intellection to take place, but he never commits himself to the view that a conceptual content needs first to be individually apprehended by the cogitative power in order to be universally apprehended by the intellect.

"ACCIDENTAL PERCEPTION" AND "COGITATIVE POWER" 295

indeed to suggest that he abides by this kind of explanation: the cogitative power is by its nature a discursive internal sense, a *ratio particularis*.[56] For, according to Jandun, the cogitative power is the very substantial form of human beings, and human beings are rational, "intelligent" animals; ergo – one might conclude – the cogitative power must somehow be rational as well, or even a source of human rationality. In fact, it is because of the rationality of the cogitative power – a rationality restricted to individual contents – that human beings can access the unique intellect and its conceptual contents, which means: universal rationality. Consequently, we just have to take into account this basic rationality of the cogitative power in order to explain why non-sensible contents are involved in human accidental perception.

From a general point of view, it is true that Jandun accounts for human accidental perception by referring to the special nature of the cogitative power, the intrinsic rationality of its operations. Nonetheless, his account turns out to be richer and more complex when he tries to figure out with more details how the cogitative power works. In particular, Jandun seems to conceive of its operation in terms of what could be described, with modern terminology, as a *mechanism of association*.[57] More precisely, he seems to conceive of the rational character of the cogitative power as a special capacity of processing the basic contents of sense perception (*sensibilia propria et communia*) automatically – a capacity which does not rest on conceptual contents delivered "top down" by the intellect, but on "bottom up" principles of association such as "similarity," "contiguity" or "repetition". Once processed by the cogitative power according to such principles, the basic contents of sense perception prove to be organized (grouped or sorted) in some meaningful way. From this point of view, the operation of the cogitative power – for instance the inductive inference described in quotation [6] – is to be understood not as an act of reflection or deliberation the physician performs consciously and willingly, but as an associative process through which a pattern of sensible properties (the sensible properties of the object presently perceived) is automatically aggregated to previously apprehended patterns of sensible properties according to principles of association. In the particular case of the physician outlined in quotation [6], the *similarity* between the "clinical conditions" of the presently

---

56   Brenet seems to assume that an account in terms of natural teleology is indeed Jandun's explanatory strategy. See Brenet, *Transferts du sujet*, p. 250 (where the operation of the cogitative power is discussed, in particular, within the context of accidental perception).

57   In the context of Scholastic philosophy, speaking of a mechanism of association is of course an anachronism. Nevertheless, the concept has a heuristic value that makes it attractive: it can be used to capture what Jandun thinks about the operation of the cogitative power, but expresses in a different, traditional vocabulary. I will come back to this point later in this section.

perceived patient (a particular pattern of sensible properties presently apprehended by the common sense) and the "clinical conditions" of dead patients who have been repeatedly perceived at a previous time (patterns of sensible properties now stored in memory) automatically leads the cogitative power to apprehend the present patient *as dead*. This apprehension requires the support not only of memory, but also of imagination: first memory has to display some previous associative clusters (something like "patient dead," "patient recovered" etc.) to which the presently apprehended sensory pattern can be confronted, e.g. with regard to similarity; then imagination has to make up a new sensory representation (image) of the present patient according to the most resembling associative cluster displayed by memory. But it is the cogitative power that somehow unifies these different elements – the pattern of sensible properties presently apprehended by the common sense, the associative clusters presented by memory, the sensory representation prompted by imagination – into a new episode of accidental perception in which a sensible *x* is, so to speak, apprehended as an *F*. At this point, as stated in quotation [6], "the physician judges by a true judgment that the person is going to die, *as if he presently perceived that the person is dying*." Needless to say, an automatic mechanism of this kind perfectly matches with the context of accidental perception in which the cogitative power usually operates.

One may resist this interpretation. In describing the function of the internal senses, and of the cogitative power in particular, Jandun does not explicitly mention any mechanism of association based on similarity or on equivalent criteria. For this reason, my interpretation might appear arbitrary. However, we have to consider that Jandun could find no explicit example of a theory of association within the Scholastic tradition. Thus, he could only describe an associative mechanism underlying accidental perception by reference to the traditional Scholastic conception of powers performing their special operations. But in the framework of his psychology it appears illegitimate to explain how non-sensible (rational) contents are involved in accidental perception by invoking the contribution of a genuinely rational power (the intellect) that cognitively "infiltrates" the cogitative power. In Jandun's framework the rational nature of the cogitative power must rather be reconstructed from the bottom up, on a pure empirical base.

Some direct evidences in favor of my interpretation can actually be found in Jandun's texts. First, immediately after having presented his example of the physician in quotation [6] and the similar example of a "good meteorologist" who, on account of the present conditions of the weather and of his previous experience, "by means of his cogitative power judges by a true and correct

"ACCIDENTAL PERCEPTION" AND "COGITATIVE POWER" 297

judgment that hail is going to fall soon, as if he saw hail falling actually," Jandun remarks:

> [8] One could also make an example from the field of possible human actions. But since these things are less certain and originate from free choice, I do not want to make any example [from this field].[58]

As Jandun suggests here, human actions requiring deliberation and free choice do not appropriately exemplify the cognitive function of the cogitative power. The reason is clear: they do not trace back to the automatism of a mechanism of association. In the case of deliberative choice, alternative actions need to be consciously pondered; this requires universal concepts in order to evaluate the different alternatives through inferences. And most importantly, the final choice must in this case not be determined by automatism. Accordingly, if Jandun rules out the cogitative power as a possible instrument for deliberative choice, this means that he conceives of the cogitative power as an automatically working power – much in line with the idea that the function of the cogitative power is based on a mechanism of association.

A second and more direct hint is to be found in the III book of the *De anima* commentary, where Jandun discuss the question "whether the cogitative soul [= power] is able to cognize material substances," essences or substantial forms of material things. Knowledge of essences is in Aristotelianism a privilege of the intellect; but Jandun's strong dependence thesis – whatever the intellect cognizes universally, the cogitative power needs first to cognize individually – commits him to the assumption that the cogitative power has first to cognize essences as well. But how can a corporeal power such as the cogitative power cognize essences, if this requires immateriality (a condition only fulfilled by the intellect)? There can be two opinions about this question, Jandun remarks in his answer. According to the first one, we have simply to assume that the cogitative power is as able to cognize essences as it is able to cognize any other kind of "intentions," non-sensible properties such as abstract qualities (goodness, malice), relations (fatherhood), action, passion etc. And if we ask why it is so, the answer can only be, once again, that "the human soul, which inheres

---

58 Jandun, *Quaestiones* II.37, p. 45va: "Similiter autem cum aliquis bonus naturalis meteorologicus cogitat de grandine futura in aestate, et per virtutem suam memorativam memoratur se vidisse post talem calorem aestivum et post talem nubem frequenter secutam fuisse grandinem, et per imaginativam imaginatur descensum grandinis, tunc per cogitativam iudicat vero et recto iudicio grandinem esse cito futuram ac si videret eam actu cadentem. Et posset poni exemplum in humanis agibilibus; sed quia illa sunt minus certa et sunt a libero arbitrio, ideo nolo exemplificare."

in the human body, is nobler than any other inherent soul and must have a power that is nobler than any powers of other animals. That power can only be the cogitative power, which reasons about things that have been apprehended particularly."[59] The second opinion is more informative and mostly suitable for the kind of interpretation I am suggesting:

> [9] The cogitative power cognizes material substances by means of their individual proper species, but [in a qualified manner, namely] insofar as the species of this kind that are received in the cogitative soul do not belong to the category of substance, but to the category of accident, for instance to the category of quality; these species nonetheless represent material substances to the extent that they are proper effects of them.[60]

Grasping an essence means, for the cogitative power, to collect a sufficient number of sensible properties that altogether represent that essence, at least to the extent to which effects represents their cause (in this case a formal cause, an essence). In this context, "to represent" does not mean "to be a direct likeness of a form" (this is the way in which *species* represent), but "to make recognizable a form indirectly."[61] Borrowing the example from John Locke, we can say that a pattern of sensible properties such as "yellow," "malleable" or "soluble in turpentine" represents the essence of *gold* to the extent to which it enables us to recognize or identify gold among other objects of experience.[62] Exactly in this way, according to Jandun, the cogitative power apprehends essences (substantial forms) of material, and even of immaterial, things, namely by assembling patterns of sensible properties which make essences recognizable. Also the intellectual (direct) grasping of essences through intelligible

---

59 Jandun, *Quaestiones* III.21, p. 68va-b: "Constat enim quod anima humana inhaerens corpori humano est nobilior omni alia anima inhaerente et debet habere aliquam virtutem nobiliorem omnibus virtutibus aliorum animalium. Et illa non est nisi cogitativa, quae ratiocinatur de rebus particulariter apprehensis."

60 Jandun, *Quaestiones* III.21, p. 68vb: "[Alia opinio posset esse quod] cogitativa cognoscit substantias materiales per species proprias individuales earum, ita tamen quod huiusmodi species receptae in anima cogitativa non sunt in genere substantiae, sed accidentis, puta in genere qualitatis, repraesenta⟨n⟩t tamen substantias materiales pro tanto quia sunt proprii effectus earum."

61 This distinction between direct and indirect apprehension of forms is suggested by Aquinas; see, e.g., *STh* I, 56.3, corp. On this topic and on Jandun's views about intentionality, see P. Rubini, "The function of the intellect: Intentionality and representationalism," in S. Schmid (ed), *Philosophy of Mind in the Late Middle Ages and Renaissance*, London, Routledge, 2018, pp. 101–124.

62 For the example of gold, see John Locke, *An Essay Concerning Human Understanding*, P.H. Nidditch (ed), Oxford, Clarendon Press, 1975, II.xxiii.10, p. 301. Locke's views about our "ideas of substances" in general are expressed in *Essay*, II.xxiii.14, p. 305.

"ACCIDENTAL PERCEPTION" AND "COGITATIVE POWER" 299

species is, in turn, based on the indirect apprehension of essences by the cogitative power:

> [10] In order for the intellect to cognize material substances it suffices that the cogitative power cognizes them by their proper accidents, particularly by operations which belong to them [= material substances] as proper accidents per se. Likewise, in order [for the intellect] to understand immaterial substances it is not necessary that the cogitative power cognizes them – this is even impossible, since a material and organic power is absolutely not able to cognize any spiritual and incorporeal thing –, but it suffices that the cogitative power apprehends proper effects of them [= of the immaterial substances], namely the perpetual and uniform motions [of the heavens].[63]

Such an indirect apprehension of essences, based on collections of sensible properties, does not require anything more than a repeated "contact" with instances of a particular essence (what we could call "experience" of a particular kind of objects) and a sensitive apparatus in which a mechanism of association can take place. On Jandun's view, the sensitive soul of human beings is an apparatus of this kind. At each new "contact" with gold, for example, the common sense apprehends a pattern of sensible properties which, in virtue of some (partial) similarity, matches other patterns of sensible properties that have been previously apprehended and are now stored in imagination and memory. Grasping the essence of gold at each new contact simply means, for the cogitative power, to ascribe the pattern that is presently apprehended to the most similar cluster, that is, to a collection of sensible properties that altogether make possible to distinguish gold from other substances with which we are confronted in experience. This indirect apprehension of essences is ultimately sufficient for the cogitative power to "recognize" or "classify" experienced individual things in a pre-conceptual way – as it is required for accidental perception.[64]

---

63 Jandun, *Quaestiones* III.21, p. 68vb: "[U]t intellectus cognoscat substantias materiales sufficit quod virtus cogitativa cognoscat eas in suis propriis accidentibus, et praecipue in suis per se et propriis operationibus, sicut ad intelligendum substantias immateriales non est necesse quod cogitativa eas cognoscat, immo est impossibile, eo quod virtus materialis et organica non potest cognoscere rem spiritualem et incorporalem omnino; sed sufficit quod cogitativa cogitet proprios effectus earum, scilicet motus sempiternos et uniformes [...]".

64 We have seen in Aquinas that the operation of the cogitative power which is fundamental for an account of accidental perception is exactly this "recognition of individuals" in experience.

4   Conclusions

In the two former sections we have seen how Thomas Aquinas and John of Jandun account for what I have called "accidental perception," a phenomenon that, within the framework of an Aristotelian theory of cognition, proves to be not less relevant than challenging. Both Aquinas and Jandun, in their accounts, focus on the operation of the cogitative power as the internal sense which in humans is specifically responsible for apprehending the non-sensible contents ("intentions") that are connected to proper sensible contents in acts of accidental perception (our most common perceptual acts). Because of their different views about the human intellect, however, our two authors conceive of the operation of the cogitative power differently. Aquinas, as we have seen, explicitly assumes an influx of the intellect which enables the cogitative power to perform a conceptual recognition of individual sensible patterns in judgments of the form "this sensible x is an individual F." On Aquinas view, acts of accidental perception actually consist in subsumptions of this kind. Therefore, it is the human capacity for (universal) conceptual cognition – the human intellect – that in the end accounts for the non-sensible contents involved in accidental perception. Aquinas' position on accidental perception can accordingly be described as a kind of intellectualistic (rationalistic) explanation that clearly restraints his general empiricism in epistemology: all non-sensible (rational) contents of human perception originate ultimately from the human intellect and not from experience itself.

By contrast – if my reading is correct – it should be appropriate to qualify Jandun's account of accidental perception as an instance of radical empiricism. The Averroist framework of his psychology prevents Jandun from tracing accidental perception back to conceptual contents floating from the intellect to the inner senses. Jandun assumes that accidental perception ultimately rests on the cogitative power's own ability to grasp non-sensible "intentions" by means of individual inferences, and he conceives of this quasi "rationality" of the cogitative power as an entirely autonomous capacity of the human sensitive soul. Since just appealing to the special nature of the human sensitive soul is not really a satisfying account, Jandun suggests a deeper explanation according to which the activity of the cogitative power is understood as an automatic mechanism of association. By this way, the whole set of non-sensible contents that the cogitative power apprehends inferentially and makes available for acts of accidental perception is supposed to originate from mere sensible contents (*sensibilia propria et communia*) simply in virtue of principles of association.

As a result, the kind of recognition of individuals that takes place in accidental perception cannot qualify, in Jandun's account, as a proper subsumption of the form "This sensible x is an individual F." Within Jandun's psychological framework the recognition of individuals performed by the cogitative power cannot be conceptual in kind; recognition of individuals can only be the result of a process in which, according to principles of association, a given pattern of sensible contents (a perceived bundle of sensible properties) is automatically grouped with other patterns of sensible contents that are stored in imagination and memory. The result is an associative classification of things experienced in acts of perception, a classification which depends on the real properties of things and, ultimately, on their essences or substantial forms. But only at the level of intellectual cognition – only after accidental perception has taken place – this associative classification receives a conceptual shape in a proper judgment of the form "This sensible x is a universal F." In other words, pre-intellectual cognition is understood as entirely pre-conceptual in Jandun's Averroist framework. As the non-sensible "intentions" grasped by the cogitative power have purely empirical origin, the cognitive operation of the cogitative power and, in turn, accidental perception are explained in a purely empirical way.

Acknowledgements

The author would like to acknowledge the funding from the European Research Council to the research project *Rationality in Perception: Transformations of Mind and Cognition 1250–1550* under the grant agreement n. 637747. Former versions of this paper have been discussed with friends and colleagues of the Department of Philosophy at the University of Helsinki as well as in the Research Seminar of the Thomas-Institut at the University of Cologne. Special thanks to Anna Tropia, who read the paper and made useful suggestions to improve it.

Bibliography

Primary Literature

Albert the Great, *De anima*, C. Stroick (ed), *Opera omnia* 7.1, Münster, Aschendorff, 1968.

Aristotle, *De anima*, D. Ross (ed), Oxford, Clarendon Press, 1961.

Averroes, *Commentarium magnum in Aristotelis De anima*, F.S. Crawford (ed), Cambridge, The Medieval Academy of America, 1953.

Avicenna, *Liber de anima seu Sextus de naturalibus*, partes IV–V, S. van Riet (ed), Leiden, Brill, 1968.

John of Jandun, *Super tres libros De anima quaestiones subtilissimae*, Venice, Iunta, 1544.

Locke, John, *An Essay Concerning Human Understanding*, P.H. Nidditch (ed), Oxford, Clarendon Press, 1975.

Thomas Aquinas, *A Commentary on Aristotle's De anima*, trans. R. Pasnau, New Haven, Yale University Press, 1999.

Thomas Aquinas, *Liber de veritate catholicae fidei contra errores Infidelium seu Summa contra Gentiles*, C. Pera (ed), Turin, Marietti, 1961–1967.

Thomas Aquinas, *Sentencia libri De anima*, Opera omnia *45.1*, Rome, Commissio Leonina, 1984.

Thomas Aquinas, *Summa theologiae*, P. Caramello (ed), Turin, Marietti, 1963.

Thomas Aquinas, *The Treatise on Human Nature: Summa theologiae Ia 75–89*, trans. R. Pasnau, Indianapolis, Hackett, 2002.

Secondary Literature

Brenet, Jean-Baptiste, "Âme intellective, âme cogitative. Jean de Jandun et la *duplex forma propria* de l'homme," *Vivarium*, vol. 46, 2008, pp. 318–341.

Brenet, Jean-Baptiste, *Transferts du sujet. La noétique d'Averroès selon Jean de Jandun*, Paris, Vrin, 2003.

De Haan, Daniel, "Aquinas on Perceiving, Thinking, Understanding, and Cognizing Individuals," in E. Băltuță (ed), *Medieval Perceptual Puzzles: Theories of Sense Perception in the 13th and 14th Centuries*, Leiden, Brill, 2020, pp. 238–268.

Hasse, Dag N., *Avicenna's "De anima" in the Latin West: The Formation of a Peripatetic Philosophy of the Soul, 1160–1300*, London, The Warburg Institut, 2000.

Klubertanz, George. P., *The Discursive Power: Sources and Doctrine of the 'Vis Cogitativa' according to Thomas Aquinas*, Saint Louis, The Modern Schoolman, 1952.

Lisska, Anthony J., *Aquinas's Theory of Perception: An Analytic Reconstruction*, Oxford, Oxford University Press, 2016.

Marmodoro, Anna, *Aristotle on Perceiving Objects*, Oxford, Oxford University Press, 2014.

Di Martino, Carla, *Ratio particularis. La doctrine des senses internes d'Avicenne à Thomas d'Aquin*, Paris, Vrin, 2008.

McClintock, Stuart, *Perversity and Error: Studies on the Averroist John of Jandun*, Bloomington, Indiana University Press, 1956.

Oelze, Anselm, *Animal Rationality: Later Medieval Theories 1250–1350*, Leiden, Brill, 2018.

Perler, Dominik, „Rational Seeing: Thomas Aquinas on Human Perception," in E. Băltuţă (ed), *Medieval Perceptual Puzzles: Theories of Sense Perception in the 13th and 14th Centuries*, Leiden, Brill, 2020 pp. 213–237

Rubini, Paolo, *Pietro Pomponazzis Erkenntnistheorie. Naturalisierung des menschlichen Geistes im Spätaristotelismus*, Leiden, Brill, 2015.

Rubini, Paolo, "The function of the intellect: Intentionality and representationalism," in S. Schmid (ed), *Philosophy of Mind in the Late Middle Ages and Renaissance*, London, Routledge, 2018, pp. 101–124.

CHAPTER 11

Peter John Olivi on Perception, Attention, and the Soul's Orientation towards the Body

André Martin

The thirteenth to fourteenth century was a remarkable period for nuanced debates over the cognitive processes of perception and thought.[1] Increasingly more often Peter John Olivi (1248–1298) has appeared as an important and innovative figure in the scholarly accounts of these debates. Olivi most explicitly saw himself as correcting some, as he called them, "Aristotelian" views on cognition that were popular at the time, especially as embodied in the so-called "species-theories" of cognition endorsed and developed by figures like Roger Bacon and Thomas Aquinas.[2] Loosely put, according to these theories, forms or "likenesses" (called "*species*") propagated from the object of cognition, through the medium, into the physical sense organs, and into the soul of the cognitive agent. Two particular issues Olivi had with these species-theories were that (i) he argued they made cognition out to be too passive a process, something one more so undergoes (being impressed with species) rather than

---

1 For the most part, I will be focusing on perceptual cognition, but much of what I say still potentially pertains to intellectual cognition too.

2 For some discussion of the influence of Aristotle and Arabic writers such as Alhazen and Avicenna on the development of species-theories, see, e.g., S. Knuutila, "Aristotle's Theory of Perception and Medieval Aristotelianism," in S. Knuuttila and P. Kärkkäinen (eds), *Theories of Perception in Medieval and Early Modern Philosophy*, Dordrecht, Springer, 2008, pp. 1–22; D. Lindberg, "Alhazen's Theory of Vision and Its Reception in the West," *Isis*, vol. 58, no. 3, 1967, pp. 321–341; A.M. Smith, "Getting the Big Picture in Perspectivist Optics," *Isis*, vol. 72, no. 4, 1981, pp. 568–589; L. Spruit, *Species intelligibilis: From Perception to Knowledge*, vol. 1: *Classical Roots and Medieval Discussions*, Leiden, Brill, 1994. To be clear, I don't want to suggest that there is one uncontested "Aristotelian" view or that all of these thinkers simply followed Aristotle (in opposition to, say, Plato). Lindberg, e.g., notes that Alhazen's and Bacon's views on the multiplication of forms or "species" can also be understood as influenced by Neo-Platonic views on the irradiation of being (from perfect to lesser) (Lindberg (ed and trans.), *Roger Bacon's Philosophy of Nature*, Oxford, Clarendon Press, 1983, pp. xxxvi–xxxix). Nevertheless, there is a historical line of influence from Aristotle to these thinkers and medieval authors like Olivi tend to label each other as being more "Aristotelian" (as they understand him) or as having stronger ties to Neo-Platonism and Augustine. Although in Olivi's case he aligns himself more with Augustine, as I'll show, he clearly shows influence from Aristotle and he is also quite critical of Augustine.

© KONINKLIJKE BRILL NV, LEIDEN, 2020 | DOI:10.1163/9789004413030_012

PETER JOHN OLIVI ON PERCEPTION

something one actively does, and (ii) Olivi argued that these species, at least at some point in the process, are unnecessary and harmful "veils" that would impede our cognitions of present objects. In contrast, Olivi argued that cognition requires an active attention or orientation (*"aspectus"*) of the soul that directly reaches out to its object.

In this paper, I wish to explain Olivi's technical notion of *"aspectus."* More specifically, I will distinguish different uses of this notion by Olivi, not all of which have been made clear in the secondary literature, in order to help resolve a *prima facie* tension in the way Olivi puts together his active theory of cognition and his direct account of cognition (or "direct realism"). In brief, the issue is that Olivi builds his active theory of cognition out of the commitment that the body cannot, strictly speaking, act as an efficient cause to produce an act of cognition in the spiritual soul; so, in order to account for soul-body interaction, Olivi will often speak of the soul having a seemingly one-way *aspectus* or orientation towards the body so that the soul can respond appropriately to changes in the body.[3] However, given Olivi's commitment to direct realism, the *aspectus* of cognition should go directly to the external object when, e.g., perceiving a present object. So, I take it Olivi must have some sort of distinction in mind between types of *aspectūs* in order to avoid contrariety and in this paper I survey the different distinctions Olivi makes in order to best explain what is going on in such a case of cognition. In short, my view is that by distinguishing between conscious/cognitive[4] and non-conscious/non-cognitive sorts of *aspectūs* in Olivi, one can understand how an *aspectus* towards inner corporeal changes can still contribute to direct cognition of external objects.[5] Moreover,

---

3 See, e.g., Olivi, *II Sent.* Q. 58, II, 484, 500; Q. 59, II, 555; Q. 72, III, 26–27, 33–34.

4 To be clear, I don't mean anything particularly strong by my use of the term "conscious." On my use of the term, a state of the soul is "conscious" insofar as it presents a subject with a distinct or indistinct experience as of something in some manner of appearance. So, on my use of the term, an occurrent act of cognition is a paradigm conscious state and not something that necessarily requires some higher-order act of explicit introspection. Although this topic warrants further discussion, I take it that much of the arguments which we will see below from Olivi against the species-theories of cognition will presuppose that Olivi considers acts of cognition to be first and foremost conscious states, presenting a subject with some content, where "knowledge" in the habitual sense can only come about afterwards (rather than as the first effect of non-conscious processes alone). For a similar point to the above, see Spruit, *Species intelligibilis,* pp. 221–223; 402 (although I think Spruit goes a bit too far in denying non-conscious processes *any* role in the causal process behind cognition for Olivi) and for further discussion of consciousness and cognition in medieval philosophy see T. Scarpelli-Cory, "Medieval Theories of Consciousness," in R. Cross and J.T. Paasch (eds), *The Routledge Companion to Medieval Philosophy*, London, Routledge, 2020.

5 My interpretation runs counter to that given by J. Toivanen, *Animal Consciousness: Peter Olivi on Cognitive Functions of the Sensitive Soul,* Jyväskylä, Jyväskylä University Printing, 2009, and

I take it that Olivi's discussion of another technical notion, the mode of connection or *"colligantia"* between soul and body, in particular provides further evidence for my interpretation.

1 Olivi and His Aristotelian and Augustinian Context

To begin, it will be useful to set up Olivi's clearest theoretical commitments by briefly explaining some of the prior views Olivi argues against and draws from; namely, I will say a bit more about the "Aristotelian" species-theories and Olivi's criticisms, as well as bring up ideas from Augustine which Olivi adopts along with those which he criticizes.

By the thirteenth century, species-theories of cognition, drawing from Aristotle along with certain Arabic developments, had become prevalent in the Latin West. The general idea behind these theories is that human cognition, at its most basic level in perception, is to be explained by a process of forms or "likenesses" (called *"species"*) propagating from the object of cognition, through the medium,[6] into the corporeal sense organs, and, thereby, into the soul of the cognitive agent;[7] higher-level cognitions like imagination or thought involve some sort of manipulation or abstraction based on these species, except perhaps in the case of self-knowledge which some of these thinkers posited to be

---

Toivanen, *Perception and the Internal Senses: Peter of John Olivi on the Cognitive Functions of the Sensitive Soul*, Leiden, Brill, 2013, as we'll discuss below.

6 A key part of these theories is that all perception, other than touch, is primarily of a sensible object at a distance from the perceiver, and nature abhors a void, so there must be something between the perceiver and her object (e.g. air/light, water, etc.): this is what is referred to as the relevant "medium." Moreover, given that species are forms, and not little bodies, they must inhere in some matter, and so the medium also plays this role. For example, the form of red in an object will generate a species of red in the most proximate point of the adjoining illuminated air, and this species generates another in the next point of the medium, and so forth, until finally the species of red reaches the external organ of the perceiver.

7 To be clear, my main concern in this paper is in explaining the causal process of cognition, i.e., how cognitions arise but not necessarily how they represent (though this issue will come up later). For more on the issue of representation in medieval philosophy, see, e.g., H.T. Adriaenssen, "Peter John Olivi on Perceptual Representation," *Vivarium*, vol. 49, no. 4, 2011, pp. 324–352; J. Brower and S. Brower-Toland, "Aquinas on Mental Representation," *The Philosophical Review*, vol. 117, 2008, pp. 193–243; J. Jacobs and J. Zeis, "Form and Cognition: How to Go Out of Your Mind," *Analytical Thomism*, vol. 80, no. 4, 1997, pp. 539–557; A. Martin, "Peter John Olivi on Reference-fixing," unpublished manuscript; C. Panaccio, "Aquinas on Intellectual Representation," in D. Perler (ed), *Intentionality in Ancient and Medieval Philosophy*, Leiden, Brill, 2001, pp. 185–201; R. Pasnau, *Theories of Cognition in the Later Middle Ages*, Cambridge, Cambridge University Press, 1997.

PETER JOHN OLIVI ON PERCEPTION 307

independent from this whole process.[8] Although a full account of these species-theories and all the variations would go beyond the scope of this paper, for our purposes it will be useful to briefly discuss how Olivi saw them as (i) being too passive and (ii) introducing some unnecessary mediators that would also threaten direct cognition of present objects. Moreover, I will primarily focus on perception, given it is arguably the most basic form of cognition and the form most relevant for Olivi's concerns.[9]

1.1 Passive vs. Active Cognition

Pertaining to (i), species-theories draw directly from Aristotle by understanding cognition under his notions of potentiality and actuality. In particular, as Aristotle understands it, perceptual cognition is brought about by the object of cognition actualizing what is (merely) potential in the cognitive power/soul (but first through actualizing the medium and then the relevant sense organ).[10] To be clear, in perceptual cognition the soul does have to be "active" in the sense of actually being able to perceive, but (i) this isn't an "activity" in the strong sense of an operation[11] and (ii) the soul is merely potential with respect

---

8 Aquinas, e.g., considers imagination and intellection to be dependent on sensation in that the senses are the origin of all the "content" in the soul (at least in this life). Avicenna, in contrast, at least thinks that self-knowledge is independent, as he argues for with his famous "floating man" thought experiment: even if one were to be born into complete darkness with no bodily sensations, Avicenna believes one could still cognize one's own existence (e.g., *Liber de anima* I.1; vol. I, pages 36–37, lines 49–68.).

9 There is room to debate, e.g., whether certain species-theorists would really consider intellectual cognition to be mostly passive given many proponents appeal to a sort of abstraction from the agent intellect (see, e.g., Spruit, 1994). Moreover, in memory, and perhaps in thought as well, Olivi is fine with saying these cognitive processes involve looking inward at mental images and not directly at external objects, so it's open to debate whether Olivi's direct realism extends beyond perception (see, e.g., H.T. Adriaenssen, "Peter John Olivi and Peter Auriol on Conceptual Thought," in R. Pasnau (ed), *Oxford Studies in Medieval Philosophy*, vol. 2, 2014, pp. 67–97).

10 See, e.g., Aristotle, *De anima*, *The Complete Works of Aristotle*, 2 vols., trans. J. Barnes, Princeton, Princeton University Press, 1984, II.5 and II.12. For further discussion, see S. Knuuttila, "Aristotle's Theory of Perception and Medieval Aristotelianism," in S. Knuuttila and P. Kärkkäinen (eds), *Theories of Perception in Medieval and Early Modern Philosophy*, Dordrecht, Springer, 2008, pp. 2–6. For now note the following passages in particular: "Sensation depends, as we have said, on a process of movement or affection from without, for it is held to be some sort of change in quality." (*De anima* II.5, 416b33–34) "Generally, about all perception, we can say that a sense is what has the power of receiving into itself the sensible forms of things without the matter, in the way in which a piece of wax takes on the impress of a signet-ring without the iron or the gold." (*De anima* II.12, 424a16–21)

11 See, e.g., what is commonly referred to as Aristotle's distinction between first and second actuality, as in his distinction between the grammarian who has gained his art but is not

to any particular object perceived (after being moved). The species-theories develop on this idea by elaborating on this process as a transmission or multiplication of forms or "species." This process is passive at least in the sense that the cognitive power/soul can be impressed with forms or "species" in virtue of the relevant sense organ being impressed. More strongly, at least for certain interpretations and especially for perceptual cognition, the impressing of the form or "species" into the cognitive power/soul is sufficient for cognition; Aquinas, e.g., expresses this when he says that "a sense's being affected is its very sensing."[12]

Olivi takes issue with the passivity in species-theories for two main reasons. The first reason is that, as a general principle, Olivi believes that the lower

---

actually practicing and the grammarian who is actually practicing his art (*De anima* II.5, 417a22–417b1), and Aquinas's distinction between activity in form alone and activity in operation. For Aquinas, consider, e.g., the following passage: "Now act is twofold; the first act which is a form, and the second act which is operation. Seemingly the word 'act' was first universally employed in the sense of operation, and then, secondly, transferred to indicate the form, inasmuch as the form is the principle and end of operation. Wherefore in like manner potency is twofold: active potency corresponding to that act which is operation – and seemingly it was in this sense that the word 'potency' was first employed – and passive potency, corresponding to the first act or the form, - to which seemingly the name of power was subsequently given. Now, just as nothing suffers save by reason of a passive potency, so nothing acts except by reason of the first act, namely the form. For it has been stated that this first act is so called from action." (*De potentia* Q. 1, a. 1, c.; cf. K. Fisher, "Thomas Aquinas on Hylomorphism and the *In-Act* Principle," *British Journal for the History of Philosophy*, vol. 25, issue 6, 2017, pp. 1053–1072.) It's also worth noting that although Aristotle often uses "activity" (ἐνέργεια) and "actuality" (ἐντελέχεια) interchangeably, it is unclear whether any case of the latter, as in the actuality of form alone, is meant to be a case of the former (see, e.g., S. Menn "The Origins of Aristotle's Concept of *Energeia*: Energeia and *Dynamis*," *Ancient Philosophy*, vol. 14, 1994, pp. 73–114).

12   Aquinas, *Summa theologiae*, P. Caramello (ed), Turin, Marietti, 1948–1950, 1a, 17.2, ad 1. Note that even if Aristotle or the species-theorists understand actually perceiving as an activity in the strong sense (as a perfection or an operation) (*De anima* II.5; cf. M. Tuominen, "On Activity and Passivity in Perception: Aristotle, Philoponus, and Pseudo-Simplicius," in J.F. Silva and M. Yrjönsuuri (eds), *Active Perception in the History of Philosophy: From Plato to Modern Philosophy*, Dordrecht, Springer, 2014, p. 61), it still holds that their general account is passive in one of the above senses where this activity of actually perceiving is (at least partially) the result of being moved from corporeal changes. Moreover, it's worth noting that although species-theorists like Aquinas still want to say the soul is the agent of cognition, (i) their explanation still depends on the object moving the soul and (ii) some thinkers, like Godfrey of Fontaines, simply concede that the object of cognition is the only agent in this scenario (*Quodlibet* IX, Q. 19; cf. A. Côté, "L'objet et la cause de la conaissance selon Godefroid de Fontaines," *Freiburger Zeitschrift für Philosophie und Theologie*, vol. 54, no. 3, 2007, pp. 407–429). There might still be some room for the "Aristotelian" to respond to all of this, but this goes beyond the scope of this paper.

PETER JOHN OLIVI ON PERCEPTION

(corporeal object) cannot act on the higher (spiritual soul). In this Olivi is drawing directly from Augustine. Augustine held a Neoplatonic ontology where spiritual entities are superior to corporeal entities and the human soul is one such spiritual entity.[13] Moreover, it was part of this view that to act upon other things is a sign of superiority and to be acted upon is a sign of inferiority. So, given this view, lower corporeal objects cannot directly act upon the spiritual soul in cognition. Instead, Augustine held that, particularly in perception, the spiritual soul actively makes images of external objects from itself (*de se-metipsa*) and in itself (*in semetipsa*).[14]

Although Olivi's ontology is more complicated than Augustine's (we'll discuss it more later), Olivi follows Augustine in making a sharp distinction between spiritual and corporeal entities, in holding that at least the cognitive powers and acts of the soul are spiritual, in denying that corporeal bodies can directly act upon the spiritual soul, and, hence, in stressing the activity of the soul in cognition. In particular, Olivi considers the cognitive powers and acts of the soul to be spiritual and simple or un-extended and distinguishes them from corporeal and extended objects like your average material objects of cognition and the "species" which they propagate in the medium and in the physical sense organs.[15] Olivi expresses these thoughts when, e.g., he says:

> For, a simple and spiritual act cannot be impressively generated (influxive gigni) by an extended and corporeal species. But every cognitive act is simple and spiritual. This is clear because [...] every being that is capable of cognition, as such, exceeds infinitely everything that lacks cognition and a power of cognizing. This is clear also from the immediate subject of an act of cognition, since, as has been said, an act or power of cognition can primarily and immediately exist only in a simple and spiritual power of the soul.[16]

---

13 For more discussion on Augustine's ontology, see, e.g., G. O'Daly, *Augustine's Philosophy of Mind*, Berkeley, University of California Press, 1987.

14 See, e.g., Augustine, *DT* 10.5.7, *DG* 12.6.33; cf. J.F. Silva and J. Toivanen, "The Active Nature of the Soul in Sense Perception: Robert Kilwardby and Peter Olivi," *Vivarium*, vol. 48, no. 3–4, 2010, pp. 248–249.

15 As scholars have noted, this distinction bares some striking similarities to Descartes' distinction between thinking things and extended things (e.g., K. Tachau, *Vision and Certitude in the Age of Ockham: Optics, Epistemology, and the Foundations of Semantics, 1250–1345*, Leiden, Brill, 1988, p. 46; Silva and Toivanen, p. 263).

16 "Quarto, quia actus simplex et spiritualis non potest influxive gigni a specie extensa et corporali. Sed omnis actus cognitivus est simplex et spiritualis. Quod clamat non solum communis ratio cognitionis, quae in tantum est nobilis ut Deo proprie ascribatur et per quam omne cognoscens, in quantum tale, in infinitum excedit omne quod caret

Elsewhere Olivi describes the simplicity of the soul in terms of "having the nature of a single subject (*habere rationem unius subjecti*)" in distinction with corporeal objects which, in themselves, are extended with disjointed parts.[17] So, in this sense the spiritual soul "exceeds infinitely" the corporeal and extended. One way to put Olivi's thought is that the spiritual soul's powers for cognition are explained or understood by its simplicity and hence inferior corporeal bodies cannot sufficiently produce or explain the cognitive powers and acts of the soul. In particular, Olivi's thought could be that cognition proper involves a simple, single conscious subject to be the cognizer, but something extended and un-unified could not have such a single conscious subject in itself.[18]

The second reason Olivi takes issue with the passivity of the species-theories of cognition is derived from experience. As Olivi points out, often our sense organs are impressed by forms from many objects, but we don't determinatively cognize any unless we actively attend to the object(s); some examples Olivi gives are that in sleep our auditory organs are impressed with sounds but we don't perceive objects so long as the mind isn't actively tending outwards to objects, and when one is strongly attending to one object, the objects in one's peripheral vision will be indistinct or fade into black.[19] So, even if forms or "species" were able to be impressed into the cognitive soul, this would be insufficient for a distinct act of cognition without the soul's active attention ("*aspectus*"). Hence, as Olivi argues, those species-theories that hold that the influx of species is sufficient for cognition must be wrong.

1.2 Direct vs. Indirect Cognition

The second relevant aspect of Olivi's criticisms of species-theories, (ii) above, is that these theories introduce some unnecessary mediators that would also

---

cognitione et potentia cognoscendi. Immo etiam clamat hoc eius immediatum subiectum, quia sicut dictum est, non potest primo et immediate esse nisi in simplici et spirituali potentia animae." (Olivi, *II Sent.* Q.73, III, 83–84; cf. Silva and Toivanen, "The Active Nature of the Soul in Sense Perception," p. 263). Translations are generally my own, though I note other translations I found helpful when relevant, such as in the above passage. Pasnau's translations, available on his website, of questions 72 and 74 were particularly useful for me, and my translations remain largely close to his. See R. Pasnau, "Peter John Olivi, *Questions on the Sentences*, Book II: Questions 72 and 74," http://spot.colorado. edu/~pasnau/research/, accessed February 2019.

17 Olivi, *II Sent.* Q. 58, II, 183; cf. Silva and Toivanen, "The Active Nature of the Soul in Sense Perception," pp. 264–266.

18 This potentially lines up with Olivi's point, which I explain later in 2.1, that corporeal objects can only be oriented towards their adjacent parts and movers but spiritual subjects can cognitively reach out to distant objects.

19 Olivi, *II Sent.* Q. 58 ad 14.11, II, 484 and Q. 73, III, 89.

PETER JOHN OLIVI ON PERCEPTION

threaten direct cognition of present objects. Olivi especially criticizes the species in the cognitive soul as conceived by the species-theories (according to his interpretation). Firstly, Olivi argues that the species in the cognitive soul are unnecessary for the representative power of a cognitive act since the act itself can suffice to represent its object; according to Olivi's own account, instead of positing some third thing logically between the cognitive act and its object, one only needs the cognitive act, "conformed" to the object, and the object itself when present.[20] Second, in particular if the "species" in the soul is supposed to function anything like an image in the mind for the soul to grasp, then Olivi thinks this would make the species in the soul the only thing one truly directly cognizes; as Olivi puts it, the species would "veil the thing and impede its being attended to in itself as something present, rather than help in attending to it."[21] To be clear, Olivi does not deny "species" in our soul to account for memory, but these are merely leftover impressions which require a prior act of cognition. Moreover, for Olivi, when these species in memory are accessed by the soul, this experience differs from when we attend to external objects as present: in the former case, we consciously attend inwards towards the species as our immediate termini, like looking at inner images, but in the latter cases, we consciously directly attend outwards. Olivi's general point is that species-theories are committed to holding that all cognition must be like the former but this is absurd.

Interestingly, despite aligning himself more with Augustine than "Aristotelian" species-theories, Olivi raises these (and other) criticisms against certain passages from Augustine as well. In particular, as was mentioned above, Augustine held that the spiritual soul actively makes its own images in perceptual cognition in and through itself. But he still needed to acknowledge that the external world plays some part such that these images wouldn't be formed arbitrarily. In some passages Augustine attempts to deal with this issue by defining sensation as "a bodily change (*passio corporis*) that is not hidden to the soul (*non latere animam*)."[22] Although there is some ambiguity in what this absence of hiddenness amounts to, Olivi criticizes the view based on either of two possible interpretations:

> Yet this formulation seems to mean that the bodily change (passio corporis) is the object that is perceived [...] Furthermore, "not hidden to the soul" (non latere animam) means only absence of hiddenness, or it means in addition to this some actual notice (notitiam) on the part of the

---

20   See, e.g., Olivi, *II Sent.* Q. 58, II, 486–487; Q. 74, III, 122–123; *Quod. I.*5 f. 64r.

21   Olivi, *II Sent.* Q. 58, II, 469; cf. Q. 74, III, 122–123.

22   Augustine, *DQA* 25.48; cf. *DQA* 23.41, *DM* 6.5.9–12.

soul. But the former cannot be true, since there cannot be absence of hiddenness when there is no noticing and since it would then not add anything real to the definition [of perception] [...] But if it means actual notice in addition to this, this actual notice means the whole essence of an act of perception. Therefore, it adds a complete act of perception to the bodily change, and not just in any way, but in such a way that the bodily change is the object of the act. Therefore, this definition has a vice of contrariety, and in addition to this it has a vice of being circular (nugationis).[23]

In other words, when Augustine says that sensation or perceptual cognition is a bodily change (caused by the object of cognition) that "is not hidden to the soul," this absence of hiddenness might either be (i) an absence of hiddenness but without an actual noticing or cognition or (ii) an actual noticing or cognition. If (i), then Olivi thinks this is nonsense and it would not help define or explain perception if the soul does not grasp the bodily change. But if (ii), then one is defining an act of cognition in terms of another act of cognition, which would lead to a regress, and in particular it would mean the bodily change is what is most immediately perceived and not the object, which, as we've seen, is repugnant to Olivi on the grounds that it denies direct cognition of present objects. So, either way, there is a problem, and Olivi laments Augustine's words here.[24]

1.3 *Augustine on Extramission Theories of Cognition*
However, as modern scholars are aware and Olivi was as well, Augustine does not express one single coherent view on cognition throughout his works. In other passages Augustine expresses the idea that the subject extends out to the object of cognition, which, on the face of it, would put one in contact with

---

23   "Et tamen in hoc dicto includi videtur quod ipsa passio sit ipsum obiectum quod sentitur [...] Hoc etiam, scilicet, non latere animam, aut dicit solam negationem latentiae aut ultra hoc dicit aliquam actualem notitiam ipsius animae. Primum autem nullo modo stare potest; tum quia negatio latentiae non potest esse ubi nulla est notitia; tum quia tunc nihil reale adderet in definitione [...] Si autem ultra hoc dicit actualem notitiam, sed illa actualis notitia dicit totam essentiam actus sentiendi. Ergo ad passionem additur totus actus sentiendi, et hoc non qualitercunque, sed ut habens ipsam passionem pro obiecto. Ergo haec definitio habet in se vitium contrarietatis et ultra hoc vitium nugationis." (Olivi, *II Sent.* Q. 58, II, 484; cf. Silva and Toivanen, "The Active Nature of the Soul in Sense Perception," p. 271; *II Sent.* Q. 74, III, 113–114, 123–124).

24   Cf. Silva and Toivanen, "The Active Nature of the Soul in Sense Perception," pp. 270–272.

PETER JOHN OLIVI ON PERCEPTION 313

more than bodily changes. At one point Olivi says that even on this Augustine
wavered in his thoughts:

> But it seems that the opinion of Augustine had been split in three, since
> partly his opinion was that corporeal rays are emitted and partly that the
> soul, while it enlivens and holds the body, without that [body] it travels
> all the way up to the location of its objects, such that at once it is beyond
> and in the body. [...] And, third, partly his opinion is that the powers of
> the soul (potentiae animae) would touch their objects through their vir-
> tual aspectus and from this they would be said in some sense to be with
> their objects.[25]

This first view was a popular one around the time of Augustine where the eyes
emitted corporeal rays in order to account for perception, in contrast with
theories that posited rays of light and/or "species" travelling only *into* the eyes.
However, Olivi regarded this view to be largely discredited by his time and to
be made superfluous by species-theories and his own view.[26] Moreover, if
these rays are simply corporeal emissions from the eyes then this involves no
extension of the cognitive powers of the soul and we still face the issue of the
soul arguably only directly cognizing bodily changes (even if caused by bodies
that were emitted by one's eyes, reaching the objects of cognition, and forming
a connection or returning). In fact, it is likely that this view of Augustine was
intended by him to go along with his questionable definition of sensation that
we saw above.

The other two views are more interesting in this regard, as they both hold
that there's some sense in which the soul directly touches (*attingere*) external
objects of cognition. The first of these two views is that the soul seemingly literally extends outwards and, as Olivi puts it, in its "essence" reaches where the
object of cognition is, but is also at the same time in the body. However, Olivi

---

25 "Quia vero opinio Augustini tripartita fuisse videtur, quia partim opinatus est radios cor-
    porales emitti et partim quod anima, dum vivitet manet in corpore, absque ipso exiret
    usque ad loca suorum obiectorum, ita quod simul esset in corpore et extra corpus. [...] Est
    etiam partim tertio opinatus quod potentiae animae per suos virtulales aspectus attin-
    gerent sua obiecta et quod ex hoc dicerentur quodammodo esse cum suis obiectis." (Olivi,
    II Sent. Q. 73, III, 61–62).
26 Olivi, *II Sent.* Q. 73, III, 60–61. Interestingly Roger Bacon, although a pioneering figure in
    the development of species-theories at the time, also awkwardly held onto a theory of the
    emission of rays from the eyes as well (see, e.g., *De multiplicatione specierum*, D.C. Lind-
    berg (ed and trans.), *Roger Bacon's Philosophy of Nature*, I, ii, lines 187–196; iii, lines 50–69).
    Olivi could have had him in mind when he regarded the fusion of these theories to be
    unnecessary.

314 MARTIN

rejects this view for a number of reasons. For example, Olivi holds that it is impossible for the powers of the soul, *qua* form, to be outside of their matter, and in this life that matter is tied to one's body; and, indeed, Olivi thinks this fits with experience in that we consciously perceive in our bodies and not outside of them.[27] On a related note, Olivi also draws from experience and rhetorically asks why we wouldn't see distant objects more clearly if we could in fact extend to them in essence as this view states.[28]

In contrast, the second of these two views is that a "virtual" attention or "*aspectus*" reaches out to the object, where the soul is not in essence or "*simpliciter* or absolutely."[29] Indeed, this is the very view that Olivi adopts himself. What exactly it means, however, is the aim of this paper to figure out.

2 More on "Aspectus" and Olivi's Positive Account of Cognition

2.1 *Various Uses of "Aspectus" by Olivi*

Let us now more directly turn to examining Olivi's central notion of "*aspectus*." "*Aspectus*" literally translates to "look" or "gaze" and it is often translated as "attention" in the secondary literature.[30] Indeed, in the cases we've seen above, Olivi does clearly use the term "*aspectus*" to express something like our modern notion of selective or focused attention; e.g., consider Olivi's active theory of cognition where one, e.g., only distinctly perceives what one is focused on.[31] However, Olivi cannot possibly have this sort of *aspectus* in mind when, in multiple passages, he also speaks of an *aspectus* the higher, common sense has on the external senses and their corresponding sense organs.[32] Take, for

---

27 Olivi, *II Sent.* Q. 73, III, 62–63. One might think that experience goes the opposite way since we perceive distant objects *qua* distant and not as if in an inner theatre; this experience is likely to have motivated thinkers like Galen and, in certain moments, Augustine to say that we perceive outside of our bodies and at the distant object. However, Olivi can very well accept this part of experience but still hold that we also still experience ourselves as remaining here and the distant objects as being there, and hence we don't experience ourselves as literally extending outwards or as having some free-floating perception outside of the soul and at the distant object.

28 Olivi, *II Sent.* Q. 73, III, 62–63.

29 Olivi, *II Sent.* Q. 73, III, 65.

30 As Toivanen, *Perception and the Internal Senses*, pp. 153–161, for one, points out, Olivi even occasionally equates the term "*aspectus*" with "*intentio*" and "*attention*," two terms that are even closer to the English term "attention" (e.g., *II Sent.* Q. 58, II, 555).

31 Olivi, *II Sent.* Q. 73, III, 89.

32 See, e.g., Olivi, *II Sent.* Q. 58, II, 484, 500; Q. 59, II, 555; Q. 72, III, 26–27, 33–34. Olivi further thinks the even higher faculty, the intellect, has this sort of *aspectus* on the common sense.

PETER JOHN OLIVI ON PERCEPTION

example, the following passage in full where Olivi addresses the issue of a sleeping agent being awoken by a loud noise:

> But perhaps you will object that someone sleeping is awakened from sleep by a strong impression or sound, and that therefore that impression or sound removed the inactiveness (consopitionem) of the power and the aversion of its aspectus, made the sensory power alert, and turned its [the power's] aspectus to itself [the impression or sound]. In reply to this one should say that the aspectūs of the sensory powers are not so totally inactive nor retracted inward by sleep as to be unable, when some object is vehemently pressing upon and offering itself to the senses, necessarily to notice it, sense it, and, through the object's terminative force, to form in itself a passive sense in such a way that, through its vehemence, the power's entire inactiveness would be expelled and the power would be called back to an alert state and aspectus. But notice – so that you do not believe that any greater difficulty is inherent in this position than in its contrary – that an affection brought about in a sense by an impression or sound could hardly be sensed and, by sensing, noticed, unless an aspectus of the power was beforehand naturally turned to that [affection]. Also, an affection cannot be impressed on the soul's powers unless the power has been made open (patula), through a prior aspectus, to its acting and its impression.[33]

Here Olivi is distinguishing between different *aspectūs* in order to answer a potential objection to his active theory of cognition: viz., if one has to actively

---

33 "Sed forte obicies quod dormiens excitatur a somno per fortem impulsum vel sonum; ergo consopitionem potentiae et aversionem sui aspectus abstulit ille impulsus vel sonus et potentiam sensitivam pervigilem fecit et ad se eius aspectum convertit. – Ad quod dicendum quod aspectus potentiarum sensitivarum non sunt sic totaliter consopiti nec per somnum ad interiora retractit quin aliquod obiectum vehementer se ingerens et offerens sensui habeant necessario advertere et sentire et ex vi terminativa obiecti sic sensum passivum in se formare quod per eius vehementiam tota consopitio potentiae expellatur et ad statum et aspectum pervigilem revocatur. Ne autem credas quod hoc plus difficultatis inferat huic positioni quam suae contrariae: attende quod passio per impulsum vel sonum facta in sensu ita parum posset sentiri et sentiendo adverti, nisi aspectus potentiae prius naturaliter esset conversus ad ipsam. In potentiam etiam animae non potest passio influi, nisi potentia per aspectum praevium facta sit patula agenti et influxui eius." (Olivi, *II Sent.* Q. 72, III, 26–27; cf. Pasnau, "Peter John Olivi, *Questions on the Sentences*, Book II: Questions 72 and 74.") Pasnau translates *"consopitio"/"consopitus"* as "unconscious(ness)" but this is a bit of a loaded translation; "sluggish(ness)" or "stupefied(ness)" would be another possible, more literal, translation choice.

attend to some specific object in order to cognize that object, and lower corporeal objects cannot directly act on the spiritual soul, then how is it that we can turn our attention to, say, a loud noise that comes from where one isn't focusing attention? This passage illustrates that for Olivi the sensory powers (here Olivi doesn't distinguish between the common sense and the external senses) have a "not so totally inactive" *aspectus* prior to any focused attention and cognition. Moreover, a corporeal affection in the sense organs is what this *aspectus* is said to be turned towards. Indeed, given Olivi's ontology, he ought to say that the spiritual soul cannot be directly acted on by the corporeal affection and thus it has to "be made open" to grasp the corporeal object; as he says at the end of this passage, this is done exactly through a "prior *aspectus*." So, Olivi expands his active theory of cognition to include a prior, different, not entirely inactive *aspectus*, directed at the corporeal organs and changes therein to explain how someone can then come to have a focused *aspectus* and thus properly perceive the external object causing the corporeal impressions.

However, how exactly are we to understand this different *aspectus*? One option is to appeal to a distinction Olivi explicitly makes between his more common use of "*aspectus*," that of focused or selective attention, which he sometimes calls "*determinativus*," from what he calls an "*indeterminatus*" or "*generalis aspectus*."[34] And indeed, Olivi also brings this distinction up in response to the issue of how an inattentive agent can come to perceive things they aren't initially focused on. Olivi's answer, at least in part, is that the spiritual soul, except when one is in deepest sleep or perhaps when one is most extremely focused,[35] has a diffuse sort of "*aspectus*" or tending outwards towards the whole perceptual hemisphere. As Olivi describes it in one text:

> [A]lthough the intellect or the power of hearing is directed forcefully to somewhere, nevertheless in the power of hearing remains some unnoticed (occulta) directedness (conversio) to the whole hemisphere – in such a way that if a vehement sound goes off somewhere, the power of

---

34 See, e.g., Olivi, *II Sent.* Q. 73, III, 68–9 and QDLA 32. Interestingly, Olivi also sometimes distinguishes the *generalis aspectus* from what he calls the "*dominativus aspectus*" (e.g. *II Sent.* Q. 58, II, 423). The *dominativus aspectus* is Olivi's notion for the will's orientation towards what it acts on, where this seems to most immediately be the body. Arguably the *dominativus aspectus* shares some relation with a determinate *aspectus*, as (i) a determinate *aspectus* appears to be voluntary for Olivi and (ii) a *dominativus aspectus* towards the body would at least be a sort of determinate *aspectus*, but they don't seem to be identical notions. I owe this point to discussion with Michael Szlachta (U of T) who has researched Olivi on the will in detail.

35 Olivi, *II Sent.* Q. 59, II, 549–550.

PETER JOHN OLIVI ON PERCEPTION

hearing perceives it quickly. The power of hearing does not need to be directed to the sound anew because the preceding unnoticed directedness suffices for perception. [...] It [viz. the power of hearing] is not directed to something in such a way that there would not remain some kind of general attention (generalis aspectus) to other things that are present or accessible to it.[36]

Above it appears Olivi is appealing to something like our experience of "diffuse attention" where, even though one is only determinately cognizing objects at the centre of one's focus, there is some degree of awareness we have towards the rest of one's perceptual hemisphere, though diminishing as it goes from the focal point. Given the phenomena Olivi is describing and his language suggesting a scale between "determinate" and "indeterminate" *aspectūs*,[37] it would appear that the *generalis aspectus* we have towards our environment is conscious, as in the case with determinate attention, just to a lesser degree (and varyingly so). Indeed, Juhana Toivanen, for one, at least on the face of it, goes for this interpretation when he says that Olivi's texts suggest that he is making a distinction between degrees of consciousness and that the *generalis aspectus* is in the periphery of our explicit consciousness.[38]

Moreover, Toivanen more broadly thinks that for Olivi the *generalis aspectus* (of the common sense) is first directed at the external senses and their corresponding sense organs, and in virtue of this one then has a *generalis aspectus*

---

36   "[...] licet intellectus vel auditus sint ad aliud fortiter conversi, nihilominus remanet in ipso auditu quedam occulta conversio ad totum emisperium ita quod si ibi fiat vehemens sonus, subito percipit illum, non preeunte aliqua nova conversione auditus ad illum, quia sufficiebat ad hoc predicta conversio occulta. [...] non est ita conversa ad alia quin remaneat sibi quidam generalis aspectus ad alia sibi presentia vel pervia." (Olivi, QDLA 32; cf. Silva and Toivanen, "The Active Nature of the Soul in Sense Perception," p. 276; cf. Q. 58 ad 14.11, II, 484).

37   Olivi, *II Sent.* Q. 73, III, 68–69.

38   Toivanen, *Animal Consciousness*, pp. 109–114; Toivanen, *Perception and the Internal Senses*, pp. 179–185. As Toivanen has pointed out to me in conversation, his 2013 book at least changes his terminology in that he prefers to speak of degrees of "attention" rather than of "consciousness." Moreover, although this isn't totally clear in the book, Toivanen tells me he thinks the (*occulta*) *generalis aspectus* is non-conscious, in a sense. The account I give below at least agrees over distinguishing conscious and non-conscious *aspectūs*. However, what's less clear is whether we agree over if this is a distinction in degree or in kind. Toivanen tells me he still wants to say this is a difference in degree in this case. I don't disagree that the soul's *aspectus* can, as it were, fall asleep into zero consciousness, but I'm not sure what it would mean to say this *aspectus*, when non-conscious, is still directed at the sense organs unless this is a non-conscious kind of orientation.

of the external world.[39] Although in the above passage Olivi only says the *generalis aspectus* is directed towards the external environment, the previous passage does mention some sort of *aspectus* towards the external sense organs and it does seem to be a similar case at hand. So, there is some textual evidence for Toivanen's interpretation that the *generalis aspectus* is a faintly conscious sort of attention the soul has on its corporeal organs, such that if changes occur there one then also somehow comes to attend to the external environment.

However, if the *aspectus* of the soul on its corporeal organs was understood solely in this way, one should worry that this would make Olivi's view too similar to the view of Augustine on the definition of sensation, which Olivi refutes. Recall from above that in certain passages Augustine seems to define perceptual cognition of external objects as the direct result of one initially and more properly attending to impressions in the body caused by the external objects; but Olivi argues against this view on the grounds that it creates an infinite regress and it would make the only direct objects of cognition our internal bodily impressions. Yet on this interpretation of Olivi, he would also be saying that perceptual cognition of external objects is somehow the result of one initially consciously attending to impressions in the body, so one might ask why these same objections don't follow.

Toivanen is not completely unaware of this worry, though he seems split in how to deal with it. At one point Toivanen, in discussing the relationship between the common sense and the external senses, remarks that Olivi cannot think that the common sense takes acts of the external senses (or, by the same reasoning, changes in the corresponding sense organs) "as *objects*" or else Olivi would threaten the direct cognition of external objects he emphasizes so much. So Toivanen thinks Olivi might actually have some sort of different, though unexplained, mechanism in mind for the soul to utilize these acts (and, by the same reasoning, corporeal impressions).[40] However, later on Toivanen explicitly says that the common sense takes acts of the external sense as *termini*, essentially the same as in the case of external objects taken as *termini*[41] and in the above passage from Q. 72 Olivi clearly says the sensory powers have some sort of *aspectus* directed at corporeal impressions.[42]

---

39   Toivanen, *Animal Consciousness*, pp. 115–120; Toivanen, *Perception and the Internal Senses*, pp. 179–191; cf. Silva and Toivanen, "The Active Nature of the Soul in Sense Perception," p. 275.

40   Toivanen, *Animal Consciousness*, pp. 104–105.

41   Toivanen, pp. 113, 119.

42   As Toivanen has brought up to me, it's possible Olivi has in mind a distinction between a first-order perception and a higher-order "perception" of perception. However, my worry here is that if only the higher-order "perception" is conscious in itself, then this goes

PETER JOHN OLIVI ON PERCEPTION

At another point Toivanen seems ready to deal with this issue by insisting that even though certain cases of cognition depends on a conscious *aspectus* directed at the external senses and their organs, Olivi can still insist that one's *aspectus* can also be directed at external things and not just the internal impressions.[43] So, in other words, Olivi's thought can just be that conscious (diffuse) attention towards corporeal impressions is just what triggers us to then turn our conscious attention more determinately to different external objects. So, this view wouldn't be necessarily circular as it isn't trying to explain all cognition, just particular cases. Moreover, it's also important for Toivanen, to avoid circularity, to insist that the attention one has towards one's external senses and organs isn't an act of cognition but a general state of the soul that is a prerequisite for an act of cognition proper; so, one isn't explaining cognition through another act of cognition.[44]

To be fair, this does seem to get this response out of major contrariety, but it also leaves us without any extra explanation for how ordinary cases of cognition grasp external objects (and as present); here it seems the *aspectus* of the soul would simply be a brute power of the soul to reach outwards. Under this interpretation, the *aspectus* of the soul wouldn't seem that different from a literal extension of the soul, which, as we've seen, Olivi denies when discussing Augustine on extramission theories. Now, perhaps another way to phrase this view is that the soul has a brute power for action at a distance; the soul doesn't literally extend but the idea could be that it doesn't have to in virtue of its simple, non-extended nature. However, even if not identical to holding a literal extension of the soul, Olivi's objections seem just as relevant. For example, if the soul can seemingly miraculously attend to distant objects then why cannot we cognize them more clearly?[45]

---

against Olivi's direct realism and this wouldn't be appealing to a non-conscious mechanism as Toivanen, *Animal counsciousness*, hints at beforehand. In general, I'm also uneasy about attributing something like a higher-order account of consciousness to Olivi, but there's a lot more that needs to be said on this (see, e.g., S. Brower-Toland, "Olivi on Consciousness and Self-Knowledge," in R. Pasnau (ed), *Oxford Studies in Medieval Philosophy*, vol. 1, 2013, pp. 136–168).

43   Toivanen, *Animal Consciousness*, pp. 117–120; cf. Toivanen, *Perception and the Internal Senses*, pp. 179–191; Silva and Toivanen, "The Active Nature of the Soul in Sense Perception," p. 277.

44   Toivanen, *Perception and the Internal Senses*, p. 186.

45   To be clear, in my account that follows there is a sense in which I wouldn't deny that the soul has a brute power to reach outwards; viz., I think it's true that for Olivi the soul has a general power, as part of its simple and spiritual nature, to consciously tend outwards (to have intentionality). Nevertheless, this leaves it open for Olivi to think that this general

320 MARTIN

Moreover, there's evidence that Olivi indeed thought that mediating corporeal "species" or impressions play some causal role in explaining how one's *aspectus* reaches external objects while we are still tied to our bodies.[46] For example, Olivi says that motions in the corporeal organs are necessary for perceptual cognition while the soul is united to its body, which could, at least in part, refer to the impressions in the sense organs.[47] At the very least Olivi is clear to insist that the reach of our *aspectus* in this life is tied to the reach of our bodies.[48]

Fortunately, there is another way to understand the *aspectus* the sensory soul has on itself and its corporeal sense organs. Toivanen interprets both as having a faint sort of consciousness, essentially on par with the conscious attention one has in determinate cognition, just of a lesser degree. In contrast, it's also possible that Olivi thought at least the *aspectus* the sensory soul has on itself and its corporeal sense organs function in an active but non-conscious sort of way to enable conscious-level attention and cognition.[49]

---

      aspectus must be determined, in part, through non-conscious causal co-operation with corporeal objects in order to constitute distinct perceptual cognitions of these objects.

46   Although it's true that Olivi thinks that separated souls, despite not having corporeal organs, can cognize and even, specifically, *sense* singular things (e.g., *QDLA* and *Quod.* I.5; cf. Toivanen, *Perception and the Internal Senses*, pp. 213–215), this doesn't rule out that corporeal species are still causally necessary in this life.

47   "Forma enim non potest ad aliud moveri vel applicari nisi per motionem suae materiae, unde visiva non potest dirigi et converti ad visibilia exterior nisi per motionem quondam spirituum in quibus fertur et organi sui." (Olivi, *II Sent.* Q. 51, II, 112).

48   See, e.g., Olivi, *II Sent.* Q. 58, II, 512; Q. 72, III, 30–33; Q. 74, III, 113–114; Q. III, III, 272–273; cf. Toivanen, *Perception and the Internal Senses*, pp. 203–206. There's some room for debate here, as I think Toivanen would raise, over whether the motions in the body which Olivi refers to in these passages are purely the result of the higher spiritual soul (e.g. in just willing the eyes to move in a direction). However, we have seen Olivi refer to impressions in the sense organs and it seems plausible to suppose that Olivi would think that is relevant to, e.g., why the eyes needs to change directions to see more (i.e. to get into causal contact with more objects). More of what follows will be relevant to this issue, though space constrains me from saying as much as I would like in this paper.

49   To be clear, I am convinced by the passages which Toivanen brings up (especially from *QDLA* 32) that Olivi would distinguish between a distinct/determinate state of attention/consciousness from a diffuse/indeterminate state of attention/consciousness; in general, it seems Olivi ought to make this distinction to avoid the implausible conclusion that we are only conscious of what we directly attend to, as if everything else was in blackness. My disagreement below is only about whether this distinction is sufficient to explain how our soul is oriented towards its lower powers/body in order to explain the causal process of cognition for Olivi.

PETER JOHN OLIVI ON PERCEPTION 321

Consider that there are passages where Olivi explicitly says that even corporeal and non-cognitive things like sense organs,[50] rays of light,[51] and fire and arrows[52] can have a sort of *aspectus*, though different from our ordinary spiritual and conscious sort of "*aspectus*" or attention. In some of these cases, Olivi considers these non-cognitive things to get their *aspectus* through the actions of cognitive agents like humans or God. For example, in one passage Olivi says that fire has an *aspectus* that inclines it upwards thanks to the divine will and similarly an arrow or stone can have an *aspectus* towards its target thanks to the will of the projector when he, e.g., tosses the stone with his own *aspectus* directed towards the target.[53] Notably in these cases, these non-cognitive things gain an *aspectus* towards *distant* things *derivatively*.

However, in other passages Olivi more interestingly distinguishes spiritual and conscious sorts of *aspectūs* and corporeal and non-conscious sorts of *aspectūs* in terms of only spiritual and conscious things being able to have a direct *aspectus* towards distant things while corporeal and non-conscious things can only, in themselves, have a direct *aspectus* towards adjacent corporeal parts.[54] Interestingly, in one of these passages Olivi also says corporeal objects cannot have an *aspectus* towards themselves either, because corporeal things cannot self-move in the same part, they can only be moved by an adjacent corporeal part.[55] So, this suggests that Olivi thinks that a corporeal *aspectus* is oriented in virtue of a causal relation, as corporeal parts can only be moved by adjacent parts and thus, Olivi argues, they can only have a direct *aspectus* towards adjacent parts.[56] This idea also appears in one of Olivi's

---

50   E.g., Olivi, *II Sent.* Q. 67, II, 618–619.

51   E.g., Olivi, *II Sent.* Q. 72, III, 36.

52   E.g., Olivi, *II Sent.* Q. 58, II, 420–421.

53   Olivi, *II Sent.* Q. 58, II, 420–421; cf. Toivanen, *Perception and the Internal Senses*, pp. 155–157.

54   E.g., Olivi, *II Sent.* Q. 51, II, 112.

55   Olivi, *II Sent.* Q. 51, II, 112.

56   To be clear, this doesn't mean that corporeal objects cannot have an *aspectus* towards distant objects indirectly in virtue of transitivity and a causal chain. This, I think, offers one interpretation of a puzzling passage where Olivi says, without refuting, "some have said that the power of the sun and of any agent acts at a distance through a virtual *aspectus* or through a virtual conversion and direction at a distance. Hence, as far as the efficacy of the virtual *aspectus* and direction is concerned, it is present to the whole medium, at a distance, extended up to the end point, beyond which it cannot act." (*II Sent.* Q. 23, I, 424; cf. Pasnau, *Theories of Cognition in the Later Middle Ages*, pp. 173–174.) Pasnau concludes from this passage that (i) there is nothing intrinsically spiritual about the *virtualis aspectus* and (ii) acknowledging B. Jansen's view, *Die Erkenntnislehre Olivis*, Berlin, Dümmlers, 1921, p. 118, that the *virtualis aspectus* is, more or less, equivalent to action at a distance. However, if the corporeal sun could truly reach out from a distance, then this would seem

objections against the species-theories of cognition.[57] Here Olivi first remarks that each species, if corporeal, must be understood as directly representing the species from which it directly propagated. But our experience of cognition is not like this: we don't only attend to the most adjacent species, rather we can have an *aspectus* directly to the distant object. So, as we've seen before, Olivi rejects the species-theories of cognition, but in such a way that he doesn't necessarily deny that corporeal things can represent/have an *aspectus* – this *aspectus* is just different from our spiritual and conscious *aspectus* and insufficient to explain it.[58]

Thus, just because corporeal species are insufficient to explain conscious level cognition, this doesn't mean the species cannot play some partial role in explaining human cognition. The above notion of a non-conscious sort of "*aspectus*" can help explain this.[59] Even though Olivi is clear that only spiritual and simple entities are capable of a higher sort of conscious *aspectus* and corporeal entities are only capable of this non-conscious sort of *aspectus* in themselves, this still leaves it open for Olivi to believe that spiritual and simple beings can also partake in this lower sort of non-conscious *aspectus*. Indeed, Olivi seemingly ought to believe this given that he believes the higher can always do what the lower can. Moreover, Olivi should be open to non-conscious

---

to contradict Olivi's distinction between corporeal and spiritual *aspectūs*. Instead what I think is more plausible is that Olivi is mainly referring to a non-conscious sort of *aspectus* (though one agents can also partake in) and that for the sun it can have an *aspectus* at a distance indirectly because it is in a causal connection that extends beyond it.

57 Olivi, *II Sent.* Q. 73, III, 84–85.

58 Tachau, *Vision and Certitude in the Age of Ockham*, p. 44, takes this to be part of Olivi's wholesale rejection of species in the medium, but an alternate explanation is that Olivi is mainly arguing that they are insufficient to explain conscious level cognition.

59 Another, more general, place where Olivi appeals to non-cognitive/non-conscious *aspectūs* occurs at the beginning of his *respondeo* of *II Sent.* Q.72, III, 6–13; as Olivi explains, he believes all cases of causal interactions between higher and lower levels requires an *aspectus* from the higher toward the lower level (e.g. between anything which is active/formal and its proper passive/material subject), whether or not there is a spiritual-corporeal asymmetry, and so Olivi's arguments about the soul having higher powers, especially above the body, (and thus the soul needs to be "open" to impressions in the lower parts) need not entirely appeal to the cognitive/conscious *aspectūs* of the soul. As we'll see below, in 2.3, Olivi even specifically speaks of the *aspectūs* of the higher powers of the soul towards the lower powers and its sense organs in the same sort of way which Olivi speaks of these non-cognitive/non-conscious asymmetries. Perhaps to a certain extent these non-cognitive/non-conscious *aspectūs* are fixed by God, and not just by causal relations, but (i) there seems to be some potential overlap here and (ii) this would still be interesting for my purposes so long as one doesn't need to appeal to the conscious *aspectūs* of a created agent (and so, give a circular account about how conscious *aspectūs* in an agent are fixed).

PETER JOHN OLIVI ON PERCEPTION 323

parts of the spiritual soul in general given that he considers habits and intellectual memories to be parts of the spiritual soul but these don't seem to be conscious, at least when they're not being exercised.[60] Furthermore, given the above passages, Olivi is at least clear to consider a non-conscious thing, especially if corporeal, to have an *aspectus* towards what it is in direct causal contact with. So, e.g., a species in the air would represent whatever prior species generated it at least *qua* cause.[61]

The general thought here is that when Olivi says that the common sense has an *aspectus* directed at the external senses and their corresponding sense organs (and the changes therein), Olivi just means that they are in a non-conscious, causal connection that makes them "open" to enabling conscious level attention and cognition. In particular, the corporeal object can propagate species through the medium and into the sense organs, each representing the last part of the process, and then the sensory powers can causally connect with the species/impressions in the sense organs to transmit some information about the object spread through the species. Following Olivi's ontology, the spiritual soul would have to be "open" to, *as it were*, allow itself to be moved for this information to transfer; or, more properly speaking, although Olivi uses this exact phrasing, the soul would be playing the efficient causal role tending towards

---

60   See, e.g., Olivi, *II Sent.* Q. 74. One should be careful here, however, in that memory species, as we've seen above, have their *aspectus* in virtue of the prior conscious cognitive act that caused them. So memory species, although not conscious in themselves, would still have an *aspectus* parasitic on a conscious *aspectus* as in the case of the arrow discussed above. But this isn't the sort of non-conscious *aspectus* I have in mind here. Indeed, Olivi is clear to distinguish other more general habits as being prior to their acts of cognition – e.g., the disposition to have a sharper vision or to be readier to investigate certain fields of knowledge more than others (*II Sent.* Q. 74, III, 117–118). So, Olivi would at least be open to admit that habits which have a more indeterminate *aspectus* can have such an *aspectus* independent from the conscious sort of *aspectus*. An *aspectus* towards one's general surroundings or corporeal organs could be this sort of habit then.

61   Moreover, in other passages, although Olivi thinks there are limits on this, he does admit that corporeal species can represent certain information about the species it is in causal contact with (and, by transitivity, the object propagating the species) such as colour (*II Sent.* Q. 74, III, 123; "Epistola ad fratrem R.," S. Piron et al. (eds), *Archivum Franciscanum Historicum*, vol 91, 1998, no. 12). This is acceptable given that Olivi more generally speaks of formal likenesses or "similitudes" as being part of his theory of representation (see, e.g., Martin, "Peter John Olivi on Reference-fixing") and there's nothing essentially conscious about two objects having a formal likeness (e.g., both species containing the form of red). So, it appears that Olivi would also be open for a non-conscious *aspectus* to be oriented towards an object it is in a causal connection with and in a certain way according to some information about the object.

324   MARTIN

the object and changing accordingly.[62] Nonetheless, in so doing, the soul can
orient a non-conscious *aspectus* at the object and take in the purely causally
derived orientation and representations of the corporeal species. At the
conscious-level, one's soul would now be "conformed" to at least have a field of
potential external objects to focus on and determinately perceive as present.
Thus, understanding the *aspectus* the sensory powers have on the sense organs
in this non-conscious way, Olivi can offer some further explanation for how
human cognition functions in this life in general and without slipping into
anything like Augustine's definition of perceptual cognition, which Olivi denies given his commitment to direct realism.[63]

2.2   *Terminative Causation*

To be clear, at this point one might ask how the soul and the corporeal organs
can be in a causal connection given that, as we've seen, Olivi thinks the corporeal, most properly, cannot act on the higher spiritual soul as an efficient cause.
At most, seemingly, Olivi refers to corporeal objects, especially the object of
cognition, as "terminative causes" of their corresponding acts of cognition.[64]
At least initially, Olivi refers to terminative causation as a sort of final cause.[65]
But, as scholars have noted, Scholastics often spoke of an object cognized or
intended as a final cause where this just trivially means that it is the object
cognized (the intentional object); indeed, sometimes it was held the object
need not even exist to be a final cause.[66] So, one might think that Olivi does not

---

62   To explain this Olivi reverses the usual analogy of a wax being impressed by an object to
      convey this sort of interaction and instead uses the analogy of wax pouring itself over an
      object to take its shape (*II Sent.* Q. 58, II, 415–416; Q. 72, III, 38; Q. 74, III, 116).

63   One might argue that there is still some tension with this passage from Olivi on Augustine
      since he seems to speak as if, should the soul not consciously notice the impressions in
      the body, then this doesn't obviously help explain cognition; so Olivi doesn't offer Augus-
      tine another way out by distinguishing types of noticing and this is suspicious. There are
      a few ways to respond here. First, I might stress that in this passage Olivi never specifically
      says the only sort of noticing of the impression the soul can have is conscious, so his point
      might only be that Augustine doesn't give us an obvious explanation for how cognition
      occurs but one could be found. Second, in general, it might just be the case that Olivi is
      holding off on giving Augustine this distinction for rhetorical purposes. Third, if Olivi in-
      deed has a conscious sense of noticing in mind, it might only be because Augustine's
      passage seems to pertain only to this sort of noticing. Finally, at the very least the alter-
      nate interpretation is also in at least some tension with this passage so at worse the two
      options are on equal ground in this regard.

64   See, e.g., Olivi, *II Sent.* Q. 72, III, 10 and 36.

65   Olivi, *II Sent.* Q. 72, III, 10 and 36.

66   Cf. R. Pasnau, *Metaphysical Themes: 1274–1671*, Oxford, Oxford University Press, 2011.

PETER JOHN OLIVI ON PERCEPTION

really mean to give much of a substantial causal role for the object of cognition or any corporeal changes in the organ when he calls any a terminative "cause."

However, Olivi nevertheless does admit that "the object can, broadly, be numbered among efficient causes." As he says in full:

> But nevertheless the object can, broadly, be numbered among efficient causes. It can be [...] because the active force of a cognitive power necessarily needs such a terminus and its termination so as to produce a cognitive act – as if the aforesaid terminus were to impress something on the cognitive force itself and on its act.[67]

That is, Olivi's point is that the object is broadly an efficient cause in that it is a necessary or, as it was sometimes also called, a "*sine qua non*" cause of a particular cognitive act.[68] Olivi's favoured analogy of a vase terminating some rays of light gives us a way to understand what he means:

> Hence, the act [of cognition] is assimilated to the object as if to its intimate terminus [...]. And one can give some example of this by referring to sunlight [...]. Because when the sun illuminates a round or triangular vase, the light which is in the vase has a round or triangular figure. It is not the case that the vase itself efficiently produced that figure in the light; it did so only terminatively.[69]

---

67 "[N]ihilominus potest large connumerari inter causas efficientes; tum quia obiectum, in quantum est talis terminus vel terminans, non habet rationem patientis aut entis possibills seu potentialis, immo potius rationem actus et entis actualis; tum quia virtus activa potentiae cognitivae sic necessario eget tali termino et eius terminatione ad hoc quod producat actum cognitivum, acsi praedictus terminus influeret aliquid in ipsam vim cognitivam et in eius actum." (Olivi, *II Sent.* Q. 72, III, 10.) As one can see, Olivi also makes another point here: "first, because the object, insofar as it is such a terminus or terminating thing, doesn't have the nature of an affected thing or a possible or potential being; rather it more has the nature of an act and an actual being." The main point here appears to be that the object of cognition is not the passive subject of change in an act of cognition, so it cannot be the material cause of cognition, and rather is something actual, as an efficient cause should be.

68 Cf. J.-L. Solère, "*Sine Qua Non* Causality and the Context of Durand's Early Theory of Cognition," in A. Speer, F. Retucci, T. Jeschke, and G. Guldentops (eds), *Durand of Saint-Pourçain and His "Sentences" Commentary: Historical, Philosophical, and Theological Issues*, Leuven, Peeters, 2014, pp. 185–227.

69 "Assimilatur igitur actus obiecto tamquam suo intimo termino [...]. Et potest huius dari qualecunque exemplum in lumine solis [...]. Cum enim sol illuminat unum vas rotundum aut triangulare, lumen quod est in vase habet figuram rotundam vel triangularem, non quod ipsum vas effective produxerit in eo hunc figuram, sed solum terminative." (Olivi, *II*

Although the vase doesn't produce the light or shape it actively on its own, it nevertheless does constrain how the rays of light fall. In modern times we are quite comfortable speaking of a vase "causing" a shadow and stopping rays of light, but Olivi, as most Scholastics, is hesitant to call the vase an "efficient (or agent) cause" only because the term is typically meant to signify the productive force of the event and that's the sun/light for Olivi (hence why Olivi says it's only "as if" the terminus was doing the "impressing"); but just because the vase isn't a causal force like an agent clearly doesn't mean the vase isn't causally relevant and Olivi recognizes that. So, the same general point holds for the object of cognition in that, like the vase, the corporeal object is also causally relevant for the act of cognition, even though the cognitive power is strictly the productive force; the object constrains the act of cognition and helps fix the act to its object. Moreover, although these passages are strictly about the object of conscious cognition, as we'll see in the next section, Olivi also describes the corporeal organs and changes therein as objects of non-conscious *aspectūs* and as terminative causes.[70]

2.3   *The Mode of Connection*

As I've argued above, there is textual evidence that Olivi distinguishes between a conscious sense of *"aspectus"* and a non-conscious sense, and, given this, it makes sense for Olivi to appeal to this in his account of cognition. In order to explain further what this non-conscious sort of *aspectus* is for Olivi, and further solidify that the common sense has this sort of *aspectus* on the external senses and their corresponding sense organs, it will be useful to turn to a another technical notion in Olivi of a "mode of connection" or *"modum colligantiae"* between the higher and the lower.

In II Sent. Q. 72, devoted to explaining how spirit and bodies interact in cognition, Olivi often speaks in a single breath of a "mode of connection" and his other technical notions where he distinguishes these thoughts from parts of the species-theories of cognition which he denies. For example, early on Olivi describes the view "of Aristotle and his followers, who say that bodies and corporeal objects act on a spirit formally conjoined to a body not only through the mode of connection (*modum colligantiae*) nor only through the mode of an

---

Sent. Q. 58, II, 414–415; cf. Adriaenssen, "Peter John Olivi on Perceptual Representation," p. 343.)

70 For more on the object of cognition as a terminative cause, see, e.g., Adriaenssen, "Peter John Olivi on Perceptual Representation;" Martin, "Peter John Olivi on Reference-fixing;" and Toivanen, *Perception and the Internal Senses*, pp. 145–150.

PETER JOHN OLIVI ON PERCEPTION

objective terminus, but also through a simple and influencing impression."[71] That is, Olivi denies, as we've seen, that the corporeal can act directly on the spiritual, and he distinguishes this view from his own where the corporeal and spiritual can interact through a mode of connection and with the object functioning as a terminative cause. Later on in this question Olivi further explains the different ways in which the corporeal and the spiritual can interact through a "natural connection" or "*naturalis colligantia*" (also called a "*colligantia potentiarum*").[72] Some illustrative, though general, examples Olivi gives are that corporeal changes can lull one to sleep sufficiently to take away one's "*generalis et indeterminatus aspectus*" in the spiritual soul and that corporeal movement of one's body can also thereby indirectly move one's spiritual soul given the natural connection between them.[73] Most relevant for our purposes, Olivi also explicitly speaks of the natural connection between sensory powers as such:

> Therefore it ought rather to be said that the act of a higher power follows the act of a lower as its object, so that the higher act is caused by the lower as by an object terminating a higher act and the first aspectus of a higher power. But still the natural connection of the powers is the cause of why the lower power's act is the terminus and connatural object of the higher.[74]

Above Olivi explicitly says the higher sensory power (e.g., the common sense) has an *aspectus* towards the lower power (e.g., the external senses), with the lower serving as a terminative cause, and this is further explained by saying that the sensory powers are in a natural connection.

One thing worth pointing out here is that Olivi is explaining all co-operations between higher and lower sensory powers, which are part of all acts of cognition. But if they could only co-operate through a conscious sort of *aspectus*

---

71 "Prima est Aristotelis et sequacium eius dicentium quod in spiritum corpori formaliter coniunctum agunt corpora et corporalia obiecta non solum per modum colligantiae nec solum per modum termini obiectivi, immoetiam per simplicem et impressivum influxum." (Olivi, *II Sent.* Q. 72, III, 13; cf. Pasnau, "Peter John Olivi, *Questions on the Sentences*, Book II: Questions 72 and 74.").

72 Olivi, *II Sent.* Q. 72, III, 30–35.

73 Olivi, *II Sent.* Q. 72, III, 32–33.

74 "Potius ergo debet dici quod actus potentiae superioris sequitur ad actum inferioris tanquam ad suum obiectum, ita quod superior actus causatur ab inferiori sicut ab obiecto terminante actum superiorem et primum aspectum potentiae superioris. Attamen naturalis colligantia potentiarum est causa quare actus inferioris potentiae est in terminum et connaturale obiectum superioris." (Olivi, *II Sent.* Q. 72, III, 33–34.).

then this threatens once again to turn all our cognitions into some indirect chain where from the seat of the common sense we only directly attend to acts of, e.g., vision, which are in turn directed towards the eyes, and so on. Second, Olivi also seems to equate the natural connection between the powers with terminative causation given that both are said to determine the *aspectus* of the higher power. Finally, as we see in Olivi's general examples of the higher and lower interacting through a natural connection, there's nothing essentially conscious about this interaction; e.g., the spirit will move along with the body automatically even if one is in deep sleep and unable to even faintly consciously attend to one's body.

Indeed, Olivi is clear that the mode of connection between the body and spirit is just part of his general account of the union between the two:

> It should further be known that the connection of a spirit to a body on account of which the movement or disposition of one overflows to another consists principally in the formal union [a] of the spirit to the body as to its matter and [b] of the body to the spirit as to its form. Only the creator can give this union to a rational spirit. But secondarily this connection consists in many powers of the soul running together in the same spiritual matter of the soul itself. In both cases, however, the identity of matter is the cause of why some effect in the soul should follow an influence directly made in the body, as if the first influence made in the body were some kind of motion on the part of soul itself. For it is a motion of the soul to the extent that it is a motion of its corporeal matter.[75]

To be brief, Olivi's general soul-body ontology consists of a mix between hylomorphism and the distinction between the corporeal and the spiritual. According to a more traditional hylomorpic account of the soul-body union, as in Aquinas, the human is a form-matter compound with the soul being the form of the body, the body being the matter of the soul. However, following prior fellow Franciscans, especially Bonaventure, Olivi makes a distinction

---

75   "Ulterius sciendum quod colligatio spiritus ad corpus propter quam motus vel dispositio unius redundat in alterum consistit principaliter in formali unione spiritus ad corpus tanquam ad suam materiam et corporis ad ipsum tanquam ad suam formam. Quae quidem unio non potest dari spiritui rationali nisi a creatore. Secundario vera consistit in concursu plurium potentiarum animae in eadem materia spirituali ipsius animae. Utrobique autem est identitas materiae causa quare ad impressionem directe factam in corpore sequatur aliquis effectus in anima, acsi prima impressio facta in corpus esset quaedam motio ipsius animae.Est enim pro tanto motio eius, pro quanto est motio suae materiae corporalis." (Olivi, *II Sent.* Q. 72, III, 34–35.)

PETER JOHN OLIVI ON PERCEPTION

between corporeal matter and spiritual matter – though corporeal matter has its associated form and spiritual matter has its associated form too. Moreover, Olivi holds that one object can have a plurality of forms. So, e.g., the human body, *qua* corporeal, has corporeal forms for, e.g., its size and shape and the spiritual matter of its soul has forms for, e.g., its intellective power and acts. What then accounts for the union between these distinct matters and, seemingly, forms? Olivi answers, first, as in the above passage, that certain corporeal and spiritual powers serve as the forms for the same spiritual matter. At this point the question might naturally arise how corporeal powers could serve as forms to spiritual matter. Elsewhere Olivi explains this by saying that this union is in virtue of the sensory soul being a form to both the corporeal matter and the spiritual matter, as e.g., vision in this life still partially takes place in the eyes and partially in the spiritual matter.[76] So, the natural connection between the soul and body is ultimately explained in terms of our sensory powers, *qua* form, having one seat in the corporeal matter of the sense organs and another seat in the spiritual matter of the soul; thus Olivi offers a bridge for how changes in the corporeal sense organs can lead to changes in the spiritual soul as he says in the above passage from Q. 72.[77]

What's important from all of this for our purposes is that Olivi explicitly says that corporeal organs and the changes therein are in a natural connection with the sensory soul, *qua* spiritual, and that this is explained in terms of a sort of hylomorphic union which doesn't seem to entail any sort of conscious *aspectus* on the part of the spiritual soul. Moreover, this natural connection appears to be expressed in terms of Olivi saying that the corporeal organs and changes therein are terminative causes for determining attention and acts of cognition (i.e. without which there would be no determination to external objects in our united state). However, Olivi's general ontology does require some sort of "prior *aspectus*"[78] to leave the spiritual soul open to changes from the corporeal, so this *aspectus* would be best understood as a non-conscious part of the natural connection and tied to a sort of terminative causation. In particular, the spiritual soul is non-consciously oriented to changes in the corporeal organs and disposed to respond appropriately with a conscious *aspectus* tending towards

---

76 Olivi, *II Sent.* Q. 58, II, 513.

77 For further discussion of Olivi's soul-body ontology, see, e.g., R. Pasnau, "Olivi on the Metaphysics of Soul," *Medieval Philosophy and Theology*, vol. 6, 1997, pp. 109–132; Toivanen, *Perception and the Internal Senses*, pp. 21–111; M. Yrjönsuuri, "The Soul as an Entity: Dante, Aquinas, and Olivi," in H. Lagerlund (ed), *Forming the Mind: Essays on the Internal Senses and the Mind/Body Problem from Avicenna to the Medical Enlightenment*, Dordrecht, Springer, 2007, pp. 59–92.

78 Olivi, *II Sent.* Q. 72, III, 26–27.

330 MARTIN

the external source of the changes; if the latter should become fixed to an object then an act of determinate cognition is completed.

Thus, the above gives us evidence that Olivi thought that corporeal species or impressions (especially in the sense organs but also, by extension, in the medium) are in some sense termini for an *aspectus* of the soul and sorts of terminative causes. Moreover, they are termini in a way that is consistent with Olivi also holding that the proper termini for ordinary cognitions are external objects, since cognition is at the conscious level and involves a different sense of termination (for a different sort of *aspectus*) than at this more basic level in the causal process of cognition.

Furthermore, this interpretation gives us a way to understand some other passages from Olivi. As mentioned above, Olivi does assert that species or motions in the corporeal sense organs are necessary for perceptual cognition in this life. In one passage Olivi expresses this by saying that: "insomuch as they [our sensory powers] are located in corporeal organs, they can have quasi-corporeal and quasi-located *aspectūs* which are, in some way, proportional to corporeal objects."[79] Olivi's thought appears to be that, given our soul's mode of connection with the body, our *aspectūs* are tied to our corporeal organs in such a way that our cognition also stretches in proportion with the reach of our corporeal organs. Given the above, this reach can be understood in terms of the reach of the causal chain between the corporeal propagation of species from the object, through the medium, and into the sense organs.[80] Thus, unlike for Augustine's view on the literal extension of the soul, we have some reason for why we cannot clearly see distant objects or those not even in our field of vision (since sufficient information isn't being delivered to us through corporeal species).[81]

In summation, on my interpretation the best way to interpret the most basic *aspectūs* the higher parts of the soul have on the external senses and changes

---

79 "Secundo vero, ratione suorum aspectuum secundum quos virtualiter protenduntur ad obiecta exteriora et corporalia; pro quanto enim sunt sitae in organis corporeis, pro tanto possunt habere aspectus quasi corporales et quasi situales et corporibus quodam modo proportionales." (Olivi, *II Sent.* Q. 58, II, 512.)

80 See especially n. 57 above for more on this thought.

81 Now, it should be admitted that there's a sense in which this bodily necessity is arguably not completely explained in that the *colligantia* between the spiritual soul and its body does appear to be a brute fact for Olivi; it's ultimately in virtue of God connecting any soul with its body that there is such a *colligantia* (*II Sent.* Q. 72, III, 34–35). Nevertheless, Olivi does at least use the familiar language of hylomorphism to attempt to describe such a connection, as we've seen above. Furthermore, the *colligantia* is still just part of the overall causal process of cognition and on my interpretation there is in fact an overall causal process.

PETER JOHN OLIVI ON PERCEPTION

in the corresponding organs is as non-conscious sorts of *aspectūs*. Conscious level *aspectūs*, on the other hand, can orient directly towards external objects,[82] in part thanks to lower-level *aspectūs* operating below consciousness. So, Olivi can hold on to his direct account of cognition while also making room for soul-body interaction which doesn't violate his active theory of cognition and soul-body ontology.[83]

Abbreviations for the Works of Peter John Olivi and Augustine

II Sent. – Olivi, *Quaestiones in secundum librum Sententiarum*, 3 vols., B. Jansen (ed), Firenze, Collegium S. Bonaventurae, 1922–1926, (question, volume, page number in the Jansen edition).

DG – Augustine, *De Genesi ad litteram libri duodecim*, J.-P. Migne (ed), Paris, Migne, 1865.

DQA – Augustine, *De quantitate animae, Sancti Aureli Augustini Opera*, sect. I, pars IV, W. Hormann (ed), Wien, Hoelder-Pichler-Tempsky, 1986.

DM – Augustine, *De musica liber VI: A Critical Edition with a Translation and an Introduction*, M. Jacobsson (ed), Stockholm, Almqvist & Wiksell International, 2002.

DT – Augustine, *De Trinitate*, W.J. Mountain (ed) with the assistance of F. Glorie, Turnhout, Brepols, 1968.

QDLA – Olivi, *Quaestio de locutionibus angelorum*, S. Piron (ed), *Oliviana* 1, 2003, http://olivianarevues.org/18, accessed February 2018.

Quod. – Olivi, *Quodlibeta quinque*, S. Defraia (ed), Grottaferrata, Collegium S. Bonaventurae, 2002.

Bibliography

Primary Literature

Aristotle, *The Complete Works of Aristotle*, 2 vols., trans. J. Barnes, Princeton, Princeton University Press, 1984.

Augustine, *De Genesi ad litteram libri duodecim*, J.-P. Migne (ed), Paris, Migne, 1865.

---

82   Though of course one can also consciously attend to one's body as well, whether diffusely or selectively.

83   I would like to thank my fellow participants in Berlin at the *Theories of Sense Perception in the 13th and 14th Centuries* conference for helpful comments on this paper as well as to the anonymous reviewer.

332 MARTIN

Augustine, *De musica liber VI: A Critical Edition with a Translation and an Introduction*, M. Jacobsson (ed), Stockholm, Almqvist & Wiksell International, 2002.

Augustine, *De quantitate animae, Sancti Aureli Augustini Opera*, sect. I, pars IV, W. Hormann (ed), Wien, Hoelder-Pichler-Tempsky, 1986.

Augustine, *De Trinitate*, W.J. Mountain (ed) with the assistance of F. Glorie, Turnhout, Brepols, 1968.

Avicenna, *Liber de anima seu Sextus de naturalibus*, S. van Riet (ed), vol. I, Leiden, Brill, 1972.

Peter John Olivi, "Epistola ad fratrem R.," S. Piron et al. (eds), *Archivum Franciscanum Historicum*, vol 91, 1998, pp. 33–65.

Peter John Olivi, "Questio de locutionibus angelorum," S. Piron (ed), *Oliviana* 1, 2003, http://olivianarevues.org/18.

Peter John Olivi, *Quaestiones in secundum librum Sententiarum*, 3 vols., B. Jansen (ed), Firenze, Collegium S. Bonaventurae, 1922–1926.

Peter John Olivi, *Quodlibeta quinque*, S. Defraia (ed), Grottaferrata, Collegium S. Bonaventurae, 2002.

Roger Bacon, *De multiplicatione specierum*, D.C. Lindberg (ed and trans.), *Roger Bacon's Philosophy of Nature*, Oxford, Clarendon Press, 1983.

Thomas Aquinas, *Summa theologiae*, P. Caramello (ed), Turin, Marietti, 1948–1950.

Secondary Literature

Adriaenssen, Han Thomas, "Peter John Olivi and Peter Auriol on Conceptual Thought," in R. Pasnau (ed), *Oxford Studies in Medieval Philosophy*, vol. 2, 2014, pp. 67–97.

Adriaenssen, Han Thomas, "Peter John Olivi on Perceptual Representation," *Vivarium*, vol. 49, no. 4, 2011, pp. 324–352.

Brower, Jeffery and Brower-Toland, Susan, "Aquinas on Mental Representation," *The Philosophical Review*, vol. 117, 2008, pp. 193–243.

Brower-Toland, Susan, "Olivi on Consciousness and Self-Knowledge," in R. Pasnau (ed), *Oxford Studies in Medieval Philosophy*, vol. 1, 2013, pp. 136–168.

Côté, Antoine, "L'objet et la cause de la conaissance selon Godefroid de Fontaines," *Freiburger Zeitschrift für Philosophie und Theologie*, vol. 54, no. 3, 2007, pp. 407–429.

Fisher, Kendall, "Thomas Aquinas on Hylomorphism and the *In-Act* Principle," *British Journal for the History of Philosophy*, vol. 25, issue 6, 2017, pp. 1053–1072.

Jacobs, John and Zeis, John, "Form and Cognition: How to Go Out of Your Mind," *Analytical Thomism*, vol. 80, no. 4, 1997, pp. 539–557.

Jansen, Bernard, *Die Erkenntnislehre Olivis*, Berlin, Dümmlers, 1921.

Knuuttila, Simo, "Aristotle's Theory of Perception and Medieval Aristotelianism," in S. Knuuttila and P. Kärkkäinen (eds), *Theories of Perception in Medieval and Early Modern Philosophy*, Dordrecht, Springer, 2008, pp. 1–22.

PETER JOHN OLIVI ON PERCEPTION

Lindberg, David, "Alhazen's Theory of Vision and Its Reception in the West," *Isis*, vol. 58, no. 3, 1967, pp. 321–341.

Martin, André, "Peter John Olivi on Reference-fixing," unpublished manuscript.

Menn, Stephen, "The Origins of Aristotle's Concept of *Energeia*: *Energeia* and *Dynamis*," *Ancient Philosophy*, vol. 14, 1994, pp. 73–114.

O'Daly, Gerard, *Augustine's Philosophy of Mind*, Berkeley, University of California Press, 1987.

Panaccio, Claude, "Aquinas on Intellectual Representation," in D. Perler (ed), *Intentionality in Ancient and Medieval Philosophy*, Leiden, Brill, 2001, pp. 185–201.

Pasnau, Robert, *Metaphysical Themes: 1274–1671*, Oxford, Oxford University Press, 2011.

Pasnau, Robert, "Olivi on the Metaphysics of Soul," *Medieval Philosophy and Theology*, vol. 6, 1997, pp. 109–132.

Pasnau, Robert, "Peter John Olivi, *Questions on the Sentences*, Book II: Questions 72 and 74," http://spot.colorado.edu/~pasnau/research/, accessed February 2019.

Pasnau, Robert, *Theories of Cognition in the Later Middle Ages*, Cambridge, Cambridge University Press, 1997.

Perler, Dominik, *Theorien der Intentionalität im Mittelalter*, Frankfurt am Main, Vittorio Klostermann, 2002.

Scarpelli-Cory, Therese, "Medieval Theories of Consciousness," in R. Cross and J.T. Paasch (eds), *The Routledge Companion to Medieval Philosophy*, London, Routledge, 2020.

Silva, José Filipe and Toivanen, Juhana, "The Active Nature of the Soul in Sense Perception: Robert Kilwardby and Peter Olivi," *Vivarium*, vol. 48, no. 3–4, 2010, pp. 245–278.

Smith, A. Mark, "Getting the Big Picture in Perspectivist Optics," *Isis*, vol. 72, no. 4, 1981, pp. 568–589.

Solère, Jean-Luc, "*Sine Qua Non* Causality and the Context of Durand's Early Theory of Cognition," in A. Speer, F. Retucci, T. Jeschke, and G. Guldentops (eds), *Durand of Saint-Pourçain and His "Sentences" Commentary: Historical, Philosophical, and Theological Issues*, Leuven, Peeters, 2014, pp. 185–227.

Spruit, Leen, *Species intelligibilis: From Perception to Knowledge*, vol. 1: *Classical Roots and Medieval Discussions*, Leiden, Brill, 1994.

Tachau, Katherine, *Vision and Certitude in the Age of Ockham: Optics, Epistemology, and the Foundations of Semantics 1250–1345*, Leiden, Brill, 1988.

Toivanen, Juhana, *Animal Consciousness: Peter Olivi on Cognitive Functions of the Sensitive Soul*, Jyväskylä, Jyväskylä University Printing, 2009.

Toivanen, Juhana, *Perception and the Internal Senses: Peter of John Olivi on the Cognitive Functions of the Sensitive Soul*, Leiden, Brill, 2013.

Tuominen, Miira, "On Activity and Passivity in Perception: Aristotle, Philoponus, and Pseudo-Simplicius," in J.F. Silva and M. Yrjönsuuri (eds), *Active Perception in the History of Philosophy: From Plato to Modern Philosophy*, Dordrecht, Springer, 2014, pp. 55–78.

Yrjönsuuri, Mikko, "The Soul as an Entity: Dante, Aquinas, and Olivi," in H. Lagerlund (ed), *Forming the Mind: Essays on the Internal Senses and the Mind/Body Problem from Avicenna to the Medical Enlightenment*, Dordrecht, Springer, 2007, pp. 59–92.

CHAPTER 12

Caesar in Bronze: Duns Scotus on the Sensation of Singular Accidents

Andrew LaZella

The story is often told that according to John Duns Scotus, individuals are intelligible *per se,* just not to us.[1] Whether due to punishment for sin, or simply the natural ordering of our powers, the mediation of the senses blocks our immediate acquaintance with individuals.[2] This account, whose plausibility I defend elsewhere, remains partial.[3] It remains partial insofar as it does not explain why our senses do not sense individual accidents. Unlike individual substances, accidents are the immediate objects of our sensory powers. So why don't the senses register individual accidents?

Understanding this fact requires a sustained treatment of how an object can move a cognitive power, and yet not move it according to the object's mode of being. Just as Caesar cast in bronze does not take on the mode of being of its medium – to employ an example from Scotus – so too our cognitive powers are assimilated to their agents, but not according to their modes of being. I will show that with sensation, which we should expect to sense singulars, this nonidentity belies a deeper metaphysical story. At its core resides a formal distinction between what Scotus calls the *ratio agentis* and the *ratio agendi.* This distinction is underwritten by his account of individuation as differentiation,

---

1 For references to the *Ordinatio* and *Lectura,* see John Duns Scotus, *Opera omnia,* C. Balic (ed), Vatican City, Vatican Polyglot Press, 1950-. For *In Metaph.,* see Scotus, *Quaestiones super libros Metaphysicorum Aristotelis,* R. Andrews, et al. (eds), St. Bonaventure, The Franciscan Institute, 1997. For *Q. de an.,* see *Quaestiones super secundum et tertium De anima,* B.C. Bazán et al. (eds), St. Bonaventure, The Franciscan Institute, 2006. Translations for *In Metaph.* will be from *Questions on the Metaphysics of Aristotle by John Duns Scotus,* 2 vols., trans. Girard J. Etzkorn and Allan B. Wolter, St. Bonaventure, The Franciscan Institute, 1997 and 1998. All other translations, unless otherwise noted, will be my own.
2 Scotus, *Ordinatio* II, d. 3, p. 2, q. 1, n. 290.
3 The current essay addresses unanswered questions from A. LaZella, *The Singular Voice of Being: John Duns Scotus and Ultimate Difference,* New York, Fordham University Press, 2019. In the Conclusion, I addressed our inability *in via* to cognize individual difference in general. I briefly noted the failure of our senses to cognize individual accidents, but did not offer an account for why this occurs. Here I attempt to give a full account.

© KONINKLIJKE BRILL NV, LEIDEN, 2020 | DOI:10.1163/9789004413030_013

which yields not just spatio-temporal instantiation, but irreplaceable singularity.

1 The Traditional Aristotelian View

Aristotle's claim from *De anima* that *senses sense individuals, the intellect understands universals* became something of a constant refrain in medieval theories of cognition.[4] Thus, to call it into question would be to challenge a basic truism. Despite its axiomatic force, however, Scotus questions and ultimately disputes both parts of the equation. While most commentaries address how the intellect can – at least in principle – cognize individuals, I will focus here on the first half of the equation: why the senses don't sense individual accidents.[5] This requires that we turn to the source, Aristotle's *De anima*.

In *De anima*, Aristotle argues that sensation depends upon an affection from without. He explains "[...] what actual sensation apprehends is individuals, while what knowledge apprehends is universals, and these are in a sense within the soul itself. That is why a man can think when he wants to but his sensation does not depend upon himself – a sensible object must be there."[6] Sensation must be of the individual because sensation is indexed to perceiving at a certain place and time. In *Posterior Analytics,* he argues that to perceive a universal would require grasping what is always and everywhere the case.[7] Rather, even if perception is of the object as qualified (*toioude*) and not of the individual itself (*tode ti*), we necessarily perceive a qualified individual at a certain place and time. We do not perceive the universal.

Consider further Aquinas's gloss:

> [...] the senses cognize the object as qualified, and not a this. For the senses' per se object is not substance and quiddity, but some sensible quality (e.g., hot, cold, white, black and other things of this kind). Qualities of this kind, however, affect singular substances existing in a determinate place and time. Thus it is necessary that that which is sensed is this something (i.e., singular substance) and that it be somewhere and now (i.e., in a determinate time and place).[8]

---

4   Aristotle, *De anima* II.5, 417b22–23. Translations of Aristotle will be from *The Collected Works of Aristotle*, 2 vols., J. Barnes (ed), Princeton, Princeton University Press, 1984.
5   LaZella, *The Singular Voice of Being*, pp. 182–187.
6   Aristotle, *De anima*, II.5.
7   Aristotle, *Posterior Analytics*, I.31.
8   "[...] sensus cognoscit aliquid tale, et non hoc. Non enim obiectum per se sensus est substantia et quod quid est, sed aliqua sensibilis qualitas, puta calidum, frigidum, album, nigrum, et

DUNS SCOTUS ON THE SENSATION OF SINGULAR ACCIDENTS

Our sensory-powers do not directly sense the individual substance or its *quiddity*, but rather its sensible qualities: white, black, hot, cold and so on. Qualities of this sort affect singular substances in a determinate location and existing at a specific time. Senses sense this something (*hoc aliquid*) or singular substance here and now.

Two factors must be highlighted. First, a purported real similarity between a cognitive power and its object underwrites this position.[9] As Aquinas further explains elsewhere: "Cognitive powers are of three grades. For one cognitive power is an act of a corporeal organ (i.e., sense). And the object of any sensitive power is a form existing in corporeal matter. And because matter of this kind is the principle of individuation, every power of the sensitive part cognizes only particulars."[10] Insofar as our sensory powers are exercised by material organs, Aquinas concludes that they cognize material (and therefore particular) objects. That is, the sensory powers as rooted in material organs can only cognize forms existing in material bodies. For example, the eyes don't see redness in general, but the redness of this apple, here and now. Thus, one sees an individual red, which brings us to the second point.

Second, Aquinas presupposes matter – or more precisely, designate matter – as the principle of individuation.[11] Matter serves to individuate both the substance and by extension its accidents; the latter – according to Aquinas – do not exist apart from their inherence in the former. Accidents are thus individuated by inhering in an individual substance, which is individuated through designate matter. Putting these two points together shows that as powers rooted in corporeal organs, sight sees the individual redness of this apple, hearing hears the individual C-flat note of this symphony, and taste tastes the individual peaty-ness of this glass of scotch. Scotus, however, will come to reject this line of reasoning. While it might be clear why we don't sense (or immediately sense) individual substances, it is unclear why Scotus would hold, counter to the venerable Aristotelian tradition, that we don't sense individual accidents.

---

    alia huiusmodi. Huiusmodi autem qualitates afficiunt singulares quasdam substantias in determinato loco et tempore existentes: unde necesse est quod id quod sentitur, sit hoc aliquid, scilicet singularis substantia, et sit alicubi et nunc, idest in determinato loco et tempore." Thomas Aquinas, *Expositio libri Posteriorum Analyticorum*, Rome, Leonine Commission, 1882, Book I, Lectio 42, Chapter 31.

9   Scotus, *Ordinatio* I, d. 3, p. 1, q. 3, n. 121. See also *Q. de an.*, q. 19, n. 16 and q. 22, nn. 26–27.

10   "Est autem triplex gradus cognoscitivae virtutis. Quaedam enim cognoscitiva virtus est actus organi corporalis, scilicet sensus. Et ideo obiectum cuiuslibet sensitivae potentiae est forma prout in materia corporali existit. Et quia huiusmodi materia est individuationis principium, ideo omnis potentia sensitivae partis est cognoscitiva particularium tantum." Aquinas, *Pars prima Summae theologiae, Opera omnia 4–5*, Rome, Ex Typographia Polyglotta, 1888–1889, I, q. 85, a. 1, resp. Hereafter *ST* I.

11   Scotus, *Q. de an.* q. 22, n. 43. Scotus seems to have in mind Aquinas, *ST* I, q. 86, a. 1, resp.

338 LAZELLA

2 Wayfarer Impediments

Scotus maintains that, in our current condition, we face an impediment to cognition, which no cause either natural or supernatural can overcome (*vincere non potest*).[12] He explains: "But what is that impediment? I respond: our intellect is not able immediately to move or be moved, unless it is first moved by something imaginable or an external sensible."[13] The intellect is not immediately moved by things, but requires the mediation of a natural action.

Our cognition differs from that of angels in an important respect: Their intellects immediately apprehend material singulars; our embodied cognition mediately apprehends such singulars through something begotten in the senses.[14] Scotus calls this "a material natural action." What is directly begotten in the senses are the sensible species of accidents. As a further consequence, not only are we not directly acquainted with material substances, so too we are not acquainted with them *as individuals*. But this is not because matter impedes intelligibility. Matter is not the principle of individuation according to Scotus.[15] Individuals are intelligible in their singularity, just not to us.[16]

Scotus speculates that even supernatural causes could not bypass this impediment. He hypothesizes that if Adam were immediately shown to him, he would not recognize that this was Adam.[17] He explains: "And in this way when I think of Adam, I do not understand the singular, because if he were shown to me intellectually, I would not know that it was he himself, but I would have a concept composed of 'man' and 'singular' [...]."[18] The issue here is not that Scotus has never seen Adam in the flesh. The same reasoning would pertain to any individual substance. Rather, unlike angels, we lack (at least currently) the cognitive mechanisms by which to register individual substances as individual.

---

12 Scotus, *Ordinatio* II, d. 3, p. 2, q. 1, n. 288.

13 "Sed quod est istud impedimentum? Respondeo: intellectus noster pro statu isto non est natus movere vel moveri immediate, nisi ab aliquo imaginabili vel 'sensibili extra' prius moveatur." Scotus, *Ordinatio* II, d. 3, p. 2, q. 1, n. 289.

14 Scotus, *In Metaph.* VII, q. 15, n. 26.

15 Scotus, *In Metaph.* VII, q. 13, nn. 40–47; *Lectura* II, d. 3, p. 1, q. 5; and *Ordinatio* II, d. 3, p. 1, q. 5.

16 Scotus, *In Metaph.* VII, q. 14, n. 26. See also *Q. de an.* q. 22, n. 17. For further discussion of this point, see LaZella, *The Singular Voice of Being*, pp. 182–187.

17 Scotus, *In Metaph.* VII, q. 13, nn. 156 and 163.

18 "[...] cum intelligo Adam, non intelligo singulare, quia si ipse intellectualiter mihi ostenderetur, nescirem quod ipse esset, sed intelligo conceptum compositum ex homine et singulari, quod est quoddam commune secundae intentionis. Talem etiam conceptum compositum habeo, intelligendo quodcumque singulare." Scotus, *In Metaph.* VII, q. 13, n. 165.

DUNS SCOTUS ON THE SENSATION OF SINGULAR ACCIDENTS

But what about accidents? Unlike the identification of individual substances, discerning between individual accidents should not be an issue.[19] Accidents *are* the immediate objects of our sensory powers. Their sensible species are begotten in the senses by the mediation of a natural action. Thus, whereas I might not be able to discriminate between this tree and that one, sight should be able to distinguish between this green and that one; hearing between this C-flat and that; or taste between this peatiness and that. But this is not the case.

Neither one of our cognitive powers (i.e., sense or intellect) can cognize the singular under its proper *ratio* of singularity.[20] Scotus proves this by means of the following argument. He invokes what Giorgio Pini has dubbed Scotus's Principle: "(SP) Something cannot be a *per se* object of a cognitive power unless that cognitive power is able to distinguish that thing from any other item of the same kind once all other items belonging to different kinds have been removed."[21] But, Scotus goes on to argue, neither the senses nor the intellect can distinguish between two singulars once all accidental distinctions such as place, figure, time, magnitude, color, and the rest have been removed. For example, we often individuate both substances and accidents by their time and place: Albert is the orange cat I saw last summer outside my house; I taste *this* peatiness here and now; I heard that C-flat note at the Berlin Symphony in March 2017, etc. But once these have been removed, my means of individual discrimination vanish.

SP asserts that a cognitive power must be able to identify its proper object and to distinguish it from others like it.[22] The fact that we can err regarding some aspect or element of an object indicates that that element is *per accidens* with respect to the power's object.[23] If one redness can be mistaken for another, then whatever we use to individuate them falls outside the scope of the proper object.

If the senses can err in registering their objects qua individual, then (per SP) the *per se* object of sensory cognition excludes individuality. Scotus states:

> The most distinct intellection of the singular seems to be of some intention [concept] which the intellect knows distinctly; but positing such

---

19   G. Pini, "Scotus on Knowing and Naming Natural Kinds," *History of Philosophy Quarterly*, vol. 26, July 2009, p. 256.

20   Scotus, *Q. de an.* q. 22, n. 26.

21   Pini, "Scotus on the Objects of Cognitive Acts," *Franciscan Studies*, vol. 66, 2008, p. 296. The principle is most clearly expressed in *In Metaph.* VII, q. 15, n. 20.

22   Pini, "Scotus on the Objects of Cognitive Acts," p. 297.

23   Scotus, *In Metaph.* VII, q. 13, n. 158.

precisely, and prescinding from [all] time differences and the various degrees of intensity as well as all other accidents ['befalling'] such an intention, it does not seem that our intellect knows how to distinguish or differentiate this intention from the intention of any other singular of the same species that may be shown to it [...].[24]

The problem is that neither the intellect nor the senses (as he goes on to argue) can distinguish between two intentions of the same species. For example, my ears can't discern between this C-flat and that one; rather our most distinct intention is of the species. Therefore, we don't sense (or understand) the individual *per se*.

Scotus invokes the following thought-experiment to defend this claim:

[T]his whiteness may be put in the same place as that whiteness, and this remains this and that remains that, because this is not this by the fact that it is in this place. Does the sense discern that in the same place there are two whitenesses, if they are equally intense? It does not.[25]

As the case of two whitenesses of equal intensity shows, our senses can't discern between the two individuals qua individual. Rather, we might individuate them *de facto* based on spatial location; but spatial location does not individuate them. Thus, if the one white were swapped out for the other while I turned away for a moment (or, more radically, if God puts two in the exact same location) I would not discern that *this* white had been replaced by *that* one.

It is crucial to recognize exactly what Scotus means by the *per se* object of the senses. Normally we don't encounter *just redness* or *just peatiness* floating on their own like the smile of the Cheshire Cat. Rather, we see the waxy smoothness of the red apple sitting on the desk across the room. I see such an accident as part of a bundle, which Scotus refers to as a *simul totum*. Our

---

24   "[...] distinctissima intellectio singularis videtur esse alicuius intentionis quam intellectus distincte cognoscit; sed posita illa praecise, amota differentia temporis, amoto alio et alio gradu intentionis, et sic de omnibus accidentibus illi intentioni, non videtur quod intellectus sciat distinguere vel discernere – si ostendatur sibi – a quacumque alia intentione singulari eiusdem speciei; ergo etc." Scotus, *In Metaph.* VII, q. 15, n. 20. See also *Lectura* II, d. 3, p. 1, q. 1, n. 24; and *Ordinatio* II, d. 3, p. 1, q. 1, n. 21.

25   "[H]aec albedo ponatur simul in loco cum illa albedine, manet ergo haec et haec, illa et illa, quia haec non est haec per hoc esse. Numquid sensus discernit in eodem loco duas esse albedines numero, si sint aeque intensae? Non." Scotus, *In Metaph.* VII, q. 15, n. 20. See also *Lectura* II, d. 3, p. 1, q. 1, n. 24; and *Ordinatio* II, d. 3, p. 1, q. 1, n. 21.

DUNS SCOTUS ON THE SENSATION OF SINGULAR ACCIDENTS

perception of such a bundle is always indexed to a "here and now," factors we often use to distinguish otherwise indistinguishable items such as office furniture, squirrels, or drops of rain. I might not be able to distinguish this from that beyond the fact that this one is here now and that one is over there.

The purpose of Scotus's thought experiment is to bracket all those additional (or *per accidens*) elements from the *per se* object to ask whether we still can individuate it. For example, if I exclude texture, time, shape, and location from the red I see, am I able to distinguish it from another of equal intensity? Scotus's response is no. Bracketing such accidents from consideration is not an elaborate bait and switch to make his case, but stems from his understanding of individuation.

Accidents cannot be individuated by other accidents, but must be individuated by some intrinsically positive principle (See section 3 below). Thus, although we may use, for example, time and space to discern a patch of redness, time and space are not its principles of individuation. They often serve as reliable indicators, but, as the possibility of bilocation suggests, one and the same individual might be in two places at once![26]

What is it that sensory cognition is missing? Here Scotus provides us with our first clue:

> [I say] that the individual difference is not known to anyone in this life, generally speaking. Proof of this is that then its difference from any other would also be known, and thus one could not err about any other shown to one intellectually without judging it [correctly] to be other. But this is false in the case of any other that is completely similar to this [...].[27]

That is, in order to cognize an individual, we must be able to discern its difference. We must cognize whatever determines it to its proper grade of singularity.[28]

If I grasped the individual difference of an accident, then I could enumerate each redness; but for now, such a precise enumeration is not possible. At best, we individuate accidents by means of external factors of differentiation such

---

26 Scotus, *In Metaph.* VII, q. 13, n. 168. For the argument that we don't sense the number of proper sensibles, see *In Metaph.* VII, q. 15, n. 21.

27 "[D]ifferentia individualis a nullo nota est in hac vita communiter. Cuius probatio est: quia tunc nota esset differentia eius ad quodcumque aliud, et ita non posset errare de quocumque alio sibi intellectualiter ostenso quin iudicaret illud esse aliud. Sed hoc est falsum de alio omnino simili [...]." Scotus, *In Metaph.* VII, q. 13, n. 158.

28 Scotus, *Q. de an.* q. 22, n. 27.

as time and space. But the question of why our sensory powers don't grasp accidents in their individuality remains.

3   Possible Explanations

One might answer that we can't distinguish accidents because we can't distinguish the substances in which they inhere. For example, because two apples remain indistinguishable as individuals to both my senses and my intellect, therefore my powers lack the means to distinguish between their accidental properties (e.g., this redness versus that one). To discern between the individual rednesses, one would need to cognize the individual apple-substances in which they inhere. Thus, although the accidents are immediate objects of my sensory powers, I do not sense them *qua this* because I lack such acquaintance with the substances in which they inhere and which account for their individuation.

But this argument does not work for Scotus. As foreshadowed above, accidents are individuated on their own apart from their inherence in substances. Scotus explains that there is a categorial coordination for each category beginning with the highest genus and ending with individuals. In other words, each category is determined (i.e., differentiated from genus into species) and ultimately individuated apart from the coordination of any other category. There is no cross-categorial pollination. Scotus states: "In every such precise coordination [i.e., category] all that pertains to that concatenation can be found there apart from any other ordered arrangement. Furthermore, each item of one ordered set is different from those of the other ordered set."[29] Everything required to move from Substance to this apple, for example, must be found in the categorial coordination of substance.

The same is true for the various categories of accidents. Against the view that only quantity is individuated *per se* and the rest of the accidents are individuated through quantity, Scotus explains:

---

29   "[…] in omni coordinatione praecise accepta inveniuntur omnia illius coordinationis, circumscripto quocumque alterius coordinationis, – praterea, quidlibet unius coordinationis est diversum a quocumque alterius coordinationis." Scotus, *Lectura* II, d. 3, a. 1, q. 4, n. 91; see also *Ordinatio* II, d. 3, p. 1, q. 4, n. 89. For the translation, see Scotus, *Early Oxford Lecture on Individuation,* trans. A.B. Wolter, St. Bonaventure, The Franciscan Institute, 2005.

DUNS SCOTUS ON THE SENSATION OF SINGULAR ACCIDENTS   343

> [...] no accident is formally singular through something of another gen-
> era [...] therefore, quality, even when it is in quantity, is not 'this' formally
> through quantity; therefore, if it is a cause of the singularity of quality,
> even proximate but extrinsic, quality can be singular without that extrin-
> sic cause.[30]

Although a quality (e.g., this red) never exists without quantity, quantity does
not individuate it. Furthermore, while *this* or any other red might in fact always
inhere in some individual substance, the redness of this apple is individuated
independently of the apple itself. Our failure to distinguish between individual
substances thus cannot explain our failure to distinguish between their individual accidents.

Perhaps, one might say, that we don't cognize accidents qua individual because accidents can operate only via some individual substance. For example,
this red might inhere in this or that apple (or even thot carpet). But I can only
perceive the redness of this red insofar as it cooperates with some individual
substantial agent (whether this one or that). And because I don't know such
individual substances, therefore my senses don't register individual accidents.

This line of reasoning, however, also doesn't explain our failure to perceive
individual accidents. As Richard Cross has shown with respect to Scotus's account of the Eucharist, not only can individual accidents migrate from substance to substance; they also can exist (and presumably act) apart from any
substance whatsoever.[31] (More on this below.) Thus, what we will come to call
their condition of acting should not require grasping their inherence in this or
that substance.[32]

If we don't sense singulars, then what do we sense? What is this redness that
my eyes see here and now if not (well), this redness here and now? The answer,
as we will see, is repeatable commonalities (section 5 below). The eyes cannot
discriminate between this red and that; the ears between this C-flat and that;
the tongue between this peatiness and that. Rather, the senses detect only a
vague commonality such that were two patches of red swapped before my
eyes, I would not be able to register the substitution. Although the most forceful

---

30   "[...] nullum accidens est singulare formaliter per aliqua alterius generis [...] qualitas ergo,
      etiam quando est in quantitate, non est 'haec' per quantitatem formaliter; igitur si est
      causa, etiam proxima sed extrinseca, singularitatis ipsius qualitatis, qualitas potest esse
      singularis sine ista causa extrinseca." Scotus, *Ordinatio* IV, q. 12, p. 1, q. 2, n. 120.
31   R. Cross, *Duns Scotus*, Oxford, Oxford University Press, 1999, p. 142.
32   Scotus, *Ordinatio* IV, d. 12, p. 2, q. unica, nn. 280–282.

344 LAZELLA

sound may strike my ears or the most beautiful red may entice my eyes, its character is repeatable. But if this is the case, why should we believe in individual accidents at all?

4 Why Believe in Individual Accidents?

The question here is why not maintain (as do opponents of contemporary trope theory) that accidental features are common and repeatable, universals not particulars. My point is not to weigh the relevance of Scotus's account vis-à-vis these contemporary debates. Rather, I seek only to acknowledge that there are good reasons to assert that accidental features are common and repeatable without any inherent thisness. And given what we have said so far about Scotus's account, namely his rejection of Aristotle's axiom plus our propensity to err in discerning singulars, it appears that he might embrace such a conclusion. So why continue to posit individual accidents?

The view that accidents are individual goes back to Aristotle's *Categories* and this position was widely accepted throughout the Middle Ages.[33] There has been, however, a shift away from it in recent times.[34] For example, in his *Nominalism & Realism,* D.M. Armstrong reviews the position of G.F. Stout as somewhat of an outlier in twentieth-century debates, a view he dubs "Particularism."[35] Stout held that two things that are both red (e.g., a curtain and a carpet) have two numerically distinct rednessess. This redness (of the curtain) is not that redness of the carpet. (He correctly adds we are not merely talking about two shades of redness.) Each red inheres in its respective subject, although it cannot be said of it. As Armstrong's discussion suggests, Stout stands as one of the few heirs to a waning Aristotelian tradition of admitting individual accidents.

Against Particularism, Armstrong first argues that there is no reason why the same bundle can't contain the same property twice. That is, if two properties resemble each other exactly, how is it that the bundle doesn't instantiate the same particular property twice? This problem is called "piling."[36] Piling is the possibility of multiple similar tropes being piled up, one upon another.

---

33 Aristotle, *Categories*, 2.

34 J.J.E. Gracia, *Individuality: An Essay on the Foundations of Metaphysics*, Albany, State University of New York Press, 1988, p. 162.

35 D.M. Armstrong, *Nominalism and Realism: Universals and Scientific Realism*, vol. 1, Cambridge, Cambridge University Press, 1978, pp. 77–88.

36 J. Shaffer, "The Individuation of Tropes," *Australasian Journal of Philosophy*, vol. 79, no. 2, 2001, pp. 247–259.

For example, not just one, but n-red tropes account for the apple's redness. Opponents of trope theory maintain that there is no causal or empirical difference between a single trope and a pile of them.[37] Against the argument from piling, anti-Particularism can simply maintain that the same particular property does not occur multiple times, but instead, there is simply one and the same universal property.

A second argument holds that Particularism offers no grounds to distinguish this particular property from that one apart from the former's universal characteristics. The yellowness of this lemon, apart from the universal property of being this shade of yellow, does not explain its distinction from the redness of this tomato. Armstrong concludes that objective properties are not individual. The redness of the carpet and the redness of the curtains are not two numerically distinct rednesses. Rather, redness is a common (or, in Armstrong's terms, a universal) property that inheres in both.

Along with these two objections, we must consider the related problem of swapping.[38] Swapping – as the image suggests – would occur if, for example, $redness_1$ (which is here) were to change places with $redness_2$ (which is there). As with piling, there seems to be no causal or empirical difference pre-swap and post-swap. Whether and to what extent Particularism can defend the existence of tropes is not our concern here. Rather, given the plausibility of rejecting the existence of individual accidents, we might ask: Due to our lack of cognition of accidents qua individual, might not Scotus embrace such a view?[39] That is, the senses don't sense singulars because they sense accidents and accidents are repeatable by nature. So why posit individual accidents at all?

The answer relies on what Scotus believes we can infer about the metaphysical structure of the world. What we can deduce about the conditions of the world at the time of sensing – what Scotus calls the *ratio agentis* – remains formally distinct from the content given by the act – the *ratio agendi*. While we can infer the necessary condition that some individual must cause such an act, which one does remains contingent. The final two sections will show that the formal reasons for sensing, or that by which a power is assimilated to its object, remains non-identical to the object's real mode of existence. This will provide

---

37 A.-S. Maurin, "Tropes," in E.N. Zalta (ed), *The Stanford Encyclopedia of Philosophy* (Winter 2016 Edition), https://plato.stanford.edu/archives/win2016/entries/tropes/, accessed July 2017.

38 D.M. Armstrong, *Universals: An Opinionated Introduction*, Boulder, Westview Press, 1989, pp. 131–132.

39 R. Cross, *The Physics of Duns Scotus: The Scientific Context of a Theological Vision*, Oxford, Oxford University Press, 2007, p. 115.

an answer to the two questions on the table: "Why believe in individual accidents at all?" and "Why don't our senses cognize accidents qua individual?"

5   The Principle of Agendi-Assimilandi

To answer these questions, recall that for Aquinas, what secured the link between our sensory powers and the object qua individual was their shared materiality. The *per se* object of the senses was the form existing in matter, or more properly speaking the qualified individual. Thus, vision sees, for example, this redness of this apple. Our sensory powers do not err regarding individuals, it seems, because both the sensory power and the object are material and matter individuates.

Scotus rejects this line of reasoning on several grounds. While we might only remind ourselves that he rejects matter as a principle of individuation, we must treat his argument that one cannot infer a certain mode of being in the object based on the mode of being of the power.[40] The fact that our sensory powers have a material basis does not warrant positing a similar mode of being for their object. Just as a bronze statue of Caesar does not take on his mode of being, so too our cognitive powers are assimilated to their agents, but not according to their modes of being.

Scotus explains:

> Now it is the case that the cognitive power, when it actually cognizes something, becomes similar to it. [...] But to conclude from this fact that the intellect itself naturally and in itself has a mode of being that is similar to that of the object or the other way around is to commit the fallacy of the consequent and of figure of speech just as the following inference is invalid: The bronze becomes similar to Caesar because it is made similar through the form that it gets. Therefore, the bronze has in itself a mode of being that is similar to Caesar's mode of being.[41]

---

40   Scotus, *Ordinatio* I, d. 3, n. 120.

41   "Nunc autem est quod potentia cognoscens assimilatur cognito. [...] sed ex hoc concludere ipsum intellectum, in se naturaliter, habere modum essendi similem modo essendi obiecti, vel e converso, est facere fallaciam accidentis et figurae dictionis; - sicut non sequitur 'aes assimilatur Caesari quia per figuram inductam assimilatur, ergo aes in se habet similem modum essendi modo essendi Caesaris.'" Scotus, *Ordinatio* I, d. 3, p. 1, q. 3, n. 122. The translation is from Scotus, *On Being and Cognition: Ordinatio 1.3*, J. van den Bercken (ed and trans.), New York, Fordham University Press, 2016.

DUNS SCOTUS ON THE SENSATION OF SINGULAR ACCIDENTS 347

This image trades on the fact that powers, like statues, can represent their object intentionally without really being the same as their objects in their modes of existence. Thus, we cannot infer an object's mode of being based on the power that cognizes it, or vice-versa. Rather, the power intends its proper object, but not necessarily according to a shared mode of being (*modus essendi*). The argument "the sensory powers become similar to their object through a received form; therefore, the sensory powers have the same mode of being as their object" commits the fallacy of the consequent. Scotus compares this to concluding that a bronze statue of Caesar has the same mode of being as the human it represents because the two share a formal likeness.[42]

The representational capacity of the senses does not include singularity as part of its proper object. (We will see the importance of Scotus's choice of the term "singularity" below.) As we have discussed, if it did, our senses could identify two distinct individuals without error. Scotus explains the reason why this is the case.[43] He states:

> It is well said that singularity is a reason or condition of an agent [ratio vel condicio agentis], but not a reason of acting [ratio agendi]. Rather, the latter is the formal nature which is similar in diverse things. And this is the account [ratio] which the generated species represents, not however the condition of the agent.[44]

Here we find a crucial distinction between the *ratio* or *principium agendi* and the *ratio* or *principium agentis*. Whereas the former encompasses only the necessary conditions for assimilation, the latter marks the object in its full grade of being. To explain why our cognitive powers do not grasp the *principium agentis*, Scotus states:

> The cause of this is the principle of acting-assimilation [principium agendi-assimilandi], because an agent intends to assimilate a patient to it, and this is especially true for cognition which comes to be through assimilation. But the principle of assimilation is not the singular as singular. Rather, the singular is more the principle of distinguishing (because singulars differ in their singularity). It is more the common nature that is

---

42 Scotus, *Ordinatio* I, d. 3, p. 1, q. 3, n. 120.
43 Scotus, *Q. de an.*, q. 22, n. 27.
44 "[...] singularitas bene est ratio vel condicio agentis, sed non est ratio agendi, immo formalis natura quae est similis in diversis; et haec est ratio quam debet representare species genita, non autem condicio agentis." Scotus, *Q. de an.*, q. 22, n. 32. See also *Ordinatio* I, d. 3, q. 1, p. 3, n. 380.

the principle of assimilation in which singulars agree. Therefore, the singular as singular is not the principle of acting in either the senses or in the intellect.[45]

Assimilation works by likening multiple things to one another on account of a common basis.[46] The principle of assimilation functions as a sort of barter principle by which different or dissimilar things are made similar or the same by means of a common term.[47] In the case at hand, cognition occurs by means of an agent assimilating a patient to it by means of a shared species, sensible or intelligible.

The *ratio agentis* eludes assimilation, however, insofar as it is a principle of individual differentiation, or singularity. Singularity here means something more than being a particular instance; rather, as we shall see, it indicates radical uniqueness.[48] Singularity remains unassimilable insofar as it shares no common ground by which it can be likened to something else. This condition, however, must be inferred from what we know about the metaphysical structure of the world. This opens a gap between the intentional object and the real object,[49] a distinction whose extra-mental basis Scotus explains by his formal distinction.

Briefly stated, the formal distinction is a more than rational distinction between two formalities or realities within one and the same thing.[50] In the case at hand, we are dealing with one and the same individual (i.e., substance or accident). But we can distinguish between the individual's common essence and its individual difference; this distinction finds ground in real and irreducible formalities or realities comprising the thing itself. Following from this,

---

45   "Cuius causa est principium agendi-assimilandi, quia agens intendit assimilare patiens sibi, et hoc specialiter est verum in cognitione quae fit per assimilationem; sed principium assimilandi non est singulare ut singulare est, immo magis [singulare est principium] distinguendi (quia in singularitate differunt [singularia]), sed magis natura communis [est principium assimilandi] in qua singularia conveniunt; igitur singulare ut singulare non est principium agendi nec in sensu nec in intellectu." Scotus, *Q. de an.*, q. 22, n. 27.

46   See, for example, Aquinas, *Liber de veritate catholicae fidei contra errores Infidelium seu Summa contra Gentiles*, C. Pera (ed), Turin, Marietti, 1961–1967, II. 46.

47   For further discussion of this issue, see also Deborah Black, "Avicenna's 'Vague Individual' and Its Impact on Medieval Latin Philosophy," in R. Wisnovsky, F. Wallis, C. Fraenkel, and J.C. Fumo (eds), *Vehicles of Transmission, Translation, and Transformation in Medieval Textual Culture*, Turnhout, Brepols, 2011, pp. 259–292, at 280.

48   Section 6 explains why. Prior to making this case below, I continue to use the more neutral "individual."

49   Scotus, *In Metaph.* I, q. 6, nn. 62–63; VII, q. 15, n. 37. *Ordinatio* I, d. 3, p. 1, q. 4, n. 238.

50   Scotus, *Ordinatio* I, d. 2, pars 2, q. 4, nn. 388–410.

DUNS SCOTUS ON THE SENSATION OF SINGULAR ACCIDENTS 349

three questions arise: First, what is the proper or *per se* object of sensation? Second, why believe in individual accidents at all? And third, if we do admit individual accidents, can Scotus avoid Armstrong's three objections?

In response to the first question, Scotus holds that the proper object of sensation is a common nature. For example, I see red, but not this red; I hear C-flat, but not this C-flat; and so on. As we saw in the passage above,[51] the species generated in the senses represents only the condition of acting, not the condition of the agent. Scotus parses the former as "the formal nature as similar in diverse things." Thus, although the things themselves might be diverse, as objects of our sensory powers they are assimilated by means of a shared likeness. Scotus claims that what I see, for example, is not this particular red, but just red.[52] This red of apple A could be swapped with that red of apple B and my sensory powers would not discern the difference. The proper object of our sensory powers enjoys a less-than-numerical unity, which Scotus dubs a commonality.

In his technical parlance, this means that the object is not yet universal, although it serves as the foundation for universals.[53] Scotus explains:

> [...] The unity of the object of the sense is not some universal unity in actuality, but is something that is one by a prior unity – namely a real unity – by which the intellect is moved to cause something common to be abstracted from this and that singular, and from singulars that are of the same species more than from singulars that are of different species. Otherwise, the universal would be a mere fiction. For apart from any act of the intellect, this white object agrees more with that white object than with something of a different genus.[54]

If the intentional object of sensation were already universal, cognition would not be about real things. Cognition would be fictitious because there are no universals *in rerum natura*.[55] Despite the object's aptitude to be predicated of several (i.e., to be universal), this is only a remote aptitude. It requires the

---

51 Scotus, *Q. de an.*, q. 22, n. 32.
52 Scotus, *In Metaph.* VII, q. 13, n. 167.
53 Scotus, *In Metaph.* I, q. 6, n. 57.
54 "[...] unitas obiecti sensus non est aliqua unitas universalis in actu, sed est aliquid unum aliqua unitate priore – scilicet reali – a qua movetur intellectus ad causandum aliquid commune abstractum ab hoc singulari et illo eiusdem speciei magis quam diversarum. Aliter universale esset fictio solum. Circumscripto enim intellectu, istud album magis convenit cum alio quam cum aliquo alterius generis." Scotus, *In Metaph.* I, q. 6, n. 22.
55 Scotus, *In Metaph.* I, q. 6, nn. 23–25; and *In Metaph.* VII, q. 15, n. 30.

consideration of the intellect to bring it into proximate aptitude. The object of sense-cognition is one object as it exists in an individual, but is itself repeatable.

While each act of sensation is about one singular only, this mode of being cannot be reflected in the content of the act. Scotus states: "Although each sense perception is about one singular, nevertheless, it is not about it as its first object, but about that one object as it exists in an individual. Otherwise, the potency and its act would not have the same object."[56] Scotus distinguishes how an act of sensation can be about a unified object as it exists in an individual without being about that singular individual itself. But does this mean our sensory powers don't cognize the individual at all? I will return to this issue below in considering the role of intuitive cognition in this process.

For the moment, what concerns us is the claim that sensation does not have the individual as its object, but rather the common nature existing in the individual. Scotus justified this claim by stating "otherwise, the potency and its act would not have the same object." Here, he seems to have in mind the following.[57] Every act of sense perception is about one singular only. (That's what exists in the world and what stimulates my sense organs; universals don't exist *in re*.) Many acts are about many singulars. (The acts are repeatable.) But these many acts stem from the same potency.[58] If, however, each sense perception had *its* own singular as its object, Scotus argues, the potency and the act could not have the same object. This is because the act would be indexed to this singular.[59] If in seeing red, I saw this red *qua this,* such an act would not share the same object with other acts of vision. Each act would have a unique and singular object and to speak of them as acts of a sensory power would be a misnomer.[60]

Underlying this account of sense perception is the metaphysical assumption that the world is populated by individual substances and accidents whose differentiation as individuals is not a mere continuation of their essence. Multiple singular objects are not mere tokens of the same type. Thus, unlike those for whom individuation adds no additional reality to the essence, individual

---

56   "Licet autem quodlibet sentire sit tantum circa singulare, non tamen ut circa primum obiectum, sed circa illud unum in singulari. Aliter non idem obiectum potentiae et actus eius." Scotus, *In Metaph.* 1. q. 6, n. 46. Scotus compares singularity as a *sine qua non* condition of the agent to quantity. *In Metaph.* 1. q. 6, nn. 62–63.

57   This issue often arises for Scotus in treating art and production. *In Metaph.* 1, q. 5, n. 18.

58   Scotus, *In Metaph.* 1, q. 6, n. 46.

59   Scotus, *In Metaph.* 1, q. 6, n. 62.

60   Scotus, *In Metaph.* 1, q. 6, n. 54.

DUNS SCOTUS ON THE SENSATION OF SINGULAR ACCIDENTS   351

difference is formally distinct from the nature and adds a real grade of being.[61] Given the formal distinction between a nature in this and its individual difference, the nature before me only happens to be caused by this one. But if the act intended the object qua singular, rather than qua its assimilable commonality, each act would not only differ, but would be diverse. This is because, as will be shown in the following section, individual differences are primarily diverse from one another. Both the power and act can find the real unity of the common nature as their *per se* and primary object.[62] But why assume that sense-perception concerns singulars in the first place? This leads us to the second point.

As we have seen, every act of sense perception is about one singular only. But the singular of which I have sensory cognition (i.e., *ratio agentis*) remains formally distinct from that which I sense (i.e., *ratio agendi*). Even if we reason to this conclusion based on metaphysical inference, why not assume that sensible accidents are multiple instantiations of a universal? This seems to be the more economical solution.

Scotus posits individual accidents based on what we can infer about the metaphysical conditions of the world.[63] Accidents operate as necessary causal components insofar as they function as principles of acting, principles of knowing substance, and as the objects of sense. For example, the heat of the hot body heats; the color of the fruit is visible; and the quantity of the body is a being. But, he states: "It's absurd to call something a principle of acting, either real action in matter or intentional action in the senses or intellect, and yet [deny] that thing some formal entity: I thereby might as well claim that a chimera acted or was sensed."[64] Accidents have their own entity and unity irreducible to that of the substance in which they inhere.[65] This extends to their individuation, which cannot be derived from substance. Otherwise, Scotus argues, a numerically identical accident could be corrupted and regenerated,

---

61   Scotus, *In Metaph.* VII, q. 13, n. 166.

62   Scotus, *In Metaph.* I, q. 6, nn. 22 and 46.

63   Scotus, *Ordinatio* IV, d. 12, p. 1, q. 1, n. 59. See Cross, *The Physics of Duns Scotus,* pp. 95–96. We have knowledge of our own soul and mental acts. *Ordinatio* I, d. 3, p. 1, q. 4, nn. 238–239.

64   "Sed trufa est dicere aliquid esse principium agendi vel actione reali in materiam vel actione intentionali in sensum vel intellectum, et non habere aliquam entitatem formalem: ita enim dicerem chimaeram agere vel sentire." Scotus, *Ordinatio* IV, d. 12, p. 1, q. 1, n. 59. Cross, *The Physics of Duns Scotus,* pp. 95–96.

65   Accidents – at least quality and quantity – are not essentially or *per se* inherent. Scotus, *Ordinatio* IV, d. 12, p. 1, q. 1, nn. 40–43, 53.

352 LAZELLA

such as when a body becomes hot, then cold, then hot again.[66] The two hot-ness-es would be numerically identical.

In principle at least, accidents must be able to operate independently of any substance.[67] In the case of the Eucharist, for example, the accidents continue to operate even when the original substance has been destroyed.[68] Scotus thus can avoid Aquinas's position such that accidents retain their individuated be-ing insofar as they previously acquired it from inhering in a substance, even though they no longer inhere in it.[69]

With respect to the third point from above, Scotus dedicates an entire ques-tion of the *Metaphysics* responding to the piling objection. He asks: Can nu-merically distinct accidents of the same species be in the same subject?[70] His answer: Imagine Agent A and Agent B encounter Patient X.[71] For example, A and B are hot agents, and X is in potency to be heated. Also, A and B are equi-potent and simultaneously encounter X. Does X receive numerically distinct accidents, one from each of its agents? Scotus speculates: "[…] the mobile can-not be moved simultaneously by two motions so as to end up with two [acci-dental forms] of the same species, although there are two actions."[72] Patient X does not receive two numerically distinct forms of heat.

We might return to the principle of agent-assimilation to explain why the *ratio* of each agent is not registered in Patient X. The principle of action is as-similation. Nature does not move according to the grade of singularity insofar as individuation differentiates.[73] This grade is not a principle of action, but limits the principle of action. Accidents are not piled because even though the accident is not individuated by its reception into a subject, nevertheless the subject is in potency to only one such accidental form.[74] Thus, two hot agents do not introduce two heats into the patient, but rather act in concert to intro-duce a single heat.[75]

Against Armstrong's second argument, we can say that there is a real and objective foundation for distinguishing the yellowness of this lemon from the

---

66   Scotus, *In Metaph.* V, q. 7, n. 43.
67   Scotus, *Ordinatio* IV, q. 12, p. 1, q. 1, n. 90.
68   Scotus, *Ordinatio* IV, d. 12, p. 3, a. 2, q. unica, n. 494.
69   See Aquinas, *ST* III, q. 77, a, 1, ad 3. Cross, *Duns Scotus*, p. 142.
70   Scotus, *In Metaph.* V, q. 7.
71   Scotus, *In Metaph.* V, q. 7, n. 83.
72   Scotus, *In Metaph.* V, q. 7, n. 84.
73   Scotus, *In Metaph.* VII, 15, n. 22.
74   Scotus, *In Metaph.* VII, 15, nn. 92–97.
75   Scotus, *In Metaph.* VII, 15, n. 98.

DUNS SCOTUS ON THE SENSATION OF SINGULAR ACCIDENTS   353

redness of that tomato in the individuals themselves.[76] But this foundation is not qua their individual differences, but qua their common natures. Scotus does not capitulate to Armstrong's view, however, because such an object – what Scotus calls a less-than-numerical unity – is not yet universal. Sense perception is about one thing which has the sort of unity that is the foundation for the unity of the universal. But color as sensed cannot itself be a universal. This is because – and here is where Scotus's view sharply departs from Armstrong's – the actual condition of an object (i.e., *condicio agentis*) is qua individual. Its condition of singularity cannot be completely separated from it.

Against the swapping objection, Scotus thus can maintain that even though we cannot cognize or discern the difference pre-swap and post-swap, the difference is *per se* intelligible. And given his arguments for the *per se* individuation of accidents, despite making no discernable difference to us, the swapping of individual accidents makes a difference in itself. In the end, the formal distinction between the *ratio agentis* and *agendi* provides cognition with an objective foundation of common natures. Cognition need not choose between adequate and objective representation, on the one hand, and mere fictional subjective thinking on the other.

6   Ultimate Individual Difference

Perhaps more than anyone else, Pini has shown how we must not confuse the objects of our cognitive acts with the study of things themselves, the latter which can be reached only by metaphysical inference.[77] In particular, Pini shows how Scotus can maintain the objectivity of our cognitive objects such that they latch on to real aspects of the world, and not mere subjective impressions, without grasping things qua individual.[78] The question Pini leaves unanswered, however, is what explains the failure of sensory cognition to register individual difference.

To the extent that he addresses this issue, he argues that it is endemic to the senses as such. He states:

> The senses are constitutionally focused on natures. They are not fine-grained enough to pick out individuals. Haeccitas non sentitur, Scotus says – and this is not just a contingent fact. No matter how developed our

---

76   Cf. Armstrong, *Nominalism and Realism*, p. 87.
77   Pini, "Scotus on the Objects of Cognitive Acts," p. 306.
78   Pini, p. 308.

senses may have been in the state of innocence, they still missed the individual differentia, probably because for Scotus the individual differentia does not have anything to do with matter.[79]

Pini's musing that our senses miss the individual difference because the individual differentia does not have anything to do with matter requires explanation, which unfortunately he does not offer.

A full explanation, I maintain, requires treating individual differences as what Scotus calls "ultimate differences." Briefly stated, an ultimate difference for Scotus is pure difference; it is a difference without a difference. He states: "An ultimate difference is so called while it does not have a difference [specifying it further] because it cannot be analyzed in a quidditative and a qualitative concept or in a determinable and determining concept. Its concept is only qualitative [...]."[80] Ultimate differences are expressed by a simply-simple concept that – insofar as it must explain difference – shares nothing in common with other ultimate differences besides their functional roles.

As we have seen, action aims at assimilation by means of a common term. As we have also seen, accidents are individuated on their own (i.e., apart from substance or other accidents). Furthermore, what individuates them is not matter, but rather ultimate individual differences (often dubbed *haecceitates*).[81] Such ultimate differences are primarily diverse from any other ultimate difference and from the quidditative terms they modify. For example, the differentiator of this red shares nothing in common either with the differentiator of that red *or* with the common reality of redness. (Recall, they are formally distinct.) Drawing these points together we can see that accidents cannot be cognized as individual because their principles of individuation are ultimate differences.

Ultimate differences instead must be grasped by simply-simple qualitative concepts. Simple-simplicity means that the concept cannot be resolved into more basic concepts; it is elemental. Qualitative concepts are ones that modify quidditative concepts; they themselves are determinative lacking any *whatness* apart from that which they determine. Our sensory powers do not cognize

---

79 Pini, pp. 309–310.

80 "'Differentia ultima' dicitur quia non habet differentiam, quia non resolvitur in conceptum quiditativum et qualitativum, determinabilem et determinantem, sed est tantum conceptus eius qualitativus [...]."Scotus, *Ordinatio* 1, d. 3, p. 1, q. 3, n. 131.

81 King correctly notes that an individual difference is not a this-ness, as the moniker "haecceitas" would indicate, but rather a "this-izer." This is because an individual difference is not itself a thing, but a differentiator. P. King, "Duns Scotus on the Common Nature and the Individual Differentia," *Philosophical Topics*, vol. 20, 1992, p. 74.

DUNS SCOTUS ON THE SENSATION OF SINGULAR ACCIDENTS 355

individuals because they don't cognize difference in the strict sense at all. The confused cognition of sensation does not distinguish between different notes or elements, but provides a rich and unresolved mixture.[82] Difference arises only once these notes have been fully resolved, which requires the work of the intellect. Difference as registered by the senses might better be called dissimilarity. Likewise, we might refer to the commonality sensed by the senses as similarity. Sensation represents its objects as similar and dissimilar, but it does not cognize difference.

Cognizing accidents qua individual difference would require that our senses be able to discern between two seemingly identical instances of one and the same nature. This requires registering not merely that some x is present here and now before me, but rather that it is this one and no other. The conjunction between a nature and an individual difference, however, is not the formal reason for sensing (*ratio formalis sentiendi*); rather, it is but a certain mode of such reason.[83] We don't sense *haec albedo* or *albedo singularis,* that is the senses do not perceive the conjunction between the nature and individual difference. True, I must sense *some* individual accident; but the fact that it is *this* one remains contingent. The conditions of the world at my time of sensing could be radically other than they happen to be and the senses would not register the difference.[84] Due to the formal distinction, what I sense (i.e., the unified object of the power) does not reflect the contingent conditions that make it possible. Our sensory powers cannot share a mode of being with their object because what individuates each one is primarily diverse from any other. Unlike those for whom a shared materiality brokered the bond between the senses and individual objects, Scotus's principle of individuation forecloses such a common exchange.

To the extent that sensation and intellection rely on assimilation, to that extent they remain constitutionally incapable of cognizing individual difference. Scotus states: "[...] from individual differences, just as from specifics, nothing can be abstracted in the first way [assimilation], because these are real 'reasons' [i.e., formalities] that are completely simple and primarily diverse; otherwise there would be an infinite regress."[85] Insofar as individual differences are ultimate, they contain but a single, primarily diverse note of

---

82   Scotus, *Ordinatio* I, d. 3, pars 1, q. 2, n. 72. Also, *In Metaph.* I, q. 6, n. 44.

83   Scotus, *In Metaph.* VII, q. 13, n. 172.

84   Scotus, *In Metaph.* V, q. 7, n. 107.

85   "Igitur a differentiis individualibus, sicut nec a specificis, nihil potest abstrahi primo modo, quia sunt rationes reales omnino simplices et primo diversae; alias processus in infinitum." Scotus, *In Metaph.* VII, q. 13, n. 166.

differentiation (what Scotus calls a "simply-simple concept"). They offer no basis for comparison. Thus, the problem is not *simply* that the senses are not granular enough to sense individual difference as Pini suggests. Rather – and even more so – the problem is how to grasp such primarily diverse pure differences in the first place.

For this reason, Scotus introduces another type of abstraction in this paragraph, one that gives rise to pure conceptual determinations.[86] This second mode of abstraction must be non-reifying because an individual is more than the form existing in matter; rather individuation is differentiation. Such abstraction peels away the various interconnected layers of the *simul totum*.[87] By abstracting out distinct notes from the hodge-podge of "substance mixed with accidents" and "accidents mixed with each other," we might eventually arrive at the individual. But Scotus is clear to state that even the intellect does not grasp the individual in its singularity, despite its *per se* intelligibility. Rather, something of a conceptual remainder or placeholder emerges from such abstraction. The modifying concepts produced from such abstraction include "individual," "incommunicable," "singular," or "this." (Recall the case of Adam above, who we conceive as "singular human.") Such concepts are placeholders in the sense that they indicate the difference, even without grasping it.

But this raises a further complication: True; singularity is not a condition of acting (only a condition of the agent that must be inferred). And true, it does not form part of the *per se* object of sensation. But are our initial acts of sensory cognition devoid of any registration of individuality? That is, do we cognize individual accidents only after such a laborious reasoning process and according to such paltry complex concepts as "individual red" or "that C-flat"?

7 Intuitive Cognition and Designate Singulars

This problem has intrigued several commentators, some of whom enlist intuitive cognition to provide an answer.[88] While most agree that intuitive cognition

---

86   Scotus, *In Metaph.* VII, q. 13, n. 166.

87   Scotus, *In Metaph.* VII, q. 15, n. 32. Wolter compares this second mode to Bertrand Russell's principle of abstraction that dispenses with abstraction. See A.B. Wolter, "Duns Scotus on Intuition, Memory, and Our Knowledge of Individuals," in M.M. Adams (ed), *The Philosophical Theology of John Duns Scotus,* Ithaca, Cornell University Press, 1990, p. 113.

88   See, for example, Wolter, "Duns Scotus on Intuition," pp. 98–122; P. King, "Thinking about Things: Singular Thought in the Middle Ages," in G. Klima (ed), *Intentionality, Cognition, and Representation in Medieval Philosophy*, New York, Fordham University Press, 2015, pp. 104–121; Pini, "Scotus on the Objects of Cognitive Acts"; J.B. South, "Scotus and the

DUNS SCOTUS ON THE SENSATION OF SINGULAR ACCIDENTS 357

does not grant access to the individual difference as such, they assign varying roles for this form of cognition.[89] Without bogging ourselves down in this debate, I might add simply that intuitive cognition at best provides an indication of singularity by registering presence and existence.

In response to the would-be objection that intellectual memory must remember the singular because it remembers something cognized here and now, Scotus responds:

> Actual existence pertains primarily to the nature. Consequently, this nature is not existing because it is formally a "this," but by reason of its being a nature. The intellect, however, intuitively knows that nature qua existing, and this cognition of an existent as existing suffices to make remembrance of it possible.

He continues:

> I deny your statement, then, that a potency in remembering knows this as this, since you only prove it knows something here and now. If by 'now' you mean existing and by "here" you mean "present in itself," I admit that it knows something as presently existing in itself. If so, I go further. "Here" and "now" are singular properties which can pertain to a nature [qua nature], not qua singular, although it is true that these properties can only pertain to something that is singular, either because it is intrinsically

---

Knowledge of the Singular Revisited," *History of Philosophy Quarterly*, vol. 19, no. 2, April 2002, pp. 125–147.

89   Scotus is clear that abstractive cognition *in principle* can grasp individuals qua individual difference as much as intuitive cognition can. Intuitive cognition does not register the nature as this, but only as existing and present. Day is an outlier on this point. Cf. S.J. Day, *Intuitive Cognition: A Key to the Significance of Later Scholastics*, St. Bonaventure, The Franciscan Institute, 1947. Where other commentators disagree is on the role of intuitive cognition in singular thought. King has argued that there is cognition of an individual without full-fledged cognition of this individual. He thus distinguishes singular thought, which grasps individuation, from *de re* thought, which grasps identity. King, "Thinking about Things," pp. 112–114. Pini, however, rejects King's argument that we can have cognition of individuals without having *de re* thought. Insofar as that which accounts for individuation, also accounts for identification, our lack of access to this principle bars us from cognition of either. Pini, "Scotus on the Objects of Cognitive Acts," p. 313. A point of general agreement, however, concerns the role of intuitive cognition in forming contingent judgments. See, for example, Wolter, "Scotus on Intuition," pp. 113–114, and Pini, "Scotus on the Objects of Cognitive Acts," pp. 311–314. For a somewhat unique approach (i.e., we can index the object to one's experience of perceiving it), see South, "Scotus and the Knowledge of the Singular Revisited," pp. 139–143.

356 LAZELLA

such [like the "haecceity"] or is joined to such. Nevertheless, they do not formally include, or essentially presuppose, singularity as the precise reason why they are there.[90]

Intuitive cognition apprehends some x as existing here and present now before me. But here and now are not properties of thisness (i.e., the ultimate individual difference) in the sense that singularity would explain them. There may be a concomitance between the two insofar as the nature exists and is present in singulars.[91] Singularity is more than hereness and nowness of the nature, but rather a condition of non-exchangeability. At best, intuitive cognition provides an indication of singularity.

What I mean by this is that in certain cases, Scotus seems to think that it is not enough to treat merely some one. While we often get by *in via* without a firm cognitive grasp of individuals in their singularity – and in fact there seems to be an advantage with having sensory powers that don't fixate on individuals in their singularity, but rather register commonalities – Scotus identifies certain areas where we must intend the difference. His arguments against singular cognition notwithstanding, he considers cases where we must develop a volitional attitude to singulars: "To the contrary are the articles of faith which are about singulars; also the act of the will which deals with a particular thing concerning which there are divine precepts and sins."[92] Faith and presumably other volitional attitudes must be directed at singular individuals and not just vague ones! In such cases, we seek to indicate a substance or accident as singular such that we mean this one and no other, even without a grasp of what

---

90   "Exsistentia actualis primo convenit naturae. Unde haec natura non est exsistens formaliter quia haec, sed per naturam. Illam autem naturam ut exsistentem intuitive cognoscit intellectus, et illa cognitio exsistentis ut exsistentis sufficit ad hoc quod eius possit esse recordatio. Cum dicis: potentia recordans cognoscit hoc ut hoc, nego, cum probas: cognoscit aliquid hic et nunc. Si intelligas per 'nunc,' exsistens, et per 'hic,' in se praesens, condedo quod cognoscit aliquid ut in se praesentialiter exsistens. Si sic ultra, hic et nunc sunt propria singularia ita quod possunt esse naturae, non ut singularis, licet non sint alicuius nisi quod est singularis singularitate intrinseca vel adiuncta. Tamen non includuunt formaliter, nec per se praesupponunt, singularitatem tanquam rationem praecisam secundum quam illa insunt." Scotus, *Ordinatio* IV, d. 45, q. 3, n. 21. For this text and translation, see Scotus, "A Treatise on Memory and Intuition from Codex A of Ordinatio IV, Distinctio 45, Question 3," trans. A.B. Wolter, *Franciscan Studies*, vol. 53, 1993, pp. 193–230.
91   Scotus elsewhere considers possible cases of bi-location. *In Metaph.* VII, q. 13, n. 167.
92   "Contra: de articulis fidei qui sunt de singularibus; ut de actu voluntatis, qui est circa rem particularem, de quo sunt praecepta divina et circa quae sunt peccata." Scotus, *In Metaph.* VII, q. 15, n. 19. For further discussion of the possibility of singular volitions according to Scotus, see LaZella, *The Singular Voice of Being*, pp. 187–191.

DUNS SCOTUS ON THE SENSATION OF SINGULAR ACCIDENTS   359

makes it so (i.e., its ultimate difference). We focus on *this* sin as opposed to that one.

We find a similar process at work in Scotus's distinction between vague versus designate singulars. Although Deborah Black has shown how this distinction becomes less prominent with his later "discovery" of intuitive cognition, the distinction provides an important perspective for understanding singular thought.[93] In *Super de anima,* Scotus distinguishes between cognizing "vague individuals," or merely attending to the nature in some supposit, as opposed to "designate ones," or adding discriminating circumstances. He explains:

> [The intellect] first represents the nature in a vague supposit, because it first offers itself to the intellect. Second, [it represents] the nature absolutely. Third, the intellect determines it [i.e. the nature] by adding those aforementioned singular circumstances. And thus it understands the designate singular, but not under a proper account of singularity, as has been said.[94]

Scotus enumerates various designated circumstances by which the intellect reconstructs the singular: for example, being here and now, with such a magnitude, figure, color, and so on. Such features are added to demarcate the individual as much as possible. Scotus insists, however, that we do not conceive the singular *sub propria ratione singularitas.*

We see this clearly with art because, Scotus tells us, art imitates nature. That is, both natural generation and productive cognition (i.e. *techne* or *ars*) aim to replicate the nature in some individual.[95] The artisan first intends to build the nature of a house in a vague supposit.[96] In this act of mere assimilation, the art itself is not directed to distinguishing between some house and this house. (Remember SP!) Some house consequently turns out to be *this* house, but only *per accidens.* The *per se* object of productive cognition (*cognitio artis*) is the nature (e.g., house), not the individual as such.

Interestingly, there are cases where cognizing the designate singular, and not just a vague particular, is crucial: medicine, for example. In the *Metaphysics,* Scotus asks whether one with experience, but lacking art, acts with more

---

93   Black, "Avicenna's 'Vague Individual,'" p. 290.

94   "Et sic primo repraesentat naturam in supposito vago, quid illud se primo offert intellectui; secundo, natura absolute; tertio, ipsam intellectus determinat, addendo sibi circumstantias singulares praedicatas. Et sic intelligit singulare signatum, non sub propria ratione singularitas, ut dictum est." Scotus, *Q. de an.* q. 22, n. 36.

95   Scotus, *Q. de an.* q. 22, n. 37.

96   Scotus, *Q. de an.* q. 22, n. 41.

certainty than her counterpart with art but no experience.[97] In other words, would you prefer a doctor with no medical training, but lots of hands on experience, over one with a top-notch education, but no experience with actual patients?

Scotus opts for the former.[98] He reasons that the artisan with art but no experience will misrecognize, or recognize less certainly, when to act and what can be done (*operabile per se*). Thus, the true expert must have experiential cognition. Scotus explains:

> In the singular about which the operation is per se there are many other things besides the individuated nature of what is common, and these many things diversify the action. One has to act toward this sick person in this place and at this time in another way than towards that sick person with the same specific infirmity at another place and at another time. But the expert knows these connections from the multiple cognition of singular instances, and knows this in itself and in regard to all that is connected with it.[99]

Productive cognition (e.g., the art of medicine) attends to human nature and the infirmity *per se* and to the patient, Callias, only *per accidens*.[100] Experience, by contrast, allows the good doctor to attend to those many things that diversify the action and the patient.

The good doctor opens, we might say, a mental file on her patient as a designate singular. Callias and his illness are not just human nature and illness existing in some supposit, as the art of medicine teaches; rather, he is *this* individual and his illness is *this* one designated according to a set of circumstances (e.g., with this medical history).[101] Thus, the good doctor acts toward this sick person in this place at this time and in another way toward the same sickness at

---

97   Scotus, *In Metaph.* I, q. 5. See also, qq. 4 and 6.

98   Scotus, *In Metaph.* I, q. 5, n. 12. Scotus responds that the one with experience acts more certainly than the one with just art. One could read the "with experience" to mean "with experience and art," but given how the question is posed, I take it to mean "with only experience."

99   "[...] in singulari, circa quod est operatio per se, multa sunt praeter naturam ipsius communis individuatam, quae multa diversificant actionem. Aliter enim oporet agere circa hunc infirmum in hoc loco et hoc tempore, quam circum illum infirmum – eadem infirmitate in specie – in alio loco et alio tempore. Ista autem annexa cognoscet expertus ex multiplicata cognitione singularium, et in se et quantum ad annexa." Scotus, *In Metaph.* I, q. 5, n. 19. Translation modified.

100   Aristotle, *Metaphysics*, I.1.

101   Cf. Aristotle, *Rhetoric*, 1.2 1356b1.

another time and place.[102] She must use whatever indications of singularity are available to her, even though cognition of this patient or that sickness eludes her grasp.

8 Conclusion

I have shown how our inability to sense individual accidents, according to Scotus, results from our inability to sense difference in a strict sense. To cognize an individual requires more than grasping some nature here and now. Rather, we must grasp this one and no other. While the senses use various make-shift measures to individuate accidents and even substances, grasping an individual in its singularity would require cognizing its individual difference. As their proper objects, the senses cognize a real, but less-than-numerical unity; individual difference is not included, as evidenced by the possibility of error. There is a formal distinction between the *ratio agendi* and the *ratio agentis*. At best, abstraction from a confused sensory input can form a conceptual remainder to indicate individual difference. While this yields rather thin conceptual content, volitional and practical attitudes can better attend to singular substances and accidents.

Bibliography

Primary Literature

Aristotle, *The Complete Works of Aristotle*, 2 vols., J. Barnes (ed), Princeton, Princeton University Press, 1984.

John Duns Scotus, "A Treatise on Memory and Intuition from Codex A of Ordinatio IV, Distinctio 45, Question 3," trans. Allan B. Wolter, *Franciscan Studies*, vol. 53, 1993, pp. 193–230.

John Duns Scotus, *Early Oxford Lecture on Individuation*, trans. Allan B. Wolter, St. Bonaventure, The Franciscan Institute, 2005.

John Duns Scotus, *On Being and Cognition: Ordinatio 1.3*, John van den Bercken (ed and trans.), New York, Fordham University Press, 2016.

John Duns Scotus, *Opera omnia*, C. Balic (ed), Vatican, Typis Polyglottis Vaticanis, 1950–.

John Duns Scotus, *Quaestiones super libros Metaphysicorum Aristotelis*, R. Andrews et al. (eds), St. Bonaventure, The Franciscan Institute, 1997.

---

102 Scotus, *In Metaph.* I, q. 5, n. 19.

John Duns Scotus, *Quaestiones super secundum et tertium De anima*, B.C. Bazán et al. (eds), St. Bonaventure, The Franciscan Institute, 2006.

John Duns Scotus, *Questions on the Metaphysics of Aristotle by John Duns Scotus*, 2 vols., trans. G.J. Etzkorn and A.B. Wolter, St. Bonaventure, The Franciscan Institute, 1997 and 1998.

Thomas Aquinas, *Expositio libri Posteriorum Analyticorum*, Rome, Leonine Commission, 1882.

Thomas Aquinas, *Liber de veritate catholicae fidei contra errores Infidelium seu Summa contra Gentiles*, C. Pera (ed), Turin, Marietti, 1961–1967.

Thomas Aquinas, *Pars prima Summae theologiae, Opera omnia 4–5*, Rome, Ex Typographia Polyglotta, 1888–1889.

Secondary Literature

Armstrong, David M., *Nominalism and Realism: Universals and Scientific Realism*, Cambridge, Cambridge University Press, 1978.

Armstrong, David M., *Universals: An Opinionated Introduction*, Boulder, Westview Press, 1989.

Black, Deborah, "'Avicenna's Vague Individual' and Its Impact on Medieval Latin Philosophy," in R. Wisnovsky, F. Wallis, C. Fraenkel, and J.C. Fumo (eds), *Vehicles of Transmission, Translation, and Transformation in Medieval Textual Culture*, Turnhout, Brepols, 2011, pp. 259–292.

Cross, Richard, *Duns Scotus*, Oxford, Oxford University Press, 1999.

Cross, Richard, *The Physics of Duns Scotus: The Scientific Context of a Theological Vision*, Oxford, Oxford University Press, 2007.

Day, Sebastian J., *Intuitive Cognition: A Key to the Significance of Later Scholastics*, St. Bonaventure, The Franciscan Institute, 1947.

Gracia, Jorge J.E., *Individuality: An Essay on the Foundations of Metaphysics*, Albany, State University of New York Press, 1988.

King, Peter, "Duns Scotus on the Common Nature and the Individual Differentia," *Philosophical Topics*, vol. 20, 1992, pp. 50–76.

King, Peter, "Thinking about Things: Singular Thought in the Middle Ages," in G. Klima (ed), *Intentionality, Cognition, and Representation in Medieval Philosophy*, New York, Fordham University Press, 2015, pp. 104–121.

LaZella, Andrew, *The Singular Voice of Being: John Duns Scotus and Ultimate Difference*, New York, Fordham University Press, 2019.

Maurin, Anna-Sofia, "Tropes," in E.N. Zalta (ed), *The Stanford Encyclopedia of Philosophy* (Winter 2016 Edition), https://plato.stanford.edu/archives/win2016/entries/tropes/.

Pini, Giorgio, "Scotus on Knowing and Naming Natural Kinds," *History of Philosophy Quarterly*, vol. 26, July 2009, pp. 255–272.

Pini, Giorgio, "Scotus on the Objects of Cognitive Acts," *Franciscan Studies*, vol. 66, 2008, pp. 281–315.

Shaffer, Jonathan, "The Individuation of Tropes," *Australasian Journal of Philosophy*, vol. 79, no. 2, 2001, pp. 247–259.

South, James B., "Scotus and the Knowledge of the Singular Revisited," *History of Philosophy Quarterly*, vol. 19, no. 2, April 2002, pp. 125–147.

Wolter, Allan B., "Duns Scotus on Intuition, Memory, and Our Knowledge of Individuals," in M.M. Adams (ed), *The Philosophical Theology of John Duns Scotus*, Ithaca, Cornell University Press, 1990, pp. 98–122.

CHAPTER 13

John Buridan on the Singularity of Sense Perception

Martin Klein

Introduction

How do we perceive things in the world? Is it true that we have sensory cognitions of them only as particulars? And if so, is the reason for this the corporeal (i.e., material) nature of sense? John Buridan's theory of sense perception is closely connected with the more general question of what role the nature of a cognitive power plays in the operations of that power. His philosophy of mind is an attempt to interpret Aristotle within a framework of incontrovertible church doctrines. While it was commonly accepted in Buridan's time that a sense is obviously a corporeal power, the nature of the human intellect posed a problem for medieval thinkers. Buridan holds that, as natural philosophers, we are better off interpreting Aristotle's ambiguous remarks on the nature of the intellect according to what Buridan takes to be the position of Alexander of Aphrodisias: since the intellect is the substantial form of the body and inheres in matter, it is as material as the soul of, say, a donkey. However, Buridan also agrees with what he calls "the truth of the Catholic faith," according to which the intellect is an immaterial form and therefore not "educed from the potency of matter"; that is, it is not the product of natural generation with matter as its breeding ground, as it were.[1]

Buridan accepts the doctrine of an immaterial intellect and incorporates it into his science of the soul, as, for instance, when he argues against a plurality of substantial forms.[2] He also admits that it is the immateriality of the intellect that makes this science so complicated when it comes to human beings.[3] At

---

1   See John Buridan, *Quaestiones in libros Aristotelis De anima secundum tertiam lecturam* bk. III q. 6 nn. 9–23. Text and translation of this work, henceforth *QDA*(3), are taken from John Buridan, *Questions on Aristotle's "On the Soul" by John Buridan: Latin Edition with an Annotated English Translation*, G. Klima, J.P. Hartman, P. Sobol, and J. Zupko (eds and trans.), Cham, Springer, forthcoming. I use the latest version from October 2018 which Professor Klima was kind enough to make available to me.
2   See Buridan, *QDA*(3) bk. III q. 17 n. 16.
3   See Buridan, *QDA*(3) bk. I q. 4 n. 16.

© KONINKLIJKE BRILL NV, LEIDEN, 2020 | DOI:10.1163/9789004413030_014

JOHN BURIDAN ON THE SINGULARITY OF SENSE PERCEPTION   365

the same time, however, he makes it very clear that philosophical arguments for the immateriality of the human soul are not conclusive. These arguments concentrate on cognitive operations that require that the intellect be immaterial, which supposedly can be shown by pointing to the fact that the operations of the senses are limited precisely because of their material nature. Consequently, Buridan's rebuttal of those arguments concentrates on the senses, which, despite their material nature, seem not to be entirely excluded from what, allegedly, only the intellect is capable of.[4]

Buridan's philosophy of mind thus appears Janus-faced, and has unsurprisingly provoked quite different interpretations. Whereas some scholars emphasize Buridan's admission of an immaterial intellect, others concentrate on those passages in which he seems to suggest that the material senses do not operate in a fundamentally different way than the intellect. And while some think that Buridan succeeds in proving that intellections can be rooted in a material cognitive subject, others hold that, if that is what he is trying to prove, his proof must fail.[5]

Buridan's own discussions of the relation between sense and intellect, as well as what modern scholars take him to be claiming, concentrate mainly on the question whether sense perception has only particulars as its objects. This is unsurprising, given that in medieval philosophy, and already in Aristotle, the distinction between singular and universal cognition marks the difference between sense and intellect.[6] Buridan distinguishes several senses in which something can be called particular or universal. The crucial sense in terms of cognition has to do with the different ways in which particulars can be *represented*. While all things in the world, such as trees, minds, and concepts of trees, exist as particulars, a concept can represent one particular tree only, and is then said to be a *singulare*, but in case it represents more than one tree it is said to be an *universale*. More precisely, to represent singularly is to refer to

---

4 See Buridan, $QDA(3)$ bk. III q. 2 nn. 17–18, which I will discuss in section three, and bk. III q. 3 nn. 14–32.

5 See exemplary the discussion between O. Pluta and J. Zupko: O. Pluta, "Persecution and the Art of Writing: The Parisian Statute of April 1, 1272, and Its Philosophical Consequences," in P.J.J.M. Bakker (ed), *Chemins de la pensée médiévale. Études offertes à Zénon Kaluza*, Turnhout, Brepols, 2002, pp. 563–585, and J. Zupko, "On Buridan's Alleged Alexandrianism: Heterodoxy and Natural Philosophy in Fourteenth-Century Paris," *Vivarium*, vol. 42, 2004, pp. 43–57.

6 See Aristotle, *De anima* II.5, 471b16–22, cited in Thomas Aquinas, *Sentencia libri De anima*, *Opera omnia vol. 45.1*, Rome, Commissio Leonina, 1984, bk. II cap. 12, p. 114, and *Physica* I.5, 189a5–8, cited in Aquinas, *In Aristotelis libros Physicorum*, *Opera omnia* 2, Rome, Commissio Leonina, 1884, bk. I cap. V lect. 10, p. 33. See also J. Hamesse (ed), *Les Auctoritates Aristotelis: Un florilège médiéval. Étude historique et édition critique*, Leuven, Publications Universitaires, 1974, p. 142, n. 27.

some object in terms of *this object here and now* without referring to any other object. To represent universally is to refer to a group of similar objects, such that it is not the case that one of these objects is more represented than the others. To have universal cognition is thus to represent many objects indifferently.[7]

In what follows I want to answer the question whether, according to Buridan, sense perception is always and necessarily the cognition of one singular object and not of many objects, and how he relates this problem to the metaphysical nature of the senses. I shall proceed by arguing against what has been recently claimed in the literature on this matter. First, regarding the *cognitive process of sense perception*, some scholars think that, although Buridan can give a natural account of the perception of material beings such as horses and dogs, his account reaches the end of the line when it comes to human beings with immaterial sensitive souls. Second, regarding the *singular and universal modes of sense perception*, some claim that Buridan shows that not only immaterial intellection but also material perception are a type of universal cognition. Third, regarding the *nature of cognitive subjects*, it has been argued that Buridan should admit that sense perception is singular essentially because of the materiality of the cognitive subject, even though he claims that the opposite is true. Against these interpretations, I will argue that Buridan gives the same explanation for sense perception in human as well as non-human animals in terms of the cognitive process (section 1); he does not claim that sense perception is a type of universal cognition (section 2); however, he is not committed to the view that the material nature of the senses is the fundamental reason for the singularity of sense perception (section 3).

1   I Spy with My Little Eye

For how Buridan understands the cognitive process of sense perception, questions 9 and 10 of book II of his commentary on *De anima* are crucial. His major

---

7   See Buridan, *QDA(3)* bk. I q. 5 nn. 7–11; Buridan, *Quaestiones super octo libros Physicorum Aristotelis (secundum ultimam lecturam): Libri I–II*, M. Streijger and P.J.J.M. Bakker (eds), Leiden, Brill, 2015, bk. I q. 7, pp. 61–63, henceforth *QP(U)*; Buridan, *In Metaphysicen Aristotelis. Quaestiones argutissimae Magistri Ioannis Buridani in ultima praelectione*, Paris, Jodocus Badius Ascensius, 1518; reprinted Frankfurt am Main, Minerva, 1964, bk. I q. 7, foll. 6vb-7ra and bk. VII q. 15, fol. 50va-b, henceforth *QM(U)*. On the several senses of singularity and universality in Buridan, see J. Zupko, "Universal Thinking as Process: The Metaphysics of Change and Identity in John Buridan's *Intellectio* Theory," in R. Keele and C. Bolyard (eds), *Later Medieval Metaphysics: Ontology, Language, and Logic*, New York, Fordham University Press, 2013, pp. 138–143.

JOHN BURIDAN ON THE SINGULARITY OF SENSE PERCEPTION 367

concern is to explain the active and passive aspects of the sensitive soul when it has an act of sensation. This problem leads him to make a sharp distinction between the reception of a sensible species and the act of sensation, and accordingly to clarify the different roles that body and soul play for perceptive states.[8]

Whereas the body *receives* a sensible species, the soul *produces* an act of perception. However, the two moments must not be confused. A sensible species is produced by a sensible object and transmitted to a sense organ. It is received only in the body or an organ or matter, but not in the soul. The body passively receives a species, which is actively produced by a perceptible object. The soul, however, is not involved at all in this process of species acquisition, neither actively nor passively: the soul neither produces the species nor receives it. The active and passive contribution of the soul for perception pertains instead to the act of sensing. The soul is active in sensing, since it produces an act of sensing; it is also passive, since it receives that act. Buridan makes clear how big the gap is between the soul forming a sensation and the body receiving a sensible species, by emphasizing that, strictly speaking, the soul is not affected by a perceptible object and that a body does not have to be ensouled to receive sensible species.[9] Nevertheless, body and soul both contribute to sensation since they each serve as the partial subject of an act of sensing. While a sensible species inheres only in the body and not in the soul, the act of sensing inheres in both the soul and the body.[10] Sense perception is therefore a process which involves the body in two crucial respects. On the one hand, every sense has an organ which receives a sensible species from something sensible. On the other hand, every act of sensation inheres in that organ in a material way, that is, it is extended throughout that organ by the extension of matter.

Within this discussion, Buridan also pays attention to the differences in sensation in human and non-human animals. These differences derive from the following commitments: first, unlike the soul of a non-human animal, the human soul is immaterial, by the authority of faith; second, in every human being there is only one soul, which is the substantial form of the body; third, the sensitive soul is a power of the soul from which it is not distinct; fourth, the actualization of this power (i.e., an act of sensation) is produced by the soul

---

8   Buridan deals with these questions in the final and an earlier redaction of his commentary. Both versions are collected in A. Pattin, *Pour l'histoire du sens agent. La controverse entre Barthélemy de Bruges et Jean de Jandun, ses antécédents et son évolution*, Leuven, Leuven University Press, 1988, pp. 241–266. For the final redaction, see Buridan, *QDA*(3) bk. II qq. 9–10.

9   See Buridan, *QDA*(3) bk. II q. 9. nn. 21 and 36.

10   See Buridan, *QDA*(3) bk. II q. 9 n. 33.

itself and received in it.[11] From these commitments it follows that in the case of human beings an act of sensation is immaterial. But how can this be reconciled with the claim that body and soul are both the subject of sensation? Buridan sees a difficulty here since it seems impossible for sensation to be extended by matter as its partial subject and at the same time to inhere in an indivisible subject, the immaterial soul:

> It is certainly true that there is a serious issue if we hold that in a human being there is a single soul. For this soul has to be intellective and indivisible, not extended by any extension of matter or subject. This unextended soul is then the sensitive and vegetative soul. Yet since sensation is supposed to be extended by the extension of the organ and matter, how can it be inherent in an indivisible subject and, as it were, drawn forth from its potency? This seems miraculous, since a form has extension only through the extension of its subject. And how too can something divisible and extended inhere in something indivisible and unextended? Well, I reply that this certainly is miraculous, since it is in a miraculous and supernatural manner that the human soul inheres in an extended body while neither being extended nor drawn forth from the potency of the matter in which it inheres, and nevertheless inheres in the whole body and in every part of it. This is quite miraculous and supernatural.[12]

Buridan explicitly admits that there is something miraculous about human perception, given that the human soul already is a product of supernatural creation. As he claims in another passage, the doctrine of the immaterial

---

11 For Buridan on the relation between soul and its powers, see *QDA(3)* bk. II q. 5; A. Wood, "Aquinas vs. Buridan on the Substance and Powers of the Soul," in G. Klima (ed), *Questions on the Soul by John Buridan and Others: A Companion to John Buridan's Philosophy of Mind*, Dordrecht, Springer, 2017, pp. 77–93; P.J.J.M. Bakker, "The Soul and Its Powers: Debates about the Powers of the Soul," in S. Schmid (ed), *The History of Philosophy of Mind: 1300–1600*, London, Routledge, 2019, pp. 63–82, at pp. 71–72.

12 See Buridan, *QDA(3)* bk. II q. 9 n. 26: "Verum est certe quod magna est dubitatio si ponamus in homine solam animam. Oportet enim istam esse intellectivam et indivisibilem, non extensam aliqua extensione materiae vel subiecti. Et tunc ista anima inextensa est anima sensitiva et vegetativa. Quomodo igitur, cum sensatio ponatur extensa extensione organi et materiae, poterit ipsa esse in subiecto indivisibili inhaerenter et tamquam educta de potentia istius? Et illud videtur mirabile, cum forma non habeat extensionem nisi extensione sui subiecti. Et quomodo etiam divisibile et extensum poterit inhaerere indivisibili et inextenso? Et certe respondeo quod hoc est mirabile, quia mirabili et supernaturali modo anima humana inhaeret corpori extenso non extensa nec de potentia materiae educta cui inhaeret, et tamen etiam toti corpori inhaeret et cuilibet parti eius. Hoc est bene mirabile et super naturam." (Translation slightly modified.)

JOHN BURIDAN ON THE SINGULARITY OF SENSE PERCEPTION

intellect simply cannot be demonstrated.[13] But since it is already impossible to explain on strictly philosophical grounds how an immaterial soul inheres in a material subject, it seems all the more inexplicable how an immaterial act of sensation of such a soul could inhere in matter.

From this metaphysical aporia, Sander de Boer observes that for Buridan human and non-human sense perception are "radically different," and concludes that "only in the non-human cases can the process be truly explained within the bounds of natural philosophy."[14] In a similar fashion, Jack Zupko comments on the passage just quoted:

> Just in case you missed it, the operation of the human sense is miraculous! [...] What this means for the psychologist is that despite the external, physiological similarities, horse sense has as much in common with human sense as a painted eye does with a real eye. The sensitive part of the human soul certainly uses a flesh-and-blood eye to see, but only insofar as it manifests the right combination of material dispositions to allow vision to take place. But the human soul is in no way extended in the eye, unlike the equine soul.[15]

According to this line of reasoning, Buridan cannot give – unlike in the case of non-human sense perception – a philosophical explanation for the cognitive process of human sense perception, because of the metaphysical difference between human and non-human sensitive souls. The question, however, is in what respect they differ, and what the difference amounts to. As I will argue, the metaphysical difference between human and non-human souls does not play a significant role in Buridan's explanation of the cognitive process of sense perception.

It is important to note where exactly Buridan sees a problem with immaterial perception. Sensation is an act which pertains to both body and soul. For

---

13   See Buridan, *QDA*(*3*) bk. III q. 3 n. 25 and bk. III q. 6 nn. 17–23.

14   S.W. de Boer, "Where Should We Discuss the Soul? On the Relation between the Doctrines of *De anima* and *De generatione et corruptione*," in G. Klima (ed), *Questions on the Soul by John Buridan and Others*, pp. 21–43, at p. 25. See also de Boer, *The Science of the Soul: The Commentary Tradition on Aristotle's "De anima," c. 1260-c. 1360*, Leuven, Leuven University Press, 2013, pp. 292–295, and de Boer, "Dualism and the Mind-Body Problem," in S. Schmid (ed), *The History of Philosophy of Mind: 1300–1600*, London, Routledge, 2019, pp. 207–228, at pp. 213–215.

15   J. Zupko, "Horse Sense and Human Sense: The Heterogeneity of Sense Perception in Buridan's Philosophical Psychology," in S. Knuuttila and P. Kärkkäinen (eds), *Theories of Perception in Medieval and Early Modern Philosophy*, Dordrecht, Springer, 2008, pp. 171–186, at pp. 180–181.

this to be the case the act of sensation must also inhere in matter, and because it inheres in matter it is divisible. The question, then, is how an act which inheres materially can also inhere in an immaterial soul, which is indivisible. Buridan proposes the following solution to this metaphysical problem: the human immaterial soul informs matter and is present throughout the body, as a whole in the whole body, and as a whole in each and every part of it; therefore, the soul, as something indivisible, also informs matter everywhere where there is an act of sensation inhering in matter. The soul, thus, although not materially extended, is coextensive with the materially inhering act of sensation. Hence, wherever an act of sensation inheres in matter, it also inheres in the soul. More precisely, matter and the immaterial soul are two distinct components of the substantial composite of the animated human body in which an act of sensation inheres both materially and immaterially, since it is brought forth from both matter and the immaterial soul as its "partial subjects." An act of sensation inheres materially on account of the material component, and is thus extended. At the same time, an act of sensation inheres immaterially on account of the immaterial component – which itself informs the material component – and is thus unextended in this partial subject.[16]

Whether this argument is convincing or not, the actual problem Buridan is responding to is how a material act of sensation can inhere immaterially in the soul. Human sensation is different from non-human sensation, since an act of the latter inheres only materially, since a non-human soul is a material form anyways. This problem of inherence, however, does not pertain to the question of how the act of sensation is actually brought forth or how the soul produces an act of sensation. About this, Buridan argues as follows:

> [S]ensation is drawn forth not only from the potency of matter, nor only from the potency of the soul, but together from the potency of the composite and on account of the whole composite and of each part, whether in a horse or in a human being. Insofar as sensation is drawn forth in a human being from the potency of the soul and the soul produces it in itself, the soul cognizes; insofar as it is drawn forth from the potency of matter, it is extended with the extension of matter.[17]

---

16 See Buridan, *QDA*(3) bk. II q. 9 n. 29.

17 Buridan, *QDA*(3) bk. II q. 9 n. 28: "[...] sensatio educitur non solum de potentia materiae nec solum de potentia animae sed simul de potentia composite et ratione totius compositi et utriusque partis, sive in equo sive in homine. Et ea ratione qua in homine educitur de potentia animae et quod anima etiam ipsam agit in se, anima cognoscit, et ea ratione qua educitur de potentia materiae ipsa, est extensa extensione materiae."

JOHN BURIDAN ON THE SINGULARITY OF SENSE PERCEPTION

To be sure, the fact that an act of sensation is produced by the soul itself is not special to humans, but pertains to any animal with perceptive powers, as we have seen. Buridan emphasizes rather that, in humans too, sensation takes place in both body and soul as partial sensitive beings. However, there is a problem that Buridan himself does not discuss: if sensation is divisible and extended, and therefore has to be brought forth from the potency of matter, the question arises how sensation can be immaterially produced in the first place. Compared with this, it is a secondary problem how an already existing material act of sensing can also inhere in an immaterial soul.

Thus, the more important question is how the inherence of an act of perception comes about in the first place: that is, how does the soul alone, not by being affected by a species, actively bring forth an act of sensation *actively*, rather than being *passively* affected by a species? Buridan does not say much about this except that the soul uses the body as an instrument on the occasion of a sensible species being passively received in the body alone. But given Buridan's strict distinction between the passive reception of a sensible species by the body and the active production of an act of sensation by the soul, this is likewise true for material souls when they produce sensations. Buridan does not think that the principles at work in perception are affected one way or another by the soul's metaphysical status. Rather, he gives an account of sensation which applies to material as well as immaterial souls. What is crucial for the cognitive process of perception is that the soul actively brings about an act of sensation, which is then received in the soul and in the relevant organ or matter. Material as well as immaterial souls use the body as an instrument in order to produce perceptions on the occasion of reception of sensible species, which in turn are produced by a sensible object and received by the organ of perception, but not by the soul.[18]

With respect to the operation of the soul, what remains rather miraculous, as it were, for both human and non-human perception is how the reception of a sensible species relates to an act of perception in the first place. Insisting on the fact that the soul is not affected either by a sensible object or by a sensible species, Buridan eventually faces the fundamental problem every active theory of sense perception struggles with: what, precisely, is the connection between the reception of a species and the formation of an act of sensation? That is,

---

18   See Buridan, *QDA*(3) bk. II q. 10 n. 27. The context of this passage makes it clear that in perception this instrumental relation also holds for non-human animals. In *QDA*(3) bk. III q. 15 n. 15, however, Buridan seems to put more emphasis on some active causal role of the species in sensation when he claims that it is "necessary for the species caused by a sensible object in the organ of sense to act together with sense in the formation of a sensation."

how are we supposed to understand the causal relation between the species and the sensation? But this question concerning all perceptive agents, whether material or immaterial, is about the cognitive process of producing an act of sensation; it is not about the subsequent metaphysical problem of how such an act could inhere materially and immaterially at the same time.

Obviously, the difference between human and non-human sense perception points to the more fundamental problem with the distinction between material and immaterial souls. Even if Buridan can arbitrate between the material and the immaterial in the production of sense perceptions, it is quite another question whether he can do the same for the representational content of these cognitive acts.

2 Universal Sense Perception: Too Good to Be True

Can an act of perception represent its object only in a singular way, or also in a universal way? As to this, question 8 of book III of Buridan's commentary on *De anima* and question 7 of book I on the *Physics* are crucial which ask whether universal cognition is prior or posterior to singular cognition. In this discussion Buridan faces the more general difficulty of whether the intellect understands only universally or also singularly, and whether the senses perceive only singularly or also universally. Buridan's discussion about the different modes of cognition is again related to the problem of material and immaterial cognitive subjects. According to Buridan, "almost all ancient commentators" – including most notably Averroes, but with the exception of Alexander of Aphrodisias – and "the Catholic faith" hold that if a cognitive subject is immaterial it necessarily cognizes only universally, and if it is material it necessarily cognizes only singularly. Therefore, since the intellect is immaterial it can have only universal understanding, and since the sense is material it can perceive objects only in a singular way.[19]

Buridan thinks that both inferences are mistaken. Against the first, he objects that this position implies that immaterial cognitive subjects are incapable of singular cognition. But this is not true, since both the human immaterial intellect and the divine intellect understand things in a singular way. In fact, God, who is supposed to be the most immaterial being, understands exclusively singularly. Therefore, as shown by both the human intellect and God, it does not necessarily follow from the fact that a cognitive subject is immaterial

---

19   See Buridan, *QDA*(3) bk. III q. 8 n. 18 and *QP*(*U*) bk. I q. 7, p. 65.

JOHN BURIDAN ON THE SINGULARITY OF SENSE PERCEPTION   373

that its acts of understanding are exclusively universal. Quite the contrary: for a cognitive subject to have an immaterial nature is compatible with having singular *and* universal cognition, or, in the case of God, exclusively singular cognition.[20]

Against the second inference from materiality to singularity, Buridan argues as follows:

> [I]t is apparent that a material and extended power properly achieves its object (*fertur bene in obiectum suum*) in a universal way, for the appetite of a horse in the form of hunger or thirst is not singularly for this sack of oats or that water, but for any indifferently, which is why it would take whichever it finds first. And the natural intention or appetite of fire for heating is not related to this or that heatable thing in a singular way, but indifferently to anything it can heat. Thus, it would heat whatever is put to it.[21]

It is not obvious how this line of reasoning should be understood, given that Buridan is now talking about sensory appetite and not cognition. But in order to make this move coherent, it is fair to assume that Buridan proceeds in a way similar to his first objection against the inference from immateriality to universal cognition. Thus, one way to understand the claim made in this passage against the inference from materiality to singularity would be that the material senses also have universal cognition in addition to singular cognition. Buridan would thus be attacking both inferences by showing that immaterial *and* material powers cognize singularly as well as universally.

---

20   Even granted that the intellect has singular cognitions, one might argue that these come about only by means of sensory input which is singular, precisely because the senses are material. Hence, when the intellect understands singularly, it does so only externally, as it were, because it uses material devices which do something the intellect could never do on its own: they lead to a cognition that is singular. Hence, in itself and without the senses, the intellect would understand only in a universal manner. However, Buridan makes it clear that the intellect itself has the power to understand singularly; see *QDA*(*3*) bk. III q. 8 nn. 19–21. Moreover, he opposes any sort of subsequent reflection of the intellect on the phantasm for it to understand singularly; see *QP*(*U*) bk. I q. 7, pp. 70–72.

21   Buridan, *QDA*(*3*) bk. III q. 8 n. 24: "... apparet quod virtus materialis et extensa fertur bene in obiectum suum modo universali, nam appetitus equi secundum famem aut sitim non est singulariter ad hanc avenam vel ad hanc aquam, sed ad quamlibet indifferenter, unde quamcumque primitus inveniret illam caperet. Et intentio naturalis vel appetitus ignis ad calefaciendum non se habet modo singulari ad hoc calefactibile vel illud, sed ad quodlibet indifferenter quod ipse posset calefacere. Ideo quodcumque sibi praesentetur, calefaceret ipsum." (Translation slightly modified). See also *QP*(*U*) bk. I q. 7, p. 66.

In fact, on the basis of this passage, several scholars take Buridan to make the sensational claim that material senses have universal cognitions. Gyula Klima, for instance, suggests that

> Buridan argues that even the obviously material cognitive and appetitive powers of brute animals should somehow have universal cognition of singulars, insofar as their cognitive and appetitive acts seem to be directed not at particular singulars, but indifferently at any singulars of a given kind. This is clear from the fact that if a horse is thirsty, it would seek out just any bucket of water to quench its thirst indifferently, and not this or that particular bucket of water.[22]

Following this line of reasoning, the argument of the thirsty horse would be that the horse does not strive for a particular portion of water but for water in general. For the argument to work, and since Buridan's objection is directed against the claim that material senses *cognize* singularly because of their material nature, Buridan is apparently claiming that the horse strives for water universally precisely because its appetition is somehow related to a universal perception of water. The horse is said to strive not for this or that particular bucket of water but indifferently for any water, for the simple reason that it has a universal cognition or representation of it – presumably some kind of imagination or memory – which inclines the horse to strive for it.

The crucial premises of this line of reasoning are that appetitions are initiated by cognitions and that the way they are directed to something conforms to the way in which something is cognized. One seeks this particular object because of a preceeding singular cognition of it, whereas to seek something generally requires a universal cognition. In fact, Buridan identifies one kind of appetite for which this is the case, which he calls "animal appetites." These can be either intellective or sensitive. On the part of the intellect, this appetite is the will; on the part of the sense, it is either desire or repugnance. Acts of animal appetite are always initiated by acts of cognition, according to which these

---

22   G. Klima, "Universality and Immateriality," *Acta philosophica*, vol. 24, 2015, pp. 31–42, at p. 36. O. Pluta argues similarly in several publications: see Pluta, "John Buridan on Universal Knowledge," *Bochumer philosophisches Jahrbuch für Antike und Mittelalter*, vol. 7, 2002, pp. 25–46, at p. 33; Pluta, "Persecution and the Art of Writing," p. 579; Pluta, "Mental Representation in Animals and Humans: Some Late Medieval Discussions," in G. Klima (ed), *Intentionality, Cognition, and Mental Representation in Medieval Philosophy*, New York, Fordham University Press, 2015, pp. 273–286, at p. 280. See also P. King, "John Buridan's Solution to the Problem of Universals," in J.M.M.H. Thijssen and J. Zupko (eds), *The Metaphysics and Natural Philosophy of John Buridan*, Leiden, Brill, 2001, pp. 1–27, at p. 8.

JOHN BURIDAN ON THE SINGULARITY OF SENSE PERCEPTION 375

appetitions can be either singular or universal. However, Buridan also emphasizes in numerous passages – including question 7 of book I of his commentary on the *Physics*, where the same argument as the one quoted above appears – that sensitive animal appetitions are always singular because sensations represent only singularly. Only intellective animal appetitions can be universally directed at something, if their preceeding intellective act of understanding is a universal representation.[23]

Thus, since a thirsty horse does not have an intellect, it can imagine water only singularly and is therefore not able to strive for it in a universal manner, at least not according to its animal appetite. But in the passage quoted above Buridan is not in fact talking about animal appetite but "natural intention or appetite." This is a different kind of appetite, which is nothing more than a universal directedness, about which Buridan argues in his commentary on the *Metaphysics* as follows:

> But there is a problem with the sensitive appetite about how an appetitive act is directed to a universal, since an act of sensing is not directed to a universal. Regarding this, it seems to me, we have to say that those appetites, such as thirst and hunger, are natural rather than animal appetites, and that they exist not mediated by cognition. Indeed, they exist unmediated by nature because of a lack of nourishment. But in order to pursue an object, an appetite is required, and cognition or memory follows. Because of this, however, it is not the case that this appetite is generated by means of this cognition or memory. But these natural appetites are not acts which are distinct from these natural appetitive powers. Therefore, they are directed at universals, just as it was said that all powers are directed at universals.[24]

---

23 See Buridan, *QP(U)* bk. I q. 7, p. 64; *QM(U)* bk. I q. 7, fol. 7rb and John Buridan, "Quaestiones supra decem libros Ethicorum Aristotelis ad Nicomachum (Quaestiones longae): Liber VI Quaestio 16," in H.-U. Wöhler (ed), *Texte zum Universalienstreit. Band 2: Hoch- und spätmittelalterliche Scholastik. Lateinische Texte des 13.–15. Jahrhunderts*, Berlin, Akademie Verlag, 1994, pp. 149–171, at p. 168, henceforth QNE. This critical edition of this particular question is preferable to the early modern print edition, cf. John Buridan, *Quaestiones Ioannis Buridani super decem libros Ethicorum Aristotelis ad Nicomachum*, Paris, Poncet de Preux, 1513, reprinted Frankfurt am Main, Minerva, 1968, foll. 131rb-132va.

24 Buridan, *QM(U)* bk. I q. 7, fol. 7rb: "Sed est dubitatio de appetito sensitivo quomodo actus appetendi sit circa universale cum actus sentiendi <non> sit circa universale. Ad hoc videtur mihi dicendum quod tales appetitus magis sunt naturales quam animales, ut sitis et fames, et non sunt mediante cognitione, immo immediate a natura propter carentiam nutrimenti. Sed ad persequendum obiectum appetitus exigitur sequens cognitio vel memoria, non tamen ideo quod ille appetitus fiat mediante cognitione illa vel memoria.

Natural appetites are distinguished from animal appetites not because they would only apply to non-animated beings, such as fire; rather, Buridan identifies them as natural because, unlike animal appetites, they are not caused or mediated by any cognition. Just as a fire does not think before it burns, a horse does not have to have an act of cognition in order to be thirsty. The reason why those natural appetites are universal is their crucial feature of always being active. As soon as a fire exists it produces heat, and it will heat whatever is near it. In this sense, it is not the case that a fire is sometimes actualized and sometimes not. The distinction between potency and act somehow breaks down. To such natural activities applies what, according to Buridan, holds for every power considered in itself and not with regard to its actualization: every power – whether material or immaterial, whether cognitive or non-cognitive – is directed at particulars in a universal manner, since it is not determined to go for this or that particular object: fire has the power to heat whatever piece of wood is in sufficient proximity to it, and thirst is quenched by whatever is drinkable.[25]

Thus, as Buridan seems to suggest in the passage just quoted, the relationship between appetitions and cognitions appears to be the following: Since animals always have a certain lack of nourishment, they have a constant natural appetite universally directed at nourishment. Once lack of nourishment reaches a certain level, this appetite can cause a representation of something nourishing; however, this representation will be a singular cognition, since it is produced in the sensory soul.[26] Finally, once something nourishing is perceived, this cognition in turn will cause an act of the animal appetite, which will be

---

Modo tales appetitus naturales non sunt actus distincti ab illis potentiis appetitivis naturalibus. Ideo sunt circa universalia sicut dictum est quod omnes potentiae sunt circa universalia." On the addition of "non" see the preliminary edition of John Buridan, *Commentary on Aristotle's Metaphysics Book I* (*v. 21 Mar 2018*), R. van der Lecq (ed), <academia .edu/36218167/John_Buridans_Commentary_on_Aristotles_Metaphysics_Book_I_v._21_ Mar_2018>, accessed February 2019, p. 32, l. 30. See also the apparatus in P. Gilbert, "Collate: A System to Aid in the Preparation of Critical Editions," Ph.D. dissertation, University of Wisconsin-Madison, 1978, p. 123. Moreover, that the "non" has to appear in the text is also clear from the passage itself and its context, since the problem arises precisely from the claim Buridan makes earlier in the same *quaestio*, namely, as we have just seen, that sense perception is de facto singular.

25   See Buridan, *QM(U)* bk. I q. 5, foll. 5vb-6rb; *QP(U)* bk. I q. 24, p. 233; *QNE* bk. VI q. 16, pp. 156–157 and bk. VII q. 8, ed Paris 1513, fol. 145ra.

26   As Buridan mentions in the quote, this becoming aware of, say, being thirsty could result in some memory of water. Again, those sensory memories are always singular, see John Buridan, *Quaestiones super libris Analyticorum Priorum*, H. Hubien (ed), typescript, n.d., <logicmuseum.com/wiki/Authors/Buridan/In_libros_posteriorum_analyticorum>, accessed February 2019, bk. II q. 20; Buridan, *Summulae: De demonstrationibus*, L.M. de

JOHN BURIDAN ON THE SINGULARITY OF SENSE PERCEPTION

singularly directed at the object inasmuch as this object has been perceived singularly.

In his objection to the traditional inference from materiality to singularity, Buridan makes the case for this basic animal striving for nourishment, which does not depend on some universal cognition. Consistent with what he repeatedly asserts, Buridan does not want to show that material sense has actual universal cognitions; rather, his argument has to be understood against the background of precisely the broad conception of intention common in medieval philosophy.[27] Buridan seems to suggest that if it is already true that non-cognitive intentional acts are universally directed despite their materiality, then it seems all the more implausible to think that perceptions are singular simply because they are acts of material powers. Whether this is a good argument, I leave undecided here. At any rate, as has become clear, Buridan nowhere actually claims that acts of perception are a type of universal cognition.[28]

3 What's the Matter with Singular Cognitions?

But why are sense perceptions singular cognitions? The crucial passages are again QDA(3) bk. III q. 8 and QP(U) bk. I q. 7. So far, Buridan has argued against the inference from immateriality to universality and materiality to singularity by showing that the intellect, despite being immaterial, cognizes both singularly and universally, and that even non-cognitive agents have intentions which are directed in a universal manner. But Buridan also thinks that the senses do not perceive objects singularly because of their material nature. To the contrary, he states:

> Third, the stated opinion [sc., the inference from immateriality to universality and materiality to singularity] seems to me to fail in claiming, with regard to the intellect's cognizing only universally and sense not cognizing except singularly, that this is because of the intellect's immateriality and lack of extension on the one hand, and sense's materiality and extension on the other. For even if one grants that the intellect is unextended

---

Rijk (ed), Groningen, Ingenium, 2001, VIII.5.4 ad 5, pp. 128–129 and QM(U) bk. II q. 2, fol. 9vb.

27 See P. King, "Mediaeval Intentionality and Pseudo-Intentionality," *Quaestio*, vol. 10, 2010, pp. 25–44, and J. Zupko, "On the Several Senses of 'Intentio' in Buridan," in G. Klima (ed), *Intentionality, Cognition, and Mental Representation in Medieval Philosophy*, pp. 251–272.

28 For a thorough discussion of this matter see my *Philosophie des Geistes im Spätmittelalter: Intellekt, Materie und Intentionalität bei Johannes Buridan*, Leiden, Brill, 2019, pp. 84–105.

and immaterial, and sense extended and material, this sort of difference in modes of apprehending, namely, between apprehending universally and apprehending singularly, does not seem to follow.[29]

How does Buridan defend this claim? After rejecting the inference from immateriality to universal cognition and from materiality to singular cognition, Buridan explains what he takes to be the actual reason for universal cognition – namely, an indifferent representation by means of which an object is cognized not distinctly from other objects. When we cognize an object, we receive species from it which are "representational likenesses" of the object. Buridan argues for some sort of transitivity of likeness between objects and representations of them in order to explain how it is possible to have general representations even though we cognize only particulars. Suppose that objects A, B, and C are similar to each other, and in general that a representation R of any given object O is similar to that object. Now, when I cognize A, not only will I have a representation R of A which is similar to it but, claims Buridan, it will be similar to B and C as well, since A is similar to B and C.[30]

Of course, the similarity between A, B, and C differs in a crucial respect from the similarity between an object and its cognition. While A, B, and C share some natural likenesses – for instance, they all have the same colour – my cognition of the colour of an object is representationally similar to the colour of the object, since in cognizing it I do not literally take on this colour. However, Buridan can relate natural likeness to representational likeness because he thinks that in general effects represent their causes, and that, at least in the case of natural kinds, objects are not just randomly similar to each other, since they are the product of natural generation and hence similar to those from which they descend. Thus, members of the same animal species share similar substantial and accidental properties and they produce similar effects (for instance, sensible species). Since donkeys are naturally similar, the species which I receive from one donkey are naturally similar to the species I would receive from any other donkey; therefore, the species are representationally similar to any other donkey.[31]

---

29   Buridan, *QDA(3)* bk. III q. 8 n. 23: "Tertio, dicta opinio apparet mihi deficere in assignando tantum quod intellectus cognoscit universaliter et sensus non nisi singulariter, quod hoc est propter immaterialitatem et inextensionem intellectus, et propter materialitatem et extensionem sensus. Nam licet concederetur intellectus inextensus et immaterialis et sensus extensus et materialis, tamen ex hoc non videtur sequi talis diversus modus apprehendendi, scilicet singulariter et universaliter." (Translation slightly modified).

30   See Buridan, *QDA(3)* bk. III q. 8 nn. 25–26.

31   See Buridan, *QDA(3)* bk. III q. 8 nn. 25–26 and *QP(U)* bk. I q. 7, pp. 66–67.

JOHN BURIDAN ON THE SINGULARITY OF SENSE PERCEPTION

But this raises the problem of how we can have singular representations at all. Wasn't the sense supposed to perceive an object only singularly? What makes the representation of a donkey singular is that we receive numerous pieces of accidental information of it – crucially, information about size and position, which enable us to demonstratively point to this object as opposed to any other. This is possible only when a *prospect*, as Buridan calls it (from *prospicio* in the literal sense of "looking out" for something), is produced by sense. In rejecting the view that it is essentially the materiality of a cognitive subject which provides this feature, Buridan clarifies the proper meaning of singular perception as follows:

> [S]omething is perceived singularly because it is perceived in the manner of something existing in the prospect (*prospectus*) of the person cognizing it. Thus, God, in fact, perceives every thing most distinctly as if he perceives them singularly because every such thing is in his prospect. But the exterior sense apprehends its object confusedly along with its magnitude and its location as if it appeared in its prospect as either long or short, as either on the left or on the right.[32]

This passage poses at least two problems. First, recall that God has only singular cognitions. However, as Buridan makes clear in his *Metaphysics* commentary, God, unlike animal sense, does not perceive objects by means of species, but in a very fancy way that is hard to imagine, namely, through his essence in a single act of self-understanding, in which every past, present, and future object is present to him.[33] God's process of cognition is thus entirely different from ours, and the comparison therefore seems not to fit well. Second, as Buridan notes in this passage, the exterior sense receives a bundle of species, and depending on how it receives them, an object appears to it. As Buridan says more explicitly in the second book of his *De anima* commentary, once the species of an object are received in, say, the right side of my eye, the object appears to be in the right corner of my "prospect."[34]

---

32 Buridan, *QP(U)* bk. I q. 7, p. 68: "... aliquid percipitur singulariter, quia percipitur per modum existentis in prospectu cognoscentis. Ideo enim Deus omnia percipit distinctissime, ac si perciperet singulariter ea, quia omnia talia sunt in prospectu eius. Sensus autem exterior obiectum suum apprehendit confuse cum magnitudine et situ ad ipsum, tamquam apparens in prospectu eius aut longe aut prope aut ad dextram aut ad sinistram." See also *QDA(3)* bk. III q. 8 n. 28.

33 See Buridan, *QM(U)* bk. VII q. 20, fol. 54ra-va and bk. XII q. 13, foll. 75rb-76rb.

34 See Buridan, *QDA(3)* bk. II q. 13 n. 15.

380   KLEIN

It therefore seems to be precisely the spatiotemporal circumstances of the object and the perceptive faculty which make this prospect possible in the first place. Material objects produce species which are received materially by a sense organ, causing the prospect Buridan is talking about. This seems to be a very material process indeed. Thus, Gyula Klima argues that this seems to contradict the objection that Buridan himself intended to make, namely, that materiality and extension are the essential reason why the sense cognizes singularly:

> For if sensory representation is singular *precisely because* it represents its object in a material fashion, encoding the distinctive, singular information about the object by its own material features, then this means that sensory representation is singular *because* it is material, that is, *its materiality implies its singularity.*[35]

This is indeed a serious objection. However, I take Buridan rather to be making here the following claims. To perceive something singularly, whether through the eye or by a divine act of cognition, what needs to be the case is the emergence of a prospect in the first place. If and only if something is perceived in a prospect is it cognized singularly. As Peter King aptly puts it, "The singularity of perception is a function of the object's presence in the perceiver's sensory field. That is, the singularity of sensitive cognition does not stem from its inherent nature or from some characteristic feature of the object, but from the circumstances in which it occurs."[36] Crucially, these circumstances can be realized differently: by a material operation – that is, by an act of perception in accordance with how species are received – or by an immaterial operation, as when God cognizes something. In both cases, Buridan emphasizes, something is cognized not because of the nature of the cognitive agent but because a prospect necessarily renders a cognition singular.

Nevertheless, it still seems to be true that in the case of human perception, once the sense receives representations of an object, it cannot but cognize that object in accordance with how the species are received, and that this is a material process. I think Buridan would not hesitate to accept the claim that for us earthly creatures, the material reception of species is necessary in order to perceive singularly. However, he also explicitly claims not only that the exterior sense perceives things singularly in accordance with how species of an object

---

35   G. Klima, *John Buridan*, Oxford, Oxford University Press, 2009, p. 82. See also Klima, "Universality and Immateriality," pp. 39–41.

36   King, "John Buridan's Solution," p. 18.

are received, but also that it is unable to abstract from the various pieces of information. Hence, it seems that if a material sense receives species it cannot but cognize things "prospectively," as it were.[37] If this is true, then Klima seems to be correct in saying that it is not just that the materiality of a perceptive power renders an act of cognition singular, but also that a power has to be immaterial in order to abstract and hence to cognize universally. For it is materiality which necessarily implies particularity.[38]

The question therefore is whether Buridan can show that a material sense also could abstract, or whether its material nature would prevent it from doing so. To abstract, very roughly, is to distinguish and to isolate all the different pieces of sensory information about an object, which are received in a very entangled way in the prospect of the cognitive subject. It means to regard separately all the information about an object which has been received by means of species being fused together: substance, colour, shape, etc. For instance, strip away all the accidental representations from the representation of the substance, and what you get is a substantial representation, which itself will represent all objects that resemble each other with regard to that subsantial information.[39]

Abstraction, Buridan says, is just one of several kinds of cognitive operation by means of which one cognition can be gained from a previous cognition in a non-discursive way. Other examples of non-discursive processing of further information would be the internal sense taking an act of external sense cognition or the internal sense gaining some normative content from what is sensible to the external senses, as when a sheep elicits an "intention" of fear when it has a wolf in its prospect.[40] Generally, perception is about further processing of information that was originally provided by means of species on whose reception it is dependent but with which it is not identical. But given that forming an act of perception is a material operation dependent on the material reception of species, the question is: To what extent could a sense power, in further processing of information, go beyond the spatiotemporal circumstances of prospective sensation? That is, could sense cognize abstractively?

Buridan claims, on the one hand, that external and internal senses effectively do not "sort out this confusion" of species; that is, they do not isolate the

---

37 See Buridan, *QDA*(3) bk. III q. 8 nn. 28–29 and n. 32.
38 As Klima points out, if cognition is necessarily singular when it is material, then by contraposition it must be that, if a cognition is non-singular, i.e., universal, it must be immaterial. See Klima, *John Buridan*, p. 82, and Klima, "Universality and Immateriality," p. 37.
39 See Buridan, *QDA*(3) bk. III q. 8 n. 30.
40 See Buridan, *QP*(*U*) bk. I q. 4, pp. 36–37.

various representations, and thus they do not abstract.[41] Only a few paragraphs later, on the other hand, he states:

> And any power that can perform an abstraction of this kind, regardless of whether it belongs to sense or intellect, can cognize universally. For this reason as well, Alexander believed that this power is material and extended in us, which he nevertheless granted should be called "intellect" in a human being, on account of its great pre-eminence over the cognitive powers of brute animals.[42]

Buridan thinks that it is generally possible for a material power to abstract, whether it be sense or intellect. However, he does not provide any proof which would directly show how sense would be able to abstract. In fact, neither external nor internal sense operates in this way. Buridan's strategy is rather to show that it is implausible to assume that the material nature of the senses is the principle reason for it.

Although Buridan thinks that the material constitution of an organ has some restrictive effect on the soul's cognitive abilities, he does not share the view that matter *absolutely* individuates forms and hence necessarily singularizes cognitions. In his metaphysics, everything is individual in itself: matter, form, composites of matter and form, and qualities of that composite.[43] Not absolutely individuating everything which is material, matter has rather different restrictive effects on corporeal powers that depend on the material structure of their organs. While it would indeed be odd to assume that an external sense, such as the power of vision, would already be capable of abstraction and hence of producing universal representations, the case might be different for the internal sense, which is much more complex in its material operations. Hence, on the assumption that matter only *gradually* restricts the scope of cognitions, Buridan has good reasons to believe that the material constitution of the sense organ does not restrict the external sense in the same way as the

---

41   See Buridan, *QDA(3)* bk. III q. 8 nn. 28–29.

42   Buridan, *QDA(3)* bk. III q. 8 n. 32: "Et quaecumque virtus potest facere huiusmodi abstractionem, sive illa sit sensus sive intellectus, illa potest universaliter cognoscere. Unde etiam Alexander illam virtutem credidit in nobis esse materialem et extensam, quam tamen in homine concessit esse vocandum intellectum, propter excellentiam nobilitatis eius super virtutes cognoscitivas brutorum."

43   See Buridan, *Quaestiones super libros De generatione et corruptione Aristotelis: A Critical Edition with an Introduction*, M. Streijger, P.J.J.M. Bakker, and J.M.M.H. Thijssen (eds), Leiden, Brill, 2010, bk. I q. 24, p. 184, and Buridan, "Tractatus de differentia universalis ad individuum," S. Szyller (ed), *Przeglad Tomistyczny, vol.* 3, 1987, pars II q. 2, p. 174.

JOHN BURIDAN ON THE SINGULARITY OF SENSE PERCEPTION

internal sense. For instance, as he shows elsewhere, an external sense can perceive colours only because of the transparent medium of the eye: the medium has to be colourless, since otherwise we would apprehend only a small part of the colour spectrum. To use a modern example: if we always used red sun glasses, the world would appear only reddish to us. However, the same condition for apprehending species of colours cannot be true for the internal sense, which Buridan locates in the heart. First, the gateway from the eyes to the heart as well as the heart itself are obviously not transparent, and yet species are propagated to and received in the organ of the internal sense. Moreover, an organ of the external sense cannot receive species of the same type and degree as a quality already inhering in the organ. When a perceptible object has the very same colour tone as our red sunglasses, we are already seeing the redness of the sunglasses, which blocks the reception of the species of red of the object. However, the internal sense must be able to receive species of external qualities which it already possesses, since I am obviously able to perceive the redness and warmth of an external object even if they are of the same degree as these qualities that already inhere in my red and warm heart. From this Buridan concludes that an intellect could, at least in principle, also understand all corporeal natures, even if it has itself a corporeal nature.[44]

This line of reasoning leads Buridan to suspect that arguments for the immateriality of the human intellect as defended by, for instance, Thomas Aquinas, are inconclusive. They might give good reasons for material restrictions of the external senses which prevent them from being able to have universal cognitions, but they seem to fail to prove that matter would generally prevent

---

[44] See Buridan, *QDA*(3) bk. III q. 2. n. 18. G. Lokert's early modern edition of Buridan's commentary, though a redaction in its own right, presents the argument from *QDA*(3) in a more intelligible manner; see John Buridan, *Quaestiones in tres libros de anima*, G. Lokert (ed), Paris, Jodocus Badius Ascensius & Conradus Resch, 1516; reprinted *Le traité de l'âme de Jean Buridan (De prima lectura)*, B. Patar (ed), Louvain-la-Neuve, Éditions de l'Institut supérieur de philosophie, 1991, bk. III q. 2, p. 662: "... virtus namque cogitativa potest cognoscere directe omne quod sensu exteriore directe et per se sentimus, et tamen sensu exteriore possemus sentire obiectum calidum in eodem gradu caliditatis, sicut est organum cogitativae. Verbi gratia, ponamus quod sit obiectum extra, ut lapis vel aqua, in eodem gradu caliditatis cum organo cogitativae, et ponamus quod manus sit frigidior, tunc ipsa percipiet caliditatem ipsius obiecto; ideo consequenter cogitativa poterit caliditatem percipere, non obstante quod habeat similem in gradu." From this Buridan concludes in *QDA*(3) bk. III q. 2 n. 18: "And so, if we assume that there is no cognitive power beyond the power that the Commentator calls cogitative and Aristotle calls the common sense, the argument made above does not entail that the intellect is without an organ and without composition, just as it does not entail this about the common sense or cogitative power." (Translation slightly modified.)

universal cognition and hence be the main reason for the singularity of sense perception.[45] Accordingly, Buridan could plausibly argue that the way the prospect of an act of internal sensation emerges and then gives rise to a singular cognition differs from the way this occurs with the external senses. Indeed, by means of the material nature of our perceptive apparatus a prospect is realized, which in turn allows a cognition to be singular. However, a prospect can be realized differently, as we can see in the case of divine cognition and the sensation of the internal sense.

The material constitution of the external sense might even make it necessary for a cognition to be singular, but it is less certain that matter in general necessarily prevents a cognitive power from having universal cognitions. Once it is granted that the prospect is realized in different ways – even if it is realized materially –, it is not implausible to assume that a material power can abstract from what we perceive prospectively. In order for a cognitive subject to cognize universally it must be able to abstract substantial features from accidental ones. This is indeed accomplished by the intellect, but as Buridan seems to suggest, it might also be possible for the interior sense, if its material make-up is sufficiently complex.[46]

4   Conclusion

Is human sense perception radically different from non-human animal perception, given that the human soul is immaterial? Does Buridan claim that sense perception is universal? Or is the material nature of sensory powers the essential reason for their cognitions being singular? The aim of this paper has been to show that what Buridan actually says about the singularity of sense perception is quite different from what scholars have hitherto taken him to

---

45   For the same reason, Buridan would object to what Klima holds more plausible in weighing Buridan's and Aquinas's position: that "just *any* material encoding" and hence "*any* material transcoding of the originally received information about the proper sensibilia in the material sensory organs will also preserve, by virtue of its materiality, the same distinctive, singular information that was encoded by the material features of these organs in the first place. Thus, the materiality of natural, cognitive representation does entail its singularity by natural necessity" (Klima, "Universality and Immateriality," pp. 40–41, my emphasis).

46   As Buridan seems to claim, the inner sense is just not powerful enough to abstract; see *QP(U)* bk. I q. 7, p. 69.

claim. Buridan does not think that an immaterial human sense cognizes in an entirely different way from the senses of non-human animal souls. Human sensation is miraculous, as Buridan says, but only insofar as it is unclear how an act of sensation can inhere materially in the body and at the same time immaterially in the soul. This does not imply, however, that the cognitive process of sensation is radically different in human and non-human animals. In both cases the soul alone produces an act of sensation, whether material or immaterial. What remains unclear – in both the human and the non-human case – is how the causal connection between the reception of a sensible species in the body and the act of sensation in the soul is to be understood.

Buridan holds that it is wrong to assume that sense perception is singular simply because of the material nature of sense powers, and points to sensory appetitions that are directed at their objects in a universal way. However, these so-called "natural appetites" are basic strivings, which are not preceded by universal perceptions, nor are they cognitive themselves. Buridan does not prove that there are universal sense perceptions, but rather points to such basic and yet universally directed material powers, which make it unlikely that the senses cognize singularly simply because of their material nature. Yet sense perception *is* singular, and in human beings too it is a partly material process involving the sense organs. But this material nature of sense is only a prerequisite for singular cognition, and not the essential reason for its singularity: first, because immaterial subjects with no organs also have singular cognitions; and second, because even if a cognitive subject is material, it might be able to abstract. Buridan does not show that they do abstract, but matter does not absolutely prevent them from doing so. Rather, matter restricts cognitive abilities depending on the level of material complexity.

What distinguishes Buridan's theory from other late medieval theories of sense perception is that he sharply differentiates the epistemological question of what it means to perceive something – that is, to cognize it singularly – from the metaphysical question of how the intentional phenomenon of singular cognition is realized. What Buridan seems to offer is a metaphysically deflationary account of cognition which is compatible with all cognitive subjects, whether material or immaterial. What matters more to him is to describe the phenomenon of different kinds of cognitive operation, such as singular cognition; what makes cognition truly singular is that something is perceived as it appears in the prospect of a cognizer, be it material or immaterial. Once metaphysical and epistemological questions about cognition come apart, Buridan can concentrate on the description of cognitive phenomena themselves. This enables him to provide a theory of cognition that can be adopted no matter what theological doctrines require one to hold about the human soul – a neat piece of Aristotelian functionalism in practice.[47]

Bibliography

Primary Literature

John Buridan, *Commentary on Aristotle's Metaphysics Book I* (*v. 21 Mar 2018*), R. van der Lecq (ed), <academia.edu/36218167/John_Buridans_Commentary_on_Aristotles _Metaphysics_Book_I_v._21_Mar_2018>, accessed February 2019.

John Buridan, *In Metaphysicen Aristotelis. Quaestiones argutissimae Magistri Ioannis Buridani in ultima praelectione*, Paris, Jodocus Badius Ascensius, 1518, Reprinted Frankfurt am Main, Minerva, 1964.

John Buridan, *Quaestiones in tres libros de anima*, G. Lokert (ed), Paris, Jodocus Badius Ascensius & Conradus Resch, 1516; reprinted *Le traité de l'âme de Jean Buridan* (*De prima lectura*), B. Patar (ed), Louvain-la-Neuve, Éditions de l'Institut supérieur de philosophie, 1991, pp. 495–695.

John Buridan, *Quaestiones Ioannis Buridani super decem libros Ethicorum Aristotelis ad Nicomachum*, Paris, Poncet le Preux, 1513, Reprinted Frankfurt am Main, Minerva, 1968.

John Buridan, *Quaestiones super libris Analyticorum Priorum*, H. Hubien (ed), Typescript, n.d., <logicmuseum.com/wiki/Authors/Buridan/In_libros_posteriorum_an alyticorum>, accessed February 2019.

John Buridan, *Quaestiones super libros De generatione et corruptione Aristotelis: A Critical Edition with an Introduction*, M. Streijger, P.J.J.M. Bakker, and J.M.M.H. Thijssen (eds), Leiden, Brill, 2010.

John Buridan, *Quaestiones super octo libros Physicorum Aristotelis* (*secundum ultimam lecturam*): *Libri I–II*, M. Streijger and P.J.J.M. Bakker (eds), Leiden, Brill, 2015.

John Buridan, "Quaestiones supra decem libros Ethicorum Aristotelis ad Nicomachum (Quaestiones longae): Liber VI Quaestio 16," in H.-U. Wöhler (ed), *Texte zum Universalienstreit. Band 2: Hoch- und spätmittelalterliche Scholastik. Lateinische Texte des 13.–15. Jahrhunderts*, Berlin, Akademie Verlag, 1994, pp. 149–171.

---

47 I want to thank all participants in the workshop "Theories of Sense Perception in the 13th and 14th Centuries," which took place in Berlin in 2017 for their comments and discussions. Special thanks to Elena Băltuță, Ian Drummond, and the anonymous referee for helpful suggestions for improving this paper in terms of language and content. Not least, I am very much indebted to Gyula Klima both for criticism and suggestions (not all of which I found myself able to heed) and for his generous permission to use the forthcoming new edition of Buridan's *QDA*(3).

John Buridan, *Questions on Aristotle's 'On the Soul' by John Buridan: Latin Edition with an Annotated English Translation*, G. Klima, J.P. Hartman, P. Sobol and J. Zupko (eds and trans.), Cham, Springer, forthcoming.

John Buridan, *Summulae: De demonstrationibus*, L.M. de Rijk (ed), Groningen, Ingenium, 2001.

John Buridan, "Tractatus de differentia universalis ad individuum," S. Szyller (ed), *Przeglad Tomistyczny*, vol. 3, 1987, pp. 137–178.

Thomas Aquinas, *In Aristotelis libros Physicorum*, *Opera omnia 2*, Rome, Commissio Leonina, 1884.

Thomas Aquinas, *Sentencia libri De anima*, *Opera omnia vol. 45.1*, Rome, Commissio Leonina, 1984.

Secondary Literature

Bakker, Paul J.J.M., "The Soul and its Powers: Debates about the Powers of the Soul," in S. Schmid (ed), *The History of Philosophy of Mind: 1300–1600*, London, Routledge, 2019, pp. 63–82.

de Boer, Sander W., "Dualism and the Mind-Body Problem," in S. Schmid (ed), *The History of Philosophy of Mind: 1300–1600*, London, Routledge, 2019, pp. 207–228.

de Boer, Sander W., *The Science of the Soul: The Commentary Tradition on Aristotle's "De anima,"* c. 1260-c. 1360, Leuven, Leuven University Press, 2013.

de Boer, Sander W., "Where Should We Discuss the Soul? On the Relation between the Doctrines of *De anima* and *De generatione et corruptione*," in G. Klima (ed), *Questions on the Soul by John Buridan and Others: A Companion to John Buridan's Philosophy of Mind*, Dordrecht, Springer, 2017, pp. 21–43.

Gilbert, Penny, "Collate: A System to Aid in the Preparation of Critical Editions," PhD dissertation, University of Wisconsin-Madison, 1978.

Hamesse, Jaqueline (ed), *Les Auctoritates Aristotelis. Un florilège médiéval. Étude historique et édition critique*, Leuven, Publications Universitaires, 1974.

King, Peter, "John Buridan's Solution to the Problem of Universals," in J.M.M.H. Thijssen and J. Zupko (eds), *The Metaphysics and Natural Philosophy of John Buridan*, Leiden, Brill, 2001, pp. 1–27.

King, Peter, "Mediaeval Intentionality and Pseudo-Intentionality," *Quaestio*, vol. 10, 2010, pp. 25–44.

Klein, Martin, *Philosophie des Geistes im Spätmittelalter: Intellekt, Materie und Intentionalität bei Johannes Buridan*, Leiden, Brill, 2019.

Klima, Gyula, *John Buridan*, Oxford, Oxford University Press, 2009.

Klima, Gyula, "Universality and Immateriality," *Acta philosophica*, vol. 24, 2015, pp. 31–42.

Pattin, Adriaan, *Pour l'histoire du sens agent. La controverse entre Barthélemy de Bruges et Jean de Jandun, ses antécédents et son évolution*, Leuven, Leuven University Press, 1988.

Pluta, Olaf, "John Buridan on Universal Knowledge," *Bochumer Philosophisches Jahrbuch für Antike und Mittelalter*, vol. 7, 2002, pp. 25–46.

Pluta, Olaf, "Mental Representation in Animals and Humans: Some Late Medieval Discussions," in G. Klima (ed), *Intentionality, Cognition, and Mental Representation in Medieval Philosophy*, New York, Fordham University Press, 2015, pp. 273–286.

Pluta, Olaf, "Persecution and the Art of Writing: The Parisian Statute of April 1, 1272, and Its Philosophical Consequences," in P.J.J.M. Bakker (ed), *Chemins de la pensée médiévale. Études offertes à Zénon Kaluza*, Turnhout, Brepols, 2002, pp. 563–585.

Wood, Adam, "Aquinas vs. Buridan on the Substance and Powers of the Soul," in G. Klima (ed), *Questions on the Soul by John Buridan and Others: A Companion to John Buridan's Philosophy of Mind*, Dordrecht, Springer, 2017, pp. 77–93.

Zupko, Jack, "Horse Sense and Human Sense: The Heterogeneity of Sense Perception in Buridan's Philosophical Psychology," in S. Knuuttila and P. Kärkkäinen (eds), *Theories of Perception in Medieval and Early Modern Philosophy*, Dordrecht, Springer, 2008, pp. 171–186.

Zupko, Jack, "On Buridan's Alleged Alexandrianism: Heterodoxy and Natural Philosophy in Fourteenth-Century Paris," *Vivarium*, vol. 42, 2004, pp. 43–57.

Zupko, Jack, "On the Several Senses of 'Intentio' in Buridan," in G. Klima (ed), *Intentionality, Cognition, and Mental Representation in Medieval Philosophy*, New York, Fordham University Press, 2015, pp. 251–272.

Zupko, Jack, "Universal Thinking as Process: The Metaphysics of Change and Identity in John Buridan's *Intellectio* Theory," in R. Keele and C. Bolyard (eds), *Later Medieval Metaphysics: Ontology, Language, and Logic*, New York, Fordham University Press, 2013, pp. 137–158.

Index of Names

Adam Buckfield   88, 135, 166, 176
Adamson, Peter   157n13, 170n52
Adelard of Bath   77n12
Adriaenssen, Han-Thomas   4n5, 95n92,
   97n100, 100n126, 101n126, 101n128,
   101n130, 102n132, 181n5, 306n7, 307n9,
   326n69
Aertsen, Jan A.   74n3, 78n19, 136n70, 175n68
Akdogan, Cemil   81n26
Al Ghazali (Algazel)   161n24
Albert the Great   5, 6, 15n11, 15n13, 17–19,
   20n22, 22n25, 22n27, 24n35, 26n40, 27,
   42n9, 48n20, 53, 54n30, 58n49, 74, 75n6,
   76, 78, 79, 81n26, 82–87, 89, 94, 97, 103,
   104, 111, 113n9, 123, 124n36, 127, 242n10,
   276, 288, 289n39290n43
Alexander of Hales   12n6, 31, 32, 169n48,
   242n10
Alhacen   6, 73, 74, 82n31, 85n48, 88, 89, 94,
   95, 97, 115, 117n17, 122, 128n45, 131n53,
   132–136, 139, 140n86, 143
Anonymi Magistri Artium   4n5, 47n17,
   47n18
Anonymous   15n11, 46, 47, 59, 77, 78, 79n21,
   84n41, 93n84, 94n85, 97n99, 157n12,
   171n56
Anzulewicz, Henryk   15n11, 75n6, 78n19,
   81n26, 82n27, 82n28
Aristotle   7, 12, 15n11, 17, 18, 31, 48, 50, 52–54,
   65, 73, 79, 82, 85, 89, 92n78, 111–113, 115,
   116, 118, 119n22, 123–125, 128n45, 129–135,
   142, 153, 157, 160n23, 161, 165–167,
   169–171, 173–175, 198, 206, 221, 233, 240,
   242–244, 247, 250, 255, 259, 269, 270,
   272, 273, 278, 286, 289n39, 304n2, 306,
   307, 308n11, 308n12, 326, 336, 344,
   360n100, 360n101, 364, 365, 383n44
Arlig, Andrew   221n20
Armstrong, David M.   344, 345, 349, 352, 353
Augustine   5, 38–46, 48, 50–52, 54–57,
   58n48, 62–65, 67n88, 70, 76, 84, 89,
   96–98, 100, 161n26, 180, 199, 304n2, 306,
   309, 311–313, 314n27, 318, 319, 324, 330

Averroes   6, 15n12, 20n22, 27n41, 29n48, 73,
   81n25, 82, 84n37, 89, 92n78, 123, 124,
   157–162, 164–168, 171, 175, 226, 288–292,
   372
Avicenna   6, 12, 13, 18, 20, 21n23, 22, 23, 24n32,
   31n53, 73, 82, 85n48, 89, 97, 115, 123, 124,
   127n43, 130n52, 161n24, 162n30,
   163, 164n38, 164n39, 223, 242, 249, 271,
   278, 304n2, 307n8

Baker, Tawrin   125n39, 134n63
Bakker, Paul J.J.M.   365n5, 366n7, 368n11,
   382n43
Băltuță, Elena   7, 93n83, 128n45, 128n47,
   131n52, 141n90, 181n3, 203n42
Bartholomeus Anglicus   78, 79n21, 88n62, 90
Bauer, Hans   131n53
Bazán, Bernardo Carlos   12n5, 65n70, 175n68,
   215n4, 216n6, 240n6, 335n1
Berkeley, George   145n105, 145n106
Bernard of Chartres   77n12
Berryman, Sylvia   79n21
Bertolacci, Amos   170n52
Beullens, Pieter   214n3
Biard, Joël   127n44
Black, Deborah   25n35, 28n48, 157n13, 159,
   242n13, 348n47, 359
Bolyard, Charles   366n7
Bonaventura   80n22
Boulter, Stephen   256n34
Boyle, Matthew   29, 30n50, 232, 233
Brenet, Jean-Baptiste   286n35, 286n36,
   289n39, 292n48, 293n52, 294n54,
   295n56
Broadie, Alexander   49n21, 184n10, 199–201
Brower, Jeffrey E.   216n7, 306n7
Brower-Toland, Susan   306n7, 319n42
Burnyeat, Myles   6, 111–113, 115, 131, 138, 145,
   153, 159, 161, 165, 166, 171, 173
Burr, David   95n93

Cameron, Margaret   31n53, 221n20
Carruthers, Peter   232n44

INDEX OF NAMES

Chalcidius 75n5, 79n21, 81
Clarke, Edwin 121n28
Constantine the African 77n11, 162n32, 163
Conti, Alessandro D. 182n8
Côté, Antoine 308n12
Cross, Richard 66n80, 305n4, 343, 345n39, 351n63, 351n64, 352n69
Cunningham, Jack P. 87n60

Day, Sebastian J. 357n89
de Boer, Sander W. 369
de Boer, Wietse 127n43
De Haan, Daniel 7, 261n44, 273n4
De Risi, Vincenzo 139n81
Decaix, Véronique 69n89, 88n62, 203n42
DeMaitre, Luke 171n55
Demange, Dominique 95n92, 97n100, 99n115
Descartes, René 113, 115n15, 126, 127, 139n81, 143, 144, 145n104, 145n105, 163, 309n15
Dewan, Lawrence 81n26, 84n37
Di Martino, Carla 12n4, 12n5, 223n26, 271n3, 273n4
Dominicus Gundissalinus 5, 20, 21, 23, 24n31, 24n35
Domininus Báñez 241n10
Donati, Silvia 17n15, 78n18, 87n59, 182n8
Dupré, Sven 125n39, 127n43
Durand of Saint-Pourçain 57n45, 58, 59n49, 59n50

Easton, Stewart C. 87n59, 87n60, 88n62
Ebbesen, Sten 88n62
Emory, Kent 74n3
Etchemendy, Matthew 175n69
Euclid 73, 76, 81n24, 82, 86, 89, 93n84, 94, 99n115, 128n45

Federici-Vescovini, Graziella 143n97
Fend, Michael 4n2
Finger, Stanley 163n33
Fish, William 102n132
Fisher, Kendall 308n11
Fletcher, Garth 29n49
Fraenkel, Carlos 25n35, 348n47
François d'Aguilon 134

Frixione, Eugenio 163n33
Fumo, Jamie C. 25n35, 348n47

Galen 76, 162n31, 163, 164, 314n27
Galfridus de Aspale 88n62
Galle, Griet 88n62, 135n66
Gauthier, René Antoine 46, 47n17, 77n13, 171n56, 175, 226, 273n5
Gibson, James 244n19, 251
Gilbert, Penny 376n24
Gilson, Étienne 127n44
Godfrey of Fontaines 49n20, 57n45, 206n45, 308n12
Göttler, Christine 127n43
Gracia, Jorge J.E. 344n34
Guldentops, Guy 181n4, 206n45, 214n3, 325n68

Hackett, Jeremiah 87n60, 88n62, 91n75, 123n34, 124n36, 136n70, 141n89
Hamesse, Jacqueline 88n62, 159n19, 365n6
Hartman, Peter John 206n45, 364n1
Hasse, Dag Nikolaus 12n4, 24n32, 74n3, 78n19, 82n31, 170n52, 223n26, 278n19
Hatfield, Gary 139n81, 144n104, 145n105
Henry of Ghent 41n2, 58n48, 64n68
Hocknull, Mark 87n60
Hoffmans, Hadelin 87n60, 91n76
Hon, Giora 122n31

Ibn Al-Haytham 115, 117n17, 132n57

Jacobi, Klaus 137n73, 226n34
Jacobs, John 306n7
Jacopo Zabarella 49n22, 125n39
Jansen, Berhnard 12n6, 57n46, 76n8, 97n100, 321n56
Jean of Jandun 7, 94n85, 141n90, 269, 271, 272, 286–301
Jeschke, Thomas 181n4, 206n45, 325n68
Johann Alsted 143
John Blund 5, 25, 27, 81n25, 84n41, 85n48
John Buridan 8, 364–385
John Duns Scotus 5, 8, 58n48, 64–68, 255, 256n34, 335–361
John of La Rochelle 5, 18, 19n18, 22n27, 24n35

INDEX OF NAMES

John of St. Thomas   242n10
John Pecham   5, 6, 54–57, 59, 60, 68, 77, 78,
   80n22, 95, 114, 116n16, 117, 120n26, 121,
   122123n34, 127–129, 133n57, 134, 140n87,
   142n95, 144n100
John Philoponus   161n24

Kahn, Charles   119n23
Kalderon, Mark E.   74n4, 75n6, 76n8, 95n92
Kärkkäinen, Pekka   4n2, 48n19, 199m36,
   304n2, 307n10, 369n15
Kaukua, Jari   13n7, 18n17, 22n26, 22n27,
   23n28, 31n53
Keele, Rondo   366n7
Kemp, Simon   29n49
Kenny, Anthony   256n34
Kepler, Johannes   125, 127n43, 143, 144
King, Peter   238n1, 255, 256n34, 258, 354n81,
   356n88, 357n89, 374n22, 377n27, 380
Klein, Martin   8
Klima, Gyula   15n13, 58n48, 238n1, 256n34,
   356n88, 364n1, 368n11, 369n14, 374,
   377n27, 380, 381, 384n45
Klubertanz, George   225n31, 261n44, 285n33
Knuuttila, Simo   4n2, 48n19, 199n36, 304n2,
   307n10, 369n15
Köhler, Theodor W.   214n1
Kretzmann, Norman   229n37, 256n34

Lagerlund, Henrik   15n13, 48n19, 137n73,
   182n8, 199n36, 256n34, 329n77
LaZella, Andrew   8, 335n3, 336n5, 338n16,
   358n92
Lemay, Richard   124n36
Lewis, David   102n132
Lička, Lukáš   5, 6, 87n58, 95n92, 97n100,
   99n115, 100n118, 128n45
Lindberg, David C.   26n39, 73n1, 73n2, 74n3,
   76n8, 77n11, 77n12, 77n13, 77n14, 79n21,
   81n26, 82n31, 85n48, 88n60, 88n62,
   89n65, 90n70, 91n72, 113n7, 114n11,
   115n12, 117n17, 117n18, 120n24,
   125, 126n40, 304n2, 313n26
Lisska, Anthony J.   20n21, 20n22, 28n46,
   181n3, 223n25, 223n28, 272n4, 279n21,
   279n22, 282n25
Locke, John   298

Lonergan, Bernard   261n44
Long, James R.   78n16, 88n62, 90n70
Loose, Patrice K.   88n60, 91n74, 91n75, 91n76,
   93n84

MacDonald, Scott   256n34
Machamer, Peter K.   91n72, 130n52
Mantovani, Mattia   5, 6, 93n83, 121n28,
   142n92, 144n102
Marenbon, John   221n20
Marmodoro, Anna   15n11, 270n2
Martin, André   7, 128n47, 306n7, 323n61,
   326n70
Matthews, Gareth B.   91n72
Maurin, Anna-Sofia   345n37
McCabe, Herbert   256n34
McClintock, Stuart   286n35
McCord Adams, Marilyn   217n10, 356n87
McDowell, John   30n50, 231, 232, 234
Menn, Stephen   308n11
Mensching, Günther   123n34
Mensching-Estakhr, Alia   123n34
Mintz, Sidney W.   15n11
Multhauf, Robert P.   121n28

Nadler, Steven   191n22, 204n44
Nemesius of Emesa   75n6, 80
Nicholas of Cusa   62n59
Nicole Oresme   58n49
Noone, Timothy B.   88n62, 90n70
Normore, Calvin   256n34
Nussbaum, Martha   112n2, 131n54, 153n1,
   153n3

O'Callaghan, John   181n3
O'Daly, Gérard   309n13
Oelze, Anselm   20n21, 139n82, 141n89, 214n3,
   224n29, 282n25
Ortúzar Escudero, Maria José   163n32
Owens, Joseph   48n20, 130n52

Panaccio, Claude   306n7
Panofsky, Erwin   133n59
Pantin, Isabelle   127n43
Pasnau, Robert   4n4, 20n21, 53n26, 53n27,
   95n92, 96n95, 97n100, 98n106, 98n109,
   100n122, 101n130, 102n132, 114, 124, 181n3,

INDEX OF NAMES

Pasnau, Robert (cont.)
  216n6, 216n7, 222n22, 273n5, 306n7,
  307n9, 310n16, 315n33, 319n42, 321n56,
  324n66, 329n77
Pattin, Adriaan   84n37, 84n41, 94n85, 159n19,
  367n8
Perler, Dominik   2n1, 4n4, 7, 12n5, 100n126,
  112n5, 113n6, 127n44, 141n90, 153n2,
  181n3, 214n2, 219n14, 220n17, 242n12,
  273n4, 282n27, 284n30, 306n7
Peter Auriol   143
Peter John Olivi   5, 6–8, 12n6, 13n9, 30, 57,
  58m48, 59–61, 62n61, 64, 68, 69, 74,
  76n8, 76n10, 77, 79, 80n22, 81, 95–104,
  304–331
Peter of Ailly   49n22
Peter Sutton   76n8, 78, 81n25
Pickavé, Martin   12n5, 58n48, 78n20,
  224n29
Pini, Giorgio   256n34, 339, 353, 354, 356,
  357n89
Piron, Sylvian   61n55, 95n92, 323n61
Plato   52, 76, 81, 82, 84, 133n61, 154n4, 304n2
Pluta, Olaf   50n23, 365n5, 374n22
Power, Amanda   87n60
Pseudo-Buckfield   105
Pseudo-Euclid   80n23
Pseudo-Grosseteste   84, 100n120
Ptolemy   73, 76, 89, 91, 93n84, 125, 128n45,
  129–136

Raizman-Kedar, Yael   87n59, 88n60, 91n72,
  91n75, 93n82, 118n19, 122n31, 123n34
Rashed, Roshdi   127n44
Retucci, Fiorella   58n49, 181n4, 206n45,
  325n68
Richard de Mediavilla   217n10, 231n41
Richard Fishacre   88n62
Richard Rufus of Cornwall   6, 7, 137n73,
  154–175
Robert Grosseteste   77, 78, 88n62, 90, 93n81,
  169n48
Robert Kilwardby   5, 7, 48–50, 52, 54, 59, 60,
  68, 128n47, 179–210
Roger Bacon   5, 6, 26, 74, 76n8, 77–79, 81,
  84n41, 87–94, 95n91, 103, 104, 114, 115n11,
  115n12, 115n14, 117, 118n19, 119–129,
  130n52, 133n57, 134–146, 162n30, 162n31,
  163, 174, 304, 313n26

Roger Marston   61–64, 68, 76n8, 78, 79n21,
  142n96
Roling, Bernd   214n3
Rorty, Amélie Oksenberg   112n2, 131n54,
  153n1, 153n3
Rosemann, Philipp   181n3
Rubini, Paolo   7, 141n20, 242n12, 289n42,
  298n61

Sabra, Abdelhamid I.   117n17, 130n52, 131n53,
  132n57, 140n86
Scarpelli-Cory, Therese   261n44, 305n4
Schmid, Stephan   298n61, 368n11, 369n14
Shaffer, Jonathan   344n36
Shapiro, Alan E.   126n39
Shapiro, Lisa   12n5, 224n29
Siebert, Harald   75n7
Silva, José Filipe   4n2, 4n5, 5, 13n7, 13n8,
  41n3, 41n4, 42n6, 42n7, 43n11, 48n19,
  58n48, 63n65, 87n58, 95n92,
  96n95, 97n99, 97n100, 101n126, 128n47,
  179n1, 190n20, 199–202, 203n42,
  206–209, 308n12, 309n14,
  309n15, 310n16, 310n17, 312n23, 312n24,
  317n36, 318n39, 319n43
Simon, Gérard   127n44, 144n101
Sirridge, Mary   198, 199, 201
Smith, Arthur D.   46
Smith, A. Mark   73n1, 74n3, 77n11, 77n12,
  88n60, 89n65, 117n17, 120n24, 120n27,
  122, 130n51, 131n53, 137n75, 304n2
Smith, C.U.M.   163n33
Solère, Jean-Luc   58n49, 181n4, 325n68
Sorabji, Richard   6, 111–113, 115, 126n42, 131,
  145, 153, 161n24
South, James B.   356n88, 357n89
Speer, Andreas   74n3, 78n19, 136n70, 175n68,
  181n4, 206n45, 325n68
Spruit, Leen   4n3, 181n3, 304n2, 305n4, 307n9
Steel, Carlos   214n3
Steneck, Nicolas H.   12n4, 81n26, 83n34
Stevenson, Lloyd G.   121n28
Stock, Michael   260n43
Stump, Eleonore   10n1, 181n3, 256n34
Summers, David   133n60

Tachau, Katherine H.   88n60, 94n86, 95n92,
  97n100, 98n106, 103n137, 137n73, 142,
  226n34, 309n15, 322n58

INDEX OF NAMES

Tellkamp, Jörg Alejandro 22n27, 25n35, 141n89, 223n25, 225n31, 226n32

Thijssen, Johannes M.M.H. 374n22, 382n43

Thom, Paul 48n19, 182n8, 199n36

Thomas Aquinas 4n5, 5–7, 10n1, 12n5, 13n7, 17n15, 20, 23, 27, 28, 29n48, 30n51, 49n20, 52–54, 80n22, 111–115, 119, 123, 126, 127, 129, 130n52, 141, 145, 153, 161, 174, 180–182, 209215–231, 233, 234, 238–266, 271–286, 288, 289, 292–294, 298n61, 299n64, 300, 304, 307n8, 308, 328, 336, 337, 346, 348n46, 352, 365n6, 383, 384n45

Thörnqvist, Christina T. 88n62

Toivanen, Juhana 4n5, 5, 13n6, 16n13, 30n52, 31n53, 43n11, 95n92, 96n95, 96n98, 97n100, 98n106, 98n109, 101n126, 101n130, 102n132, 131n52, 199n36, 200n39, 208n49, 305n5, 309n14, 309n15, 310n16, 310n17, 312n23, 312n24, 314n30, 317–320, 321n53, 326n70, 329n77

Tuominen, Miira 308n12

Turnbull, Robert G. 91n72, 130n52

Verger, Jacques 87n59

Wallis, Faith 25n35, 348n47

Weijers, Olga 87n59

Weisberg, Michael 173n62

Weisheipl, J. Athanasius 81n26

William of Auvergne 5, 25, 43–45, 50, 55n35, 161

William of Conches 77n12, 78n19, 97n100

William of Ockham 57n45, 62n61, 143, 217n10, 219n14, 220n15, 255, 256n34

Winkler, Norbert 83n34

Wippel, John 239n4

Wisnovsky, Robert 25n35, 348n47

Witelo 6, 95, 114, 117, 121n28, 122, 128, 133n57, 134, 138n76, 143

Wittgenstein, Ludwig 254

Wolfson, Harry A. 81n25, 131n52

Wolter, Allan B. 335n1, 342n29, 356n87, 356n88, 357n89, 358n90

Wood, Adam 368n11

Wood, Rega 6, 124n36, 137n73, 154n4, 167n44, 173n62, 175n69

Wright, Wayne 11n3

Yrjönsuuri, Mikko 4n2, 13n7, 13n8, 42n6, 96n95, 128n47, 308n12, 329n77

Zanin, Fabio 143n97

Zavalloni, Roberto 216n6, 231n41

Zeis, John 306n7

Zupko, Jack 364n1, 365n5, 366n7, 369, 374n22, 377n27

Index of Concepts

Abstraction 26n40, 93, 113, 159, 166, 167, 258, 285, 286, 306, 307n9, 356n87, 361, 381, 382n42

act
of cognition 274, 275, 305, 309–312, 319, 323n60, 324–327, 329, 374, 376, 380, 381
of perception 1, 30, 46, 142, 269, 273, 274, 280, 312, 367, 371, 372, 380, 381
of sensation 49, 50, 350, 367–372, 385
visual 76, 86, 92n80, 94, 98–104

activity
causal 83, 118, 191
of perception 97
of the soul 57, 60, 61, 96, 128n47, 200, 201, 209, 309
rational 213, 219, 227–230
visual 75, 99

actuality 47, 53, 64, 153, 172, 173, 190, 307, 308n11, 349

affection 42, 50–52, 54, 57, 61, 67, 75, 96, 128, 193, 194, 197, 202, 204, 208, 209, 227, 250, 281, 307n10, 315, 316, 336

agent sense 69, 84n37

Aristotelianism/Aristotelian 3, 5–8, 17, 27, 49, 53, 64, 70, 73, 79n21, 81–83, 85–87, 92–94, 103, 111, 112, 114, 115n15, 116, 135, 142, 153, 154, 170, 174, 180, 181, 190n20, 213, 215, 238–241, 243, 255, 271, 277, 279, 297, 300, 304, 306, 311, 336, 337, 344, 386

attention 8, 42n6, 51, 52, 59–61, 66, 75, 80, 87, 98–104, 127, 128n45, 128n47, 129, 159, 194, 195, 201, 202, 205, 207–209, 244, 254, 305, 310, 314, 316–321, 323, 329

Augustinianism/Augustinian 3, 5, 38, 42n8, 43, 50, 54n32, 57, 58n49, 61, 65, 67, 68, 69n89, 70, 93n84, 100, 161, 180, 181, 200, 306

awareness 19, 21n24, 26n40, 41, 42, 43n10, 45, 50, 52, 61, 112, 140, 145, 146, 156, 159, 160, 174, 193, 244, 317

being
human 7, 20, 23, 24n33, 27, 28, 41n5, 44, 45n13, 55, 129, 132, 139, 140, 142, 173, 182, 189, 213–218, 220, 222–225, 227, 229, 230, 231n41, 232, 233, 235, 238, 240, 242, 245, 247, 250, 260, 261, 265, 271, 272, 275, 276, 277n16, 280, 281, 283, 285–288, 292, 293, 295, 299, 364, 366–368, 370, 382, 385
living 39, 51, 58, 118, 146
rational 229
spiritual 54, 93, 124, 125, 154, 155, 160–162, 166, 167, 169, 171–174, 185

body 3, 38–43, 45, 50–55, 57, 59, 63, 70, 76, 83, 89, 90, 92, 97, 100, 113, 120, 121, 124n36, 128, 135, 138, 139, 145n104, 146, 158, 162–164, 171, 179n1, 183–185, 188, 190–197, 202–209, 217, 220, 221, 230, 240, 253, 257, 271, 292, 293, 298, 305, 306, 313, 314, 316n34, 318, 320, 322n59, 324n63, 326–331, 351, 352, 364, 367–371, 385

brain 117, 119–121, 123, 138, 144, 162, 163, 225, 243, 271

capacity 27, 32, 34, 41, 43–45, 50n23, 55–57, 67, 80, 83, 118, 119, 139n82, 158, 160, 202, 248, 262, 272, 277n16, 286, 290, 293, 295, 300, 347

category 130n52, 136, 175, 243, 244, 290, 298, 342, 344

cause
efficient 46, 48–50, 52, 53n28, 57, 60–62, 69, 70, 101, 102, 104, 182, 183, 185, 187–191, 195–198, 200, 202–206, 305, 323–325
final 324
formal 298
material 53n28, 163, 325n67
terminative 60, 61, 101, 102, 104, 324, 326–330
sine qua non 7, 179, 198, 200, 201, 205, 206, 209, 325

change
bodily 48, 50, 192–197, 203, 311–313
material 114–117, 119, 122, 127, 128, 131, 138, 164, 174
spiritual 111–114, 123, 153, 164, 167–169

cogitation 241, 242, 265, 291, 293

cognition
abstractive 357
animal 250, 282

INDEX OF CONCEPTS

intellectual   4, 239, 247, 255, 258–261, 265, 271, 285, 286, 294, 301, 304n1, 307n9
intuitive   350, 356–359
colour   1, 5, 6, 10, 14–19, 25, 26n40, 32, 39, 42, 43, 53, 77, 83, 85, 86, 87n59, 89, 92, 93n83, 109, 112–114, 116–119, 121, 123, 125–132, 134–136, 138, 139, 141, 142, 144–146, 148, 150, 155, 157, 160, 161, 166–169, 173, 174, 223, 233, 234, 243–247, 249, 253, 254, 269, 270, 275, 323n61, 339, 351, 353, 359, 378, 381, 383
consciousness   96, 145, 160, 201, 305n4, 317, 319n42, 320, 331

disposition   30, 45, 65, 172, 173, 195, 323n60, 328, 369
dualism   41, 96

essence   20, 29, 34, 44, 53, 60, 84, 119, 142, 165, 218, 220n17, 229, 239, 271, 283–286, 292, 297–299, 301, 312–314, 348, 350, 379
excitation   44, 46, 48, 54, 55, 57, 59, 62–64, 67n88, 69
extramission   6, 17n15, 73–83, 84n41, 85, 87, 89–104, 128n45, 132, 169n48, 312, 319
eye   6, 13, 15, 31, 32, 41n5, 47, 51, 66, 73, 75–77, 79–81, 83, 85, 86, 88–92, 95, 96, 99, 101n126, 103, 104, 111–120, 125–127, 128n45, 129, 131, 132, 142, 144, 145, 160, 166, 182, 191, 207, 208, 217, 274, 313, 320n48, 328, 329, 337, 343, 344, 366, 369, 379, 380, 383

faculty   1, 5, 8, 11, 15, 30, 31, 116, 129, 137, 138, 141, 142, 157, 160, 164, 170, 171, 190, 220–222, 229–231, 255n34, 271, 281, 283, 314n32, 380
  cognitive   53, 68, 189, 271, 283, 288, 293
  rational   7, 220–222, 225, 227, 228, 229n38, 230, 235, 292
  sensitive/sensory   7, 131n52, 141n91, 142, 155, 156, 170, 172, 189, 220–222, 227, 229, 230, 233, 272, 275, 282, 292n47
form
  accidental   181n5, 352
  substantial   3, 181n5, 216, 220, 290, 292, 293, 295, 297, 298, 301, 364, 367
function   5, 11, 12, 15, 17n14, 18, 21, 22, 30, 32, 33, 99, 104, 118, 131n52, 163, 164, 195, 197n30, 215–218, 220, 226, 238, 271, 272,

276, 277, 288, 289, 293, 296, 297, 311, 320, 324, 348, 380
  cognitive   11, 288, 292, 297
  psychological   11, 14, 30

hearing   65, 113, 116, 142, 168n47, 169, 213, 246, 247, 316, 317, 337, 339
heart   162, 216, 271, 283
hylomorphism   52, 113, 119, 139, 240, 272, 292, 328, 329, 330n81

imagination   20, 21n24, 22–24, 26, 29, 137, 158, 188–190, 222, 234, 238, 241–243, 245, 246, 249, 260, 279–281, 288–291, 296, 299, 301, 306, 307n8, 374
impression   52, 56, 57n46, 59, 69, 87, 98, 115, 119, 126, 128n48, 188, 191, 280, 311, 315, 316, 318–320, 322n59, 323, 324n63, 327, 330, 353
instinct   138, 140, 141n91, 145n104, 193, 194, 203, 224, 280–282
intellect
  agent   242n11, 243, 285, 286, 307n9
  possible   7, 238, 241, 242n11, 243
  practical   261
intentionality   40, 41, 53, 66, 67, 85, 112, 114, 154, 161n24, 166, 168, 192n24, 194, 197, 201, 203–205, 210, 223n28, 298n61, 319n45, 324, 347–349, 351, 377, 385
intromission   6, 73, 74, 76n8, 77, 78, 79n21, 80, 83, 85, 88–91, 94–96, 99, 104, 132

light   6, 54, 55, 75, 76, 81, 84–86, 89, 94, 113, 114, 116–123, 125–127, 128n47, 129, 131, 132, 134–136, 141, 144, 146, 167–171, 174, 194, 195, 207, 208, 285, 306n6, 313, 321, 325, 326

matter   3, 39–43, 50, 53, 54, 85, 93, 100, 111, 113, 118, 123, 125, 165, 166, 171, 184, 193, 194, 199, 204, 217, 239, 243, 258, 259, 265, 306n6, 307n10, 314, 328, 329, 337, 338, 346, 351, 354, 356, 364, 366–371, 382–385
medium   46–49, 59, 65, 68, 83, 84n41, 85, 90, 92, 93, 97, 100, 112, 118, 121–125, 127n45, 155, 157–161, 163, 167, 171, 172, 174, 186, 304, 306, 307, 309, 321n56, 322n58, 323, 330, 335, 383

memory   22n27, 30n51, 32, 62, 135n68, 137,
     158, 222, 226n33, 229, 238, 240, 241, 243,
     245, 246, 249, 260, 279, 280, 283,
     288–291, 296, 299, 301, 307n9, 311,
     323n60, 357, 374, 375, 376n26
mind   40, 43, 44, 113, 139, 140, 145n104, 153,
     184, 232, 255n34, 261, 262, 310, 311, 314,
     318, 324n63, 364, 365
modality   18, 21, 48, 116, 122, 135, 269, 274

Neoplatonism/Neoplatonic   3, 113, 161, 164,
     175, 309
nerve   92n77, 93n80, 117, 119–121, 137, 143, 160

pain   20, 89, 277
passion   39, 230, 251–253, 297
perceiver   16, 19, 28, 43n10, 57, 75, 79, 80, 86,
     87, 90, 98, 103, 112, 114, 115, 119, 128n45,
     131, 132, 135, 140, 142, 145, 160, 234, 270,
     273, 306n6, 380
perceiving as   5, 10–12, 14, 16, 18, 19, 25, 26, 29,
     33, 34, 130n52
Perspectivists   6, 87, 114–122, 126, 127n44, 128,
     133n57, 143, 144–146
phantasia/phantasm   115n14, 214, 222, 223,
     227, 230, 234, 241, 249, 259, 260, 261n44,
     276n14, 279–282, 284–286, 288, 290n43,
     373n20
potency/potentiality/potential   49, 53n28,
     54, 56, 57, 65, 83, 84, 93, 99, 123, 156, 162,
     166, 172, 173, 181–183, 190, 197, 199, 202,
     206, 217, 221, 229n38, 307, 308n11,
     310n18, 313, 324, 350, 352, 357, 364, 368,
     370, 371, 376
power
   causal   190, 192
   cogitative/vis cogitativa   7, 20, 21n24,
     30n51, 138, 139, 216, 222–227, 229, 234,
     238, 241, 243, 245–257, 260–265, 269,
     271–276, 280–286, 288–301, 383n44
   cognitive   5, 12, 33, 45, 46, 48, 59, 61, 64,
     66, 67, 101, 238, 242, 245–247, 256–258,
     260, 265, 270, 273, 276, 278, 289, 292,
     307–310, 313, 325, 326, 335, 337, 339, 346,
     347, 364, 383n44, 384
   intellectual   10, 19, 20, 27, 29, 248, 251, 257,
     259, 272, 286
   natural   44, 203, 204

rational   222, 296
sensitive/sensory power   47, 48, 49, 63,
     84, 92, 94, 96, 98, 247, 248, 254, 258, 275,
     276–278, 315, 316, 318, 323, 324, 327, 329,
     330, 335, 337, 339, 342, 346, 347, 349,
     350, 354, 355, 358, 384
   visual   46, 47, 54, 83–86, 90, 92, 93, 96, 98,
     100–102, 104
psychology   10, 11, 14, 15, 29–31, 33, 88, 118,
     137n73, 139, 238n1, 239, 240, 242, 255,
     258, 265, 271, 272, 293n53, 296, 300

realism   10, 17, 248, 273, 305, 307n9, 319n42,
     324
reflection   100, 118, 146, 167, 192, 197, 202–205,
     260, 261n44, 295, 373n20
representation   3, 21, 22, 45, 50, 52, 56, 57, 68,
     86, 87, 89, 100, 222, 279, 286, 306n7,
     323n61, 324, 347, 353, 372, 374–376,
     378–382, 384n45
   sensory   214, 222, 279n22, 285, 286, 296,
     380

sensation   11, 25, 45n13, 46n16, 49, 50, 55, 65,
     66, 69n89, 94, 111, 117n17, 138, 160, 161,
     163, 164, 170, 171, 175, 193, 223n28, 238,
     240, 243–249, 251, 253–255, 257, 307n8,
     307n10, 311–313, 318, 335, 336, 349, 350,
     355, 356, 367–372, 375, 381, 384, 385
sense
   common   15, 17, 18, 21, 26, 29, 31, 32, 116,
     117, 120, 130, 131n53, 134, 137, 142, 157, 158,
     160, 170, 171, 222, 234, 278–282, 288, 289,
     291, 296, 299, 314, 316–318, 323, 326–328,
     383n44
   external   5–7, 11, 14–17, 26n40, 31, 32,
     48n18, 120, 222, 223, 224n28, 238,
     242–248, 271, 273, 278, 279, 287, 288, 314,
     316–319, 323, 326, 327, 330, 381–384
   inner/internal   5, 11, 12, 14, 21n24, 30,
     31n53, 32, 33, 48n18, 88, 128, 131n52, 222,
     223, 226n33, 226n34, 234, 241–243, 248,
     258, 260, 271, 275, 276, 277, 278n19, 279,
     280, 282, 288–291, (290n43), 293–296,
     300, 306, 381–384
   organ   8, 31, 41, 42, 43n10, 46–57, 58n46,
     59, 63, 64, 66, 68, 69, 73, 75, 80, 83, 90,
     92, 93, 100, 104, 111–114, 117–120, 123,

INDEX OF CONCEPTS

125–129, 138, 141, 142, 144, 146, 155, 156,
158–160, 162, 163, 165, 167, 169, 171–173,
180n3, 183–186, 190, 191, 201–205, 216,
218, 220, 224, 262, 270, 271, 276, 278, 281,
304, 306–310, 314, 316–321, 322n59,
323–326, 329, 330, 331, 337, 350, 367,
368, 371, 380, 382, 383, 384n45, 385

sensible

common   6, 18, 116, 128–136, 139–142,
144–146, 170, 243, 273, 287

proper   6, 15, 25, 26n40, 53, 116, 118,
123n35, 128n47, 130n51, 131, 139, 141n91,
142, 144–146, 243, 263, 273, 287, 300,
341n26

sight   11, 13, 26n40, 79, 86, 90, 92n80, 94n89,
96–98, 104, 112, 113, 116, 118, 122, 128n45,
129, 130n51, 131n52, 132, 133, 135, 137, 142,
144n103, 145, 167, 169, 214, 223, 224n28,
225, 230, 246, 247, 254, 337, 339

smell   5, 16, 20, 141, 173, 214, 223, 224n28, 233,
234, 249, 269

soul

animal   40, 385

human   38, 45n13, 184, 185, 220, 221, 292,
293, 297, 309, 365, 367–370, 384, 386

rational   54, 55n34, 138, 139, 214–217, 219,
222, 240, 271, 285

sensitive/sensory   7, 11, 26, 31, 49, 51, 52,
61, 63, 79, 119, 131n52, 138, 139, 141n91,
142, 145n104, 162, 179, 183, 185–200,
202–209, 213–216, 218–220, 222, 271, 272,
275, 276, 277, 282, 289, 292, 299, 300,
320, 329, 366, 367, 369, 376

spiritual   96, 305, 309–311, 316, 320n48,
323, 324, 327, 329, 330n81

vegetative   213, 216–218, 220, 368

species

intelligible   239, 259, 285, 286

sensible   49n22, 50, 57, 58n46, 59, 172,
182–186, 188, 190–192, 194–197, 202–205,
338, 339, 367, 371, 378, 385

spirit   59, 75, 121, 122, 124n36, 125, 143,
162–164, 326, 328

stimulus   57, 66, 201, 207–209

Stoicism/Stoic   3, 75, 129, 132

Substance   11, 15–17, 19–22, 23n28, 24–28, 38,
159, 169, 175, 216, 272n4, 273, 274,
298n62, 299, 336, 337, 339, 342, 343, 351,
352, 354, 356, 358, 361, 381

corporeal   114, 182

incorporeal   155

immaterial   258, 299

individual   13, 14, 16, 29, 287, 335,
337–339, 343, 350

material   243, 255, 257, 297–299, 338

spiritual   83

taste   5, 10, 18–21, 24, 25, 112, 141, 155, 169, 246,
274, 337, 339

teleology   51, 222, 294, 295n56

touch   75, 97, 98, 112, 113, 116, 129, 130n51,
131n52, 134, 135, 141, 142, 144n103, 145,
169, 174, 306n6, 313

universals   10, 20, 27, 29, 246–248, 252–254,
255n34, 256n34, 259, 262, 265, 281, 291,
292, 301, 336, 344, 345, 349–351, 353,
365, 366, 372, 375

vision   5, 6, 38, 53, 73–77, 79–82, 84–91,
92n80, 93–98, 100–104, 113–116, 117n17,
118–120, 122, 123, 125, 127, 129, 134–137,
138n78, 141–143, 144n103, 145n104, 167,
169n48, 173, 175, 182, 206, 240, 242–244,
264, 274, 280, 291, 310, 323n60, 328–330,
346, 350, 369, 382

Printed in the United States
By Bookmasters